# *Enuma Elish*

**The Library of Babylonian Literature**

Series editors: Edited by Johannes Haubold, Sophus Helle, Enrique Jiménez, and Selena Wisnom

The Library of Babylonian Literature makes the main works of Akkadian literature available in an accessible format, with state-of-the-art essays on each text by leading scholars in ancient religion, Assyriology, and ancient Near Eastern studies. Each volume contains a transcription and a translation of the poem, as well as a rich introduction and a series of essays that will act as a companion to the text, guiding new readers through its most important facets.

Essays cover literary history, narrative structure, genre, intertextuality and allusions, political significance, and reception in and beyond the ancient world (including where applicable its influence on the Hebrew Bible and Classical literature). The essays also look at poetics, performance, authorship, materiality, gender, and sexuality.

These books open up the rich treasures of Akkadian poetry to a larger readership while also laying the groundwork for further literary analyses of the work. The Library of Babylonian Literature moves the field of Assyriology towards a more mature engagement with stylistic studies, close readings, narrative analyses, and poetic reflections.

This series is for researchers in ancient religion and Assyriology as well as adjacent disciplines, such as religious studies, classics, biblical studies, ancient Near Eastern studies, and comparative and world literature. The series will benefit graduate and undergraduate students, scholars, and audiences with an interest in the religion of the ancient world.

# *Enuma Elish*

## *The Babylonian Epic of Creation*

Edited by Johannes Haubold, Sophus Helle,
Enrique Jiménez, and Selena Wisnom

BLOOMSBURY ACADEMIC
LONDON • NEW YORK • OXFORD • NEW DELHI • SYDNEY

BLOOMSBURY ACADEMIC
Bloomsbury Publishing Plc
50 Bedford Square, London, WC1B 3DP, UK
1385 Broadway, New York, NY 10018, USA
29 Earlsfort Terrace, Dublin 2, Ireland

BLOOMSBURY, BLOOMSBURY ACADEMIC and the Diana logo
are trademarks of Bloomsbury Publishing Plc

First published in Great Britain 2025



Series Design: Stefan Killen
Cover image: Deep blue Lapis lazuli rock (c) Damian Pawlos/istock



A catalogue record for this book is available from the British Library.

A catalogue record for this book is available from the Library of Congress.

ISBN: HB: 978-1-3502-9716-6
PB: 978-1-3502-9719-7
ePDF: 978-1-3502-9717-3
eBook: 978-1-3502-9718-0

Series: The Library of Babylonian Literature

Typeset by Integra Software Services Pvt. Ltd.

To find out more about our authors and books visit www.bloomsbury.com
and sign up for our newsletters.

# Contents


List of Contributors vii
Preface: Introducing the *Library of Babylonian Literature* x
Acknowledgments xi

Part One *Enuma Elish*

Introduction *Sophus Helle* 3

*Enuma Elish*
Transcription by *Adrian C. Heinrich* and translation by *Sophus Helle* 25

Part Two The History of the Epic

1 Marduk and the battle with the sea: On the dating of *Enuma Elish* *Enrique Jiménez* 99
2 *Enuma Elish* in cult and ritual performance *Céline Debourse* 115
3 The cuneiform reception of *Enuma Elish* *Frances Reynolds* 129
4 *Enuma Elish* outside the cuneiform tradition *Eckart Frahm* 151
5 Monstrous mothers and metal bands: *Enuma Elish* today *Gina Konstantopoulos* 166

Part Three Major Themes

6 Marduk's elevation: A masterpiece of political thought *Gösta Gabriel* 181
7 Divine rhetoric: *Enuma Elish* on communication and emotion *Johannes Haubold* 198
8 A mirror for queens: Gender, motherhood, and power in *Enuma Elish* *Karen Sonik* 215
9 *Enuma Elish*, knowledge of the heavens, and world order *Francesca Rochberg* 237

Part Four Poetics and Hermeneutics

10 Soothing the sea: Intertextuality and lament in *Enuma Elish* *Selena Wisnom* 259

11 The shape of water: Content and form in *Enuma Elish* *Sophus Helle* 279

12 The sound of creation: The revolutionary poetics of *Enuma Elish* *Piotr Michalowski* 296

13 Marduk's names and cuneiform hermeneutics *Marc Van De Mieroop* 320

Index 333

# Contributors

**Céline Debourse** is Assistant Professor in Near Eastern Languages and Civilizations at Harvard University, USA. She is an Assyriologist specializing in the languages, history, and religion of Babylonia during the first millennium BCE, with a focus on the final centuries of cuneiform culture. Her work draws on a broad spectrum of methods and disciplines, from rigorous philological analysis, through historical criticism and literary studies, to the application of sociological and anthropological theories. She furthermore aims to embed Babylonia in wider Near Eastern history and to foster dialogues between Assyriology and other disciplines.

**Eckart Frahm** is Professor of Near Eastern Languages and Civilizations at Yale University, USA. His research interests focus on Assyrian and Babylonian history, cuneiform scholarly texts, and the connections between literature, religion, and politics in ancient Mesopotamia and Israel. Frahm is the (co-)author or (co-)editor of nine books, among them, most recently, *Assyria: The Rise and Fall of the World's First Empire* (2023). He is the director of the *Cuneiform Commentaries Project* (http://ccp.yale.edu) and has served as an expert witness in a number of high-profile cases of trafficking in cultural artefacts from the Middle East.

**Gösta Gabriel** is an Assyriologist and head of an independent junior research group (Emmy Noether-Gruppe) at the Freie Universität Berlin, Germany. His research focuses on mythological narratives (in literary and other sources) and the ways in which they convey ancient ideas and discourses. He has worked intensively on *Enuma Elish* (a monograph was published in 2014, followed by several articles). More recently, he has been working on the *Sumerian King List* and is preparing a book on the early tradition of the hero Gilgamesh and the ways in which this figure had been shaped and repeatedly reinterpreted.

**Johannes Haubold** is Professor of Classics at Princeton University, USA. He has published widely on contact and exchange between the literatures of ancient Greece and Mesopotamia (e.g. *Greece and Mesopotamia: Dialogues in Literature*, 2013); and on the Chaldean movement and its roots in Babylonian celestial scholarship (e.g. ed., with John Steele and Kathryn Stevens, *Keeping Watch in Babylon: The Astronomical Diaries in Context*, 2019).

**Sophus Helle** is a postdoctoral researcher at Princeton University, USA. He holds a PhD in Comparative Literature from Aarhus University and has translated the Babylonian epic *Gilgamesh* (2021) and the Sumerian poems attributed to Enheduana (2023), accompanying both translations with in-depth studies of the texts. He has published on the recurrent narrative structures, poetic forms, authorship, gender and sexuality, and modern reception of cuneiform poetry. He is also a freelance correspondent for the Danish newspaper *Weekendavisen*, writing on premodern literature and history more broadly.

**Enrique Jiménez** is Chair of Ancient Near Eastern Literatures at LMU, Germany, and the winner of a 2017 Sofja Kovalevskaja Award. He specializes in the literature and scholarly texts from ancient Mesopotamia, in particular from the first millennium BCE. He is PI of the *electronic Babylonian Literature* platform (http://www.ebl.lmu.de/).

**Gina Konstantopoulos** is Assistant Professor in Assyriology and Cuneiform Studies in the Department of Near Eastern Languages and Cultures at the University of California Los Angeles, USA. She works on religion and magic in Mesopotamia, Sumerian and Akkadian literature, and the modern reception of the ancient Near East. Her publications include *The Divine/Demonic Seven and the Places of Demons in Mesopotamia* (2023) and the co-edited volume *The Shape of Stores* (2023). She has previously held research positions at the Institute for the Study of the Ancient World, the University of Helsinki, and the University of Tsukuba.

**Piotr Michalowski** is George G. Cameron Professor Emeritus of Ancient Mesopotamian Civilizations at the University of Michigan, USA. He studied at the University of Warsaw and at Yale University (PhD 1976). His research interests focus on many aspects of the cultures of Mesopotamia, including languages, linguistics, literatures, poetics, mythology, history, historiography, politics, pedagogy, as well as music and urbanism.

**Frances Reynolds** is Shillito Fellow and Associate Professor of Assyriology in the Faculty of Asian and Middle Eastern Studies at the University of Oxford, UK. She is also a Senior Research Fellow at The Queen's College, University of Oxford. Her broad research area is the intellectual history, literature and religion of Mesopotamia in the first millennium BCE. Her second book, *A Babylon Calendar Treatise: Scholars and Invaders in the Late First Millennium BC* (2019), reflects her focus on Babylon and Marduk's Esagil temple. Through research, graduate supervision and teaching, she seeks to understand texts in their ancient settings.

**Francesca Rochberg** is Catherine and William L. Magistretti Distinguished Professor of Near Eastern Studies Emerita in the Department of Middle Eastern Languages and Cultures at the University of California, Berkeley, USA. She is the author of the recent monographs *Before Nature: Cuneiform Knowledge and the History of Science* (2016) and *Worldmaking and Cuneiform Antiquity: An Anthropology of Science* (forthcoming).

**Karen Sonik** is a cultural historian specializing in the ancient Near East. She is the author of numerous works on Sumerian and Akkadian narratives and editor of *The Routledge Handbook of Emotions in the Ancient Near East* (with U. Steinert, 2023); *Art/*

*ifacts and ArtWorks in the Ancient World* (2021), *Journey to the City: A Companion to the Middle East Galleries at the Penn Museum* (with S. Tinney; 2019), *The Materiality of Divine Agency* (with B. Pongratz-Leisten; 2015), and *Contemporary Approaches to Mesopotamian Literature: How to Tell a Story* (with D. Shehata; Brill, forthcoming).

**Marc Van De Mieroop** is Miriam Champion Professor of History at Columbia University, USA, and director of its Center for the Ancient Mediterranean. He has published numerous books and articles on various aspects of ancient Near Eastern history, Egyptian history and World History with interests ranging from socio-economic and political history to intellectual history. He has also written extensively on historical methodology as it applies to his field of study. His most recent books, *Philosophy before the Greeks: The Pursuit of Truth in Ancient Babylonia* (Princeton University Press, 2015) and *Before and After Babel: Writing as Resistance in Ancient Near Eastern Empires* (Oxford University Press, 2023), investigate the underlying principles of Babylonian hermeneutics and their relationship to the various writing systems of the ancient Near Eastern world. He has received various fellowships including from the Guggenheim Foundation, the ACLS, the NEH, and the Internationales Forschungszentrum Kulturwissenschaften in Vienna.

**Selena Wisnom** is Lecturer in the Heritage of the Middle East at the University of Leicester, UK. She is a specialist in the literary and cultural interpretation of cuneiform sources, particularly literature, poetics and intellectual history. As a playwright she has written three plays set in ancient Assyria, and adapts Babylonian verse forms for poetry in English. Her book *Weapons of Words: Intertextual Competition in Babylonian Poetry* was published in 2020, and *The Library of Ancient Wisdom* is forthcoming with Penguin and University of Chicago Press.

# Preface: Introducing the *Library of Babylonian Literature*

The Editors

Babylonian literature is a treasure trove of poetic gems, but only a few are known outside the discipline of Assyriology. While students of world literature may have heard of *Gilgamesh*, they are often surprised to discover that Babylonian poetry is much richer and more diverse than the fame of this single text would suggest. The *Library of Babylonian Literature* (*LBL*) aims to make the major works of literature in the Akkadian language more accessible to new readers, while helping scholars to study them and artists to adapt them.

Each volume in the series is divided into three parts. The first introduces readers to a specific work of Akkadian literature, offering basic guidance on its structure, history, and main themes. The second provides a transcription of the Akkadian text, based on the platform *electronic Babylonian Literature* (*eBL*), and a facing translation into English. Significant points of textual uncertainty and variation are noted, but readers wishing to learn more about spellings, variant readings, and editorial challenges should refer to the online *eBL* editions, to which the *LBL* acts as a companion series. The third part offers a selection of specially commissioned essays by leading scholars in the field that both survey current scholarship and advance it in new directions, serving as a state-of-the-art companion to the ancient work under discussion.

The Babylonian epic *Enuma Elish* inaugurates the series. Throughout the first millennium BCE, it was central to Babylonian religion, culture, and politics – even when its worldview met with criticism and resistance. It is the best attested poem among what survives of Akkadian literature, and it had a pronounced impact on neighbouring cultures, as evidenced by several Greek texts as well as the biblical book of Genesis. The intellectual sophistication and rich poetic patterning of *Enuma Elish* help to articulate the premise that animates this whole series: Babylonian literature rewards sustained, attentive engagement, not only at the level of individual lines and phrases but also in terms of the broader vision of the world embedded in each text. It is our hope that the series will expand our understanding of what Akkadian poetry is and reveal its treasures to contemporary readers.

# Acknowledgments

This work is published open access with funding from Princeton University and LMU Munich.

Extracts from the following sources are not covered by the book's Creative Commons licence. All rights in this material are reserved. For permission to re-use, please contact the copyright holder.

Assadi and Naamneh (2018); Bardazzi (2014); Baruchi-Unna (2013); Beaulieu (2021); Betegh (2002); Buccellati (1990); Brikmann (1998/2000);Civil (1979); Cohen (1988); Cohen (2013); Chicago Assyrian Dictionary; Crisostomo (2019); Dalley (2002); Dissection (2006); Dirven (1999); Foster (2005;) Falkenstein (1931); Felski (2011); Frahm (2013); Frahm and Jiménez (2015); Frahm, Frazer and Jiménez (2013–2022); Frymer-Kensky (1992); Gabriel (2018); Gabriel (2018b); Gabriel (2014); Glaister (2020); Geller (2014); Geller (2018); George (1991); George (1992); Grayson (1975); Grayson (2014); Gunkel's (1895); Helle (2020); Helle (2023); Hallo (2004); Haubold (2013); Horton (1993); Hobbes (2002); Horowitz (2014); Hunger (1976); Jacobsen (1976); Kämmerer and Metzler (2012); Köcher (1978); Kvanvig (2011); Lambert (1963); Lambert (1980); Lambert (1986); Lambert (1984); Lambert (1994); Lambert (1998); Lambert (2013); Loisel (2016); Livingstone (1986); Maiwald (2022);Metzler (2012); MNB (1848); Notley (2001); Nabû-mushesi; Oppenheim (1974); Peterson (1999); Pongratz-Leisten (1994);Reiner (1985); Reiner and Pingree (1981); Reynolds (2019); Rochberg (2009); Rochberg (2010); Rubio (2013); Scurlock and Andersen (2005); Sommer (2000); Sonik (2020); Steinkeller (1999); Sparks (2007); Solomon (2012); Smith (1876); Taylor and Cartwright (2011); Thomas (1954); Tolkien (1936); Tolkien (1966); von Soden (1953); von Soden (1955); Edubdubabba (K 1356); Wasserman (2006); Winters (2020); Wisnom (2020); Woloch (2003); Woloch (2006); Zgoll (2019).

# Part One

# *Enuma Elish*

# Introduction

Sophus Helle

*Enuma Elish* marks a turning point in Babylonian culture. It is no exaggeration to say that, in cuneiform literature and religion, there is a time before and a time after the composition of *Enuma Elish*. It is the cuneiform poem of which most manuscripts survive, attesting to its importance among the scribes of the first millennium BCE, and it would come to be ritually performed every year during the Babylonian New Year festival, the *akītu* (see Debourse in this volume). The changes it wrought to the cultures of ancient Iraq can be summarized in one sentence: it established the divine supremacy of Marduk and Babylon.

At the outset of the second millennium BCE, the cuneiform pantheon was ruled by a triad of gods – the king of the gods Enlil, their forefather Anu, and the creator god Ea – and Enlil's city of Nippur, while it was never the region's most powerful political entity, was seen as the *axis mundi*, the midpoint of the universe. The following centuries saw a gradual shift that culminated in the political programme of *Enuma Elish*: the poem formulated, cemented, and perhaps accelerated the advent of a new worldview in which Babylon was the centre of the universe and its god Marduk the king of the cosmos.[1] Beginning with the military conquests of the Babylonian king Hammurabi (*r. c.* 1792–1750 BCE), Babylon gradually established itself as the main seat of power in southern Iraq. With the composition of *Enuma Elish*, which probably took place at the end of the second millennium BCE (see Jiménez in this volume), this development found a parallel in the cultural, literary, and religious sphere: Enlil was ousted from divine supremacy and Anu and Ea were sidelined by Marduk, the new king of the gods. *Enuma Elish* justifies Marduk's supremacy, explaining that he earned it by vanquishing the primordial sea Tiamat and creating the universe as we know it from her corpse.[2] It is unclear whether *Enuma Elish* reflects changes that had already taken place or whether it was the work of a pro-Marduk religious avant-garde that sought to promote this agenda (see Jiménez in this volume), but either way, its legacy was enduring: it formulated the Marduk-centric worldview that would shape cuneiform literature for the following millennium.

However, this should not be taken to mean that the epic's worldview was universally accepted. On the contrary, we can take *Enuma Elish* to mark a moment of seminal change precisely because of the reactions it provoked, many of them critical (for the epic's ancient reception, see Reynolds and Frahm in this volume).[3] As detailed below, counternarratives to *Enuma Elish* were produced by at least one Babylonian poet, by Assyrian ideologues after the sack of Babylon in 689 BCE, and by Jewish authors during the Babylonian captivity of the sixth century BCE. That is, both those who conquered and those who were conquered by Babylon, as well as some Babylonians themselves, responded to *Enuma Elish* by using its poetic language and sweeping vision to fashion an alternative worldview in response. It is a testament to the poem's power that even those who fought it did so on its own terms (see Reynolds, Frahm, and Helle in this volume).

The following pages will lay out the plot and narrative structure of the epic, and the literary language and poetic style in which it is written. I then sketch out the epic's literary history (which is explored in more detail in Part One of this volume), briefly describing its origins, reception, and state of preservation. I summarize the history of modern scholarship on the epic and the major themes that recur in the chapters of this volume, and conclude by introducing the translation and transcription. Before launching into this discussion, one key question of terminology must be addressed. Here and throughout the volume, *Enuma Elish* will be referred to as an 'epic'. An epic is conventionally defined as 'a long narrative poem in elevated style recounting the deeds of a legendary or historical hero',[4] and *Enuma Elish* abides by every element of that definition. It is, at least by cuneiform standards, long (with 1,095 lines, it is the second-longest Akkadian poem, after *Gilgamesh*); it is a narrative poem; and it centres on the deeds of the heroic god Marduk. However, some scholars have resisted the application of 'Western' literary categories – including the term 'epic' – to cuneiform poetry, arguing that these categories inevitably skew our perception of ancient texts (e.g. Michalowski 2010; see also the references collected in Kämmerer and Metzler 2012: 2–4). For example, viewing *Enuma Elish* as an epic may focus our attention on the narrative portions of the poem and away from the hymnic recitation of Marduk's names with which it ends (in the second half of Tablet VI and most of Tablet VII), which according to Marc Van De Mieroop in this volume contains 'the point of the entire poem': Thomas Kämmerer and Kai Metzler point to this passage as a non-narrative and hence 'hymnic' rather than 'epic' section of the text (Kämmerer and Metzler 2012: 3). Likewise, some scholars have objected against the traditional titling of the poem as 'The Epic of Creation', arguing that this name reflects a stereotypically Western obsession with origins that risks overshadowing the poem's main theme – the supremacy of Marduk (e.g. Michalowski 1990: 383; Vanstiphout 1992: 52; and the overview and references in Kämmerer and Metzler 2012: 4–6).

In this volume, we have decided to retain the term 'epic', given how well the text fits the criteria by which the genre is defined. We believe that 'epic' can be a useful and flexible cross-cultural category, and the list of Marduk's names is in fact an apt illustration of that reach. Long lists and catalogues are an established feature of the epic genre, appearing in many epics from around the world, from the Greek *Iliad* to the Sanskrit *Mahabharata* (Reitz, Lämmle and Wesselmann 2019). When *Enuma Elish* is included in the category of epics, such similarities are brought to the fore. That is, instead of defining 'epics' in the terms set up by the Homeric poems and other Western texts and treating every new addition to the category with suspicion, we can allow texts such as *Enuma Elish* to expand and transform our understanding of what an epic is.

## Story and structure

Like most cuneiform literary works, *Enuma Elish* took its ancient title from its incipit, that is, the first words of the text. And like most cuneiform incipits, these words were not randomly chosen but introduce a key theme of the work: *enūma eliš* means 'When above', setting the action of the story in the distant past and in an elevated sphere. This past, we soon learn, is the oldest past possible – a time before gods, names, destinies, and fixed shapes. In the beginning, all that exists are two primordial seas, Apsû and Tiamat, and the first generation of gods are born from the confluence of their waters (I 1–9). The seven Tablets[5] of the epic track a transformation from this initial state of absolute fluidity to an ordered, strictly hierarchical world that has Babylon at its centre and Marduk as its king.

The first generation of gods is followed by more divine births, a process that culminates in the birth of Ea, whose massive strength and superior intellect set him apart from his ancestors (I 15–20). In a motif that recurs across cuneiform literature, the noise of the younger gods disturbs the sleep of the primordial seas within whose waters they live, infuriating Apsû to the point that he decides to kill his offspring (I 21–40).[6] He ignores Tiamat's protests, listening instead to his flattering minister Mummu (I 41–54), but Ea hears of his schemes and seizes the initiative, pacifying Apsû and Mummu with a magic spell before binding and killing them (I 55–70). Ea then carries out the first truly creative act of the poem: he shapes Apsû – once a shapeless expanse of water – into a definite region of the world, making his corpse into a home in which Ea will dwell with his wife Damkina (I 71–8). To a Babylonian audience, this development would have come as no surprise: Apsû was the name of a mythical subterranean lake from which freshwater was thought to rise and in which Ea lived.

Ea's act of creation concludes the first episode of the poem. As many scholars have noted, the narrative section of *Enuma Elish* is divided into two parallel acts: Ea's battle against Apsû and his subsequent act of creation are mirrored and expanded by his son Marduk's battle against Tiamat and creation of an all-encompassing cosmic order from Tiamat's corpse.[7] The first episode thus lays out the narrative template that the rest of the story will develop on a much grander scale. The two episodes are bound together by exact lexical parallels, especially the line, 'After he had bound and slain his foes' (*ištu lemnīšu ikmû isādu*, I 73 = IV 123), which describes first Ea's and then Marduk's triumph (Katz 2011: 129). As Gösta Gabriel (2014: 189–91) shows in his study of the epic, the parallels between Ea's and Marduk's actions repeatedly stress the latter's superiority: Marduk surpasses his father, and by implication all other gods, at every turn. The epic thus adapts a recurrent motif in cuneiform literature – a division of the narrative into two acts, of which the second mirrors and expands the first (Helle 2020) – to bring out Marduk's supremacy, which is the poem's constant concern.[8]

Marduk's birth, at the exact midpoint of Tablet I (I 81–2), is followed by a panegyric extolling his might and incomprehensible nature (I 83–104). But this hymn soon gives way to the next crisis of the poem: Marduk's youthful play with the four winds roils the waters of Tiamat, disturbing the peace of an unnamed group of gods who take their complaint to their primordial mother (I 105–24). Again, it is worth noting that at this point, the entire universe, outside of the Apsû that has become Ea's home, consists of Tiamat's endless expanse, in which the gods live. When Marduk's winds send waves through her waters, he thus disturbs the home of all the gods except Ea and his family in the Apsû. Tiamat, provoked by the accusation that she did not stand by Apsû in his moment of need, is roused into action. She gives birth to an army of monsters with which she plans to wipe out Marduk and Ea's lineage of gods, which is currently ruled by their ancestor Anshar (I 125–46). Tiamat chooses one of the disgruntled gods, Qingu, as her partner and general of her army, granting him the Tablet of Destinies that lends power to his decrees (I 147–62). As the Anshar gods scramble to respond to this new threat, their messages to each other repeat the description of Tiamat's army three more times in Tablets II and III. While these repetitions can be off-putting to modern readers, they would have been more poetically effective in an ancient aural performance, building up dramatic tension and the perceived threat of Tiamat's army (Wisnom 2023). Furthermore, as argued by Johannes Haubold in this volume, the repetitions effectively safeguard the flow of communication among the Anshar gods, preventing the silence that would signal total social breakdown and building up agreement within the divine circle: the repetitions thus mark stages in an evolutionary process that will eventually yield the 'institutional scaffolding' of Babylonian kingship, including counsellors, messengers, and an advising assembly.

Anshar is enraged at Ea, because as he sees it, it was Ea's killing of Apsû that provoked Tiamat's anger (II 49–56). Ea manages to soothe him with an eloquent speech (II 57–70, see Haubold in this volume), and takes it upon himself to defeat Tiamat with another magic spell (II 71–80). However, he is overwhelmed by her power and fails, and when Anshar sends Ea's father Anu to attempt a reconciliation, Anu fails too, casting the Anshar gods into despair (II 81–126). This motif, in which several characters attempt and fail to carry out the task that will be eventually completed by the main character of the story, has deep roots in cuneiform literature, stretching back to Sumerian poetry.[9] Realizing that the crisis affords him a unique opportunity, Ea encourages Marduk to step forth and volunteer to take on Tiamat (II 127–34), which Marduk promptly does. But he also makes an extraordinary demand: in return for defeating Tiamat, he requests universal kingship (II 135–62). Anshar assents to gathering the gods in their place of assembly, the Ubshu-ukkinnaku (III 1–10), and amid much merriment and drinking (III 129–36), the gathered gods ratify Marduk's power in a speech that, as Gösta Gabriel argues in this volume, formulates an implicit theory of kingship, including a set of reciprocal obligations (IV 1–18). As a final test of the efficacy of his words, they create a constellation and ask Marduk to destroy and recreate it by the power of his speech, which he does (IV 19–28). Marduk then arms himself and sets off for battle (IV 35–62).

The battle between Marduk and Tiamat is placed midway through the poem, in Tablet IV. After Marduk confounds Qingu and the rest of the army by the sheer force of his presence (IV 65–70), he and Tiamat rouse each other to combat with mutual provocations (IV 71–92). In the end, the battle is short: Marduk traps Tiamat in his mighty net and unleashes his wind – his weapon of choice – into her mouth, paralysing her. He then shoots an arrow into her heart, binds her, and smothers her (IV 93–104). He quickly despatches her army of monsters, taking all of them prisoners, and reclaims the Tablet of Destinies from Qingu (IV 105–22). After announcing his victory to the rest of the Anshar gods, Marduk proceeds to shape Tiamat's corpse into the world that we see around us, splitting her into two halves, which will become the skies and the earth, respectively (IV 123–40). Tiamat is essentially turned inside out, creating an air bubble within her expansive waters: that bubble is the cosmos we inhabit (Wisnom forthcoming). Heaven and earth are positioned on top of the Apsû, yielding a tripartite structure, with each layer ruled by one of the traditional heads of the pantheon: Anu in the heavens, Enlil on earth, and Ea in the Apsû (IV 141–6; on the shape of the Babylonian cosmos, see Horowitz 2011).

Having established the broad outlines of the cosmos at the end of Tablet IV, Marduk hones in on the specifics in Tablet V, which is the least well-preserved part of the epic. First, he creates the pattern of the months, the year, and the night-sky, as detailed by Francesca Rochberg in this volume (V 1–52). The Babylonians envisaged the stars, the Moon, the Sun, the visible planets, and the constellations as the astral manifestations of the gods, which was one way in which the gods were present in the world – one of their 'modes of existence', as it were (Rochberg 2009). Marduk, for example, was simultaneously an omnipotent deity, the cult statue in his temple, a character in mythological stories, and several stars in the night-sky, most notably the planet Neberu (see Rochberg in this volume on the identity of that planet). By organizing the night-sky, Marduk thus creates the heavenly stations and paths that the astral manifestation of the gods will travel. He then turns to the earth, moulding Tiamat's limbs into geographical features: her breasts become mountains, rivers flow from her eyes, her tail becomes the bond between heaven and earth, and so on (V 53–66). Finally, after a second confirmation of his kingship (V 109–16), Marduk builds his city, Babylon, at the centre of the newly organized cosmos and makes it the seat of his kingship and of the gods' assembly (V 117–30).

Tablet VI opens with Marduk's decision to create humankind, borrowing and reworking a scene from the older Babylonian epic *Atra-hasis* (see Wisnom in this volume). In that epic, the lower gods revolt against the higher gods, protesting against the burden of labour that had been imposed on them during the creation of the world, but Ea defuses the standoff by creating humankind to take over the work, allowing the gods to rest. In *Enuma Elish*, Marduk anticipates this problem and creates humanity, placing the burden of work on our shoulders and so allowing the gods to enjoy our offerings in a state of permanent ease. Only afterwards does he divide the gods into a higher and a lower rank, thus preventing the crisis we see in *Atra-hasis* (VI 1–46; Wisnom 2020: 124–8). In *Atra-hasis*, humanity is created jointly by Ea and the mother goddess Belet-ili, but in the more misogynist account we find in *Enuma Elish*, it is created by two male gods after the killing and brutal dismemberment of the cosmic mother Tiamat (Helle 2020; for the gender politics of *Enuma Elish*, see Sonik in this volume). In return for freeing them from labour, the gods create Marduk's main temple in Babylon, the Esagil (VI 47–69), and gather there for a second scene of merriment and drinking, in which Marduk's power is reaffirmed once more (VI 70–120).

At this banquet, the gods grant Marduk fifty names, each of which is matched by a corresponding destiny that Marduk is to fulfil. The enumeration of names and destinies begins in Tablet VI (VI 121–66) and lasts until the end of Tablet VII (VII 1–144), in yet another creative adaptation of a long-lasting trope of cuneiform literature, in which narratives end with a climactic list.[10] The number of Marduk's names is highly significant: fifty was traditionally the divine number of Enlil, so by assuming fifty names, Marduk also assumes Enlil's traditional position as king of the gods – explicitly so at the end of the list, where Enlil gives Marduk his own name, 'Lord of the Lands' (*bēl mātāti*, VII 136; Röllig 1957–1971: 500). Shortly thereafter, Marduk is referred to as 'the Enlil of the gods' (*enlil ilī*, VII 149), that is, the leader of the pantheon. A key premise of the list of Marduk's names is that the relation between the names and the accompanying destinies is not arbitrary; rather, the two are seen as expressions and extensions of one another (see Van De Mieroop and Helle in this volume). In some instances, the link between them is obvious (in his role as Malah, name no. 29, Marduk is to be a ferryman, because *malaḫḫu* means 'ferryman' in Akkadian, VII 76–7); in many cases, the link relies on the Sumerian meaning of the name, as explained in the notes to the translation. Further, one of the two commentaries to the epic, Commentary II, traces linguistic associations between the names and each word of the accompanying fate, as explained by Van De Mieroop in this volume.

The epic ends with a brief epilogue (VII 143–62), describing how the names were revealed to an anonymous author who refers to himself as 'the first one' (*maḫrû*): he recited the epic before Marduk, receiving his approval, and then wrote it down so that it could be passed on to future generations. This epilogue is yet another instance of the epic reworking a traditional trope of cuneiform literature: as noted by Benjamin Foster, many Akkadian poems end by describing their own composition, but *Enuma Elish* is particularly insistent on presenting its author as merely the first in a chain of scribes and scholars who will carry the text through time (Foster 1991: 21–3; Helle 2023b: 93–107; Cancik-Kirschbaum and Wagensonner 2017). The epic glorifies the deeds of Marduk and the supremacy of Babylon one final time and spells out its ambitions that it will be transmitted into the far future – ambitions that did, by and large, come true.

## Style and prosody

*Enuma Elish* is one of the most stylistically impressive poems in Akkadian (see the stylistic analyses in Vanstiphout 1992; Kämmerer and Metzler 2012: 55–71; Gabriel 2014). It combines an erudite vocabulary, an intricate patterning of sounds, and unusual syntactical arrangements to create an extraordinarily vivid linguistic landscape. One of its main poetic devices is assonance and alliteration, as in the phrase *lišāna liškunū ina qerêti lišbū* ('let there be conversation, let them sit down for a feast', III 8), with its triple repetition of *liš*, or the spectacular line *naḫlapta apluḫta pulḫāti ḫalip-ma* ('He was clad in an armoured garment of dread', IV 57), with its fourfold play on the consonants *ḫ*, *l*, and *p*, which Lambert (2013: 475) considered 'unique in Akkadian poetry'. The text brims with wordplay, as in striking expressions like *libbuš lippuš* ('let her heart relax', II 100), or the phrase *rummi kiṣrīša* ('Disband her troops', II 93), which literally means 'unknot the bond', playing on the double meanings of the word *kiṣru*: 'troops' and 'knot'.

As with Akkadian poetry in general, *Enuma Elish* has no fixed rhyme scheme; end rhymes are rare and their significance is unclear.[11] Internal rhymes are more common, especially in conjunction with parallelism, chiasmus, and other stylistic features, as in the line *urriš lā šupšuḫāku mūšiš lā ṣallāku* ('By day I have no rest, by night no sleep', I 38), where two words ending in *-iš* parallel two words ending in *-āku*. A particularly telling example is the line that describes the first clash between Tiamat and Marduk: *šašmiš itlupū qitrubū tāḫāziš* (they 'entwined in single combat, closing in for the fray, IV 94). The entwining of the gods is mirrored by the chiastic construction of the line, where the two nouns ending in *-iš* bracket two verbs with the vowel structure *i-u-ū*. Such elaborate arrangements of sense, sound and syntax are found throughout the poem. Two particularly interesting sets of wordplay revolve around the syllables *mu* and *lu*. The first is discussed in this volume by Michalowski, who shows that the epic evokes the fluid origins of the world through an extended set of puns on the sound *mu*, which in Akkadian means 'water'. Likewise, the passage in which Marduk announces the creation of humankind repeats the syllable *lu* fourteen times in just six lines (and the consonant *l* a further eight times in the same lines, VI 5–10), because in Sumerian, it means 'human' (**lu**$_2$). Through these bilingual puns, which filter Sumerian sense through Akkadian sounds, the epic instils in the mind of the reader a deep association between words and thing: the author of the epic saw the linguistic fabric of Sumerian, Akkadian and cuneiform as an inextricable part of creation itself, as shown in more detail by Helle, Michalowski, and Van De Mieroop in this volume.

Many of these word games are made possible by the poetic language in which the text is written, Standard Babylonian, a version of the Akkadian language that, much like Homeric Greek, was never actually spoken but was used for poetry, royal inscriptions, and other 'elevated' compositions. Standard Babylonian is characterized by a free word order (as opposed to the subject-object-verb order that is the norm in Akkadian), as well as archaizing grammatical forms and an expanded vocabulary (Hecker 1974). But even by the standards of Standard Babylonian poetry, *Enuma Elish* is exceedingly fond of rare words. To take just one, particularly significant example, the word used at the very beginning of the poem to describe the uncreated world, *ammatu* 'ground' (I 2), is found only here and in one other Akkadian text, *Ludlul*, which may have borrowed it from *Enuma Elish*: the text avoids using the more common term 'earth' (*erṣetu*) until the earth is created in V 62.[12] The text also deploys unusual syntactical constructions, such as 'Janus sentences' in which one grammatical element is part of two different clauses that are placed on either side of it. For example, when Apsû declares that he will kill his children, he says: *lušḫalliq-ma alkassunu lusappiḫ* ('I will destroy their ways, disrupt them!', I 39), with the noun *alkassunu*, 'their ways', serving as the object of both verbs. In the translation that accompanies the edition by Kämmerer and Metzler (2012: 315–549), Janus sentences are marked by commas in brackets around the central grammatical element.

As well as playing with sound, *Enuma Elish* also plays with the way it is written, using the polyvalence of the cuneiform script to arrange its signs in striking ways. The phrase 'to the gods', *ana ilī*, is rendered in several cases as the sign DINGIR repeated three times: first in the phonemic reading *an*, abbreviating *ana*, and then as the reduplicated sign dingir, meaning *ilu*, 'god', with the reduplication being one possible way of indicating a plural form. This play with the multiple meanings of cuneiform signs and the blend of Sumerian and Akkadian discussed above reaches a climax in the list of Marduk's names, in which these strategies are deployed to spectacular effect, as detailed by Van De Mieroop in this volume.

It is unclear whether Akkadian poetry employed a regular prosodical pattern, since Akkadian metre remains poorly understood (see the study of metre in *Enuma Elish* in Lambert 2013: 17–34). The opening lines of *Enuma Elish*, to which I return below, have repeatedly served as a 'prosodical guinea pig': several scholars have used them to test their models of how Akkadian poetry is to be scanned (Buccellati 1990: 125–8; West 1997: 187; Helle 2014: 69–71; Wisnom 2015: 499–500). Despite this uncertainty, two things are clear. Most but not all lines of Akkadian poetry end on a stressed syllable followed by an unstressed one, that is, a trochaic ending, suggesting that the metrical structure of Akkadian poetry, if it existed, was based on stress rather than syllable length (see Lambert 2013: 18–20). Second, many but again not all lines display a strong middle caesura, that is, a division into two half-lines. According to the most prevalent school of thought, such half-lines can be further subdivided into two 'beats', which are loosely defined as significant semantic units: the poem would thus alternate between four-beat lines, in which the caesura is readily apparent, and three-beat lines, in which it is not.[13] Moreover, most lines can be grouped into couplets, and sometimes, but less consistently, those couplets combine to form quatrains.

A particularly prominent feature of *Enuma Elish*, and of cuneiform poetry in general, is the extensive parallelism between half-lines in a line, lines in a couplet, and couplets in a quatrain. Borrowing a phrase from biblical criticism, the grammatical parallelism between half-lines is often referred to as *parallelismus membrorum*, but it is worth noting that, just as in Hebrew poetry, the parallelism is often combined with chiasm and other forms of contrast, yielding elegant patterns of symmetry and reversal. Consider this speech by Apsû, in which he declares his murderous intentions to Tiamat:

*imtarṣam-ma alkassunu elīya*
*urriš lā šupšuḫāku mūšiš lā ṣallāku*
*lušḫalliq-ma alkassunu lusappiḫ*
*qūlu liššakin-ma i niṣlal nīnu*

Their ways disturb me.
By day I have no rest, by night no sleep.
I will destroy their ways, disrupt them!
Let silence be settled, so that we may sleep.

(I 37–40)

I have already noted the rhyming parallelism of the second line and the Janus construction of the third, but the elegance of the speech lies especially in the way it concatenates different elements into larger wholes. The second and fourth lines are both divided into two half-lines (making them 'four-beat lines') with a clear parallel both internally and between them (note the recurrence of the word *ṣalālu*, 'sleep'). The first and third lines also mirror each other, as they both consist of three words (making them 'three-beat lines'), the second of which is *alkassunu*, 'their ways'. This parallelism between the couplets is offset by a reversal in their meaning: the first couplet describes Apsû's problem and the second his infanticidal solution, with the implicit contrast between the sleep he craves and the violence he plans structuring the speech (on this theme, see Machinist 1983, 2005). This arrangement is typical of the text, which likes to build up its poetic structure through a dynamic set of parallels and contrasts that tie smaller elements into progressively larger units – up to and including the level of the plot, which as noted above, relies on both the contrast and the symmetry between Ea's defeat of Apsû and Marduk's much grander defeat of Tiamat.

## Literary history

The literary origins of *Enuma Elish* are shrouded in two controversies. The first concerns its date of composition, as discussed by Enrique Jiménez in this volume. Some scholars, notably Stephanie Dalley (1997), have argued for an early date, namely the Old Babylonian period (the eighteenth to seventeenth century BCE) when Babylon first rose to political prominence. The majority view, however, is that the epic dates to the late second millennium BCE, that is, either the final years of the Kassite dynasty (which ended in 1155 BCE) or the subsequent dynasty, called Isin II (which lasted until *c.* 1022 BCE). Wilfred G. Lambert (1964) argued that the poem was composed under the most famous king of the Isin II period, Nebuchadnezzar I (1125–1104 BCE). The Kassite dynasty was brought to the point of collapse by an invasion from neighbouring Elam: in 1155 BCE, the Elamite king Kutir-Nahhunte (dates unclear) raided Babylon and abducted Marduk's cult statue, bringing it to his capital Susa in what is now western Iran. Some four decades later, *c.* 1110 BCE, Nebuchadnezzar I successfully raided Susa and retrieved Marduk's statue, bringing it back to Babylon and thereby restoring the city's main cult. Lambert argued that this event, which would have been of paramount significance to the Babylonian clergy, prompted the composition of *Enuma Elish*, and while there is little direct evidence to support his claim, it has proven popular among Assyriologists. The evidence presented by Jiménez in this volume sets the latest possible date of composition for the epic (the *terminus ante quem*) during the reign of King Marduk-nadin-ahhe (1099–1082 BCE), just after Nebuchadnezzar.

The second controversy about the epic's origins is the degree to which it draws on mythological influences from the Western edges of the cuneiform world, especially the Ugaritic cycle of stories about the god Baal, which also includes a battle between the main god and the sea – a motif that is unknown in previous Sumerian and Akkadian literature. Some scholars have identified even more specific literary parallels between *Enuma Elish* and these Western texts (see the overview in Ayali-Darshan 2020: chap. 4, with references to previous literature). Others, including Piotr Michalowski in this volume, have resisted this idea, pointing instead to possible Babylonian and Sumerian origins for the myth of the battle against the sea. Simply put, it has been deemed strange that *Enuma Elish* should be both the most Babylonocentric text in the cuneiform record and the one that displays some of the clearest indications of influence from neighbouring traditions – but that is exactly what makes the possibility so intriguing.

While we do not know exactly when *Enuma Elish* came into being, it was almost certainly composed by a scholar from Babylon who was steeped in the cuneiform tradition and had a connection with Marduk's main temple, the Esagil. While it is possible in principle that more than one scholar collaborated on the epic, the author refers to himself in the epilogue as 'the first one' in the singular (*maḫrû*, VII 145 and 157), and describes how he recited the text before Marduk (I follow the original text in using masculine pronouns to refer to the author). He also expresses the hope that it will be discussed by the wise and the learned (VII 157 and 146, respectively), implying a religious and scholarly context for the composition. Choosing not to identify himself, the author emphasizes that he is merely a link between Marduk himself and the scribal chain that will pass the text through time (Foster 1991: 31; Cancik-Kirschbaum and Wagensonner 45–8).

Similarly, while the degree of Western influence on *Enuma Elish* is debated, the influence from other cuneiform compositions is abundantly clear. As Selena Wisnom discusses in this volume, *Enuma Elish* is an intertextually voracious poem, and its allusions to other texts are often complex and competitive: it uses older myths, especially those about the warrior god Ninurta, to show off Marduk's superior powers. The epic also refers to non-narrative texts, such as ritual lamentations (see Wisnom in this volume) and the god lists that formed the template for the list of Marduk's names (Seri 2006).

Over the course of the first millennium BCE, *Enuma Elish* achieved a remarkable popularity among cuneiform scribes and scholars (see Reynolds in this volume), as shown by the surviving manuscripts of the epic. The most recent edition of the text by the *electronic Babylonian Literature* project is based on 116 manuscripts, 71 school tablets, and 18 further fragments, as well as 27 manuscripts of commentaries (see below) and 56 quotations in other texts, for a total of 288 textual sources – an exceptional number in cuneiform literature.[14] As is often the case for Akkadian texts, the largest single find-spot for manuscripts of *Enuma Elish* is the Assyrian capital city Nineveh, which boasts forty-seven manuscripts and fragments (Lambert 2013: 3–4): most of these come from the royal archives, the so-called 'Library of Assurbanipal' (for a critique of this concept, see Robson 2019: chap. 2). These tablets were produced for the imperial court and are works of great craftmanship and scribal skill. By contrast, most of the thirty manuscripts and sixty-seven school tablets from Babylonia were illegally excavated and thus cannot be sourced to a specific location; a great number of them probably came from Babylon (Lambert 2013: 4). The numerous Babylonian school tablets show how central the epic was to the educational system of the period. It often appears on excerpt tablets where a few lines of the epic are copied next to lines from works such as *Ludlul* and other hymns to Marduk, as students familiarized themselves with canonical works of cuneiform literature by writing out small sections of them (Gesche 2000).

As is again typical of cuneiform literature, the sources are not evenly distributed among the epic's seven Tablets. The manuscripts, school tablets, and further fragments are arrayed as follows: sixty for Tablet I, thirty for Tablet II, sixteen for Tablet III, thirty for Tablet IV, eighteen for Tablet V, twenty-four for Tablet VI, and twenty-seven for Tablet VII. The scribes' interest seems to have focused on the first Tablet, as is almost universally the case with cuneiform literature (Oppenheim 1977: 243; see also Reynolds in this volume). They also valued the battle between Tiamat and Marduk in Tablet IV and the list of Marduk's names in the last two Tablets. The relative dearth of manuscripts for Tablets II and III is offset by the repetitiveness of their contents, which allows us to reconstruct most of the missing passages. Tablet V, meanwhile, was both less popular and less repetitive, making it much more difficult to reconstruct. Still, compared to other cuneiform compositions, *Enuma Elish* is remarkably well preserved.

As well as being popular with the ancient scribes, the epic was much quoted in other sources, as detailed by Frances Reynolds in this volume. It was also the subject of two commentaries, known today as 'Commentary I' and 'Commentary II'. The first glosses rare words in the text and links the narrative to ritual activities; the second, which is analysed by Van De Mieroop in this volume, seeks to explain the deeper significance of Marduk's names. As noted by Eckart Frahm in this volume, the first commentary seems at various points to offer an interpretation of the text that favours an Assyrian perspective, as when it identifies the nurse raising Marduk in I 86 with the Assyrian goddess Ishtar of Nineveh.

The reception of *Enuma Elish* in Assyria was fraught to say the least. After the Assyrian king Sennacherib razed Babylon in 689 BCE to punish the city for an uprising five years earlier that had led to the death of his son, the scholars at his court made a concerted effort to wipe Babylon off the mythological map (see Reynolds, Frahm, and Helle in this volume). A new recension of *Enuma Elish* was composed, in which Marduk was replaced by Ashur, the main Assyrian god, and Babylon by the city of Assur (Frahm 2010: 8–10). A mysterious text known as the 'Marduk Ordeal' may also date to this period: it reads scenes from the epic against the grain, turning its celebration of Marduk into a bitter criticism (see Reynolds in this volume). However, after the death of Sennacherib, his successor Esarhaddon rebuilt Babylon and restored its cult, ushering in the heyday of the epic's popularity, as noted by Lambert (2013: 464). Whether they embraced or resisted it, Assyrian scholars never ignored *Enuma Elish.*

Meanwhile, the epic continued to hold a central position in the Babylonian school curriculum as well as the city's most important religious ritual, the *akītu*, or New Year's festival. Céline Debourse in this volume discusses the gradual and complicated process by which *Enuma Elish* came to be tied to the occasion that marked the beginning of the new year and reaffirmed Marduk's supremacy over the cosmos. Yet even within Babylonia, *Enuma Elish* met with resistance. The Babylonian epic *Erra and Ishum*, which was composed during the first half of the first millennium BCE, has often been read as engaging in a creative and critical dialogue with *Enuma Elish*, adapting, or even reversing, many of its claims (see Machinist 2005; Frahm 2010; Wisnom 2020: chap. 6; and Reynolds in this volume). While *Enuma Elish* ends with the establishment of a permanent world order ruled by Marduk, *Erra* depicts the god of war Erra unleashing a catastrophic conflagration that Marduk is powerless to prevent. *Erra* can be read as claiming that a peaceful order can never be established once and for all, as *Enuma Elish* seems to imply, but must instead be constantly renewed (for this reading of *Erra*, see George 2013).

The last dateable manuscript of *Enuma Elish* was written, according to its colophon, on 5 May 495 BCE, during the reign of Darius the Great (9 Ayyāru, regnal year 27; Hunger 1968: 124, no. 422). But as shown by Reynolds in this volume, quotations of the epic in other texts indicate that it continued to be studied intensely, though in increasingly narrow circles, during the Late Babylonian period, when Babylon had fallen under the rule of the Persian, Seleucid, and Parthian empires. A particularly important testament to the epic's ongoing popularity comes from the Babylonian writer Berossus. In the third century BCE, in the aftermath of the Greek takeover of Babylon, Berossus sought to summarize cuneiform culture for a Greek audience, and his retelling of *Enuma Elish* speaks to the creativity and cleverness with which he adapted the story to suit Greek philosophical tastes (Haubold 2013; Frahm in this volume).

In fact, echoes of *Enuma Elish* continued to resound for a strikingly long time. It is generally assumed that, when the cuneiform script ceased to be used during the first century CE, practically all knowledge of cuneiform literature was lost as well – see, for example, the argument by Andrew George (2003: 54–70) that the story of *Gilgamesh* did not survive the death of the cuneiform script in any substantial form. But in the sixth century CE, the Greek philosopher Damascius wrote a remarkably accurate summary of the first episode of *Enuma Elish*, drawing on Eudemus of Rhodes, who was active in the fourth century BCE, showing that some memory of the epic persisted. The ancient reception of *Enuma Elish* outside cuneiform cultures, including Damascius, is treated in detail by Frahm in this volume. *Enuma Elish* also makes notable appearances in the ritual architecture of Palmyra and in the Hebrew Bible, where it appears as a recurrent foil to the text's monotheistic message. Indeed, when *Enuma Elish* was rediscovered in the 1870s, it was its influence on Greek literature and on Genesis that first garnered attention. It is well known among Assyriologists that the British Prime Minister William Gladstone attended the lecture at which *Gilgamesh* was first presented, but Gladstone (1890: 129–32) also deserves credit for his lucid reflections on the relation between *Enuma Elish* and Homer, published in 1890, between two of his stints as prime minister. Likewise, the influence of *Enuma Elish* upon the Hebrew Bible – a topic that has since grown into an academic subfield in its own right (see the overview and references in Frahm 2013) – ignited a fierce debate soon after the epic first appeared in translation, as I discuss below. Even 3,000 years after its composition, *Enuma Elish* still held the power to provoke.

## History of scholarship and overview of the volume

That modern readers saw a connection between *Enuma Elish* and the Hebrew Bible is apparent from the title of its first translation into a modern language: George Smith, best known as the discoverer of *Gilgamesh*, translated the epic as *The Chaldean Account of Genesis* (1875), 'Chaldean' being the name for Babylonian culture used by Classical writers. Karen Sonik in this volume surveys the text editions of the epic that would appear over the next century and a half, culminating in the magisterial edition by Lambert that was published posthumously in 2013. Alongside the German edition by

Thomas Kämmerer and Kai Metzler that had appeared the preceding year, Lambert's book continues to form the basis for most studies of the text. However, as of 2023, the most up-to-date edition of the epic is the one published by the *electronic Babylonian Literature* (*eBL*), the digital project to which the *Library of Babylonian Literature* acts as a companion series.[15] The *eBL* corpus contains freely accessible, continuously updated online editions of the major works of cuneiform literature, using newly developed algorithms to locate even the smallest fragments of literary texts. These editions are accompanied by English and Arabic translations, an online dictionary and sign list, metrical analyses, and links to photographs and drawings of the tablets.

Turning from the reconstruction of the epic to its reception, modern readers of *Enuma Elish* initially placed a strong emphasis on cosmogony, as evidenced by the titles of early publications such as Smith's *Chaldean Account of Genesis* (1875), Leonard King's *The Seven Tablets of Creation* (1902), and Alexander Heidel's *The Babylonian Genesis* (1942). Essentially, they understood the epic in light of the biblical story of creation, but this reading of the text soon led to problems of its own. Friedrich Delitzsch (1902) caused an uproar in theological circles when he claimed that the Hebrew Bible was in large part a retelling of originally Babylonian myths, casting doubt over the divine origins of the Bible and depicting its Jewish authors – in increasingly anti-Semitic terms – as beholden to what he saw as their racially purer Babylonian predecessors. The ensuing controversy, known as the 'Bibel-Babel Streit', engulfed the learned circles of Germany at the time and even reached the emperor Wilhelm II, who took a keen interest in the debate (Lehmann 1994; Arnold and Weisberg 2002). At around the same time, a less contentious, but equally influential claim was put forth by another German philologist, Hermann Gunkel (1895). While Gunkel did not see Genesis as merely rewriting *Enuma Elish*, he did argue that one could only understand the latter in relation to the former. Specifically, he argued that *Enuma Elish* and other mythological parallels revealed the logic behind the narrative of Genesis: creation was only possible after a violent 'battle against chaos' (*Chaoskampf*), in which the main deity, as a representative of order, had to defeat an aquatic agent of chaos (on the history and legacy of this idea, see Scurlock and Beal 2013 and Sonik in this volume).

While recent scholarship has resisted Gunkel's reading of *Enuma Elish* (see e.g. Sonik 2013), it continues to be influential outside academic circles: the anti-feminist pop psychologist Jordan Peterson (1999: 108–28) treats the battle between Marduk and Tiamat as supposed evidence for a deeply embedded archetypal conflict between a 'masculine' principle of order and a 'feminine' principle of chaos. The most important rejoinder to this view is that, far from a universal feature of the human psyche, the misogynistic worldview displayed by *Enuma Elish* was the result of a specific historical development. Tellingly, Peterson (1999: 100) incorrectly refers to *Enuma Elish* as 'the oldest written creation myth we possess', obscuring the (gendered) history of the text by placing it at the beginning of recorded literature. As argued by Tikva Frymer-Kensky (1992), the ancient Near East saw a dramatic shift in gender relations around the middle of the second millennium BCE, which meant, among other things, that hitherto influential goddesses and priestesses were marginalized. *Enuma Elish* – which displays some of the most explicit sexism in cuneiform literature (Helle 2020) – was composed in the aftermath of this transition.

After the initial focus on cosmogony, *Enuma Elish* came to be read during the second half of the twentieth century as first and foremost a political document. Early stirrings of this development came in 1943, when the Danish Assyriologist Thorkild Jacobsen published an essay claiming that Mesopotamian culture had once, in some deep prehistoric time, been democratic, and only moved towards monarchical rule in later periods. Jacobsen (1943) alleged that a memory of this ancient democratic society was preserved in Sumerian and Babylonian myths, including *Enuma Elish*, in which Marduk's power is depicted as legitimate because it is ratified collectively by the gods' assembly (for an up-to-date reading of the relation between autocracy and collective decision-making in *Enuma Elish*, see Gabriel in this volume). While the substance of Jacobsen's argument has been called into doubt (see e.g. Gabriel 2014: 316–9), his article can still be appreciated as a historical document in its own right: Jacobsen defended his PhD in Copenhagen in September 1939, just as Hitler invaded Poland. One year later, Denmark would fall under Nazi occupation, with Jacobsen himself having moved to Chicago. For Jacobsen, the democratic election of an autocratic ruler was not an ancient development to be studied dispassionately, but a recent trauma.

Despite its shortcomings, Jacobsen's article inaugurated a series of political readings of the epic,[16] eventually yielding the scholarly consensus with which this introduction began: *Enuma Elish* is now generally seen as establishing Marduk's supremacy among the gods in the wake of Babylon's rise to power. This consensus is crystallized in Gösta Gabriel's recent study of the epic, which seeks to show that *Enuma Elish* is throughout guided by a single goal: affirming Marduk's supremacy in every way, especially by demonstrating that the world order which ancient readers saw around them was a reflection of Marduk's creativity and power (Gabriel 2014). Another key aspect of the political reading that has dominated studies of *Enuma Elish* over the past decades was formulated by Lambert. As he emphasized (Lambert 2013: 464), it would be a mistake to read the epic as if it contained '*the* Babylonian cosmology': Lambert was adamant that this was not the case. Without denying the importance of the epic, he repeatedly emphasized that *Enuma Elish* was only one account among several that were current in ancient Babylonia, and that its claims should be situated in a specific historical context (which, according to Lambert, was the resurgence of Babylonian pride during the reign of Nebuchadnezzar I). Highlighting the political agenda and historical context of the epic thus also means recognizing that its message was not accepted at all times or by all ancient scribes.[17]

Given this scholarly consensus, it is not surprising that political themes weave through the chapters of this volume. Gabriel shows that the speeches by which Marduk is elevated to universal power contain an implicit theory of kingship that is essentially contractarian, meaning that it relies on mutual obligations between ruler and subject. Wisnom looks at how *Enuma Elish* draws on older cuneiform works, such as *Anzû* and *Atra-hasis*, in a bid to prove the superiority of Marduk over Enlil and his son Ninurta. Rochberg turns to the astrological sections of the epic to show that these also reflect an emphasis on Marduk's absolute power: the cosmos is depicted as consisting of a set of symmetries and regularities that express, on a global scale, the cosmic order which Marduk imposed after his victory over Tiamat. Sonik highlights the gendered dimensions of the epic's political claims, depicting it as (among other things) a royal family drama and a 'mirror for queens', that is, a reflection on whether women can wield legitimate political power. Debourse traces the complicated historical process whereby *Enuma Elish* became central to the cult of Marduk; Reynolds shows how the poem's programmatic elevation of Marduk, Babylon, and the Esagil temple to absolute supremacy resonated with and were resisted by cuneiform scholars; and Frahm looks at how, ironically, the text's obsessive focus on Marduk's superiority helped to make it popular outside of Babylon, as authors from numerous backgrounds engaged critically with its ideas.

However, the volume also brings other aspects of the text into clearer relief. Two themes that recur across the chapters are *the power of language* and *the poetics of water*. The importance of language to the epic is announced in its very first line, 'When heaven on high had not been named' (*enūma eliš lā nabû šamāmū*, I 1): the world before creation is depicted as a world in which names did not yet exist. Michalowski shows that *Enuma Elish* developed a new literary language that was ground-breaking in the cuneiform tradition and that aimed to reproduce, in poetic form, the sound of creation. I argue that *Enuma Elish* conceives of creation in linguistic terms, as the simultaneous emergence of words, shapes, and destinies from an original fluid state: the epic thus tracks a transition from the formlessness of water to the order of language. Van De Mieroop builds on the premises set out in these two chapters to explore how Babylonian scholars interpreted the epic, arguing that they saw the text of *Enuma Elish* as holding the epistemological key that would unlock the structure of the created cosmos. If language is infused in *Enuma Elish* with a profoundly creative power, it also has the power to soothe emotions and reconcile conflicts – at least up to a point. Haubold reads *Enuma Elish* as both a rhetorical masterpiece and a reflection on rhetorics, arguing that the epic establishes an ideal of good counsel which keeps emotional excesses in check: such excesses must be controlled by eloquence if possible and by violence if necessary. Likewise, Wisnom looks at how the epic draws on the genre of lamentation literature to depict Marduk attempting and failing to soothe Tiamat, demonstrating both the power of language to calm emotions and the limits of that power.

Wisnom also highlights another theme explored in this volume: the poetics of water. Ritual lamentations often compare the god that is to be appeased with an angry sea, and as Wisnom notes, *Enuma Elish* literalizes that image: Tiamat is the angry sea personified, and since everything sprang from her according to the cosmology of *Enuma Elish*, water is a constant preoccupation of the text. Michalowski argues that the epic mimics the murmuring sound of water and uses the Sumerian word **mu** ('water') to recreate the aural landscape of creation; while I detail the conceptual contrast between water and language, form, and fate that structures the narrative. Intriguingly, an interest in water also runs through the history of its reception, from the early quotation examined by Jiménez that connects Marduk to the watery *aganutillû*-disease; through the anti-Marduk invective presented in the Assyrian composition *Marduk's Ordeal*, which, as noted by Reynolds, repeatedly mentions water in its distortion of *Enuma Elish*; all the way to some of the most recent adaptations, such as the video games and music albums discussed by Konstantopoulos. Both the epic and the readers who have responded to it through the ages thus display a sustained interest in water, this strange material that is at once ubiquitous and shapeless, necessary for survival and potentially destructive. Indeed, an interest in water may become more central to the study of *Enuma Elish* in the decades to come: just as Jacobsen's study of the epic's 'primitive democracy' was motivated by the fight against fascism during the Second World War, so the consequences of the climate crisis, including water shortages and rising sea levels, may lead scholars to reconsider the poetic significance of water across the ages.

## Note on the text

As noted above, the transcription is based on the edition in *eBL*, which was prepared by Adrian C. Heinrich with contributions by Zsombor J. Földi and Enrique Jiménez. A *transcription* of an Akkadian text renders it as a sequence of words, while a *transliteration* renders it as a sequence of cuneiform signs, and it is the former convention that has been adopted here: readers who wish to read a transliteration of the text, including a synoptic overview of the differences between the preserved manuscripts, are advised to consult the *eBL* website. The transcription printed here flags only the most significant textual variants in the notes. For example, line I 40 is given by eleven manuscripts as 'Let silence be settled, so that we may sleep' (*qūlu liššakin-ma i niṣlal nīnu*), but one manuscript from Assur has instead '(so that) you may rest by night' (*mūšiš lū nēḫet*). Likewise, words rendered in round brackets are omitted by some manuscripts. Square brackets contain words or parts of words that are missing from all preserved manuscripts but can be plausibly restored; while ellipses mark either missing words that cannot currently be restored (if they are placed inside square brackets) or signs that are preserved but cannot be deciphered (if square brackets are not present).

The translation presented here leans towards semantic equivalence, meaning that it does not seek to reproduce the poetic patterns and elaborate lexicon described in the section on style. The translation also aims, whenever possible, to render key Akkadian terms with the same English word. For example, a crucial word in the beginning of the narrative is *dalāḫu*, which can mean 'to disturb, to worry', and, when applied to water, 'to muddy, to roil'. The epic leans on this double meaning by using it to describe both Tiamat's waters being disturbed by the gods and her mood becoming gradually more enraged, drawing a direct link between her psychological and physical states. To preserve this ambivalence, the word *dalāḫu*, including its various grammatical derivations, has throughout been translated as 'trouble' or 'troubled'. However, the translation still aims to be readable and accessible to non-specialists, so the highly compact Akkadian lines have been transformed into more straightforward English sentences. One consequence is that, as is often the case with English translations of Akkadian and Sumerian texts, individual lines tend to become much longer in English than in the original. An instructive example is line I 4, 'and the creative force Tiamat, who gave birth to them all' (*mummu tiāmtu mu'allidat gimrīšun*), which consists of just four words in Akkadian but eleven in English. The notes to the translation explain unclear words or passages, mark uncertainties in the reconstruction or interpretation of the text, present other possible translations, flag significant double meanings, give the literal meaning of idiomatic phrases, and the like. The essays that follow occasionally deviate from the main translation to highlight aspects of the original that are particularly relevant to their argument; these alterations are marked by the phrase 'translation modified'.

*Enuma Elish* responded fiercely to the stories that came before it, as it sought to establish Marduk's preeminence over his divine precursors, and it inspired fierce responses in its turn. These reactions were not what its author had in mind when he declared himself 'the first one' in a chain of scribal transmission that would reach far into the future: in reality, the chain turned out to include a series of critical responses and counter-responses, such as the Assyrian recension and the epic of *Erra*. And yet, by the irony of history, it is precisely this chain that secured the epic's place in world literature more firmly than even the most dedicated scribal compliance ever could: *Enuma Elish* first gained notoriety in the modern world because Genesis was written in direct response to it, and the epic continues to provoke passionate responses to this day, as the survey offered by Konstantopoulos in this volume confirms. I began this introduction by saying that, in cuneiform cultures, there is a time before and a time after *Enuma Elish*. By that logic, we are still living in the time after *Enuma Elish*, as its influence, especially as mediated through the Hebrew Bible, continues to resonate through world literature. As Michalowski puts it in this volume: 'indirectly, its echoes reached many other languages, resounding with us to this day'. This volume aims to make the source of these echoes ring loudly once again.

## Notes

1 See Lambert (1964), Vanstiphout (1992: 37–61), and Gabriel (2014) with further reading. On the question of whether *Enuma Elish* reflected an ideological change that had already taken place or accelerated it, see Jiménez in this volume.

2 In most manuscripts, the name Tiamat is rendered ᵈti-GEME, with GEME being a logogram meaning *amtu*, 'slave woman, servant woman'. As reflected in the transcription, we take this spelling to render an Akkadian pronunciation *tiāmtu*, but in translation, we retain the traditional English form 'Tiamat'.

3 The seminal study of *Enuma Elish*'s ancient reception, from which the following examples are drawn, is Frahm (2010).

4 *Merriam-Webster.com*, s.v. 'epic'.

5 Assyriologists distinguish between 'tablets', which are the physical manuscripts on which the story survives, and 'Tablets', which are the subdivisions of the story that were written on one tablet each, corresponding to the songs of a classical epic or the episodes of a modern TV series; see Helle (2023a).

6 The episode bears a strong similarity to the cuneiform story of the Flood, unleashed upon humanity by the god Enlil to quell the noise that was keeping him awake. For this motif, see, among others, Michalowski (1990: 385–8) and Heffron (2014).

7 Oppenheim (1977: 214); Vanstiphout (1992: 47); Katz (2011: 129–30); Helle (2020: 195–8); and Gabriel (2014: 182–97), with further references.

8 It is worth noting that, in *Enuma Elish* as in many other of the works that employ this trope, the crisis of the second act emerges as an unintended consequence of the solution to the crisis of the first: by killing Apsû and resolving the first conflict, Ea lays the foundation for the second and much larger conflict with Tiamat. Likewise,

by creating humanity in the first act of *Atra-hasis*, Ea unintentionally creates the problem of noise that will lead to the crisis of the second act: the Flood.

9 The trope of 'the search for the right character' was highlighted by Jane Gordon in a paper at the 68th Rencontre Assyriologique Internationale at Leiden. *Enuma Elish*'s use of this trope is inflected by its allusion to *Anzû*, in which three gods fail to fight Anzû, just as Ea and Anu fail to confront Tiamat; see Wisnom in this volume.

10 See Wisnom in this volume for the similar endings of *Anzû* and *Enuma Elish*; other climatic lists include *Lugal-e*, the *Exaltation of Inana*, and, arguably, Tablet XII of *Gilgamesh*.

11 See e.g. the four lines ending in *-ša* in I 41–4, followed by four lines ending in *-šu* in I 51–4. The symmetry seems deliberate, but *-ša* and *-šu* are, respectively, the feminine and masculine third-person pronominal suffixes and thus very common, including at the end of lines, making their significance less clear.

12 I would like to thank Johannes Haubold for pointing this out to me. The dating of both *Ludlul* and *Enuma Elish* is unclear, meaning that the word's direction of travel – if indeed it was a direct borrowing – is unclear.

13 For this system of metrical analysis, see Buccellati (1990) as well as the more straightforward presentation in George (2003: 162–5).

14 This overview is taken from the *eBL* website, https://www.ebl.lmu.de/corpus/L/1/2. The eighteen 'further fragments' here refer to fragments that can be identified as having been part of one of the 116 manuscripts, but cannot physically be joined with it.

15 This edition can be accessed at https://www.ebl.lmu.de/corpus/L/1/2.

16 Notable entries in this tradition of political readings include Jacobsen (1976: chap. 6), Lambert (1964), Michalowski (1990), Vanstiphout (1992), and Katz (2011). See also the overview of scholars highlighting either the cosmogonic or the political focus of the epic in Kämmerer and Metzler (2012: 4–6).

17 Tellingly, the last sentence of Lambert's (posthumously published) book on *Enuma Elish* reads: 'The traditional tolerance and mutual respect of the various cities did not completely disappear, and even in Babylon itself there were those who preferred forms of the myth other than those which our author tried to canonize' (Lambert 2013: 465). It is clear that Lambert resisted the epic's centripetal force – that is, its attempt to establish itself as the singular, hegemonic Babylonian myth – to the very end.

## Bibliography

Arnold, B. T. and D. B. Weisberg (2002), 'A Centennial Review of Friedrich Delitzsch's "Babel und Bibel" Lectures', *Journal of Biblical Literature*, 121 (3): 441–57.

Ayali-Darshan, N. (2020), *The Storm-God and the Sea: The Origin, Versions, and Diffusion of a Myth throughout the Ancient Near East*, trans. Liat Keren, Orientalische Religionen in der Antike 37, Tübingen: Mohr Siebeck.

Buccellati, G. (1990), 'On Poetry – Theirs and Ours', in T. Abusch, J. Huehnergard, and P. Steinkeller (eds), *Lingering over Words: Studies in Ancient Near Eastern Literature in Honor of William L. Moran*, Harvard Semitic Studies 37, 105–34, Atlanta: Scholar's Press.

Cancik-Kirschbaum, E. and K. Wagensonner (2017), 'Abschrift, Offenbarung, Sukzession: Autoritätsnarrative in der Textkultur Mesopotamiens', in A.-B. Renger and M. Witte (eds), *Sukzession in Religionen*, 33–54, Berlin: De Gruyter.

Dalley, S. (1997), 'Statues of Marduk and the Date of Enūma eliš', *Altorientalische Forschungen*, 24: 163–71.
Delitzsch, F. (1902), *Babel und Bibel: Ein Vortrag*, Leipzig: J. C. Hinrichs.
Foster, B. R. (1991), 'On Authorship in Akkadian Literature', *Annali dell'Istituto universitario orientale di Napoli*, 51: 17–32.
Frahm, E. (2010), 'Counter-Texts, Commentaries, and Adaptations: Politically Motivated Responses to the Babylonian Epic of Creation in Mesopotamia, the Biblical World, and Elsewhere', *Orient: Reports of the Society for Near Eastern Studies in Japan*, 45: 3–33.
Frahm, E. (2013), 'Creation and the Divine Spirit in Babel and Bible: Reflections on mummu in Enūma eliš I 4 and rûaḥ in Genesis 1:2', in D. S. Vanderhooft and A. Winitzer (eds), *Literature as Politics, Politics as Literature: Essays on the Ancient Near East in Honor of Peter Machinist*, 97–116, Winona Lake: Eisenbrauns.
Frymer-Kensky, T. (1992), *In the Wake of the Goddesses: Women, Culture, and the Biblical Transformation of Pagan Myth*, New York: Free Press.
Gabriel, G. (2014), *'enūma eliš' – Weg zu einer globalen Weltordnung: Pragmatik, Struktur und Semantik des babylonischen 'Lieds auf Marduk'*, Orientalische Religionen in der Antike 12, Tübingen: Mohr Siebeck.
George, A. R. (2003), *The Babylonian Gilgamesh Epic: Introduction, Critical Edition, and Cuneiform Texts*, 2 vols, Oxford: Oxford University Press.
George, A. R. (2013), 'The Poem of Erra and Ishum: A Babylonian Poet's View of War', in H. Kennedy (ed.), *Warfare and Poetry in the Middle East*, 39–71, London: I. B. Tauris.
Gesche, P. D. (2000), *Schulunterricht in Babylonien im ersten Jahrtausend v. Chr.*, Alter Orient und Altes Testament 275, Münster: Ugarit-Verlag.
Gladstone, W. E. (1890), *Landmarks of Homeric Study: Together with an Essay on the Points of Contact between the Assyrian Tablets and the Homeric Text*, London: Macmillan and Company.
Gunkel, H. (1895), *Schöpfung und Chaos in Urzeit und Endzeit: Eine religionsgeschichtliche Untersuchung über Gen 1 und Ap Joh 12*, Göttingen: Vandenhoeck & Ruprecht.
Haubold, J. (2013), '"The Wisdom of the Chaldeans": Reading Berossos, Babyloniaca Book 1', in J. Haubold, G. B. Lanfranchi, R. Rollinger, and J. M. Steele (eds), *The World of Berossos*, Classica et Orientalia 5, 31–45, Wiesbaden: Harrassowitz Verlag.
Hecker, K. (1974), *Untersuchungen zur akkadischen Epik*, Alter Orient und Altes Testament 8, Kevelaer: Butzon & Bercker.
Heffron, Y. (2014), 'Revisiting "Noise" (rigmu) in Atra-ḫasīs in Light of Baby Incantations', *Journal of Near Eastern Studies*, 73 (1): 83–93.
Heidel, A. (1942), *The Babylonian Genesis: The Story of Creation*, Chicago: University of Chicago Press.
Helle, S. (2014), 'Rhythm and Expression in Akkadian Poetry', *Zeitschrift für Assyriologie*, 104 (1): 56–73.
Helle, S. (2020), 'The Two-Act Structure: A Narrative Device in Akkadian Epics', *Journal of Ancient Near Eastern Religions*, 20 (2): 190–224.
Helle, S. (2023a), 'Tablets as Narrative Episodes in Babylonian Poetry', in S. Helle and G. Konstantopoulos (eds), *The Shape of Stories: Narrative Structures in Cuneiform Literature*, Cuneiform Monographs 54, 93–111, Leiden: Brill.
Helle, S. (2023b), 'The Return of the Text: On Self-Reference in Cuneiform Literature', *Journal of Cuneiform Studies*, 75: 93–107.
Horowitz, W. (2011), *Mesopotamian Cosmic Geography*, Mesopotamian Civilizations 8, Winona Lake: Eisenbrauns.

Hunger, H. (1968), *Babylonische und assyrische Kolophone*, Alter Orient und Altes Testament 2, Neukirchen-Vluyn: Butzon und Bercker.
Jacobsen, T. (1943), 'Primitive Democracy in Ancient Mesopotamia', *Journal of Near Eastern Studies*, 2 (3): 159–72.
Jacobsen, T. (1976), *The Treasures of Darkness: A History of Mesopotamian Religion*, New Haven: Yale University Press.
Kämmerer, T. R. and K. A. (2012), Metzler, *Das babylonische Weltschöpfungsepos 'Enūma elîš'*, Alter Orient und Altes Testament 375, Münster: Ugarit-Verlag.
Katz, D. (2011), 'Reconstructing Babylon: Recycling Mythological Traditions toward a New Theology', in E. Cancik-Kirschbaum, M. van Ess, and J. Marzahn (eds), *Babylon: Wissenskultur in Orient Und Okzident*, Topoi 1, 123–34, Berlin: De Gruyter.
King, L. W. (1902), *The Seven Tablets of Creation, or the Babylonian and Assyrian Legends Concerning the Creation of the World and of Mankind*, vol. 2, Luzac's Semitic Text and Translation Series 12–13, London: Luzac and Co.
Lambert, W. G. (1964), 'The Reign of Nebuchadnezzar I: A Turning Point in the History of Ancient Mesopotamian Religion', in W. S. McCullough (ed.), *The Seed of Wisdom: Essays in Honour of T.J. Meek*, 3–13, Toronto: University of Toronto Press.
Lambert, W. G. (2013), *Babylonian Creation Myths*, Mesopotamian Civilizations 16, Winona Lake: Eisenbrauns.
Lehmann, R. G. (1994), *Friedrich Delitzsch und der Babel-Bibel-Streit*, Orbis Biblicus et Orientalis 133, Göttingen: Vandenhoek und Ruprecht.
Machinist, P. (1983), 'Rest and Violence in the Poem of Erra', *Journal of the American Oriental Society*, 103 (1): 221–6.
Machinist, P. (2005), 'Order and Disorder: Some Mesopotamian Reflections', in S. Shaked (ed.), *Genesis and Regeneration: Essays on Conceptions of Origins*, 31–61, Jerusalem: The Israel Academy of Sciences and Humanities.
Michalowski, P. (1990), 'Presence at the Creation', in T. Abusch, J. Huehnergard and P. Steinkeller (eds), *Lingering over Words: Studies in Ancient Near Eastern Literature in Honor of William L. Moran*, Harvard Semitic Studies 37, 381–96, Atlanta: Scholars Press.
Michalowski, P. (2010), 'Maybe Epic: The Origins and Reception of Sumerian Heroic Poetry', in D. Konstan and K. A. Raaflaub (eds), *Epic and History*, 7–25, Chichester: Wiley-Blackwell.
Oppenheim, A. L. (1977), *Ancient Mesopotamia: Portrait of a Dead Civilization*, ed. E. Reiner, rev. edition, Chicago: University of Chicago Press.
Peterson, J. B. (1999), *Maps of Meaning: The Architecture of Belief*, London: Routledge.
Reitz, C., C. Scheidegger Lämmle and K. Wesselmann (2019), 'Epic Catalogues', in C. Reitz and S. Finkmann (eds), *Structures of Epic Poetry*, 1, 653–726, Berlin: De Gruyter.
Robson, E. (2019), *Ancient Knowledge Networks: A Social Geography of Cuneiform Scholarship in First-Millennium Assyria and Babylonia*, London: UCL Press.
Rochberg, F. (2009), '"The Stars Their Likenesses": Perspectives on the Relation between Celestial Bodies and Gods in Ancient Mesopotamia', in B. N. Porter (ed.), *What Is a God? Anthropomorphic and Non-Anthropomorphic Aspects of Deity in Ancient Mesopotamia*, 41–92, Winona Lake: Eisenbrauns.
Röllig, W. (1957–1971), 'Götterzahlen', *Reallexikon der Assyriologie und vorderasiatischen Archäologie*, 3: 499–500.
Scurlock, J. and R. H. Beal (eds, 2013), *Creation and Chaos: A Reconsideration of Hermann Gunkel's* Chaoskampf *Hypothesis*, University Park: Penn State University Press.

Seri, A. (2006), 'The Fifty Names of Marduk in Enūma eliš', *Journal of the American Oriental Society*, 126 (4): 1–13.
Smith, G. (1875), *The Chaldean Account of Genesis, Containing the Description of the Creation, the Fall of Man, the Deluge, the Tower of Babel, the Times of the Patriarchs, and Nimroud; Babylonian Fables, and Legends of the Gods; from the Cuneiform Inscriptions*, London: Sampson, Low, Marston, Scarle and Rivingston.
Sonik, K. (2013), 'From Hesiod's Abyss to Ovid's rudis indigestaque moles: Chaos and Cosmos in the Babylonian "Epic of Creation"', in J. Scurlock and R. H. Beal (eds), *Creation and Chaos: A Reconsideration of Hermann Gunkel's* Chaoskampf *Hypothesis*, 1–25, University Park: Penn State University Press.
Vanstiphout, H. L. J. (1992), 'Enuma Elish as a Systematic Creed: An Essay', *Orientalia Lovaniensia Periodica*, 22: 37–61.
West, M. L. (1997), 'Akkadian Poetry: Metre and Performance', *Iraq*, 59: 175–87.
Wisnom, S. (2015), 'Stress Patterns in Enūma Eliš: A Comparative Study', *Kaskal*, 12: 485–502.
Wisnom, S. (2020), *Weapons of Words: Intertextual Competition in Babylonian Poetry; A Study of 'Anzû', 'Enūma Eliš', and 'Erra and Išum'*, Culture and History of the Ancient Near East 106, Leiden: Brill.
Wisnom, S. (2023), 'The Dynamics of Repetition in Akkadian Literature', in S. Helle and G. Konstantopoulos, *The Shape of Stories: Narrative Structures in Cuneiform Literature*, Cuneiform Monographs 54, 112–43, Leiden: Brill.
Wisnom, S. (forthcoming), 'Like a Dried Fish: The World According to *Enuma Elish*'.

*Enuma Elish*

Transcription by Adrian C. Heinrich and translation by Sophus Helle

# Tablet I

*enūma eliš lā nabû šamāmū*
*šapliš ammatu šuma lā zakrat*
*apsûm-(ma) rēštû zārûšun*
*mummu tiāmtu mu'allidat gimrīšun*
*mûšunu ištēniš iḫiqqū-ma*
*gipāra lā kiṣṣurū ṣuṣâ lā šē'ū*
*enūma ilū lā šūpû manāma*
*šuma lā zukkurū šīmāti lā šīmū*
*ibbanû-ma ilū qerebšun*
*laḫmu (u) laḫāmu uštāpû šuma izzakrū*
*adi irbû išīḫū*
*anšar (u) kišar ibbanû-(ma) elīšunu atrū*
*urrikū ūmī uṣṣibū šanāti*
*ānu apilšunu šānin abbīšu*
*anšar ānu bukrašu umaššil-ma*
*u ānu tamšīlašu ulid nudimmud*
*nudimmud ša abbīšu šālissunu šū-ma*
*palkâ uznī ḫasis emūqīn puggul*
*guššur ma'diš ana ālid abīšu anšar*
*lā īši šānina ina ilī atḫêšu*
*innendū-ma atḫû ilū anu[k]kū*
*ešû tiāmtam-ma naṣīršunu ištappu*
*dalḫūnim-ma ša tiāmti karassa*
*ina šu'āri šūdurū qereb andurunna*
*lā našir apsû rigimšun*
*u tiāmtu šuqammumat ina maḫrīšun*
*imtarṣam-ma epšetašun elīšun*
*lā ṭābat alkassunu šunūti …*

# Tablet I

When heaven on high had not been named[1]
and the ground below was not given a name,
primordial Apsû, who fathered them,
and the creative force[2] Tiamat, who gave birth to them all,
were mingling together their waters:
they had not yet bound meadows or lined the reedbeds.[3]
When none of the gods had been brought forth,
had not been given names and had not decreed destinies,
then were the gods created within them.
Lahmu and Lahamu were brought forth and called by name.
When they had grown big, grown tall,
Anshar and Kishar were created, greater than them.
They lengthened their days, expanded their years.
Anu, their firstborn, rivalled his fathers.[4]
Anshar made Anu, his child, like him,[5]
and Anu gave birth to his likeness in turn – Nudimmud.[6]
Nudimmud: he was the leader among his fathers,
vast of mind, perceptive, massive in strength,
much mightier than Anshar, who had fathered his father,
he had no rival among the gods his brothers.
They joined together, the brothers, the gods,[7]
and confused Tiamat as their clamour kept growing,
troubling Tiamat's belly,[8]
and with their games spreading grief in Andurunna.[9]
Apsû did not still their noise,
and Tiamat was silent before them:
their doings disturbed her,
their ways were not pleasant, but …[10]

1 The first nine lines of the poem are among the most discussed passages of Akkadian literature, and the syntax of the text allows for different interpretations. See Sophus Helle and Piotr Michalowski in this volume.
2 Akk. *mummu*, which is later used as a name for Apsû's servant.
3 Southern Iraq consisted of a checkerboard of canals and fields: without land or the reed-covered banks, the water was able to mix freely; see Buccellati (1990: 125). On the grammar and the other possible translations of this line, see Haubold (2017: 221–8).
4 Here and throughout the text, the word *abu* 'father' is also used to mean 'ancestor'.
5 Or: 'Anu, his child, became like Anshar'.
6 A learned name for the god Ea.
7 Babylonian recension adds: 'the Anunnaki'.
8 The word *karšu* means 'mind' as well as 'belly', so the disturbance can be both physical and mental. Tiamat's belly is here the watery expanse where the gods live.
9 A cosmological location of uncertain nature. Its use in this context is partly motivated by a pun on the preceding word *šūdurū*, 'spreading grief'.
10 The widely accepted reading *igammela*, 'she was lenient', seems less likely in light of recent manuscripts; see Fadhil and Jiménez (2021: 216).

*inūšu apsû zār ilī rabûti*
*issī-ma mummu sukkallašu izakkaršu*
*mummu sukkallu muṭīb kabattīya*
*alkam-ma ṣēriš tiāmti i niddin milk[a]*
*illikū-ma qudmiš tiāmti ūšibū*
*amâti imtallikū aššu ilī bukrīšun*
*apsû pâšu īpušam-ma*
*ana tiāmti ellītam-ma izakkarši*
*imtarṣam-ma alkassunu elīya*
*urriš lā šupšuḫāku mūšiš lā ṣallāku*
*lušḫalliq-ma alkassunu lusappiḫ*
*qūlu liššakin-ma i niṣlal nīnu*[1]
*tiāmtu annīta ina šemêša*
*īzuz-ma iltasi elu ḫarmīša*
*issī-ma marṣiš uggugat ēdiššīša*
*lemutta ittadi ana karšīša*
*mīnâ nīnu ša nibnû nušḫallaq-ma*
*alkassunu lū šumruṣat-ma i nišdud ṭābiš*
*īpul-ma mummu apsâ imallik*
*sukkallu lā māgiru milik mummīšu*
*ḫulliqam-ma abī alkata ešīta*
*urriš lū šupšuḫāt(a) mūšiš lū ṣallāt(a)*[2]
*iḫdūšum-ma apsû immerū pānūšu*
*aššu lemnēti ikpudū ana ilī mārīšu*
*mummu ītedir kišāssu*
*ušbam-ma birkāšu unaššaq šâšu*
*mimmû ikpudū (ina) puḫruššun*
*ana ilī bukrīšunu uštannûni*
*išmûnim-ma ilū idullū*
*qūla iṣbatū*[3] *šaqummiš ušbū*
*šūtur uzna itpēšu tele'û*
*ea ḫasis mimmāma iše''â šibqīšun*
*ibšimšum-ma uṣurāti kalâ*[4] *ukīnšu*
*unakkilšu šūtura tâšu ella*
*imnūšum-ma ina mê ušapšiḫ*
*šitta irteḫīšu ṣalil ṭūbātiš*

[1] Var.: *mūšiš lū nēḫet.*
[2] Var.: [...] *nēḫet.*
[3] Var.: *qūlu iššakin.*
[4] Var.: *uṣurat kalî.*

Then Apsû, who had fathered the great gods,
called Mummu, his minister, and said to him:
'Mummu, minister who soothes my mood!
Come, let us take counsel with Tiamat.'
They went and sat down, facing Tiamat,
to confer about the gods their children.
Apsû worked his words,
saying loudly[11] to her, to Tiamat:
'Their ways disturb me.
By day I have no rest, by night no sleep.
I will destroy their ways, disrupt them!
Let silence be settled, so that we may sleep.'
When Tiamat heard this,[12]
she was angry and screamed at her lover.
She screamed, disturbed, alone in her rage,
for he had cast evil upon her mind.[13]
'What! Should we destroy what we ourselves created?
Disturbing as their ways may be, let us bear them with good grace.'
Mummu replied and gave counsel to Apsû,
and his Mummu's counsel was that of a devious minister:
'Destroy, my father, their confused way,
that by day you may rest, by night you may sleep.'
Apsû was pleased with him, his face lighted up,
because he had plotted evil against the gods his sons.
Mummu embraced his neck,
sitting on his lap and kissing him.
What they plotted in their assembly
was repeated to the gods their children:
the gods listened and panicked,[14]
then turned quiet[15] and sat in silence.
The supremely clever, wise, and skilled
Ea, who perceives all things, found out their scheme:
against it he fashioned a comprehensive plan, fixing it firmly,
and devised his supreme, sacred spell.
He recited it, granting him rest in the water:
sleep poured over him and he slumbered soundly.

[11] Unclear. Alt.: 'saying to the pure Tiamat'.

[12] Tiamat's reaction is described in four metrically linked lines: they all end with the syllable *ša*, have eleven syllables, and begin and end with an amphibrach.

[13] Unclear. Alt.: 'she pushed the evil down in her mind,' or, 'she took the evil into her mind.' As noted above, the word *karšu*, 'mind', can also mean 'belly'.

[14] The phrase *ilū idullū*, 'the gods panicked', foreshadows the phrase *dullu ilī*, 'the toil of the gods', which in VI 8 is used to explain why humanity must be created: to free the gods from the burden of work.

[15] Lit.: 'they seized quietness'.

*ušaṣlil-ma apsâ reḫi šitta*
*mummu tamlāku dalāpiš kūru*
*ipṭur riksīšu ištaḫaṭ agâšu*
*melammīšu itbala ea ūtaddiq*
*ikmīšū-ma apsâ ināraššu*
*mummu ītašar elīšu iptarka*
*ukīn-ma eli apsî šubassu*
*mummu ittamaḫ ukāl ṣerressu*
*ištu lemnīšu ikmû isādu*
*ea ušzizzu ernittašu eli gārîšu*
*qerbiš kummīšu šupšuḫiš inūḫ-ma*
*imbīšum-ma apsû u'addû ešrēti*
*ašruššu gipārašu ušaršid-ma*
*ea u damkina ḫīratuš ina rabbâti ušbū*
*ina kiṣṣi šīmāti atman uṣurāti*
*lē'û lē'ûti apkal ilī bēlu ittarḫi*
*ina qereb apsî ibbani marduk*
*ina qereb elli apsî ibbani marduk*
*ibnīšū-ma ea abūšu*
*damkina ummašu ḫaršassu*
*ītinniq-ma ṣerrēt ištarāti*
*tārīt ittarrûšu pulḫāti ušmalli*
*šamḫat nabnīssu ṣarir nīš īnīšu*
*uṭṭulat ṣītašu gašir ištu ulla*
*īmuršū-ma ānu bānû abīšu*
*irīš immir libbašu ḫidûta imla*
*uštaṣbīšum-ma šunnât ilūssu*
*šušqû ma'diš elīšunu atar mimmûšu*
*lā lamdā-ma nukkulā minâtūšu*
*ḫasāsiš lā naṭâ amāriš pašqā*
*erba īnāšu erba uznāšu*
*šaptīšu ina šutābuli gīru ittanpaḫ*
*irtebû erbu'ā ḫasīsa*

He made Apsû slumber, sleep was poured over him,
while the councillor Mummu was put into a waking stupor.
He untied his sash, stripped off his crown,
took away his frightful aura[16] and put it on himself.
He bound Apsû and killed him,
he turned to Mummu and locked him up.[17]
He founded his home upon Apsû,
Mummu he seized, holding his leash.
After he had bound and slain his foes,
declaring triumph over his adversaries,
Ea rested calmly within his chamber,
and called it Apsû, 'that makes known the shrines'.[18]
There he founded his sanctuary[19]:
Ea and his wife Damkina lived in splendour.
In the chapel of fates, the temple of plans,
the expert of experts, the sage of the gods, the Lord, was conceived.
Within Apsû, Marduk was created,
within sacred Apsû, Marduk was created.
His father Ea created him,
Damkina, his mother, delivered him.
He suckled at the breasts of goddesses
and the nurse who raised him infused him with dreadfulness:
his form flourished, the flick of his eyes flashed bright,
his growth was manly, he was mighty from the start.
Anu, who had created his father, saw him:
he exulted, lighting up, his heart full of joy.
He perfected him, so that his divinity became different:
he is truly eminent, supreme among them in every way.
His proportions cannot be known, they are intricate,
impossible to understand, difficult to look on.
Four are his eyes and four his ears,
fire[20] flares up when his lips flit.
His four ears grew great,[21]

16 The *melammu* was an aura of fear-inducing brilliance that surrounded deities, demons, and similar beings.

17 Unclear. Alt.: 'he (Marduk) laid him (Mummu) across him (Apsû)'; that is, Mummu's body would be used as a latch to keep Apsû's waters in place. For the first part of the line, see Fadhil and Jiménez (2021: 217).

18 The second half of the line is an etymographic reading of the name 'Apsû'; see Marc Van De Mieroop in this volume.

19 The word for 'sanctuary', *gipāru*, was used in I 6 with the meaning 'meadow'.

20 Lit.: 'Girra', the Fire God.

21 The word for 'ears', *ḫasīsu*, also means 'intellect, perception', so the size of Marduk's ears refers to the scope of his understanding.

*u īnā kīma šuāti ibarrâ gimrēti*
*ullū-ma ina ilī šūtur lānšu*
*mešrêtūšu šuttuḫā ilitta šūtur*
*māri'utu māri'utu*
*māri šamšu šamšu ša il[āni]*
*labiš melammī ešret ilī šaqîš etpur*
*pulḫātu ḫamšāssina elīšu kamrā*
*ibnī-ma šār erbetti u'allid ānu*
*qātuššu umallâ mārī limmell[ū]*
*ibšim-(ma) epra meḫâ ušazbal*
*ušabši agâm-ma idallaḫ tiāmta*
*dalḫat tiāmtum-ma urra u mūša idulla*
*ilū lā šupšuḫū izzabbilū šārīša*
*iktapdū-ma karšussunu lemutta*
*ana tiāmti ummīšunu šunu izzakrū*
*enūma apsâ ḫarmaki inārū-ma*
*iduššu lā tallikī-ma qâliš tušbī*
*ibnī-ma šār erbetti ša puluḫti*
*šudluḫū*[5] *karšakī-ma ul niṣallal nīnu*
*ul ibši libbukki apsû ḫarmāki*
*u mummu ša ikkamû ēdiš*[6] *ašbāti*
*ištu ūmi attī dulluḫiš tadullī*
*u nīnu ša lā nisakkipu ul taremmīnâši*[7]
*amrī sarmā'ni ḫummurā īnātūni*
*ḫuṣbī abšāna lā sākipa i niṣlal nīnu*
*epšī tāḫāza gimillašunu tirrī*
*mi[mm]û*? *šunu ibšimū ana zāqīqi šuknī*
*išmē-ma tiāmtu amātu iṭīb elša*
*mimmû attunu tuštaddinā i nīpuš ūma*
*isḫurūšim-ma ilū qerebša*

[5] Var.: *ša šudluḫ.*
[6] Var.: *lā ēdiš.*
[7] Var.: [. . .] *i niṣlal nīni.*

and his eyes likewise discern everything.[22]
He stands tall among the gods, supreme in form,
his limbs are enormous, supreme from birth.[23]
*Mari-utu, Mari-utu,*
son of the Sun, Sun of the gods![24]
He was dressed in the frightful aura of ten gods, enveloped up high,[25]
and fifty dreads[26] were heaped upon him.
Anu created the four winds, giving birth to them
and handing them to him: 'Let my son play!'[27]
He fashioned dust and let the tempest carry it,
creating waves[28] and troubling Tiamat.
Tiamat was troubled, day and night she tossed about,
the gods had no rest, they were burdened? by each wind.
Plotting evil in their minds,
they said to their mother Tiamat:
'When they killed your lover Apsû,
you did not rally to his side but sat in silence.
Now he has created the four winds of dread:
your belly is troubled and we cannot sleep.[29]
He was not in your heart, you lover Apsû,
nor was Mummu, whom they bound: now you sit alone.
Since that day, you have been making trouble, tossing about,
and as for us, who cannot lie still – you do not love us.
Behold our burden, our eyes have shrivelled up!
Break this relentless yoke,[30] so that we may sleep.
Make war, avenge them!
Consign all that they planned to oblivion.'[31]
Tiamat listened, she found the speech good:
'All that you advised, let us do it today.'
The gods assembled inside her,

22 Alt.: 'his eyes are like them (i.e., four), they perceive everything', or 'his eyes, like him (i.e., Anu), perceive everything'.

23 Alt.: 'his character is supreme', or, 'his descent is supreme'.

24 An untranslatable set of wordplays on Marduk's name; see Piotr Michalowski in this volume.

25 Unclear. Alt., reading *itbur*: 'exalted in strength'.

26 Like the *melammu* (for which see the note to I 68), the 'dreads', *pulḫātu*, are fear-inducing cloaks that envelop divine beings.

27 Alt.: 'My son, let them play!'

28 The word *agû*, 'flood wave', can also mean 'crown', hinting at Marduk's later assumption of kingship.

29 As noted for I 23, Tiamat's body is where the gods live, meaning that when her water is roiled, the gods cannot lie still.

30 The yoke is described as *lā sākipu*, 'which does not move away', i.e. 'relentless'. But two lines earlier, in I 120, the word *sakāpu* is used in the meaning, 'to lie still', so that the two opposite senses, 'to lie still' and 'to move away', appear in quick succession and are both negated, yielding an elegant symmetry.

31 The reconstruction of the first part of line, proposed by Fadhil and Jiménez (2021: 218), is still uncertain. The phrase *ana zaqīqi šuknī*, here translated 'consign them to oblivion', can also mean 'turn them into ghosts'.

*[lemn]ēti uštaḫḫazū an ilī bānîšun*
*immasrūnim-ma iduš tiāmti tebûni*
*ezzū kapdū lā sākipū mūša u imma*
*[na]šû tamḫāra nazarbubū labbū*
*ukkinna šitkunū-ma ibannû ṣūlāti*
*ummu ḫubūr pātiqat kalāma*
*ušraddi kakka lā maḫra ittalad mušmaḫḫī*
*zaqtū-ma šinnī lā pādû attā'ī*
*imta kīma dāmi zumuršunu ušmalli*
*ušumgallī nadrūti pulḫāti ušalbiš-ma*
*melammī uštaššâ iliš umtaššil*
*āmiršunu šarbābiš liḫḫarmim*
*zumuršunu lištaḫḫiṭam-ma lā ine''ū irassun*
*ušziz bašma mušḫušša u laḫāma*
*ugalla uridimma u girtablīla*
*ūmī dabrūti kulīla u kusarikka*
*nāš kakki lā pādû lā ādirū tā[ḫāz]i*
*gapšā têrētūša lā maḫrā šinā-ma*
*appūnā-ma ištēn-ešret kīma šuāti uštabši*
*ina ilī bukrīša šūt iškunūši puḫra*
*ušašqi qingu ina birīšunu šâšu ušrabbīš(u)*
*ālikūt maḫri pān ummāni mu'errūt puḫri*
*našê kakkī tiṣbutu dekû ananta*
*šūt tamḫāri rab sikkattūti*
*ipqid-ma qātuššu ušēšibaššu ina karri*
*addi tâka ina puḫur ilī ušarbīka*
*malikūt ilī gimrassunu qātukka ušmalli*
*lū šurbâtā-ma ḫā'irī ēdû attā*
*lirtabbû zikrūka eli kalîšunu anukkī*
*iddinšum-ma tuppi šīmāti iratuš ušatmiḫ*
*kataduggûka lā innennâ likūn ṣīt pîka*
*innana qingu šušqû leqû ānūti*
*an ilī mārīša šīmata ištīma*
*epšu pîkunu gīra liniḫḫa*
*imtuk kitmuru*[8] *magšara lišrabbib*

[8] Var.: *ina k[itmuri]*.

driven to evil against the gods who created them.
They drew together,[?] rising at Tiamat's side,
angry, plotting, not lying still by night or by day,
ready for battle, wrathful, seething,
they set up a council to bring about conflict.
Mother Noise,[32] who fashions all,
supplied invincible weapons, giving birth to *mushmahhu*-serpents,
sharp of teeth and merciless of fang,[?]
and filling their bodies with poison for blood.
The ferocious *ushumgallu*-serpents she dressed in dread,
arming them with frightful auras and making them like gods:
'May those who look upon them meekly collapse,
may their bodies keep charging and never turn back.'
She enlisted *bashmu*-serpents, *mushhusshu*-serpents, *lahamu*-men,
*ugallu*-demons, lion-men, scorpion-men,
fierce demons, fish-men and *kusarikku*-bisons:
they carried merciless weapons, no fear had they of war.
Her orders were formidable, no one could oppose them:
she truly created eleven such beings.
Among the gods her children, who made up her assembly,
she elevated Qingu: it was him she made greatest among them.
To lead the army, command the assembly,
carry weapons, engage, call for combat,
the way of war,[?] the general's rank –
with this she entrusted him, seating him upon a throne:
'I have cast a spell on you, making you great in the gods' assembly,
the command of all the gods I have put into your hands.
You are the greatest, you alone will be my lover.
May your word be greatest among all the Anunnaki.'
She gave him the Tablet of Destinies and fixed it to his chest[33]:
'May your pronouncements be unaltered, your utterance firm.'
After Qingu had been raised up and received dominion,
he fixed the fates of the gods her sons:
'May the working of your words quench fire
and your amassed poison subdue the strong.'

[32] For this meaning of the word *ḫubūru* in the present context, see Michalowski (1990: 386–6).
[33] Lit.: 'made him hold it to his chest'.

# Tablet II

*ukappit-ma tiāmtu pitiqša*
*tāḫāza iktaṣar ana ilī niprīša*
*aḫrâtaš eli apsî ulammin tiāmtu*
*ananta kī iṣmidu ana ea iptašrū*
*išmē-ma ea amāta šuāti*
*kummiš ušḫarrir-(ma) šaqummiš ušba*
*ištu imtalkū-ma uzzašu inūḫu*
*muttiš anšar abīšu šū uštardi*
*īrum-ma maḫru abi ālidīšu anšar*
*mimmû tiāmtu ikpudu ušannâ ana šâšu*
*abī tiāmtu ālittani izerrannâti*
*puḫra šitkunat-ma aggiš labbat*
*isḫurūšim-ma ilū gimiršun*
*adi ša attunu tabnâ idāša alkū*
*immasrūnim-ma iduš tiāmti tebûni*
*ezzū kapdū lā sākipū mūša u imma*
*našû tamḫāra nazarbubū labbū*
*ukkinna šitkunū-ma ibannû ṣūlāti*
*ummu ḫubūr pātiqat kalāma*
*ušraddi kakka lā maḫra ittalad mušmaḫḫī*
*zaqtū-ma šinnī lā pādû attā'ī*
*imta kīma dāmi zumuršunu ušmalli*
*ušumgallī nadrūti pulḫāti ušalbiš-ma*
*melammī uštaššâ iliš umtaššil*
*āmiršunu šarbābiš liḫḫarmim*
*zumuršunu lištaḫḫiṭam-ma lā ine''ū irassun*
*ušziz bašma mušḫušša (u) laḫāma*
*ugalla uridimma u girtablīla*
*ūmī dabrūti kulīla u kusarikka*
*nāš kakki lā pādû lā ādirū tāḫāzi*
*gapšā têrētūša lā maḫrā šinā-ma*
*appūnā-ma ištēn-ešret kīma šuāti uštabši*
*ina ilī bukrīša šūt iškunūši puḫra*
*ušašqi qingu ina birīšunu šâšu ušrabbīš*
*ālikūt maḫri pān ummāni mu'errūt puḫri*
*našê kakkī tiṣbutu dekû ananti*
*[šū]t tamḫāri rab sikkatūti*

# Tablet II

Tiamat gathered those she had fashioned,
braiding battle for the gods her offspring:
from then on, Tiamat did more evil than Apsû.
It was revealed to Ea that she had prepared for a clash.[34]
Ea heard these words,
he was struck dumb within his chamber and sat down in silence.
After he had taken counsel and his anger had calmed,
he went straight to stand before Anshar, his father.[35]
He came into the presence of Anshar, who had fathered his father,
and repeated to him all that Tiamat had plotted.
'My father! Tiamat, who gave birth to us, repudiates us:
she has convened an assembly, seething with rage.
Every god has rallied to her,
even those you[36] created walk by her side.
They drew together[?], rising at Tiamat's side,
angry, plotting, not lying still by night or by day,
ready for battle, wrathful, seething,
they set up a council to bring about conflict.
Mother Noise, who shapes all,
supplied invincible weapons, giving birth to *mushmahhu*-serpents,
sharp of teeth and merciless of fang[?],
and filling their bodies with poison for blood.
The ferocious *ushumgallu*-serpents she dressed in dread,
arming them with frightful auras and making them like gods:
"May those who look upon them meekly collapse,
may their bodies keep charging and never turn back."
She enlisted *bashmu*-serpents, *mushhusshu*-serpents, *lahamu*-men,
*ugallu*-demons, lion-men, scorpion-men,
fierce demons, fish-men and *kusarikku*-bisons:
they carried merciless weapons, no fear had they of war.
Her orders were formidable, no one could oppose them:
she truly created eleven such beings.
Among the gods her children, who made up her assembly,
she elevated Qingu: it was him she made greatest among them.
To lead the army, command the assembly,
carry weapons, engage, call for the clash,
the way of war[?], the general's rank –

[34] Alt.: 'how she had harnessed (her forces) for the clash'.
[35] See note to I 14.
[36] Plural.

*[ip]qid-ma qātuššu ušēšibaššu ina karri*
*[a]ddi tâka ina puḫur ilī ušarbīka*
*[ma]likūt ilī gimrassunu qātukka ušmalli*
*lū šurbâtā-ma ḫā'irī ēdû attā*
*[li]rtabbû zikrūka eli kalîšunu anukkī*
*iddinšum-ma tuppi šīmāti iratuš ušatmiḫ*
*kataduggûka lā innennâ likūn ṣīt pîka*
*innana qingu šušqû leqû ānūti*
*an ilī mārīša šīmata ištīma*
*epšu pîkunu gīra liniḫḫa*
*imtuk kitmuru magšara lišrabbib*
*išmē-ma anšar amātu magal dalḫat*
*ū'a ištasi šapassu ittaška*
*e[zz]et kabtassu lā nāḫat karassu*
*eli ea bukrīšu šagīmašu uštaḫḫaḫ*
*mārī ša tegrû tuqunta*
*mimmâ ēdukka tēpušu itašši attā*
*ta'īram-ma apsâ tanāra*
*u tiāmtu ša tušāgigu ali māḫirša*
*āšiš milki rubê tašīmti*
*bānû nēmeqi ilu nudimmud*
*amāt tapšuḫti siqar tanēḫi*
*anšar abāšu ṭābiš ippal*[9]
*abī libbu rūqu mušimmu šīmti*
*ša šubšû (u) ḫulluqu bašû ittīšu*
*anšar libbu rūqu mušimmu šīmti*
*ša šubšû (u) ḫulluqu bašû ittīšu*
*inimmê ātammūka surriš nūḫam-ma*
*kī amāt dumqi ēpušu šudud libbukka*
*lām anāku apsâ anāram-ma*
*mannu ītamar-ma inanna annâti*
*lām urriḫam-ma uballû šuāti*
*lū šâši ušḫalliqa minû bašī-ma*
*išmē-ma anšar amātu iṭīb elšu*
*ipšaḫ libbašū-ma ana ea izakkar*
*mārī epšētūka iliš naṭ[â-m]a*
*ezza meḫṣa lā maḫra tele''e …*
*ea ep[šētūk]a iliš [naṭâ]-ma*
*ezza meḫ[ṣa lā maḫr]a tele''e …*

[9] Var.: [*ea*] *pâšu ī*[*pušam-ma*].

with this she entrusted him, seating him upon a throne:
"I have cast a spell on you, making you great in the gods' assembly,
the command of all the gods I have put into your hands.
You are the greatest, you alone will be my lover.
May your word be greatest among all the Anunnaki."
She gave him the Tablet of Destinies and fixed it to his chest:
"May your pronouncements be unaltered, your utterance firm."
After Qingu had been raised up and received dominion,
he fixed the fates of the gods her sons:
"May the working of your words quench fire
and your amassed poison subdue the strong.'"
Anshar heard these words, and they were very troubling:
'Woe,' he cried, and bit his lip.
His mind was angry, his heart had no rest,
his roar was unleashed[37] on Ea, his child.
'My son, who spurred on this conflict,
now bear the responsibility for all that you, alone, have done!
You attacked Apsû and killed him,
but Tiamat, whom you enraged – where is her match?'
The master of counsel, prince of shrewdness,
creator of wisdom, the godly Nudimmud,
with soothing words and calming speech
gently answered his father Anshar:
'My father, deep heart, fixer of fates,
with whom creation and destruction lie:
Anshar, deep heart, fixer of fates,
with whom creation and destruction lie.[38]
I will recite to you a word, be calm for a moment,[39]
accept in your heart that I did a good deed.
Before I killed Apsû,
who could have seen what is happening now?
If, before hurrying to put him down,
I had destroyed her, what would have happened?'[40]
Anshar listened, the speech pleased him,
his heart found rest and he spoke to Ea:
'My son, your doings suit a god,
you are capable of … an angry, invincible strike.
Ea, your doings suit a god,
you are capable of … an angry, invincible strike.

[37] Alt.: 'was spent'.

[38] The parallel couplets, of which the second identifies the addressee by name, are typical of the hymnic genre and seem to function as a mark of respect.

[39] Alt.: 'soon you shall be calmed'. Note that term here translated as 'word', *enimmû*, is a rarefied Sumerian loanword.

[40] On the grammar and alternative translations of this line, see Haubold (2017: 228–36).

*alik-ma muttiš tiāmti tēbâša šup[šiḫ]*
*uggassa lū (...) šūṣ[ât sur]riš ina šiptī[ka]*
*išmē-ma zikr[ī abīšu] a[nšar]*
*iṣbat ḫarrānš[ū]-ma uruḫšu uštar[di]*
*illik ea šibqūš tiāmti iše''âm-ma*
*[uš]ib ušḫarrir-ma itūra arkiš*
*[īr]um-ma maḫru ba'ūli anšar*
*[un]n[en]na iṣbatam-ma izakkaršu*
*[abī] ūtattir-ma tiāmtu epšetaša elīya*
*mālakša eše''ē-ma ul imaḫḫar šiptī*
*gapšā emūqāša malât adīr[a]*
*puḫra dunnunat-ma ul iyârši mam[man]*
*lā našir tukkaša šebâm-m[a]*
*ādur-ma rigmaša atūra arkiš*
*abī ē tuštāniḫ tūr šupurši*
*emūqā sinništi lū dunnunā ul mala ša zikri*
*rummi kiṣrīša milkaša supuḫ attā*
*lām qātīša ummidu ana muḫḫīni*
*anšar uzzuziš išassi*
*ana āni mārīšu šū izakkar*
*aplu kannû kašūšu qarrādu*
*ša gapšā emūqāšu lā maḫār tēbûšu*
*aruḫ-ma muttiš tiāmti iziz attā*
*šupšiḫ kabtataš libbuš lippuš*
*šummā-ma lā šemâta amātka*
*amāt unnenni atmēšim-ma šī lippašḫa*
*išmē-ma zikrī abīšu anšar*
*iṣbat ḫarrānšū-ma uruḫšu uštardi*
*illik ānu šibqūš tiāmti iše''âm-ma*
*ušib ušḫarrir-ma itūra arkiš*
*īrum-ma maḫru abi ālidīšu anšar*
*unnenna iṣbatam-ma izakkaršu*
*abī ūtattir-ma tiāmtu [epšetaša] elīya*
*mālakša eše''ē-ma ul imaḫḫar šiptī*
*gapšā emūqāša malât adīra*
*puḫra dunnunat-ma ul iyârši mamman*
*lā našir tukkaša š[eb]âm-ma*
*ādur-ma rigmaša atūra arkiš*
*abī ē tuštāniḫ tūr šupurši*
*emūqā sinništi lū dunnunā ul mala*[10] *ša zikri*
*rummi kiṣrīša milkaša supuḫ attā*

10 Var.: [*lā? dun*]*nunā ma*[*la?*].

Go before Tiamat, bring rest to her revolt,
may her rage soon be driven out by your spell.'
He heard the speech of Anshar his father,
he took the road and made straight along the path.
Ea went to find out Tiamat's scheme,
but stopped, dumbstruck, and turned back.
He came into the presence of lordly Anshar,
making obeisance as he spoke to him:
'[My father,] Tiamat's doings are beyond me.
I found out her course, but my spell is no match for her.
Her strength is formidable, she is full of fearsomeness,
she is powerful in the assembly – no one can attack her!
Undiminished, her roar resounded against me,
I became afraid of her noise and so turned back.
My father, do not despair, send another against her!
Great as a woman's strength may be, it is no match for a man's.
Disband her troops, disrupt her stratagem,
before she lays her hands on us.'
Anshar screamed in anger,
and spoke to Anu, his son:
'Loyal heir, warlike hero,
whose strength is formidable, whose attack is invincible,
hurry – you must stand before Tiamat!
Bring rest to her mind, let her heart relax,[41]
and if she does not listen to your words,
speak words of obeisance that she may relent.'
He heard the speech of Anshar his father,
he took the road and made straight along the path.
Anu went to find out Tiamat's scheme,
but stopped, dumbstruck, and turned back.
He came into the presence of lordly Anshar,
making obeisance as he spoke to him:
'My father, Tiamat's doings are beyond me.
I found out her course, but my spell is no match for her.
Her strength is formidable, she is full of fearsomeness,
she is powerful in the assembly – no one can attack her!
Undiminished, her roar resounded against me,
I became afraid of her noise and so turned back.
My father, do not despair, send another against her!
Great as a woman's strength may be, it is no match for a man's.
Disband her troops, disrupt her stratagem,

[41] Note the wordplay *libbuš lippuš*, 'let her heart relax'.

*lām qātīša ummidu ina muḫḫīni*
*ušḫarrir-ma anšar qaqqara inaṭṭal*
*ikammam ana ea unāš qaqqassu*
*paḫrū-ma igīgū kalīšunu anukkū*
*šaptāšunu kuttumā-ma qâliš uš[bū]*
*ilu ayyûm-ma ul iyâr …*
*maḫāriš tiāmti ul uṣṣi ina šaptī[šu]n*
*u bēlu anšar abi ilī rabûti*
*kamil libbašū-ma ul išassi mamman*
*aplu gašru mutirru gimilli abīšu*
*ḫā'iš tuqmāti marduk qardu*
*ilsī-ma ea ašar pirištīšu*
*ka'inimmak libbīšu ītammīšu*
*marduk milka šeme abīka*
*attā-ma mārī munappišu libbīšu*
*muttiš anšar qitrubiš ṭeḫē-ma*
*epuš pīka izuzzu amārukka niḫḫa*
*iḫdū-ma bēlu ana amât abīšu*
*iṭḫē-ma ittaziz maḫariš anšar*
*īmuršū-ma anšar libbašu ṭubbāti imla*
*iššiq šaptīšu adīrašu uttessi*
*abī lā šuktumat pite šaptuk*
*lullik-ma lušamṣâ mala libbīka*
*anšar lā šuktumat pite šaptuk*
*lullik-ma lušamṣâ mala libbīka*
*ayyû zikru tāḫāzašu ušēṣīka*
*u tiāmtu ša sinnišat(u) iyârka ina kakki*
*abī bānû ḫidi u šūlil*
*kišād tiāmti urruḫiš takabbas attā*
*anšar bānû ḫidi u šūlil*
*kišād tiāmti urruḫiš takabbas attā*
*alik mārī mūdû gimir uzni*
*tiāmta šupšiḫ ina têka elli*
*rikab ūmī urruḫiš šutardī-ma*
*pānušša lā uttakkašū tīr arkāniš*
*iḫdū-ma bēlu ana amāt abīšu*
*īliṣ libbašū-ma ana abīšu izakkar*
*bēlū ilī šīmāt ilī rabûti*
*šummā-ma anāku mutīr gimillīkun*
*akammi tiāmtam-ma uballaṭ kâšun*

before she lays her hands on us.'
Anshar was dumbstruck, staring at the ground,
nodding and shaking his head at Ea.[42]
All the Igigi and the Anunnaki were assembled,
with sealed lips they sat in silence.
None of the gods would attack [ ]
or go forth to face Tiamat at the order of his lips,[43]
and Anshar, the Lord, father of the great gods,
was furious in his heart and did not call on anyone.
The mighty heir, avenger of his fathers,
who hastens into battle, Marduk the hero:
Ea called him to a secret place,
to speak the word in his heart.[44]
'Marduk, listen to the counsel of your father,
you are my son, who relaxes his heart.
Draw near and go before Anshar,
work your words and stand up, let him see you and find calm.'
The Lord rejoiced at the words of his father,
he drew near and stood in the presence of Anshar.
Anshar saw him, his heart filled with pleasure,
he kissed his lips and dispelled his fear.
'My father, do not seal but part your lips.
I will go and fulfil your heart's desires.
Anshar, do not seal but part your lips.
I will go and fulfil your heart's desires.
Which man has brought his battle against you?
Or is Tiamat, a woman, attacking you with a weapon?
My father, creator, rejoice and be happy!
Soon you will trample on Tiamat's neck.
Anshar, creator, rejoice and be happy!
Soon you will trample on Tiamat's neck.'
'Go, my son, who knows all reason,
bring Tiamat to rest with your sacred spell.
Ride the storm, make straight for her, be quick,
and with its steadfast front, make her turn back!'[45]
The Lord rejoiced at the words of his father,
his heart was glad, and to his father he said:
'Lord of gods, fate of the great gods,
if I am to be your avenger,
to bind Tiamat and save your lives,

42 Alt.: 'he gnashed his teeth at Ea.'
43 Lit.: 'they did not go forth before Tiamat by his lips.'
44 As in II 65, the text here uses a rarified Sumerian loanword, *ka'inimmaku*, to describe Ea's speech.
45 The line is unclear. Alt.: 'if her face cannot be repelled, turn around', or, 'turn to her back'.

*šuknā-ma puḫra šūterā ibâ šīmtī*
*ina ubšukkinnakki mitḫāriš ḫadîš tišbā-ma*
*epšu pîya kīma kâtunū-ma šīmata lušīm-ma*
*lā uttakkar mimmû abannû anāku*
*ai itūr ai innenâ siqar šaptī*

then convene an assembly and pronounce a supreme fate for me.
Sit together in joy, in the Ubshu-ukkinnaku,[46]
and let the working of my words, like yours,[47] fix fates.
What I create shall not be changed,
the command of my lips shall not be altered or reversed.'

[46] The gods' place of assembly.
[47] Alt.: 'instead of yours'.

# Tablet III

*anšar pâšu īpušam-ma*
*ana kaka sukkallīšu amāta izakkar*
*kaka sukkallu muṭīb kabattīya*
*ašriš laḫmu (u) laḫāmu kâta lušpurka*
*šite"â mūdâta tiṣbura tele"e*
*ilī abbīya šūbika ana maḫrīy[a]*
*lībukūnim-ma ilī nagabšun*
*lišāna liškunū ina qerêti lišbū*
*ašnan līkulū liptiqū kurunna*
*ana marduk mutīr gimillīšunu lišīmū šīmta*
*i'ir alik kaka qudmīšunu iziz-ma*
*[mi]mmû azakkarūka šunnâ ana šâšun*
*anšar-[(ma)] mārūkunu uma"iranni*
*[têre]t libbīšu ušaṣbiranni yâti*
*[umma ti]āmtu ālittani izerrannâti*
*[puḫra šit]kunat-ma aggiš labbat*
*isḫurūšim-ma ilū gimiršun*
*adi ša attunu tabnâ idāša alkū*
*immasrūnim-ma iduš tiāmti tebûni*
*ezzū kapdū lā sākipū mūša u imma*
*našû tamḫāra nazarbubū labb[ū]*
*ukkinna šitkunū-ma ibannû ṣūlā[ti]*
*ummu ḫubūr pātiqat kalā[ma]*
*ušraddi kakka lā maḫra ittalad mušmaḫ[ḫī]*
*zaqtū-ma šinnī lā pādû attā'[ī]*
*imta kīma dāmi zumuršunu ušmal[li]*
*ušumgallī nadrūti pulḫāti ušalbiš-[ma]*
*melammī uštaššâ iliš umtaš[šil]*
*āmiršunu šarbābiš liḫḫar[mim]*
*zumuršunu lištaḫḫiṭam-ma lā ine"ū irass[un]*
*ušziz bašma mušḫušša u laḫā[ma]*
*ugalla uridimma u girtablī[la]*
*ūmī dabrūti kulīla u kusari[kka]*
*nāš kakki lā pādû lā ādirū tāḫ[āzi]*
*gapšā têrētūša lā maḫrā šinā-[ma]*
*appunnāma ištēn-ešret kīma šuāti ušt[abši]*
*ina ilī bukrīša šūt iškunūši [puḫra]*
*ušašqi qingu ina birīšu[nu šâšu] ušra[bbīš]*
*ālikūt maḫri pān ummāni mu'errūt puḫri*

# Tablet III

Anshar worked his words
and said this to Kaka, his minister:
'Kaka, minister who soothes my mood!
Let me send you to where Lahmu and Lahamu are.
You know how to find your way, you are skilled in recitation:
have the gods, my fathers, brought into my presence.
Let every one of the gods be brought here,
let there be conversation,[48] let them sit down for a feast.
Let them eat grain,[49] let them drink ale,
and let them fix a fate for Marduk, their avenger.
Be off! Go, Kaka, and stand before them,
and repeat to them all that I will say to you:
"Anshar, your son, has dispatched me here
and made me recite the decree of his heart:
'Mother Tiamat, who gave birth to us, has spurned us:
she has convened an assembly, seething with rage.
Every god has rallied to her,
even those whom you created walk by her side.
They drew together[?], rising at Tiamat's side,
angry, plotting, not lying still by night or by day,
ready for battle, wrathful, seething,
they set up a council to bring about conflict.
Mother Noise, who shapes all,
supplied invincible weapons, giving birth to *mushmahhu*-serpents,
sharp of teeth and merciless of fang[?],
and filling their bodies with poison for blood.
The ferocious *ushumgallu*-serpents she dressed in dread,
arming them with frightful auras and making them like gods:
"May those who look upon them meekly collapse,
may their bodies keep charging and never turn back."
She enlisted *bashmu*-serpents, *mushhusshu*-serpents, *lahamu*-men,
*ugallu*-demons, lion-men, scorpion-men,
fierce demons, fish-men and *kusarikku*-bisons:
they carried merciless weapons, no fear had they of war.
Her orders were formidable, no one could oppose them:
she truly created eleven such beings.
Among the gods her children, who made up her assembly,
she elevated Qingu: it was him she made greatest among them.
To lead the army, command the assembly,

[48] Lit.: 'let them set up the tongue' (an unusual phrase to create the assonance between *lišāna*, 'tongue', *liškunū*, 'let them set up', and *lišbū*, 'let them sit down').

[49] Lit.: 'Ashnan', the goddess of grain.

*našê kakkī tiṣbūtu [dekû ananti]*
*[šūt] tamḫāri rab sik[katūti]*
*[ipqid]-ma qātuššu ušēšibaš[šu ina karri]*
*[add]i tâka ina puḫur ilī ušarbīka*
*[ma]likūt ilī gimrassunu qātu[kka ušmalli]*
*[lū] šurbâtā-ma ḫā'irī ēd[û attā]*
*lirtabbû zikrūka eli kalîšunu anu[kkī]*
*iddinšum-ma tuppi šīmāti iratuš ušatmiḫ*
*kataduggûka lā innennâ likūn ṣīt pî[ka]*
*innanu qingu šušqû leqû [ānūti]*
*an ilī mārīša šīmata išti[ma]*
*epšu pîkunu gīra liniḫḫa*
*imtuk kitmuru*[11] *magšara lišrabbib*
*ašpur-ma āna ul ile''â maḫārša*
*nudimmud īdur-ma itūra arkiš*
*i'ēr marduk apkal ilī mārūkun*
*maḫāriš tiāmti libbašu âra ubla*
*epšu pîšu ītamâ ana yâti*
*šummā-ma anāku mutīr gimillīkun*
*akammi tiāmtam-ma uballaṭ kâšun*
*šuknā-ma puḫra šūterā ibâ šīmtī*
*ina ubšukkinnakki mitḫāriš ḫadîš tišbā-ma*
*epšu pîya kīma kâtunū-ma šīmata lušīm-ma*
*lā uttakkar mimmû abannû anāku*
*ai itūr ai innenâ siqar šaptīya*
*ḫumṭānim-ma šīmatkunu arḫiš šīmāšu*
*lillik-(ma) limḫura nakarkunu danna*
*illik kaka urḫašu ušardī-ma*
*ašriš laḫmu u laḫāmu ilī abbīšu*
*uškēn-ma iššiq qaqqara maḫaršun*
*īšir izzaz izakkaršun*
*anšar-(ma) mārūkunu uma''iranni*
*têret libbīšu ušaṣbiranni yâti*
*umma tiāmtu ālittani izerrannâti*
*puḫra šitkunat-ma aggiš labbat*
*isḫurūšim-ma ilū gimiršun*
*adi ša attunu tabnâ idāša alkū*
*immasrūnim-ma iduš tiāmti tebûni*
*ezzū kapdū lā sākipū mūša u imma*
*našû tamḫāra nazarbubū labbū*
*ukkinna šitkunū-ma ibannû ṣūlāti*
*ummu ḫubūr pātiqat kalāma*
*ušraddi kakka lā maḫra ittalad mušmaḫḫī*

[11] Var.: *ina kitmuri*.

carry weapons, engage, call for the clash,
the way of war[?], the general's rank –
with this she entrusted him, seating him upon a throne:
"I have cast a spell on you, making you great in the gods' assembly,
the command of all the gods I have put into your hands.
You are the greatest, you alone will be my lover.
May your word be greatest among all the Anunnaki."
She gave him the Tablet of Destinies and fixed it to his chest:
"May your pronouncements be unaltered, your utterance firm."
After Qingu had been raised up and received dominion,
he fixed the fates of the gods her sons:
"May the working of your words quench fire
and your amassed poison subdue the strong."
I sent Anu, but he could not face her,
Nudimmud was afraid and so turned back.
Marduk, sage of the gods, your son, came forward,
his heart has compelled him to set out against Tiamat.
He worked his words and said to me:
"If I am to be your avenger,
to bind Tiamat and save your lives,
then convene an assembly and pronounce a supreme fate for me.
Sit together in joy, in the Ubshu-ukkinnaku,
and let the working of my words, like yours, fix fates.
What I create shall not be changed,
the command of my lips shall not be altered or reversed."
Hurry here and quickly fix your fate for him,
that he may go and face your powerful enemy."'
Kaka went and made straight along the path
to where Lahmu and Lahamu were, the gods his fathers.
He bowed low and kissed the ground before them,
then stood up straight and said to them:
'Anshar, your son, has dispatched me here
and made me recite the decree of his heart:
"Mother Tiamat, who gave birth to us, has spurned us:
she has convened an assembly, seething with rage.
Every god has rallied to her,
even those you created walk by her side.
They drew together[?], rising at Tiamat's side,
angry, plotting, not lying still by night or by day,
ready for battle, wrathful, seething,
they set up a council to bring about conflict.
Mother Noise, who shapes all,
supplied invincible weapons, giving birth to *mushmahhu*-serpents,

*zaqtū-ma šinnī lā pādû attā'ī*
*imta kīma dāmi zumuršunu ušmalli*
*ušumgallī nadrūti pulḫāti ušalbiš-ma*
*melammī uštaššâ iliš umtaššil*
*āmiršunu šarbābiš liḫḫarmim*
*zumuršunu lištaḫḫiṭam-ma lā ine''ū irassun*
*ušziz bašma mušḫušša u laḫāma*
*ugalla uridimma u girtablīla*
*ūmī dabrūti kulīla u* [*kusarik*]*ka*
*nāš kakki lā pādû lā ādirū tāḫāzi*
*gapšā têrētūša lā maḫrā šinā-ma*
*appunnāma ištēn-ešret kīma šuāti uštabši*
*ina ilī bukrīša šūt iškunūši puḫra*
*ušašqi qingu ina birīšunu šâšu ušrabbīš*
*ālikūt maḫri pān ummāni mu'errūt puḫri*
*našê kakkī tiṣbūtu* [*dekû*] *ananti*
*šūt tamḫāri rab sikkatūti*
*ipqid-ma qātuššu ušēšibaššu ina karri*
*addi tâka ina puḫur ilī ušarbīka*
*malikūt ilī gimrassunu qātukka ušmalli*
*lū šurbâtā-ma ḫā'irī ēdû attā*
*lirtabbû zikrūka eli kalîšunu anukkī*
*iddinšum-ma tuppi šīmāti* [*iratuš ušatmiḫ*]
*kataduggûka lā i*[*nnennâ likūn ṣīt pîka*]
*innanu qingu šušq*[*û leqû ānūti*]
*an ilī mārīša šī*[*mata ištīma*]
*epšu pîkunu gī*[*ra liniḫḫa*]
[*imtuk kitmuru*[12] *magšara lišrabbib*]
*ašpur-ma ānu ul i*[*le''â maḫārša*]
*nudimmud īdur-ma i*[*tūra arkiš*]
*i'ēr marduk apkal* [*ilī mārūkun*]
*maḫāriš tiāmti li*[*bbašu âra ubla*]
*epšu pîšu ī*[*tamâ ana yâti*]
*šummā-ma anāku m*[*utīr gimillīkun*]
*akammi tiāmtam-m*[*a uballaṭ kâšun*]
*šuknā-ma puḫra š*[*ūterā ibâ šīmtī*]
*ina ubšukkinnakki m*[*itḫāriš ḫadîš tišbā-ma*]
*epšu pîya kīma k*[*âtunū-ma šīmata lušīm-ma*]
*lā uttakkar mimmû abannû* [*anāku*]
*ai itūr a*[*i inn*]*enâ siqar š*[*aptīya*]
[*ḫ*]*umṭānim-ma šīmatkunu arḫiš* [*šīmāšu*]
[*l*]*illik-ma limḫura nakarkunu danna*

[12] Var.: *ina kitmuri*.

sharp of teeth and merciless of fang[?],
and filling their bodies with poison for blood.
The ferocious *ushumgallu*-serpents she dressed in dread,
arming them with frightful auras and making them like gods:
'May those who look upon them meekly collapse,
may their bodies keep charging and never turn back.'
She enlisted *bashmu*-serpents, *mushhusshu*-serpents, *lahamu*-men,
*ugallu*-demons, lion-men, scorpion-men,
fierce demons, fish-men and *kusarikku*-bisons:
they carried merciless weapons, no fear had they of war.
Her orders were formidable, no one could oppose them:
she truly created eleven such beings.
Among the gods her children, who made up her assembly,
she elevated Qingu: it was him she made greatest among them.
To lead the army, command the assembly,
carry weapons, engage, call for the clash,
the way of war[?], the general's rank –
with this she entrusted him, seating him upon a throne:
'I have cast a spell on you, making you great in the gods' assembly,
the command of all the gods I have put into your hands.
You are the greatest, you alone will be my lover.
May your word be greatest among all the Anunnaki.'
She gave him the Tablet of Destinies and fixed it to his chest:
'May your pronouncements be unaltered, your utterance firm.
After Qingu had been raised up and received dominion,
he fixed the fates of the gods her sons:
'May the working of your words quench fire
and your amassed poison subdue the strong.'
I sent Anu, but he could not face her,
Nudimmud was afraid and so turned back.
Marduk, sage of the gods, your son, came forward,
his heart has compelled him to set out against Tiamat.
He worked his words and said to me:
'If I am to be your avenger,
to bind Tiamat and save your lives,
then convene an assembly and pronounce a supreme fate for me.
Sit together in joy, in the Ubshu-ukkinnaku,
and let the working of my words, like yours, fix fates.
What I create shall not be changed,
the command of my lips shall not be altered or reversed.'
Hurry here and quickly fix your fate for him,
that he may go and face your powerful enemy.'"

*išmû-ma laḫmu (u) laḫāmu issû elīta*
*igīgū napḫaršunu inūqū marṣiš*
*mīnâ nakrā adi iršû ṣibit ṭ[ēmīn]i*
*lā nīdi nīni ša tiāmti epiš[taš]*
*iggaršūnim-ma illa[kūni]*
*ilū rabûtu kalīšunu mušimmū [šīmāti]*
*īrubū-ma muttiš anšar imlû [ḫidûta]*
*innašqū aḫu u aḫu ina puḫri [...]*
*lišāna iškunū ina qerêti [ušbū]*
*ašnan īkulū iptiqū kur[unna]*
*arsa matqa usanninū rāṭīšu[n]*
*šikra ina šatê ḫabṣu zum[ra]*
*ma'diš egû kabattašun ītel[ṣū]*
*ana marduk mutīr gimillīšunu išimmū šīm[ta]*

Lahmu and Lahamu listened and cried out loud,
all the Igigi wailed, disturbed:
'What is this enmity, that she has taken action against us?
We did not know the doings of Tiamat.'
They rose up[50] and went,
all the great gods, the fixers of fates,
they came in before Anshar and were filled with joy.
They kissed one another in the assembly [of the gods,]
they made conversation and sat down for a feast.
They ate grain and drank ale,
they filled their gullets with sweet confections.[51]
As they drank the beer, they felt elated in their bodies,
they were wholly relaxed and their mood grew glad.
They fixed a fate for Marduk, their avenger.

[50] The meaning of *garāšu* is unclear; one ancient commentary glosses it as *tebû*, 'to rise up'.
[51] The line is unclear, presenting several problems. The word for 'gullet' is *rāṭu*, literally 'pipe'.

# Tablet IV

*iddûšum-ma parak rubûti*
*maḫariš abbīšu ana malikūti irme*
*attā-ma kabtāta ina ilī rabûti*
*šīmatka lā šanān siqarka ānu*
*marduk kabtāta ina ilī rabûti*
*šīmatka lā šanān siqarka ānu*
*ištu ūmim-ma lā innennâ qibītka*
*šušqû u šušpulu šī lū qātka*
*lū kīnat ṣīt pîka lā sarār siqarka*
*mamman ina ilī itûkka lā ittiq*
*zanānūtu eršat*[13] *parak ilī-ma*
*ašar sāgīšunu lū kūn ašrukka*
*marduk attā-ma mutirru gimillīni*
*(i) niddinka šarrūta kiššat kal gimrēti*
*tišab-ma ina puḫri lū šaqât amātka*
*kakkūka ai ippalṭû lira''isū nakirīka*
*bēlu ša taklūka napištašu gimil-ma*
*u ila ša lemnēti īḫuzu tubuk napšassu*
*ušzizzū-ma ina birīšunu lumāša ištēn*
*ana marduk bukrīšunu šunu izzakrū*
*šīmatka bēlu lū maḫrat ilī-ma*
*abātu (u) banû qibi liktūnā*
*epšu pîka li''abit lumāšu*
*tūr qibīšum-ma lumāšu lišlim*
*iqbī-ma ina pîšu i''abit lumāšu*
*itūr iqbīšum-ma lumāšu ittabni*
*kīma ṣīt pîšu īmurū ilū abbūšu*
*iḫdû ikrubū marduk-ma šarru*
*uṣṣibūšu ḫaṭṭa kussâ u palâ*
*iddinūšu kakka lā maḫra dā'ipu zayyāri*
*alik-ma ša tiāmti napšatuš puru'-ma*
*šārū dāmīša ana busrati libillūni*
*išīmū-ma ša bēli šīmatuš ilū abbūšu*
*uruḫ šulmi (u) tešmê uštaṣbitūš ḫarrāna*
*ibšim-(ma) qašta kakkašu u'addi*
*mulmulla uštarkiba ukīnši matna*

[13] Var.: *zanānūt kiššat.*

# Tablet IV

They set up a princely throne dais for him
and he took his place before his fathers, ready for kingship.
'You are the most important among the great gods,
your fate is unrivalled, your command is like Anu's.[52]
Marduk, you are the most important among the great gods,
your fate is unrivalled, your command is like Anu's.
From this day onward, your command shall be unaltered:
to raise high and bring low, this shall be in your hand.
May your utterance be firm and your command never false,
none among the gods shall transgress your bounds.
The daises of the gods are in need of support:
where their temples stand, may yours too be established.[53]
You, Marduk, are now our avenger:
we have given you kingship over the entire world, all of it.
Sit down in the assembly, may your word be raised high,
may your weapons never miss, may they crush your enemies.
Lord! Spare the life of those who trust in you,
but blot out the life of the god who chooses evil.'
They set up among them one constellation,
and said to him, to Marduk their child:
'Your fate, Lord, shall equal the gods:
command destruction or creation, and it shall be done.
At the working of your words, let the constellation be destroyed,
command again and let the constellation be made whole.'
He commanded, and at his word the constellation was destroyed,
he commanded again and the constellation was created anew.
When the gods his fathers saw the effect of his utterance,[54]
they rejoiced and acclaimed: 'Marduk is king!'
They equipped him with a sceptre, throne, and kingly staff,
and gave him an invincible weapon that brings down rivals.
'Go and slit Tiamat's throat,
let the winds bear off her blood as happy news.'
The gods his fathers fixed a fate for the Lord,
and set him on the road, a path of safety and success.
He fashioned a bow and appointed it to be his weapon,
he mounted an arrow and fixed it firmly on the string.

52 Lit.: 'your command is Anu', in a reference to Anu's traditional status as a moral authority among the gods.

53 Alt.: 'May the place of their temples be established in your place.' The line may thus refer either to the establishment of cellas to Marduk within the temples of other gods, or, conversely, to the establishment of temples to all the gods in Marduk's city of Babylon.

54 Lit.: 'saw his utterance'.

*iššī-ma miṭṭa imnašu ušāḫiz*
*qašta u išpata iduššu īlul*
*iškun berqa ina pānīšu*
*nabla muštaḫmiṭa zumuršu umtalli*
*īpuš-ma sapāra šulmû qerbiš tiāmta*
*erbetti šārī ušteṣbita lā aṣê*[14] *mimmîša*
*šūta iltāna šadâ amurra*
*iduš sapāri uštaqriba qīsti*[15] *abīšu āni*
*ibni imḫulla šāra lemna meḫâ ašamšūta*
*šār-erbetti šār-sebetti imsuḫḫa šār-lā-maḫār*
*ušēṣâm-ma šārī ša ibnû sebettīšun*
*qerbiš tiāmti šudluḫu tebû arkīšu*
*iššī-ma bēlu abūba kakkašu rabâ*
*narkabta ūma lā maḫra galitta irkab*
*iṣmissim-ma erbet naṣmadī idušša īlul*
*šaggiša lā pādâ rāḫiṣa mupparša*
*patûni šaptī šinnāšunu našâ imta*
*anāḫa lā īdû sapāna lamdū*
*ušziz imnuššu tāḫāza rašba u tuqunta*
*šumēla ananta dā'ipat kala muttendī*
*naḫlapta apluḫta pulḫāti ḫalip-ma*
*melammī rašubbāti apir rāšuššu*
*uštēšir-ma bēlu urḫašu ušardī-ma*
*ašriš tiāmti ša uggugat pānuššu iškun*
*ina šaptīšu tâ ukalla*
*šammi imta bullî tamiḫ rittuššu*
*ina ūmīšu idullūšu ilū idullūšu*
*ilū abbūšu idullūšu ilū idullūšu*
*iṭḫē-ma bēlu qabluš tiāwati ibarri*
*ša qingu ḫā'irīša iše''â šibqīšu*
*inaṭṭal-ma eši mālakšu*

[14] Var.: *ana lā aṣê*.
[15] Var.: *an*[*a qīšti*].

He took up a club, grasping it with his right hand,
and hung the bow and quiver at his side.
He placed lightning at his front
and infused his body with a blazing flame.
He made a net with which to trap Tiamat,
preparing the four winds, so that none of her would escape:
the south wind, north wind, east wind, west wind.
He set this net at his side, the gift of Anu his father.[55]
He created the evil wind,[56] the tempest, the dust storm,
the fourfold wind, the sevenfold wind, the whirlwind, the invincible wind.
He released the winds he had created, all seven of them,
they rose up behind him to trouble Tiamat's inside.
The Lord took up the Flood, his great weapon,
and mounted the invincible, terrifying storm chariot.
He harnessed to it a team of four, and hung the reins at its side:
the Slaughterer, the Merciless, the Trampler, the Airborne.
Their lips were parted, their teeth bore poison,
they did not know tiredness but had learned to lay waste.
At his right he stationed daunting war and battle,
and at his left a clash to bring down all conspirators.
He was clad in an armoured garment of dread[57]
and crowned on his head with awe-inspiring auras.
The Lord set out and made straight along the path,
he turned his face toward the raging Tiamat.
He held a spell on his lips,
in his hand he grasped a plant to smother poison.
On that day they thronged around him, the gods thronged around him,
the gods his forbears thronged around him, the gods thronged around him.[58]
The Lord drew near and examined Tiamat's battle lines,[59]
he found out the schemes of her lover Qingu.
As he looked on, his advance was confused,[60]

55 The line seems to imply that the net is (at least partially) made out of the four winds gifted to Marduk by Anu. Alt.: 'he set (the winds) at his side, by the net,' or, 'he set (the winds) at the side of the net.'

56 The text adds *šāra lemna*, 'evil wind', as a gloss to *imḫulla*, literally translating the Sumerian loanword. The gloss became part of the main text, but it must be removed for the count of winds to come out as seven.

57 The line displays a particularly remarkable pattern of consonance: *naḫlapta apluḫti pulḫāti ḫalip-ma* (*ḫlp / plḫ // plḫ / ḫlp*).

58 The couplet displays a heavy consonance around the sounds *l*, *š*, *i*, and *u*: *ina ūmīšu idullūšu ilū idullūšu / ilū abbūšu idullūšu ilū idullūšu.*

59 Alt.: 'Tiamat's centre', or 'waist'.

60 The lines display a remarkable ambiguity, as they withhold the subject of the stanza – Qingu or Marduk? – until the last line. The stanza also plays on the previous scenes of Ea and Anu, who were – like Qingu but not like Marduk – overwhelmed by the sight of their opponent. Note also the pun on *mālakšu*, 'his advance', which suggests *malakšu*, 'his king'.

*sapiḫ ṭēmašū-ma seḫât epšessu*
*u ilū rēṣūšu ālikū idīšu*
*īmurū-ma qarda ašarēda niṭilšun īši*
*iddi t[âš]a tiāmtu ul utār kišāssa*
*ina šaptīša lullâ ukalla sarrāti*
*… ša bēli ilū tebûka*
*… ipḫurū šunu ašrukka*
*[iššī]-ma bēlu abūba kakkašu rabâ*
*[a]na tiāmti ša ikmilu kīam išpurš[i]*
*mīnâ ṭubbâti eliš našâtī-ma*
*u kapid libbakī-ma dekê ananta*
*issû mārū abbīšunu idaṣṣū*
*u attī ālittašunu tazerrī rēma*
*tabbî qingu ana ḫā'irūtīki*
*ana lā simātīšu taškunīš ana paraṣ ānūti*
*ana anšar šar ilī lemnēti tešê-ma*
*u ana ilī abbīya lemuttaki tuktinnī*
*lū ṣandat ummātki lū ritkusū šunu kakkūki*
*endīm-ma anāku u kâši i nīpuš šašma*
*tiāmtu annīta ina šemêša*
*maḫḫūtiš ītemi ušanni ṭēnša*
*issī-ma tiāmtu šitmuriš elīta*
*šuršiš malmališ itrurā išdāša*
*imanni šipta ittanaddi tâša*
*u ilū ša tāḫāzi uša''alū šunu kakkīšun*
*innendū-ma tiāmtu (u) apkal ilī marduk*
*šašmiš itlupū qitrubū tāḫāziš*

his mind disrupted, his doings disarrayed,
and likewise the gods his allies who walked at his side,
saw the hero, the vanguard, and their sight was obscured.
Tiamat cast her spell, she did not look away,[61]
she held untruth and lies on her lips:
'[ ] Lord of the gods, your onslaught,[62]
they assembled on their [own,?] but they are with you!'[63]
The Lord took up the Flood, his great weapon,
and to Tiamat, who acted conciliatorily,[64] sent this message:
'Why are you raised up in kindness
while plotting within your heart and rousing conflict?
The children cried out and harassed their fathers,
but you, who gave birth to them, refused mercy.
You named Qingu as your lover
and unrighteously assigned him dominion.
You pursued evil against Anshar, the king of the gods,[65]
and firmly established wickedness against the gods, my fathers.
Your army may be prepared, your weapons arrayed,[66]
but join me here: let you and me engage in single combat.'
When Tiamat heard this,
she became like an ecstatic, her mind was deranged.
Tiamat cried out, fiercely and loudly,
she shook all over, down to her depths.[67]
She was reciting an incantation, she kept chanting her spell,
while the gods were whetting their weapons for battle.
They joined together,[68] Tiamat and the sage of the gods, Marduk,
entwined in single combat, closing in for the fray.[69]

[61] Lit.: 'she did not turn back her neck'.

[62] The exchange between Marduk and Tiamat (IV 73–8) can be understood in two different ways. The option chosen here is that Tiamat pretends to flatter Marduk, who sees through her ruse and rebuffs her. Alternatively, one can read Tiamat's (fragmentary) words as a provocation, leading to a translation such as '"The gods have risen up against you, they assembled in their [] are they with you?" The Lord took up the Flood, his great weapon, and to Tiamat, who was furious, sent this message: "Why are you truculent and raised up high, plotting in your heart and rousing conflict?"'

[63] Lit., 'they assembled in their [place,?] they are in your place.'

[64] The choice between the two options, as described in the previous note, hinges on the parsing of this word as either *igmilu*, 'to act agreeably' or *ikmilu*, 'to be angry'.

[65] The title 'king of the gods' works as a reversed reading of Anshar's name: the two signs AN and ŠAR$_2$ are interpreted as DINGIR, 'god', and *šarru*, 'king', respectively.

[66] Alt.: 'May your army be readied, may your weapons be girt, and then … '

[67] Lit.: 'deeply, entirely, her foundations shook'.

[68] The text uses the same word, *innendū*, 'to join together', which in I 21 describes the gods meeting for a celebration: in stark contrast, Tiamat and Marduk here meet in battle.

[69] The entwining of the two gods is mirrored at the level of syntax and sound through the chiastic construction of the line *šašmiš itlupū qitrubū tāḫāziš*, where the two nouns ending in *-iš* bracket the two similar-sounding verbs.

*ušparrir-ma bēlu sapārašu ušalmīši*
*imḫulla ṣābit arkati pānušša umtaššir*
*iptē-ma pīša tiāmtu ana la'ātīša*
*imḫulla uštēriba ana lā katām šaptīša*
*ezzūtu šārū karšaša iṣānū-ma*
*innesil libbašā-ma pâša ušpalki*
*issuk mulmulla iḫtepi karassa*
*qerbīša ubattiqa ušalliṭ libba*
*ikmīšī-ma napšatuš uballi*
*šalamtaš iddâ elīša izzaza*
*ištu tiāmta ālik pāni ināru*
*kiṣrīša uptarrira puḫurša issapḫa*
*u ilū rēṣūša ālikū idīša*
*ittarrū iplaḫū usaḫḫirū alkassun*
*ušeṣṣû-ma napšatuš eṭēra*
*nīta lamû naparšudiš lā le'û*
*īsiršunūtī-ma kakkīšunu ušabbir*
*sapāriš nadû-ma kamāriš ušbū*
*endū tubqāti malû dumāmī*
*šēressu našû kalû kišukkiš*
*(u) ištēn-ešret nabnīti šūt pulḫāti ṣa'nū*
*milla gallê ālikū kirdip imnīša*
*ittadi ṣerrēti idīšunu ukassi*
*qadu tuqmātīšunu šapalšu ikbus*
*u qingu ša irtabbû ina birīšun*
*ikmīšū-ma itti uggê šuātu imnīšu*
*īkimšū-ma tuppi šīmāti lā simātīšu*
*ina kišibbi iknukam-ma irtuš itmuḫ*
*ištu lemnīšu ikmû isādu*
*ayyāba mutta'da ušāpû šūrīšam*
*ernitti anšar eli nakirī kalîš ušzizzu*
*nizmat nudimmud ikšudu marduk qardu*
*eli ilī kamûti ṣibittašu udannin-ma*
*ṣēriš tiāmti ša ikmû itūra arkiš*
*ikbus-ma bēlu ša tiāmti išissa*
*ina miṭṭīšu lā pādî ulatti muḫḫa*
*uparri'-ma ušlāt dāmīša*
*šāra iltāna ana busrati uštābil*

The Lord spread out his net, trapping her,
he unleashed in her face the evil wind that held the rear.
Tiamat opened her mouth to swallow it,
he forced the evil wind inside her, so that she could not close her lips.
The angry winds bloated her belly,
her inside was congested, her mouth gaped wide.
He shot an arrow and it pierced her belly,
gashed her entrails, and gouged her heart.
He bound her and smothered her life,
he threw down her corpse and stepped upon it.
After he had killed Tiamat, their leader,
her troops scattered, her assembly dispersed,
and the gods her allies who walked at her side,
trembled in dread and turned back in retreat.
They fled,[?] so as to save their lives,
but they were surrounded on all sides, they could not escape.
He locked them up, he smashed their weapons,
they were thrown into the net, they slumped into the trap,
they sunk into a corner, they were full of weeping,
they bore his punishment, they were held captive.
The eleven creatures, those that brimmed with dread,
the throng[?] of demons who walked at her right hand as helpers,
he put a leash on them and chained their arms,
he trampled them beneath him, together with their rancour.
As for Qingu, who had become the greatest among them:
he bound him and counted him among the gods of death.
He took from him the Tablet of Destinies that he unrightly held,[70]
sealed it and fixed it to his own chest.
After he had bound and slain his foes,
had … the mighty enemy,
had declared triumph for Anshar over all his opponents,
and had fulfilled Nudimmud's desire, Marduk the hero
strengthened his hold over the captive gods,
and then turned back[71] to Tiamat, whom he had bound.
The Lord trampled upon the depths of Tiamat,
and split open her head with his merciless club.
He slit the vessels of her blood
and had the North Wind bear it off as happy news.

[70] The opening words of this and the preceding line form a neat symmetry: *ikmīšū-ma*, 'he bound him', and *īkimšū-ma*, 'he took from him'. This line also contains a key pun on the words *šīmāti*, 'destinies', and *lā simatīšu*, 'not his right'.

[71] The phrase *itūra arkiš*, 'he turned back', is an ironic repetition of its appearance in II 82 and 105, where it signalled Ea's and Anu's failures: here, it marks Marduk's triumph over Tiamat, as he begins to manipulate her body.

*īmurū-ma abbūšu iḫdû irīšū*
*igisê šulmāna ušābilū šunu ana šâšu*
*inūḫ-ma bēlu šalamtaš ibarri*
*šerkuppa uzāz ibannâ niklāti*
*iḫpīšī-ma kīma nūn maštê ana šinīšu*
*mišluššа iškunam-ma šamāmī uṣṣallil*
*išdud maška maṣṣara ušaṣbit*
*mêša lā šūṣâ šunūti umta''ir*
*šamê ībir ašrata iḫīṭam-ma*
*uštamḫir meḫret apsî šubat nudimmud*
*imšuḫ-ma bēlu ša apsî binûtuššu*
*ešgalla tamšīlašu ukīn ešarra*
*ešgalla ešarra ša ibnû šamāmī*
*ānu enlil u ea māḫāzīšun ušramma*

His fathers saw it, rejoiced and exulted:
they had gifts and presents brought to him in turn.
The Lord grew calm and examined her corpse
to carve up the watery mass[72] and create artful things.
He split her in two, like a dried fish,
set half of her up as a roof above heaven,[73]
stretched out her skin and appointed a watch,
ordering them not to let her waters escape.
He crossed[74] the sky, inspected the firmament,
and made it a counterpart of the Apsû, the home of Nudimmud.
The Lord measured out the shape of the Apsû,
and founded the Eshara, the image of Eshgala.
In the Eshgala, in the Eshara he created, and in heaven,
he installed Anu, Enlil and Ea in their temples.[75]

72 The rare word *serkuppu* seems to mean 'marsh', or the like. The commentary *Malku* II 37 equates it with Tiamat, but that association is probably based on this line. The word was previously read *kūbu*, 'foetus'.

73 Lit.: 'he set half of her up, he roofed heaven.' This can be taken to mean that Tiamat's watery body was stretched out above the heavens, or that the heavens were made out of Tiamat's upper half as a roof over the world.

74 The description of Marduk as 'crossing' (*ebēru*) the sky foreshadows his identification with Jupiter, in Akkadian Neberu, for which see the note on VII 124.

75 The text envisions three layers, each organized around a central location and ruled by a god (who are listed in chiastic order): the Eshgala ('Great Shrine') in the Apsû, ruled by Ea; the Eshara ('House of the Universe') on earth, ruled by Enlil; and the heavens, ruled by An. For discussion, see Livingstone (1986: 79–81), Horowitz (1998: 113–4) and Lambert (2013: 476). Note that Eshara can also be written as Esharra, and Eshgala as Eshgalla.

# Tablet V

*ubaššim manzāza ana ilī rabûti*
*kakkabī tamšīlšunu lumāšī ušziz*
*u'addi šatta miṣrāti umaṣṣir*
*šinšeret arḫī kakkabī šulu[š]ā ušziz*
*ištu ūmī ša šatti uṣṣ[ir]u uṣurāti*
*ušaršid manzāz nēberi ana uddû riksīšun*
*ana lā epēš anni lā egû manāma*
*manzāz enlil u ea ukīn ittīšu*
*iptē-ma abullāti ina ṣēlī [k]ilallīn*
*šigarī udannina šumēla u imna*
*ina kabattīšā-ma ištakan elâti*
*nannāra uštēpâ*[16] *mūša iqtīpa*
*u'addīšum-ma šuknat mūsi ana uddû ūmī*
*arḫīšam lā naparkâ ina agê uṣṣir*
*ina rēš arḫim-ma napāḫi elâti*
*qarnī nabâta ana uddû zakāri ūmī*
*ina sebūti agâ [ma]šla*
*[š]apattu lū šutamḫurāt(a) mišil [arḫī]šam*
*e[n]ūma šamšu ina išid šamê ina[ṭṭal]ūka*
*in[a s]imti šutakṣibam-ma bini arkāniš*
*bub[bul]u ana ḫarrān šamši šutaqrib-ma*

[16] Var.: [*nannāra kakk*]*abšu*.

# Tablet V

He fashioned stations for the great gods[76]
and established the constellations, the images of the stars.
He marked out the year, drawing its outline,
and established the twelve months, with three stars each.[77]
After he had planned out the year,[78]
he fixed Neberu's station to mark the bonds between the stars,[79]
and so that they would not err or be remiss in any way,
he fixed alongside it the stations of Enlil and Ea.[80]
He then opened gates in both her ribs,
and reinforced the bolts to the right and to the left.[81]
He placed her liver in the heights of heaven
and brought forth the Moon, entrusting the night to him,
appointing him as the night-time jewel, so as to distinguish the days.
Monthly and without fail, he ennobled him with a crown[82]:
'At the beginning of each month, light up the height of heaven![83]
You shine with horns to mark the naming of the days.[84]
On the seventh day, you will have your crown halved,
on the fifteenth, halfway through each month, you shall be matched:
when Shamash can see you on the horizon,[85]
then reach your full size at the fitting time, and reverse your form.[86]
On the day of disappearance, approach the path of Shamash,

[76] Each god was thought to have an astral manifestation – a star or planet, the sun, or the moon. The *manzāzū*, 'stations', of the gods are the orbit of their astral manifestation through the night-sky.

[77] Alt: 'he established three stars for each of the twelve months.' For discussion, see Horowitz (1998: 115, 155–6).

[78] Alt: 'the days of the year'. The phrase *ištu ūmī*, 'after', includes the word 'day' (*ūmī*), which is the object of Marduk's next act of creation.

[79] Neberu is Jupiter, Marduk's astral manifestation.

[80] The 'path of Enlil' and 'path of Ea' refer to the zone north and south of the ecliptic, which was identified as the 'path of Anu'.

[81] These are the bolts of the gates through which the sun, the moon, and the stars pass as they rise and set; see Horowitz (1998: 266–7).

[82] Alt.: 'he (the Moon) departed with a crown', or, 'he (Marduk) drew on a crown'.

[83] Alt.: 'When the New Moon shines upon the height of heaven'.

[84] The word *nabâta*, 'you shine', could also mean 'you are named'; the association is strengthened by the occurrence of *zakāru*, 'naming', in the same line, just as the two words *nabû* and *zakāru* are juxtaposed in the epic's opening couplet.

[85] Shamash was the Sun God. The text states that half-way through the month, the sun and moon should stand in opposition to each other, with both visible at opposite ends of the horizon.

[86] Lit.: 'create (yourself) backwards'. The word *šutakṣubu*, 'reach fullness', can also be understood to mean 'wane'.

*[ina šalā]šê*[17] *lū šutamḫurāt(a) šamša lū šannāt(a)*
*… […] … itta ba'i uruḫša*
*… [… š]utaqribā-ma dīna dīn[ā]*
*… […] … šamaš tummâta d[âka] ḫabāla*
*… […] … yât[i]*
*… […] … […]*
*… […]*
*ša[maš … ]*
*ina … […]*
*lū nadn[aššu …]*
*attā u š[âšu …]*
*ai ibbašī-ma … […]*
*šunu lū šul[lumū …]*
*ina taqtī[t … …]*
*bubbulu libb[aši …]*
*ištu têrēti … […]*
*uṣurāti pāni … […]*
*ibnī-ma ūma […]*
*šattu lū šutamḫ[urat …]*
*ina zagmukki […]*
*šattu ina … […]*
*lū kayyānamm[a …]*
*šigar āṣīt[i …]*
*ištu ūmi … […]*
*maṣṣarāt mūši u i[mmi …]*
*rupuštu ša tiāmti […]*
*[marduk] ibtaši[m …] … […] …*
*ikṣur-ma ana erpēti ušasbi'*
*tebi šārī šuznunu kaṣāṣa*
*šuqtur imbari kamār imtīša*
*u'addī-ma ramānuš ušāḫiz qāssu*
*iškun qaqqassa … […] išpuk*
*nagba uptettâ mê ittešbi*
*iptē-ma ina īnīša pur[atta] idiglat*
*naḫīrīša upt[e]ḫḫâ … ītezba*

[17] Var.: *ša [ina šalāšê]*.

on the thirtieth day, you shall be matched with Shamash.[87]
[ ] the sign, walk its path.
Approach [ ] give verdicts,[88]
[ ] Shamash, conflict,[89] murder, and wrongdoing,
[ ] me,
[ ]
[ ]
Shamash [ ]
In [ ]
It shall be given [ ]
You and he [ ]
Let there be no [ ]
They shall be restored [ ]
At the end of [ ]
On the day of disappearance, let there be [ ]
After [he had given] the decrees [ ]
The plans [ ]
He created the day [ ]
Let the year be matched [ ]
On the New Year [ ]
The year in [ ]
Let there be constant [ ]
The bolt on the exit [ ]
After [ ]
The watches of night and day[90] [ ]
Tiamat's spit [ ]
Marduk[91] created [ ]
He bound it together and made it swirl as clouds.
To raise the winds, to make the rain fall,
to make the fog billow, to heap up her poison,[92]
this he appointed to himself, grasping it with his hand.
He set up her head, he heaped up [ ]
He flung open a chasm, it filled up with water,
he let the Euphrates and Tigris flow from her eyes,
he plugged her nostrils, leaving behind [ ]

87 The word *šutamḫuru*, used in V 18 to describe the opposition of sun and moon, is here used to describe their conjunction, as the moon is in line with the sun and so invisible. Note that the use of this word to describe conjunction and opposition is unique to *Enuma Elish*.
88 The word 'verdicts', *dīnu*, here likely refers to the astral omens produced by the planets.
89 Alt.: 'Shamash, restrict murder and wrongdoing!'
90 Day and night were divided into three 'watches' each.
91 The line is only preserved in an Assyrian manuscript, which as described by Frances Reynolds and Eckart Frahm in this volume consistently replaces Marduk's name with that of Ashur.
92 It is unclear what Tiamat's 'poison', *imtu*, refers to; an explanation may have been supplied by the missing lines.

*išpuk ina ṣertīša š[ad]î bērūti*
*namba'ī [u]ptalliša ana babāl[i] kuppī*
*egir zibbassa durmāḫ[i]š urakkis-ma*
*[…] … apsâ šapal šēpuššu*
*[iškun ḫ]allīša retât šamāmī*[18]
*[mišil]ša uṣṣallila erṣeta uktinna*
*[ … š]ipra libbuš tiāmti ušasbi'*
*[ušparri]r sapārašu kalîš uštēṣi*
*iptiq-ma šamê u erṣeti …*
*[…] rikissunu-ma epiš kunnūni*
*ištu pelludêšu uṣṣiru ubaššimu parṣ[īšu]*
*[ṣerr]ēti ittadâ ea uštaṣbit*
*[tuppi š]īmāti ša [qi]ngu īkimu ubillam-ma*
*rēš tāmarti itbala ana āni iqtīša*
*… ša tāḫāzi īlulu ītaprūš*
*… irtedâ ana maḫar [ab]bī[šu]*
*[u] ištēn-ešret nabnīssa ša tiāmtu ibnû …*
*[kakk]īšun iḫtepâ īsir šēpuššu*
*ibnī-ma ṣalmī[šunu ina bāb] apsî uša[ṣbit]*
*[aḫ]râtaš lā immaššâ [š]ī lū ittu*
*īmurū-[ma] il[ū k]arassunu ḫa<dîš> irišš[ū]*
*[la]ḫmu u laḫāmu kalîšunu abbūšu*
*[īd]iršum-ma anšar šar šulma ušāpīšu*
*[ān]u enlil u ea uqa''išūš qīšāti*
*ummu damkina ālittašu ušālilšu*
*ina ebbi tuqsiqqê pānīšu ušnammir*
*ana usmî ša tāmartaša ana busrati ubla*
*[iqī]pšum-ma šukkallūt apsî paqāda ešrēti*
*[pa]ḫrū-ma igīgū kalîšunu uškinnūš*
*anunnakkū mala bašû unaššaqū šēpīšu*
*[…] … puḫuršunu labāniš appi*
*[…] … izzizū iknušū annāma šarru*
*[…] … abbūšu išbû lalâšu*
*išmē-ma bēlu … ubbuḫu turbu' šašmi*
*… […] ēma taḫūqūši*
*ḫašurra … […] zumuršu ušal[bak]*
*ūtediq-ma [tēd]īq rubûtī[šu]*

[18] Var.: [*iškun ḫa*]*llī ša imitta*? *retât šamāmī*.

He heaped her breasts into lofty mountains,
he bored springs to carry the well-water,[93]
he twisted her tail, tying it up as the Durmahu,[94]
[ ] Apsû beneath his feet.
[He set up] her groin, keeping heaven in place[95]:
he made a roof out of her second half, founding the earth.[96]
After he had completed his work inside Tiamat,
he spread open his net, he let everything out.
He formed heaven and earth [ ]
[ ] their bonds [ ] firm.
After he had drawn up his ordinances, fashioned his rituals,
he laid out reins and had Ea take hold of them.[97]
The Tablet of Destinies which Qingu had snatched and carried off,
he took as a foremost trophy and gifted it to Anu.
[ ] of battle he hung, setting it on his head.
[ ] he led before his fathers,
and the eleven beings that Tiamat had created [ ]
he broke their weapons, he bound them to his feet.
He created statues of them, installing them at Apsû's gate:
'Let them be a sign, never to be forgotten.'
The gods saw it and their hearts exulted with joy –
Lahmu, Lahamu and all his fathers.
Anshar embraced him and recited greetings for the king,[?]
Anu, Enlil, and Ea gave him gifts.
Mother Damkina, who gave birth to him, cried out with joy over him,
she lit up his face with a spotless divine robe.
To Usmû, who brought him the happy news of her gift,
he entrusted the ministry of the Apsû and care of the sanctuaries.
The Igigi assembled and all bowed low before him,
the Anunnaki, every one of them, kissed his feet.
[ ] their gathering to pay him obeisance,
[they drew near,] stood, and bowed: 'This is the king!'
his fathers [ ] and drank their fill of his beauty,
The Lord listened [ ] still covered in the dust of the fray.
'[ ] wherever you advance[?] against her.'
He anointed his body with cedar oil [ ]
He dressed himself in a lordly garment,

[93] Marduk here punctures Tiamat's skin to access the water on the other side.
[94] Literally 'the Mighty Bond', Durmahu was the cosmic bond that held together heaven and earth.
[95] The word for 'keeping in place', *retû*, most commonly refers to driving in pegs.
[96] In this reading, Tiamat's second half becomes the earth, which acts as a roof above the Apsû. Alt.: '(The first) half of her being roofed, he fixed firm the earth.'
[97] The line refers to the cuneiform concept of the world or the country being controlled by metaphorical reins that are held by the gods or the king.

*[mela]mmī šarr[ūti] agâ rašubb[ati]*
*iššī-ma miṭṭa imnašu ušāḫi[z]*
*[ … šu]mēla ukt[īl]*
*iškun eli … […]*
*… [eli mušḫuš]ši šēpīšu ušarš[id]*
*ušpar šulmi u tešmê iduššu [īlul]*
*[…] … […]*
*ištu melammī […]*
*azamilšu apsû rašubb[atu …]*
*šūšub kīma … […]*
*ina emāši ašt[îšu …]*
*ina simakkīšu […]*
*ilū mala bašû […]*
*laḫmu (u) l[aḫām]u […]*
*īpušū-ma pâšunu i[zakkarū ana i]lī igīgī*
*pānâ-ma [mardu]k māru narāmni*
*inanna šarrakun qibīssu qālā*
*šanû izzakrū-ma iqbû puḫuršun*
*lugaldimeranki'a zikrašu šuāšu tiklāšu*
*enūma ana marduk iddinū šarrūta*
*ka'inimmak dumqi u tešmê šuāšu izzakrū*
*ištu ūmi attā lū zānin parakkīni*
*mimmû attā taqabbû i nīpuš nīni*
*marduk pâšu īpuš-ma iqabbi*
*ana ilī abbīšu amāta izzakkar*
*elēnu apsî šubat ḫašmāni*
*meḫret ešarra ša abnû anāku elkun*
*šapliš ašrati udannina qaqqarša*
*lūpuš-ma bīta lū šubat lalêya*
*qerbuššu māḫāzašu lušaršid-ma*
*kummī luddâ lukīn šarrūtī*
*enūma ištu apsî tellâ ana purussê*
*ašruššu lū nubattakun ana maḫār(i) puḫrīkun*
*enūma ištu šamāmī turradā ana pur[ussê]*
*ašruššu lū nubattakun ana maḫār(i) puḫrīkun*
*lubbī-ma šumšu bābi[li] bītāt ilī rabûti*

a frightful aura of kingship and an awe-inspiring crown.
He took up his club, grasping it with his right hand,
[ ] he held in his left.
He set up [ ]
[ on the *mushhusshu*-serpent] he planted his feet,
the staff of safety and success he hung at his side.
[ ]
After [ ] the frightful aura,
His sack, the Apsû, an awe-inspiring [ ]
seated like [ ]
in the sanctum of his throne [ ]
in his cella [ ]
Every one of the gods [ ]
Lahmu and Lahamu [ ]
worked their words and said to the Igigi-gods:
'Marduk was once our beloved son,
now he is your king – obey his command!'
Then they said, speaking together:
'Lugal-Dimmer-Ankia[98] is his name – trust in him!'
When they had given kingship to Marduk,
they recited an oration of goodness and success for him:
'From now on, you shall provide for our sacred throne-daises,
and whatever you command, we will do!'
Marduk worked his words and spoke,
saying these words to the gods his fathers:
'Above the Apsû, the home of *hashmanu*,[99]
opposite the Eshara, which I built for you,
beneath the firmament, whose surface I made strong,
I will build a house. Let it be my beautiful home!
Inside it, I will found its temple,
I will appoint my chamber and make firm my kingship.
When you come up from the Apsû to make decisions,
let this be your place of repose before your assembly.
When you come down from the heavens to make decisions,
let this be your place of repose before your assembly.
I will name it 'Babylon, Houses of the Great Gods.'[100]

[98] 'King of the gods of heaven and earth'.

[99] The word *ḫašmānu* refers to an unidentified precious stone of a blueish (and so sea-like) colour.

[100] The name of Babylon, *Bābili*, was most often etymologized as *bāb ilī*, 'gate of the gods'. The text here replaces 'gate' with 'houses', probably based on the graphic similarity between the signs ka$_2$, *bābu*, 'gate', and e$_2$, *bītu*, 'house'.

*isinnu qerbuš … […] … ippušū šī nubattu*
*i[šmû-ma ilū abb]ūšu annâ q[abâ]šu*
*… […] …*
*eli mimma ša ibnâ qātāka*
*man[nu … ] … īši*
*eli qaqqari ša ibnâ qātāka*
*man[nu … ] … īši*
*[bābili] ša tazkura šumšu*
*aš[ruššu nubatt]ani idi dārišam*
*… [ … sa]ttukkani libillūni*
*… […] …*
*manāma šiprīni ša … […]*
*ašruššu […] mānaḫtaš […] …*
*iḫdû […] … […] …*
*ilū … […] …*
*ša īd[û … ] ukillūš(u) kakka*
*iptē-[ma pâšu ukalla]mšunūti nūra*
*… [ … qab]âšu eninnu*
*[u]špal[ki … ] … parṣī*
*[…] … […]*
*… […] … […]*
*uškinnūšum-ma ilū iqabbûšu*
*ana lugaldimeranki'a bēlīšunu [šun]u [izzakrū]*
*pānâ-ma bēlu māru n[arāmni]*
*inanna šarrani … […]*
*ša … […] uballiṭ[ūnâši]*
*… [ … mel]ammī mi[ṭṭi] u ušpa[ri]*
*līpuš eṣr[ēti (…) k]ala u[mmâ]nūt[i]*
*[…] … […] … nīnu*

within it [ ] we shall hold a festival, that of repose.'
The gods his fathers heard his command,
[ ]
'Over everything that your hands have created,
who has [ ]
Over the earth that your hands have created,
who has [ ]
In Babylon, which you have named,
lay out our place of repose for all time!
[ ] let them bring us our regular offerings,
[ ]
Whoever [ ] our tasks [ ]
In this place [ ] his toil [ ]'
They rejoiced [ ]
The gods [ ]
He who knows [ ] granted them a weapon,
He opened [his mouth and revealed] to them the light,
[ ] his command was supreme,
he broadened [ ]
[ ] … [ ]
[ ]
The gods bowed low before him and spoke to him,
they said to Lugal-Dimmer-Ankia, their lord:
'Lord, you were once our beloved son,
now you are our king [ ]
who [ ] saved our lives,
[ ] frightening aura, club, and staff,
Let him make plans [ ] every expertise,
[ ] we [ ]'

# Tablet VI

*[mar]duk zikrī ilī ina šemêšu*
*[ub]bal libbašu ibannâ niklāti*
*[ep]šu pîšu ana ea iqab[bi]*
*[ša] ina libbīšu uštāmû inaddin milka*
*dāmī lukṣur-ma eṣemta lušabšī-ma*
*lušziz-ma lullâ lū amēlu šumšu*
*lubnī-ma lullâ amēla*
*lū emdū dulli ilī-ma šunu lū pašḫū*
*lušannī-ma alkakāt ilī lunakkil*
*ištēniš lū kubbutū-ma ana šina lū zīzū*
*īpulšū-(ma) ea amāta iqabbīšu*
*aššu tapšuḫti ša ilī ušannâššu ṭēma*
*linnadnam-ma ištēn aḫūšun*
*šū li''abbit-ma nišū lippatqā*
*lipḫurūnim-ma ilū rabûtu*
*[š]a anni linnadin-ma šunu liktūnū*
*marduk upaḫḫir-ma ilī rabûti*
*ṭābiš uma''ar inaddin têrta*
*epšu pîšu ilū upaqqūšu*
*šarru ana anunnakkī amāta izakkar*
*lū kīnam-ma maḫrû nībūkun*
*kināti atamâ inimmâ ittīya*
*mannum-ma ša ibnû tuqunta*
*(u) tiāmta ušbalkitū-ma ikṣuru tāḫāza*
*linnadnam-ma ša ibnû tuqunta*
*arnuššu lušaššâ pašāḫiš tušbā*
*īpulūšū-ma igīgū ilū rabûtu*
*ana lugaldimeranki'a malik ilī bēlāšun*
*qingum-ma ša ibnû tuqunta*
*(u) tiāmta ušbalkitū-ma ikṣuru tāḫāza*
*ikmûšū-(ma) maḫriš ea ukallūšu*
*anna īmidūšū-ma dāmīšu iptar'ū*
*ina dāmīšu ibnû amēlūta*
*īmid dulli ilī-ma ilī umtaššir*

# Tablet VI

When Marduk heard the speech of the gods,
his heart compelled him to create artful things.
He spoke the work of his words to Ea,
what he thought in his heart, he offered in counsel:
'I will weave blood, I will bring about bone,
and I will make a creature[101] – let his name be 'Human'.
I will create the human creature,
that the toil of the gods be imposed upon them, so that the gods may rest.
I will artfully change the ways of the gods,
let them be honoured as one but divided in two.'
Ea answered, he spoke these words,
relating to him his plan to bring rest to the gods:
'Let one of their brothers be given up,
let him be destroyed, so that people might be fashioned.
Let the great gods assemble,
let the guilty be given up, so that the gods might retain their position.'
Marduk assembled the great gods,
he pleasantly proclaimed orders and gave decrees.
The gods heeded the working of his words,
the king spoke these words to the Anunnaki:
'Let your previous naming of me be proven true,[102]
and declare true words to me!
Who was it that created conflict,
made Tiamat revolt and wove a war?
Let him who created conflict be given up to me,
he shall bear his punishment while you sit and rest.'
The Igigi, the great gods, gave him their answer,
to Lugal-Dimmer-Ankia, counsellor of the gods, their Lord:
'It was Qingu who created conflict,
made Tiamat revolt and wove a war.'
They bound him and held him before Ea,
they imposed the punishment upon him and slit his veins.
From his blood, he created humankind,
imposed the toil of the gods on them, setting the gods free.

[101] The word *lullû* seems to refer to humans that are, in one way or another, not fully formed. Alternatively, it may simply be a learned Sumerianizing term for 'human'. Here it forms part of an elaborate pun on the syllable *lu*, which links the being created by Marduk (*lullû* and *amēlu*, 'human,' which is $\mathbf{lu}_2$ in Sumerian) and the verbal forms used to describe its creation (*lukṣur*, *lušabši*, *lušziz*, *lū amēlu šumšu*, and so on).

[102] Lit.: 'be firm.' This may be a reference to the gods naming Marduk Lugal-Dimmer-Ankia, which as noted above means 'King of the gods of heaven and earth'. Alt.: 'Let your first speech be true', or, 'your previous speech was indeed true.'

*ištu amēlūta ibnû ea eršu*
*dulla ša ilī īmidūni šâšu*
*šipru šū lā naṭû ḫasāsīš*
*ina niklāti ša marduk ibnâ nudimmud*
*marduk šarru ilī uza''iz*
*ana anunnakkī gimrassunu eliš u šapliš*
*u'addi ana āni têrētuš naṣāra*
*ḫamšat šušši ina šamê ukīn maṣṣarta*
*uštašnī-ma alkakāt erṣeti u'aṣṣir*
*ina šamê u erṣeti nēr uštēšib*
*ištu têrēti napḫaršina uma''iru*
*ana anunnakkī ša šamê u erṣeti uza''izu isqāssun*
*anunnakkū pâšunu īpušū-ma*
*ana marduk bēlīšunu šunu izzakrū*
*inanna bēl ša šubarrâni taškunū-ma*
*mīnû dumqâni ina maḫrīka*
*i nīpuš parakka ša nabû zikiršu*
*kummuk lū nubattani i nušapšiḫ qerbuš*
*i niddi parakka nēmeda ašaršu*[19]
*ina ūmi ša nikaššada (i) nušapšiḫ qerbuš*
*marduk annīta ina šemêšu*
*kīma ūmi immirū zīmūšu ma'diš*
*epšā-ma bābili ša tērišā šipiršu*
*libnassu lippatiq-ma parakka zuqrā*
*anunnakkū itrukū alla*
*šattu ištât libittašu iltabnū*[20]
*šanītu šattu ina kašādi*
*ša esagil meḫret apsî ullû rēšīšu*
*ibnû-ma ziqqurrat apsî elīta*
*ana āni enlil ea u šâšu ukinnū šubta*
*ina tarbâti maḫaršunu ušibam-ma*
*šuršiš ešarra inaṭṭala qarnīšu*

[19] Var.: *ša nimmidu ašaršu.*
[20] Var.: *šattu ana ištâti libittašu iltebnū.*

After the wise Ea had created humankind
and imposed upon them the toil of the gods –
this deed is impossible to understand,
Nudimmud created by the artfulness of Marduk! –
King Marduk divided the gods,
all of the Anunnaki, above and below.
To guard the decrees of Anu, he appointed
three hundred[103] gods, stationing them as a watch in heaven.
He did the same again, designing the ways of the Netherworld[104]:
six hundred gods he settled in heaven and in the Netherworld.
After he had proclaimed each one of his decrees,
dividing the shares of the Anunnaki in heaven and in the Netherworld,
the Anunnaki worked their words,
and said to Marduk, their Lord:
'Now, Lord, you who established our freedom,
what shall be our service to you?
We will make you a throne-dais, whose name shall be much spoken,
your chamber shall be our place of repose, we shall rest within it.
We shall set up a throne-dais and make it bear an altar[?],
when we come there, we shall rest within it.'
When Marduk heard this,
his face lit up very bright, like the daylight:
'Build Babylon, the work you desired.
Let its brickwork be fashioned and its throne-dais raised high!'
The Anunnaki swung the hoe,
for one year they prepared the bricks.
When the second year arrived,
they raised up the top of the Esagil,[105] the Apsû's counterpart.
They built the soaring ziggurat of the Apsû,
and established homes for Anu, Enlil, Ea, and him.
In splendour he sat down before them,
his horns pointing to the Eshara's foundation.[106]

[103] Lit. 'five times sixty'.

[104] The word *erṣetu* is used throughout the text in the sense 'earth', though it can also mean 'Netherworld' – the latter sense seems more appropriate here.

[105] The Esagil ('House Whose Head is High') was Marduk's main temple in Babylon.

[106] Gods were crowned with horns as a marker of their divinity. Here, Marduk's horns face or point (literally, 'look', *naṭālu*) towards the Eshara. One possible interpretation is that Babylon is beneath the Eshara, which should then be taken as the lower heavens, ruled by Enlil, as opposed to the upper heavens, ruled by Anu: in that case, Marduk's horns would be facing upwards towards the Eshara. Alternatively, Babylon may be located opposite the Eshara (as stated in V 120) on a horizontal plane, meaning that Marduk's horns would be pointing forward towards it. It is also possible to interpret the horns as a figurative description of the temple's pinnacle, so that the line would be stating that the Esagila's top is level with the foundations of the lower heavens: 'its pinnacle was facing the Eshara's foundation', or, 'he looked at its pinnacle, which was as high as (lit., like) the Eshara's foundation.'

*ištu esagil īpušū šipiršu*
*anunnakkū kalīšunu parakkīšunu ibtašmū*
*ḫamšat šušši igīgū ša šamāmī u nēr ša apsî kalīšunu paḫrū*

*bēlu ina paramāḫi ša ibnû šubassu*
*ilī abbīšu qerītašu uštēšib*
*annâ bābili šubat narmîkun*
*nugâ ašruššu ḫidûtašu tišbā-ma*
*ušibū-ma ilū rabûtu*
*zarbāba iškunū ina qerīti ušbū*
*ištu nigûta iškunū qerebšu*
*ina esagil rašbi ītepušū šunu taqribta*
*kunnā têrētu napḫaršina uṣurātu*
*manzāz šamê u erṣeti uza"izū ilū gimrassun*
*ilū rabûtu ḫamšāssunu ušibū-ma*
*ilī šīmāti sebettīšunu ana purussê uktinnū*
*imḫur-ma bēlu qašta kakkašu maḫaršun iddi*
*sapāra ša īteppušu īmurū ilū abbūšu*
*īmurū-ma qašta kī nukkulat binûta*
*epšēt īteppušu inaddū abbūšu*
*iššī-ma ānu ina puḫur ilī iqabbi*
*qašta ittašiq šī lū mārtī*
*ibbī-ma ša qašti kīam šumīša*
*iṣu arik lū ištēnum-ma šanû lū kāšid*
*šalšu šumša kakkab qašti ina šamê ušāpi*
*ukīn-ma gisgallaša itti ilī atḫêša*
*ištu šīmāti ša qašti išīmu ānu*
*iddī-ma kussê šarrūti ša ina ilī šaqâta*
*ānu ina puḫur ilī šuāšu uštēšibši*
*ipḫurūnim-ma ilū rabûtu*
*šīmat marduk ullû šunu uškinnū*
*uzakkirū-ma ana ramānīšunu arāra*
*ina mê u šamni itmû ulappitū napšāti*
*iddinūšum-ma šarrūt ilī epēša*
*ana bēlūt ilī ša šamê u erṣeti šunu uktinnūšu*
*ušātir-ma anšar asarluḫi ittabi šumšu*

After they had completed their work on the Esagil,
all the Anunnaki fashioned their throne-daises.
The three hundred Igigi of heaven and the six hundred of the Apsû, all of them were assembled.[107]
In the throne-room that they had created as his home, the Lord
seated the gods his fathers for his banquet.
'This is Babylon, your place of residence.
Sing merrily here, sit down amid its joyfulness!'
The great gods sat down:
they set up beer mugs and sat down for the banquet.
After they had made merry inside it,
inside the formidable Esagil, they performed a ritual.
Each decree and design was now firm,
and all the gods divided into their stations in heaven and earth.[108]
The fifty great gods sat down,
and fixed the authority of the seven gods of fate.[109]
The Lord received his weapon, the bow, and laid it before them.
The gods his fathers saw the net he had made,
they saw how artful the construction of the bow was,
and his fathers praised the work he had done.
Anu lifted it and spoke in the assembly of the gods,
kissing the bow: 'This is my daughter!'[110]
He named her, and these were the names of the bow:
'Longwood' was the first, the second was 'Striker,'
her third name was 'Bow Star', he brought her forth in heaven,
and made firm her orbit with the gods her brothers.
After Anu had fixed the fate of the bow,
he set up a throne of kingship that was exalted among gods,
and Anu seated her there in the gods' assembly.
The great gods assembled,
exalted Marduk's fate and bowed low.
They took a solemn oath,[111]
swearing with water and oil and crossing their throats.
They gave him the right to exercise kingship over the gods,
they fixed firm his lordship over the gods of heaven and earth.
Anshar made him supreme and gave him his name Asarluhi.

[107] This reference is inconsistent with the description given in VI 43–4, where Marduk settles 300, not 600, gods in the Netherworld, not the Apsû.
[108] Here and throughout Tablet V, the text draws a connection on the level of both sound and meaning between *zâzu*, 'to divide', and *manzāzu*, 'station'.
[109] Lit.: 'they made firm the gods of the fates, the seven of them, for decision(-making).'
[110] The word 'bow', *qaštu*, is gendered feminine in Akkadian.
[111] Lit.: 'they recited a curse on themselves (if they should break the oath).'

*ana zikrīšu qabê i nilbin appa*
*epšu pîšu ilū lipiqqūšu*
*qibītuššu lū šūturat eliš u šapliš*
*lū šušqū-ma māru mutīr gimillīni*
*enūssu lū šūturat šānina ai irši*
*līpuš-ma rē'ût ṣalmāt qaqqadi binâtuššu*
*aḫrâtaš ūmī lā mašê*[21] *lizakkirā alkassu*
*likīn ana abbīšu nindabê rabûti*
*zāninūssun līpuša lipaqqida ešrēssun*
*lišēṣin qutrinnī ti'āšina lišreššа*
*tamšīl ina šamê īteppušu ina erṣeti līteppuš*
*li'addī-ma ṣalmāt qaqqadi palāḫiššu*[22]
*ba'ūlātu lū ḫissusā ilašina lizzakrā*
*epšu pîšu ištariš lipiqqā*
*nindabû linnašâ ilašina ištaršin*
*ai immašâ ilašina likillā*
*mātīšina lišteppâ parakkīšina lītepšā*
*lū zīzā-ma ṣalmāt qaqqadi ilī*
*nâši mala šuma nibbû šū lū ilni*
*i nibbī-ma ḫamšā šumīšu*
*alkatuš lū šūpât epšetuš lū mašlat*[23]
*marduk ša ištu ṣītīšu ibbûšu abūšu ānu*
*šākin mirīti u mašqīti muṭaḫḫidu urîšun*

*ša ina kakkīšu abūbi ikmû šāpûti*
*ilī abbīšu īṭiru ina šapšāqi*
*lū māru šamši ša ilī*[24] *nebû šū-ma*
*ina nūrīšu namri littallakū šunu kayyāna*
*nišī ša ibnû šikitta napša*
*dulli ilī īmidū-ma šunu ippašḫū*
*banâ abāta napšura enēna*
*lū bašī-ma nannûššu lū naplusū šunu šâšu*[25]
*marukku lū ilu bānûšunu šū-ma*
*muṭīb libbi anunnakkī mušapšiḫu igīgī*
*marutukku lū tukulti māti āli u nišīšu*
*šâšū-ma*[26] *litta''idāšu nišū aḫrâtaš*
*meršakušu eziz (u) muštāl sabuš (u) tayyār*

[21] Var.: *ana lā mašê.*
[22] Var.: *[palāḫu] šâšu.*
[23] Var.: *alkātuš lū šūpâ epšētuš lū mašlā.*
[24] Var.: *ša ina il[ī].*
[25] Var.: *lū bašī-ma ullânuššu lū naplusū šunu ana šâšu.*
[26] Var.: *ana šâšū-ma.*

'When his name is spoken, let us do obeisance,
let the gods heed the working of his words.
May his command be supreme above and below,
may the son, our avenger, be raised high,
may his dominion be supreme, may he have no rival.
Let him shepherd the black-headed people,[112] his creatures,
and forever after, without forgetting, they shall recount his ways.
Let him establish great food offerings for his fathers,
let him be their provider, let him care for their sanctuaries.
Let him make the incense waft and their shrines exult.
As he has done in heaven, let him do alike on earth.[113]
Let him show the black-headed people how to worship him:
let the populace revere and call on their god,
at the working of his words, let them heed their goddess.
Let food offerings be brought! Their god, their goddess,
may they not be forgotten: they shall remember their god.
May their sacred precincts come into being, may their throne-daises be built.[114]
Let the black-headed people be divided as to gods,
but for us, whatever we may call him, he shall be our god.
Let us give him fifty names,
so that his ways may be brought forth, and likewise his doings.
(1) Marduk is what his father Anu named him at birth,
he who supplies pastureland and watering holes, who makes their stables flourish,
who captured the renegades with his weapon, the Flood,
rescuing the gods his fathers from anguish.
He is truly the son, Sun of the gods, luminous is he:
let them walk unceasingly in his bright light.
On the people he created, the breathing beings,
he imposed the toil of the gods, so that they could rest.
Creation and destruction, forgiveness and punishment
exist at his command: let them look upon him.
(2) Marukka: he is truly the god who created them,
who pleased the Anunnaki and brought rest to the Igigi.
(3) Marutukku is truly the trust of the land, the city, and his people:
forever after, the people shall be mindful of him.
(4) Mershakushu: angry but considerate,[115] irate but relenting,

[112] Literally 'the black of head', a common Akkadian designation for humanity.

[113] The following passage is not fully clear, but it seems to describe Marduk's creation of religious division on earth, just as he had previously divided the gods into the Anunnaki and the Igigi. Through their reverence of Marduk, the human population is made to revere their own local god or goddess, which are then shown to be aspects (or names) of Marduk (see VII 119–20).

[114] The line is unclear; the odd phrasing is probably meant to allow for a pun between *lištēpâ*, 'let them be brought forth', and *lītepšā*, 'let them make (for themselves)'.

[115] Literal translation of Sumerian **mer**, 'angry', **ša$_4$-kuš$_2$-u$_3$**, 'deliberate'.

*rapaš libbašu lā'iṭ karassu*
*lugaldimeranki'a šumšu ša nibbû*[27] *puḫurni*
*zikrī pîšu nušašqû eli ilī abbīšu*
*lū bēl ilī ša šamê u erṣeti kalîšun*
*šarru ana taklimtīšu ilū lū šu'durū eliš u šapliš*
*nari-lugaldimeranki'a šumšu ša nizkuru āšir ilī kalāma*

*ša ina šamê u erṣeti ittaddû šubatni ina pušqi*
*ana igīgī u anunnakkī uza''izu manzāza*
*ana šumīšu ilū lištar'ibū linūšū ina šubti*
*asarluḫi šumšu ša ibbûšu abūšu ānu*
*šū lū nūru ša ilī gešṭû dannu*
*ša kīma šumīšū-ma lamassi ilī u māti*

*ina šašmi danni īṭeru šubatni ina pušqi*
*asarluḫi-namtila šanîš ibbû ilu mušneššu*
*ša kīma binûtīšū-ma ikširu kala ilī abtūti*
*bēlu ša ina šiptīšu elleti uballiṭu ilī mītūti*
*mu'abbit egrūti zā'irī i nibbûšu*
*asarluḫi-namru ša innabû šalšiš šumšu*
*ilu ellu mullilu alaktīni*
*šulušā šumīšu ibbû anšar laḫmu u laḫāmu*
*ana ilī mārīšunu šunu izzakrū*
*nīnū-ma šulušā nittabi šumīšu*
*kī nâšī-ma attunu šumīšu zukrā*
*iḫdû-(ma) ilū išmû siqaršun*
*ina ubšukkinnakki uštaddinū šunu milkassun*
*ša māri qarrādi mutīr gimillīni*
*nīnu ša zānini i nulli šumšu*
*ušibū-ma ina ukkinīšunu inabbû šīmāti*
*ina mēsī nagbašunu uzakkirūni šumšu*

[27] Var.: *lša šumšu i nimbû.*

his heart is wide, his mind encompasses all.
(5) LUGAL-DIMMER-ANKIA is the name we gave him in our assembly,
whose commands we have raised higher than the gods his fathers.
He is truly the Lord of all the gods of heaven and earth,
the king at whose revelations the gods above and below are distressed.
(6) NARI-LUGAL-DIMMER-ANKIA is his name that we spoke, he who marshals all the gods,[116]
who in a time of need laid out homes for us in heaven and earth
and divided the stations among the Igigi and Anunnaki.
Let the gods tremble at his name, let them quake in their homes!
(7) ASARLUHI is his name that his father Anu gave him:
he is truly the light of the gods, a strong warrior,
who, in accordance with his name, is the *lamassu*-spirit of the gods and the land,[117]
who in an arduous fray, in times of need, saved our home.
(8) Asarluhi they secondly named NAMTILA: the life-giving god,[118]
who, in accordance with his name's form, revived the broken gods.
The Lord who with his sacred spell restores dead gods,
he who breaks twisted rivals – let us proclaim his name!
(9) Asarluhi they thirdly gave the name NAMRU[119]:
the pure god who purifies our ways.'[120]
Anshar, Lahmu, and Lahamu each gave him three of his names,
they then spoke to the gods their sons:
'We have each given him three of his names,
now you, like us, call him by his names!'
The gods rejoiced, they listened to the speech,
in the Ubshu-ukkinnaku they exchanged counsel:
'Of the heroic son, our avenger,
of our provider – let us extol the name!'
They sat down in their council and pronounced his fates,
with full ceremonial rites, they called him by his names.

[116] Indirect translation of the Sumerian **na-RI**, 'marshal', **lugal-dimmer-ankia**, 'king of the gods of heaven and earth'.

[117] The *lamassu* was a guardian spirit that ensured one's well-being and success. The phrase 'according to his name' implies a direct link between the name and the associated epithet, but the connection between the sign ASAR and the *lamassu* is unclear.

[118] Several of Marduk's names receive further additions; in these cases, one can understand the additions as independent names ('Asarluhi they secondly named Namtila') or as compound constructions ('They secondly named him Asarluhi-Namtila'). The 'life-giving god' refers to the Sumerian meaning of **namtila**, '(he) of life'.

[119] Lit.: 'The Bright'.

[120] The text interprets the name *namru*, 'bright', as 'ritually pure', *ellu*, and links it with the verbal form *ullullu*, 'to make ritually pure'. This also yields a striking consonance: *ilu ellu mullilu*.

## Tablet VII

*asarre šārik mērešti ša israta ukinnu*
*bānû ê u qê mušēṣû urqīti*
*asaralim ša ina bīt milki kabti šūturu milikšu*
*ilū ūtaqqû adīršu aḫzū*
*asaralimnunna karūbu nūr abi ālidīšu*
*muštēšir têrēt āni enlil (u) ea (u) nin[š]īku*
*šū-(ma) zāninšunu mu'addû isqī[š]un*
*ša šukūssu ḫegalla uṣṣapa ana māti*
*tutu bān tēdištīšunu š[ū]-ma*
*lillil sāgīšunū-ma šunu lū pašḫū*
*libnī-ma šipta ilū linūḫū*
*aggiš lū tebû linē'ū [irass]un*
*lū šušqû-ma ina puḫur ilī ēdiššīšu*
*mamman ina ilī šuāšu lā umdaššalšu*
*tutu zi'ukkina napišti ummāni šanîš izzakrū*
*ša ukinnu ana ilī šamê ellūti*
*alkassun iṣbatū-(ma) u'addû manzāssun*
*ai immaši ina apâti epšetašu liktilla*

*tutu ziku šalšiš imbû mukīl tēlilti*
*il šāri ṭābi bēl tašmê u magāri*
*mušabši ṣimri (u) kubuttê mukīn ḫegalli*
*ša mimmâni īṣa ana ma'dî utirru*
*ina pušqi danni nīṣinu šāršu ṭāba*
*liqbû litta''idū lidlulū dalīlīšu*
*tutu agaku ina rebî lišarriḫā abrātu*
*bēl šipti elleti muballiṭ mīti*
*ša ana ilī kamûti iršû tayāra*
*abšāna enda ušassiku eli ilī nakirīšu*
*ana padîšunu ibnû amēlūta*
*rēmēnû ša bulluṭu bašû ittīšu*
*likūnā-ma ai immašâ amâtūšu*
*ina pî ṣalmāt qaqqadi ša ibnâ qātāšu*
*tutu tuku ina ḫamši tâšu ella pāšina littabbal*
*ša ina šiptīšu elleti issuḫu nagab lemnūti*

## Tablet VII

(10) Asari, giver of farmland, who established the watered fields,
creator of grain and flax, who brings forth plants.
(11) Asar-Alim, whose superb advice is honoured in the house of counsel,
the gods pay heed and learn to fear him.
(12) Asar-Alim-Nuna, the blessed, light of the father who gave birth to him,
who directs the decrees of Anu, Enlil, and Ea the Prince,[121]
he is their provider, who appoints their shares,
his field[122] increases the abundance of the land.
(13) Tutu is he who brings about their restoration,
let him purify their shrines so that they may rest.
Let him create a spell that the gods may be calmed:
though they rise up enraged, let them turn back!
He is truly raised high, unique in the assembly of the gods,
no one among the gods can rival him.
(14) Tutu was secondly called Zi-Ukkina, the life of his peoples,[123]
who firmly established[124] holy heaven for the gods,
who took hold of their ways and appointed their stations:
may he not be forgotten among the teeming people, they shall keep his deeds in mind.
(15) Tutu was thirdly named Ziku, he who maintains purifications,
god of the pleasant wind, lord of success and obedience,
who creates riches and wealth, establishes abundance,
and turns all our shortage into plenty.
His pleasant wind we inhaled[125] in times of dire need:
let them command that he be ever extolled, let them sing his praises!
(16) Let humanity fourthly glorify Tutu as Agaku,
the lord of the sacred spell, who revives the dead,
who had mercy on the bound gods,
who removed the yoke that the gods, his enemies, had to bear,
and, to spare them, created humankind.
The merciful one, with whom revival lies,
let his words be made firm and unforgotten
in the mouths of the black-headed people, whom his hands created.
(17) Tutu is fifthly Tuku: let their mouths carry his sacred incantation,[126]
he who uprooted all the evil ones with his sacred spell.

[121] The use of Ea's title *ninšīku*, 'prince', refers back to the element **nun**, 'prince', in the name.
[122] Alt.: 'coronet'.
[123] Sumerian **zi**, 'life', **ukkina**, 'of the assembly'.
[124] The word for 'firmly established', *ukinnu*, echoes the name Zi-Ukkina.
[125] The line refers back to the literal meaning of the name: **zi**, 'breath', **ku**$_3$, 'holy'.
[126] Sumerian **tu**$_6$, 'incantation', **ku**$_3$, 'holy'.

*šazu mūdê libbi ilī ša ibarrû karša*
*ēpiš lemnēti lā ušēṣû ittīšu*
*mukīn puḫri ša ilī muṭīb libbīšun*
*mukanniš lā māgirī ṣulūlšun rapšu*
*mušēšir kitti nāsi[ḫ] itgura dabāba*
*ša sartu u ki[tt]u umtassâ ašruššu*
*šazu zisi mušeb[b]i tēbî šanîš litta"idū*
*mukkiš šuḫarrati ina zumur ilī abbīšu*
*šazu suḫrim šalšiš nāsiḫ ayyābī gimiršunu ina kakki*

*musappiḫ kipdīšunu muterru šāriš*
*muballi napḫar raggī mala iyârūš(u)*
*ilū lištallilū šunu ina puḫri*
*šazu šuḫgurim ina rebî šākin tašmê ana ilī abbīšu*

*nāsiḫ ayyābī muḫalliq niprīšun*
*musappiḫ epšētīšunu lā ezēb mimmêšun*
*lizzakir*[28] *liqqabi šumšu ina māti*
*šazu zaḫrim ina ḫamši lištaddinū arkûtu*
*muḫalliq nagab zāmânī lā māgirī kalîšun*
*ša napḫar ilī munnabtī ušēribu ešrētiš*
*likūn-ma annû zikiršu*
*šazu zaḫgurim ina šešši appūna kalîš lištamrū*
*ša napḫar ayyābī uḫalliqu šū tāḫāziš*
*enbilulu bēlu mudeššûšunu šū-ma*
*dannu nabûšunu šākin taklīmi*
*ša rîta mašqīta uštešššeru ukinnu ana māti*

*berāti upattû uza"izu mê nuḫši*
*enbilulu epadun bēl namî u atê šanîš lizzakrū*

62a *gugal šamê (u) erṣeti mukinnu absinni*
62b *ša mērešta elleta ukinnu ina ṣēri*
*īka u palga uštešššeru uṣṣiru apkīsa*
*enbilulu gugal gugal miṭrat ilī linādū šalš[i]š*

[28] Var.: *lū zakir.*

(18) Shazu is he who knows the gods' hearts,[127] who examines their minds, who lets no evildoer flee,
he who makes firm the assembly of gods, who soothes their hearts,
who subjugates the disobedient, vast protection of the gods,
who administers justice and uproots twisted speech,
with whom falsehood and truth are told apart.
(19) Shazu they shall secondly praise as Zisi, he who silenced rebels,[128]
who expelled paralysis from the bodies of the gods his fathers.
(20) Shazu is thirdly Suhrim, who with his weapon uprooted each and every enemy,[129]
who disrupted their plots and turned them into mere wind,
who smothered all the wrongdoers, every one that marched against him:
Let the gods always cry out in joy in their assembly!
(21) Shazu is fourthly Shuhgurim, he who established success for the gods his fathers,
who uprooted the enemies[130] and destroyed their offspring,
who disrupted their doings and made no exceptions:
Let his name be spoken and proclaimed in the land!
(22) Shazu shall fifthly be discussed by future generations as Zahrim,
he who destroys every rebel,[131] all the disobedient,
who brought each of the fugitive gods back into their shrines:
Let this name be firm!
(23) Further, Shazu shall sixthly be extolled everywhere as Zahgurim,
he who in war destroyed every adversary.[132]
(24) En-Bilulu, the Lord who abundantly provided for them,[133] is he,
the strong one whom they chose, who establishes sacrifices,
who sets aright the grasslands and watering holes, making them reliable for the country,
who opened channels, meting out abundant water.
(25) Enbilulu shall secondly be called Epadun, lord of pasture and flooding,
watchman of waterways in heaven and earth, who established furrows,[134]
who established sacred farmland upon the steppe,
who sets aright canals and dikes, marking out the furrows.
(26) Enbilulu shall thirdly be praised as Gugal, watchman of the gods' waterways,[135]

[127] Sumerian **ša$_{3}$**, 'heart', **zu**, 'to know'.
[128] Sumerian **zi**, 'to rise', **si**, 'to silence'.
[129] Sumerian **suḫ**, 'to uproot', **erim$_{2}$**, '(enemy) troops'.
[130] Sumerian **suḫ**, 'to uproot', **gu$_{2}$**, 'totality', **erim$_{2}$**, '(enemy) troops'.
[131] Sumerian **zaḫ**, 'to destroy', **erim$_{2}$**, '(enemy) troops'.
[132] Sumerian **zaḫ**, 'to destroy', **gu$_{2}$**, 'totality', **erim$_{2}$**, '(enemy) troops'.
[133] Sumerian **en**, 'lord', **bi-lu-lu**, 'makes abundant'.
[134] The line refers back to the literal meaning of the name: **e**, 'canal', **pa$_{5}$**, 'irrigation ditch', **dun**, 'to dig'.
[135] Sumerian **gu$_{2}$-gal**, 'canal inspector'.

*bēl ḫegalli ṭuḫdi išpikī rabûti*
*šākin mešrê munaḫḫiš dadmē*
*nādin šu'i mušabšû ašnan*
*enbilulu ḫegal mukammir ḫegalli ana nišī rebîš liqbû*

*mušaznin nuḫši eli erṣeti rapašti mudeššû urqīt[i]*

*sirsir šāpik šadî elēnuš tiāmti*
*šālil šalamta tiāmta ina kakkīšu*
*muttarrû māti rē'ûšina kīnu*
*ša šarkūš(u) mērešu šukūsu šer'u*
*ša tiāmta rapašta*[29] *ītebberu uzzuššu*
*kī titurri ītettequ ašar šašmīša*
*sirsir malaḫ ina šanî imbû šī lū kīam*
*tiāmtu rukūbšū-ma šū malāḫša*
*gil muštappik karê tīlī bitrûti*
*bānû ašnan u laḫri nādinu zēr māti*
*gilima mukīn ṭurri ilī bānû kināti*
*rappu lā'issunu mušaṣbitu damqā[ti]*
*agilima šaqû nāsiḫ agê āšir šalgi*
*bānû erṣeti eliš mê mukīn elâti*
*zulum mu'addi qerbeti ana ilī pālik binûti*
*nādin isqī (u) nindabê pāqidu ešrēti*
*mummu bān šamê (u) erṣeti mušēšir parsi*
*ilu mullil šamê u erṣeti šanîš zulummu*
*ša ana dunnīšu ina ilī šanû lā mašl[u]*
*gišnumunab bānû napḫar nišī ēpišu kibrāti*
*ābit ilī ša tiāmti ēpiš nišī ina mimmêšun*
*lugalabdubur šarru sāpiḫ epšet tiāmti nāsiḫu kakkī[ša]*

*ša ina rēši (u) arkati duruššu kunnu*
*pagalgu'enna ašarēd napḫar bēlī*[30] *ša šaqâ emūqāšu*
*ša ina ilī aḫḫīšu šurbû etel napḫaršun*
*lugaldurmaḫ šarru markas ilī bēl durmāḫi*
*ša ina šubat šarrūti šurbû ana ilī ma'diš ṣīru*

[29] Var.: *ša ina tiāmti rapašti.*
[30] Var.: *napḫar bēl ilī.*

lord of abundance, plenty, and great grain-heaps,
who sets up riches, making the settlements prosper,
who gives wheat, bringing grain into being.
(27) Enbilulu shall fourthly be proclaimed as Hegal, who piles up plenty for the people,[136]
who rains prosperity on the wide earth and makes plants grow in abundance.
(28) Sirsir, who heaped up mountains upon Tiamat,
who despoiled Tiamat's corpse with his weapon,[137]
leader of the land, their steadfast shepherd,
he to whom farmland, field, and furrow were granted,
who in his anger is always crossing vast Tiamat,
like a bridge always crossing the site of their fray.
(29) Sirsir they secondly named Malah[138]: let it be so!
Tiamat is his vessel, he is her sailor.
(30) Gil, who heaps up barley in enormous mounds,
creator of grain and flocks of sheep, giver of the land's seed.
(31) Gilima, who made firm the bonds between gods, creator of stability,
the neck stock that restrains them, yet gives good things.
(32) Agilima, the exalted, who tore off the crown, who marshals the snow,
who created earth above the water and made firm the height of heaven.
(33) Zulum, who appointed meadows for the gods, dividing up creation,
who gives out shares and food offerings, who cares for the shrines.
(34) The creative force[139] who made heaven and earth, who guides the lost,
the god who purifies heaven and earth, is secondly Zulummu,
whom no other god can rival in strength.
(35) Gish-Numun-Ab, creator of all people, maker of the world regions,
who destroyed the gods of Tiamat and made the people out of them.
(36) Lugal-Ab-Dubur, the king who disrupted the doings of Tiamat, who uprooted her weapon,
whose foundation is firm,[140] both before and behind.
(37) Pagal-Guena, the vanguard of all lords,[141] whose strength is exalted,
who is mightiest among the gods his brothers, noblest of them all.
(38) Lugal-Durmah, king of the bond between gods, lord of Durmahu,[142]
who is the greatest in his royal home, much exalted above the other gods.

136 Sumerian **he$_2$-gal**, 'plenty.'

137 The phrase *šâlil šalamta Tâmti*, 'who despoiled Tiamat', displays a particularly elegant construction: the first two words begin with *šal*, the last two words end with *-mt-*, with *šalamta* acting as a hinge between the two sounds.

138 Lit.: 'The Sailor'.

139 The word used here is *mummu*, as also applied to Tiamat in I 4.

140 The line refers back to the meaning of the element **dubur** in Sumerian, 'foundation'.

141 Sumerian **pa$_4$**, 'ancestor' (here interpreted as 'foremost'), **gal**, 'great', **gu$_2$**, 'totality', **en-a**, 'of lords'.

142 The line presents two interpretations of the name, one taking the word Durmah as a cosmic location (see note on V 59), one translating the Sumerian **lugal**, 'king', **dur**, 'bond', **maḫ**, 'mighty'.

*aranunna mālik ea bān ilī abbīšu*
*ša ana alakti rubûtīšu lā umaššalu ilu ayyumma*
*dumuduku ša ina duku ūtaddašu šubassu ellet*
*dumuduku ša (ina) balīšu purussâ lā iparrasu lugalduku*
*lugalšu'ana šarru ša ina ilī šaqâ emūqāšu*
*bēlu emūq āni ša šūturu*[31] *nibût anšar*
*irugga šālil gimrīšunu qerbiš tiāmti*
*ša napḫar uzni iḫmumu ḫasīsa palkû*
*irqingu šālil qingu ayyābiš tāḫāzi*
*muttabbil têrēt napḫari mukīn bēlūti*
*kinma muma''ir napḫar ilī nādin milki*
*ša ana šumīšu ilū kīma meḫê išubbū palḫiš*
*dingiresiskur šaqîš*[32] *ina bīt ikribi lišib-ma*
*ilū maḫruššu lišēribū kadrâšun*
*adi erebšun(u) imaḫḫarūni*
*mamman ina balīšu lā ibannâ niklāti*
*erba ṣalmāt qaqqadi binâtuššu*
*ela šâšu ṭēmi ūmīšina lā iyadda ilu mamman*
*gīru mukīn āṣât kakki*
*ša ina tāḫāz tiāmti ibannâ niklāti*
*palkâ uzni itpēša ḫasīsi*
*libbu rūqu ša lā ilammadū ilū gimrāssun*
*addu lū šumšu kiššat*[33] *šamê līrim-ma*
*ṭābu rigmašu eli erṣeti lirtaṣṣin*
*mummu erpēti lištakṣibam-ma*
*šapliš ana nišī ti'ûta liddin*
*ašaru ša kīma šumīšū-ma īšuru ilī šīmāti*

[31] Var.: *bēl emūqān ṣīrāti šūt[uru]*.
[32] Var.: *ša šaqîš*.
[33] Var.: *ša kiššat*.

(39) ARA-NUNA, counsellor of Ea, creator of the gods his fathers,[143]
whose princely ways no other god at all can rival.
(40) DUMU-DUKU, whose sacred home in Duku is ever renewed for him,
son of Duku, without whom Lugal-Duku makes no decision.[144]
(41) LUGAL-SHUANA, the king whose strength is exalted among gods,[145]
lord, strength of Anu, who was made supreme, chosen by Anshar.
(42) IR-UGA, who ravaged them[146] all within Tiamat,
who gathered all wisdom and is vastly intelligent.
(43) IRQINGU, who ravaged Qingu,[147] his adversary$^?$ in war,
who guides the decrees of the universe and establishes lordship.
(44) KINMA,[148] commander of all the gods, who gives counsel,
at whose name the gods shake in fear, as before a storm.
(45) DINGIR-E-SISKUR: let him dwell exalted in the house of blessings,[149]
let the gods bring in their offerings before him
as long as he received their gifts.
No one can create artful things without him,[150]
the four regions of the black-headed people are his creation.
Apart from him, no god at all knows the meaning of their days.
(46) GIRRU,[151] who makes firm the sharpness$^?$ of weapons,
who in the war against Tiamat created artful things,
vast of mind, skilled in perception,
deep of heart, whom all the gods together cannot understand.
(47) ADAD[152] shall be his name: let him span the fullness of heaven.
Let his sweet voice thunder upon the earth,
may the creative force of the clouds reach its fullness[153]
and give sustenance to the people below.
(48) ASHARU, who, in accordance with his name, marshals the gods
of fate,[154]

[143] As noted by Lambert (2013: 489), the two parts of the line interpret the Sumerian name differently. The word **nuna** is read 'of the prince', meaning 'of Ea' (see note to VII 6), while **a-ra$_2$** is analysed first as 'advisor', then as 'begetter'.

[144] The name **dumu-du$_6$-ku$_3$** means 'son of the Holy Hill'. The 'Holy Hill', **du$_6$-ku$_3$**, could refer to several sacred locations; **lugal-du$_6$-ku$_3$**, 'king of the Holy Hill', probably refers to Ea.

[145] Shuana is a learned name for Babylon, yielding the apparent meaning 'King of Babylon'. But the text instead interprets the name as **lugal**, 'king', **šu**, 'strength', and **an-a**, read either 'of An' as in the following line, or **diĝir**, 'of the gods'.

[146] Sumerian **ir**, 'ravage', **ug$_5$-a**, 'of the dead'.

[147] Though the name Irqingu probably had a different origin, unconnected to Qingu, it is analysed here as Sumerian **ir**, 'ravage', **qingu**, 'of Qingu'.

[148] Kinma is a variant spelling of Qingu, meaning that Marduk here takes on the name of his defeated enemy.

[149] Sumerian **e$_2$**, 'house', **siskur**, 'blessings'. The E-siskur was the *akītu* house in Babylon; for the *akītu*, see Céline Debourse in this volume.

[150] Alt: 'no one but him can create artful things.'

[151] Girra was the god of fire.

[152] Adad, or Addu, was the god of storms.

[153] The line is unclear. The word translated as 'creative force' is *mummu*. Alt: 'may the *mummu* of the clouds subside', or, 'may the *mummu* (i.e., the downpour) diminish the clouds'.

[154] The Akkadian word *ašāru* means 'to marshal'.

*kullat kal nišī šū lū pāqid*
*nēberu nēberet šamê (u) erṣeti lū tamiḫ-ma*
*eliš u šapliš lā ibberū liqe''ûšu šâšu*
*nēberu kakkabšu ša ina šamê ušāpû*
*lū ṣābit kunsaggêšunu šâšu lū palsūšu*
*mā ša (ina) qerbiš tiāmti ītebbiru lā nâḫiš*
*šumšu lū nēberu āḫizu qerbīšu*
*ša kakkabī šamāmī alkassunu likīn-ma*
*kīma ṣēni lirtaʾʾâ ilī gimrašun*
*likmi tiāmta napištaša lisīq u likri*
*aḫrâtaš nišī labāriš ūmī*
*liššī-ma lā uktāl lirēq ana ṣâti*
*aššu ašra ibnâ iptiqa dannina*
*bēl mātāti šumšu ittabi abu enlil*[34]
*(ina) zikri igīgū ibbû nagabšun*
*išmē-ma ea kabattašu ittangi*
*mā ša abbīšu ušarriḫū zikiršu*
*šū kīma yâtī-ma ea lū šumšu*
*rikis parṣīya kalīšunu libēl-ma*
*gimri têrētīya šū littabbal*
*ina zikri ḫamšā ilū rabûtu*
*ḫamšā šumīšu imbû ušātirū alkassu*
*liṣṣabtū-ma maḫrû likallim*
*enqu (u) mūdû mitḫāriš limtalkū*
*lišannī-ma abu māra lišāḫiz*
*ša rēʾî u nāqidi lipattâ uznīšun*
*lā iggī-ma ana enlil ilī marduk*
*māssu liddeššâ šū lū šalma*
*kīnat amāssu lā enât qibīssu*
*ṣīt pîšu lā uštepêl ilu ayyumma*
*ikkelemmū-ma ul utār kišāssu*

[34] Var.: [*bēl mātāti*] *ša abu enlil imb*[*ûšu*].

he is indeed the caretaker of the totality of all people.
(49) NEBERU shall hold the crossing between heaven and earth:
they shall not cross above or below but wait for him.[155]
Neberu is his star that he brought forth in heaven,
it is he who has seized their crossing point.[156] Let them look upon him,
saying: 'He who unceasingly crosses back and forth inside Tiamat:
let his name be Neberu, he who seized her waist![157]
Let him make firm the ways of the heavenly stars,
let him herd all the gods like sheep.
Let him bind Tiamat, let her breath be kept short and shallow[158]:
for future people, for days to come,
may he carry on and not be held back, may he roam forever.'
(50) Because he created the firmament and fashioned the ground,
Father Enlil gave him his name 'LORD OF THE LANDS'.
All the names that the Igigi had called him:
Ea heard them and his mood grew merry.
He said: 'He whose name was glorified by his fathers,
let his name, like mine, be Ea.
Let him control the entire range of my rituals,
let him be in charge of all my decrees.'
With the fiftieth title, the great gods
gave him his fifty names, and so made his path supreme.[159]
Let them be grasped, let 'the first one' reveal them,[160]
let the wise and the learned discuss them together,
let the father repeat them and make the son grasp them,
let them open the ears of shepherd and herdsman.[161]
He who does not neglect the Enlil[162] of the gods, Marduk:
his land shall prosper, he shall be safe.
His word is firm, his order does not change,
and no god whatever can overturn his utterance.
If he glowers in anger, he will not budge,

155 Neberu is Jupiter, Marduk's planet; see note on V 6. The word *nēberu* means 'crossing'.

156 The meaning of *kunsaggû* is unclear; it is glossed in a commentary as 'front-rear' and appears in other texts in the meaning 'staircase'. Here, it seems to refer to Jupiter's control over the other stars and planets.

157 The couplet makes a double pun on the words *ebēru*, 'to cross', and *qerbu*, both 'waist' and 'inside'.

158 The text seems to interpret Jupiter's orbit as a rope that continually constricts Tiamat.

159 The word *zikru* can be taken either as a synonym of *šumu*, 'name', as in the translation offered here, or as meaning 'utterance' or 'pronouncement' (compare VII 160), which would yield the alternative translation, 'With fifty pronouncements, the great gods gave him his fifty names.'

160 Here and in VII 157, the 'first one', *maḫrû*, seems to be an oblique reference to the author of the epic.

161 The 'shepherd', *rē'û*, was a common metaphor for rulers, so the line can be read as a reference to the king.

162 A reference to Enlil's traditional position as king of the gods, which has now been taken over by Marduk.

*ina sabāsīšu uzzašu ul imaḫḫaršu ilu mamman*
*rūqu libbašu rapaš karassu*
*ša annu (u) gillatu maḫaršu bā'û*
*taklimti maḫrû idbubu pānuššu*
*išṭur-ma ištakan ana šemî arkûti*
*šīmat marduk ša u[ll]û ilū igīgū*
*ēma mû iššattû šumšu lizzakrū*
*inannam-ma zamāru ša marduk*
*ša tiā[mta i]kmû-(ma) ilqû šarrūta*
*[(...) ān]u enlil (u) ea [(...)] bēlet-ilī [...]*
*[ ... i]na bābili (u) esagi[l ... ]*

when his anger is inflamed, no god can face him,
his heart is deep, his mind is wide,
whoever has committed crimes or sins must pass before him.
This is the revelation that 'the first one' recited before him,
wrote down and set up for future generations to hear:
the fate of Marduk, whom the Igigi exalted.
Wherever water is drunk, may his name be invoked.
This now is the song of Marduk,
who bound Tiamat and received kingship.
[ ] Anu, Enlil, and Ea, [ ] Belet-ili [ ]
[ ] in Babylon and the Esagil [ ][163]

[163] The final two lines of the text are only present in Babylonian manuscripts, not in the Assyrian ones: they may have been added later to the Babylonian version, or expunged from the Assyrian one. See Fadhil and Jiménez (2021: 227–8).

## Bibliography

Buccellati, G. (1990), 'On Poetry – Theirs and Ours', in T. Abusch, J. Huehnergard, and P. Steinkeller (eds), *Lingering over Words: Studies in Ancient Near Eastern Literature in Honor of William L. Moran*, Harvard Semitic Studies 37, 105–34, Atlanta: Scholars Press.

Fadhil, A. A. and E. Jiménez (2021), 'Literary Texts from the Sippar Library II: The Epic of Creation', *Zeitschrift für Assyriologie und Vorderasiatische Archäologie*, 111: 191–230.

Haubold, J. (2017), 'From Text to Reading in Enūma Eliš', *Journal of Cuneiform Studies*, 69: 221–46.

Horowitz, W. (1998), *Mesopotamian Cosmic Geography*, Mesopotamian Civilizations 8, Winona Lake: Eisenbrauns.

Lambert, W. G. (2013), *Babylonian Creation Myths*, Mesopotamian Civilizations 16, Winona Lake: Eisenbrauns.

Livingstone, A. (1986), *Mystical and Mythological Explanatory Works of Assyrian and Babylonian Scholars*, Oxford: Clarendon Press.

Michalowski, P. (1990), 'Presence at the Creation', in T. Abusch, J. Huehnergard, and P. Steinkeller (eds), *Lingering over Words: Studies in Ancient Near Eastern Literature in Honor of William L. Moran*, Harvard Semitic Series 37, 381–96, Atlanta: Scholars Press.

# Part Two

# The History of the Epic

1

# Marduk and the battle with the sea: On the dating of *Enuma Elish*

Enrique Jiménez

The anthropologist Robin Horton (1993: 250–1) compares the paradox of belief systems that are constantly changing, but which are perceived as static by their participants, to a game of Grandmother's Footsteps. In this game, 'Grandson mov[es] a little at a time when Grandma's back is turned, but always tak[es] care to be still when Grandma rounds on him.' In Horton's comparison, which he applies to oral societies, Grandma takes the shape of written sources, the absence of which enables Grandson (cultural innovation) to move more or less freely. In literate cultures, such as the Mesopotamian one, Grandma turns around almost constantly, so Grandson's movements are much more restricted.

Grandma's permanent watch means that creativity, particularly in religious contexts, often seeks to disguise itself as tradition, and so to go unnoticed. A religious text, such as *Enuma Elish*, would not present itself as a new creation but rather as a traditional text, however revolutionary its ideas may be (see e.g. Piotr Michalowski in this volume). For the modern critic, this means that the language of the text is essentially undatable, since any feature that might serve to date it can be either taken as diagnostic or explained away as archaism or affectation. Some ostensibly diagnostic grammatical features have been detected in *Enuma Elish*, most importantly the fact that the adverbial ending *-iš* is exclusively used in its directive sense and not the comparative sense it acquires after *c.* 1300 BCE, in the Middle Kassite period. Some critics have used this feature to date the text's composition to the first half of the Kassite period (the fifteenth and fourteenth centuries BCE), before texts such as *Ludlul* ('The Poem of the Righteous Sufferer') and the Standard Babylonian version of *Gilgamesh*.[1] However, one could simply take this use as a deliberate archaism, that is, an attempt to reflect the conventions of older literary language to give the epic a patina of venerability.

The same principle applies to the contents of the text. Any religious development reflected in the text can be explained as a historical fact and thus a commonly accepted opinion at the time of its composition, or disregarded as a revolutionary agenda promoted by a small group of scholars who wished to present their sectarian views as a *fait accompli*. The elevation of Marduk to the head of the Babylonian pantheon – one of the most remarkable developments in the history of Mesopotamian religion and the central subject matter of *Enuma Elish* – was taken by Wilfred Lambert as the *conditio sine qua non* for the composition of the text. In Lambert's view, the historical exaltation of Marduk must have preceded the poem devoted to celebrating it, and since that elevation was only concluded during the Isin II dynasty (twelfth–eleventh century BCE), that is the earliest possible date for its composition (Lambert 1964; 2013: 248–77; Sommerfeld 1982: 182–9; Nielsen 2018: 163–85). However, as first noted by Walter Sommerfeld (1982: 174–81),[2] the poem may instead reflect the agenda of some Babylon theologians who wished to present the patron god of Babylon as the head of the pantheon well before this became a widely accepted position: if so, a date of composition in a preceding period, such as during the Kassite domination of Babylon (fifteenth to mid-twelfth century BCE), would be more likely (Sommerfeld 1982: 180–1; see also Katz 2011: 124–5). Syncretistic hymns, which present all major gods as aspects or names of another god, probably represent manifestos of this sort, since the theological views they espouse were never universally accepted (Fadhil and Jiménez 2022: 254–6).[3] Nothing precludes an understanding of the epic's agenda as the manifesto of a religious movement rather than the reflection of a development that had already taken place. If this is the case, the message of the poem offers no chronological anchor point for its composition.

Both the contents and language of *Enuma Elish* – and indeed of any Near Eastern religious text – are therefore largely undatable to modern critics. Even in the rare cases in which religious and linguistic developments can be glimpsed through the jalousie of traditional ideas and language, one can take them either at face value or as emulations of older models – as Grandson freezing at Grandmother's gaze. It is no surprise, then, that the dating of Babylonian literary texts often relies on preconceived ideas about the genesis and transmission of Akkadian literature.

Cuneiform palaeography, another potential source of information, is not an exact science, and the lack of any comprehensive reference manual means that Assyrian palaeography is particularly underdeveloped. Nevertheless, attempts have been made at dating the oldest-looking manuscripts from Assur based on their script, suggesting either that they stem from the reign of Assurnasirpal II (883–859 BCE) or the turn of the second to the first millennium BCE (respectively, Köcher *apud* Lambert 2013: 4 and Maul *apud* George 2005/2006: 87 fn. 15). While either of these dates may well be correct, they would postdate the alleged composition of the epic by several centuries. Moreover, although one may assume that a few centuries must have intervened between the composition of a Babylonian poem and its adoption and transmission in Assyria, too little is known about the transmission of Babylonian literature in Assyria in the second half of the second millennium BCE to establish even an approximate transmission period (see also Gabriel 2021).

It has traditionally been assumed that Babylonian literature saw two periods of heightened creativity – the Old Babylonian (in the first half of the second millennium BCE) and the Middle Babylonian (in the second half of the second millennium) – and the composition of most Babylonian literary texts is typically dated to one of these two periods. It is conventionally assumed that the texts that were transmitted to the 'periphery' (Hattusha, Amarna, Emar, Ugarit) or copied on Middle Babylonian school tablets were composed during the Old Babylonian period: the absence of *Enuma*

*Elish* and *Ludlul* from 'peripheral' and Middle Babylonian school tablets thus suggests that they were not composed during the Old Babylonian period. This is an argument *ex silentio*, but given how popular *Enuma Elish* became in school tablets of the first millennium BCE, its complete absence from Middle Babylonian tablets is most easily explained by a later date of composition (see also Bartelmus 2018: 40 n. 75).

The traditional perception of the last third of the second millennium BCE as 'perhaps the most creative period in Babylonian literature' ('die vielleicht schöpferischste Periode der babylonischen Literatur'; von Soden 1953: 22) has meant that the composition of many works for which no evidence exists has been ascribed to this time, based on often fragile logic. However, the dearth of literary tablets in this period precludes any claim to certainty: in fact, new findings have occasionally overturned these assertions. For example, the hymn 'Ferocious Lord' ('Marduk 1'), one of the most popular hymns to Marduk in the Babylonian schools of the first millennium BCE, was generally assumed to be of Kassite date until an Old Babylonian manuscript of it was identified; and the fact that an excerpt of it has now been found on a Kassite school tablet means that it was already a classic in that period.[4] Assigning the composition of literary works to the Kassite period is thus a riskier practice than traditionally acknowledged.

Lambert, the most influential scholar of Babylonian literature of the twentieth century, often indulged in this practice, including in the case of 'Ferocious Lord', which he dated without much evidence to the Kassite period. But when it came to *Enuma Elish*, Lambert formulated a meticulously constructed argument according to which the text was penned during the rule of Nebuchadnezzar I (1125–1104 BCE) to celebrate the reinstatement of Marduk's statue to the Esagil after the king's victorious campaign against the Elamites.[5] This argument – essentially a response to the Old Babylonian dating of the poem that was still common in the 1950s – has gained considerable traction and is now widely accepted. But since there is no external evidence linking *Enuma Elish* to Nebuchadnezzar's Elamite campaign or any other aspect of his reign, Lambert's proposal remains, at best, 'a strong circumstantial case' (Brinkman 1998/2000: 194).

Establishing the date of composition of the epic is of utmost importance for understanding the history of Babylonian literature, so the question cannot simply be disregarded as unanswerable. There are, in fact, several texts for which a date of composition can be established, and these dates are especially valuable in examining the possible influences of one text over another. The protagonist of *Ludlul* is a historical character known to have lived during the reign of Nazi-Maruttash (1307–1282 BCE), so the composition of the poem must coincide with or postdate the life of that person (Fadhil and Jiménez 2019: 161–2). The similarities of 'Ferocious Lord' with *Ludlul* must thus be explained as the result of the former influencing the latter, not the other way around.

Regrettably little external evidence is available in the case of *Enuma Elish*. If an author or authors were given credit for the epic in the Mesopotamian tradition, their names have not yet been recovered. Though the epic is cited in many commentaries and other scholarly texts (Frahm 2011: 105; Fadhil and Jiménez 2021: 228; and Frances Reynolds in this volume), they all postdate its alleged date of composition by several centuries. In fact, the many quotations of the epic in the royal inscriptions of the

Assyrian kings are the oldest evidence of the text's circulation: only with these texts are we 'on somewhat safer grounds for establishing a *terminus ante quem* for [the epic's] origins' ('Auf etwas sichererem Boden für die Ermittlung eines Terminus ante quem für die Entstehung [des Epos]'; Kämmerer and Metzler 2012: 18). However, the epic only gained in popularity during the Sargonic period, so the oldest quotation of it that has so far been identified appears in an inscription of the Assyrian king Sargon II (721–705 BCE; Kämmerer and Metzler 2012: 40–3).[6]

This chapter will discuss the oldest available external evidence for dating *Enuma Elish*, evidence that has so far escaped attention in the secondary literature. In Tablet IV of the epic, we read: 'The angry winds bloated her belly, her inside was congested, her mouth gaped wide' (*ezzūtu šārū karšaša iṣānū-ma / innesil libbašā-ma pâša ušpalki*, IV 99–100). The phrase 'to fill the belly' (*karša ṣânu*) is very rare: it is attested only once outside *Enuma Elish*, in an inscription on a boundary stone (so-called *kudurru*) of a king of the Isin II dynasty, Marduk-nadin-ahhe (1099–1082 BCE), the younger brother and second successor of Nebuchadnezzar I. The *kudurru* was reportedly found in Babylon, near the Esagil temple, in the mid-nineteenth century (Reade 1987: 48). In the text's curse section, one of the formulae asks Marduk to fill the belly of anyone who damages the inscription with the *aganutillû*-disease: 'Let Marduk, king of heaven and earth, bloat his belly with indissoluble *aganutillû*-disease!' (*marūtuk*(damar.utu) *šar*(lugal) *šamê*(an-*e*) *u erṣeti*(ki-*tì*) *a-ga-nu-til-la-a ša ri-ki-is-su / la ip-paṭ-ṭa-ru li-ṣa-an ka-ra-as-su*, ii 25; BM 90841; Paulus 2014: 540). The phrase 'to fill the belly' (*karša ṣânu*), consists of two relatively rare words, whose combination is known only in Marduk-nadin-ahhe's inscription and in *Enuma Elish*. The strong association of the *aganutillû*-disease with Marduk, and the watery character of the disease itself, which will be discussed in detail below, makes the connection between *Enuma Elish* and the curse formula almost inescapable. The distribution patterns of the phrase fit even the strictest criteria for establishing a direct quotation (as opposed to a more general literary topos; see e.g. Jiménez 2017: 81; Matuszak 2021: 30–7), so the line can indeed be considered a quotation from *Enuma Elish* – and the oldest quotation of it yet known.

## Marduk and the water disease

The connection between the *aganutillû*-disease and Marduk became commonplace at the end of the Kassite dynasty: in almost all its appearances before the first millennium BCE, the disease is linked to Marduk.[7] A curse invoking Marduk's *aganutillû*-disease first appears in an inscription of the Kassite king Marduk-apla-iddina I (1171–1159 BCE),[8] and from this point onwards, Marduk is always made responsible for this disease. All *kudurrus* from the Isin II period that mention the disease link it with Marduk: it appears in the inscriptions of Marduk-nadin-ahhe (1099–1082 BCE) such as the one cited above[9] and in those of other rulers of the same dynasty.[10] Later, curses addressed to Marduk invoking the *aganutillû*-disease appear in boundary inscriptions of rulers from the tenth, eighth, and seventh centuries BCE,[11] in a Neo-Assyrian colophon,[12] and in curse formulae of Neo-Babylonian administrative documents.[13] The disease is also one of the dire punishments that Marduk will inflict on oath-breakers according to an inscription of Assurbanipal.[14]

It thus seems reasonable to assume that the association between the *aganutillû*-disease and Marduk began in the second millennium and continued into later periods. In the first millennium, however, several other gods are also associated with it (see n. 7). In particular, Esarhaddon's 'Vassal Treaties' (*SAA* 2, no. 6, l. 522), a text full of a 'totally unexpected wealth of unparalleled imagery in the curses' (Lambert 1980: 98), makes not Marduk, but Ea, 'king of the Apsû, lord of the underground waters', responsible for it. Perhaps the association between *aganutillû* and Marduk was no longer understood and a more appropriate god (Ea) was made responsible for the 'water disease'.

In short, it is evident that in Babylonia, at least from the end of the Kassite period onward, Marduk was perceived as responsible for the disease called *aganutillû*, in the same way that, for example, the moon god Sîn was held responsible for leprosy. The reasons why Marduk should be associated with this disease will be explored below.

## The water disease

Several Babylonian speculations on the meaning of the word *aganutillû* are preserved, all of which try to explain its meaning according to its first syllable, A, 'water'. The curse formula in Esarhaddon's 'Vassal Treaties' glosses the word *aganutillû* as 'unwholesome water' (*mû*(A) *lā*(NU) *balāṭi*(TI-LA); *SAA* 2, 6: 521), while the inscription by Assurbanipal glosses it as 'full water' (*mû malûtu*). A commentary on the medical compendium *Sagig* provides three alternative interpretations:

1) 'full of water' (*malâ mê*);
2) 'will not have / live to see a future' (*arkāt lā bašê / balāṭi*, by virtue of the equivalences **a-ga** = *arkatu*, **nu** = *lā*, **ti-la** = *bašû*, *balāṭu*); and
3) 'unending treasure of *water*' (*makkūr* ⌜A?⌝meš *lā qatû*, on account of (**níĝ**)-**ga** = *makkūr*, **a** = *mû*, **nu** = *lā*, and **til** = *qatû*; George 1991: 148–9, 56).

Further, the equation *aganutillû* = 'full of water' (*ma-la-a me-e*), is attested in numerous lexical lists from the Old Babylonian period onwards.[15] It is on account of this equation that the disease has traditionally been identified as dropsy.[16] In divinatory texts,[17] the disease is cited alongside skin diseases (such as *šaḫaršubbû*, *kiṣṣatu*, and *ṣennītu*), suggesting that it too is a type of skin disease.

The association of the *aganutillû*-disease with water was also used for medical diagnosis, as the disease was thought to indicate that the patient will die on a rainy day: 'If the upper part of the stomach protrudes, he has no fever but his sense is confused: it will develop into *aganutillû* and he will die one day when there is a downpour' (*šumma*(diš) *rēš*(sag) *libbī*(šà)-*šú za-qir umma*(kúm) *lā*(nu) *īšu*(tuku) *ṭēm*(umuš)-*šú inakkir*(kúr-kúr)-*šú ana*!(šú) *a-ga-nu-til-le-e iturraš*(gur)-*šum-ma ina ūm*($u_4$-*um*) *tīk*(bi-iz) *šamê*(an-*e*) *imât*(gam), *Sagig* XIII 16; Schmidtchen 2021: 517 and 40–1, where a different emendation is adopted). Naturally, the indication that the patient will die on a rainy day must relate to the watery nature of the disease. It is thus abundantly clear that, already in the Old Babylonian period, the disease was thought to produce or be characterized by an excess of water.

According to a medical treatise from Uruk that classifies diseases according to the organs they affect, or in which they originate, the disease 'full of water' (⸢*ma-li*⸣ *me-e*) originates 'from the mouth of the stomach' (*ultu pī karši*, *SpTU* 1, 43, l. 12; following the reading by Geller 2014: 3; the text was recently re-edited by Böck 2022). According to another medical text, the accumulation of wind in the 'mouth of the stomach' of a patient may develop into a disease called *šīqu*: 'If a man has the "mouth" of his belly filled with wind and it evolves into the *šīqu*-disease: until the wind that fills his chest goes downwards (that is, towards his rectum) and the man heals, … ' (*šumma*(diš) *amēlu*(na) *šá-a-ri ina pī*(ka) *kar-ši-šú in-né-sil-ma ana ši-i-q*[*u* ø] *i-tu-raš-ši a-di šāru*(im) *šá ina irtī*(gaba)-*šú in-né-sil ana* ⸢*šap*⸣-[*liš*] ⸢*pānī*(igi)-*šú išakkanū*(gar-*nu*)-⸢*ma amēlu*(lú)⸣ *i-bal-lu-ṭu*, BM 76510, l. 1–3).[18] According to this text, then, the wind accumulated in 'the mouth of the belly' may be the cause of a *šīqu*-disease, which will heal once the wind that fills the belly 'goes downwards', that is, towards the rectum. The *šīqu*-disease is an illness whose nature cannot be precisely identified, but whose name ('watering') suggests that it is related to fluid retention.[19] The Uruk medical treatise places the *šīqu*-disease among those pertaining to the lungs, immediately before the disease *šāru*, 'flatulence', and thus seems to confirm the link that is implied in the diagnostic text between the *šīqu*-disease and 'wind' inside the body (i.e. meteorism).

In short, according to these medical texts, the presence of water in the organism may be due to the action of the wind accumulated in the 'mouth of the stomach'. This is precisely the effect of the 'evil winds' that fill Tiamat's 'stomach' (*karšu*, IV 99) and that cause her 'innards' (*libbu*, IV 100) to be 'congested' (*innesil*, IV 100) and her mouth to be opened. The description of the winds' effect on Tiamat's body thus follows well-known medical descriptions of how 'wind' (*šāru*) affects a patient's intestinal tract (see also Jiménez 2022). This also seems to be the course of the *aganutillû*-disease: the 'abundance of water' that 'congests' (*esēlu*) the patient seems to be created by the 'wind' in their stomach.

## Marduk and the sea

When formal curses ask the gods to punish those who break oaths, defile buildings, and the like, the evils that are requested of each god are not arbitrary, but based on their respective functions. For instance, the healing goddess Gula is asked to inflict wounds that are untreatable by physicians, the storm god Adad to send destructive storms, and the moon god Sîn to inflict leprosy upon those who harm the inscription – skin diseases being associated with the moon in many cultures around the world.[20] The connection between the *aganutillû*-disease and Marduk is not as straightforward. Indeed, the realm of Marduk in general is not as clearly defined as that of Adad, Gula, or Sîn: besides his association with Babylon, Marduk's personality only includes such features as are characteristic of the so-called 'universal gods', that is, deities 'lacking any clear individual traits and without any specific domain' (as Steinkeller 1999: 114 fn. 36 writes about Enlil). Nothing seems to connect the patron of Babylon to any particular disease,[21] so the fact that the *aganutillû*-disease is almost exclusively connected with Marduk calls for an explanation.

The form that the theomachy (the battle between gods) takes in *Enuma Elish* is peculiar. Instead of sending the winds towards the enemy, blinding or otherwise paralysing them, as Ninurta does with Anzû and Gilgamesh with Humbaba, Marduk directs the winds *into* Tiamat so as to immobilize her. The peculiarities of Tiamat's defeat may be due to her not being fully anthropomorphized in *Enuma Elish*[22]: for example, it has been proposed that Marduk uses the winds to create a tidal wave to 'disturb' Tiamat.[23] Although the description of the battle in *Enuma Elish* does not seem to have meteorological connotations, and Tiamat is affected by Marduk's winds in the same way as the patients of the medical texts, the fact remains that Tiamat in *Enuma Elish* is never anthropomorphized to the same extent as monsters in other cuneiform poems, such as Anzû in the eponymous epic. Whereas in *Anzû*, the winds sent by Ninurta have a clear target, the bird's feathers, in *Enuma Elish* the winds of Marduk face an almost shapeless enemy. The situation is reminiscent of the most conspicuous borrowing of *Anzû* into *Enuma Elish*: that of the wind which in *Anzû* carries off the bird's feathers after the battle to bring good tidings to the gods, and which in *Enuma Elish* seems to carry off Tiamat's blood (Lambert 1986: 59; Jiménez 2013: 344–61; Wisnom 2020: 75–8; and Wisnom in this volume). In this case, the absence of feathers on Tiamat's body forces the author of *Enuma Elish* to modify the motif and adapt it to Tiamat's description: blood is indeed the most appropriate liquid – liquid being Tiamat's element – to prove someone's death. Similarly, Tiamat's lack of feathers makes it necessary to modify the motif of the winds plucking the feathers of the enemy, which was the key to the monster's defeat in *Anzû* (see Wisnom in this volume).

Tiamat's aquatic nature does not seem to be reflected in the action of the winds. However, it is probable that her watery aspect holds the key to the curse under consideration: it is difficult to imagine any other reason for Marduk's association with *aganutillû*-disease than the fact that Tiamat, the sea, is defeated at his hands (on the significance of water in *Enuma Elish*, see also Sophus Helle and Piotr Michalowski in this volume). Defeating Tiamat effectively put Marduk in charge of the 'Water Disease', as evidenced by the phrase from *Enuma Elish* being used to describe the *aganutillû*-disease in Marduk-nadin-ahhe's inscription.

The motif of the battle between a storm god and the sea – the central theme of *Enuma Elish* – is unknown in Sumerian literature. In Akkadian literature, it is almost unknown until the Kassite period, and shortly afterwards it is also attested in Ugarit; some have argued that it entered Babylonian literature from the West.[24] Even if it appeared independently in Mesopotamia, establishing the date of its first appearance is crucial for determining when *Enuma Elish* was composed. As argued above, the attribution of the 'Water Disease' to Marduk can be taken as the earliest evidence for the existence of this myth in Babylonia. The intertextual connection between the cosmic battle in *Enuma Elish* and the curse formula seems to confirm that the motif is one and the same. In our present state of knowledge, we can say that the story of Marduk's battle with the sea made its first appearance in Babylonia during the late Kassite or early Isin II period.

It is difficult to determine whether *Enuma Elish* already existed at this time. The *terminus ante quem* is now the reign of Marduk-nadin-ahhe (1099–1082 BCE). Before the terminal phase of the Kassite period, Marduk appears frequently in curse formulae of *kudurru*-inscriptions relating to general evils, such as death, evil, and famine.[25] But significantly, when the *aganutillû*-curse first appears in a *kudurru*-inscription, during the reign of the Kassite ruler Meli-Shipak (1186–1172 BCE), it is attributed to Sîn; in the same text, Marduk is called upon to enact curses of a more general nature.[26] With Meli-Shipak's son and successor, Marduk-apla-iddina I (1171–1159 BCE), Marduk begins to be associated with *aganutillû*-disease, but not yet systematically: at least one text is known from this time in which *aganutillû* is associated with several gods.[27] Subsequently, during the Isin II dynasty, Marduk is systematically associated with the *aganutillû*-disease, in the inscriptions of Enlil-nadin-apli (1103–1100 BCE) and Marduk-nadin-ahhe (1099–1082 BCE), Nebuchadnezzar I's immediate successors.

## Conclusions

Because of the conservative nature of Near Eastern religious literature, the modern critic can use neither the contents of *Enuma Elish* nor its language to date its composition: only external evidence can be used. Unfortunately, in the case of *Enuma Elish*, there is little external evidence beyond its quotations in the inscriptions of Neo-Assyrian kings. This chapter has contributed to the discussion of *Enuma Elish*'s date by analysing what appears to be the oldest quotation of the epic, namely a curse formula in a *kudurru*-inscription from the reign of Marduk-nadin-ahhe (1099–1082 BC). In this curse, a line of *Enuma Elish* is used to summon the god Marduk to inflict a disease called *aganutillû* on anyone who disrespects the inscription.

The curse formula linking Marduk to the *aganutillû*-disease first gained in popularity in inscriptions of the Kassite period. The disease is described as 'Water Disease' in Mesopotamian texts, so Marduk's association with it probably derived from his defeat of the sea in Babylonian mythology. Moreover, the description of Tiamat's defeat in *Enuma Elish* has clear echoes of medical texts that describe the effects of wind (Marduk's weapon of choice) on the patient. The motif of Marduk's defeat of the sea also makes its first appearance in Mesopotamian literature during the Kassite period.

The development of the *aganutillû*-formula in Kassite-period *kudurru*-inscriptions suggests that Marduk's role as the conqueror of the sea first emerged in the thirteenth or twelfth century BCE, coinciding with the end of the Kassite dynasty and the beginning of the Isin II dynasty. *Enuma Elish* is commonly believed to have been composed during the reign of Nebuchadnezzar I (1125–1104 BCE), and although Nebuchadnezzar I's role in its final composition remains hypothetical, this study supports the idea that the threads which would be woven into the epic were being spun at this time.

## Further reading

The elevation of Marduk to the head of the Mesopotamian pantheon, which took place in the final centuries of the second millennium BCE, is one of the most remarkable religious developments in ancient Near Eastern history. Sommerfeld (1982) conducted a monographic study of it, while other authors (Tenney 2016; Jiménez 2019) have discussed different aspects of this development. On the dating of *Enuma Elish*, see the informative summaries provided by Dina Katz (2011) and by Thomas Kämmerer and Kai Metzler (2012), as well as the classic works by Lambert (1964, 2013: 248–77) on the topic and the responses it generated (see also Dalley 1997; Nielsen 2018: 163–85). On *Enuma Elish*'s dependence on other epics, especially *Anzû*, see the studies by Lambert (1986) and Selena Wisnom (2020).

## Notes

1 The argument was already used by Schott (1926: 69–71), who dated the text to the Neo-Assyrian period. Von Soden (1933: 128–30) used it to suggest an Old Babylonian date of composition, a view he later abandoned. See also the discussion in Sommerfeld (1982: 175 fn. 2) and Kämmerer and Metzler (2012: 16–17). On possible Old Babylonian occurrences of *-iš* with a comparative force, see Lambert (1984: 6) and Streck and Wasserman (2008: 350).

2 See also the response by Lambert (1984: 4–6) and the literature cited in Kämmerer and Metzler (2012: 20). Kämmerer and Metzler (2012: 21) describe the Epic as a 'permanent performative process' ('permanente[r] performative[r] Prozeß'), in which the elevation of Marduk is 'both asserted and also thereby effected' ('sowohl behauptet als auch zugleich damit bewirkt').

3 Lambert (1984: 4) resists the idea that 'this new "Marduk theology" was being shouted from the rooftops already under the Cassite kings', but his scepticism seems unwarranted in view of these texts.

4 A Kassite date of composition was defended by Lambert (1960: 48). The Old Babylonian manuscript is BM 78278 (*CT* 44, 21 = *CTL* 1, 81), see Fadhil and Jiménez (2019: 162). The Middle Babylonian excerpt, Bab 36657, was identified by Bartelmus (2016: 99 and 161).

5 See the literature cited in the Further Reading section.

6 On further possible quotations of the epic in inscriptions by Sargon II, see Renger (1986: 127) and Fuchs (1994: 292 fn. 64).

7 Only on five occasions are gods other than Marduk associated with the *aganutillû*-disease:

(1) With Sîn in the oldest attestation of the curse, in the *kudurru* 'Meli-Shipak 1' (Sb 22, 1186–72 BCE): 'May Sîn burden him with insolvable *aganutillû*-disease' ($^{d}$*suen (…) a-gá-nu-til-la-a ša rikissu lā ippaṭṭaru lišeššīšu*, vi 41–6; Paulus 2014: 376–7).

(2) With several gods in the *kudurru* 'Marduk-apla-iddina I 1' (Sb 26, 1171–59 BCE): 'may they infect him with *aganutillû*-disease' (*a-gá-nu-til-la-a lišamriṣūšū-ma*, vi 20; Paulus 2014: 435).

(3) With Shamash (?) in an anti-witchcraft ritual (Abusch and Schwemer 2011: 272, no. 8.3, §1 l. 10).

(4) With Ea, in Esarhaddon's 'Vassal Treaties' (see below).

(5) With Nabû and Nissaba in a Late Babylonian colophon (BM 42282+ o. 5; see Lawson 1997: 72–3).

8 'Marduk-apla-iddina I 6' (Sb 169): 'Let [Marduk], the sage of heaven and earth, burden him with [...] ... *aganutillû*-disease' ([*marūtuk ap*]*kal šamê u erṣeti* [o o (o)] x-*ni a-ga-nu-til-la* [*liša*]*ššīšū-ma*, iii 11′–13′; Paulus 2014: 467).

9

(1) 'Marduk-nadin-ahhe 1' (*Caillou Michaux*): 'Let Marduk, the great lord, burden him with indissoluble *aganutillû*-disease' (*marūtuk bēlu rabû a-ga-nu-ti-la-a rikissu lā paṭīra lišeššīšu*, iii 13; Paulus 2014: 535).
(2) 'Marduk-nadin-ahhe 2' (BM 90841), cited in the main text (ii 25; Paulus 2014: 514).
(3) 'Marduk-nadin-ahhe 3' (BM 90840, tenth year of his reign): 'Let Marduk, the great lord, [burden him] with indissoluble *aganutillû*-disease' (*marūtuk bēlu rabû a-ga-nu-til-la-*[*a*] *riksu lā paṭīra* [*lišeššīšu*], iii 31–2; Paulus 2014: 546).
(4) 'Marduk-nadin-ahhe 4' (IM 90585, thirteenth year of reign), 'Let Marduk, the great lord (...) burden him with indissoluble *aganutillû*-disease' (*marūtuk bēlu rabû* (...) *a-ga-nu-til-la-a ša rikissu lā ippaṭṭaru lišeššīšū-ma*, vi 29–33; Paulus 2014: 558).

10

(1) 'Enlil-nadin-apli 2' (BM 102485, *r.* 1103–00): 'Let king Marduk, [...] lord of the lands, [burden him] with *aganutillû-disease*, his severe punishment" (*marūtuk* (...) *a-ga-nu-t*[*i-la-a*] / *šēressu rabīta* [*lišeššīšu*], v 4–6; Paulus 2014: 527).
(2) 'Marduk-shapik-zeri 1' (IM 74651, *r.* 1081–69 BCE): 'Let Marduk, the great lord, inflict him with indissoluble *aganutillû*-disease' (*marūtuk šar šamê u erṣeti* (...) *a-ga-nu-ti-la-a* [*š*]*a rikissu lā paṭīru lišaršīšū-ma*, ii 18–9; Paulus 2014: 577).

11

(1) 'Nabû-mukin-apli 1' (BM 90835, twenty-second year of Nabû-mukīn-apli, *r.* 978–43 BCE): 'Let [Marduk], the king of the gods, [...] with indissoluble *aganutillû*-disease' ([*marūtuk*] *šar ilī* (...) *ina a-ga-nu-tìl-e ša rikissu lā paṭ*[*īra* ... ], ii 39–41; Paulus 2014: 625).
(2) 'Marduk-apla-iddina II 1' (VA 2663, *r.* 721–10 BCE): 'Let Marduk (and ... ) burden him with his heavy punishment, the *aganutillû*-disease' (*marūtuk* (...) *šēressu kabta*[sic] *a-ga-nu-til-la-a lišaššûšū-ma*, v 40–3; Paulus 2014: 699).
(3) 'Shamash-shuma-ukin 3' (BM 130827, *r.* 667–48 BCE, second year of his reign): '[Let] Marduk, the great lord (...) [inflict him with indissoluble *aganutillû*-disease], [his heavy] punishment' (*marūtuk bēlu rabû* [*aganutillâ ša rikissu*] *lā paṭāru šēr*[*essu kabitta lišaršīšū-ma*], r. 2–3; Paulus 2014: 741; Slanski 2003: 223).
(4) Note also the inscription by Sîn-sharra-usur, governor of Ur during the time of Shamash-shumu-ukin: 'Let Marduk, the great lord (...) inflict him with *aganutillû*-disease, his indissoluble punishment' (*marūtuk bēlu rabû* (...) *a-ga-nu-til-la-a šēressu ša lā paṭāru lušaršīš*, l. 10–12; Frame 1995: 259 no. 2001).

12 *LKA* 109: '[...] *aganutillû*-disease [...] from the hand of Marduk' ([ ... *i*]*na qātī marūtuk a-ga-nu-til-la-a* [...], r. 17; Hunger 1968: 68 no. 194; Maul 1994: 477).

13 As has been observed, the few known curses in Neo-Babylonian administrative documents are similar to the execratory sections of *kudurrus*, from which they probably derive; see Owen and Watanabe (1983: 39), Jursa (2005: 15), and Sandowicz (2012: 109). On curses in Neo-Babylonian documents invoking *aganutillû* in connection with Marduk, see Sandowicz (2012: 122):

(1) HS 452 (Nippur, Marduk-apla-iddina II, *r.* 721–10, 703 BCE): 'Let Marduk, the great lord (...) inflict him with *aganutillû*-disease, his heavy punishment'

(*marūtuk bēlu rabû a-ga-nu-til-la-a šēressu kabitta lišaršīš*, l. 26–7; Krückmann 1933: no. 8; Sandowicz 2012: 435).

(2) FLP 1386 (Nippur (?), Esarhaddon, *r*. 680–69 BCE): 'Let Marduk, the great lord (...) inflict him with *aganutillû*-disease, his heavy punishment' (*marūtuk bēlu rabû a-ga-nu-t[il-la-a] šēressu kabitta lišaršīš*, l. 27–8; Owen and Watanabe 1983: 39–43; Sandowicz 2012: 435).

(3) BM 113927 (Ur, Shamash-shuma-ukin): 'Let Marduk, the great lord, burden him with indissoluble *aganutillû*-disease' (*marūtuk bēlu rabû a-ga-nu-til-la-a ša lā paṭāru lišaššīš*, l. 22–3; Sandowicz 2012: 446).

(4) *Drevnosti vostočnyja* I (Uruk, Shamash-shuma-ukin, *r*. 667–48 BCE): 'Let Marduk, the great lord (...) inflict him with indissoluble *aganutillâ*-disease, his heavy punishment' (*marūtuk bēlu rabû [aganutillâ riksa] lā paṭāru šēres[su kabittu lišaršīš]*, 2; Weidner 1952/1953: 43–5; Sandowicz 2012: 447).

(5) *UET* 4, 171 (Ur): Let Mushteshir-habli (a weapon of Marduk) '*inflict* him with indissoluble *aganutillû*-disease!' (*a-ga-na*[sic]*-tal*[sic]*-lâ-a ša lā paṭāri šuššânni*, 16–17; Sandowicz 2012: 400).

14 'Nabu-shuma-eresh, the governor (*sc.* of Nippur), who did not keep the oath, was burdened with *aganutillû*-disease, (i.e.) abundant water. And on Marduk-shuma-ibni, his general, who had instigated him, who had plotted insidiousness against Urtaki, Marduk, the king of the gods, inflicted his severe punishment' (*nabû-šuma-ēreš šandabakku lā nāṣir adê iššī a-ga-nu-til-la-a mê*(A[meš]) *ma-lu-u-ti marduk-šuma-ibni šūt rēšīšu mušadbibšu ša lemuttu ušakpidu ana urtaki ēmissu marūtuk šar ilī šērtašu rabītu*, Ashurbanipal 3 IV 56–63 // Ashurbanipal 6 v 73–87; Borger 1996: 96, 223; Novotny and Jeffers 2018: 67, 90, 125, 49). Although the first sentence does not state who is responsible for the disease, it seems clear from the second sentence that it is Marduk. As noted by Oettinger (1976: 71–3), dropsy is invoked in a Hittite text as punishment for the oath-breaker, perhaps reflecting a Babylonian influence. Oettinger finds parallels in the Vedas and consequently suggests that the Mesopotamian curse is of Indo-European origin, perhaps brought to Mesopotamia by the Kassites. He further claims that the curse derives from the custom of swearing by water.

15 See the *Chicago Assyrian Dictionary*, s.v. *agannutillû*, and the *Pennsylvania Sumerian Dictionary*, s.v. **a-ga-la-ti-la**, for references in lexical lists. The earliest attestation appears in the 'Old Babylonian List of Diseases'; Landsberger (1967: 79).

16 Thus for example Delitzsch (1896: 16, 'Wassersucht'); Bezold (1926: 15, 'Wassersucht'); *Akkadisches Handwörterbuch*, s.v. *aganutillû* ('Wassersucht'); the *Chicago Assyrian Dictionary*, s.v. *agannutillû* ('dropsy'); the *Pennsylvania Sumerian Dictionary*, s.v. **a-ga-la-ti-la** ('dropsy'); Biggs (1969: 102, 'dropsy'); Oppenheim (1978: 15:645, 'dropsy'); and Scurlock and Andersen (2005: 254, 'generalized swelling or edema [anasarca]').

17 See *Shumma Alu* XXI 23, Freedman (1998: 310–11); or *Iqqur Ipush* §41′ 16, Labat (1965: 106–7), which predicts that a man will die of dropsy and will not be buried.

18 The text is unpublished; l. 1–2a are quoted in Stol (2006: 107 fn. 20).

19 According to Geller (2014: 8), it would be 'excessive "moisture"'. Köcher (1978: 24) glosses the name as '[e]ine schwere, nässende Krankheit, die (auch) die Lippen befällt', following *Akkadisches Handwörterbuch*, s.v. *šīqu*. For Scurlock and Andersen (2005: 42), it would be a 'phlegm'; according to p. 688 fn. 84, it would be 'colored sputum'.

20 On curses invoking the Storm God, see Schwemer (2001: 435–9) and Grätz (1998). On curses involving Gula, see Böck (2013: 22–4). On the role of the Moon God in curses, see Watanabe (1984) and Hätinen (2021: 255–70).

21 Although Marduk's early identification with Asalluhi, the god of Kuara (a city near Eridu), made him the son of Ea, god of Eridu and lord of the waters, Marduk did not inherit from his putative father a close connection with water.

22 As noted by Lambert (1994: 104): 'Tiāmat is not uniform in the Epic of Creation. At times she is presented as a solid-bodied monster, at other times as a mass of water. The author is conflating two traditions. Berossus combined the two traditions more systematically: he presents Tiāmat advancing against Marduk as a woman yet at the same moment as a body of water so that monsters are swimming inside her!'

23 Thus Reiner (1985: 63–4): 'The winds which accompanied Marduk were intended to throw waves, for Tiamat is the sea: the text says, "to disturb the bosom of Tiamat"'. On the relation between Tiamat's defeat and anthropomorphism, see also Sophus Helle in this volume.

24 See the classic studies by Jacobsen (1968) and Durand (1993: 42–3 and passim). The latter author claims that the motif is of Amorite origin, but this supposed Amorite origin was challenged by Lambert (1994: 111–13), who believes that both the Amorite and Mesopotamian myths 'descended from a common prehistoric tradition spread very widely from the Indus Valley to the Aegean, and that borrowing from the known Syrian tradition into the Babylonian world is not proven or probable'.

25 E.g. in:

(1) 'Kadashman-Harbe I 1' (YBC 2242, fifteenth–fourteenth century BCE; iii 30ff; Paulus 2014: 299).
(2) 'Nazi-Maruttash 2' (Sb 21, 1305–1280 BCE): 'let him pour out his life like water!' (*napištašu kīma mê litbuk*, iii 30–5; Paulus 2014: 328). Perhaps this is a precursor of the *aganutillû*-curse.
(3) 'Meli-Shipak 1' (Sb 22, 1184–70 BCE; vi 29–40; Paulus 2014: 376), mentioned in n. 7 no. 1.
(4) 'Meli-Shipak 2' (BM 90829; iii 13; Paulus 2014: 386).

Before the Kassite period, Marduk's presence among the gods summoned to curse the damager of an inscription is more sporadic. Both Leick (1976: 66) and Sommerfeld (1982: 77) note that, despite Marduk's prominent role in the prologue of the Code of Hammurapi, he does not appear among the gods invoked in the curses section.

26 E.g., 'Meli-Shipak 1' (Sb 22), 'let him inflict upon him his great punishment, hunger' (*bubūta šērtašu rabīta limmissū-ma*, vi 33–4; Paulus 2014: 376).

27 See above, n. 7 no. 2.

## Bibliography

Abusch, T. and D. Schwemer (2011), *Corpus of Mesopotamian Anti-Witchcraft Rituals*, Ancient Magic and Divination 8, Leiden: Brill.

Bartelmus, A. (2016), *Fragmente einer großen Sprache: Sumerisch im Kontext der Schreiberausbildung des kassitenzeitlichen Babylonien*, 2 vols, Untersuchungen zur Assyriologie und Vorderasiatischen Archäologie 12, Berlin: De Gruyter.

Bartelmus, A. (2018), 'Formale Besonderheiten mittelbabylonischer Schülertafeln', in E. Cancik-Kirschbaum and B. Schnitzlein (eds), *Keilschriftartefakte: Untersuchungen zur Materialität von Keilschriftdokumenten*, Berliner Beiträge zum Vorderen Orient 26, 63–94, Glabdeck: PeWe-Verlag.

Bezold, C. (1926), *Babylonisch-assyrisches Glossar*, Heidelberg: Winter Verlag.

Biggs, R. D. (1969), 'Medicine in Ancient Mesopotamia', *History of Science*, 8: 94–105.
Böck, B. (2013), 'Medicinal Plants and Medicaments Used for Conception, Abortion, and Fertility Control in Ancient Babylonia', *Journal Asiatique*, 301: 27–52.
Böck, B. (2022), 'The Babylonian Ars medica and the Uruk text SpTU I 43', *Orientalistische Literaturzeitung*, 117 (4–5): 297–305.
Borger, R. (1996) *Beiträge zum Inschriftenwerk Assurbanipals: Die Prismenklassen A, B, C= K, D,E, F,G, H, J und T sowie andere Inschriften*, Wiesbaden: Harrassowitz.
Brinkman, J. A. (1998/2000), 'Nebukadnezar I', *Reallexikon der Assyriologie und Vorderasiatischen Archäologie*, 9: 192–4.
Dalley, S. (1997), 'Statues of Marduk and the Date of Enūma eliš', *Altorientalische Forschungen*, 24: 163–71.
Delitzsch, F. (1896), *Assyrisches Handwörterbuch*, Leipzig: Hinrichs.
Durand, J.-M. (1993), 'Le mythologème du combat entre le Dieu de l'Orage et la Mer en Mésopotamie', *MARI: Annales de Recherches Interdisciplinaires*, 7: 41–61.
Fadhil, A. A. and E. Jiménez (2019), 'Literary Texts from the Sippar Library I: Two Babylonian Classics', *Zeitschrift für Assyriologie und Vorderasiatische Archäologie*, 109: 155–76.
Fadhil, A. A. and E. Jiménez (2021), 'Literary Texts from the Sippar Library II: The Epic of Creation', *Zeitschrift für Assyriologie und Vorderasiatische Archäologie*, 111: 191–230.
Fadhil, A. A. and E. Jiménez (2022), 'Literary Texts from the Sippar Library III: Eriš šummi, a Syncretistic Hymn to Marduk', *Zeitschrift für Assyriologie und Vorderasiatische Archäologie*, 112: 229–74.
Frahm, E. (2011), *Babylonian and Assyrian Text Commentaries: Origins of Interpretation*, Guides to the Mesopotamian Textual Record 5, Münster: Ugarit-Verlag.
Frame, G. (1995), *Rulers of Babylonia from the Second Dynasty of Isin to the End of Assyrian Domination (1157–612 B.C.)*, The Royal Inscriptions of Mesopotamia, Babylonian Periods 2, Toronto: University of Toronto Press.
Freedman, S. M. (1998), *If a City Is Set on a Height: The Akkadian Omen Series šumma ālu ina mēlê šakin*, i: *Tablets 1–21*, Occasional Publications of the Samuel Noah Kramer Fund 17, Philadelphia: University Museum.
Fuchs, A. (1994), *Die Inschriften Sargons II. aus Khorsabad*, Göttingen: Cuvillier Verlag.
Gabriel, G. (2021), 'Der assyrische Raub des *Enūma elîš* und weitere Überlegungen zur Textdatierung', *Nouvelles assyriologiques brèves et utilitaires*, 2021 (2): 114–17, no. 47.
Geller, M. J. (2014), *Melothesia in Babylonia: Medicine, Magic, and Astrology in the Ancient Near East*, Science, Technology, and Medicine in Ancient Cultures 2, Berlin: De Gruyter.
George, A. R. (1991), 'Babylonian Texts from the Folios of Sidney Smith. Part Two: Prognostic and Diagnostic Omens, Tablet I', *Revue d'assyriologie et d'archéologie orientale*, 85: 137–67.
George, A. R. (2005/2006), 'The Tower of Babel: Archaeology, History and Cuneiform Texts', *Archiv für Orientforschung*, 51: 75–95.
Grätz, S. (1998), *Der strafende Wettergott: Erwägungen zur Traditionsgeschichte des Adad-Fluchs im Alten Orient und im Alten Testament*, Bonner Biblische Beiträge 114, Bodenheim: Philo.
Hätinen, A. (2021), *The Moon God Sîn in Neo-Assyrian and Neo-Babylonian Times*, dubsar 20, Münster: Zaphon.
Horton, R. (1993), *Patterns of Thought in Africa and the West: Essays on Magic, Religion and Science*, Cambridge: Cambridge University Press.
Hunger, H. (1968), *Babylonische und assyrische Kolophone*, Alter Orient und Altes Testament 2, Neukirchen-Vluyn: Neukirchener Verlag.

Jacobsen, T. (1968), 'The Battle between Marduk and Tiamat', *Journal of the American Oriental Society*, 88: 104–8.

Jiménez, E. (2013), *La imagen de los vientos en la literatura babilónica*, PhD thesis: Universidad Complutense de Madrid.

Jiménez, E. (2017), *The Babylonian Disputation Poems: With Editions of the Series of the Poplar, Palm and Vine, the Series of the Spider, and the Story of the Poor, Forlorn Wren*, Culture and History of the Ancient Near East 87, Leiden: Brill.

Jiménez, E. (2019), 'Marduk', *Encyclopedia of the Bible and Its Reception*, 17: 885–7.

Jiménez, E. (2022), 'Der Gott Marduk und die Winde der Flut: Oder, wie Marduk Tiamat besiegte', in A. Höfele and B. Kellner (eds), *Naturkatastrophen: Deutungsmuster vom Altertum bis in die Neuzeit*, 65–81, Leiden: Brill, 2022.

Jursa, M. (2005), *Neo-Babylonian Legal and Administrative Documents: Typology, Contents and Archives*, Guides to the Mesopotamian Textual Record 1, Münster: Ugarit-Verlag.

Kämmerer, T. R. and K. A. Metzler (2012), *Das babylonische Weltschöpfungsepos Enūma elîš*, Alter Orient und Altes Testament 375, Münster: Ugarit-Verlag.

Katz, D. (2011), 'Reconstructing Babylon: Recycling Mythological Traditions toward a New Theology', in E. Cancik-Kirschbaum, M. van Ess and J. Marzahn, *Babylon: Wissenskultur zwischen Orient und Okzident*, 123–34, Berlin: De Gruyter.

Köcher, F. (1978), 'Spätbabylonische medizinische Texte aus Uruk', in C. Habrich, F. Marguth and J. H. Wolf (eds), *Medizinische Diagnostik in Geschichte und Gegenwart: Festschrift für H. Goerke zum sechzigsten Geburtstag*, 17–39, Munich: Werner Fritsch.

Krückmann, O. (1933), *Neubabylonische Rechts- und Verwaltungsttexte*, 2 vols, Texte und Materialien der Frau Professor Hilprecht Collection 2–3, Leipzig: Hinrichs.

Labat, R. (1965), *Un calendrier Babylonien des travaux des signes et mois (Séries iqqur īpuš)*, Paris: Librairie Honoré Champion.

Lambert, W. G. (1960), 'Three Literary Prayers of the Babylonians', *Archiv für Orientforschung*, 19: 47–66, pls. VIII–XXIII.

Lambert, W. G. (1964), 'The Reign of Nebuchadnezzar I: A Turning Point in the History of Ancient Mesopotamian Religion', in W. S. McCullough (ed.), *The Seed of Wisdom: Essays in Honour of T.J. Meek*, 3–13, Toronto: University of Toronto Press.

Lambert, W. G. (1980), 'Introduction to Akkadian', in J. H. Eaton, *Horizons in Semitic Studies: Articles for the Student*, 91–9, Birmingham: Department of Theology.

Lambert, W. G. (1984), 'Studies in Marduk', *Bulletin of the School of Oriental and African Studies*, 47: 1–9.

Lambert, W. G. (1986), 'Ninurta Mythology in the Babylonian Epic of Creation', in K. Hecker and W. Sommerfeld, *Keilschriftliche Literaturen*, Compte Rendu de la Rencontre Assyriologique Internationale 32, Berliner Beiträge zum Vorderen Orient 6, 55–60, Berlin: Dietrich Reimer Verlag.

Lambert, W. G. (1994), 'A New Look at the Babylonian Background of Genesis', in R. S. Hess and D. T. Tsumura (eds), *'I Studied Inscriptions from Before the Flood': Ancient Near Eastern, Literary, and Linguistic Approaches to Genesis 1–11*, 96–113, Winona Lake: Eisenbrauns.

Lambert, W. G. (2013), *Babylonian Creation Myths*, Mesopotamian Civilizations 16, Winona Lake: Eisenbrauns.

Landsberger, B. (1967), *The Series ḪAR-ra = ḫubullu: Tablet XV and Related Texts*, Materialien zum sumerischen Lexikon 9, Rome: Biblical Institute Press.

Lawson, J. N. (1997), '"The God Who Reveals Secrets": The Mesopotamian Background to Daniel 2.47', *Journal for the Study of the Old Testament*, 74: 61–76.

Leick, G. (1976), *Die akkadischen Fluchformeln des 3. und 2. Jahrtausends*, PhD thesis: Karl Franzens Universität Graz.

Matuszak, J. (2021), *'Und du, du bist eine Frau?!': Editio princeps und Analyse des sumerischen Streitgesprächs 'Zwei Frauen B'*, Untersuchungen zur Assyriologie und Vorderasiatischen Archäologie 16, Berlin: De Gruyter.

Maul, S. M. (1994), *Zukunftsbewältigung: Eine Untersuchung altorientalischen Denkens anhand der babylonisch-assyrischen Löserituale (Namburbi)*, Baghdader Forschungen 18, Mainz: Von Zabern.

Nielsen, J. P. (2018), *The Reign of Nebuchadnezzar I in History and Historical Memory*, London: Routledge.

Novotny, J. R. and J. Jeffers (2018), *The Royal Inscriptions of Ashurbanipal (668–631 BC), Aššur-etal-ilāni (630–627 BC), and Sîn-šarra-iškun (626–612 BC), Kings of Assyria*, Royal Inscriptions of the Neo-Assyrian Period 5, Winona Lake: Eisenbrauns.

Oettinger, N. (1976), *Die Militärischen Eide der Hethiter*, Studien zu den Bogazköy-Texten 22, Wiesbaden: Harrassowitz.

Oppenheim, A. L. (1978), 'Man and Nature in Mesopotamian Civilization', in C. C. Gillispie (ed.), *Dictionary of Scientific Biography*, 15 (1), 634–66, New York: Scribner.

Owen, D. I. and K. Watanabe (1983), 'Eine neubabylonische Gartenkaufurkunde mit Fluchen aus dem Akzessionsjahr Asarhaddons', *Oriens Antiquus*, 22: 37–48.

Paulus, S. (2014), *Die babylonischen Kudurru-Inschriften von der kassitischen bis zur frühneubabylonischen Zeit: Untersucht unter besonderer Berücksichtigung gesellschafts- und rechtshistorischer Fragestellungen*, Alter Orient und Altes Testament 51, Münster: Ugarit-Verlag.

Reade, J. E. (1987), 'Babylonian Boundary-Stones and Comparable Monuments in the British Museum', *Annual Review of the Royal Inscriptions of Mesopotamia Project*, 5: 47–9.

Reiner, E. (1985), *Your Thwarts in Pieces, Your Mooring Rope Cut: Poetry from Babylonia and Assyria*, Michigan: University of Michigan.

Renger, J. (1986), 'Neuassyrische Königsinschriften als Genre der Keilschriftliteratur: Zum Stil und zur Kompositionstechnik der Inschriften Sargons II. von Assyrien', in K. Hecker and W. Sommerfeld, *Keilschriftliche Literaturen*, Compte Rendu de la Rencontre Assyriologique Internationale 32, Berliner Beiträge zum Vorderen Orient 6, 109–28, Berlin: Dietrich Reimer Verlag.

Sandowicz, M. (2012), *Oaths and Curses: A Study in Neo- and Late Babylonian Legal Formulary*, Alter Orient und Altes Testament 398, Münster: Ugarit-Verlag.

Schmidtchen, E. (2021), *Mesopotamische Diagnostik: Untersuchungen zu Rekonstruktion, Terminologie und Systematik des babylonisch-assyrischen Diagnosehandbuches und eine Neubearbeitung der Tafeln 3–14*, Die babylonisch-assyrische Medizin in Texten und Untersuchungen 13, Berlin: De Gruyter.

Schott, A. (1926), *Die Vergleiche in den akkadischen Königsinschriften*, Mitteilungen der Vorderasiatisch-Aegyptischen Gesellschaft 30 (2), Leipzig: Hinrichs.

Schwemer, D. (2001), *Die Wettergottgestalten Mesopotamiens und Nordsyriens im Zeitalter der Keilschriftkulturen: Materialien und Studien nach den schriftlichen Quellen*, Wiesbaden: Harrassowitz.

Scurlock, J. and B. R. Andersen (2005), *Diagnoses in Assyrian and Babylonian Medicine: Ancient Sources, Translations, and Modern Medical Analyses*, Champaign: University of Illinois Press.

Slanski, K. E. (2003), *The Babylonian Entitlement* narûs *(kudurrus): A Study in Form and Function*, ASOR Books 9, Boston: American Schools of Oriental Research.

Sommerfeld, W. (1982), *Der Aufstieg Marduks: Die Stellung Marduks in der babylonischen Religion des zweiten Jahrtausends v. Chr.*, Alter Orient und Altes Testament 213, Neukirchen-Vluyn: Butzon & Becker Kevelaer.

Steinkeller, P. (1999), 'On Rulers, Priests and Sacred Marriage', in K. Watanabe (ed.), *Priests and Officials in the Ancient Near East: Papers of the Second Colloquium on the Ancient Near East, The City and Its Life, Held at the Middle Eastern Culture Center in Japan (Mitaka, Tokyo)*, 103–37, Heidelberg: Winter Verlag.

Stol, M. (2006), 'The Digestion of Food According to Babylonian Sources', in L. Battini and P. Villard (eds), *Médecine et médecins au Proche-Orient ancien: Actes du Colloque International organisé à Lyon les 8 et 9 novembre 2002, Maison de l'Orient et de la Méditerranée*, BAR International Series 1528, 103–19, Oxford: British Archaeological Reports.

Streck, M. P. and N. Wasserman (2008), 'The Old Babylonian Hymns to Papulegara', *Orientalia*, 77: 335–58.

Tenney, J. S. (2016), 'The Elevation of Marduk Revisited: Festivals and Sacrifices at Nippur During the High Kassite Period', *Journal of Cuneiform Studies*, 68: 153–80.

von Soden, Wolfram (1933), 'Der hymnisch-epische Dialekt des Akkadischen', *Zeitschrift für Assyriologie und Vorderasiatische Archäologie*, 41: 90–183.

von Soden, Wolfram (1953), 'Das Problem der zeitlichen Einordnung akkadischer Literaturwerke', *Mitteilungen der Deutschen Orient-Gesellschaft*, 85: 14–26.

Watanabe, K. (1984), 'Die literarische Überlieferung eines babylonisch-assyrischen Fluchthemas mit Anrufung des Mondgottes Sîn', *Acta Sumerologica*, 6: 99–119.

Weidner, E. F. (1952/1953), 'Keilschrifttexte nach Kopien von T. G. Pinches: Aus dem Nachlass veröffentlicht und bearbeitet. 1. Babylonische Privaturkunden aus dem 7. Jahrhundert v. Chr.', *Archiv für Orientforschung*, 16: 35–46.

Wisnom, S. (2020), *Weapons of Words: Intertextual Competition in Babylonian Poetry; A Study of 'Anzû', 'Enūma Eliš', and 'Erra and Išum'*, Culture and History of the Ancient Near East 106, Leiden: Brill.

2

# *Enuma Elish* in cult and ritual performance

Céline Debourse

The text of *Enuma Elish* is in essence a performative text, as the epilogue makes clear by referring to it as the 'song of Marduk' (*zamāru ša Marduk*, VII 161). A variety of contexts for the performance of the poem can be imagined, but our sources attest mainly to a cultic setting (Gabriel 2014: 70–101). Many of the extant manuscripts of *Enuma Elish* were written or owned by priests-scholars who were ritual experts, and the texts' storage in temple libraries indicates a connection to the religious sphere. Cultic handbooks explicitly mention the recitation of (parts of) the epic during rituals, and cuneiform commentaries draw direct parallels between *Enuma Elish* and several rituals in the cult of Marduk. Most commonly, modern scholars associate *Enuma Elish* with the cult of Marduk in what is called a *myth-ritualist* way. The myth-and-ritual school of thought holds that there is an inextricable connection between myth and ritual, with one strongly influencing the other: either a myth is derived from ritual action, or a ritual reenacts a given myth (see the introduction and critiques in Segal 2004).

The main cultic setting of *Enuma Elish* is generally considered to be the *akītu* or New Year Festival that was celebrated at the beginning of Nisannu, the first month of the Babylonian calendar.[1] During this multi-day festival, the gods of the land were brought to the capital, from where the king led them in procession to the *akītu* temple that was located outside the city walls. Before setting out and upon their return to the city a few days later, the divine assembly decreed the destinies of the king and the country for the forthcoming year. Scholars have most often explained the meaning of the *akītu* festival in light of *Enuma Elish*. This myth-ritualist interpretation was formulated already at the beginning of the twentieth century and remains pervasive in current scholarship (Zimmern 1906). However, this concept is not without its problems, as shown by the ongoing debate about how exactly the ritual and the poem relate to one another. Today, the ritualization of *Enuma Elish* at the New Year is usually studied under three broad headings: re-enactment, shared plotlines, and recitation. In the following, I will discuss each interpretation before proposing a more suitable model for how to understand the relation between *Enuma Elish* and the *akītu* festival. Thus, instead of studying the relation between *Enuma Elish* and the *akītu* as a unified or monolithic concept within cuneiform culture, I propose to pay more attention to the socio-historical influences on this relationship, so as to allow for a more dynamic vision on the role of *Enuma Elish* in cult and ritual.

## *Enuma Elish* and the *akītu*

The Mesopotamian *akītu* or New Year festival was celebrated in some form or other for more than two millennia. The details of its performance, such as the deities involved and the rituals observed, depended on the time and place where the festival took place.[2] In modern scholarship, the focus often lies on the *akītu* festival observed in the capital city, Babylon, in which the god Marduk was the main divine protagonist. The constant and defining ritual element of the *akītu* was the procession of gods from the centre of the city to a special *akītu* temple that lay outside the city walls. The meanings of this central ritual lie at the core of modern scholarship on the festival and continue to be a matter of debate (Debourse 2022a: 25–32; see also Black 1981; Sommer 2000). In what follows, I discuss the most prominent interpretations, which revolve around the myth-ritualist connection between the *akītu* and *Enuma Elish*.

Early twentieth-century scholarship thus suggested that, during the New Year festival, the story of *Enuma Elish* was re-enacted in a cultic drama. At that time the text known as the *Marduk Ordeal*, which I discuss below, was thought to be part of *Enuma Elish*: the two were read together as one story about Marduk's death and resurrection. Within that framework, the *akītu* festival was seen as a dramatic reproduction of this 'passion of Marduk', who supposedly died before returning triumphant (Sommer 2000, with further references). With the insight that the *Marduk Ordeal* was not a chapter of *Enuma Elish* – and there was thus no 'passion' plot – came the need for a new interpretation (von Soden 1955).

Nevertheless, today's myth-ritualist understanding of the *akītu* and *Enuma Elish* has its roots in this early scholarship. The idea of a ritual re-enactment continued to be defended by Wilfred Lambert (1963: 190), who held that 'in the annual *akītu* festival Marduk's battle and victory over Tiamat was symbolized.' According to Lambert, the first procession of the *akītu* festival – from the god's main temple in Babylon to the *akītu* temple outside the city – represented Marduk and his allies going into battle against Tiamat. The confrontation between the two then took place inside the *akītu* temple, which Marduk left triumphantly during the second procession, which led back into the city. Lambert's understanding of the ritual as a cultic drama was largely based on the description of the cultic architecture found in an inscription of the Assyrian king Sennacherib (704–681 BCE) and in the topographical list *Tintir*, both of which are discussed below. More recently, the idea of a cultic drama has been rejected, as there is no unambiguous evidence that such a re-enactment ever took place (van der Toorn 1991; Pongratz-Leisten 1994: 74).

An alternative interpretation is that the ritual follows the plotline of *Enuma Elish*. According to this scenario, the festival would not be a direct representation of the epic but a conceptual parallel to it. Beate Pongratz-Leisten (1994: 74–8), for example, reads both ritual and epic as *rites of passage*, in which Marduk goes through the stages of separation, liminality, and incorporation (van Gennep 1909). In *Enuma Elish*, Marduk goes from being a young god elected by the divine council (separation) to becoming the warrior who battles the primordial being Tiamat (liminality) to assuming the position of ruler among gods (incorporation). In the *akītu* festival, this same sequence is expressed by the gods going in procession from the centre of the city to its hinterland (separation), where they remain for a few days in the *akītu* temple (liminality), before subsequently returning inside the city walls (incorporation). As such, Pongratz-Leisten argues, both myth and ritual serve to re-establish order.[3] While in the epic this sequence takes place *in illo tempore*, the ritual confirms that order on a yearly basis in the here and now (Eliade 1949 [1954]: 55–6). According to a similar interpretation, Annette Zgoll has described the relation between *Enuma Elish* and the *akītu* festival as 'interactional'[4]: not only are they both an expression of the same rite of passage leading to the same outcome, the epic and the festival also follow the same course of action, meaning that the two can be compared in structural terms. Zgoll argues that specific rituals that took place during the *akītu* festival find parallels in key events in *Enuma Elish*: for example, the double decreeing of destinies during the festival has been related to the double gathering of gods that establish Marduk's accession to divine kingship in the epic (III 129–38 and VI 80–122; Zgoll 2006: 41–4).

Finally, scholars have stressed that *Enuma Elish* was recited during the *akītu* festival. The recitation of the poem during the festival is mentioned in several sources, including ritual instructions from the Hellenistic period which state that on the fourth day of Nisannu, 'the high priest recites *Enuma Elish* from its beginning until its end to Bel' (MNB 1848 ii 22–24; Debourse 2022a: 145; Bel, Akkadian for 'lord', was used as a byname for Marduk in this period). I return to this point below.

One may notice a certain arbitrariness in how the relation between *Enuma Elish* and the *akītu* festival is interpreted, which raises the question of whether the close association between poem and ritual was indeed as prominent and universal as has been claimed (see also Gabriel 2014: 70–1). One problem is the history and development of both the *akītu* festival and *Enuma Elish* respectively. The origins of the festival lie in the third millennium BCE in the city of Ur, where the *akītu* was celebrated biannually in honour of the moon god Nanna (Cohen 2015: 99–106). While *Enuma Elish* may have its roots already in the early second millennium BCE (see below), the poem as we know it had not yet been composed when the *akītu* festival was first celebrated (Black 1981: 50), so if a direct connection between them exists, it must have been forged later. *Enuma Elish* and the *akītu* were not natural expressions of the same idea; instead, the meaning of one was artificially mapped onto the other.

Furthermore, one should be wary of direct structural comparisons between the plotline of the poem and the ritual schedule of the *akītu* festival. While the storyline of *Enuma Elish* had been standardized by the ninth century BCE at the latest, the schedule of the *akītu* festival continued to change throughout the first millennium BCE (Debourse 2022a: 36–89). While the festival may have included ritual events that are reminiscent of episodes in *Enuma Elish*, a direct schematic comparison cannot be upheld. In short, the relation between poem and ritual is fraught with problems.

Perhaps the most important argument against an inherent connection between the two is the importance of Nabû in the festival. Nabû was Marduk's son, who lived in

Babylon's sister city Borsippa (Kämmerer and Metzler 2012: 44–5). The participation of Nabû in the *akītu* festival is one of its central elements, as attested already by an Old Babylonian letter (Kraus 1972: 16–17, no. 168). In his royal inscriptions, the Neo-Assyrian king Sargon II (722–705 BCE) is said to have led both Marduk and his son in the *akītu* procession (e.g. Fuchs 1994: 156, 332), and the Neo-Babylonian evidence for Nabû's central role in the festival is overwhelming: royal inscriptions refer to kings renovating the stations of Nabû's procession during the *akītu* festival; administrative texts from Nabû's temple in Borsippa indicate that the deity travelled yearly around the time of the festival, presumably to join his father Marduk in Babylon (Waerzeggers 2010: 119–34); and the Babylonian chronicles emphasize the need for Nabû's presence at Babylon during the *akītu* festival, repeatedly noting that 'Nabû did not come from Borsippa for the procession of Bel and Bel did not come out' (e.g. the *Akitu Chronicle*; Grayson 1975: no. 16). The preparation of Nabû's cella Ezida in Esagil and the deity's arrival by barge are also described in the Hellenistic (331–141 BCE) ritual texts relating to the New Year (Debourse 2022a: 271–6). Finally, the tradition of Marduk and Nabû leading the *akītu* procession was preserved outside the Mesopotamian heartland, as shown by a reference in the Hebrew Bible (Isaiah 46: 1–2; Schaudig 2008),[5] and a relief on the Temple of Bel in first-century-CE Palmyra (Dirven 1997). Clearly, Nabû's participation in the *akītu* festival had a long tradition, but Nabû plays no role whatsoever in *Enuma Elish*. Since *Enuma Elish* is the story of Marduk's elevation, it emphasizes his exclusive position amongst the gods, suppressing all mention of his son (Gabriel 2014: 406–10 and *passim*). This discrepancy is too large a factor to ignore, and as such it represents a crucial argument against seeing too close a connection between them.

In summary, the role of *Enuma Elish* in cult, and specifically in the *akītu* festival, is not as straightforward as is often presumed. Most likely, the meaning of the epic was conceptualized differently in different contexts, and while it is clear that *Enuma Elish* played a lasting central role in Marduk's cult, the ways in which it was ritualized changed over time.

## Myth and ritual under the Sargonids

The most unambiguous evidence for an ancient myth-ritualist understanding of *Enuma Elish* and the *akītu* festival comes from a specific historical context, Assyria under the reign of Sargon and his successors (721–609 BCE). At that time, scholars were concerned with creating texts that exposed the – in their eyes – inextricable link between epic and festival. The most explicit source in this regard is a cultic commentary that explains rituals enacted during the *akītu* festival in light of mythical episodes, most prominently those from *Enuma Elish* (K 3476, Livingstone 1989: no. 37). For example, the commentary refers to 'the king, who opens the *ḫarû*-vessel in the race' and identifies him with 'Marduk, who bound Tiamat with his winds' (K 3476, obv. 18; for the reading of the line, see Zgoll 2006: 59). In this instance, the king is equated with Marduk and the ritual act he performs with Marduk's binding of Tiamat, as related in

*Enuma Elish* (IV 103 and VII 162). A similar type of association is evident in a text known as the *Marduk Ordeal* (Livingstone 1989: nos 34–5; see also Frahm 2011: 349–60 and Frances Reynolds in this volume). This text resembles a cultic commentary in the sense that it interprets rituals in terms of myths, but the mythical references are not, despite what the text itself claims (Assur version, l. 54), to *Enuma Elish* proper, but rather seems to be a spoof on the original poem that transformed it from a story of Marduk's rise to power into a story of his downfall.

Aside from the cultic commentaries, the idea of the *akītu* being a ritual expression of *Enuma Elish* was also expounded on an architectural and visual level, in particular witnessed by one inscription of King Sennacherib, where he describes how he built the *akītu* temple in Assur, naming it 'Temple Where Tiamat Is Put to Death' (Eabbaugga) and Ashur's cella within it 'Temple That Makes the Host of Tiamat Tremble' (Edubdubabba; K 1356; Pongratz-Leisten 1994: 75; Grayson 2014: no. 160). Moreover, Sennacherib claimed to have depicted the battle against Tiamat on the door of this temple. In this inscription, Sennacherib therefore directly compares the *akītu* procession with Ashur's battle against Tiamat.

Two complementary trends in Assyrian scholarship may help explain why the myth-ritualist link between *Enuma Elish* and the *akītu* festival came to be fully realized under Sargonid rule. The first is the adoption and adaptation – or 'Assyrianization' – of Babylonian theological and cultic elements after the destruction of Babylon by the Assyrian king Sennacherib (689 BCE; Frahm 1997: 222–4, 282–8, 2011: 349–60; Pongratz-Leisten 2015: 418; and Reynolds, Eckart Frahm, and Sophus Helle in this volume). Essentially, concepts that were connected to the Babylonian deity Marduk were transferred to the Assyrian head of the pantheon, Ashur, in order to legitimate and strengthen the latter's position as supreme god. This included a rewriting of *Enuma Elish* with Ashur's name instead of Marduk's and the introduction of the *akītu* festival to the Assyrian capital Assur (Pongratz-Leisten 1997; Maul 2000; Barcina 2017; see also Reynolds in this volume). The latter was accompanied by large-scale building works, e.g. the building of the *akītu* temple outside Assur's city walls, as well as by the production of new ritual handbooks, and this 'Assyrianization' seems to have established a stronger connection between *Enuma Elish* and the *akītu* festival.

A second, related process in Assyrian scholarship was the ritualization of the mythology of warrior deities, which most likely culminated during the reign of Sennacherib (Pongratz-Leisten 2015: 379–447). This entailed a reconceptualization of Assyrian state rituals to focus on the person of the king and establish the ruler as the centre of the empire. Both new and existing rituals were associated with mythical traditions revolving around various warrior deities who defeated the forces of chaos, so it was only natural that Marduk's battle against Tiamat in *Enuma Elish*, with its ritual counterpart in the *akītu* festival, gained a central role in this new discourse.

In sum, the strong myth-ritualist connection between *Enuma Elish* and the *akītu* festival was fully established by Late Assyrian scholars in an attempt to strengthen the position of their king and their own god, Ashur. While this does not exclude the existence of a similar, earlier Babylonian tradition, it becomes evident in our sources only at this time.

## Conveying meaning in the cult of Marduk

The evidence from Babylonia regarding the significance of *Enuma Elish* to the cult of Marduk is much more nuanced. Generally speaking, there is less evidence for a special connection between *Enuma Elish* and the *akītu* festival; instead, the epic seems to have been of importance to the cult of Marduk more broadly, including the *akītu* as one of several rituals. While *Enuma Elish* is not the only story that affirms Marduk's role as the prime deity of Babylon, it does seem to have held an unparalleled relevance for his cult.

An early connection between *Enuma Elish* and the cult of Marduk has been suggested on the basis of a ritual text known as BM 29638 (Wasserman 2006; Pongratz-Leisten and Knott 2021). This text, which dates to the mid-second millennium BCE, outlines the ritual details of Marduk's travel by boat to an unspecified temple where he receives offerings and recitations.[6] Although such divine travel may have occurred in connection with an *akītu* festival, the ritual specificities of the text and the lack of thematic correspondences with other ritual texts for the Babylonian *akītu* festival made its primary editor 'hesitant to link this text with the *akītu* ceremony' (Wasserman 2006: 210). The reverse of the tablet is particularly relevant, as it provides a detailed account of the items given as offerings to Marduk by the *tāriātum*, 'nurses'. It is the use of the term *tārītu*, 'nurse', that forms a link to *Enuma Elish*, where it is said that 'the nurse who raised him infused him with dreadfulness' (*tārītu ittarrušu pulḫata ušmalli*, I 86). The word *tārītu* is most prominently attested during the late third and early second millennium BCE (Pongratz-Leisten and Knott 2021: 29). Moreover, the appearance of a 'nurse' in cultic contexts is rare, making the connection noteworthy.

Pongratz-Leisten and Elisabeth Knott (2021: 31) argued that, since the role of the *tārītu* as nursemaid for royal children – divine and human – was more firmly established during the Old Babylonian period than in later periods, it is most likely that the mythical trope of Marduk's *tārītu* originated at that time. The ritual text BM 29638, in which special attention is given to the *tārītu*s and their offerings to Marduk, may be taken as a witness to this. In other words, this motif of Marduk being raised by a *tārītu* most likely developed during the Old Babylonian period and took root simultaneously in the cult of Marduk and in the myths that revolve around this deity. The fact that no cultic texts from the first millennium refer to this specific 'nurse' suggests that this is an early development.[7]

More direct evidence for the use of *Enuma Elish* in the context of Marduk's cult dates to the first millennium BCE, which saw the composition of texts meant to explain ritual actions in light of myth and, conversely, mythical tropes in terms of ritual. While these texts fall in line with the Assyrian myth-ritualist texts discussed above, they differ from them in two ways: first, they mostly engage with Marduk's theology rather than with Ashur's, and second, they do not solely relate to the *akītu* festival but to the cult of Marduk at Babylon more broadly.

This is illustrated by Commentary I, an exegetical text that explains lines from *Enuma Elish*, most often by relating them to ritual elements (Frahm and Jiménez 2015; see also Frahm 2011: 113–14 and Lambert 2013: 135–8). The composition is known from both Assyrian and Babylonian recensions that date between the seventh and fifth centuries BCE (Frahm and Jiménez 2015: 297–9). The Assyrian versions use distinctly Assyrian tropes. No manuscripts from Babylon itself are known, and the text features non-Babylonian deities such as Ishtar of Nineveh and Zababa. It therefore remains unclear where the commentary originated, and likely different traditions were interwoven at different times and places.[8] However, almost all rituals and cultic elements that are associated with lines from the poem can be placed within Greater Babylon (meaning Babylon, Borsippa, and Kish; see the overview in Frahm and Jiménez 2015: 332). Moreover, all deities mentioned in the text are known either to have had sanctuaries in Babylon or to have participated in rituals there.[9] Among the rituals mentioned in the commentary are several that were part of the *akītu* festival, such as Bel's entrance into the *akītu* temple and Nabû's presence at the decreeing of destinies. However, the *akītu* festival is not the main concern of the commentary, as it includes references to other instances of divine travel and involves other divine protagonists.

Moreover, despite its Babylon-centred cultic background, the commentary's theology departs from that of *Enuma Elish* by relating several lines of the poem to deities other than Marduk. This creates an odd situation: while specifically Babylon-centred rituals are related to lines from *Enuma Elish*, the focus is on cultic acts that do not solely involve Marduk, meaning that the commentary challenges the main message of *Enuma Elish* and 'its insistence that Marduk alone is in charge' (Frahm and Jiménez 2015: 333). At the same time, the commentary's effort to challenge this idea is indicative of how central *Enuma Elish* was to Marduk's cult in the first place.

Just as ritual actions were imbued with meaning by their association with mythical action, so were ritual spaces related to the story of *Enuma Elish*. In the topographical list *Tintir*, which provides theological explanations for religious buildings and topographical features of Babylon, it is said that 'the seat of Bel on which Bel sits (is called) Tiamat' (*tiamat šubat bēl ša bēl ina muhhi ašbu*; *Tintir* II 1; George 1992: 44–5). The list is not concerned with explaining why Marduk's seat is called this, but the implication is clear to anyone familiar with the story of *Enuma Elish*: it refers to Marduk's victory over Tiamat. Moreover, there is little doubt that the 'seat' in question was located within the precinct of Marduk's temple Esagil, most likely in the inner cella Eumusha, and that this was thus Marduk's regular abode.[10] In the same vein, a famous seal, meant to be hung around the neck of the cult statue, depicts Marduk in anthropomorphic form standing on the waters of the sea, which may once again be interpreted as a reference to his victory over Tiamat (Zgoll 2006: 54–5).

In sum, in Babylonia during the first millennium BCE, *Enuma Elish* was one of the primary frameworks within which the cult of Marduk was contextualized and conceptualized. This connection between the deity's most important myth and his cult may have stretched back even further in time, but there is almost no evidence to show this. Links between epic and ritual were not limited to the *akītu* festival but pervaded the cult of Marduk as a whole, including both ritual actions and ritual space. Moreover, adopting *Enuma Elish* as a conceptual framework did not prevent other deities from being worshipped even as Marduk was envisaged as the supreme deity of the pantheon.

## The ritual recitation of *Enuma Elish*

The prominence of *Enuma Elish* in the cult of Marduk is most strongly underscored by the fact that the poem was recited to him during rituals (Zgoll 2006: 48–53; Gabriel

2014: 70–101). As far as we know, these recitations took place in the privacy of the god's cella and were sometimes, but not always, accompanied by ritual actions. Within this context, *Enuma Elish* was no different from other texts that were spoken to Marduk, such as lamentations and hymns, except for its greater length. However, *Enuma Elish* was the only narrative, mythical poem to occupy such a prominent role in the cult. Citations from other mythical texts could be found in prayers, but only *Enuma Elish* is known to have been recited in its entirety (Maiwald 2021; Debourse 2022a: 296–302). Because of its recitation in the cult, some have termed *Enuma Elish* a 'ritual text', that is, a text that was primarily conceptualized within the context of cult (Maiwald 2021: 195–6).

The recitation of the poem is attested in several sources dating to the first millennium BCE, most of which place the event on the fourth day of the first month, Nisannu (*Marduk Ordeal*, Assur version, l. 34; Livingstone 1989: no. 34; the New Year Festival text MNB 1848 ii 22–4; Debourse 2022a: 145). It was therefore long seen as peculiar to the *akītu* festival, which took place precisely during the first days of Nisannu. One Late Babylonian ritual text, however, mentions the recitation of (part of) the poem during a ritual that took place on the fourth day of the ninth month, Kislimu:

> While it [a mixture of beer mash and water] is being sprinkled in front of Bel, the singer (will recite) *Enuma Elish* to Bel. At 'To Usmû, who brought him the happy news of her gift' [V 83], the *mār šalāli* (a cultic functionary) will raise a palm frond and put it on a silver tablet opposite Bel.[11]

The fact that *Enuma Elish* was recited to Marduk at different moments throughout the year fits well with the general importance of the poem in the god's cult, not only at the *akītu* festival (see also Cancik-Kirschbaum 1995: 14, n. 34; Linssen 2004: 81, n. 425). However, the idea that the recitation of the poem at the New Year was of greater importance than at other moments persists in modern scholarship. According to Zgoll, the recitation of *Enuma Elish* can be paralleled to the Christian motif of the Last Supper: a ritual commemorating the Last Supper is performed during every mass, in the form of communion, but it is most prominently remembered on Maundy Thursday during the Holy Week (Zgoll 2006: 50–1). In a similar vein, Zgoll claims, *Enuma Elish* was generally important to Marduk's cult, but it was specifically celebrated at the New Year during the *akītu* festival. This proposal seems attractive, but it involves the risk of drawing potentially problematic parallels between Christian and Babylonian rituals. However, it should not be dismissed completely, either, for there is indeed a considerable overlap in the significance of *Enuma Elish* and the *akītu* festival, as both were meant to celebrate Marduk's kingship (though both also held other meanings; Zgoll 2006: 51–2).

## Marduk and *Enuma Elish* in Late Babylonian times

*Enuma Elish* continued to be of prime importance to the cult of Marduk in Late Achaemenid and Hellenistic Babylon (484–141 BCE), when the epic was integrated into a new discourse that revolved around the absolute centrality of Babylon, Esagil, and Marduk (Jursa and Debourse 2020; Debourse 2022a: 337–420, see also Reynolds in this volume). When Babylon fell under the rule of foreign kings, such as the Persians and Seleucids, who did not care much for Babylonian deities and their worship, the local priesthood engaged in the creation of new texts in which they asserted their own importance. This Late Babylonian priestly literature gave an unprecedented centrality to Marduk, who went from being the supreme deity of Babylon to becoming almost the sole deity of the city. The focus of Babylon's cult became narrower, including only Marduk and his inner circle and excluding such deities as Anu and Enlil. This Late Babylonian tendency towards *oligolatry*, that is, the active worship of a limited group of deities, can partly be explained as a reaction to the new socio-political situation of foreign rule. Indeed, we see it paralleled in the other large hub of cuneiform culture of that period, the southern Babylonian city of Uruk, where there was a similarly sharp focus on one deity and his court, in this case the god Anu (Krul 2018; Debourse 2022a: 320–1).

Within this context, *Enuma Elish*'s message that Marduk ruled supreme was radicalized further: Marduk was the supreme deity not just because he had defeated Tiamat and created the universe, but also because he had subsumed the power of the former divine rulers Anu and Enlil within his own. In other words, the focus came to be on Marduk's *exclusive* power in contrast to the former heads of the Mesopotamian pantheon. As such, it should not surprise us that *Enuma Elish* remained highly popular in Babylon, as attested by the abundance of manuscripts from the Late Babylonian libraries of the Esagil temple.[12] By contrast, the rich textual record of contemporary Uruk has yielded only a few manuscripts of *Enuma Elish*. This can be explained by the fact that a story about Marduk's absolute rulership would have been incongruous with the cult of Anu as it was practised there, which treated Anu rather than Marduk as the highest god (Lambert 2013: 4, 123).

The new emphasis on *Enuma Elish* comes to the fore most clearly in the cultic contexts in which the poem is mentioned. In the Hellenistic ritual texts for the New Year Festival, the high priest is instructed to recite *Enuma Elish* to Marduk in its entirety, as discussed above. While the recitation of the poem during the festival is already attested in earlier periods, the ritual text casts it in a new light by stating that 'as long as he is reciting *Enuma Elish* to Bel, the front of the crown of Anu and the seat of Enlil will remain covered' (MNB 1848 ii 24–26; Debourse 2022a: 144–7). The covering of these deities' symbols while the account of Marduk's rise to power was being recited emphasized Marduk's supremacy over those other gods and simultaneously affirmed Babylon's superiority over the cities of these gods, Anu's Uruk and Enlil's Nippur.[13]

A similar use of *Enuma Elish* in a ritual context that emphasizes the dominance of Marduk and his city Babylon, albeit in a different way than in the New Year Festival texts discussed above, can be found in a cultic text called *The Babylon Calendar Treatise* (l. iii 12–13; Reynolds 2019). This text generally adopts a more traditional reading of *Enuma Elish* as the story of Marduk's battle with Tiamat and Qingu. In the way of a cultic commentary, the *Treatise* uses the story of *Enuma Elish* to explain why certain rituals would be effective in countering predictions of invasion and destruction of Babylon.[14] This is made clear in the introduction of the *Treatise*, which states that when 'a cultic functionary did not perform the rites ... Tiamat organized battle, [plotted] evil against the gods, her offspring' (Reynolds 2019: 188–9). While the rituals upon which the *Treatise* comments are performed in reaction to specific predictions of doom, they are thus also framed more broadly within the story of *Enuma Elish*.

In other words, the *Treatise*'s logic is as follows: the invasion of Babylon is predicted by astrological omens and rituals are performed to prevent these predictions from coming true; the effectiveness of these rituals is explained by reading the elements of both the predictions and the rituals against the background of *Enuma Elish*, which states that Marduk is victorious over the forces of chaos, and therefore the rituals are successful. The *Treatise* thus confirms the message of *Enuma Elish*, namely the supremacy of Marduk and Babylon, over and over (Debourse 2022b).

In sum, in Late Achaemenid and Hellenistic Babylon, *Enuma Elish* became part of a discourse centred around the pre-eminence of Babylon and the corresponding supremacy of Marduk. This discourse was an apologetic reaction to the socio-political context in which the Marduk priesthood found itself at the time: Babylon was no longer the centre of a great empire but was ruled by foreign kings who did not care much about Marduk. At the same time, Babylon had to contend for royal favour with the other large hubs of cuneiform culture, Uruk (with its city god Anu) and Nippur (with its city god Enlil). The surviving priesthood therefore emphasized Marduk's role as a triumphant king who had defeated his enemies and taken the throne from his divine rivals, which is reflected in the way in which the epic was used in rituals. *Enuma Elish* thus remained of central importance for the cult of Marduk while also gaining a new set of political and religious connotations.

## Conclusion

As the main story of Marduk's ascent to kingship, *Enuma Elish* occupied a place of primary importance within the context of Marduk's cult, as shown by the fact that it is the only mythical, narrative poem that was recited to the deity. Its relevance was not limited to the *akītu* festival, but encompassed all aspects of the cult, including rituals and cultic architecture. The poem provided one of the primary frameworks for understanding the theology of Marduk, and as such, it imbued rituals connected to Marduk with mythical meaning. The exact ways in which this connection was conceptualized changed across space and time, as exemplified by the Late Assyrian readings and adaptations of *Enuma Elish*, which were designed to bolster a new ideology centred on Ashur and the Assyrian king, in contrast to for example, the Hellenistic ritual practices that sought to establish Marduk's superiority over Anu and Enlil. While the exact origins of the close relationship between *Enuma Elish* and the cult of Marduk remain obscure, it persisted until the very end of cuneiform culture.

## Further reading

General introductions to *Enuma Elish* and the *akītu* festival, including further references, can be found in the works of Céline Debourse (2022a), Annette Zgoll

(2006), and Beate Pongratz-Leisten (1994). Gösta Gabriel (2014) examines *Enuma Elish* as a performative text, and Pongratz-Leisten (2015) discusses the ritualization of the warrior god during the Neo-Assyrian period. For cultic commentaries on *Enuma Elish*, see the works of Eckart Frahm (2011), Frahm and Enrique Jiménez (2015), and Wilfred Lambert (2013). Fran Reynolds (2019) provides a complete edition of the *Babylon Calendar Treatise*, along with a discussion of its engagement with *Enuma Elish*. Finally, a methodological approach to the study of Mesopotamian creation myths in ritual performance was presented by Kerstin Maiwald (2021), but note that *Enuma Elish* is largely excluded from her work.

## Notes

1 For an introduction to the *akītu* festival and its interpretations, see Debourse (2022a) and Zgoll (2006) with further references. See also Reynolds (2021).

2 It should be noted that '*akītu*' is often studied as a monolithic concept rather than as a historically dynamic phenomenon. For a critical evaluation of the scholarship on this topic, see Debourse (2022a: 9–35).

3 Pongratz-Leisten (1994: 75): 'The intention of both myth and ritual during the New Year Festival is to explain and confirm the existing order and re-establish Babylon as centre of the cult' (translation by the author).

4 Zgoll (2006: 41–4, 58) uses the word 'interactional' (*interaktional*, related to 'intertextual') to indicate that both the poem and the ritual share the same course of *action* leading to the same outcome.

5 These verses refer to a procession of Marduk and Nabû in the form of their divine statues, which topple and fall over. Schaudig (2008) has argued that this expresses a prophecy given on the occasion of the New Year Festival.

6 As Wasserman (2006: 207) observes, the text does not give instructions (it contains only one verbal form), but instead 'offers an outline for the ceremonial event, by designating generally the time, place, agents, paraphernalia and *recitanda* – but not *agenda* – of the ritual'. Most likely, Marduk was visiting one of his own temples; see Pongratz-Leisten and Knott (2021: 30).

7 However, the line in *Enuma Elish* is quoted in the first millennium BCE commentary on *Enuma Elish* I–VII, where the 'nurse' is identified with Ishtar of Nineveh; see below.

8 According to Frahm (2011: 114), the commentary was based on Assyrian models. But his later opinion is more nuanced; see Frahm and Jiménez (2015: 333).

9 Ishtar of Nineveh thus had her own temple Egishuranki in Babylon, and Madanu had a shrine in the Esagil temple, see George (1992: 324–5, 396–7). Zababa and Mar-biti appear in rituals set in Babylon: BM 32206+, Çağırgan and Lambert (1991–93); and BM 41239, George (2000). The commentary also seems to betray an interest in the cult of Babylon specifically when it interprets the line, 'Tutu is he who brings about their restoration' (VII 9) with the comment, 'because of the gods of the cultic centres […], who / which … in Babylon' (*aššu ilī ša māhāzī* [(…)] *ša ina Bābili* […], l. 43′); Frahm and Jiménez (2015: 309).

10 George (1992: 268–9). Note that a Neo-Assyrian text takes this line and turns it into an *akītu*-related explanation: 'Bel who during the *akītu* festival (or, in the *akītu* temple) sits on Tiamat' (*bēl ša ina akīt ina qabal tamti ašbu*, Frahm, Frazer and Jiménez 2013–2022).

11 BM 32206+ ii 17–20; Çağırgan and Lambert (1991–93: 92); translation by the author. The text continues with a reference to Asari, which probably relates to *Enuma Elish* VII 10, but the poor state of preservation prevents a proper understanding of the line.

12 The attribution of manuscripts of *Enuma Elish* to these libraries is based on museum archaeology; see Clancier (2009: 105–213).

13 Elsewhere, the ritual text cites a line from the poem *Enmeshara's Defeat*, which states that 'Uruk and Nippur are burnt and defeated', referring to the destruction of those cities' temples and cult. Here too, the text affirms the dominance of Marduk over Anu and Enlil and of Babylon over Uruk and Nippur (DT 15 ii 29–35; Debourse 2022a: 104–5, 296–300). For *Enmeshara's Defeat*, see Lambert (2013: 281–98), Gabbay (2018: 25–31).

14 Aside from mythological explanations, the Treatise also uses astrological predictions to explain why certain rituals should be performed (Reynolds 2019: 39).

## Bibliography

Barcina, C. (2017), 'The Conceptualization of the *akītu* under the Sargonids: Some Reflections', *State Archives of Assyria Bulletin*, 23: 91–129.

Black, J. (1981), 'The New Year Ceremonies in Ancient Babylonia: "Taking Bel by the Hand" and a Cultic Picnic', *Religion*, 11 (1): 29–59.

Çağırgan, G. and W. G. Lambert (1991–3), 'The Late Babylonian Kislīmu Ritual for Esagil', *Journal of Cuneiform Studies*, 43/45: 89–106.

Cancik-Kirschbaum, E. (1995), 'Konzeption und Legitimation von Herrschaft in neuassyrischer Zeit', *Die Welt des Orients*, 26: 5–20.

Clancier, P. (2009), *Les bibliothèques en Babylonie au Ier millénaire avant J.-C.*, Alter Orient und Altes Testament 363, Münster: Ugarit-Verlag.

Cohen, M. E. (2015), *Festivals and Calendars of the Ancient Near East*, Bethesda: CDL Press.

Debourse, C. (2022a), *Of Priests and Kings: The Babylonian New Year Festival in the Last Age of Cuneiform Culture*, Culture and History of the Ancient Near East 127, Leiden: Brill.

Debourse, C. (2022b), 'Late Babylonian Temple Ritual Texts with Cultic Commentaries: Aspects of Form and Function', *Wiener Zeitschrift für die Kunde des Morgenlandes*, 112: 347–65.

Dirven, L. (1997), 'The Exaltation of Nabû: A Revision of the Relief Depicting the Battle Against Tiamat from the Temple of Bel in Palmyra', *Die Welt des Orients*, 28: 96–116.

Eliade, M. (1949 [1954]), *Cosmos and History: The Myth of the Eternal Return*, trans. W. R. Trask, New York: Harper and Brothers.

Frahm, E. (1997), *Einleitung in die Sanherib-Inschriften*, Archiv für Orientforschung Beiheft 26, Vienna: Selbstverlag des Instituts für Orientalistik der Universität Wien.

Frahm, E. (2011), *Babylonian and Assyrian Text Commentaries: Origins of Interpretation*, Guides to the Mesopotamian Textual Record 5, Münster: Ugarit-Verlag.

Frahm, E. and E. Jiménez (2015), 'Myth, Ritual, and Interpretation: The Commentary on Enūma eliš I–VII and a Commentary on Elamite Month Names', *Hebrew Bible and Ancient Israel*, 3: 293–343.

Frahm, E., M. Frazer, and E. Jiménez (2013–22), 'Commentary on Marduk's Address to the Demons A 16', *Cuneiform Commentaries Project*. Accessed 24 July 2022, at https://ccp.yale.edu/P461327. DOI: 10079/g4f4r4b.

Fuchs, A. (1994), *Die Inschriften Sargons II. aus Khorsabad*, Göttingen: Cuvillier.

Gabbay, U. (2018), 'Drums, Hearts, Bulls, and Dead Gods: The Theology of the Ancient Mesopotamian Kettledrum', *Journal of Ancient Near Eastern Religions*, 18: 1–47.

Gabriel, G. (2014), *'enūma eliš': Weg zu einer globalen Weltordnung; Pragmatik, Struktur und Semantik des babylonischen 'Lieds auf Marduk'*, Orientalische Religionen in der Antike 12, Tübingen: Mohr Siebeck.

George, A. R. (1992), *Babylonian Topographical Texts*, Orientalia Lovaniensia Analecta 40, Leuven: Peeters.

George, A. R. (2000), 'Four Temple Rituals from Babylon', in A. R. George and I. Finkel (eds), *Wisdom, Gods, and Literature: Studies in Assyriology in Honour of W. G. Lambert*, 259–99, Winona Lake: Eisenbrauns.

Grayson, A. K. (1975), *Assyrian and Babylonian Chronicles*, New York: Locus Valley Augustin.

Grayson, A. K. (2014), *The Royal Inscriptions of Sennacherib, King of Assyria (704–681 BC), Part 2*, Royal Inscriptions of the Neo-Assyrian Period 3 (2), Winona Lake: Eisenbrauns.

Haubold, J. (2019), 'History and Historiography in the Early Parthian Diaries', in J. Haubold, J. Steele and K. Stevens (eds), *Keeping Watch in Babylon: The Astronomical Diaries in Context*, 269–93, Leiden: Brill.

Jursa, M. and C. Debourse (2020), 'Late Babylonian Priestly Literature from Babylon', in P. Dubovský and F. Giuntoli (eds), *Stones, Tablets, and Scrolls: Periods of the Formation of the Bible*, Archaeology and Bible 3, 253–81, Tübingen: Mohr Siebeck.

Kämmerer, T. and K. Metzler (2012), *Das babylonische Weltschöpfungsepos Enūma elîš*, Alter Orient und Altes Testament 375, Münster: Ugarit-Verlag.

Kraus, F. R. (1972), *Altbabylonische Briefe in Umschrift und Übersetzung*, vol. 5, Leiden: Brill.

Krul, J. (2018), *The Revival of the Anu Cult and the Nocturnal Fire Ceremony at Late Babylonian Uruk*, Culture and History of the Ancient Near East 95, Leiden: Brill.

Lambert, W. G. (1963), 'The Great Battle of the Mesopotamian Religious Year: The Conflict in the Akītu House (A Summary)', *Iraq*, 25 (2): 189–90.

Lambert, W. G. (2013), *Babylonian Creation Myths*, Mesopotamian Civilizations 16, Winona Lake: Eisenbrauns, 2013.

Linssen, M. (2004), *The Cults of Uruk and Babylon*, Cuneiform Monographs 25, Leiden: Brill.

Livingstone, A. (1989), *Court Poetry and Literary Miscellanea*, State Archives of Assyria 3, Helsinki: Helsinki University Press.

Maiwald, K. (2021), *Mesopotamische Schöpfungstexte in Ritualen: Methodik und Fallstudien zur situativen Verortung*, Mythological Studies 3, Berlin: De Gruyter.

Maul, S. (2000), 'Die Frühjahrsfeierlichkeiten in Aššur', in A. George and I. Finkel (eds), *Wisdom, Gods and Literature: Studies in Assyriology in Honour of W. G. Lambert*, 389–420, Winona Lake: Eisenbrauns.

Pongratz-Leisten, B. (1994), *Ina šulmi īrub: Die kulttopographische und ideologische Programmatik der akītu-Prozession in Babylonien und Assyrien im I. Jahrtausend v. Chr.*, Baghdader Forschungen 16, Mainz: Von Zabern.

Pongratz-Leisten, B. (1997), 'The Interplay of Military Strategy and Cultic Practice in Assyrian Politics', in S. Parpola and R. Whiting (eds), *Assyria 1995: Proceedings of the 10th Anniversary Symposium of the Neo-Assyrian Text Corpus Project, Helsinki, September 7–11, 1995*, 245–52, Helsinki: The Neo-Assyrian Text Corpus Project.

Pongratz-Leisten, B. (2015), *Religion and Ideology in Assyria*, Studies in Ancient Near Eastern Records 6, Berlin: De Gruyter.

Pongratz-Leisten, B. and E. Knott (2021), 'The Old Babylonian Ritual Text BM 29638, *Enūma eliš*, and Developments in Marduk's Cult', *Nouvelles assyriologiques brèves et utilitaires*, 2021 (1): 27–33, no. 13.

Reynolds, F. (2019), *A Babylon Calendar Treatise: Scholars and Invaders in the Late First Millennium BC; Edited with Introduction, Commentary and Cuneiform Texts*, Oxford: Oxford University Press.

Reynolds, F. (2021), 'Politics, Cult, and Scholarship: Aspects of the Transmission History of Marduk and Tiʾamat's Battle', in A. Kelly and C. Metcalf (eds), *Gods and Mortals in Early Greek and Near Eastern Mythology*, 58–79, Cambridge: Cambridge University Press.

Schaudig, H. (2008), '"Bel Bows, Nabû Stoops!" The Prophecy of Isaiah xlvi 1–2 as a Reflection of Babylonian "Processional Omens"', *Vetus Testamentum*, 58: 557–72.

Segal, R. (2004), *Myth: A Very Short Introduction*, Oxford: Oxford University Press.

Sommer, B. (2000), 'The Babylonian Akitu Festival: Rectifying the King or Renewing the Cosmos?', *Journal of Ancient Near Eastern Studies*, 27: 81–95.

van der Toorn, K. (1991), 'The Babylonian New Year Festival: New Insights from the Cuneiform Texts and Their Bearing on Old Testament Study', in J. A. Emerton (ed.), *Congress Volume, Leuven 1989*, 331–44, Leiden: Brill.

van Gennep, A. (1909), *Les rites de passage*, Paris: Éditions Nourry.

von Soden, W. (1955), 'Gibt es ein Zeugnis dafür, daß die Babylonier an die Wiederauferstehung Marduks geglaubt haben?', *Zeitschrift für Assyriologie und vorderasiatische Archäologie*, 51: 130–66.

Waerzeggers, C. (2010), *The Ezida Temple of Borsippa*, Achaemenid History 15, Leiden: Nederlands Instituut voor het Nabije Oosten.

Wasserman, N. (2006), 'BM 29638: A New Ritual to Marduk from the Old Babylonian Period', *Zeitschrift für Assyriologie und vorderasiatische Archäologie*, 96: 200–11.

Zgoll, A. (2006), 'Königslauf und Götterrat: Struktur und Deutung des babylonischen Neujahrsfestes', in E. Blum and R. Lux (eds), *Festtraditionen in Israel und im Alten Orient*, 11–80, Gütersloh: Gütersloher Verlagshaus.

Zimmern, H. (1906), 'Zum babylonischen Neujahrsfest', *Berichte über die Verhandlungen der Königlich Sächsischen Gesellschaft der Wissenschaften, Phil.-hist. Klasse*, 58 (3): 126–56.

3

# The cuneiform reception of *Enuma Elish*

Frances Reynolds

*Enuma Elish* remained a touchstone and a rich intellectual resource for cuneiform scholars for about a thousand years. The supremacy of Marduk, his city Babylon, and his temple Esagil were embedded in the poem, and scholars used the poem to promote this worldview. At times, when political, theological, or cultic realities conflicted with the poem's ideology, cuneiform scholars reinterpreted it to conform with their current priorities. The composer of the epilogue of *Enuma Elish* set out a programme for the poem's written and oral transmission and reception (VII 145–59) and this corresponds closely to the realities of the poem's circulation. Even scholars who reinterpreted the poem could allude to the model in the epilogue.

As a didactic poem about Marduk's supremacy, *Enuma Elish* functioned as a paradigm for divine and human kingship (see Gösta Gabriel in this volume). As a result, the poem was linked with temple rituals, especially in the cult of the god Marduk in Babylon and, through cultural appropriation, in the cult of the god Assur in the city of Assur. In the earlier period, the focus was on rituals where the king participated, principally the *akītu* ritual in the New Year festival in the first month Nisannu (see Céline Debourse in this volume). In this ritual the statue of the chief god temporarily left his city in a controlled ritual to secure the land's good fortune during the year ahead. In the Late Babylonian period, the imperial kings of Babylonia were more remote, and scholars connected the poem with non-royal rituals, while nostalgically looking back to a more glorious past.

Akkadian texts written on clay tablets provide nearly all the evidence for the cuneiform reception of *Enuma Elish*. Babylonian and Assyrian scholars used the poem as a tool for interpreting other works, concepts, and phenomena. The intellectual endeavour of transmitting, quoting, and interpreting the poem continued until the final centuries of the first millennium BCE. The sources often accord with *Enuma Elish* and its Marduk theology, but scholars also reinterpreted the poem to align with political, theological, and cultic developments. Warfare and in particular the looting of Marduk's principal statue from the Esagil, whether actual or feared, played a major role in shaping the poem's reception. This can be seen in the war poem *Erra and Ishum*, in the religious reforms of the Assyrian king Sennacherib after his sack of Babylon, and in the Late Babylonian calendar treatise on rituals against Babylonia's invasion.

The relative status of other gods compared to Marduk resulted in major changes in the poem's reception. While Marduk was the supreme god in earlier Babylonia, the god Assur held this role in Assyria, driving Assyrianized responses to the poem. The increased status of Marduk's son Nabû in the first millennium BCE was also an influential factor, and the poem may have been rejected in Babylon itself during Nabonidus' short-lived promotion of the god Sîn. Variations between the gods worshipped in different Babylonian cities meant that, in the first millennium, Marduk's supremacy became increasingly regional and in the Late Babylonian period it was restricted to northern Babylonia with Babylon as the epicentre. The cities of Nippur and Uruk, with their worship of Enlil and Anu respectively, rejected the poem. In the Late Babylonian period, the intellectual networks of Babylon's cuneiform scholars had shrunk dramatically, and they were marginalized politically within externally imposed empires.

Scholars quoted *Enuma Elish* in different contexts. Quotation in commentaries on *Enuma Elish* enabled rich scholarly interpretations of the poem, which could accord with traditional Marduk theology or Assyrianized theology. Four other compositions quoting or citing the poem serve as case studies for exploring what *Enuma Elish* could mean to ancient scholars. A work from earlier Babylonia quotes *Enuma Elish* as part of interpreting Marduk's names in Babylon's *akītu* festival. The explanatory work called *Marduk's Ordeal*, which can be associated with Sennacherib, and a scholar's letter to his successor, the Assyrian king Esarhaddon, attest to contrasting responses. *Marduk's Ordeal* subverts the poem as part of reinterpreting Babylon's *akītu* festival to humiliate Marduk and promote Assyria's state god Assur; but the letter quotes the poem to hold up Marduk as a model for Esarhaddon, although probably in the service of Babylonian factionalism. Finally, a Late Babylonian calendar treatise quotes and alludes to the poem in its interpretation of rituals in the Esagil cult as bulwarks against enemy attack. This treatise portrays Marduk as the victorious warrior king who is analogous to Babylonia's human king, but this analogy had become a vehicle for nostalgic Babylonian aspiration during a time of marginalization.

After an overview of previous research, I compare the poem's own programme for its circulation as set out in the epilogue to the realities of its transmission. Following some brief remarks on kingship ideology, I outline the poem's reception history: Babylonian reception in earlier sources, Neo-Assyrian reception, and Babylonian reception in later sources. This outline takes account of key developments in contemporary politics, theology, and temple cult. Focusing on quotations, I finally give a brief overview of commentaries on *Enuma Elish* and four case studies of compositions that quote or cite the poem to illustrate its changing meanings to ancient scholars.

## Previous research

This section gives a broadly chronological overview of some of the relatively recent research on the cuneiform reception of *Enuma Elish*. The publications included here contain further bibliography, which gives access to the earlier scholarship.

In two books Alasdair Livingstone (1986, 1989) edited and discussed six works quoting and alluding to *Enuma Elish* that remain key to the poem's reception. The explanatory compendium *Inamgishhurankia* may be a Babylonian composition (Livingstone 1986: 22–5, 40–2; see also Francesca Rochberg in this volume), while the other works are Neo-Assyrian: Assurbanipal's hymn to Marduk and his wife (Livingstone 1989: no. 2); three compositions interpreting royal ritual, including *Marduk's Ordeal* (Livingstone 1989: no. 34, 35, 37, 40); and an explanatory compendium with cosmogonic and ritual material (Livingstone 1989: no. 39). More important primary sources followed: Galip Çağirgan and Wilfred G. Lambert (1991–1993: 96) published the first edition of a text describing previously unknown ritual in Babylon in the ninth month Kislimu with the recitation of *Enuma Elish* and ritual interpretation quoting the poem; Simo Parpola (1993: no. 112 and 365) re-edited two letters from scholars to the Assyrian king that quote and allude to *Enuma Elish*; and Petra Gesche (2000: 177–8, 808) published Neo- and Late Babylonian school texts quoting *Enuma Elish*, identified as the most frequently quoted literary text in the curriculum.

In two versions of a seminal and wide-ranging study, Eckart Frahm (2010; 2011: 345–68) discussed politically driven responses to *Enuma Elish* in and beyond Mesopotamia from 900 BCE to 500 CE. He analysed the poem *Erra and Ishum* as a Babylonian counter-text to *Enuma Elish*, and, in a survey of the Neo-Assyrian reception of *Enuma Elish*, he focused on reinterpretations that promote the god Assur, including an Assyrianized version of the poem and *Marduk's Ordeal*. Concerning Babylonia in the Neo- and Late Babylonian periods, Frahm argued that the poem's promotion of Marduk and Babylon could sustain its popularity in that city but could also have a negative impact, including in the city of Uruk. The revised version of Frahm's study includes a focus on three text commentaries, two of them on *Enuma Elish*, and elsewhere in the book he discusses commentaries and other texts related to the poem (Frahm 2011: 105, 112–17, 355–60, 470; see also 2010: 10–12). Frahm's analysis remains central to understanding the poem's reception.

Within three years, three important books on *Enuma Elish* were published. Thomas Kämmerer and Kai Metzler (2012: 23–33, 355–60) edited the poem and included analysis of the Assyrianized version. They gave an overview of the textual reception, including *Marduk's Ordeal*, school texts, commentaries on the poem, a related lexical text, allusions in Neo-Assyrian royal inscriptions, and ritual recitations in Babylon in the first month, Nisannu, and the ninth month, Kislimu (p. 33–45). Their notable overview of the iconographic reception of the poem includes a cylinder seal made for a statue of Marduk and a description of an *akītu* house gate in the city of Assur (p. 45–9). Lambert (2013) used more textual sources both in his edition of *Enuma Elish* and in his contextual study. Besides sections on the versions of and commentaries on *Enuma Elish*, his discussion of related texts ranged from ritual recitations of the poem to quotations and allusions in other works, including ritual explanatory texts and royal inscriptions (p. 4–9, 135–42, 187–90, 197–8, 202–47, and *passim*). The book listed commentary entries and quotations for specific lines after the edition of each Tablet (p. 60, 72, 82–3, 94, 106, 120, 134). Lambert also edited the *Defeat of Enutila, Enmeshara, and Qingu* and the *Exaltation of Nabû*, two Babylonian narrative works relevant to the transmission of *Enuma Elish*, including the depiction of Nabû and Ninurta as warriors under Marduk's authority (p. 281–98, 326–9, 346–9). He also published (though in cuneiform copy only) a new source for a list of Marduk's names during the Babylon *akītu* festival that quotes *Enuma Elish* (p. 106, 134, 187, pl. 41). Gösta Gabriel (2014: 29–106) investigated the ancient locations and dates of the sources of the poem and analysed the epilogue.

The first key online resource for the reception of *Enuma Elish* is the *Cuneiform Commentaries Project* (*CCP*), initiated by Frahm.[1] This project published a searchable electronic database of Mesopotamian text commentaries with introductory material, bibliography, many tablet photographs, and some annotated editions. The texts relevant to this chapter, some of which are published by *CCP* for the first time, are commentaries on *Enuma Elish* and commentaries on other works that quote the poem.[2] Building on these advances, Frahm and Enrique Jiménez (2015) published the first full editions of the commentary on *Enuma Elish* I–VII and an explanatory text on Elamite month names with quotations of the poem.

In a study of Assyrian religion and ideology, Beate Pongratz-Leisten (2015: 179–80, 188–91, 306–21, 407–34) shed new light on the Neo-Assyrian reception of *Enuma Elish* and discussed allusions to the poem in royal inscriptions and texts describing and interpreting state rituals, including the *akītu* ritual in the city of Assur.[3] She concluded that the central ritual role of the king as conqueror of chaos assimilated Marduk's role in the Babylon *akītu* ritual and involved symbolic gestures representing acts of conquest (Pongratz-Leisten 2015: 432–4; 2017: lxxiii–lxxv).

New knowledge was also gained about the poem's reception in and beyond Babylonia. In his doctoral thesis, Jiménez (2013) identified complex networks of intertextuality and allusions to *Enuma Elish* in *Erra and Ishum*, lexical sources, curse formulas, and royal inscriptions, including the earliest direct allusion to the poem.[4] Selena Wisnom (2020: 182–215) published another important study of intertextuality that included allusions to *Enuma Elish* in *Erra and Ishum*. In a book on a Babylon calendar treatise, I published the first full edition of this Late Babylonian work (Reynolds 2019), which interprets rituals in the Esagil cult in order to boost the temple's elite. Marduk, Tiamat, and Qingu are depicted as analogues to the kings of Babylonia, Elam, and Subartu, respectively, and thus the battle in *Enuma Elish* is the subject of poetic narrative, unattested elsewhere, and gives rise to other quotations of and numerous allusions to the poem (Reynolds 2019: 12–17, 39–45, 50–4, 73–5). Building on recently available Late Babylonian sources, and focusing on the priorities of the Esagil's scholars, I also published a wider survey of the impact of politics and cult on the reception history of Marduk and Tiamat's battle, and urged greater consideration of non-textual transmission through ritual practices and heavenly bodies (Reynolds 2021: 77–8).

The second transformative online project is the *Electronic Babylonian Literature* (*eBL*) project, directed by Jiménez.[5] This project has already revolutionized access to cuneiform sources of the poem and works that quote and allude to it. At the time of writing, the core *eBL* Corpus of electronic editions includes *Enuma Elish* I–VII (L.I.2) and *Erra and Ishum* I (L.I.5). The manuscript sources listed for *Enuma Elish* include quotations in other works, notably the expanded corpus of Babylonian school tablets. The accompanying *eBL* Fragmentarium, an electronic database of cuneiform tablet pieces with sophisticated search functions, includes most of the manuscript sources listed in the Corpus editions and a wealth of other material.[6]

The best resource for understanding the impact of the god Nabû on the reception of *Enuma Elish* is Zachary Rubin's (2021) doctoral thesis. Drawing on the *eBL* project, Anmar Fadhil and Jiménez (2021) published first editions of three manuscripts of *Enuma Elish* from a library in the city of Sippar, recovering most of the two final lines of the epilogue, and supplemented Lambert's lists of quotations of the poem. Continuing to publish the Sippar tablets, they edited a new hymn to Marduk and identified it as a manifesto for his absorption of other gods in the form of a pastiche of *Enuma Elish* (Fadhil and Jiménez 2022).

In her book on Babylon's New Year festival, Céline Debourse (2022: 90–176, 296–300, 331–2) re-edited the festival ritual texts, which specify the recitation of *Enuma Elish* in the first month Nisannu, and concluded that these texts are Late Babylonian compositions, written when the festival was largely only a cultural memory. She argued that *Enuma Elish* was more relevant for the Neo-Assyrian New Year festival and reframed the ritual texts as Late Babylonian priestly literature, produced by Esagil priests as self-validation without the need for ritual enactment (Debourse 2022: 41–2, 46–7, 255–62, 399–420). However, the relative scarcity of texts from Babylonia in the earlier first millennium BCE should be taken into account.[7]

New primary sources continue to be published, including a piece of *Marduk's Ordeal* from excavations in Nineveh (MacGinnis et al. 2022). Research on the cuneiform reception of *Enuma Elish* will continue to break new ground.

## Transmission and reception according to *Enuma Elish*

The epilogue in *Enuma Elish* VII 145–64 contains instructions about the poem's proper transmission and reception (Gabriel 2014: 81–101). The epilogue stipulates that Marduk's names listed in Tablets VI–VII should be grasped and that the *maḫrû*, 'the first one', should reveal them (VII 145). The first scholar to know the poem is discussed below. As onward oral and written transmission, *enqu*, 'the wise one', and *mūdû*, 'the learned one', should discuss the names; *abu*, 'the father', should repeat them and teach them to *māru*, 'the son', signifying scribal training; and finally the ears of *rē'û*, 'the shepherd', and *nāqidu*, 'the herdsman', should be opened, referring to the oral instruction of the Babylonian king by these scholars (VII 146–8). If the king does not neglect Marduk, king and land shall prosper (VII 149–50); this probably refers to royal ritual in Babylon's New Year festival in the month of Nisannu. Reinforcing the necessity for proper behaviour, the heart of the epilogue is a description of Marduk as omnipotent, unrelenting in his anger, and omniscient of wrongdoing (VII 151–6).

The epilogue then revisits the theme of the poem as *taklimtu*, 'a revelation', by 'the first one', now explaining that he recited it before Marduk, wrote it down, and deposited it for future generations to hear (VII 157–8). According to this origin myth, the poem's author is an elite cultic functionary and cuneiform scholar who recited the poem in front of Marduk's statue in the Esagil. Once written down, the poem was to be recited or sung in onward oral transmission through future generations. As a further framing device, the epilogue returns to the transmission of Marduk's destiny and name (VII 159–60) before the poem is summarized as *zamāru ša marūtuk*, 'a song of Marduk', who conquered Tiamat and assumed kingship (VII 161–2). One tablet from a library excavated in Sippar and another tablet likely to be from Sippar, both probably dating to the sixth century BCE, include two partially legible final lines mentioning senior gods, Babylon, and the Esagil (VII 163–4); but a Neo-Assyrian tablet from Huzirina in south-eastern Turkey, datable to the eighth or seventh century BCE, ends with a double ruling and does not include these two lines.[8] Whether these two lines predate or postdate the Neo-Assyrian tablet, they offer a distinctively Babylonian closing reference to Marduk's Esagil cult in Babylon.

This skilfully composed epilogue sets out the author's aspirations for the transmission and reception of the poem. Scribal and cultic practice shaped and realized these aspirations. As shown below, the realities of the poem's reception match the epilogue's programme: oral and written transmission and interpretation, including scribal training and the poem's recitation in the Esagil's cult; the importance of Marduk's names; the poem's role in securing Marduk's favour and well-being for the human king and his land; the centrality of Babylon and the Esagil with its scholars and cultic experts; and the predominant roles of Marduk as victor and king. Two compositions that subvert traditional *Enuma Elish* probably close with material about their transmission that alludes to the epilogue: the Babylonian poem *Erra and Ishum*; and *Marduk's Ordeal*, a hostile Assyrian interpretation of Babylon's New Year festival.[9] Within the framework of Sennacherib's religious reforms (for which see Eckart Frahm and Sophus Helle in this volume), the wider realities of the poem's transmission still correspond to the epilogue's programme, albeit with the replacement of Marduk by the god Assur. The Assyrianized version of *Enuma Elish* VII has not survived but this could have included a version of the epilogue centred on the god Assur and his city Assur.

## The reception of *Enuma Elish*: Kingship ideology

The poem's cuneiform reception is intrinsically related to ancient Mesopotamian politics and their impact on theology and cult, including those members of the elite who were both scholars and ritual experts. Of fundamental importance is the poem's role as an origin myth and charter for the supremacy of Marduk, Babylon, and the Esagil, and for the supremacy of Babylonia's human king as Marduk's analogue. The poem expresses Marduk's supremacy by portraying him as a king who is both a victorious warrior and the creator of the world. The list of Marduk's names in *Enuma Elish* VI–VII celebrates his absorption of other gods and affirms his sovereignty (Gabriel 2014: 170–6; in this volume, see Marc Van De Mieroop on the role of the names and Gösta Gabriel on the political philosophy of the poem).

The harnessing of *Enuma Elish* as the source of analogies between the human king and the victorious divine king, and between human and divine enemies, in pursuit of scholars' interests and state or regional security continued into the Late Babylonian period. The New Year *akītu* festival in Babylon in the first month Nisannu and its relationship with Marduk's defeat of Tiamat and *Enuma Elish* is of fundamental importance (Reynolds 2021: 64–7; Debourse 2022: 255–62; on the use of *Enuma Elish* in the *akītu* festival, see Céline Debourse in this volume). In this festival, Marduk's principal cult statue, accompanied by the king as his human analogue, traditionally made a return journey from the Esagil to the *akītu* house outside Babylon as part of an annual affirmation of divine and human kingship. This controlled ritual journey of Marduk's statue from the Esagil was interpreted as signifying his battle victory over Tiamat, and the festival secured Babylonia's well-being for the year ahead. As part of his religious reforms after the destruction of Babylon, Sennacherib transferred this festival to Assyria's state god Assur and his city Assur.

Neo-Assyrian letters and royal inscriptions reflect a direct relationship between scholars and the king centred on a palatial hub (Pongratz-Leisten 2015: 30–8, 448–67). By the Late Babylonian period, this model had disappeared. Babylonia's imperial rulers, the Achaemenid, Hellenistic, and Arsacid kings, were more remote and scholars in their temple communities were more inward-looking. Esagil scholars elaborated the analogy between victorious Marduk and the Babylonian king, but these ideas were now rooted in nostalgia rather than political or cultic reality, as demonstrated in the Babylon calendar treatise (see the case study below).

## Evidence for the reception history of *Enuma Elish*

The following outline of the poem's reception highlights the impact of politics, theology, and cult; it does not aim to be exhaustive, especially not in the case of allusions. The sources from Babylonia and Assyria are divided into two chronological phases. The first phase runs until the fall of the Neo-Assyrian empire around 612 BCE; I consider first the Babylonian and then the Assyrian sources from this phase. The second phase encompasses other sources from Babylonia until the end of cuneiform scholarship. For each category, I examine first reception that is aligned with the theology of Marduk's supremacy, then reception that adapted this theology.

What constitutes evidence for the reception of *Enuma Elish*? The onward transmission of a composition through copying and curating it on clay tablets shows scholars' continued interest in the work. Besides versions of the poem itself, scholars also quoted and alluded to it in other works. Creating a new composition that quoted or alluded to the poem shows scholars' innovation and productivity. Cuneiform texts on clay tablets are thus the principal evidence for the poem's reception. Both scribes and tablets were mobile, so tablets can be found in secondary settings. The number of available cuneiform tablets from Babylonia in the earlier period of the poem's reception is relatively low compared to the wealth of tablets from the Neo-Assyrian and later Babylonian periods. Nearly all the Babylonian tablets come from northern Babylonia and most of them entered the British Museum's Sippar and Babylon Collections in the late nineteenth century CE and they are usually unprovenanced and undated (Reade 1986; see also Leichty, Finkel, and Walker 2019). The terms 'Sippar Collection' and 'Babylon Collection' correspond to the find-spots of most of the tablets, but each collection also includes tablets from different northern Babylonian cities. Most tablets in the Sippar Collection come from the late seventh to early fifth centuries BCE, during the Neo-Babylonian Dynasty and early Achaemenid periods, and most tablets in the Babylon Collection are Late Babylonian, from the late Achaemenid into the Arsacid period, chiefly from tablet collections associated with the Esagil (Clancier 2009: 185–213). Without archaeological contexts or dates on the tablets, tablet-dating criteria include museum registration numbers, cuneiform sign forms, and the spelling of words. Undated tablets in the Sippar and Babylon Collections are included under later evidence, although some of them, including school tablets, may be contemporary with the Neo-Assyrian period. Reproducing earlier works was a core element of cuneiform scholarship, so the date of a tablet is often later than the date when the work on it was composed. Dates of composition are usually unknown, with proposals based on textual content (see Enrique Jiménez in this volume). In particular, works attested only on Assyrian and/or later Babylonian tablets can represent compositions, ideas, or practices that already existed in earlier Babylonia when the available evidence is relatively scant.

## Babylonian reception in earlier sources

The overall picture is of the faithful transmission of *Enuma Elish* and its embedded theology, but the poem was also adapted in response to political, theological, and cultic concerns. In northern Babylonian cities, four Neo-Babylonian manuscripts of *Enuma Elish* and a pyramidal school extract text quoting the poem have clear excavation contexts (to varying degrees) and may all date to this earlier period (Gabriel 2014: 49, 54–8).

There is scattered evidence in other works for the onward transmission of *Enuma Elish* that accords with the poem's doctrine of Marduk's supremacy, including his conquest of Tiamat and creation of the heavens. The sources from Babylonia in this earlier period are relatively scarce but they are supplemented by works first attested on Neo-Assyrian tablets that are identified as earlier Babylonian compositions.[10] A curse formula in an inscription of the Babylonian king Marduk-nadin-ahhe (1099–1082 BCE) contains the earliest-known direct allusion to the poem, and this relates to Marduk's conquest of Tiamat (Jiménez 2013: 316; see also Jiménez in this volume). A Babylonian composition interpreting the outward procession in Babylon's *akītu* festival in Nisannu quotes *Enuma Elish* in the exposition of names given to Marduk (see the case study below). A text commentary on *Enuma Elish* VII may have been composed in Babylon (see below for overviews of commentaries). Babylonian compositions may also include a text commentary on another work that quoted a name of Marduk and the explanatory treatise *Inamgishhurankia* that quoted from Marduk's creation of the heavens.[11]

Babylonian politics, theology, and cult resulted in three types of divergence in the poem's reception. As a reflection on war and disruption, the Babylonian poem *Erra and Ishum* was probably composed in the ninth or eighth century BCE and had a wide circulation in Assyria and later Babylonia (Jiménez 2013: 161–2, 196–8, 203–6, 251–5, 268–72; Wisnom 2020: 159–61, 182–215). The poet used allusion to subvert

*Enuma Elish* and portray Marduk as a gullible king of the gods who lost control to the war god Erra. Because Erra persuaded Marduk to have his cult statue refurbished, this statue left its normal home in the Esagil and Marduk's kingship was suspended. Despite promising to maintain stability during the interregnum, Erra unleashed war and destruction until reined in by the god Ishum. The closing passage of the poem concerns its onward transmission, including via singers, scribes, and scholars in oral discussion, and alludes to the epilogue of *Enuma Elish* (Frahm 2011: 349; Wisnom 2020: 238–40). *Erra and Ishum* provides a theological rationale for war and portrays the presence and proper maintenance of Marduk's principal statue in the Esagil as essential for Babylonia's peace and stability. Despite Marduk's gullibility as a plot device, I would argue that this poem aimed to promote Marduk and his Esagil cult as essential for state security.

Speculative theology promoting Marduk that went beyond *Enuma Elish* was a second cause of divergence. The hymn *Erish Shummi* can be identified as a Babylonian work composed before the eighth century BCE and there is evidence of circulation in Assyria and later Babylonia (Fadhil and Jiménez 2022). It speculatively awards the names, and thereby the identities, of other gods to Marduk and emulates *Enuma Elish* in terms of the structure in Tablets VI–VII and some vocabulary.

A third factor was the increased importance of the god Nabû, Marduk's son, in Babylonia and Assyria during the first millennium BCE. *Enuma Elish* does not mention Nabû, but the poem's theology was reinterpreted to boost Nabû's status through partial syncretism with Marduk, although Marduk continued to exist as a separate god, sometimes superior to his son. Two works on tablets from Assur that were probably composed in Babylonia exemplify this. A hymn to Nabû drew on the theology of *Enuma Elish* and the structure and vocabulary of Tablets VI–VII, including a quotation from *Enuma Elish* VII, to support reallocating a name of Marduk to Nabû (Ebeling 1953: no. 16, l. 9, quoting *Enuma Elish* VII 35; Lambert 2013: 147–8; Rubin 2021: 184–6).[12] In a narrative termed the *Exaltation of Nabû*, Marduk retains his supremacy, but he celebrates Nabû's dominance over Tiamat in Babylon's New Year *akītu* festival (Lambert 2013: 346–9, 509–10; Reynolds 2021: 68–9).

## Neo-Assyrian reception

The Neo-Assyrian reception of *Enuma Elish* also displays varying degrees of adherence to or adaptation of the poem in response to political, theological, and cultic developments.[13] Assur was the state god of Assyria and head of the Assyrian pantheon in the Neo-Assyrian period and this directly conflicted with Marduk's supremacy in *Enuma Elish*. Some Neo-Assyrian compositions still aligned, at least broadly, with Marduk's roles as a warrior and cosmic creator in the poem, although the Assyrian king replaced the Babylonian king as Marduk's human analogue. However, in the most extreme form of cultural appropriation, some works directly replaced Marduk with Assur. This new, Assyrianized response to the Babylonian poem can be attributed to religious reform by the Assyrian king Sennacherib after his sack of Babylon and removal of Marduk's principal cult statue.

Manuscripts of the Babylonian version of *Enuma Elish* from Neo-Assyrian cities are plentiful, but only two school tablets quoting the poem are known, both excavated in the city of Assur and datable to the seventh century BCE.[14] Other works attest to the onward transmission of *Enuma Elish* in at least broad agreement with the poem's theology. Allusions to the poem have been identified in Assyrian royal inscriptions from at least the time of Sargon II until Assur-etel-ilani, one of the last Assyrian kings (e.g. Frame 1995: no. B.6.35.2; Jiménez 2013: 425–6, 431; Pongratz-Leisten 2015: 179–80, 189, 306–21). These passages are understood to reference Marduk's creation of the heavens and battle victory in *Enuma Elish*, often in analogies with the Assyrian king, but they usually occur within the framework of Assur's supremacy. A Babylonian scholar's letter encouraged the Assyrian king Esarhaddon to defeat his enemies like Marduk by quoting *Enuma Elish* (see the case study below). Marduk's expanded role as a warrior resulted in works alluding to Marduk's defeat of Tiamat and Qingu, but also other conquests beyond the scope of *Enuma Elish*. A hymn dedicated by the Assyrian king Assurbanipal to Marduk alludes to *Enuma Elish* in its subject matter and vocabulary (Livingstone 1989: no. 2). It celebrates Marduk as supreme god, including his victories over Tiamat, Qingu, and Anzû, as well as his creation of the heavens and the Esagil. Marduk's repertoire of enemies is also extended in Neo-Assyrian works interpreting rituals (Livingstone 1989: no. 37 and 40). Quotation concerning his creation of the heavens occurs in a treatise interpreting Elamite month names that is probably an Assyrian composition (Frahm and Jiménez 2015: 338–43, A 15, quoting *Enuma Elish* V 24; the sources come from Nineveh and Achaemenid Babylon). Marduk theology aligned with *Enuma Elish* is mixed with Assyrianized interpretation in some works, including a commentary on *Enuma Elish* I–VII.[15]

In the most extreme Assyrian reactions to the poem, *Enuma Elish* and Babylon's *akītu* festival in the first month Nisannu were culturally appropriated and reinterpreted to serve Neo-Assyrian political and religious agendas, including the direct replacement of Marduk and his human analogue the Babylonian king by the god Assur and the Assyrian king (Frahm 2010: 8–13; 2011: 349–56; Pongratz-Leisten 2015: 416–26; Debourse 2022: 40–7; see also Eckart Frahm in this volume). This ideological endeavour probably dates to the reign of the Assyrian king Sennacherib after his sack of Babylon and removal of Marduk's statue in 689 BCE; he also mapped Babylon's *akītu* festival in Nisannu onto the city of Assur as part of his religious reforms. An Assyrianized version of *Enuma Elish* itself is attested on two tablets from the city of Assur and one tablet from Nineveh.[16] One of the tablets from Assur was found in the house of a family of cult singers, together with a tablet of the traditional version of *Enuma Elish* (Pedersén 1986: 2:N3.37, 2:N3.38). In the repurposed version, Assur, Assyria's state god, replaced Marduk, Babylonia's state god, and consequent changes included the city of Assur, called Baltil, replacing Babylon. A fragmentary letter from a scholar to the Assyrian king, possibly Esarhaddon, quotes Assyrianized *Enuma Elish*, apparently in relation to the scholar's dream about the enthroned king with a tablet of Assyrianized *Enuma Elish* IV in front of him (Parpola 1993: no. 365, l. 10′–12′, quoting Assyrianized *Enuma Elish* IV 17; for discussion, see Parpola 1983: no. 288). I would suggest that this letter may hold up Assur in Assyrianized *Enuma Elish* as a model for the Assyrian king concerning the proper treatment of loyal subjects. The battle in

Tablet IV of the Assyrianized *Enuma Elish* is also transmitted via cultic topography and iconography. Sennacherib's new *akītu* house outside the city of Assur had ceremonial names celebrating Tiamat's defeat and a bronze gate depicting Sennacherib, the battle-ready god Assur as his divine analogue, and Assur's opponent Tiamat (Grayson and Novotny 2014: no. 160). A ritual interpretation work known as *Marduk's Ordeal* gives an Assyrianized interpretation of Babylon's *akītu* festival in Nisannu to Marduk's detriment that mentions the singing of *Enuma Elish* before Marduk's statue and also cites the poem (see the case study below).

## Babylonian reception in later sources

Scholars continued to promote Marduk and the Esagil until the final stages of cuneiform culture. However, politics and the localized cults of Babylonian cities meant that this promotion was a regional phenomenon in northern Babylonia with Babylon as the epicentre. In the Late Babylonian period scholars deployed the poem to assert the continued centrality of Marduk's cult at the Esagil despite Babylonia's reduced status as a province within externally imposed Achaemenid, Hellenistic, and Arsacid empires. The Late Babylonian reception of *Enuma Elish* was part of an intellectual response by scholars, especially those associated with the Esagil, to the marginalization of Babylon and their increased remoteness from the king (Reynolds 2019: 12–17, 22–3; Reynolds 2021: 71–6; Debourse 2022: 399–403). The scholars' nostalgic and self-referential assertions that Marduk's Esagil cult was essential for Babylonia's security, including the retention of Marduk's statue in the Esagil, are an instance of ancient clericalism. The Babylonian sources considered here include quotations of the poem in numerous school extract texts, as well as commentaries on other works. In ritual and explanatory texts, as well as narratives about the gods, *Enuma Elish* was associated with a range of rituals and gods in Babylon, although Marduk's cult at the Esagil remained the principal focus.

Most tablets are unprovenanced and undated, but they can be attributed to northern Babylonia, chiefly the cities of Sippar and Babylon, in the Neo-Babylonian Dynasty period (626–539 BCE) and the Late Babylonian period (539 BCE – first century CE), when Babylonia was ruled by the Achaemenid, Hellenistic, and Arsacid empires. The nature of these tablets and the scarcity of sources from earlier Babylonia mean that some of the reception features discussed in this section may have been earlier innovations.

Politics and cultic variation between and within Babylonian cities affected the transmission of the poem. Manuscripts of *Enuma Elish* from northern Babylonia are datable to the Neo-Babylonian Dynasty and the Late Babylonian period, although excavation contexts and dated tablets are relatively rare.[17] Two excavated manuscripts from the city of Uruk are the only direct evidence from southern Babylonia for manuscripts or quotations of the poem (Gabriel 2014: 60–2).[18] Frahm has argued that these tablets date to the period of control by the Neo-Babylonian dynasty, after which Marduk theology centred on Babylon conflicted with Uruk's new focus on the god Anu and his cult (Frahm 2010: 17–18; 2011: 361–2; Krul 2018: 16–19). In royal inscriptions, allusions to *Enuma Elish* have been identified in texts of the Neo-Babylonian kings Nabopolassar and Nabonidus, but only before the latter's short-lived promotion of Sîn in Marduk's stead (Da Riva 2013: no. 2.2.7 C32, i 15-16; Jiménez 2013: 438–42).

School tablets from northern Babylonia were a major vector for the poem's regional transmission. Teachers dictated extracts from *Enuma Elish* and other works for trainee scribes to write down. The *eBL*'s Fragmentarium has expanded the known corpus of school tablets quoting *Enuma Elish* to seventy-two, with more to follow.[19] In the later first millennium BCE, the northern Babylonian school curriculum was focused on Marduk. This was part of an intellectual drive to promote and embed Marduk's theology, including the supremacy of Marduk, the Esagil, and Babylon. The teachers' choice of school extracts as a way of transmitting knowledge not only gave exposure and prestige to the poem and its theology, but also reflected and reinforced relationships between *Enuma Elish* and a network of other compositions. The school texts demonstrate that the poem was part of the intellectual apparatus of scholars and a key element in knowledge transfer, both oral and written, between scholars and their pupils. The school curriculum was fundamental to scribes who went on to reproduce and compose texts and teach pupils of their own. *Enuma Elish* is by far the most frequently quoted literary text on school tablets; and most instances are on the tablets from the Babylon Collection, which can usually be attributed to collections linked with the Esagil (see Gesche 2000: 808 for examples; on the Babylon Collection, see above). *Enuma Elish* I–VII are all quoted, but Tablet I is the most popular. Typically, an *Enuma Elish* passage of about six lines is accompanied by other extracts from literary and lexical texts, the latter expounding the meaning of specific words. The literary texts most frequently combined with the poem are the exorcistic series *Udughul*, 'Evil Demons', including a section known as 'Marduk's Address to the Demons', and the *Prayer to Marduk 2*.[20] As argued by Jiménez (2022: 4, 6–7, 29), in the first millennium BCE *Enuma Elish* was not quoted in school texts from the central Babylonian city of Nippur, because this city promoted its own local gods, led by Enlil and his son Ninurta.[21]

The onward transmission of *Enuma Elish* to promote Marduk theology in northern Babylonia is also chiefly attested in text commentaries and works relating to ritual. As well as composing new works, later scholars reproduced earlier works that quoted or alluded to the poem.[22] A written text commentary could draw on a combination of oral teaching and written sources (Gabbay 2016: 13–83). Commentators used techniques such as wordplay, number-play, and analogy to interpret existing compositions (Frahm 2011: 59–85). Evidence for the continued use of *Enuma Elish* as an interpretative tool includes its quotation in text commentaries.[23] Compared to the school tablets discussed above, text commentaries are a more advanced form of knowledge transfer between teachers and junior scholars or within a group of scholars. However, the remarks about school tablets and knowledge transmission through quotation also apply here. As with school texts, nearly all the commentaries quoting *Enuma Elish* are on unprovenanced Babylonian tablets, mostly in the British Museum's Sippar and Babylon Collections (see above). One Babylon Collection tablet is datable to around the end of the second century BCE.[24] Some commentaries interpret specific works: the lexical series *Aa*[25]; the list of divine names dubbed the *Weidner God List*[26]; and the medical series *Sagig*.[27] Others are based on combinations of extracts from different works, often literary ones.[28] The list of Marduk's names in *Enuma Elish* VI–VII, which itself employed many commentary techniques, was quoted seven times, making Tablet VII the most popular tablet, but scholars also quoted Tablets I and III–VI of the poem. Commentaries quoting *Enuma Elish* also quoted other literary texts. The formative effect of the scribes' education is shown by an overlap with the texts quoted in the northern Babylonian school curriculum.[29] The commentaries on *Aa* quoted *Enuma Elish* to illustrate the meaning of specific words in context; in other commentaries, the relationship between the base text and the quotation is more elaborate.[30] Some of the more complex techniques used by scholars in commentaries are discussed in the case studies below.

In addition to text commentaries, works on Late Babylonian tablets that describe and interpret rituals attest to the late transmission of *Enuma Elish.* Scholars used the poem to promote Marduk's supremacy in Babylon, sometimes also undermining the chief gods of Nippur and Uruk in competitive theology. In a description of the New Year festival in Nisannu on day 4, a cultic functionary narrates *Enuma Elish* to Marduk's cult statue in the Esagil while Anu and Enlil, the chief gods of Nippur and Uruk, are ritually disempowered (Debourse 2022: 138, 144–7, l. 280–4 [ii 22–6]; see also Debourse in this volume). Early on day 5, prayers to Marduk's cult statue include addressing the god in astral form as Tiamat's conqueror (Debourse 2022: 139, l. 309 and 313 [iii 9 and 13], see also p. 308–9, 311; see further Reynolds 2019: 45, 358–60, 376–9). In a description of a ritual at the Esagil on day 4 of the ninth month, Kislimu, a cult singer is said to narrate *Enuma Elish* to Marduk's cult statue (Çağirgan and Lambert 1991–1993: 96, l. 62–4). From this oral quotation of the whole poem, Usmû's bringing of Damkina's gift to her victorious son Marduk in *Enuma Elish* V 83 is said to be analogous to a priest's offering of a palm frond to Marduk's statue. In the Babylon calendar treatise, the interpretation of rituals in the Esagil cult as averting foreign invasion includes quotations from and allusions to *Enuma Elish* (see the case study below).[31] These works can be understood as examples of Late Babylonian priestly literature: self-validatory compositions by scholars associated with the Esagil (Debourse 2022: 399–403).

## Quoting and citing *Enuma Elish*: Case studies

Why am I quoting quotes? In the footsteps of ancient Mesopotamian scholars, I am aiming to transmit knowledge and support contentions, in this case about the reception of *Enuma Elish.* Quotation adds authority to both the source and recipient texts. The intentions of the author of the recipient text shape the selection and deployment of quotations. Ancient scholars dictated quotations from *Enuma Elish* to train scribes and embed Marduk theology; they quoted *Enuma Elish* in commentaries on the poem as a basis for interpreting it; and they quoted and alluded to the poem in other compositions as an explanatory tool, usually to interpret other works or aspects of theology or ritual. Other compositions rarely mention *Enuma Elish* by name, and quotations of the poem are usually unmarked. This chapter distinguishes literal or near-literal quotations from allusions. However, modern definitions of quotation vary in their strictness and allusions can be more nebulous, although Wisnom (2020: 11–15) adopted the helpful criteria proposed by Oliver Taplin of prominence, coherence, and purpose (see also Fadhil and Jiménez 2022: 256–7).

Two commentaries on *Enuma Elish* are known. One interprets selected lines from *Enuma Elish* I–VII and is attested by six Neo-Assyrian tablets, five from 'Assurbanipal's Library' in Nineveh and one from the city of Assur, all datable to the seventh century BCE, as well as by three Babylonian tablets from the British Museum's Sippar Collection (Frahm and Jiménez 2015: 293–333; CCP 1.1.A with 1.6; see also Frahm in this volume). As the editors note, Marduk's names attract the most comment, but other recurring themes include the creation of the world and aspects of nature, such as the sun and moon, as well as divine feasting and gift-giving. While Babylon's *akītu* ritual in the first month Nisannu is mentioned, the commentary also refers to ritual in other months and gods linked with other Babylonian and Assyrian cities, sometimes in Assyrianizing interpretations: perhaps the author, a cuneiform scholar versed in cult practices, came from the Babylonian city of Nippur and wrote the commentary in Assyria (Frahm and Jiménez 2015: 330–3). The second commentary on selected lines of *Enuma Elish* VII is attested on two Neo-Assyrian tablets from 'Assurbanipal's Library' in Nineveh datable to the seventh century BCE (Lambert 2013: 139–42; CCP 1.1.B; on this commentary, see Marc Van De Mieroop in this volume). It interprets names awarded to Marduk through wordplay and is an expression of the Marduk theology centred on his city Babylon, where it may have been composed. There is no evidence that any commentaries on *Enuma Elish* were composed in the Late Babylonian period, but this may just be an accident of discovery.

The following four case studies explore works quoting or citing the poem that illustrate some of the most interesting developments in its reception. A Babylonian explanatory text lists a short sequence of Marduk's names during his statue's procession from the Esagil to the *akītu* house outside Babylon on day 8 of Nisannu during the New Year festival, and these names are closely related to *Enuma Elish* and the list of Marduk's fifty names in Tablets VI–VII.[32] In the entry on Marduk's fourth name, Sirsir, the explanatory text reads 'He sits on … in Maumusha and his name is Sirsir: When he tramples Tiamat, "Tiamat is his vessel, he is [her] sailor." When(?) [he(?) tramples(?).]' (*ina libbi* [giš]MÁ.UMUŠ.A *ina muḫḫi* … […] … *uššabma Sirsir šumšu / Tiamat kī ikabbasu / Tiamat rukūbšūma šū malā*[*ḫš*]*a kī ika*[*bbasu*(?)], l. 6–8).[33] The text makes an assertion, also known from other works, that Marduk is called Sirsir when his statue is in his barge called Maumusha during the procession to Babylon's *akītu* house (Lambert 1997: 79–80, l. 10). The explanatory text justifies this assertion by linking it to Marduk's defeat, literally his 'trampling', of Tiamat and by quoting *Enuma Elish* VII 77. In *Enuma Elish* this line is part of the entry on Marduk's name Malah ('Sailor') that is awarded to the god under his preceding name Sirsir (VII 70–7; this includes earlier interpretation of Marduk's victory over Tiamat that references her watery nature). Interpreting the processional barge as Tiamat and interpreting Marduk's statue as the sailor on board is a way of interpreting this ritual journey as signifying Marduk's victory over Tiamat. This interpretation is tailored to a specific stage of the *akītu* festival and is also theologically appropriate, since Tiamat was the deified sea. While there is overall agreement between the poem and the explanatory text, the latter lists only a short sequence of names of specific ritual significance and is far more concise.

Therefore, in the entry on Marduk's name Sirsir the material drawing on *Enuma Elish* is abbreviated and does not specify Malah as a name of Marduk. The explanatory text refers to the transport of Marduk's statue in the Maumusha in the final stages of the outward procession to the *akītu* house (on the barge's arrival there, see Da Riva 2022). Although the details are unclear, other evidence also suggests that this ritual journey was interpreted as signifying Marduk's defeat of Tiamat (Reynolds 2021: 65–6). In a more damaged entry concerning day 10 of Nisannu, the same explanatory text quotes *Enuma Elish* V 81–2 about the goddess Damkina hailing and dressing her son Marduk after his victory over Tiamat and this constitutes further evidence for Marduk's post-battle recovery and celebration in Babylon's *akītu* house. This explanatory text is thus important Babylonian evidence from the earlier first millennium BCE for the explicit linkage of Babylon's New Year *akītu* festival with *Enuma Elish*.

The second case study is a specifically marked quotation or citation of *Enuma Elish* in a Neo-Assyrian subversive work that reinterprets Babylon's New Year festival in Nisannu to disempower Marduk and promote the god Assur (Livingstone 1989: no. 34 and 35; Frahm 2011: 352–4; see also Frahm 2010: 12–13). This ritual interpretation work, dubbed *Marduk's Ordeal* by modern scholars, is unusually written in the Neo-Assyrian dialect and probably dates from Sennacherib's reign, after his sack of Babylon in 689 BCE. The Assur version is attested on two tablets from that city, one from the main temple of the god Assur and one from the house of a family of exorcists, as well as on one tablet from the North-west Palace in the city of Kalhu (Postgate 1973: no. 268; Pedersén 1986: 2:N1.121, N4.453). The Nineveh version is known from seven tablets from that city, one of which was excavated in 2022 (MacGinnis et al. 2022). According to both versions, *Enuma Elish* that is sung before Marduk's cult statue in Nisannu concerns his imprisonment, in what is clearly an Assyrianizing subversion of the ritual and the poem (Livingstone 1989: no. 34, l. 34; no. 35, l. 11, 28). As part of this Assyrianizing agenda, both versions claim to quote or cite *Enuma Elish* about the primeval creation of the god Anshar and the later creation of Marduk. The Assur version reads: 'The garment which is on him (i.e., Marduk), about which it says as follows: "It is water." They are lies. It said in *Enuma Elish* – When heaven (and) earth were not created, Anshar [came into existence]. When city and house existed, he (i.e., Marduk) came into existence. – It is the water which is on Anshar' (*šer'itu ša ina muḫḫīšu ša iqabbûni mā mû š*[*u*]*nu sili'āte šina / šū ina libbi enūma eliš iqṭibi kī šamê erṣeti lā ibbanûni anšar it*[*tabši*] */ kī ālu u bētu ibšûni šū ittabši mû ša ina muḫḫi anšar*, l. 53–5).[34] To add weight to the claim, the text specifically marks *Enuma Elish* as the source of the assertion about Anshar and probably also the assertion about Marduk.[35] However, this is not a case of quotation from the poem. The assertion about Anshar is a highly abbreviated paraphrase of *Enuma Elish* I 1–12, but the assertion about Marduk conflicts with the poem, where Marduk is created long before the creation of the earth, mankind, Babylon, or the Esagil. This passage aims to disempower Marduk by portraying him as a very junior god, coming into existence when the world was well established, in contrast to primeval Anshar who could legitimately be associated with Apsû and Tiamat as the primordial creator gods (I 3–4). Given the references to water and the nature of *Marduk's Ordeal*, this subversive passage presumably aims to oust Marduk from his role as Tiamat's conqueror. Both versions of *Marduk's Ordeal* close with curses on anyone who does not disseminate the composition, referring to both written and oral transmission. This can be seen as a subversive response to the epilogue of *Enuma Elish*, as suggested by Frahm (2011: 353–4).

The third instance is in a letter found at Nineveh and it is marked as being the words of the great gods to Marduk, although *Enuma Elish* is not specified (identified in Parpola 1983: 286). The Babylonian scholar Bel-ushezib, who was probably from Nippur but living in Nineveh, wrote to Sennacherib's son and successor Esarhaddon (680–669 BCE), and drew on Marduk's enthronement scene, quoting *Enuma Elish* IV 8: 'The great gods spoke to Bel, as follows: "To raise high and bring low, [this shall be] in your hand". You are Marduk of the people. Bel as destinies decreed [...], your joys. [The king, my lord, should] act just like Bel. Make the high low and [raise] the low [high].' (*ilānū rabûtu / ana Bēl iqtabû umma šušqû u šušpulu / [šī l]ū qātukka Marduk ša nišī attā Bēl akî šīmāti / [ ... ta]šīlātīka iltēm akî ša Bēl maḫru / [šarru bēlī lī]puš šaqû šuppil u šapli [šušqi]*, r. 29–33; Parpola 1993: no. 112; translation mine). This passage follows Bel-ushezib's warnings to the king about unrest and conspiracy in Babylonia, involving the governor of Nippur called Shumu-iddin (Fabritius 1999; Luukko 2011). Bel-ushezib encourages the king to model himself on Marduk in his exercise of sovereign power. He draws an analogy between the great gods' awarding of the sovereign power to promote and demote to Marduk as divine king and Marduk's decreeing of a good destiny for Esarhaddon as human king. In accord with this analogy, Bel-ushezib encourages Esarhaddon to act like Marduk and exercise his sovereignty to demote and promote his subjects. The reversed order, with demotion first, and the earlier warnings suggest that this pro-Assyrian Babylonian scholar, who regularly wrote to Esarhaddon, was encouraging the king to crush the Babylonian rebels. Esarhaddon did not espouse the Assur-centred religious reforms of his father Sennacherib but was instead committed to restoring Babylon after its sack. Bel-ushezib deployed the traditional Marduk kingship ideology of *Enuma Elish* for very specific political objectives in direct communication with this Assyrian king. He subverted the poem by drawing an analogy between Marduk and the Assyrian king and directing this against his fellow Babylonians, who were probably opposed to his own interests in Nippur as well as the interests of the Assyrian state.

The final case study is a condensed account of Tiamat and Marduk's battle and its aftermath in the Late Babylonian calendar treatise. This is attested on three tablets from Babylon and reinterprets non-royal rituals at the Esagil in different months of the year as preventing the invasion of Babylonia and the looting of Marduk's statue from the Esagil (Reynolds 2019). It is probable that this Late Babylonian treatise was composed in the Hellenistic period and that it was still being copied around 170 BCE (Reynolds 2019: 13–17, 111–20). A section that may concern the second month Ayaru includes this passage of narrative poetry:

*mulmul issukma i*[*ḫtepi karassu*]
[*ša Qing*]*u ḫāmirīšu ina kakki lā gamāl i*[*tt*]*akis kišāds*[*u*]
[*ultu*] *Tiamat ikmû ilqû šarrūssu*

*[u tuppi] šīmāti ša Qingu itmuḫu qātuššu*
*[ṣalmīš]unu ibnīma Bāb Apsî ušaṣbit*
*[aḫrataš ū]mū ana lā mašê epšēti Tiamat*

He shot an arrow and [broke open her (i.e. Tiamat's) belly],
he cut through the neck of [Qingu], her consort, with a merciless weapon.
[After(?)] he defeated Tiamat, took his sovereignty,
[and(?)] secured in his hand the [Tablet of] Destinies of Qingu,
he made [images] of them (i.e. Tiamat's monsters) and installed them in the Gate of the Apsû,
so that the deeds of Tiamat be not forgotten [in future] days.
(i 1′–6′; Reynolds 2019: 190–1, 238–44)

This concise account is related to selected events in *Enuma Elish* IV–V, and its structure and vocabulary allude to this much longer poem. The first line, although restored, is an almost literal quotation of *Enuma Elish* IV 101, and there are especially close relationships between the third line and VII 162 in the epilogue and between the final two lines and V 75–6. It is significant that the second and fourth lines about Qingu are less closely related to *Enuma Elish*: in the treatise Marduk kills Qingu in battle, but in *Enuma Elish* the Igigi gods kill him after the conflict to enable mankind's creation. The treatise links the allusion to Tiamat's defeat in the epilogue of *Enuma Elish* with the defeat of Qingu. However, the epilogue only mentions Tiamat.

The treatise's overall focus is on Babylonia's defeat of two historic foreign enemies, Elam and Subartu, the latter signifying Assyria. This traditional terminology harks back to past invasions of Babylonia, when Marduk's statue was looted, especially by the Elamites in the twelfth century BCE before it was retrieved by Nebuchadnezzar I (Reynolds 2019: 70–101; see Enrique Jiménez in this volume). The treatise draws a complex analogy between Babylonia's conflict with Elam and Subartu, on the one hand, and Marduk's conflict with Tiamat and Qingu, on the other. This two-enemy model explains the treatise's innovations about Qingu. Related material in the treatise includes a condensed poetic narrative about the build-up and onset of Marduk's battle; wordplay interpreting Tiamat and Qingu as Elam and Subartu respectively; quotes from *Enuma Elish* about the battle; and elaborate interpretations of heavenly bodies as representing the three combatants (Reynolds 2019: 39–45, 50–4, 73–5).

It is striking that this treatise from the late first millennium BCE still used *Enuma Elish* as its model for divine and human kingship. Late Babylonian kings were more remote in terms of both ritual participation and contact with the scholars and ritual experts associated with the Esagil, the community where this treatise was composed and copied. This nostalgic work harks back to the days of Babylonian sovereignty when the Esagil's cult specialists were seen as essential for the king's well-being and for state security. The treatise was self-validation by scholars in response to the realities of the Esagil's marginalization in provincial Babylonia under remote imperial rulers (Reynolds 2019: 12–17, 22–3; 2021: 72–6).

The cuneiform reception of *Enuma Elish* changed over the centuries but, despite the poem's varying fortunes, Marduk's victory and Tiamat's deeds remained a powerful paradigm: they were certainly not forgotten.

## Further reading

The following are recommended as further reading, with more detailed references in the discussion above. The online *eBL* project has published a corpus of Akkadian literature, including an edition of *Enuma Elish* (L.I.2) that lists quotations, as well as a wealth of cuneiform tablets in the Fragmentarium. An online corpus of Akkadian commentaries with accompanying resources is available online through the *CCP* project. Frahm (2010; 2011: 345–68) assessed politically motivated responses to the poem in and beyond Mesopotamia, including an Assyrian focus. Lambert (2013) offered editions of *Enuma Elish*, the *Defeat of Enutila, Enmeshara, and Qingu*, and the *Exaltation of Nabû* and collected extensive material attesting to the cuneiform reception of *Enuma Elish*. Elsewhere, I (Reynolds 2021) analysed the broad transmission history of Marduk and Tiamat's battle, paying particular attention to Babylonian sources, and published and contextualized a Late Babylonian calendar treatise that quoted and alluded to the poem (Reynolds 2019). Frahm and Jiménez (2015) edited and discussed a commentary on *Enuma Elish*. Pongratz-Leisten (2015, 2017) analysed Neo-Assyrian royal inscriptions and ritual texts that attest to the reception of *Enuma Elish*. Debourse (2022) assessed the New Year festival and its relationship to the poem, especially in the Late Babylonian period. Fadhil and Jiménez (2022) edited and discussed a Marduk hymn, identified as a pastiche of *Enuma Elish*.

## Notes

1 Eckart Frahm et al., Cuneiform Commentaries Project (2013–23), https://ccp.yale.edu/.

2 CCP 1.1.A, with 1.6, and 1.1.B (on *Enuma Elish*); CCP 3.1.12.A; 3.1.u32; 4.1.4.B; 6.1.9.B; 6.1.10.B; 6.1.13.A; 6.1.13.B.a; 6.1.16.A.a; 6.7.A; 7.1.1; 7.1.6.A (ritual interpretation); 7.2.u27; 7.2.u92; 7.2.u93.

3 For a slightly revised version of chap. 10, see Pongratz-Leisten (2017: xxxi–lxxv). More speculatively on royal inscriptions of Assurbanipal, see Crouch (2013).

4 P. 161–2, 196–8, 203–6, 251–5, and 268–72 for *Erra and Ishum*; p. 247 for lexical material; p. 316–22 for curse formulas; and p. 425–6, 431, and 438–42 for royal inscriptions.

5 Enrique Jiménez et al., Electronic Babylonian Library Project (2018–23), https://www.ebl.lmu.de/. As noted there, future plans include data-mining the *eBL* corpus for intertextual parallels.

6 As well as the school tablets, newly accessible sources include three commentaries quoting *Enuma Elish* (*eBL* Fragmentarium BM 36978 (L.I.2 SB I BabaNBQuo1); BM 36848 + 37521 (L.I.2 SB VII BabaLBQuo2); BM 41071 + 41171 (L.I.2 SB VII BabaLBQuo5)) and a new source for *Marduk's Ordeal* (*eBL* Fragmentarium 1882,0323.4).

7 For related discussion of another corpus of texts, see Frahm (2011: 26–7).

8 Fadhil and Jiménez (2021: 227–8); *eBL* L.I.2 SB VII SipNB1, BabaNB2, HuzNA1a.

9 On *Erra and Ishum*, see the section on Babylonian reception in earlier sources; on *Marduk's Ordeal*, see the case study.

10 The commentary on *Enuma Elish* VII; CCP 3.1.12.A; *Inamgishhurankia*; *Erra and Ishum*; *Erish Shummi*; and three compositions focused on Nabû (see outline below).

11 CCP 3.1.12.A.a(+)b, i 12 (quoting *Enuma Elish* VII 57) is attested on a Nineveh tablet; see also *eBL* Fragmentarium K 2281. *Inamgishhurankia* (Livingstone 1986: 22–5, l. 11, 24, quoting V 17, 21, respectively) is attested on Nineveh tablets, one dated to 683 BCE, as well as a tablet attributable to Babylon, dated 488 BCE. On *Inamgishhurankia*, see Francesca Rochberg in this volume.

12 See the Neo-Assyrian treatise on Nabû on a tablet from Nineveh *eBL* Fragmentarium K 104, r. 54–6 (quoting *Enuma Elish* I 101–2 on Marduk's names); Lambert (2013: 164; I propose: r. 54 *ma-ri-u*$_2$*-tu*$^{\text{la!}}$); Rubin (2021: 165–6).

13 The following compositions were also in circulation in Assyria but are discussed above under Babylonian reception: commentary on *Enuma Elish* VII; CCP 3.1.12.A; *Inamgishhurankia*; *Erra and Ishum*; *Erish Shummi*; and three compositions focused on Nabû.

14 *eBL* L.I.2 lists of manuscripts. For the school tablets, see *eBL* L.I.2 SB 1 AssNASch1, AssNASch2; Lambert (1960: 356–7).

15 See below for an overview of commentaries on the poem. Another 'mixed' work is a Neo-Assyrian explanatory compendium that alludes to the poem and quotes it concerning Marduk's creation of the world from Tiamat's corpse (Livingstone 1989: no. 39, r. 2, quoting *Enuma Elish* IV 137). The interpretations of ritual extend Marduk's conquests beyond Tiamat and Qingu; present Ninurta as the analogue to the Assyrian king; and include Assyrianized interpretations (Frahm 2011: 355; Pongratz-Leisten 2015: 409, 446). See also Eckart Frahm in this volume.

16 *eBL* L.I.2 SB I AššNA5, III AššNA1, V NinNA; Kämmerer and Metzler (2012: 26–33, 355–60).

17 Four excavated tablets from the Sippar Library probably date from the sixth century BCE (Gabriel 2014: 58–60; Fadhil and Jiménez 2021). Excavated tablets from Kish and Meturan may post-date the fall of Assyria (see above on earlier sources). An *Enuma Elish* tablet in the British Museum's Babylon Collection is probably dated to the twenty-seventh year of Darius I, 495 BCE (Gabriel 2014: 37–8; *eBL* L.I.2 Colophons SB I BabaLB1).

18 Scholarly tablets found at Uruk very rarely mention Tiamat and Qingu, and then not as Marduk's conquests (Reynolds 2019: 30, 40, 292, 365, 370).

19 *eBL* L.I.2 listed for *Enuma Elish* SB 1–7 with notations BabaNBSch, SipLBSch1, SipNBSch1; Gesche (2000: 174–83).

20 E.g. *eBL* L.I.2 SB 1 BabaNBSch1, BabaNBSch4, BabaNBSch9, BabaNBSch13, BabaNBSch18, BabNBSch 19. See *eBL* L.III.3 Marduk's Address to the Demons; Oshima (2011: 216–70). More work remains to be done on relationships between all the texts involved.

21 As with Uruk, scholarly tablets from Nippur very rarely mention Tiamat and Qingu and then not as Marduk's conquests (Reynolds 2019: 30, 40, 292, 370).

22 *Inamgishhurankia*, *Erra and Ishum*, and *Erish Shummi* are included under Babylonian reception in earlier sources; a treatise on Elamite month names and a commentary on *Enuma Elish* I–VII under Neo-Assyrian reception.

23 For a list of *Enuma Elish* quotations, see Fadhil and Jiménez (2021: 228); *eBL* Fragmentarium BM 41071 + 41171.

24 *eBL* Fragmentarium BM 41071 + 41171, r. 7′–10′; see CCP 3.4.1.A.i.

25 CCP 6.1.9.B, l. 14′ (quoting I 139); 6.1.10.B, r. 18′ (quoting I 22); 6.1.13.A, l. 4 (quoting VII 62); 6.1.13.B.a, r. 15 (quoting VI 148); 6.1.16.A.a, l. 7 (quoting III 129).

26 CCP 6.7.A, l. 11′ (quoting IV 82).

27 CCP 4.1.4.B, l. 14 (quoting IV 101).

28 CCP 7.1.1, r. 3–5 (quoting VI 151–3); 7.2.u93, l. 3 (quoting VII 5); *eBL* Fragmentarium BM 41071 + 41171, r. 3′–4′ (quoting VII 143–4).

29 As an example, some text commentaries quote *Enuma Elish* with 'Marduk's Address to the Demons' and/or the *Prayer to Marduk 2* (CCP 7.2.u93, l. 1, 3, 9; *eBL* Fragmentarium BM 36848 + 37521, l. 3′–5′; BM 66956 + 76066 + 76498, l. 12′–18′, 26′–33′). On these works in the school curriculum, see above.

30 For an example of a commentary quoting *Enuma Elish* in more complex exegesis, see CCP 4.1.4.B, l. 14 (quoting IV 101); Jiménez (2013: 331–4).

31 For a further example of a Late Babylonian explanatory text related to gods and ritual that quotes the poem, see CCP 7.1.6.A.a and 7.1.6.A.b, l. 27, 31 (quoting I 60, VII 35). I would suggest that one tablet attesting to the *Defeat of Enutila, Enmeshara, and Qingu* may be another example (Lambert 2013: 328–9, BM 47530, l. 2–6, quoting I 22–6).

32 The two duplicate sources are: a tablet excavated in Babylon and dating to the seventh century BCE (Cavigneaux 1981: no. 79.B.1/30, l. 8, 12–13; 1999: 385–91; see Al-Mutawalli 1999: 191–4); and a Babylon Collection tablet copied from a Babylon source (Lambert 2013: pl. 41; *eBL* Fragmentarium BM 38706 + 39843, l. 8, 11–2).

33 Based on *eBL* Fragmentarium BM 38706 + BM 39843 (transliteration); translation mine. *eBL* L.I.2 SB VII 77 BabaLBQuo3 suggests reading l. 8 to give a marked quotation, although the phrasing would be unusual (Gabbay 2016: 201–63).

34 Livingstone (1989: no. 34, l. 53–5; translation mine; see also no. 35, l. 44–5); MacGinnis et al. (2022: 34, l. 6′, with the variant *kī annî iqṭibi*).

35 On *šū ina libbi enūma eliš iqṭibi* possibly expressing the agency of scripture, see Gabbay (2016: 260–1).

## Bibliography


Al-Mutawalli, N. (1999), 'A New Foundation Cylinder from the Temple of Nabû ša ḫarê', *Iraq*, 61: 191–4.

Çağirgan, G. and W. G. Lambert (1991–1993), 'The Late Babylonian Kislīmu Ritual for Esagil', *Journal of Cuneiform Studies*, 43–5: 89–106.

Cavigneaux, A. (1981), *Textes scolaires du Temple de Nabû ša Harê*, Baghdad: State Organization of Antiquities and Heritage.

Cavigneaux, A. (1999), '*Nabû ša ḫarê* und die Kinder von Babylon', in J. Renger (ed.), *Babylon: Focus mesopotamischer Geschichte, Wiege früher Gelehrsamkeit, Mythos in der Moderne*, 2. Internationales Colloquium der Deutschen Orient-Gesellschaft 24.–26. März 1998 in Berlin, 385–91, Saarbrücken: Saarbrücker Druckerei und Verlag.

Clancier, P. (2009), *Les bibliothèques en Babylonie dans la deuxième moitié du 1er millénaire av. J.-C.*, Alter Orient und Altes Testament 363, Münster: Ugarit-Verlag.

Crouch, C. L. (2013) 'Ištar and the Motif of the Cosmological Warrior: Assurbanipal's Adaptation of Enuma Elish', in R. P. Gordon and H. M. Barstad (eds), *'Thus Speaks Ishtar of Arbela': Prophecy in Israel, Assyria, and Egypt in the Neo-Assyrian Period*, 129–41, Winona Lake: Eisenbrauns.

Da Riva, R. (2013), *The Inscriptions of Nabopolassar, Amēl-Marduk and Neriglissar*, Studies in Ancient Near Eastern Records 3, Berlin: De Gruyter.

Da Riva, R. (2022), 'BM 40757: Marduk's Arrival at the Akītu Temple on the 8th of Nisannu', *Zeitschrift für Assyriologie*, 112: 107–23.

Debourse, C. (2022), *Of Priests and Kings: The Babylonian New Year Festival in the Last Age of Cuneiform Culture*, Culture and History of the Ancient Near East 127, Leiden: Brill.

Ebeling, E. (1953), *Literarische Keilschrifttexte aus Assur*, Berlin: Akademie-Verlag.

Fabritius, K. (1999), 'Bēl-ušēzib', in K. Radner (ed.), *The Prosopography of the Neo-Assyrian Empire 1/II B-G*, 338–9, Helsinki: Neo-Assyrian Text Corpus Project.

Fadhil, A. A. and E. Jiménez (2021), 'Literary Texts from the Sippar Library II: The Epic of Creation', *Zeitschrift für Assyriologie*, 111: 191–230.

Fadhil, A. A. and E. Jiménez (2022), 'Literary Texts from the Sippar Library III: "Eriš šummi", A Syncretistic Hymn to Marduk', *Zeitschrift für Assyriologie*, 112: 229–74.

Frahm, E. (2010), 'Counter-Texts, Commentaries, and Adaptations: Politically Motivated Responses to the Babylonian Epic of Creation in Mesopotamia, the Biblical World, and Elsewhere', *Orient*, 45: 3–33.

Frahm, E. (2011), *Babylonian and Assyrian Text Commentaries: Origins of Interpretation*, Guides to the Mesopotamian Textual Record 5, Münster: Ugarit-Verlag.

Frahm, E., and E. Jiménez (2015), 'Myth, Ritual, and Interpretation: The Commentary on Enūma eliš I–VII and a Commentary on Elamite Month Names', *Hebrew Bible and Ancient Israel*, 4: 293–343.

Frahm, E., E. Jiménez, M. Frazer, and K. Wagensonner (2013–2023), Cuneiform Commentaries Project. At https://ccp.yale.edu/.

Frame, G. (1995), *Rulers of Babylonia From the Second Dynasty of Isin to the End of Assyrian Domination (1157–612 BC)*, The Royal Inscriptions of Mesopotamia: Babylonian Periods 2, Toronto: University of Toronto.

Gabbay, U. (2016), *The Exegetical Terminology of Akkadian Commentaries*, Culture and History of the Ancient Near East 82. Leiden: Brill.

Gabriel, G. (2014), *'enūma eliš' – Weg zu einer globalen Weltordnung*, Orientalische Religionen in der Antike 12, Tübingen: Mohr Siebeck.

Gesche, P. D. (2000), *Schulunterricht in Babylonien im ersten Jahrtausend v. Chr.*, Alter Orient und Altes Testament 275, Münster: Ugarit-Verlag.

Grayson, A. K. and J. Novotny (2014), *The Royal Inscriptions of Sennacherib, King of Assyria (704–681 BC), Part 2*, The Royal Inscriptions of the Neo-Assyrian Period 3 (2), Winona Lake: Eisenbrauns.

Jiménez, E. (2013), 'La imagen de los vientos en la literatura babilónica', doctoral thesis. Universidad Complutense de Madrid.

Jiménez, E. (2022), *Middle and Neo-Babylonian Literary Texts in the Frau Professor Hilprecht Collection, Jena*, Texte und Materialien der Hilprecht Collection 13, Wiesbaden: Harrassowitz.

Kämmerer, T. R. and K. A. Metzler (2012), *Das babylonische Weltschöpfungsepos 'Enūma elîš'*, Alter Orient und Altes Testament 375, Münster: Ugarit-Verlag.

Krul, J. (2018), *The Revival of the Anu Cult and the Nocturnal Fire Ceremony at Late Babylonian Uruk*, Culture and History of the Ancient Near East 95, Leiden: Brill.

Lambert, W. G. (1960), *Babylonian Wisdom Literature*, Oxford: Oxford University Press.

Lambert, W. G. (1997), 'Processions to the Akītu House', *Revue d'Assyriologie et d'archéologie orientale*, 91: 49–80.

Lambert, W. G. (2013), *Babylonian Creation Myths*, Mesopotamian Civilizations 16, Winona Lake: Eisenbrauns.

Leichty, E., I. L. Finkel, and C. B. F. Walker (2019), *Catalogue of the Babylonian Tablets in the British Museum Volumes 4–5*, Münster: Zaphon.

Livingstone, A. (1986), *Mystical and Mythological Explanatory Works of Assyrian and Babylonian Scholars*, Oxford: Clarendon Press.

Livingstone, A. (1989), *Court Poetry and Literary Miscellanea*, State Archives of Assyria 3, Helsinki: Helsinki University Press.

Luukko, M. (2011), 'Šumu-iddina', in H. D. Baker (ed.), *The Prosopography of the Neo-Assyrian Empire 3/II Š-Z*, 1292–3, Helsinki: Neo-Assyrian Text Corpus Project.

MacGinnis, J., S. Parpola, A. Juboori, and M. Danti (2022), 'A Fragment of the Marduk Ordeal from the Mašqi Gate in Nineveh', *State Archives of Assyria Bulletin*, 28: 29–38.

Oshima, T. (2011), *Babylonian Prayers to Marduk*, Orientalische Religionen in der Antike 7, Tübingen: Mohr Siebeck.

Parpola, S. (1983), *Letters from Assyrian Scholars to the Kings Esarhaddon and Assurbanipal, Part II*, Alter Orient und Altes Testament 5 (2), Kevelaer: Butzon & Bercker.

Parpola, S. (1993), *Letters from Assyrian and Babylonian Scholars*, State Archives of Assyria 10, Helsinki: Helsinki University Press.

Pedersén, O. (1986), *Archives and Libraries in the City of Assur Part 2*, Studia Semitica Upsaliensia 8, Uppsala: Almqvist och Wiksell.

Pongratz-Leisten, B. (2015), *Religion and Ideology in Assyria*, Berlin: De Gruyter.

Pongratz-Leisten, B. (2017), 'The Assyrian State Rituals: Re-invention of Tradition', in S. Parpola (ed.), *Assyrian Royal Rituals and Cultic Texts*, xxxi–lxxv, Helsinki: Neo-Assyrian Text Corpus Project.

Postgate, J. N. (1973), *The Governor's Palace Archive*, Cuneiform Texts from Nimrud 2, London: British School of Archaeology in Iraq.

Reade, J. E. (1986), Introduction: Rassam's Babylonian Collection: The Excavations and the Archives', in E. Leichty (ed.), *Catalogue of the Babylonian Tablets in the British Museum Volume 6*, xiii–xxxvi, London: British Museum.

Reynolds, F. (2019), *A Babylon Calendar Treatise: Scholars and Invaders in the Late First Millennium BC*, Oxford: Oxford University Press.

Reynolds, F. (2021), 'Politics, Cult and Scholarship: Aspects of the Transmission History of Marduk and Ti'amat's Battle', in A. Kelly and C. Metcalf (eds), *Gods and Mortals in Early Greek and Near Eastern Mythology*, 58–79, Cambridge: Cambridge University Press.

Rubin, Z. M. (2021), 'The Scribal God Nabû in Ancient Assyrian Religion and Ideology', PhD dissertation, Brown University.

Wisnom, S. (2020), *Weapons of Words: Intertextual Competition in Babylonian Poetry; A Study of 'Anzû', 'Enūma Eliš', and 'Erra and Išum'*, Culture and History of the Ancient Near East 106, Leiden: Brill.

4

# *Enuma Elish* outside the cuneiform tradition

Eckart Frahm

*Enuma Elish*, the Babylonian 'Epic of Creation', is in many respects a rather insular and parochial text. Its protagonist, the god Marduk, completely outshines everyone else. The other deities starring in the text feature as little more than Marduk's ancestors, admirers, or as villains serving as *materia virtutis gloriaeque* ('sources of valour and glory') for him. In the end, when Marduk receives his fifty names, other great Mesopotamian gods such as Ea, Adad, and Enlil morph into mere aspects of his all-encompassing divine self. Finally, only one Mesopotamian urban centre is mentioned in the text: Marduk's holy city of Babylon, which is celebrated as the navel of the world. Given this almost obsessive focus on one single god and the city in which he was worshipped, it is no wonder that for some modern scholars, *Enuma Elish* should be classified as not an epic but a hymn: a poem about the One, rather than the many.[1]

Given the text's narrow outlook, one may wonder why it is that, from the very beginning, *Enuma Elish* was studied not only in Babylon and its satellite cities, where the cult of Marduk was centred, but also in other places, both within and outside the cuneiform world, and even beyond the lifespan of cuneiform culture. But that is clearly what happened. The earliest copies of the epic, which can be dated on palaeographic grounds to the ninth century BCE, are not from Babylon but from the Assyrian city of Ashur; the largest number of library tablets of *Enuma Elish* comes from seventh-century Nineveh, likewise in Assyria; and offshoots of the epic circulated in Syria and even in the Greek world well into the first centuries CE.

Somewhat paradoxically, it may be that an important reason for the widespread appeal of the text was exactly what made it, at the same time, so 'provincial': the enthusiasm with which it celebrated the autocracy of a single god. Western Asia experienced two crucial transformations during the first millennium: the rise of empires ruled by all-powerful monarchs and – undoubtedly related to that rise – henotheistic and to some extent monotheistic reconceptualizations of the divine. *Enuma Elish* provided a convenient blueprint for both phenomena, leading Neo-Assyrian imperial kings to pepper their inscriptions, which celebrated their unfettered authority, with quotes from and allusions to the text; and inspiring local elites all over the region to model the exaltation of their patron deities on theological ideas expressed in it (for the former, see, e.g. Weissert 1997: 191–202; for the latter, Oelsner 1994: 489–94).

Another selling point for the epic was that it offered an unusually intriguing account of how the cosmos – in its well-ordered, final iteration – came into being. Combining proto-philosophical reflections with dramatic battle scenes, it seems to have spoken to intellectuals and commoners alike. That both groups were among the text's target audience is explicitly stated in the epic itself. The final passage about Marduk's fifty names proclaims, 'Let the wise and the learned discuss them together, let the father repeat them and make the son grasp them, let them open the ears of shepherd and herdsman' (VII 146–8).[2] Such lofty directives were not merely aspirational: on the tablets written by Late Babylonian students as part of their elementary education, no literary text appears more frequently than *Enuma Elish* (Gesche 2000: 177–8). Recitations of the text in the course of important cultic festivals gave it additional cultural cachet. One of these ritual celebrations, the Babylonian New Year (or *akītu*) festival, had, like the epic, a major impact on religious life outside Babylonia.[3]

The 'export' of *Enuma Elish* and the Babylonian *akītu* festival to other places required their adaptation to local customs. Within Babylonia, the text of the epic was remarkably stable; the many manuscripts inscribed with it display very few semantically significant variants.[4] But even here, evidence can be found for the existence of religious discourses that questioned important premises of the text. Especially its portrayal of Marduk as both king of the gods and heroic conqueror of the forces of chaos was apparently met with surprisingly limited enthusiasm. Traditionally, these two roles were strictly divided in Mesopotamian religion: in Nippur, they were held by the stately god Enlil and his dashing son Ninurta, respectively. The citizens of Babylon, rather than accepting that Marduk, as outlined in *Enuma Elish*, had assumed the qualities of both deities, continued to long for a god who was youthful and vigorous, and found that god in Marduk's son Nabû. Although not mentioned a single time in the epic, Nabû played an important role in the Babylonian *akītu* festival (Debourse 2022: 23–5, 262–76, and passim), and a variety of Neo- and Late Babylonian texts portray him – and not Marduk – as the world's saviour and as a Ninurta-like slayer of primeval monsters (Lambert 2013: 275–7, 281–98, 326–9; Agnethler et al. 2022: 205–22).

If the seemingly rigid theology of *Enuma Elish* could be adapted to specific spiritual needs in Babylon, the centre of the Marduk cult, one would expect that such adaptation – of the epic, but also of the cultic framework in which it was recited – was even more common elsewhere. A cuneiform commentary known from manuscripts from Ashur, Nineveh, and Sippar, but not from Babylon, supports this assumption. The commentary correlates verses from *Enuma Elish* with myths and rituals associated with deities such as Nabû, Madanu, Zababa, Mar-biti, and even Ishtar of Nineveh, none of whom is mentioned in the epic. The treatise thus 'remythologizes' the story told in *Enuma Elish*, repudiating its 'Marduk First' ideology and espousing instead the spirit of a Mesopotamian religious *koiné* that the Babylonocentric message of the epic itself does not actually endorse (Frahm and Jiménez 2015).[5]

## The *akītu* festival beyond Babylon

The city of Ashur, the religious centre of the Assyrian Empire, became the setting of one of the best-documented attempts to adjust *Enuma Elish* and the *akītu* festival to local needs and customs. Caught in a love-hate relationship with Babylonia, Assyria had for centuries borrowed features of Babylon's religious culture, while at the same time trying to dominate its southern neighbour politically. Between 729 and 626 BCE, during the heyday of Assyrian power, the tensions produced by these conflicting interests erupted into a series of particularly violent military altercations between the two kingdoms. After crushing an anti-Assyrian rebellion in 689 BCE, the Assyrian king Sennacherib (704–681 BCE) destroyed large parts of Babylon (see also Sophus Helle in this volume). But he remained so obsessed with Babylonian culture that he decided, in the aftermath of the attack, to transfer key elements of Babylon's religious infrastructure to Assyria, repurposing them for the greater glory of his empire (for the following, see Frahm 2011: 349–57). It was a brazen act of cultural cannibalism.[6] Sennacherib refashioned the cultic landscape of Ashur after the model of Babylon and introduced a new *akītu* festival, celebrated – like the Babylonian one – at the beginning of the first month of the year. He also decreed that *Enuma Elish* should serve as the festival's 'cultic legend'. But it was a modified version of the epic, one in which the god Ashur (written An-šár, after the name of Marduk's primeval great-grandfather, Anshar) replaced Marduk, and the city of Ashur (under its ceremonial name Baltil) took the place of Babylon (Lambert 1997: 77–80). The rituals performed in the course of Sennacherib's new *akītu* festival in Ashur had a particularly Assyrian flavour as well: they included numerous deities, such as Amurru, Tishpak, and Sherua, who did not play any role in the Babylonian festivities (Pongratz-Leisten 1994: 115–31). Along with Ashur, Tiamat, and the 'creatures inside her', these gods and goddesses were depicted on the newly fashioned bronze gate erected in the entrance to Sennacherib's *akītu* house in Ashur, as revealed by a cuneiform tablet describing the gate (Grayson and Novotny 2014: 222–5).[7]

Ashur's sacred infrastructure suffered massive destruction during the brutal attack on the city by the Medes in 614 BCE. Two years later, when Nineveh was conquered by the combined forces of the Medes and the Babylonians, the Assyrian Empire came to an end, and the use of cuneiform writing in Assyria was abandoned. But despite all the mayhem, the celebration of the *akītu* festival in Ashur somehow continued. Many centuries after the fall of the empire, during the second century CE, inscriptions scratched by worshippers into pavement slabs within the precinct of a new, Parthian-era Ashur temple not only paid homage to Ashur and his wife Sherua, the old patron deities of the city, but also specified the dates on which the pilgrims visited the sanctuary. The first twelve days of the month of Nisannu, the very time when Assyria's imperial kings had celebrated the *akītu* festival, were particularly popular for worship at the temple (see most recently Livingstone 2009: 151–8).

It is not certain that the *akītu* festival celebrated in Ashur during the Late Parthian period still drew on the story told in *Enuma Elish*. But for other cities outside Babylonia – and beyond the sphere of cuneiform culture – there is compelling evidence that the story did stay alive and informed local cult practices. In the caravan city of Palmyra, located some 600 kilometres west of Babylon in the Syrian desert, the ruins of a large temple dedicated to the god Bel have yielded fragments of a bas-relief from the temple's peristyle that looks very much like a pictorial representation of the central battle scene described in *Enuma Elish*. The relief, which dates to *c.* 80 CE, shows, on the left, a god riding in a chariot getting ready to shoot arrows from his bow. His target, in the centre of the image, is a monster with a female torso and snake-like legs. A male deity on horseback and in military garb, flanked by other gods and goddesses, approaches the monster from the left. Despite the absence of epigraphs identifying these figures, the scene was soon interpreted as a visual representation of the divine battle against Tiamat, although with some deviations from its description in *Enuma Elish*. Bel-Marduk can be identified with the god in the chariot and Tiamat with the ophidian monster in the centre. The god on the horse, as has persuasively been argued by Lucinda Dirven, is most likely Bel-Marduk's son Nabû – who is not mentioned in *Enuma Elish*, but who was credited with heroic feats elsewhere and was demonstrably worshipped in Palmyra. The other figures to the left must be various local Palmyrene deities (for a discussion and drawing of the relief, see Dirven 1997).

Several indications strengthen this interpretation. The main deity worshipped in Palmyra was initially known as 'Bol', but later, apparently in a deliberate attempt to make him more like the Babylonian god Bel-Marduk, the Palmyrene priests rechristened him 'Bel'. His temple was consecrated in 32 CE on the sixth day of Nisan, that is, during the time when the Babylonian *akītu* festival had traditionally taken place; and like in Parthian Ashur, many pious inscriptions found at Palmyra were dated to the first days of the month of Nisan (Dirven 1997: 99–100). The scene shown on the Palmyra relief is, moreover, highly reminiscent of the depiction of the Assyrian version of *Enuma Elish* on the gate of Sennacherib's new *akītu* house in Ashur, as described in the cuneiform text mentioned above.

Palmyra was apparently not the only city to the west of Babylonia where (modified) versions of the story told in *Enuma Elish* were integrated into local cults well into the Common Era. A Syriac treatise known as 'The Acts of Sharbel', usually dated to the fifth century CE, discusses festivities in the city of Edessa (the predecessor to modern Urfa in southern Turkey) that were held on the eighth day of Nisan. The text claims that the whole population was assembled in the sacred precinct in the city centre, and so were 'all the deities: Nebo and Bel and their companions'. The Syriac 'Chronicle of Joshua the Stylite' confirms that such a festival was celebrated in Edessa during the late fifth century CE and adds the interesting observation that it was on this very occasion that 'the pagan myths used to be recited' (Dirven 1997: 113, n. 71).

## *Enuma Elish* in Neoplatonic philosophy

The chronicle's last remark raises the question of whether the text of *Enuma Elish*, presumably in an Aramaic rendering, was still known (and publicly disseminated) in Late Antiquity. Given the epic's many wordplays and 'etymographic' puns, both of which only work in Akkadian and cuneiform, the existence of a literal translation in some other language may not seem likely; but it is highly plausible that somewhat less faithful retellings circulated outside Mesopotamia. There is, in fact, unequivocal evidence for this in a text from about the same time as the aforementioned Syriac works: the Greek treatise 'Problems and Solutions Concerning First Principles' (ἀπορίαι καὶ λύσεις περὶ τῶν πρώτων ἀρχῶν) by the Neoplatonic philosopher Damascius (see the translation in Ahbel-Rappe 2010). This important Late Antique thinker, born around

460 CE in Damascus, was the last director of the Platonic Academy in Athens, which was closed by the Byzantine Emperor Justinian in 529 CE. In a passage dealing with approaches to the origins of the world in the Orphic tradition and in various eastern religions, Damascius writes:

> Among the barbarians, the Babylonians appear to pass over the idea of a single principle in silence and instead to assume two principles of the universe, Tauthe and Apason, making Apason the husband of Tauthe, and calling her the mother of the gods. From these was born an only-begotten child (παῖς), Moumis, who, it seems, brought about the intelligible world (τὸν νοητὸν κόσμον) from the first two principles. The same parents also gave rise to another generation, Dache and Dachos, and yet another, Kissare and Assoros, who in turn had three sons, Anos, Illinos, and Aos. Aos and Dauke begot a son called Belos, who they say is the demiurge.
>
> (Translation, with minor adjustments, after Haubold 2013: 36)

This concise account is remarkably close to, albeit not identical with, the theogony found at the beginning of *Enuma Elish*. Tauthe is Tiamat and Apason Apsû; Mummu reappears as Moumis and Laḫmu and Laḫamu as Dache and Dachos (with the change of the first consonant caused by the graphic similarity of the Greek letters lambda (Λ) and delta (Δ)); Kissare and Assoros are Kishar and Anshar (or perhaps Ashur, identified with the latter in Assyria); Anos is Anu, Aos and Dauke are Ea and Damkina, and Belos, needless to say, can be identified with Bel-Marduk, the main hero of the epic. There are also a few deviations from *Enuma Elish*. Damascius mentions the female member of each proto-divine couple first; Moumis is identified as a child of the first couple and considered, in a distinctly Neoplatonic allegorical reading, the originator of the 'intelligible world'; and Anu (Anos), who is unaccompanied in the theogony in Tablet I of the epic, is mentioned alongside Enlil (Illinos) and Ea (Aos), with the three of them forming a triad that was well-known from Mesopotamian religion and is also occasionally referenced in *Enuma Elish*, though not in Tablet I.[8] Damascius' goal in his treatise is to explore the interrelations of the elements of the highest levels of the Neoplatonic 'ontological hierarchy', the different gradations of being from the mundane to the sublime; and he is looking for (and finding) such elements in the theo-cosmogonies – the gods and cosmic forces – of other traditions, including the Babylonian one (Betegh 2002: 339).

Damascius also draws on the 'Chaldean Oracles', a Greek philosophical-spiritual treatise with alleged Babylonian origins that was popular among certain Neoplatonists. The fifth-century CE Neoplatonic philosopher Proclus discusses the 'Oracles' as well (Spanu 2020).[9] Among other things, Proclus claims that they explained the name of the Syro-Mesopotamian god Adad as comprising a sequence of two *ad*s, each meaning 'one' and standing for the One in the ontological hierarchy, while their combination in *Adad* represented the 'intelligible creator of the world' (note that Syriac 'one' is *ḥad*; see Talon 2001: 274; Ahbel-Rappe 2010: 477). Though the 'Chaldean Oracles' were not composed before the third century CE, it is noteworthy that one of the fifty names assigned to Marduk in *Enuma Elish* is Adad (VII 119–21a), and that this name is associated two verses later with 'Mummu' – Damascius' intelligible being that brought forth the νοητὸς κόσμος (Betegh 2002: 342–3). Even more striking is the fact that a cuneiform commentary on Marduk's fifty names from the seventh century BCE interprets the verses in question by deriving the element *ad* from Adad and translating it (in allusion to *mummu*) as *ummu*, 'mother'.[10] Proclus' note on Adad, inspired by the 'Chaldean Oracles', and Damascius' remark about Mummu, are in other words, much more consistent with the theology outlined in *Enuma Elish* and cuneiform discourses about the epic than they may appear at first.[11] A closer look at the role Mummu plays in *Enuma Elish* further confirms this point. Throughout the epic, Mummu is portrayed as a dynamic, creative, intelligent force. Later in the text, as the plot unfolds, this force appears in the form of a personal manifestation, Apsû's cunning vizier, who is defeated and appropriated by Ea, the crafty god. At the beginning, however, where his name, without divine determinative, is juxtaposed with that of Tiamat, Mummu represents what looks like an abstract principle very much in line with Damascius' and other Neoplatonists' ideas: a primeval intelligence that sets the process of creation in motion (Talon 2001: 267–8; Frahm 2013: 104–12; both with references to earlier literature).

Given Damascius' origin in Syria, his alleged visits to various Syrian temples, and his studies in the Egyptian city of Alexandria, his interest in 'eastern wisdom' does not come as a surprise. However, Damascius claims that he received his information on the Babylonian and other eastern theo-cosmogonies not from some eastern priests but from the Greek philosopher Eudemus of Rhodes, a student and 'companion' of Aristotle, who was active in Athens and Rhodes in the second half of the fourth century BCE (Wehrli 1955). Though Damascius paraphrases Eudemus rather than quoting him, meaning that he could have culled portions of his account from some other sources, scholars generally assume that Damascius' Babylonian cosmogony was indeed taken from Eudemus, possibly from a work on the history of theology that included a synoptic collection of various ancient creation stories (Betegh 2002: 354).[12] What exactly Eudemus' own sources were remains unknown.[13]

## Berossus's account of creation

Eudemus' short outline of the cosmogonic narrative found in *Enuma Elish* was composed some 1500 kilometres from where the epic had originated. And yet, in several respects it is more accurate than a summary of the epic that was written a generation or two after Eudemus in Babylon itself. The author of that summary, a priest of Bel by the name of Berossus, flourished during the first decades of the Hellenistic period, when in the wake of Alexander's eastern conquests a new dynasty of Greek-speaking rulers, the Seleucids, had assumed power in Babylonia.[14] Berossus' treatise, known as the *Babyloniaca* and like Eudemus' work written in Greek,[15] was dedicated to a Seleucid king by the name Antiochus, either Antiochus I (281–261) or Antiochus II (261–246).[16] Berossus' goal was to familiarize his new foreign overlords with Babylonian history, culture, and religion, and – in line with Egyptian claims that 'you Greeks are always children'[17] – show them how much older and thus more venerable Babylonian civilization was than the cultural foundations of the Greek world.

Berossus' original work is lost, and all that is left of it are second- or third-hand quotations from it in a variety of later, mostly Jewish and Christian writings. Most if not all of them draw on a first-century BCE summary of the text by the Greek scholar Alexander Polyhistor. Despite this problematic textual history, the basic outline of Berossus' work is clear (for the following, see Verbrugghe and Wickersham 1996: 43–6). Book 1 of the *Babyloniaca* began with a description of the geography of Babylonia, before zooming in on the region's early history. Berossus' account claims that many different people had settled there, initially living 'without discipline and order, like wild animals'. One day, however, a strange monster by the name of Oannes – half-fish and half-human – emerged from the sea to raise mankind out of this primitive stage. Oannes taught his primeval companions everything from agriculture to mathematics and writing, so that 'since this time, nothing further has been discovered'. Just as importantly, he also told them how the world had come into being.

At the beginning, Oannes claimed, the universe had been 'only darkness and water', but then some 'wondrous beings' materialized and engendered others: men with two or four wings and two faces, others with goat legs or horses' feet, bulls with human heads, and many more. Images of them were allegedly still preserved in the temple of Bel, i.e. Marduk, during Berossus' time. The primeval mistress of this chaotic host was 'a woman named Omorka, who in Chaldean is named Thalatth,[18] but in Greek her name is translated as Thalassa (i.e., Sea) or, with the same value of the letters in the name, Selene (i.e., Moon)'. Against this woman 'rose Bel and cut her in half'. From the two halves of his victim, he fashioned the earth and the heavens, destroying the 'creatures inside her'. However, according to Berossus, all this was just an 'allegory' foreshadowing what came next: the creation of human beings. The extant text provides two versions of how this crucial event happened. According to the first, 'when all was water and only the monsters were in it, the god (Bel) cut off his own head, and the other gods mixed the flood of blood with earth and created men'. In the second version, Bel 'cut through the darkness', separating the sky from the earth. The monsters, 'unable to endure the strength of the light', were destroyed, and Bel, 'seeing the empty and barren region',[19] ordered one of the other gods to 'cut off his own head and mix earth with the flowing blood' to create men.

Book 1 of the *Babyloniaca* apparently also mentioned that Bel surrounded Babylon with a wall, and included information on the stars and planets and on Babylonian festivals. Books 2 and 3 covered Babylonian history from the legendary antediluvian king to the Flood and then down to Berossus' own times.

Already a casual look at Berossus' creation story reveals some conspicuous parallels with *Enuma Elish*. The sea-like female creature at the beginning of time is clearly modelled on Tiamat; the 'creatures inside her'[20] can be identified with the hybrid monsters that fight at Tiamat's side in the epic; and Bel's creation of the world out of his female opponent's body echoes the plot of *Enuma Elish* too. Even the fact that Berossus' creation story is told by Oannes – who was identified with the antediluvian sage Adapa in Late Babylonian tradition – is in line with the epic. As has repeatedly been observed, *Enuma Elish*'s claim, in VII 145 and 157–8, that someone named 'the first one' (*maḫrû*) 'revealed' (*kullumu*) and 'recited' (*dabābu*) the text and had it 'put into writing' (*šaṭāru*) for the benefit of 'later generations' (*arkūtu*) may well be an allusion to Adapa-Oannes, though this is not explicitly stated in the epic.[21]

There are, however, also pronounced differences between Berossus' creation story and the one told in *Enuma Elish*. Tiamat is neither called 'Omorka' nor identified with the moon in the epic; darkness and light play no major role in it; and the strange story of Bel taking off his own head so that human beings can be created from his blood has no counterpart in the epic either. Unlike Eudemus, Berossus does not mention Apsû and Mummu, nor does he list the various divine generations that succeed them. Modern scholars have proposed different explanations for these deviations. Some have argued for the existence of variant cuneiform versions of the epic on which Berossus might have drawn (Dalley 2013), though with the exception of Sennacherib's Assyrian recension there is no clear evidence for such texts. Others have claimed that Berossus was deeply steeped in Greek philosophical thinking and amalgamated Babylonian with Greek lore to reach his target audience, the Seleucid elite, more effectively. For example, Berossus' reference to primeval creatures that were two-faced, male and female, and human- as well as animal-like, could have been inspired by the work of the pre-Socratic philosopher Empedocles.[22] A third possible scenario is that Berossus' account includes interpolations made by later authors, especially Jewish and Christian ones, who wished to make his text more compatible with their own doctrines. Berossus' alleged claim that at the beginning there was not only water but also darkness could thus have been added to better align the text with the statement in the first creation account in Genesis: 'and darkness covered the face of the deep (or, the sea)' (Genesis 1.2; see the discussion in Horowitz 1998: 133). Finally, as argued especially by Paul-Alain Beaulieu (2021), Berossus may have 'reinterpreted' the creation account in *Enuma Elish* by drawing on arcane (and partially oral) inner-Babylonian traditions. Described by Seneca as an 'interpreter of Bel' ('Berosos qui Belum intepretatus est', *Naturales Quaestiones* 3.29.1),[23] he may have seen himself as a late successor of the culture hero and antediluvian 'intellectual' Oannes-Adapa, the 'first one' to 'expound' the text. Berossus' identification of Thalatth (i.e. Tiamat) with the moon-goddess Selene, for example, might be traced to a cuneiform text, known from Hellenistic times, that claims that an image of Tiamat could be seen on the face of the moon (Beaulieu 2021: 156).[24] It is beyond the scope of this chapter to establish which of these scenarios comes closest to the truth, but it should be stressed that they are not mutually exclusive. The various 'idiosyncrasies' that have been noted in Berossus' account can have multiple different causes.

## *Enuma Elish* and the first creation account in the Hebrew Bible

Even though neither Eudemus (as attested via Damascius) nor Berossus quotes the epic by its ancient title, divine names and other details leave no doubt that both authors had *Enuma Elish* in mind when summarizing what they knew about Babylonian beliefs regarding the origins of the world. Another ancient creation account, the one found in Genesis 1–2.4, represents a more complicated case.[25] It is the most famous and influential creation story of all, and while it lacks overt parallels with *Enuma Elish*, there are still several striking similarities between the two texts.

The Genesis 1 account begins with a short introductory statement about the universe in its primeval, chaotic state, and God's transformative role in putting an end to that situation by creating the world. The process, described in the following verses, takes a period of seven days and includes the separation of light and darkness; the fashioning of a celestial firmament; the division of land and sea; the emergence of vegetation; the placing of heavenly bodies onto the sky; the creation of animals in the sea, the air, and on land; and, on day six, the creation of human beings. By giving all things and creatures names, God establishes their specific identity. On the seventh day, having finished his work, God rests from his exertions.

It is all but obvious that this story is in several respects quite different from the one told in *Enuma Elish*. In Genesis 1–2.4, an almighty deity is in charge from the very beginning. There is no sea- or dragon-like female creature of massive proportions that must first be defeated. The biblical god creates the cosmos without access to any primeval organic matter, while Marduk has to use the body of his slain opponent to do so; and no other gods or monsters appear in the biblical account. But ever since the first edition of *Enuma Elish* was published, tellingly entitled 'The Chaldean Account of Genesis' (Smith 1875), scholars have also found overlaps between the two accounts. These include the importance of naming and 'separating' in the creation process (notably, *Enuma Elish* begins with the verse 'When heaven on high had not been named'); the references to earth, sky, water, and sea at the beginning of the two accounts; the (otherwise rather un-biblical) idea that the heavenly bodies can serve as 'signs'[26]; the correspondence between the seven tablets into which *Enuma Elish* is divided and the seven days of creation in the biblical account; and the fact that in both accounts the creation of human beings (described in Tablet VI of *Enuma Elish* and ascribed to the sixth day in the biblical text) is followed by divine rest.[27]

Since first lines always stand out (even more so if they deal with 'first things'), it is noteworthy that the first verses of *Enuma Elish* and the creation account in Genesis share a particularly large number of features, marked in bold below.

*Enuma Elish* I 1–5 (translation modified)

**When** the **heavens** (***šamāmū***) on high had not been named
and the **earth** below not given a name,
**primordial** (***rēštû***) Apsû, who fathered them,
and the **creative force** (*mummu*) **Tiamat**, who gave birth to them all,
were mingling together their **waters**.

Genesis 1.1-2 (NRSV, translation modified)

In the **beginning** (***b<sup>e</sup>-rēšīt***) (**when**) God created the **heavens** (***šāmayim***) and the **earth**, (but) the **earth** was (still) a formless void and darkness covered the face of **the sea**/the deep (***t<sup>e</sup>hôm***), and God's **(creative) spirit** (*rûaḥ*) swept over the face of the **waters**.

To be sure, quite a few of the elements highlighted here are found in other creation accounts as well (as pointed out, with many examples, by Bauks 1997). But the sheer quantity of correspondences (some of which are exact on the lexical level) makes it hard to deny the likelihood of some genetic relationship between the two accounts. What is particularly striking is that both refer to some kind of 'creative spirit' (*mummu* in *Enuma Elish* and *rûaḥ* in the biblical account) as being engaged in the creation process (Frahm 2013). As discussed above, the involvement of an intelligent abstract force in the Babylonian creation account was also stressed by Eudemus/Damascius, suggesting that later students of the epic considered it a particularly important feature of the text.

In contrast to Berossus and Eudemus, the 'priestly author' credited by modern scholars with the composition of the first creation account in the Bible was not interested in summarizing and explaining the Babylonian *Epic of Creation*. What he produced instead can be characterized as a 'counter-story' to the epic, aimed at thoroughly demythologizing it and implicitly criticizing some of its central tenets (Sparks 2007). It remains unclear when he wrote the account and whether he had access to the original version of *Enuma Elish* or to some later adaptation of it. Genesis 1 might have been composed in Babylon during the time of the 'Babylonian exile', when many members of the Judean elite, in the wake of their deportation from Jerusalem in 597 BCE, must have come across the main works of Babylonian literature; but since the epic was apparently known outside Babylonia as well, the biblical author could also have encountered it elsewhere and at some later point. Other segments of the so-called 'Primeval History' – the historical 'prologue' of the Hebrew Bible in Genesis 1–11 that is set in Mesopotamia – seem likewise based on literary models from the cuneiform world.[28] The story of Adam and Eve may draw on *Gilgamesh* and *Adapa* (which might also have influenced the 'Enoch episode' in Genesis 5); the Cain and Abel story on the *Theogony of Dunnu*; the genealogies in Genesis 5 on the 'Dynastic Chronicle' or some similar text; the short tale of the Nephilim on motifs from *Gilgamesh*; and the biblical Flood story on the Babylonian Flood narrative as it is known from *Atra-hasis* and *Gilgamesh*.[29]

## Conclusion

*Enuma Elish* circulated outside Babylonia for more than a millennium. Various versions of the epic provided the mythological background for cultic rituals in cities stretching from seventh-century BCE Ashur through first-century CE Palmyra to fifth-century CE Edessa. In the third century BCE, the Babylonian priest Berossus wrote a summary of the text that focused on the wondrous and the heroic, to impress an outside audience: the new rulers of the Seleucid Dynasty. The author of the first creation account in the Bible, in contrast, speaking to an inner audience – those who believed in the god of Israel – used the epic as a template for a thoroughly revised version of how the world had come into being. And in yet another take on *Enuma Elish*, the fifth-century CE philosopher Damascius, drawing on the work of his fourth-century BCE predecessor Eudemus, gave a detailed account of the beginning of the text in order to demonstrate the existence of early eastern analogues for his own conception of the 'ontological hierarchy'. Although it is traceable only through fragmentary and secondary evidence, the legacy left by the Babylonian *Epic of Creation* outside the cuneiform world was a strong one. Clearly, this remarkable text, its theo-ideological rigidity notwithstanding, had a powerful message to convey that left a significant impact on a great variety of people.

## Further reading

On the reception of *Enuma Elish* in Babylonia and Assyria, see Reynolds (2021) as well as Reynolds in this volume. For evidence from Palmyra and Edessa for a continuing interest during the first centuries of the common era in stories about Marduk's (and Nabû's) battles, and religious festivities based on them, see Dirven (1997). The *akītu* festival in Parthian Ashur is discussed by Livingstone (2009). For the creation account communicated and discussed by Eudemus and Damascius and its close links to *Enuma Elish*, see Talon (2001); for its philosophical underpinnings, see Betegh (2002). For Berossus, see the volume *The World of Berossos* (2013), with contributions by Dalley and Haubold specifically dealing with *Enuma Elish*; Beaulieu (2021) and George (2021) cover similar ground. The epic's possible relationship with the biblical creation account in Genesis 1–2.4 is discussed by Sparks (2007) and Frahm (2013).

## Notes

1 See, e.g. Michalowski (1990: 383–4). In this essay, I will refer to *Enuma Elish* as an 'epic' – the text identifies itself as the 'song of Marduk' (*zamāru ša Marduk*, VII 161), but it also recounts the 'epic' story of his rise to power.

2 I see no reason to posit, as other scholars have, that 'shepherd' and 'herdsman' are metaphors for the king in these lines.

3 For the relation between *Enuma Elish* and the *akītu* festival, see Céline Debourse in this volume. For the latest editions of the texts describing the ritual acts performed in the course of these festivals, see Çağırgan and Lambert (1991–93) and Debourse (2022, with discussion of the recitation of *Enuma Elish* on p. 255–62). Debourse emphasizes the fluid nature of Babylonian cult rituals and their adaptability to political and cultural change.

4 Note that the last two lines of the epic found in Babylonian copies seem to be absent in Assyrian ones; see Fadhil and Jiménez (2021: 220–8).

5 For general overviews of the reception history of *Enuma Elish*, see Frahm (2011: 345–68), and, with a focus on Babylonia, Reynolds (2021: 58–79). See also Frances Reynolds in this volume.

6 I owe this term to Eli Tadmor.

7 It is noteworthy that the Assyrian version of *Enuma Elish* does not mention any of these deities, a discrepancy between myth and ritual similar to the one found in Babylon. On the connection between myth and ritual, see also Debourse in this volume.

8 See IV 146, V 80, VI 64, VII 6, VII 163; see also V 8, VII 136, VII 149.

9 The original text of the *Oracles* is lost, and Proclus' 'commentary' too is only known from excerpts.

10 For this (not completely certain) reading, which was first proposed by Enrique Jiménez, see Frahm (2013: 106–7). Sumerian **ad** is usually translated not *ummu*, 'mother', but *abu*, 'father'. For the commentary on Marduk's names, see Marc Van De Mieroop in this volume.

11 At the risk of overinterpreting the evidence, it is tempting, in this context, to revisit the spelling AD.AD for *abbū*, 'fathers', which is found in several manuscripts of *Enuma Elish* (see I 14, IV 27.33.64.79.84, V 72.78.89.118.131, VII 13). That such writings, anticipating the 'Chaldean Oracles', were meant to also invoke the god Adad cannot be proven, but it does seem possible.

12 In Betegh's view, the alternative – that the passage stems from a 'doxographical digression' in a systematic work of Eudemus, possibly his *Physics* – is less likely.

13 Already in the nineteenth century, a verse in Homer's *Iliad* – 'Okeanos, origin of the world, and mother Tethys' (*Iliad* 14.201) – has been compared to the characterization of Apsû and Tiamat (~Tethys?) in the first lines of *Enuma Elish*; for discussion, see West (1997: 147–8, 375–6) and Lardinois (2018: 895–919). However, the parallel does not seem specific enough to suggest that Homer drew directly on some version of *Enuma Elish*.

14 For a recent collection of essays on Berossus and his work, see Haubold et al. (2013). For Berossus as 'a scholar between two worlds', see Stevens (2019: 94–120).

15 Geller (2012: 101–9) has argued that the text was originally written in Aramaic and only later translated into Greek; but other scholars have not accepted this view. See e.g. Beaulieu (2021: 158, n. 5) and Stevens (2019: 95, n. 1).

16 Editions of the *Babyloniaca* are listed by Beaulieu (2021: 147, n. 2). In the following, I use Verbrugghe and Wickersham (1996: 13–91). For the date of the work, see most recently van der Spek (2018: 138–40). Bach (2013: 157–62) has suggested that Berossus is to be identified with Bēl-rē'ûšunu, the high priest of the Esagil temple in 258 BCE. This would make a later date more likely, but the identification is not certain and has been questioned, for example, by Stevens (2019: 114–19).

17 As reported in Plato's *Timaeus* (22a), this is what an Egyptian priest had allegedly said to Solon.

18 As many scholars have observed, the Greek is probably corrupt here. Originally, Berossus must have provided a name closer to Babylonian *Tiamat*.

19 The passage is reminiscent of the reference to 'Tohu wa-bohu' in Genesis 1.2, but it should be noted that 'barren' is an emendation – the text actually has 'fertile'. Haubold (2013: 41) accepts the original reading and assumes that the passage refers to the Babylonian soil's potential for cultivation.

20 The same expression is used in Sennacherib's text about the bronze gate of the *akītu* house; see above.

21 See, most recently, Beaulieu (2021: 150–3, 166–7), who argues (although some uncertainty remains) that the name Oannes goes back to **umun**, the word for *bēl(u)*, 'Lord', in the Sumerian Emesal dialect.

22 Thus Haubold (2013: 38); but see Beaulieu (2021: 154–5) for an attempt to establish a Mesopotamian background for the passage.

23 For the Assyrian and Babylonian commentary tradition of the first millennium BCE, see Frahm (2011).

24 For some of the lesser-known cuneiform sources Berossus might have used, see also Dalley (2013) and George (2021: 185–98).

25 The secondary literature on the first creation account in the Bible is enormous and cannot be summarized here. For a particularly detailed study, see Bauks (1997).
26 See Genesis 1.14 and *Enuma Elish* V 23. Hebrew *'ôtôt* corresponds to Akkadian *ittu*, plural *ittātu*.
27 In the biblical account, this is of course also an aetiology for the Shabbat.
28 Recent studies on the sources, Mesopotamian and otherwise, of the Primeval History include, among many others, Carr (2020) and Hendel (2005: 23–36).
29 Of course, much of this remains debated, as a scholarly consensus on the main sources of the Primeval History is not at hand. The Nephilim episode has recently been linked to a Graeco-Philistine source; see Scodel (2021: 169–84). I will discuss the possible but unexplored connection between the story of Cain and Abel and the 'Theogony of Dunnu' in a forthcoming article.

## Bibliography


Agnethler, H., E. Gogokhia, E. Jiménez, A. Pilloni, and A. Setälä (2022), 'Eine spätbabylonische synkretistische Hymne an Nabû', *Journal of Cuneiform Studies*, 74: 205–22.

Ahbel-Rappe, S. (2010), *Damascius' Problems and Solutions Concerning First Principles*, Oxford: Oxford University Press.

Bach, J. (2013), 'Berossos, Antiochos und die Babyloniaka', *Ancient West and East*, 12: 157–80.

Bauks, M. (1997), *Die Welt am Anfang: Zum Verhältnis von Vorwelt und Weltentstehung in Gen 1 und in der altorientalischen Literatur*, Wissenschaftliche Monographien zum Alten und Neuen Testament 74, Neukirchen-Vluyn: Neukirchener Verlag.

Beaulieu, P.-A. (2021), 'Berossus and the Creation Story', *Journal of Ancient Near Eastern History*, 8: 147–70.

Betegh, G. (2002), 'On Eudemus Fr. 150 (Wehrli)', in I. Bodnár and W. M. Fortenbaugh (eds), *Eudemus of Rhodes*, 337–57, New Brunswick: Transaction Publishers.

Çağırgan, G. and W. G. Lambert (1991–1993), 'The Late Babylonian Kislimu Ritual for Esagil', *Journal of Cuneiform Studies*, 43–45: 89–106.

Carr, D. M. (2020), *The Formation of Genesis 1–11: Biblical and Other Precursors*, Oxford: Oxford University Press.

Dalley, S. (2013), 'First Millennium BC Variation in Gilgamesh, Atrahasis, the Flood Story and the Epic of Creation: What Was Available to Berossos?', in J. Haubold, G. B. Lanfranchi, R. Rollinger, and J. M. Steele (eds), *The World of Berossos*, Classica et Orientalia 5, 165–76, Wiesbaden: Harrassowitz Verlag.

Debourse, C. (2022), *Of Priests and Kings: The Babylonian New Year Festival in the Last Age of Cuneiform Culture*, Culture and History of the Ancient Near East 127, Leiden: Brill.

Dirven, L. (1997), 'The Exaltation of Nabû', *Die Welt des Orients*, 28: 96–116.

Fadhil, A. A. and E. Jiménez (2021), 'Literary Texts from the Sippar Library II: The Epic of Creation', *Zeitschrift für Assyriologie und Vorderasiatische Archäologie*, 111: 191–230.

Frahm, E. (2011), *Babylonian and Assyrian Text Commentaries: Origins of Interpretation*, Guides to the Mesopotamian Textual Record 5, Münster: Ugarit-Verlag.

Frahm, E. (2013), 'Creation and the Divine Spirit in Babel and Bible: Reflections on *mummu* in *Enuma Elish* I 4 and *rûah* in Genesis 1:2', in D. S. Vanderhoof and

A. Winitzer (eds), *Literature as Politics, Politics as Literature: Essays on the Ancient Near East in Honor of Peter Machinist*, 97–116, Winona Lake: Eisenbrauns.

Frahm, E. and E. Jiménez (2015), 'Myth, Ritual, and Interpretation: The Commentary on Enūma eliš I–VII and a Commentary on Elamite Month Names', *Hebrew Bible and Ancient Israel*, 3–4: 293–343.

Geller, M. J. (2012), 'Berossos on Kos from the View of Common Sense Geography', in K. Geus and M. Thiering (eds), *Common Sense Geography and Mental Modelling*, Max-Planck-Institut für Wissenschaftsgeschichte Preprints 426, 101–9, Berlin: Max-Planck-Institut für Wissenschaftsgeschichte.

George, A. R. (2021), 'Berossus and Babylonian Cosmogony', in A. Kelly and C. Metcalf (eds), *Gods and Mortals in Early Greek and Near Eastern Mythology*, 185–98, Cambridge: Cambridge University Press.

Gesche, P. (2000), *Schulunterricht in Babylonien im ersten Jahrtausend v. Chr.*, Alter Orient und Altes Testament 275, Münster: Ugarit-Verlag.

Grayson, A. K. and J. Novotny (2014), *The Royal Inscriptions of Sennacherib, King of Assyria (704–681 BC), Part 2*, Royal Inscriptions of the Neo-Assyrian Period 3 (2), Winona Lake: Eisenbrauns.

Haubold, J. (2013), '"The Wisdom of the Chaldeans": Reading Berossos, Babyloniaca Book 1', in J. Haubold, G. B. Lanfranchi, R. Rollinger, and J. M. Steele (eds), *The World of Berossos*, Classica et Orientalia 5, 31–45, Wiesbaden: Harrassowitz Verlag.

Haubold, J., G. B. Lanfranchi, R. Rollinger, and J. M. Steele (eds, 2013), *The World of Berossos*, Classica et Orientalia 5, Wiesbaden: Harrassowitz.

Hendel, R. (2005), 'Genesis 1–11 and Its Mesopotamian Problem', in E. S. Gruen (ed.), *Cultural Borrowings and Ethnic Appropriations in Antiquity*, 23–36, Stuttgart: Steiner.

Horowitz, W. (1998), *Mesopotamian Cosmic Geography*, Mesopotamian Civilizations 8, Winona Lake: Eisenbrauns.

Lambert, W. G. (1997), 'The Assyrian Recension of Enūma Eliš', in H. Waetzoldt and H. Hauptmann (eds), *Assyrien im Wandel der Zeiten*, Compte rendu de la Rencontre Assyriologique lnternationale 39, Heidelberger Studien zum Alten Orient 6, 77–80, Heidelberg: Heidelberger Orientverlag.

Lambert, W. G. (2013), *Babylonian Creation Myths*, Mesopotamian Civilizations 16, Winona Lake: Eisenbrauns.

Lardinois, A. (2018), 'Eastern Myths for Western Lies: Allusions to Near Eastern Mythology in Homer's Iliad', *Mnemosyne*, 71: 895–919.

Livingstone, A. (2009), 'Remembrance at Ashur: The Case of the Dated Aramaic Memorials', in M. Luukko, S. Svärd, and R. Mattila (eds), *Of God(s), Trees, Kings, and Scholars: Neo-Assyrian and Related Studies in Honour of Simo Parpola*, 151–8, Helsinki: Finnish Oriental Society.

Michalowski, P. (1990), 'Presence at the Creation', in T. Abusch, J. Huehnergard, and P. Steinkeller (eds), *Lingering Over Words: Studies in Ancient Near Eastern Literature in Honor of William L. Moran*, Harvard Semitic Studies 37, 381–96, Atlanta: Scholars Press.

Oelsner, J. (1994), 'Henotheistische Tendenzen in der spätbabylonischen Religion?', in H. Preissler and H. M. Seiwert (eds), *Gnosisforschung und Religionsgeschichte: Festschrift für Kurt Rudolph zum 65. Geburtstag*, 489–94, Marburg: Diagonal.

Pongratz-Leisten, B. (1994), *Ina šulmi īrub: Die kulttopographische und ideologische Programmatik der akītu-Prozession in Babylonien und Assyrien im 1. Jahrtausend v. Chr.*, Mainz: Verlag Philipp von Zabern.

Reynolds, F. (2021), 'Politics, Cult, and Scholarship: Aspects of the Transmission History of Marduk and Ti'amat's Battle', in A. Kelly and C. Metcalf (eds), *Gods and Mortals in Early Greek and Near Eastern Mythology*, 58–79, Cambridge: Cambridge University Press.

Scodel, R. (2021), 'Heroes and Nephilim: Sex between Gods and Mortals', in A. Kelly and C. Metcalf (eds), *Gods and Mortals in Early Greek and Near Eastern Mythology*, 169–84, Cambridge: Cambridge University Press.

Smith, G. (1875), *The Chaldean Account of Genesis*, London: Sampson Low, Marston, Scale and Rivingston.

Spanu, N. (2020), *Proclus and the Chaldean Oracles: A Study on Proclean Exegesis, with a Translation and Commentary of Proclus' Treatise on Chaldean Philosophy*, London: Routledge.

Sparks, K. L. (2007), '*Enūma elish* and Priestly Mimesis: Elite Emulation in Nascent Judaism', *Journal of Biblical Literature*, 126: 625–48.

Stevens, K. (2019), *Between Greece and Babylonia: Hellenistic Intellectual History in Cross-Cultural Perspective*, Cambridge: Cambridge University Press.

Talon, P. (2001), '*Enūma Eliš* and the Transmission of Babylonian Cosmology to the West', in R. M. Whiting (ed.), *Mythology and Mythologies: Methodological Approaches to Intercultural Influences*, Melammu Symposia 2, 265–78, Helsinki: Neo-Assyrian Text Corpus Project.

Van der Spek, R. J. (2018), 'Debates on the World of Berossus', *Zeitschrift für altorientalische und biblische Rechtsgeschichte*, 24: 137–51.

Verbrugghe, G. P. and J. M. Wickersham (1996), *Berossos and Manetho, Introduced and Translated: Native Traditions in Ancient Mesopotamia and Egypt*, Ann Arbor: University of Michigan Press.

Wehrli, F. (1955), *Eudemus von Rhodos*, Die Schule des Aristoteles: Texte und Kommentar 7, Basel: Schwabe.

Weissert, E. (1997), 'Creating a Political Climate: Literary Allusions to Enūma Eliš in Sennacherib's Account of the Battle of Halule', in H. Waetzoldt and H. Hauptmann (eds), *Assyrien im Wandel der Zeiten*, Compte rendu de la Rencontre Assyriologique Internationale 39, Heidelberger Studien zum Alten Orient 6, 191–202, Heidelberg: Heidelberger Orientverlag.

West, M. L. (1997), *The East Face of Helicon*, Oxford: Oxford University Press.

# 5

# Monstrous mothers and metal bands: *Enuma Elish* today

Gina Konstantopoulos

For a text concerned with beginnings, *Enuma Elish* commands a remarkable range of, if not endings, at least afterlives. The text lives on through these resonances, echoes that manifest as it is interpreted in cultures and contexts outside of its Mesopotamian origin. It reaches across boundaries established by distance and time; or, most often, both. In some instances, *Enuma Elish* resurfaces close to its Mesopotamian origin, influencing material in ancient Greek or biblical contexts. These echoes, such as they appear, are considered in detail in the contribution by Eckart Frahm in this volume. My own focus is on later resonances, on how *Enuma Elish* resurfaces, sometimes in a very different form, in modern reception.[1]

The nature of our reception of *Enuma Elish* – with early references found in Greek and biblical material, and then little to be seen until the latter half of the nineteenth century CE – is an expected and inevitable consequence of the nature of Mesopotamia's own cultural transmission and the survival of Mesopotamia itself. The early references to *Enuma Elish* were able to pull on lines of influence that directly connected back to the sources themselves. *Enuma Elish,* especially with its use in the *akītu,* or New Year's, festival, had a particularly long reach, with the latest references dating to the Seleucid period (see Céline Debourse in this volume). Later references, however, had to wait for the rediscovery of the text of *Enuma Elish* itself and its subsequent translation. We thus see a considerable gap between the earliest examples of reception and this later group. As a whole, most examples will track back to the source text itself, rather than branching out along lines of influence, pulling from the works that were influenced and impacted by *Enuma Elish*, to thereafter develop their own influences in turn.

It is these later examples of reception that I will focus on in my paper; however, we find here yet another division within this later and more limited sub-set of receptions. First, we have works that represent a reception of the text of *Enuma Elish* as a whole. These examples respond to the major themes of the text, or use specific lines of the composition, either in the original Akkadian or in translation. This is the direct reception most often seen in the use of *Enuma Elish* by a number of (often Nordic) metal bands, for example.[2] Amongst the metal bands using *Enuma Elish* in their songs, I would also reference here the Spanish Gothic/Power metal band Enuma

Elish (2003–13), which took its name from the text and whose music often invoked Mesopotamian or biblical themes; the Spanish Pagan black metal band Itnuveth, whose 2020 album *Enuma Elish* included a similarly titled song; the German death metal band Eridu, with the song 'Enuma Elish' belonging to their own eponymous 2023 album. Eridu's entire 2023 album pulls on the themes of the text, and will be discussed in greater detail further on in this paper.[3]

The second type of reception draws on individual elements of the text, principally invoking specific figures from its narrative, refashioning them to fit a purpose that may be quite distinct from their original function or form. This approach is most often seen with the use (or rather, reuse) of the figures of Tiamat, Apsû (as a concept more than as a being), and Marduk. The last of these three is, of course, a deity of importance and standing that reaches far beyond the text of *Enuma Elish*. For Tiamat and Apsû, as well as the occasional addition of figures such as Qingu, their prominence is primarily established through *Enuma Elish* alone, and thus the case for tying any later appearances to the core text is more straightforward.

A final avenue of reception studies lies in considering the manifestations (or echoes) of *Enuma Elish* as seen in present-day Iraq and its wider modern communities. The ancient has an undeniable impact on and power in the present, for both modern Iraqis and the wider communities and peoples (Assyrian, Chaldean, and others) living in Iraq or primarily in diaspora.[4] Though a full study of reception works in the modern Iraqi – or even, more broadly, Arabic – context is beyond the scope of this present study, I would nevertheless speak briefly on the subject. As elsewhere, *Gilgamesh* remains the most popular focus for works of modern reception, and *Enuma Elish* is much less frequently seen. The modern Iraqi poet Saadi Yousef references both, with each text serving as the focal point of different works, in the poem entitled 'Home of Delights' and the poetical play *When on High*. The latter draws a clear link to the opening lines of *Enuma Elish*, and the creation myth continues to serve as inspiration: in one passage, Yousef describes the creation of the world from Tiamat's corpse, moving beyond the details provided in the original poem to describe the creation of the Tigris and Euphrates rivers (Assadi and Naamneh 2018: 53). As with other forms of reception, *Enuma Elish* serves here as a launching point for unique interpretations.

## Complete echoes and early histories

By and large, the reception of the text relies on the accessibility, or at least existence, of translations from its original Akkadian. As a major literary work, and moreover a work with a clear degree of crossover and engagement with both biblical and Classical spheres, *Enuma Elish* attracted attention from the earliest days of Assyriological scholarship. Tablets belonging to the library of the Neo-Assyrian ruler Assurbanipal (*r.* 669–631 BCE) were excavated by the British Museum from the site of Nineveh in the mid-nineteenth century CE. These became some of the earliest-known modern-day exemplars of the text and were published in handcopy in 1902.[5] However, the epic itself had been accessible to the scholarly public for several decades before the tablets were themselves published. In 1876, George Smith published the earliest translation of the text, presented under the title *The Chaldean Account of Genesis,* thus drawing on its biblical links.[6] Such a title may have reflected the author's own interest, but it was also a shrewd marketing scheme: public attention was focused on how the then-recent Assyriological discoveries overlapped with, and provided context for, the Bible (Bohrer 2003: 99–102). Further translations followed Smith's edition, including German editions by Peter Jensen (in both 1890 and 1900) and by Friedrich Delitzsch (in 1896).[7]

Other editions and translations of *Enuma Elish* soon followed. I will discuss here only the translations that are most relevant to the aims of this study.[8] Many of the subsequent publications of the text incorporated new finds, filling in some of the previously existing lacunae in the text, which remains incomplete. For later editions, their major contribution lay in translating the text into another language, allowing it to reach a new modern audience – or a less modern one, in the case of Antonius Deimel's (1912) translation of the text into Latin. The next major editions were completed by D. D. Luckenbill (1921) and by Stephen Langdon (1923). Both publications included a number of new sources from recent excavations at the city of Assur.

These developments were swiftly followed by several translations, including into German (Ebeling 1926) and French (Labat 1935). Subsequent English translations maintained the link to the biblical material in their framing and, often, titles: Alexander Heidel's 1942 edition was entitled *The Babylonian Genesis* and included a discussion of both related Mesopotamian material, principally other cosmological texts, and biblical parallels. *Enuma Elish* was also used as an Assyriological teaching text, with a composite cuneiform handcopy edition of the text for students to practise working with both the Akkadian language and cuneiform script used to write it (Lambert and Parker 1966; Talon 2005).

Recent scholarship, particularly of the last decade, has seen a further increase in editions of *Enuma Elish.* The most recent 'authoritative' text edition of the poem was published by Wilfred Lambert in 2013, but had been long in coming: one can find references to the edition as a work in progress throughout decades of Lambert's scholarship, and, though it was completed before his death, the work was published posthumously (Lambert 2013). Lambert's work is chronologically bookended by two extensive studies on the epic, both in German: an edition by Thomas Kämmerer and Kai Metzler (2012) and a study by Gösta Gabriel (2014). The text has also, over the years, been translated into an increasing number of languages, including Italian, Spanish, and Japanese (Furlani 1958; Peinado 2008; Tsukimoto 2022). This scholarly attention has increased the reach of *Enuma Elish* to a degree that is, with the exception of *Gilgamesh,* unmatched amongst Mesopotamian material. In turn, that reach has resulted in a wide variety of responses and receptions to the text in popular culture.

## Responding and restaging: The text as a whole

With the historical stage now set, I turn to receptions of *Enuma Elish* that respond to the text as a whole or to its major themes. Once the work was relatively accessible to a popular, non-academic audience, works of modern and popular reception could react to it in various ways, and through a variety of interpretative means and media.

In general, translations and receptions of a work range in how closely they adhere to – or how far and creatively they stray from – the original text. Mesopotamian texts have only recently, in the most part, reached the stage of integration that seems to prompt full-on creative (re)interpretations, as well as fully derivative works. Here, the former may be taken to mean translations or editions that function as fully independent creative works and do not necessarily seek as their main aim to communicate a translation of the original work. Within the Classical sphere, we may consider as a model of reinterpretation works such as Derek Walcott's epic poem *Omeros* or Alice Oswald's 2011 *Memorial*, which the author describes as an 'excavation' of the *Iliad*.

For Mesopotamian material, this level of integration is typically, and primarily, seen with works responding to the *Epic of Gilgamesh*.[9] This is unsurprising, given the overall popularity of *Gilgamesh*. The text is also the Mesopotamian text that most frequently finds a home on the stage, with a number of theatrical reinterpretations and restagings.[10] Despite this, theatrical attention has been focused on other Mesopotamian texts – and contexts, as seen in a trio of Sargonid-set plays by Assyriologist Selena Wisnom.[11] As a setting, Mesopotamia has not received the level of attention given to ancient Egypt, to say nothing of ancient Greece or Rome. However, we may still find references to specific texts, as well as the setting as a whole, in film or on stage.

This includes *Enuma Elish*: in 2016, a theatrical performance of the epic was staged near Munich. It was brought to the stage through the collaboration between a local theater group, Meta Theater Group, and the Assyrian Mesopotamian Association of Augsburg. Following its performance in Munich, the play travelled to perform in the cities of Augsburg and Wiesbaden, reaching a larger audience (BarAbraham 2016). Unfortunately, the production was relatively small in scale and circulation. It received substantially less attention than most productions of *Gilgamesh*, and as a result we have less detailed information about its particulars. Much must be divined from the few reviews of the production, and they detail a play that remained close to the original text in most regards.

Moving to a genre connected to theater, we also see *Enuma Elish* surface in modern poetry.[12] The text serves as inspiration and connective thread for some of the work of American poet Alice Notley, including, most notably, the poem 'Enuma Elish' (2001). It focuses in particular on the figure of Tiamat as the place of watery, cosmic, creation, but also deals with the text as an organic whole as a frame for engaging with the role of human choice against cosmic creation: 'I don't want a choice at all I want fundament / stop thinking / float script E's so pretty / enuma elish / riding the first flood itself, of bitter chaotic water / (and what a tangy aftertaste) / not the second flood god-sent but the first flood a god itself' (Notley 2001: 30–2).

Notley (2001: 31) considers the full scope of creation, but in her poem, the endless abyss serves to centre the individual, directly referencing the poem's opening lines: '*Enuma elish la nabu shamamu* .../"when there was no heaven, no earth, no height, no depth, no name ... " / wasn't I there partaking how lovely with you.' The poem continues by directly referencing Tiamat, invoking the idea of the primordial, watery chaos as an underground pool that reflects the subject back to themselves. Similarly, we see the Iraqi poet Saadi Yousef's work invoke Tiamat alongside the text's opening lines, as it describes a primordial, pre-creation world without name, shape, or form: 'There was blindness / Blindness / Blindness. / There was nothing but water' (Assadi and Naamneh 2018: 54).

Even the works that respond to the poem as a whole tend to highlight certain figures or quote particular passages. As with Notley's poem, the quoted lines tend, in the vast majority of instances, to come from the text's opening lines:

*enūma eliš lā nabû šamāmū*
*šapliš ammatu šuma lā zakrat*
*apsûm-ma rēštû zārûšun*
*mummu tiāmtu mu'allidat gimrīšun*
*mûšunu ištēniš iḫiqqū-ma*
*gipāra lā kiṣṣurū ṣuṣâ lā šē'ū*
*enūma ilū lā šūpû manāma*
*šuma lā zukkurū šīmāti lā šīmū*
*ibbanû-ma ilū qerebšun*

When heaven on high had not been named
and the ground below not given a name,
primordial Apsû, who fathered them,
and the creative force Tiamat, who gave birth to them all,
were mingling together their waters:
they had not yet bound meadows or lined the reedbeds.
When none of the gods had been brought forth,
Had not been given names and had not decreed destinies,
Then were the gods created within them.

(I 1–9)

Aside from being the opening lines of a creation myth – a genre of text often, understandably and by design, obsessed and associated with 'first things' – these lines create a compelling picture on their own. Readers who are less familiar with other Mesopotamian creation texts may read in them a greater novelty, if not outright uniqueness, than should necessarily be attributed to them, given how frequently similar tropes and imagery are found in other creation texts from Mesopotamia, both Sumerian and Akkadian.[13]

This is not to undercut the extraordinary nature of *Enuma Elish*, or the power and importance of the text, but merely to highlight that *Enuma Elish* is, in the end, one creation story amidst many in Mesopotamia. But within that cosmological milieu, it gained a standing like none other, and notably, expressed that prominence in both its original, ancient circulation and its modern reception. In its original context (as well as earlier receptions) the epic had notable political implications, but modern reception finds resonances with the core imagery of beginnings, of primordial creation, that is found in its opening lines.[14]

Although some other Mesopotamian creation myths make an appearance – including, notably and regrettably, the use of *Atra-hasis* in conspiracy theories about ancient aliens – the allure of the opening lines of *Enuma Elish* has proven especially strong. This is the case, for example, in modern musical compositions.[15] A number of classical compositions take the epic as inspiration, including a 2010 piano piece by composer Marc Yeats entitled 'Enûma Eliš'; the prologue of Vladimir Ussachevsky's 'Three Scenes from the Creation', also entitled 'Enuma Elish'; and English composer Carl Vine Symphony no. 6, which included the passage 'Enuma Elish' following its prelude. The works by both Ussachevsky and Vine include a choir singing passages in Akkadian taken directly from the epic, and again especially from its opening lines.

The other, far more prominent musical reception of *Enuma Elish* is in the metal genre. The connection between Mesopotamian material and bands belonging to the various metal sub-genres (principally death metal, black metal, and heavy metal) has its roots in another entanglement. Sumerian material, including the Sumerian/Akkadian exorcistic series *Udughul* ('Evil Demons'), was incorporated in several of H.P. Lovecraft's works of cosmic horror and in later extensions of his universe, such as the *Necronomicon*, a book that Lovecraft described in his fiction and that was later written by other authors.[16] These connections are clearly seen in some of the earlier examples of black metal, such as the song 'Apzu', by the band Apsu, from their 1995 album, which invokes a mix of Mesopotamian material (the steppe, Dumuzi, Uruk, Nineveh) and direct references to the *Necronomicon* (Rosa 2020: 109). Later music may be inspired by a closer connection to and more direct knowledge of Mesopotamia itself, as with Canadian death metal band Deathlehem's song 'Epic of Creation', which details a number of key points from *Enuma Elish* over its fifty-six verses (Gabrieli 2023: 293–4). Similarly, the 2023 album *Enuma Elish*, by the band Eridu, traces the full arc of the epic throughout its ten tracks. The album opens with the songs 'Cosmogony' and 'Enuma Elish', the latter of which includes lyrics directly quoted, in translation, from the epic. It continues to depict the uprising of Tiamat and the creation of Marduk ('Reign Supreme', 'Defiling the Tablet of Destinies'); Marduk's victory and his establishment of the cosmos ('The Great Divide', 'Constructing the Realms of Nebiru'); the slaying of Qingu and the creation of mankind ('Clay, Blood, and Vengeance'); and an abbreviated recitation of the fifty names of Marduk, who is then finally praised once again ('The 50 Names of Marduk', 'Let Them Call on His Name'). As with their previous album, *Lugalbanda*, the band incorporates the narrative of the text as a whole.

Moving away from music, though not entirely, we also find lines of influence between *Enuma Elish* and video games. The opening lines of *Enuma Elish*, as well as the themes they embody, recur in one of the more interesting examples of the epic's modern reception, namely the adventure video game *Abzû*, created by Giant Squid Studios and released in 2016 for both console and PC. *Abzû* is a difficult game to categorize. The player is never in any danger of death or even of damage, so to speak, and there are no enemies to conquer or 'bosses' to defeat.[17] Instead, the player navigates a vast ocean, exploring and solving various puzzles. Along the way, they encounter the ruins of a long-ago civilization, though the glyptic writing used on these ruins does not resemble cuneiform. The name of the game itself is a combination of the Sumerian (Abzu) and Akkadian (Apsû) renderings of the name for the cosmic freshwater abyss that appears in the opening lines of *Enuma Elish*. It is through the mingling of the waters of Apsû and Tiamat that life is first created, and fittingly, the waters that the player explores in *Abzû* are filled with life, and the main objective in the game is to fully restore life to the vast ocean. In many ways, the game is a spiritual cousin to Thatgamecompany's 2012 release *Journey*, where the player traversed a vast desert landscape.

The two games share the same composer – Austin Wintory – but their soundtracks diverge, as *Abzû's* music is one of its strongest and most direct links to *Enuma Elish*. The soundtrack is primarily orchestral, though certain tracks also feature choral accompaniment. The individual songs have titles that generally fall into one of two camps: either common-to-obscure marine animals or direct references to *Enuma Elish*. The latter includes several songs with Akkadian lyrics, such as 'And the Earth Did Not Yet Bear a Name', 'Heaven Was Not Named', and 'No Destinies Ordained'. Other titles in this category allude to *Enuma Elish* more obliquely, such as 'To Know, Water', and 'Chaos, the Mother', which echo Apsû and Tiamat, respectively. The Akkadian lyrics, which are again taken from the first nine lines, play a crucial role, with the composer remarking that, for him, 'the choir was representative of the Abzû; the kind of ethereal or otherworldly force … the choir [becomes] more and more revealed, the more life that you spread. And the text that serves as the spiritual jumping-off point for the whole game becomes increasingly also revealed' (Glaister 2020). As such, the text of *Enuma Elish* serves as a critical lyric thread, a leitmotif weaving through the game as a whole.

The range of these references highlights the flexible nature of *Enuma Elish*, the universal appeal of its core themes, and the different uses to which both may be applied. Since its earliest translations, the text has become enmeshed in other contexts, connecting first and foundationally to the Bible. From there, its core themes of creation and the idea of its own antiquity inspired and influenced a wide variety of different works, in increasingly modern media.

## Excerpted receptions: Tiamat

Though the examples above have targeted specific lines or quoted passages of *Enuma Elish*, they have generally also utilized the entire text; or at least, they have considered and integrated the broader themes of the text as a whole: creation, chaos, the primordial, a cosmic battle. The incorporation of the entire text is the most frequently and variably attested type of reception, but it is not the only one. Striking figures from *Enuma Elish* may take on lives of their own, appearing in works that are, save the inclusion of that figure, entirely distinct from the source text. This form of reception centers on one figure: Tiamat, who has enjoyed a long 'afterlife' in several video and role-playing games. To a lesser degree, we also see independent works focused on Marduk, who maintains a wider context and significance as an important Mesopotamian deity, but nevertheless manifests in ways that directly connect to his role in *Enuma Elish*.

As with *Enuma Elish* as a whole, Tiamat has received some sustained attention from the realm of heavy metal, including, notably, the Swedish metal band Tiamat, which formed in Stockholm in 1987. Another Swedish band, Dissection, makes continued references to Tiamat in their third and final studio album, *Reinkaos*. In the song 'Black Dragon', Tiamat is one of several monstrous beings, set amidst figures like Jormungand, Leviathan, and Typhon, and detailed with lyrics that suggest a knowledge of *Enuma*

*Elish*: 'Tiamat Queen of the formless deep – The Eleventh seal is now broken / Hark to your children's invocations and awaken from your dreadful sleep.' Another song on this album, 'Dark Mother Divine', highlights the idea of a monstrous feminine, an imagery that Tiamat is often associated with in this form of reception (Xiang 2018). The Japanese mobile game *Fate/Grand Order* depicts Tiamat as both a powerful goddess and a monstrous, demonic figure, with both roles repeated in the subsequent anime (*Fate/Grand Order – Absolute Demonic Front: Babylonia*). *Fate/Grand Order* is one part of a much larger franchise, *Fate/Stay Night*, which pulls strongly on Mesopotamian material in general.[18]

The notions of monstrosity and chaos come together in one of Tiamat's longest-running appearances in modern reception, as the five-headed draconic goddess who spawned all evil dragons in the *Dungeons & Dragons* role-playing game franchise. First designed and published by Gary Gygax and Dave Arneson in 1974, the game has remained in publication ever since, evolving over time to its current iteration, the fifth edition. *Dungeons & Dragons* is a grab-bag of influences, as shown especially by the denizens of its iconic *Monster Manual*. One example is the monstrous Demogorgon, which was recently made popular by the Netflix series *Stranger Things*. The term potentially (if possibly mistakenly) originates in Greek mythology, for all that *D&D* depicts the figure as an '18-foot reptilian hermaphroditic humanoid' (Solomon 2012: 33).

Tiamat was presented with complete in-game description and statistics for the first time in the *D&D* supplemental volume *Deities and Demigods*, first published in 1980, which provided full information about the figure and thus allowed for her to be incorporated into the player-built campaigns (Redman et al. 2002).[19] From this volume, we learn that she resides on the plane known as Baator, a hellish realm that takes many of its geographic notes from Dante's *Inferno*. Tiamat most often appears as a five-headed dragon, with each head representing one of the types of evil chromatic dragon (red, blue, green, black, and white) that are found in the wider *Dungeons & Dragons* universe. Her anthropomorphic manifestation is that of an alluring woman, allowing Tiamat to represent both the trope of monstrous progenitor and that of feminine seduction (Redman et al. 2002: 93).[20] *Deities and Demigods* was notable for a number of reasons: like its predecessor, a volume entitled *Gods, Demigods, and Heroes,* it represented the first major attempt to provide religions for an interactive fantasy game. The volumes drew heavily on comparative mythology, pulling from a wide range of different – including non-Western – religious traditions. During the 'Satanic Panic' of the 1980s, conservative evangelicals saw such influences as evidence that *Dungeons & Dragons* fostered an interest in occult practices among its players (Laycock 2015: 65–6).

The association between *Dungeons & Dragons* and the occult highlights the prominent place of monstrous themes in much of Tiamat's modern reception. Within the text of *Enuma Elish*, Tiamat functions as a cosmic force, giving birth to both gods and monsters. Her monstrous nature, as well as her standing as a primordial force, generally carries over into her modern reception, but is often transfigured in various ways. Most notably, modern receptions break from the source material by assigning her seductive features. Her anthropomorphic avatar in *Dungeons & Dragons* is that of an alluring woman, who may use her physical appearance as one of the weapons in her arsenal. Given that Tiamat lacks any primary engagement with human figures in the original text, seductive or otherwise, the presence of these qualities is a thoroughly modern invention. Their addition represents the roles which Tiamat finds herself in, some of which bring her much closer to direct human engagement. This aspect may also represent an overlap with Ishtar, who is undoubtedly the most famous female figure from Mesopotamia, and with whom such alluring qualities are strongly associated.

## Conclusion

As this study, however brief, has demonstrated, *Enuma Elish* continues to hold significance long after Mesopotamia itself. Indeed, the text endures beyond the end of cuneiform culture – or even the active memory of such by those cultures connected to or immediately following Mesopotamia in the first millennium BCE. The gap in the understanding of cuneiform and the Akkadian language had inevitable consequences on the subsequent transmission and reception of *Enuma Elish*. The text appears as a more immediate influence in Greek sources and biblical material that existed as contiguous or even concurrent with Mesopotamia, but later receptions had to wait for the eventual rediscovery of cuneiform texts and the decipherment of Akkadian in the latter half of the nineteenth century CE. Once the text was translated into modern languages, principally English and German, it became accessible to a modern audience, leading to its wider circulation and the eventual growth of its reception.

This reception falls into two major categories. The first category, within which most examples of reception fall, responds to the text of *Enuma Elish* as a whole, connecting to its general overall themes of creation and its place as one of the earlier well-known creation stories. These examples of reception may pull more directly on certain aspects of the text, to be sure, and when they quote directly from the text, it is almost invariably from the poem's opening lines, whether in the original Akkadian or in translation. Here, reception ranges from heavy metal to poetry to classical compositions to video games and Japanese animation. The second category of reception largely severs the connection between modern representation and original text, allowing certain aspects of *Enuma Elish* to exist independently, acquiring a life quite of their own. As seen most prominently with the figure of Tiamat, this avenue of reception allowed for a more varied and unique form of modern reception, evolving well away from the original text. Although Tiamat's roots, and some of her key characteristics, may still link her to her primordial origins, the monstrous dragon-queen found in *Dungeons & Dragons* and other examples of popular culture may claim her own identity.

## Further reading

On the place of *Enuma Elish* outside of Mesopotamian contexts, see Eckart Frahm in this volume; the importance of the *akītu* festival and *Enuma Elish's* place within it is discussed by Céline Debourse (2022), as well as in her contribution to this volume.

The early nineteenth-century reception of Mesopotamian material is discussed most comprehensively in a three-volume study by Kevin McGeough (2015). For a specific overview of the connection between Assyriological scholarship and biblical studies, see the survey by Fink and Konstantopoulos (2024). The modern reception of *Enuma Elish* is also discussed by Silvia Gabrieli (2023), while Daniele Federico Rosa (2020) presents an overview of the use of Mesopotamian material by modern metal bands. On the nature of Tiamat, see a summary of her femininity and monstrosity by Xiang (2018), and a survey of her overall character by Sonik (2010).

## Notes

1 The reception of *Enuma Elish* has been the focus of a recent study by Gabrieli (2023). I will avoid duplicating in depth her findings and focus primarily on representations of *Enuma Elish* that are not discussed in her article. The instances of the reception of *Enuma Elish* that are detailed in her work – principally appearances in certain popular venues, such as the Japanese anime and mobile game series Fate/Grand Order – will be referenced only in passing.

2 See the discussion of the use of *Enuma Elish* by metal bands in Gabrieli (2023: 293–5), as well as the more general overview of the use of Mesopotamian material in black metal in Rosa (2020).

3 Eridu's 2019 album, *Lugalbanda*, presents a retelling, of sorts, of the Lugalbanda duology, with songs that discuss the conflict between Uruk and Aratta for the favour of the goddess Inana ('Inanna's Favour' and 'Enmerkar') and others that follow Lugalbanda's own journey through the wilderness ('The Cavern') and the cosmic, astral battle he witnesses ('Astral Warfare'), before returning to the overarching conflict ('The Siege of Aratta').

4 On the construction of modern Assyrian and Chaldean identities, and links to ancient Mesopotamia, see the overview in Hanoosh (2016). On modern Iraqi culture and its links to its past, see Al-Musawi (2006).

5 Tablets such as K 5419c, K 8522, and K 8526 were all published by L. W. King in CT 13. The last of these three is a particularly noteworthy copy of the text, as it contains its famous opening lines, with the first seven lines of the text nearly entirely preserved.

6 Smith (1876) published *Enuma Elish* along with a number of other just-discovered epics and myths of Mesopotamia, including early renderings of the Deluge found in stories concerning the exploits of 'Izdubar' (or rather, Gilgamesh).

7 For a summary of early scholarly work on *Enuma Elish*, see the brief overview in Heidel (1951: 2–3).

8 This limitation also aims to avoid reduplicating previous scholarship. See the more exhaustive summary of prominent editions of *Enuma Elish* in Gabrieli (2023: 292, fn. 45 and 46).

9 For a summary of the reception of *Gilgamesh*, see Ziolkowski (2012), Pryke (2019), Helle (2021: vii–xxx), as well as recent 'retellings' such as Lewis (2018).

10 See, for example, Zeynep Avcı's 1996 retelling of *Gilgamesh* (Uçar-Özbirinci 2010). See also the staging of the epic as a one-man show by playwright David Novak in 2008 (Mann 2008).

11 These plays include *Ashurbanipal: The Last Great King of Assyria*, *Esarhaddon: The Substitute King*, and a third play about the murder of Sennacherib (Wisnom 2016).
12 In modern poetry, both *Gilgamesh* and *Enuma Elish* may be outstripped in popular reference by the figure of Enheduana, whose own standing as the 'world's first author' has given her prominence and ideological standing; see Konstantopoulos (2021).
13 On the broader corpus of creation stories in Mesopotamia, particularly their connection to Mesopotamian thought, see van Dijk (1964).
14 On the political implications and interpretations of *Enuma Elish*, see the discussion in Frahm (2010).
15 On the use of the Akkadian text of *Atra-hasis* by 'ancient aliens' and 'ancient astronaut theory', principally in the works of Zecharia Sitchin, see Winters (2020: 240–2). Sitchin and ancient astronaut theory is discussed within the context of science fiction in Nuruddin (2006: 134–8).
16 See Rosa (2020: 107–11) for a discussion of the connection between Mesopotamia, Lovecraft, and black metal. On the use of Mesopotamian material in the Lovecraft and the *Necronomicon*, see Konstantopoulos (2023).
17 The player's robotic 'diver' avatar does take physical damage near the end of the story, becoming degraded and worn, but this is an integral part of the narrative rather than a reflection of damage inflicted through gameplay. Because the diver is robotic, the player is similarly unconcerned with breathing in the underwater environment, removing yet another restriction on play.
18 These connections are discussed in full in Gabrieli (2023: 295–7). The ancient Near East has, at times, served as the setting for other works of Japanese manga and anime: the manga *Red River* or *Anatolia Story*, written and drawn by Chie Shinohara, ran for twenty-eight collected volumes from 1995 to 2002. The series, which centred on a Japanese high-school girl time-travelling to the Hittite empire, proved popular, with millions of volumes in circulation.
19 Tiamat is opposed by her brother and twin, Bahamut, the deity of good dragons. The name of Bahamut is taken from the great fish that supports the upper levels of the earth and cosmos in Islamic cosmography.
20 Tiamat's character was expanded on in several tie-in books also set within the general 'universe' of D&D. This is more popularly seen in the *Dragonlance* trilogy by Margaret Weiss and Tracey Hickman between 1984 and 1985, with several other works branching off from the original trilogy.

# Bibliography

Al-Musawi, M. (2006), *Reading Iraq: Culture and Power in Conflict*, London: I.B. Taurus.

Assadi, J. and M. Naamneh (2018), 'Intertextuality in Arabic Criticism: Saadi Yousef's Mobile Model as an Example', *Advances in Language and Literary Studies*, 9 (6): 49–56.

BarAbraham, A. (2016), 'Enuma Elish: A Modern Creation Myth for Courage and Renewal', *Bethnahrin.de*, 18 July 2016, https://bethnahrin.de/2016/07/18/enuma-elish-a-modern-creation-myth-for-courage-and-renewal/.

Bohrer, F. N. (2003), *Orientalism and Visual Culture: Imagining Mesopotamia in Nineteenth-Century Europe*, Cambridge: Cambridge University Press.

Debourse, C. (2022), *Of Priests and Kings: The Babylonian New Year Festival in the Last Age of Cuneiform Culture*, Culture and History of the Ancient Near East 127, Leiden: Brill.

Deimel, A. P. (1912), '*Enuma Eliš' sive Epos Babylonicum de Creatione Mundi*, Rome: Pontifical Biblical Institute.

Ebeling, E. (1919), *Keilschrifttexte aus Assur religiösen Inhalts*, Leipzig: J. C. Hinrichs.

Ebeling, E. (1926), 'Babylonisch-assyrische Texte, erster Teil: Religiöse Texte, erster Abschnitt; Mythen und Epen I: Die Schöpfung', in H. Gressmann (ed.), *Altorientalische Texte zum Alten Testament*, 108–29, Leipzig: De Gruyter.

Ebeling, E. (1939), *Die siebente Tafel des akkadischen Weltschöpfungsliedes Enuma Eliš*, Osnabrück: Zeller.

Fink, S. and G. Konstantopoulos (2024), 'Assyriology Meets Biblical Studies', in M. Nissinen and J. Jokiranta (eds), *Changes in Sacred Texts and Traditions: Methodological Encounters and Debates*, SBL Resources for Biblical Study, 235–53, Atlanta: SBL Press.

Frahm, E. (2010), 'Counter-texts, Commentaries, and Adaptations: Politically Motivated Responses to the Babylonian Epic of Creation in Mesopotamia, the Biblical World, and Elsewhere', *Orient*, 45: 3–34.

Furlani, G. (1958), *Miti babilonesi e assiri*, Firenze: Sansoni.

Gabriel, G. (2014), '*enūma eliš' – Weg zu einer globalen Weltordnung: Pragmatik, Struktur und Semantik des babylonischen 'Lieds auf Marduk'*, Orientalische Religionen in der Antike 12, Tübingen: Mohr Siebeck.

Gabrieli, S. (2023), 'Enuma Elish: A Glorious Past and a Curious Present', in C. Meccariello and J. Singletary (eds), *Uses and Misuses of Ancient Mediterranean Sources: Erudition, Authority, Manipulation*, SERAPHIM 12, 285–301, Tübingen: Mohr Siebeck.

Glaister, D. (2020), 'ScruffyMusic: Crafting the Ocean in the Music of Abzû (feat. Austin Wintory)', YouTube video, 39: 59. 26 June 2020. https://www.youtube.com/watch?v=0S8WGtbYvSg.

Hanoosh, Y. (2016), 'Minority Identities Before and After Iraq: The Making of the Modern Assyrian and Chaldean Appellations', *Arab Studies Journal*, 24 (3): 8–40.

Heidel, A. (1951), *The Babylonian Genesis: The Story of Creation*, 2nd edn, Chicago: University of Chicago Press.

Helle, S. (2021), *Gilgamesh: A New Translation of the Ancient Epic*, New Haven: Yale University Press.

Kämmerer, T. R. and K. A. Metzler (2012), *Das babylonische Weltschöpfungsepos Enūma Elîš*, Alter Orient und Altes Testament 375, Münster: Ugarit-Verlag.

King, L. W. (1902), *The Seven Tablets of Creation, or the Babylonian and Assyrian Legends Concerning the Creation of the World and of Mankind*, London: Luzac and Co.

Konstantopoulos, G. (2021), 'The Many Lives of Enheduana: Identity, Authorship, and the "World's First Poet"', in S. Fink and K. Droß-Krüpe (eds), *Presentation and Perception of Powerful Women in the Ancient World*, Melammu Workshops and Monographs 4, 7–76, Münster: Zaphon.

Konstantopoulos, G. (2023), 'An Excellent Day for an Exorcism: Mesopotamian Demons in the Horror Genre', in M. Kleu (ed.), *Antikenrezeption im Horror*, 127–39, Essen: Oldib-Verlag.

Labat, R. (1935), *Le poème babylonien de la creation*, Paris: Adrien-Maisonneuve.

Lambert, W. G. (2013), *Babylonian Creation Myths*, Mesopotamian Civilizations 16, Winona Lake: Eisenbrauns.

Lambert, W. G. and S. B. Parker (1966), *Enuma Eliš: The Babylonian Epic of Creation; The Cuneiform Text*, Oxford: Clarendon Press.

Langdon, S. H. (1923), *The Babylonian Epic of Creation: Restored from the Recently Recovered Tablets from Aššur; Transcription, Translation, and Commentary*, Oxford: Clarendon Press.

Laycock, J. P. (2015), *Dangerous Games: What the Moral Panic over Role-Playing Games Says about Play, Religion, and Imagined Worlds*, Berkeley: University of California Press.

Lewis, J. (2018), *Gilgamesh Retold*, London: Carcanet Classics.

Luckenbill, D. D. (1921), 'The Ashur Version of the Seven Tablets of Creation', *American Journal of Semitic Languages and Literatures*, 38 (1): 12–35.

Mann, B. S. (2008), '"Gilgamesh": Pushing the Boundaries in Story and Performance', *Storytelling, Self, Society*, 5 (1): 55–9.

McGeough, K. (2015), *The Ancient Near East in the Nineteenth Century: Appreciations and Appropriations*, Sheffield: Sheffield Phoenix Press.

Notley, A. (2001), *Disobedience*, New York: Penguin.

Nuruddin, Y. (2006), 'Ancient Black Astronauts and Extraterrestrial Jihads: Islamic Science Fiction as Urban Mythology', *Socialism and Democracy*, 20 (3): 127–65.

Peinado, F. L. (2008), *Enuma Elish: Poema babilónico de la creación*, Madrid: Trotta.

Pryke, L. M. (2019), *Gilgamesh*, London: Routledge.

Redman, R., S. Williams and J. Wyatt (2002), *Deities and Demigods*, Dungeons & Dragons Supplement, Renton: Wizards of the Coast.

Rosa, D. F. (2020), 'Ye Go to Thy Abzu: How Norwegian Black Metal Used Mesopotamian References, Where It Took Them from, and How It Usually Got Them Wrong', in L. Verderame and A. Garcia-Ventura (eds), *Receptions of the Ancient Near East in Popular Culture and Beyond*, 105–15, Atlanta: Lockwood Press.

Smith, G. (1876), *The Chaldean Account of Genesis: Containing the Description of the Creation, the Fall of Man, the Deluge, the Tower of Babel, the Destruction of Sodom, the Times of the Patriarchs, and Nimrod*, New York: Scribner, Armstrong and Co.

Solomon, J. (2012), 'Boccaccio and the Ineffable, Aniconic God Demogorgon', *International Journal of the Classical Tradition*, 19 (1): 31–62.

Sonik, K. (2010), '*Daimon*-Haunted Universe: Conceptions of the Supernatural in Mesopotamia', PhD dissertation, University of Pennsylvania.

Talon, P. (2005), *The Standard Babylonian Creation Myth Enūma Eliš: Introduction, Cuneiform Text, Transliteration, and Sign List with a Translation and Glossary in French*, State Archives of Assyria Cuneiform Texts 4, Helsinki: University of Helsinki.

Tsukimoto, A. (2022), バビロニア創世叙事詩エヌマ・エリシュ, Tokyo: Pneumasha.

Uçar-Özbirinci, P. (2010), 'A Woman Playwright's Revision of a Legendary Epic: Zeynep Avcı's *Gilgamesh*', *Tulsa Studies in Women's Literature*, 29 (1): 107–23.

Van Dijk, J. J. (1964), 'Le motif cosmique dans la pensée sumérienne', *Acta Orientalia*, 28: 1–59.

Winters, R. (2020), 'Ancient Aliens, Modern Cosmologies: Zecharia Sitchin and the Transformation of Mesopotamian Myth', in L. Verderame and A. Garcia-Ventura (eds), *Receptions of the Ancient Near East in Popular Culture and Beyond*, 237–47, Atlanta: Lockwood Press.

Wisnom, S. (2016), 'Bringing Assyria to the Stage', *Altorientalische Forschungen*, 43 (1–2): 203–7.

Xiang, Z. (2018), 'Below Either/Or: Rereading Femininity and Monstrosity Inside *Enuma Elish*', *Feminist Theology*, 26 (2): 115–32.

Ziolkowski, T. (2012), *Gilgamesh among Us: Modern Encounters with the Ancient Epic*, Ithaca: Cornell University Press.

Part Three

# Major Themes

6

# Marduk's elevation: A masterpiece of political thought

Gösta Gabriel

Names play a central role in the story of *Enuma Elish*.[1] They are present from the very beginning until the very end. The text begins with the absence of names as a means of *not-yet*. It concludes with fifty (and then two more) names bestowed on the divine king, Marduk. Throughout the story, names and naming play a vital role in the narrative. However, naming is also central to the history of the poem's modern rediscovery and study. Since Leonard King's (1902) first edition of the text under the title 'Seven Tablets of Creation', the aspect of creation has been central to modern designations of the text, such as 'the Babylonian Genesis' (Heidel 1951), 'the Babylonian Creation Myth' (Talon 2005), and 'the Babylonian Epic of Creation' (Lambert 2008, 2013).[2] Like the performative nature of names in the ancient narrative, these modern names have proved effective. There are many studies of the creation theme in the poem,[3] but only a few (e.g. Jacobsen 1946, 1976; Sonik 2008; Gabriel 2014: 317–92) focus on Marduk's rise to kingship,[4] although it is widely accepted that the focus of the text is his elevation rather than creation.[5] As Jacobsen (1976: 183) notes, for example, 'the story's final goal is certainly Marduk's attaining to the position of permanent king of the universe'.

Jacobsen reads the text as a progression from 'primitive democracy' to Marduk's kingship, a view that has proved influential (see, e.g. Bartash 2010). However, the monarchical principle is embedded in the story from the very beginning (Kämmerer and Metzler 2012: 6; Gabriel 2014: 316–9; Wisnom 2020: 115–9). The narrative revolves around the legitimation of a new king, not around radical changes in the political system. It is no wonder, then, that the text ends[6] with the statement that what the audience has heard is a song about Marduk who has 'received kingship' (*ilqû šarrūti*, VII 162) – 'kingship' being the very last word of the poem (see also Jacobsen 1976: 183; Gabriel 2014: 219–20; Seri 2017: 836).

In this chapter I will bring this aspect of the song back to the centre of research. First, I will reconstruct the various steps in Marduk's accession to the throne, then I will explore the underlying ideas that together form a political argument that artfully legitimizes the new divine king. Finally, I will examine how this argument relates to the philosophical concept of *contractarianism*, that is, the idea that a ruler's claim to power is based on a (sometimes implicit) contract with his subjects. As I will argue, *Enuma Elish* is the first-known example of this political argument in world history.

## Marduk's rise to power

Marduk's elevation to kingship runs like a thread through the narrative of *Enuma Elish* and consists of a series of gradual steps. In total, the divine assembly convenes three times to elevate Marduk: before his battle with Tiamat (first elevation), after his victory and subsequent creation of the cosmic order (second elevation), and in the newly built city of Babylon (third elevation). In this section I will analyse the nature of each step, beginning with a brief account of the state of affairs before Marduk's accession.

When Marduk is born, a number of important events have already taken place. Some gods have come into being through the mingling of Apsû's and Tiamat's waters; there has been a first conflict between the gods and Apsû, the primordial father and first king. He planned to exterminate the gods, but Ea killed him instead, and created the first cosmic body from the royal corpse. Here, in the groundwater ocean, Ea made a home for himself and his wife. Ea's regicide is not without political consequences. The text tells us that Ea took the insignia of power from the dead Apsû (I 67–8), but it does not say that Ea himself became king (see especially Gabriel 2014: 320 n. 19). Given the line of succession, it would not have been his turn anyway: much later in the text (IV 83), we learn that the gods were at that point ruled by Anshar,[7] who was two generations older than Ea.[8] Furthermore, the gods split into two groups, one following Anshar and the other following the primordial mother Tiamat (Dietrich 2006: 143; Bartash 2010: 1103; Gabriel 2014: 320–1). Since Ea belongs to the first group, we can say that one faction forms around the regicide and the other around the queen dowager.

This is the political landscape into which Marduk is born, as a member of Anshar's party. Marduk's actions then trigger a conflict between the two factions, as he disturbs Tiamat by playing with the winds given to him by his grandfather Anu. Tiamat's subjects then call her to action with two arguments: to restore silence and to avenge her husband's murder (I 113–24). Tiamat responds by gathering her troops, creating monsters, and installing a new king, Qingu. This god appears on the scene seemingly out of nowhere, with no claim to power based on descent; his only legitimacy is his marriage to the widow queen (Sonik 2008: 742 and 2009: 92; Gabriel 2014: 328). Having organized her party, Tiamat now seeks to annihilate the other faction: Marduk's games have led to a civil war between the gods. Anshar learns of the existential threat and sends first Ea, the regicide, and then Ea's father Anu to defeat the deadly enemy, but both fail, conceding that the opponent is too strong for them. In this desperate situation, Ea turns to his son and asks him to volunteer to fight. This results in Marduk's exaltation, as he demands a high price for his commitment: divine kingship (II 156–62). He does not mention 'kingship' (*šarrūtu*) directly, but rather paraphrases what he wants, demanding the ability to decree destiny by speech alone and stating that this power should be equal to any verdict of the divine assembly, the highest political body. This would also mean that the assembly could not alter anything created by his command. This transfer of power must be made by the divine assembly itself, as it is the only body with the power and legitimacy to do so. Marduk also wants an unchangeable 'destiny' (*šīmtu*, II 158) and demands that the gods 'name' (*nabû*, II 158) his new status, thus linking his political elevation to the act of naming (Gabriel 2014: 330-1, see also Marc Van De Mieroop in this volume). As we shall see below, this act of naming will serve to make the transfer of power permanent. After King Anshar has consented to Marduk's demands, the gods gather to elevate him and grant his request.

## The treaty (first elevation)

Marduk's first elevation is the defining moment of his ascent, setting out the path that Marduk and the other gods will follow until he finally achieves absolute kingship. Not surprisingly, this section is one of the most elaborate in the entire poem.

The gods of Anshar's party gather and hold a banquet, eating and drinking until they are full and their spirits are lifted. In this mood they erect a throne for Marduk and speak to him. It is noteworthy that this is the speech of the divine assembly constituted as a political body, making it the highest possible verdict in the cosmos: as the last line of Tablet III puts it 'they decreed destiny for Marduk […]' (*ana* $^{d}$*marūtuk* […] *išimmū šīm*[*ta*], III 138). Such a divine decree is immutable; its every word instantly becomes reality. In the terminology of speech act theory, it constitutes a *declarative* speech act, meaning that it creates the reality it describes (comparable to the announcement of a priest, 'I now pronounce you husband and wife'; see Gabriel 2018a: 166). In turn, the gods' decree confers on Marduk the power of performative speech, as demonstrated shortly afterwards, when Marduk destroys and then recreates a constellation by speech alone (IV 21–6).

The decree of the divine assembly consists of sixteen lines (IV 3–18) and falls into two parts. The first grants Marduk the power to decree fates, like the divine assembly itself. The Akkadian term *šīmtu* (often translated 'fate' or 'decree') has a double meaning here, designating both the gods' *decree* on behalf of Marduk and Marduk's new *power to decree destinies* for others (Gabriel 2014: 259–60). The passage ends with the sentence: 'No god shall be allowed to transgress your bounds' (*mamman ina ilī itûkka lā ittiq*, IV 10), emphasizing that the assembly will have no power to overrule his decisions. With this decree, Anshar's faction fulfils Marduk's original demands – except for the assignment of a name to his new status. However, this is only the first part of the assembly's speech.

In the second part (IV 11–18), the gods turn the unilateral verdict into a bilateral agreement, defining the rights and duties of the future ruler in relation to his subjects – that is, what Marduk can and must do with the power delegated to him. These ideas are arranged in three concentric circles. In the middle of the second speech, the gods announce Marduk's new kingship: 'Let us give you kingship over the whole of the entirety of everything. Sit down in the assembly, your word shall be (the most) exalted there!' (*(i) niddinka šarrūta kiššat kal gimrēti / tišab-ma ina puḫri lū šaqât amātka*, IV 15–6, translation modified). The pleonasm 'over the whole of the entirety of everything' (*kiššat kal gimrēti*) indicates that Marduk's royal power knows no bounds. Tellingly, this is the first time the text uses the word 'kingship' (*šarrūtu*), a political climax already anticipated by the use of the terms 'rulership' (*rubûtu*, IV 1) and 'sovereignty' (*malikītu*, IV 2) immediately preceding the divine decree.[9] Finally, the gods' call in IV 16 for Marduk to sit in the assembly refers to the throne erected for him there, alluding to his enthronement.

A first circle is then laid around this nucleus:

*marduk attā-ma mutirru gimillīni*
...
*kakkūka ai ippalṭû lira"isū nakirīka*

Marduk, you are our avenger.
...
Your weapons shall not to miss, they shall smite your enemies.
(IV 13 and 16, translation modified)

In line VI 16 the gods reinforce Marduk's qualities as a warrior. Both lines link his kingship to his duty to defeat Tiamat and her army. The gods grant Marduk kingship only on the condition that he save them. Stefan M. Maul and Annette Zgoll have argued that Marduk's status after the first elevation resembles that of a Roman *dictator*: he would have absolute power, but only for a limited time (Maul 2004: 46; A. Zgoll 2006: 65–6). I would read the lines slightly differently: Marduk's reign is not temporary, but conditional.

Further evidence for this reading can be found in the second and final circle of the assembly's decree. Here the gods further define the ideal of good kingship, adding a second set of conditions to Marduk's elevation:

*zanānūtu eršat parak ilī-ma*
*ašar sāgīšunu lū kūn ašrukka*
...
*bēlu ša taklūka napištašu gimil-ma*
*u ila ša lemnēti īḫuzu tubuk napšassu*

Provision is the desire of the cult pedestals of the gods.
The place of their shrines is to be permanent in your place.
...
Lord, spare the life of the person who trusts in you,
But spill the life of the god who planned evil.
(IV 11–12 and 17–18, translation modified)

The two sections of this circle address different topics. Lines IV 11–2 deal with the problem of sustenance: the gods are as hungry and thirsty as humans, so they need to be fed. It is the king's duty to see to this and to provide for the gods. They also need places of worship, which are also places where they receive their sustenance. Marduk must provide the gods with such shrines in his yet-to-be-built home.

This line, IV 12, has often been misunderstood in Assyriological scholarship,[10] based on a parallel to another Akkadian narrative, *Anzû*,[11] in which the assembled gods promise the divine hero Ninurta that he will be worshipped in all the sanctuaries of the other gods (Annus 2001: 23). Lambert (2008: 45; 2013: 87) saw the same idea in line IV 12, but there is no evidence for this expansionist notion in *Enuma Elish*. On the contrary, its worldview is centralized and centripetal (Gabriel 2014: 384–5). Accordingly, only a concentric movement towards the centre of the world makes sense, as we see more clearly once Babylon is built (VI 69–71, see also below). In *Enuma Elish*, therefore, it is the other gods who are worshipped in Marduk's sanctuary, not the other way around.

The second part of the outer circle deals with the balance between mercy and punishment. Marduk must not use force against obedient subjects, but bloodshed is necessary to deal with enemies of the state. This notion of justice is central to a stable polity, as it helps to create order: the king's subjects know that they can trust him not to abuse his power, but rebellion and all other forms of political destabilization are clearly sanctioned. The outer circle thus shows that Marduk's elevation is not limited to the immediate threat of Tiamat, but intended to be permanent. The circular structure also represents an ingenious combination of form and content: it places Marduk's kingship at the centre and surrounds it with royal duties, so that the reader has to pass through these circles and thus through the conditions twice.

This arrangement places a double emphasis on Marduk's obligations and subtly indicates the conditionality of his elevation without using an explicit conditional term such as 'if' (*šumma*). Marduk's first elevation also determines the further course of events in the poem, paving the way for his absolute kingship: in order to fulfil the gods' demands, he will

- defeat Tiamat (IV 93–104);
- establish legal procedures to ensure royal justice (VI 17–32);
- instruct Ea to create humans to provide for the gods (VI 33–8); and
- allow the gods to erect their cult pedestals in his city of Babylon (VI 68–9).

## Submission and naming (second elevation)

After defeating Tiamat, Marduk builds the world out of her corpse, or rather, he adds two cosmic bodies to the groundwater ocean Apsû that his father Ea had previously created. Marduk also determines the movement of the night-sky, giving his kingdom a spatial and temporal order. When he returns from the battlefield and his cosmogonic work, the divine assembly convenes again. For the first time in the text, the gods of Anshar's party bow to him and thus submit to his rule:

*[pa]ḫrū-ma igigū kalîšunu uškinnūš*
*anunnakkū mala bašû unaššaqū šēpīšu*
*[innendū]*⸢*ma*⸣ *puḫuršunu labāniš appa*
*[maḫriš]u izizū iknušū annâma šarru*

All the Igigi were ⸢assembled⸣ and bowed to him.
All the Anunnaki kissed his feet.

They all [gathered] in order to show submission (lit., 'to touch the nose').
They stood [before] him, they bowed down, (exclaiming): 'Here, the king!'
(V 85–88; transcription and translation modified)

It is important that all the gods of Anshar's party submit to Marduk, as emphasized by the threefold repetition of the terms for 'all' (*kalîšunu*, V 85; *mala bašû*, V 86; *puḫuršunu*, V 87). In addition, the complimentary designations Igigi and Anunnaki are used to show that every single god of Anshar's party is involved, and the text uses a variety of terms to signal their submission: The gods 'bowed to him' (*uškinnūš*, V 85), 'kissed his feet' (*unaššaqū šēpīšu*, V 86), came together 'to show submission' (*labāniš appa*, V 87), and 'bowed down' (*iknušū*, V 88). The passage concludes with the exclamation 'Here: the king!' (*annâma šarru*, V 88), which places the term 'king' (*šarru*) at the end as its logical climax. Furthermore, this exclamation represents a further decree confirming Marduk's fulfilment of the first condition laid down for his kingship: he has saved the gods of Anshar's party from Tiamat's assault.

In an unfortunately fragmentary passage (V 89–106), Marduk is then clothed in royal robes and given a crown, sceptre, and other insignia.[12] The two oldest gods, Lahmu and Lahamu, then confirm his royal status. The second elevation ends with two declarative speech acts by the divine assembly:

*lugaldimeranki'a zikrašu šuāšu tiklāšu*
*enūma ana marduk iddinū šarrūta*
*ka'inimmak dumqi u tešmê suāšu izzakrū*
*ištu ūmi attā lū zānin parakkīni*
*mimmû attā taqabbû i nīpuš nīni*

'Lugal-Dimmer-Ankia is his name. In him – trust in him!'
When they had bestowed kingship on Marduk,
They spoke to him an incantation of goodness and success:
'From this day forth, you are truly the provider of our cult pedestals.
All that you command, we will do.'
(V 112–6, translation modified)

The first line (V 112) is an act of divine name-giving. As such, the content of the name becomes a true and lasting statement about the name-bearer. Since the Sumerian Lugal-Dimmer-Ankia means 'king of the gods of heaven and earth', the name makes Marduk's kingship eternal. Accordingly, the next line (V 113) summarizes its effect: The gods bestowed kingship on Marduk, or more precisely, bestowed it on him forever. In the next speech (V 115–16), Marduk is reminded of his royal obligations to provide for the gods, although the gods emphasize that they, as his subjects, will assist him in this endeavour.

The second elevation is followed by an account of the measures taken by Marduk to ensure the continued fulfilment of his royal duties as laid down in the treaty. This passage displays another elaborate circular structure (Gabriel 2014: 200–18), comprising a total of 108 lines (V 117–VI 68). It consists of six parts. In the first three, Marduk explains what he intends to create: Babylon, humankind, and justice. He then executes these three in reverse order: Justice, humankind, and Babylon. Although much of the end of Tablet V is fragmentary, the course of events can be deduced with relative certainty.

First, Marduk presents his vision for Babylon, referring to the city as 'the houses of the great gods' (*bītāt ilī rabûti*, V 129), echoing the gods' reminder of his role as their provider, who must grant them places of worship in his city. But to fully provide for them, crops must be grown, canals dug, and dykes built, as the audience would have known from another mythical song, *Atra-hasis* (Machinist 2005: 44 n. 30; Gabriel 2014: 367–9, 388–90; Wisnom 2020: 126–8). Despite the incomplete preservation of Tablet V, the use of the term 'toil' (*mānaḫtu)* in V 142 suggests that the link between work and exhaustion, which is a key motif of *Atra-hasis*, is also present in *Enuma Elish*. This work then is not something the gods are prepared to do.

Marduk then develops his ingenious plan to create humanity as a cosmic working class. He calls this being *lullû* ($\mathbf{lu}_2$-$\mathbf{lu}_7^{\mathrm{lu}}$, VI 6), and explains the meaning of this name: the sequence /lulu/ can be understood as an Akkadian-Sumerian phrase, *lū* $\mathbf{lu}_2$, where $\mathbf{lu}_2$ stands for Akkadian *amēlu*. The resulting Akkadian phrase, *lū amēlu*, is spelled out immediately afterwards, as an exegesis of the term *lullû*. It can be translated as 'He shall be the *amēlu*', or, 'He is truly the *amēlu*.'[13]

This sentence would be strange if we understood *amēlu* in its conventional sense as 'man, human'. In the context of the cosmic division of labour, however, the word has a different meaning: 'worker, bearer of the burden of labour' (Gabriel 2018b: 187). According to this mythical view, which is also evident in the creation of humanity in *Atra-hasis*, the meaning 'human' is derived from this primary meaning: in the world as we know it, humans fulfil the role of workers. What is more, they were created for this very purpose.

The creation of humanity, however, requires divine blood as the main ingredient, as the audience would again have known from *Atra-hasis*, which presents Marduk with another problem. The solution is to turn the killing of a god into a just judgement, the fair punishment for a crime. The criminal is the one who led Tiamat's party against Anshar and his faction, but Marduk neither names Qingu as the culprit nor passes the sentence. He merely appoints a panel of judges to decide the punishment for Tiamat's faction. This appointment is the turning point in this circular structure, as the plan is put into action. The judges find Qingu guilty and execute him, and his blood is then used to create humankind, who will take on the burden of labour, thus freeing the gods from work (VI 34).

The text does not specify which gods are freed, but it is clear from the context. Originally, the defeated gods of Tiamat's faction were destined to work for the victorious gods of Anshar's faction. When the judges find Qingu guilty, these gods are released from their guilt; and when humankind is formed from his blood, they are also freed from the burden of labour. Their liberation is thus twofold. As a result, the rift between the gods that followed Apsû's death is healed: both factions are reunited as equal subjects under their new king, Marduk, making him the first true successor to Apsû, since Anshar and Qingu only ruled over the gods of their respective parties.

After Marduk has given each of his subjects a home, the gods volunteer for one last task: to build Marduk's home, Babylon. It will serve as a place of rest for the gods, who will gather there regularly. The construction of Babylon ends with the erection of pedestals for each god in the city (VI 68). Marduk has now fulfilled the final obligation of his royal contract. By appointing the judges and commanding them to give a fair verdict, he has established a system that guarantees justice by creating the law and its procedures (Gabriel 2014: 215–17). By creating humankind, he ensured that the gods would always be provided for without risking a rebellion among the working gods, as seen in *Atra-hasis*. Through these measures, law and humankind, he also allowed the hostile gods to re-enter the divine polity, healing the political wound caused by the killing of Apsû. Moreover, Babylon serves as a place of worship and becomes the new meeting place for the divine assembly. All this makes Babylon the centre of the world, a place of provision and worship, and the seat of both the divine assembly and its new king.

Again, the circular structure artfully combines form and content, showing us that things are complicated – that everything is connected, as the solution to one problem leads to another. A smart mind is needed to find a comprehensive solution and to fulfil the duties of kingship. Furthermore, Marduk's solution does not take the form of a trial-and-error approach, as in *Atra-hasis*, where several solutions – including the cataclysmic Flood – are tried, each failing in turn, until a working solution is found (Gabriel 2018b). Instead, we follow Marduk's deliberations as he thinks things through, and only after he has found a solution to each problem does he take action. Marduk is thus shown to be a deliberate, thoughtful king, who acts when he knows the consequences of his decisions, in stark contrast to Enlil's rash decisions in *Atra-hasis*, which for a long time only bring suffering to the gods and the people (see also Selena Wisnom in this volume).

## Self-curse and naming (third elevation)

After the construction of Babylon, Marduk summons the gods to his city. Another banquet is held, possibly a celebration of the inauguration of the capital, but also a prelude to Marduk's third and final elevation. There are four reasons why a third elevation is necessary. First, Marduk has only now fulfilled the final requirements of the contract from his first elevation, by establishing provisions and a system of justice. Second, the assembly takes place in the new world capital. Third, only the gods of Anshar's party have endorsed Marduk's kingship, and the third assembly marks the first time that all the deities have come together: it is the political body of the reunited gods, more important and influential than the previous partial assemblies. When they bow to Marduk (VI 96), it is the whole of the divine world that submits to his rule, leading to the fourth point: The gods 'elevate' (*ullû*, VI 96) Marduk's 'destiny' (*šīmtu*, VI 96); that is, they give him an even higher status than he had before. One aspect of this new, even higher status is that the gods curse themselves by swearing an oath and touching their throats (VI 97–8). The gods thus swear allegiance to Marduk and impose a prophylactic punishment on themselves should they break their oath.[14] In this case, they would die of their self-imposed curse, as expressed by the seizing of their throats. From now on the gods can only exist as subjects of Marduk. No divine existence is possible beyond subordination to the divine king's rule.

Anshar then gives Marduk another new name, Asarluhi, which the text interprets as referring to Marduk's status as king of gods and humans (VI 101–11). After this, the assembly first gives Marduk fifty names, then Enlil and Ea transfer their own names to Marduk. Ea describes the name transfer as follows: 'He is like me, Ea – Ea shall be his name. May he rule the complex of all my cultic orders, may he, yes he, permanently control all my directives' (*šū kīma yâtima* ᵈ*ea lū šumšu / rikis parṣīya kalîšunu libēlma / gimri têrētiya šū littabbal*, VII 140–2, translation modified). Ea observes that his son has the same qualities as himself, an identity that results in the transfer of the name Ea from father to son. That is, since Marduk has Ea's qualities (among his many other qualities), he should also have his name. As a result, Marduk also comes to rule over Ea's realm, replacing his father as the master of cultic and ritual practices. Ea thus merges with Marduk in both name and function. The fusion is elegantly expressed by an *apokoinou*, a stylistic device that places the name Ea in the middle of line VII 140, making it part of both the first half of the line ('He is like me, Ea') and the second ('Ea shall be his name'). 'Ea' is thus an expression of both the qualities and the name of the two gods. The same logic applies to the transfer of Enlil's epithet 'Lord of the Lands' (*bēl mātāti*, VII 136): the qualities and competences of the original name-bearer are absorbed by Marduk, as he becomes the lord of the lands. Indeed, the transmission of the fifty names by the fifty great gods works in the same way, meaning that Marduk assumes the power of the entire divine assembly. All political power now rests with him alone. There are only two kinds of gods: the subjects and Marduk. Louis XIV's dictum, 'L'état, c'est moi', applies with cosmic force to Marduk – he has become the eternal, absolute ruler of the gods and the universe.

So Jacobsen was half right to identify a change in the political system over the course of the poem. The text is indeed about 'how monarchy evolved and gained acceptance as a unifier of the many divine wills in the universe' (Jacobsen 1976: 191), but it is not a progression from primitive democracy to monarchy, but from monarchy limited and balanced by the divine assembly to absolute kingship.

## The argumentative challenge

*Enuma Elish* is a response to an implicit challenge. In the second millennium BCE, Marduk experienced an unprecedented rise from one god among many to the new divine king of Babylonian society. However, there was already a ruler of the gods, Enlil, leading to the question: How could Marduk's kingship be legitimate when there was an older and therefore more venerable tradition of another divine king? Moreover, this is the first time that cuneiform sources report the installation of a new divine king. The procedures for enthroning a human king were known, but the enthronement of a divine ruler was uncharted territory.

In response to to this challenge, the new myth of *Enuma Elish* first places its action at the very beginning of space and time, meaning that there can be nothing older than the events narrated in this story: the new myth thus claims to be the oldest and hence most venerable tradition. Second, it establishes the idea of a first world ruler, Apsû, and a line of succession derived from him: a sequence of first-born sons (Sonik 2008: 741–3; Seri 2012: 9–10; Gabriel 2014: 358–9). This idea is marked by the term 'heir, first-born son' (*aplu*) which is used to describe the relationship between Anshar and Anu (I 14) and between Ea and Marduk (II 127). These uses of the term can be read metonymically, as also shaping the relationship between the other male members of Apsû's family. A direct line of succession from the very first king to Marduk is thus established: Apsû, (Lahmu,[15]) Anshar, Anu, Ea, Marduk. Although the story does not mention Enlil, it clearly attacks him. First, the text shows that there was a divine king before Enlil, so he is not the first and his claim to power is not self-evident. Second, Enlil is not part of the line of first-born sons, so he cannot have a legitimate claim to power. He is more like Qingu, who came from nowhere. By association, Enlil would also be a usurper. The avoidance of Enlil's name at the beginning of the text thus speaks louder than many words.

Here, one might ask why the story did not put Marduk in Apsû's place, which would have simplified the argument by making Marduk the king of the gods and the world since the beginning of time and space. We can only speculate about the motives of the author(s), but it is possible that they wanted to reflect Marduk's historical rise. Just as Marduk had become increasingly important in Babylonian society, Marduk undergoes a process of elevation in the story. Marduk is thus part of the line of succession in *Enuma Elish*, but is placed at the end of it. Furthermore, Marduk is described as the most competent of the gods, meaning that the story poses a new question: How can the most capable deity, who also has a legitimate claim to the throne by descent, become king? The text's answer is to create a problem that only the most competent deity can solve, namely the existential crisis of Tiamat's civil war, which Ea and Anu fail to end. Since Anshar is unable to save the gods, the incumbent king and his possible successors all prove incapable of rising to the challenge. This situation is the narrative lever that allows for Marduk's ascent. Even though it is the only logical consequence of the predicament created by the author(s), Marduk's elevation is still a delicate matter, and a great deal of thought and effort is put into the process.

First, it is important that Marduk not only possesses outstanding abilities, but is also able and willing to use these abilities for the benefit of the gods, as shown by his defeat of Tiamat and his creation of the system of justice and provision. His cosmogonic activities and his healing of the divine schism also show that his deeds are always directed to the benefit of his subjects. He is portrayed as a deliberate king who acts only when he fully understands the challenge, and the story emphasizes that concentrating all power in his hands is the best solution for all. The implicit argument is that absolutism is the most desirable political system as long as it gives power to the best and the fairest, that is, Marduk.

The process is delicate, however, as regards not only Marduk's actions but also those of the other gods. The nature of their actions is a crucial aspect of his legitimacy. First, it is important that they act voluntarily in elevating him. Although there is an emergency that pushes them in a certain direction, this pressure does not come from Marduk, but from the situation itself. Every time they elevate Marduk, they do so voluntarily. This is true for the deities of Anshar's party during the first two elevations, and for those of Tiamat's party during the third: they participate in this elevation after being freed from guilt and the burden of labour. In addition, all gods are elated, emphasizing the voluntary nature of their political choices.

Furthermore, the gods make Marduk king by making themselves his subjects; his ascension is a consequence of their subjugation. In the first exaltation, the gods grant

Marduk the supreme power to determine destinies, a power that the divine assembly cannot overturn, thus submitting to his rule. In the second elevation, all the Anshar gods bow to him, a scene rendered in four lines (V 85–8) that effectively describes their submission. After this gesture they exclaim: 'Here, the king!' (*annâma šarru*, V 88). This sequence of events suggests that his royal status is a result of their voluntary subjugation. The same is true of the third elevation, in which the reunited gods curse themselves, meaning that from now on they can only live as his subordinates.

The gods' subjugation thus goes hand in hand with their renunciation of power, most clearly in the third elevation, where the gods renounce their existence beyond his rule and transfer their names, and with them all their powers, to Marduk. Ea is particularly explicit in giving Marduk his original authority to rule the cultic orders. Ea, Enlil, and the divine assembly are thus merged into Marduk: he absorbs all their individual competences and qualities (Jacobsen 1976: 191; Gabriel 2014: 374–6). What remains of the gods is their existence as his subjects. All power is transferred to the new absolute king, Marduk.

But who is the addressee of this complex argument and what do we know about the place of the text in Babylonian society (see Frances Reynolds in this volume)? To begin with the second question: The epilogue to the song makes it clear that it was originally understood as a *Geheimwissen* text. As such, it was to be circulated only among the priests of Marduk and the king (Gabriel 2014: 84–94).[16] Moreover, the song is said to have been recited before Marduk before it was put down in writing (VII 157). The audience was thus an exclusive circle consisting of the priestly elite in Babylon, the human king, and the divine king.

For the priests of Marduk, the text represents a piece of self-validation, giving them a crucial function in the highly centralized realm of Marduk's rule. It also gives them the upper hand over the priesthood of Enlil, who, according to *Enuma Elish*, is an illegitimate ruler. For the human king, it is empowering because the story places him at the centre of the cosmos: he is responsible for Marduk's royal duties in the human world, namely ensuring justice and providing for the gods. Moreover, the centripetal concept of Marduk's cosmos frees the Babylonian king from the need to build a large empire. There is no need to wage war to spread influence; the centre is self-sufficient and everything tends towards it. Finally, the story legitimizes Marduk as the 'new' and only true king of the gods, strengthens his grip on the throne, displaces Enlil, and subjugates the other gods. Enlil is therefore another implicit addressee: although he is largely left out of the story, this silence is itself effective. He is placed outside the line of succession, emphasizing the fundamental illegitimacy of his claim to power. Moreover, the text creates a world in which Marduk can never be removed from his throne: any rebellious deity would die instantly of their self-curse. Finally, the transfer of names also means that the transfer of power cannot be undone: Marduk's absolutism is eternal.

## Cuneiform contractarianism

As I have argued, Marduk's elevation works through a contract between the prospective king and his subjects, in which the future subjects relinquish their own powers and transfer them to Marduk. Both elements of this argument for Marduk's legitimacy are typical of the philosophical approach of *contractarianism* (Gabriel 2014: 376–80), a concept best known from early modern thinkers such as Hobbes, Rousseau, or Kant and their *social contract theory*.

The idea of legitimizing political power through a contract is often based on a thought experiment that posits a plausible fictional or historical situation, often referred to as the 'state of nature'. Since the parallels between *Enuma Elish* and Hobbes' version of the social contract are particularly striking, I will focus on his ideas as presented in *Leviathan* (1651). Hobbes describes the 'state of nature' as characterized by a constant civil war between people (*bellum omnium contra omnes*, 'the war of all against all'). However, people seek peace and security. So, to overcome the terrible state of war, they agree on a treaty in which they transfer all their power to a political centre, the Leviathan:

> The only way to erect such a Common Power, as may be able to defend them from the invasion of Forraigners, and the injuries of one another, and thereby to secure them in such sort, as that by their owne industrie, and by the fruites of the Earth, they may nourish themselves and live contentedly; is, to conferre all their power and strength upon one Man, or upon one Assembly of men, that may reduce all their Wills, by plurality of voices, unto one Will.
>
> (Hobbes 2002: chap. 17)

This is almost exactly what happens in *Enuma Elish*. The gods of Anshar's faction find themselves in a civil war that threatens their very existence, and so they transfer all their individual competences and political power to a single centre, Marduk. The result of Hobbes' thought experiment is an absolute monarchy,[17] and the same is true of *Enuma Elish*.

Hobbes could not have known about *Enuma Elish*, so the question is why similar lines of thought can be found in texts several thousand kilometres and nearly 3,000 years apart. The answer may be found in the situations that prompted the two texts. Instead of the established doctrine of divine right, Hobbes wanted to find a new legitimatizing argument for the current political system, one that did not derive from God; the argument had to be built on the level of human beings. The solution was a contract between humans and the renunciation of individual power in favour of a stable political order.

The authors of *Enuma Elish* faced a similar challenge: in seeking to legitimize a new divine king, there was no supra-divine level to appeal to. Instead, the argument had to be constructed on a single level, that is, among the gods. As a result, similar forms of comprehensive political thought are present in both texts, the mythical song and the philosophical treatise. The difference in form and format can be explained by the particularities of each tradition. Hobbes constructs an explicitly fictional 'state of nature' as the starting point for his thought experiment. While the civil war between Anshar's gods and the followers of Tiamat may have been historical in emic terms, from a modern perspective it can also be understood as a thought experiment, that is, a deliberate construction of a situation for the purpose of presenting a legitimation argument (albeit limited by the boundaries that restrict the use of a venerable mythical tradition). In terms of the structure of the argument, there is little difference between *Leviathan* and *Enuma Elish*. As a result, *Enuma Elish* can be seen as the first known formulation of a social contract argument in the history of political thought.

## Summary

*Enuma Elish* is a stylistic masterpiece, an intricately woven text. Part of its artistry is the high degree of deliberation in the political argument: it creates a complex line of thought to legitimize Marduk's rule. To this end, the author(s) have created specific situations that make Marduk's rise to kingship a necessary, legitimate outcome, presenting an implicit argument that combines crucial elements of social contract theory with ideas of inheritance and meritocracy. Only people in the line of succession can become kings, and only the best of the best should be king; so the story constructs an existential crisis in which the current king and the potential successors fail. The situation can only be resolved by the best of the gods, Marduk. His gradual ascension is based on a treaty between him and his future subjects, who (of their own free will) gradually transfer all their power to Marduk, eventually making him an eternal, absolute ruler.

That the text makes this argument means that there could be a counter-argument: this is Enlil's traditional claim to divine power. The mythical story thus proves to be an 'ideological battleground' (C. Zgoll 2019: 440)[18] between the competing kings, Marduk and Enlil, and invalidates any potential claim by Enlil by placing him outside the political succession traced back to the world's first king, Apsû. Since there can be no (hi)story earlier than the beginning of the world, *Enuma Elish* makes any Enlil-centred counter-narrative impossible. Reading *Enuma Elish* in this way reveals the complex thinking that went into its design. Several ideas of legitimation are elegantly interwoven to create the strongest possible argument in Marduk's favour. *Enuma Elish* is thus not only a poetic masterpiece, but also a masterpiece of political thought.

## Further reading

The political dimension of *Enuma elish* was first studied by Thorkild Jacobsen (1946; 1976: 165–92). Although some of his findings are questionable from the perspective of more recent scholarship, his studies are still a good read. Karen Sonik (2008) compares the various divine rulers (from Apsû to Marduk), their qualities, and the nature of their claims to power. The intertextual dimension of political argumentation is partly discussed in Selena Wisnom's book *Weapons of Words* (2020), especially in the context of the relationship between Marduk and Enlil. Finally, the most comprehensive study of political thought in *Enuma elish* has been presented by Gösta Gabriel (2014: 317–92), who analyses in particular the many different arguments supporting Marduk's claim to divine kingship.

## Notes

1 See Sophus Helle and Marc Van De Mieroop in this volume.
2 For an overview of the history of the text's modern names, see Seri (2012: 4–5).
3 There is not enough space here to mention them all. Among the most recent ones are Lambert (2013: 169–201) and Haubold (2017: 222–8).
4 Jacobsen first approached the idea of a change in the political system in mythology and historical reality in a more general sense in 1943 (Jacobsen 1943). For a recent evaluation of Jacobsen's approach see Machinist (2016).
5 E.g. Michalowski (1990: 383), A. Zgoll (2006: 51), Groneberg (2009: 134), Wilcke (2010: 22), Frahm (2011: 112), Krebernik (2012: 81), and Lambert (2013: 147).
6 Two additional lines (VII 163–4) mentioning An, Enlil, Ea, and Belet-ili as well as Babylon and Marduk's temple Esangila are attested by two younger manuscripts; see Lambert (2013: 132), Fadhil and Jiménez (2021: 225). The divine tetrad – An, Enlil, Ea, and Belet-ili – is never mentioned in *Enuma Elish*. Furthermore, Belet-ili is entirely absent from it, raising the suspicion that these two lines are later additions.
7 This line is particularly revealing as it draws a contrast between Qingu as the illegitimate and Anshar as the legitimate divine king.
8 There is no explicit information in the text as to why the male member of the first divine generation, Lahmu, is not considered in this context.
9 This is especially true of the term 'sovereignty' (*malikītu*, IV 2), since this is described as the goal of the verdict: 'for sovereignty' (*ana malikīti*).
10 Exceptions to this rule include Kämmerer and Metzler (2012: 201) and Gabriel (2014: 333).
11 Lambert (1986: 55–60). A more recent and comprehensive study on the intertextual relations between *Enuma Elish* and *Anzû* can be found in Wisnom (2020: 66–104).
12 This scene is much more elaborate than that of Marduk's first elevation, where he also receives a throne, sceptre, and crown (IV 29).
13 This is another line that is regularly misunderstood. Translators usually overlook the fact that the particle *lū* does not come before *šumšu* ('his name'), but before *amēlu*: *lū amēlu šumšu* (VI 6). If the word referred to *šumšu*, it would have to come directly before it. It can therefore only refer to *amēlu*, and is thus part of the name. See also Gabriel (2018b: 206–7).
14 For the gesture of touching the throat in the context of swearing an oath, see e.g. Weeks (2004, 24–6, 123).
15 Lahmu is somehow passed over in the line of succession, but the text does not tell us why.
16 *Pace* Oppenheim (1947: 207–38), Lambert (1984), and Frahm (2011: 346).
17 To be precise, the Leviathan can have any form of government, but Hobbes favours absolutist kingship.
18 Wisnom (2020) notes the same competitive nature as a key aspect of Mesopotamian poetic *texts*. However, Christian Zgoll's point is more fundamental, since he observes that this is central to any mythical *Erzählstoff* (*narrative material*), regardless of its medial representation (text, image, ritual, … ), implying that it is independent of the textual genre.

## Bibliography

Annus, A. (2001), *The Standard Babylonian Epic of Anzu: Introduction, Cuneiform Text, Transliteration, Score, Glossary, Indices and Sign List*, State Archives of Assyria Cuneiform Texts 3, Helsinki: The Neo-Assyrian Text Corpus Project.

Bartash, V. (2010), '*Puḫru*: Assembly as a Political Institution in *Enūma eliš* (Preliminary Study)', in S. Loesov, L. E. Kogan, S. Tishchenko, and N. Koslova (eds), *Language in the Ancient Near East: Proceedings of the 53^e Rencontre Assyriologique Internationale*, 2 vols, Babel und Bibel 4, 1083–108, Winona Lake: Eisenbrauns.

Dietrich, M. L. (2006), 'Das *Enūma eliš* als mythologischer Grundtext für die Identität der Marduk-Religion Babyloniens', in M. L. Dietrich and T. Kulmar (eds), *Significance of Base Texts for the Religious Identity: Die Bedeutung von Grundtexten für die religiose Identität*, Forschungen zur Anthropologie und Religionsgeschichte 40, 135–63, Münster: Ugarit.

Fadhil, Anmar A. and E. Jiménez (2021), 'Literary Texts from the Sippar Library II: The Epic of Creation', *Zeitschrift für Assyriologie und Vorderasiatische Archäologie*, 111 (2): 191–230.

Frahm, E. (2011), *Babylonian and Assyrian Text Commentaries: Origins of Interpretation*, Guides to the Mesopotamian Textual Record 5, Münster: Ugarit.

Gabriel, G. I. (2014), '*enūma eliš*' – *Auf dem Weg zu einer globalen Weltordnung: Pragmatik, Struktur und Semantik des babylonischen 'Lieds auf Marduk'*, Orientalische Religionen in der Antike 12, Tübingen: Mohr Siebeck.

Gabriel, G. I. (2018a), 'Decreeing Fate and Name-giving in *Enūma eliš*: Approaching a Fundamental Mesopotamian Concept with Special Consideration of the Underlying Assumptions and of the Condition of Possibility of Human Knowledge', in P. Attinger, A. Cavigneaux, C. Mittermayer, and M. Novák (eds), *Text and Image: Proceedings of the 61^e Rencontre Assyriologique Internationale*, Orbis Biblicus et Orientalis Series Archaeologica 40, 163–78, Leuven: Peeters.

Gabriel, G. I. (2018b), 'An Exemplificational Critique of Violence: Re-reading the Old Babylonian Epic Inūma ilū awīlum (a.k.a. Epic of Atramḫasīs)', *Journal of Ancient Near Eastern History*, 5 (2): 179–213.

Groneberg, B. (2009), 'Aspekte der "Göttlichkeit" in Mesopotamien: Zur Klassifizierung von Göttern und Zwischenwesen', in R. G. Kratz and H. Spieckermann (eds), *Götterbilder, Gottesbilder, Weltbilder*, vol. 1: *Ägypten, Mesopotamien, Persien, Kleinasien, Syrien, Palästina*, 2nd edn, Forschungen zum Alten Testament 2, Reihe 17/18, 131–65, Tübingen: Mohr Siebeck.

Haubold, J. (2017), 'From Text to Reading in *Enūma Eliš*', *Journal of Cuneiform Studies*, 69: 221–46.

Heidel, A. (1951), *The Babylonian Genesis: The Story of Creation*, 2nd edn, Chicago: University of Chicago Press.

Hobbes, T. (2002 [1651]), *Leviathan or The Matter, Forme and Power of a Commonwealth Ecclesiasticall and Civil*, ed. E. White and D. Widger. Available at: https://www.gutenberg.org/files/3207/3207-h/3207-h.htm, last accessed on 15 August 2022.

Jacobsen, T. (1943), 'Primitive Democracy in Ancient Mesopotamia', *Journal of Near Eastern Studies*, 2 (3): 159–72.

Jacobsen, T. (1946), 'The Cosmos as a State', in H. Frankfort and H. A. Groenewegen-Frankfort (eds), *The Intellectual Adventure of Ancient Man: An Essay on Speculative Thought in the Ancient Near East*, 125–84, Chicago: Chicago University Press.

Jacobsen, T. (1976), *The Treasures of Darkness: A History of Mesopotamian Religion*, New Haven: Yale University Press.
Kämmerer, T. and K. A. Metzler (2012), *Das babylonische Weltschöpfungsepos Enūma elîš*, Alter Orient und Altes Testament 375, Münster: Ugarit.
King, L. W. (1902), *The Seven Tablets of Creation, or the Babylonian and Assyrian Legends Concerning the Creation of the World and Mankind*, 2 vols, London: Luzac and Co.
Krebernik, M. (2012), *Götter und Mythen des Alten Orients*, München: Beck.
Lambert, W. G. (1984), 'Studies in Marduk', *Bulletin of the School of Oriental and African Studies*, 47 (1): 1–8.
Lambert, W. G. (1986), 'Ninurta Mythology in the Babylonian Epic of Creation', in K. Hecker and W. Sommerfeld (eds), *Keilschriftliche Literaturen: Ausgewählte Vorträge der XXXII. Rencontre Assyriologique Internationale*, Berliner Beiträge zum Vorderen Orient 6, 55–60, Berlin: Reimer.
Lambert, W. G. (2008), 'Mesopotamian Creation Stories', in M. J. Geller and M. Schipper (eds), *Imagining Creation*, Studies in Judaica 5, 15–59, Leiden: Brill.
Lambert, W. G. (2013), *Babylonian Creation Myths*, Mesopotamian Civilizations 16, Winona Lake: Eisenbrauns.
Machinist, P. (2005), 'Order and Disorder: Some Mesopotamian Reflections', in S. Shaked (ed.), *Genesis and Regeneration: Essays on Conceptions of Origins*, 31–61, Jerusalem: The Israel Academy of Sciences and Humanities.
Machinist, P. (2016), '*The Intellectual Adventure of Ancient Man*: Revisiting a Classic', in K. A. Raaflaub (ed.), *The Adventure of the Human Intellect: Self, Society, and the Divine in Ancient World Cultures*, 29–72, Malden: Wiley Blackwell.
Maul, S. M. (2004), 'Altorientalische Schöpfungsmythen', in R. Brandt and S. Schmidt (eds), *Mythos und Mythologie*, 43–53, Berlin: Akademie.
Michalowksi, P. (1990), 'Presence at Creation', in T. Abusch, J. Huehnergard and P. Steinkeller (eds), *Lingering over Words: Studies in Ancient Near Eastern Literature in Honor of William L. Moran*, Harvard Semitic Studies 37, 381–96, Atlanta: Scholars Press.
Oppenheim, A. L. (1947), 'Mesopotamian Mythology I', *Orientalia Nova Series*, 16: 207–38.
Seri, A. (2012), 'The Role of Creation in *Enūma eliš*', *Journal of Ancient Near Eastern Religions*, 12: 4–29.
Seri, A. (2017), 'Some Notes on *enūma eliš*', *Journal of the American Oriental Society*, 137 (4): 833–8.
Sonik, K. (2008), 'Bad King, False King, True King: Apsû and His Heirs', *Journal of the American Oriental Society*, 128 (4): 737–43.
Sonik, K. (2009), 'Gender Matters in *Enūma Eliš*', in J. Scurlock, R. H. Beal and S. Holloway (eds), *In the Wake of Tikva Frymer-Kensky*, Gorgias Précis Portfolios 4, 85–101, Piscataway: Gorgias Press.
Talon, P. (2005), *The Standard Babylonian Creation Myth Enūma eliš: Introduction, Cuneiform Text, Transliteration, and Sign List with a Translation and Glossary in French*, State Archives of Assyria Cuneiform Texts 4, Helsinki: The Neo-Assyrian Text Corpus Project.
Weeks, N. (2004): *Admonition and Curse: The Ancient Near Eastern Treaty/Covenant Form as a Problem in Inter-Cultural Relationships*, Journal for the Study of the Old Testament, Supplement Series 407, London, New York: T&T Clark International.
Wilcke, C. (2010), 'Altmesopotamische Weltbilder: Die Welt mit altbabylonischen Augen gesehen', in P. Gemeinhardt and A. Zgoll (eds), *Weltkonstruktionen: Religiöse*

*Weltdeutung zwischen Chaos und Kosmos vom Alten Orient bis zum Islam*, Orientalische Religionen in der Antike 5, 1–28, Tübingen: Mohr Siebeck.

Wisnom, S. (2020), *Weapons of Words: Intertextual Competition in Babylonian Poetry; A Study of 'Anzû', 'Enūma Eliš' and 'Erra and Išum'*, Culture and History of the Ancient Near East 106, Leiden: Brill.

Zgoll, A. (2006), 'Königslauf und Götterrat: Struktur und Deutung des babylonischen Neujahrsfestes', in E. Blum and R. Lux (eds), *Festtraditionen in Israel und im Alten Orient*, Veröffentlichungen der Wissenschaftlichen Gesellschaft für Theologie 28, 11–80, Gütersloh: Gütersloher Verlagshaus.

Zgoll, C. (2019), *Tractatus mythologicus: Theorie und Methodik zur Erforschung von Mythen als Grundlegung einer allgemeinen, transmedialen und komparatistischen Stoffwissenschaft*, Mythological Studies 1, Berlin: De Gruyter.

7

# Divine rhetoric: *Enuma Elish* on communication and emotion

Johannes Haubold

The spoken word has an elemental force in *Enuma Elish*. It names the powers that rule our world (I 1–10) and fixes them in place through solemn pronouncements (I 160, II 160, etc.). It is used to cast spells (I 59–65, 153–4, etc.); it creates and destroys (IV 19–26). Without it, the world as we know it could not exist.

Yet speech is also a form of communication, with a social valence of which ancient Babylonians were keenly aware. We see this in the moments of stunned silence that punctuate their mythological narratives. In *Anzû*, the gods are dumbfounded when they learn that the monstrous thunderbird has usurped the government of the world (I 83–4). Similar silences greet the arrival of major bad news in *Enuma Elish* (I 57–8, II 5–6, II 119–26). When speech resumes, it is not merely to address a specific impasse but also to reconstitute the networks of communication and collective action that sustain all forms of communal life. How these networks function is a question that *Enuma Elish* poses with great insistence, as it traces the emergence of order from chaos over the course of the text.

Like other Babylonian thinkers, the poet of *Enuma Elish* conceives the world in autocratic terms. Autocracies, the military historian Lawrence Freedman (2022) reminds us, tend to perform poorly under strain, because they restrict the flow of information, sideline experts, and shut down debate, with fatal consequences for all involved. Ensuring effective communication is thus a perennial challenge for autocratic regimes, and Babylonian thinkers, who considered kingship (*šarrūtu*) the only form of government worth exploring in any detail, took that challenge very seriously. Indeed, much of what we now call Babylonian 'literature' focuses precisely on how to maintain effective communication within fixed hierarchies, from canonical classics such as *Gilgamesh* to self-consciously counter-canonical works like the *Dialogue of Pessimism*.[1]

Within this textual ecology, *Enuma Elish* occupies a special place, not just because it considers kingship in its purest form – before it descended to earth and became tainted with human frailty – but also because it was arguably the most influential of all Babylonian narrative texts. As Gösta Gabriel (2014) has shown, the poem's thematic focus and *Sitz im Leben* make *Enuma Elish* that society's quintessential statement about kingship as an institution and an idea. By the same token, *Enuma Elish* also offers in-depth analysis of political communication as Babylonian thinkers understood it. Over half the poem consists of direct speech,[2] but more important than the sheer number of spoken lines is the significance attached to them. That, in a nutshell, is the topic of this chapter.

## Shouting and plotting

Like other cosmogonies, *Enuma Elish* describes how order emerged from chaos. Its treatment of communication mirrors this arc: we begin with a chaotic burst of noise (I 21–4)[3] that culminates in a first moment of communicative breakdown.[4] By contrast, the poem ends with an extended passage of harmonious unisono speech in which the gods acclaim their newly minted king (VI 121–VII 136). As well as illustrating the potential of the spoken word to unify society under one ruler, this acclamation mobilizes the hermeneutic techniques of cutting-edge Babylonian scholarship (see Marc Van De Mieroop in this volume). The gods now speak the language of Babylonian religious experts and thus co-opt those experts to the ongoing project of upholding cosmic order, on earth as in heaven.

The portrayal of speech at the end of *Enuma Elish* contrasts sharply with the noisy quarrels that open proceedings in Tablet I. The gods have just been born and with their hubbub disturb Apsû and Tiamat. Tiamat, we hear, bears this disturbance in silence (I 26), but Apsû calls for his minister:

*inūšu apsû zār ilī rabûti*
*issī-ma mummu sukkallašu izakkaršu*
*mummu sukkallu muṭīb kabattīya*
*alkam-ma ṣēriš tiāmti i niddin milk[a]*

Then Apsû, who had fathered the great gods,
called Mummu, his minister, and said to him:
'Mummu, minister who soothes my mood!
Come, let us give counsel before Tiamat.'

(I 29–32, translation modified)

After hinting that this is where the main narrative starts (the adverb *inūšu*, 'then, at that point' marks the transition[5]), we hear the first speech in the history of the world. It is an order to a subordinate who 'soothes' or 'pleases' his master (*muṭīb kabattīya*). Whether pleasing a superior will guarantee successful communication in the long term remains to be seen. For now, what matters is Apsû's business with Tiamat: he proposes to 'give counsel', and this communicative plan, hatched at the very dawn of time, will turn out to become a leitmotif of the epic as a whole. Here is how the poet develops it:

*amâti imtallikū aššu ilī bukrīšun*
*apsû pâšu īpušamma*
*ana tiāmti ellītam-ma izakkarši*
*imtarṣam-ma alkassunu elīya*

*urriš lā šupšuḫāku mūšiš lā ṣallāku*
*lušḫalliq-ma alkassunu lusappiḫ*
*qūlu liššakin-ma i niṣlal nīni*

They conferred about the gods their children.
Apsû worked his words,
saying loudly to her, to Tiamat:
'Their ways disturb me.
By day I have no rest, by night no sleep.
I will destroy their ways, disrupt them!
Let silence be settled, so that we may sleep.'

(I 34–42, translation modified)

Several points stand out about this passage. First, the poet introduces 'conferring' or 'taking counsel' (*imtallikū*) as a new form of communication. The aim is not now to announce a predetermined course of action but to agree a joint way forward in a situation where hierarchies are less clearly marked and consensus cannot be taken for granted. That raises the rhetorical stakes and explains why Apsû's second speech receives an elaborate introduction.[6] Indeed, Apsû himself chooses his words carefully: two lines describe the problem as he sees it, a third how he proposes to address it, while the last line sketches the intended outcome. Everything about the speech is clearly and rationally arranged. This, by contrast, is how Tiamat responds:

*tiāmtu annīta ina šemêša*
*īzuz-ma iltasi elu ḫarmīša*
*issī-ma marṣiš uggugat ēdiššīša*
*lemutta ittadi ana karšīša*
*mīnâ nīnū ša nibnû nušḫallaq-ma*
*alkassunu lū šumruṣat-ma i nišdud ṭābiš*

When Tiamat heard this,
she was angry and screamed at her lover.
She screamed, disturbed, alone in her rage,
for he had cast evil upon her mind.
'What! Should we destroy what we ourselves created?
Disturbing as their ways may be, let us bear them with good grace.'

(I 41–6)

Tiamat is right, at least in principle: children do indeed disturb their parents' sleep, but that is no reason to kill them.[7] To underscore the point, she asks the first rhetorical question in the history of the world. Tiamat also seems right to treat counsel as a shared endeavour, in line with the poet's own use of the reciprocal Gt-form *imtallikū* in the framing narrative (I 34). Apsû had largely ignored this aspect of counselling, opting instead to focus on his own grievances (*elīya*, 'me'; *lā šupšuḫāku*, 'I cannot rest'; *lā ṣallāku*, 'I cannot sleep'; *lušḫalliq-ma*, 'I shall destroy'; *lusappiḫ*, 'I shall scatter') and acknowledging Tiamat's perspective only as an afterthought (*i niṣlal nīni*, 'so that we may sleep'). Despite having initiated the conversation, Apsû barely includes Tiamat in his thinking and does not seem keen to hear from her at all. Tiamat, by contrast, uses plural forms throughout her short speech (*nīnu*, 'we'; *ša nibnû*, 'what we have created'; *nušḫallaq*, 'we destroy'; *i nišdud*, 'let us bear'). She clearly has the common good in mind. Nonetheless, she too fails to communicate successfully, ending up isolated (note her description in I 43 as *ēdiššīša*, 'alone') and ignored by her partner. Of course, she disagrees with Apsû, but the problem is not simply what she says but how she says it: taking the 'evil' of Apsû's proposal to heart (I 44), Tiamat loses control over her emotions and hence the ability to communicate effectively. She is livid with rage, she shouts and screams (I 42–3). Karen Sonik has written compellingly about Gilgamesh's failure to control the 'storm of his heart' (*ūm libbīšu*, Standard Babylonian *Gilgamesh* I 97). His unbridled willfulness, she suggests, comes at the expense of reasoned argument and the process of deliberation (*milku*) that it enables. The protagonist's failure in this regard stands out sharply against the positive example of characters who do manage to contain themselves:

> It is perhaps unsurprising, in a narrative peopled by heroes, gods, monsters, and Others … that the emotions on display are towering, complex, and capable of overwhelming all other considerations. What is striking, for the purposes of this study, is that there yet exist characters in the narrative who explicitly resist (at times at least) acting on emotion and impulse alone, who pause to take (and give) counsel. These figures stand in explicit contrast in the narrative to those (enormously destructive) characters who do not demonstrate such resistance, control, or self-regulation.
>
> (Sonik 2020: 396)

With some qualifications, what Sonik says about the treatment of affect and counsel in *Gilgamesh* applies also to *Enuma Elish*. Here too we see some characters give free rein to their emotions while others compose themselves and uphold the protocols that sustain effective communication. In fact, the poem draws a clear distinction between the representatives of chaos (Tiamat, Apsû, Mummu, the rebel gods), who are prone to emotional and communicative dysfunction, and the champions of order (chiefly Ea and Marduk), who are not.[8] Tiamat's outburst sets the tone for the former group and puts us on a path towards communicative breakdown.[9]

Enter Mummu, the cosmic blueprint of the flatterer. Clever and adaptable (the word *mummu* means something like 'intelligence, craft'; see Sophus Helle in this volume), he simply echoes what his master proposed.[10] True enough, he says, these noisy children should simply be killed. Apsû responds enthusiastically, taking Mummu onto his lap and kissing him, as though posing for a snapshot of a happy couple (I 53–4).[11] In fact, Apsû should be wary, for Mummu only *appears* to be a good minister. Someone who truly pleases his master (*muṭīb kabatti*, I 31) should not always be saying what the master wants to hear. Quite the contrary, in fact. Mummu's flattery turns him, in the words of the poet, into a *sukallu lā māgiru*, a 'devious' or 'disagreeable' minister (I 48).

The upshot is another dysfunctional form of counsel. Mummu may not be emotional himself, but he manipulates Apsû's emotions to the point where he 'delights' (*iḫdūšum-ma*, I 51) in what is 'evil' (*lemnēti*, I 52). 'Counselling' (*imallik*, I 47) thus turns into 'plotting' (*ikpudū*, I 52), a concept that, in the further course of the narrative, will become associated, first and foremost, with Tiamat and her army of monsters (I 111, 130, II 10, etc.). We see here the beginnings of a theory of communication which places the ideal of proper 'counsel' (*malāku, mitluku, milku*) between the emotional excess of the speaker on the one hand and the emotional manipulation of the listener on the other. Unchecked anger gives rise to dysfunctional forms of speech, isolating the advisor and nullifying even the most sensible suggestion they may have (such as not to kill one's own children). Unchecked flattery, on the other hand, isolates the recipient and makes him vulnerable to serious misjudgement (such as deciding to kill one's own children). In Tablet II the god Ea will model how a good adviser steers a course between these extremes, conquering his own anger and soothing that of his superior. First, however, we witness yet another example of crooked speech, one that takes emotional manipulation to a new level. It too receives an elaborate introduction: 'Plotting evil in their minds, they said to their mother Tiamat' (*iktapdū-ma karšussunu lemutta / ana tiāmti ummīšunu šunu izzakrū*, I 111–12). These lines introduce the extraordinary speech that unleashes Tiamat's rebellion. Like the flattery of Mummu, it is described as a 'plot' (*kapādu*), though the label is now employed upfront, with no pretense that counsel was ever being sought or given.

Contrast how the poet describes Tiamat's response: 'Tiamat listened, she found the speech good: "All that you advised, let us do it today"' (*išmē-ma tiāmtu amātu iṭīb elša / mimmû attunu tuštaddinā i nīpuš ūma*, I 125–6). What the poet introduced as an act of 'plotting' (*kapādu*) appears to Tiamat as a piece of advice (*šutaddunu*; note that she avoids the more positively charged language of *malāku*); and what the poet called 'evil' (*lemuttu*) seems to her 'good' (*ṭâbu*). Good and evil clashed in Apsû and Tiamat's initial exchange ('he had cast evil upon her mind', *lemutta ittadi ana karšīša*, I 44; 'let us bear them with good grace', *i nišdud ṭābiš*, I 46), until Apsû was taken in by the words of a flatterer (I 51–2). Now, the rebels turn an outright evil into an unqualified good. The poet warns his readers that the spoken word can do that too, that it can bring about an *Umwertung aller Werte*, in Nietzsche's famous phrase, a 'revaluation of all values', that destroys even the most fundamental social bonds. We have reached a key inflection point in the text. This is where Tiamat renounces her previous attempt to protect her children and sets about murdering them instead. It is a truly astonishing turn of events – and it hinges on this one speech.

How does one persuade a mother to kill her own children? The rebels begin by stating two accepted facts. First, Tiamat failed to come to Apsû's aid when he was slain (I 113–14). Second, Anu gave the four winds to Marduk, unsettling Tiamat and the gods inside her (I 115–16). So far, so accurate. Indeed, the rebels call the poet himself to witness, quoting verbatim from his own account (note I 115a = 105a). But already the ground begins to shift beneath our feet, for the description of the gods' predicament in the very next line ('we cannot sleep', *ul niṣallal nīnu*, I 116), aligns suspiciously with Apsû's own earlier longing for rest ('so that we may sleep', *i niṣlal nīnu*, I 40). From here, two issues get increasingly conflated, when in fact they ought to be kept separate: Tiamat's relationship with her spouse and her relationship with her children.

While it is arguably true to say that Apsû was not 'in Tiamat's heart' when he was killed (I 117–18), it seems something of a leap to conclude that she does not love her children (I 120). By confusing the love of a spouse with that of a mother, the rebel gods set a powerful emotional trap. What mother can listen with equanimity to her children claiming that she does not love them? Not Tiamat, who agrees to kill the other gods (in fact also her children) in an accommodating response to the rebels' wishes (which is how a mother's love for her children is often expressed). Apsû set a precedent for violent action, and so the rebels channel him one more time, now quoting him verbatim ('so that we may sleep', *i niṣlal nīnu*, I 122 ~ *i niṣlal nīnu*, I 40). Having identified with their father in this way, they demand the violence that was always his preferred course of action. Tiamat has already dismissed this as evil: how can parents murder their own children (I 45)? Yet, that is what she now concludes should happen next (I 126).

## Deliberating, reporting, soothing

So far, we have witnessed the power of the spoken word to unsettle, distort, and antagonize. There is no lack of brilliant speakers in these early exchanges in *Enuma Elish*, but they misuse the power of speech to further their nefarious ends. Words, however, can also be a force for good and, as we embark on our journey from chaos to order, the poet shows us how to soothe emotions rather than excite them; transmit accurate information rather than spread lies; and build community rather than start wars.

It falls to Ea to initiate this process of recovery, for he is the first to learn that Tiamat has mustered an army. His immediate response is appalled silence: 'Ea heard these words, he was struck dumb within his chamber and sat down in silence' (*išmē-ma ea amātu šuāti / kummiš ušḫarrir-(ma) šaqummiš ušba*, II 5–6). Clearly, this is a serious crisis, but the gods can only take measures if the threat is communicated to them. Three things must happen to make this possible. First, Ea must steady himself and 'take counsel' to calm his 'anger' (II 7). Next, he must report what he has learned, as indeed he does by 'repeating' (*šunnû*) verbatim the poet's own long description of Tiamat's army (II 11–48). Repetition is a characteristic feature of Babylonian storytelling, but here it serves the more specific purpose of illustrating Ea's prowess as a messenger: not one detail of what has occurred is changed or omitted. Finally, Ea must deal with his superior's reaction. This proves to be the most challenging part of his mission, for Anshar is understandably appalled by what he hears. Again, we note the by now familiar mechanism whereby extreme emotion leads to a breakdown in communication:

*išmē-ma anšar amātu magal dalḫat*
*ū'a ištasi šapassu ittaška*
*e[zz]et kabtassu lā nāḫat karassu*
*eli ea bukrīšu šagīmašu uštaḫḫaḫ*

Anshar heard these words, and they were very troubling:
'Woe,' he cried, and bit his lip.
His mind was angry, his heart had no rest,
his roar was unleashed on Ea, his child.

(II 49–52)

Anshar's response recalls that of Tiamat in Tablet I: he is furious with Ea, he rages and shouts. In response, Ea must steady Anshar's nerves, appealing to his emotional capacity (his *libbu rūqu* or 'deep heart') and assuring him that he is still in charge (II 61–4). One might call this flattery, in the sense that it is what Anshar needs to hear, but crucially Ea does *not* echo his superior's analysis of the situation. In fact, he insists that Anshar is wrong, and that matters could be far worse (see the detailed discussion in Haubold 2017).

Anshar is impressed with Ea's 'soothing speech' (*amāt tapšuḫti*, II 59), as we can tell from the poet's concluding comment: 'Anshar listened, the speech pleased him, his heart found rest and he spoke to Ea (*išmē-ma anšar amātu iṭīb elšu / ipšaḫ libbašū-ma ana ea izakkar*, II 71–2). If we compare this with Tiamat's reaction to the murderous speech of her children (*išmē-ma tiāmtu amātu iṭīb elša / mimmû attunu tuštaddinā i nīpuš ūma*, I 125–6), we notice an obvious difference between the two passages: while Anshar's reaction matches the tone and purpose of what he hears (*iṭīb*, II 71 ~ *ṭābiš*, 60; *ipšaḫ libbašū-ma*, 72 ~ *amāt tapšuḫti*, 59), Tiamat's reaction does not (*iṭīb*, I 125 ≠ *lemutta*, I 111; *tuštaddinā*, 126 ≠ *iktapdū-ma*, 111). There is a lesson here which will not have been lost on Babylonian readers of the poem: lest we end up like Tiamat we must become competent *listeners* as well as speakers. *Enuma Elish* teaches how to evaluate as well as manipulate the spoken word. What is at issue is not just rhetorical skill, but an entire system of communication.

## Breaking the silence

Tiamat had responded to conflict with shouting, Mummu with flattery. Ea resists both temptations, and with his 'soothing speech' helps Anshar regain the initiative. After soothing his master, Ea is dispatched to perform the same operation on Tiamat ('bring rest to her revolt', *tēbâša šup*[*šiḫ*], II 77). Tiamat, however, will not be placated (II 79–118): the communicative resources that enabled Ea to relay the crisis will not be sufficient to resolve it.[12]

Another moment of perplexed silence ensues, the most extended in the text (II 119–26). Only Ea can break the spell (II 129), with an intervention so powerful that the poet graces it with the rare Sumerian loanword *ka'inimmaku*, 'binding utterance' (II 130).[13] At issue is another piece of advice (*milku*), but this time it is couched in the language of traditional Babylonian instruction literature ('Marduk, listen to the counsel of your father', *marduk milka šemi abīka*, II 131). In effect, what we see here is Ea inventing an entire new genre of literature. We may think, for instance, of the classic composition known from its incipit as *Šimâ milka* ('Listen to the counsel'), in which a father counsels his son (Cohen 2013: 81–128).[14] Ea, the poet has us know, created the template for this kind of text, and he did so under specific circumstances, and for a specific purpose.

And with that, the silence is broken once and for all: there will be no further moments of speechlessness in the poem. Henceforth, communication flows freely throughout the divine community. 'Go before Anshar and work your words' (*muttiš anšar qitrubiš ṭeḫē-ma / epuš pīka*, II 133–4), Ea urges Marduk, echoing the formula used to introduce direct speech in Babylonian literature, 'he worked his words' (*pâšu īpuš-ma*), as if to re-launch the very idea of communication. Marduk obliges and devotes much of his own discourse to unsealing Anshar's lips (*pite šaptuk*, II 139 and 141). Anshar in turn requests verbal prowess from Marduk (II 150), who replies in kind by asking that the gods make a formal declaration, or *Festsprechung*, of his supreme destiny ('pronounce a superb fate for me', *šūterā ibâ šīmtī*, II 158; for this important concept, see Gabriel 2014: 249–68). And the point of that? To endow him with special powers of speech ('the command of my lips shall not be altered or reversed', *ai itūr ai innenâ siqar šaptīya*, II 162). Speech permeates these exchanges, giving rise to more speech, entire new genres of speech, and leaving in its wake the institutions that uphold society as if by a process of verbal sedimentation.

All this builds towards the moment when Marduk is proclaimed king (IV 1–18), but first the news of Tiamat's rebellion must travel one more time. It is worth pausing at this point to consider how that motif develops over the course of Tablets II–III. It all began with a piece of news that had neither source nor destination (II 5). The poet refrained from quoting it verbatim and did not describe it as a 'report' (the verb *šunnû*, 'report', is not used in II 4–5). The second phase of the transmission process involved a named character (Ea) accurately conveying to a named superior (Anshar) the facts of the matter as the poet had reported them. Careful repetition is now required, along with significant work of reassurance and advice to guide the superior's response. The third phase marks a further step in this potted history of information sharing. The message itself is now reframed as a superior's 'instructions' (*[têre]t libbīšu*, III 14) to his officers on how to deal with the crisis. An expert is charged with 'repeating' the instructions ('repeat to them all that I will say to you', *[mi]mmû azakkarūka šunnâ ana šâšun*, III 12), but accuracy alone is no longer sufficient. Kaka must also be a skilled communicator ('you are skilled in recitation', *tiṣbura tele''e*, III 5) and must authorize his message with reference to that skill: 'Anshar, your son, has dispatched me here and made me recite the decree of his heart' (*anšar-(ma) mārūkunu uma''iranni / têret libbīšu ušaṣbiranni yâti*, III 13–14 and 71–2). Compare *ušaṣbiranni* here with *tiṣbura* in III 5, both derived from the same speech verb *ṣabāru*: Kaka's performance corresponds closely to his area of expertise, and that is what makes him truly a 'minister who soothes his master's mood' (*sukkallu muṭīb kabattīya*, III 3, translation modified). Mummu, who held the same title earlier in the text (I 31), had taken it upon himself to reinterpret 'counselling' (*malāku*) as 'plotting' (*kapādu*). Kaka knows to stick to his task.

Every aspect of this reframed message is significant: the fact that a superior presents it as an order to a subordinate; that an expert messenger delivers it; that it is textualized twice in a row and so can be 'tracked'. Most significant of all is what happens next. When Kaka's message reaches Lahmu and Lahamu, the elders of the gods and their foremost representatives, they too are appalled by what they hear (III 125–8). However, far from allowing the community to lapse into silence, they lay on a veritable feast of communication. At their behest, the gods gather and make merry, eat, drink, talk ('they made conversation', *lišāna iškunū*, III 133), and then appoint Marduk king. It is in the assembly of the gods (III 132), formally convened here for the first time with Anshar in the chair (III 131), that Ea's news reaches its destination. Speech, the poet tells us, flows as freely here as the beer that lubricates it (III 134–8). The details are not recorded but the outcome is, and it brings precisely the determination that Marduk requested (III 138, IV 3–18; cf. Gabriel 2014: 141–3 and Gabriel in this volume): kingship is now his ('we have given you kingship', *niddinka šarrūta*, IV 14), and in the way the gods bestow it, we glimpse the structures of monarchic government that will be fleshed out in the rest of the poem.[15]

## Confrontation

The story of Tiamat's rebellion illustrates the importance of information flow in Babylonian society – a flow that must be safeguarded until it reaches its destination in the assembly (Bartash 2010; Ballesteros-Petrella 2017). Special powers of insight, self-restraint, and persuasion are required of those who are charged with upholding this process. As a school text, *Enuma Elish* helped budding scribes develop those qualities, but all the intelligence-gathering in the world comes to nothing if it does not result in decisive action. This is properly the task of the king, and it involves words as well as deeds, as the poet illustrates by prefacing Marduk's combat with Tiamat with an extensive battle of words. Here is Tiamat's opening salvo:

*iddi t[âš]a tiāmtu ul utār kišāssa*
*ina šaptīša lullâ ukalla sarrāti*
*… ša bēli ilū tebûka*
*… ipḫurū šunu ašrukka*

Tiamat cast her spell, she did not look away,
she held untruth and lies on her lips:
'[ ] Lord of the gods, your onslaught,
They assembled on their [own,?] but they are with you!'

(IV 71–4)

Marduk has just 'scanned' Tiāmat's army (*barû*, IV 65), in a display of visual control that marks him out among all other characters in *Enuma Elish*.[16] The rebel gods attempt to return his gaze but are defeated, their vision utterly confounded (IV 70). At this point, Tiamat shifts the confrontation to the realm of language and casts her spell (IV 71). Tiamat used her spell to elevate the usurper Qingu (I 153–4 and *passim*), so it has already played a crucial role in the poem. Now she turns it against Marduk, but rather than offer a description that to Babylonian readers might have suggested an actual spell, the poet reports a brief speech by Tiamat. The text is fragmentary at this point, and restoration has proved controversial. However, Marduk protests that Tiamat tries to deceive him with friendly words while plotting violence in her heart (IV 77–8).[17] This, it would seem, is the substance of her spell, which she first cast in IV 71 and continues casting (in an iterative verbal form known as the Gtn-stem) in IV 91.

Marduk responds by calling things by their name: despite appearances, Tiamat is bent on violence (IV 77–8), and to illustrate the depth of her treachery, Marduk recapitulates her story as others in the poem had done before him. On Marduk's retelling, Tiamat has flouted the social roles of mother (79–80), spouse (81–2), and loyal subject of the king ('you pursued evil against Anshar, the king of the gods', *ana anšar šar ilī lemnēti tešê-ma*, IV 83). These acts of defiance culminate in her challenging the male line of succession that leads to Marduk ('and firmly established wickedness against the gods, my fathers', *ana ilī abbīya lemuttaki tuktinnī*, IV 84). Marduk can thus claim a personal stake in the matter but, just as importantly, he is called to enforce social norms in his capacity as king. For that, sound judgement is required, and the ability to get to the bottom of even the murkiest of problems and social constellations. Apsû was bamboozled by a devious minister, Tiamat by a cabal of plotting courtiers. Marduk retains a clear view of roles and responsibilities, exposing to scrutiny even the innermost thoughts of those involved (IV 78). The case for violence could not be made more transparently or dispassionately: Marduk's invitation, 'let you and me engage in single combat' (*i nīpuš šašma*, IV 86), is the logical conclusion to a logical speech.

To Marduk's ostentatiously controlled discourse, effectively a judicial enquiry by other means, Tiamat responds with the most chaotically violent outburst in the entire text (IV 87–90). 'Her mind was deranged' (*ušanni ṭēnša*, IV 88), the poet tells us, even her body no longer obeyed her (IV 90). Before the first physical blow is struck, Marduk has landed a *rhetorical* blow from which his opponent can no longer recover. That too is part of what the spoken word can do. It can soothe and heal, but it can also wound like a powerful weapon – like Marduk's Flood weapon in fact, which he raises up just as he dispatches his message to Tiamat (IV 75–6).

In all this, the ability of speech to engage the emotions remains paramount. Already Mummu had appreciated this when he clouded Apsû's judgement with flattery. The rebel gods appreciated it too, when they convinced Tiamat to feel good about the one thing in the world that should make no mother feel good. These are impressive feats of rhetoric, but Marduk trumps them all, both in the immediate impact he has on his listener and in terms of the long-term benefits he secures for his community. Mummu and the rebel gods managed to prevail in the short term, but their rhetoric was ultimately self-defeating. Marduk enjoys more stable success because, the poet suggests, he combines rhetorical skill with an unwavering sense of right and wrong, a sense that is grounded in his understanding of social roles (mother, father, child, spouse, king, subject) and the expectations that attach to them. Like other forms of juridical discourse in ancient Babylon, his judgement of Tiamat suggests a constitution in a nutshell, that is to say, it encapsulates a normative view of how society functions and how we must therefore live our lives. Indeed, *Enuma Elish* as a whole sketches the contours of kingship as an institution and a way of life and derives from this a set of norms which those tasked to uphold the system must adopt and defend. Its programme of rhetorical education – for that is indeed what the poem offers its readers – is an indispensable part of this larger project.

## Royal counsel and expert advice

After defeating Tiamat and creating the world from her body, Marduk orders the affairs of the gods. He begins the process by announcing a plan:

*[mar]duk zikrī ilī ina šemîšu*
*[ub]bal libbašu ibannâ niklāti*
*[ep]šu pîšu ana ea iqabbi*
*[ša] ina libbīšu uštāmû inaddin milka*

When Marduk heard the speech of the gods,
his heart compelled him to create artful things.
He spoke the work of his words to Ea,
what he thought in his heart, he offered in counsel.

(VI 1–4)

Marduk is here responding to a speech by his fellow gods which is too fragmentary for analysis (V 151–8). We can, however, still make out that it contained a request (note 'let him make plans', *līpuš eṣr[ēti]*, V 157), to which Marduk responds by offering 'counsel', *milka* (VI 4). This crucial word last featured in Tablet II, when Ea urged Marduk to 'listen to the counsel of [his] father' (II 131). Like any good student of Babylonian didactic literature, Marduk followed the advice and took on Tiamat. Now, he is in a position to offer counsel of his own[18]:

*dāmī lukṣur-ma eṣemta lušabšī-ma*
*lušziz-ma lullâ lū amēlu šumšu*
*lubnī-ma lullâ amēla*
*lū emdū dulli ilī-ma šunu lū pašḫū*
*lušannī-ma alkakāt ilī lunakkil*
*ištēniš kubbutū-ma ana šina lū zīzū*

'I will weave blood, I will bring about bone,
and I will make a creature – let his name be "Human".
I will create the human creature,
that the toil of the gods be imposed upon them, so that the gods may rest.
I will artfully change the ways of the gods,
let them be honoured as one but divided in two.'

(VI 5–10)

There are unmistakable parallels between this speech and that of Apsû in Tablet I. Not only are they framed in similar ways (compare I 32 *i niddin milk*[*a*] and VI 4 *inaddin milka*) but the tone and content are also similar: Marduk too wants respite after a period of turmoil, and like Apsû he speaks almost entirely in the first-person singular. Indeed, the poet connects the first-person verb forms *lukṣur*, *lušabši*, *lušziz*, etc., to the Akkadian word for 'human being' (*amēlu*, spelled lú in some manuscripts) by way of an elaborate pun: *lu-* ('I will'), *lū* ('let there be'), lú/*amē<u>lu</u>* ('man'), lú.u$_{18}$.lu ('human creature'; for a similar play on the syllable *mu*, see Piotr Michalowski in this volume). Marduk too certainly insists on his sovereign will. Unlike Apsû, however, he does so in a way that is both theologically meaningful (*pašāḫu*, 'be at peace', rather than mere *ṣalālu*, 'sleep') and in the interest of the community at large ('so that [the gods] may rest', *<u>šunu</u> lū pašḫū*, VI 8). Crucially, he also listens to advice:

*īpulšū-ma ea amāta iqabbīšu*
*aššu tapšuḫti ša ilī ušannâšu ṭēma*
*linnadnam-ma ištēn aḫūšun*
*šū li''abbit-ma nišū lippatqā*
*lipḫurūnim-ma ilū rabûtu*
[*š*]*a arni linnadin-ma šunu liktūnū*

Ea answered, he spoke these words,
relating to him his plan to bring rest to the gods:
'Let one of their brothers be given up,
let him be destroyed, so that people might be fashioned.
Let the great gods assemble,
let the guilty be given up, so that the gods might retain their position.'

(VI 11–16)

Ea's reply to Marduk is headlined by the Akkadian word *ṭēmu*, a complicated notion ranging in meaning from 'intelligence' (both in the sense of 'information' and 'understanding') to 'command', 'plan', 'counsel', 'decision', and even 'characteristic' or 'essence'.[19] The last time we encountered *ṭēmu* in *Enuma Elish* was in connection with the rebel Qingu losing the plot (IV 68) and Tiamat losing her mind (IV 87–8). Now it features in the context of communal deliberation, with the aim of planning not war but lasting peace.[20]

Ea's intervention would not have come as a surprise to Babylonian readers. They knew from the popular Babylonian poem called *Atra-hasis*, which told the story of human creation and the Flood, that he, not Marduk, knew how to make human beings from the flesh of a slaughtered god.[21] Ea handles this delicate situation in an exemplary fashion. His proposals are substantial, he certainly does not flatter Marduk. But in order not to embarrass him, he refrains from articulating an opinion of his own, preferring instead to speak in impersonal volitional forms and keeping to the passive N-stem: *linnadnam*, 'let (one of their brothers) be given up'; *li''abbit* 'let (him) be destroyed', *lippatqā*, 'let (people) be fashioned', etc.[22]

That is one point. The other is that Ea concentrates on social process, and specifically on how Marduk's plan can be embedded in the life of the community: the gods should assemble, convict the perpetrator, and then be confirmed in their roles. Gösta Gabriel points out that we see here the making of something akin to a constitutional monarchy among the gods (Gabriel 2014: 355–92 and Gabriel in this volume). But Ea's system does not rest on checks and balances, the point is not to oppose one political will with others. In the end, there is only *one* will, prompted by the community, articulated by the king, and mediated by his advisors. This synthesis rests on an interlocking system of discourses that include obeisance ('bowed low', *uškinnūšum*, V 151), 'counsel' (*milku*, VI 4), and expert advice ('plan', *ṭēmu*, VI 12). As king, Marduk responds to the community and formulates a plan ('he offered in counsel', *inaddin milka*, VI 4), but we need Ea, the expert counsellor ('master of counsel', *āšiš milki*, II 57) who first introduced Marduk to the concept of *milku* (II 131), to salvage the plan by injecting a timely dose of *ṭēmu*.[23]

We can assume, I think, that Ea, not Marduk, would have been of most immediate interest to those who studied and transmitted *Enuma Elish* in ancient Babylon (for the identity of this group, see Gabriel 2014: 70–106 and Reynolds in this volume). He modelled for them the roles of messenger, counsellor, and expert advisor which they themselves expected to fulfil from time to time. In these capacities, he showed them how to inform, placate, and advise relevant stakeholders, even from a position of relative weakness. Ea is of course a major figure in the epic; he is certainly not 'weak' in absolute terms. But, crucially, he never engages in physical violence, is never elevated to kingship, and does not command an army.[24] His main achievements derive, rather, from his ability to soothe and placate ('granting rest', *ušapšiḫ*, I 63; 'soothing words', *amāt tapšuḫti*, II 59; 'his heart found rest', *ipšaḫ libbašū-ma*, II 72; 'to bring rest to the gods', *aššu tapšuḫti ša ilī*, VI 12). When in Tiamat he encounters an opponent who will not be soothed, he must defer to the king.

## Conclusion

William Hallo (2004: 25) once noted that 'cuneiform literature does not, as in the case of classical literature, provide us with a neatly prepackaged corpus of theoretical prescriptions or practical illustrations of the art of persuasion in public speaking'. I have argued that this statement requires some rethinking. While it is true that cuneiform writers did not produce rhetorical handbooks or collect model speeches in the way their classical peers did, they did offer 'practical illustrations' of what the spoken word could achieve, and they did so in ways that suggest considerations of a more theoretical kind.

*Enuma Elish* was crucial in shaping a specifically Babylonian communicative agenda, both because of its subject matter and because of the central place it occupied in Babylonian culture. As order emerges from chaos over the course of the text, dysfunctional forms of communication such as 'shouting' (*šasû*) and 'plotting' (*kapādu*) give way to the proper exercise of 'counsel' (*milku*) among characters who accept their place in society, contain their emotions, and know to distinguish good from evil. Within this arc, the early tablets of *Enuma Elish* introduce both the ideal of communication through counsel and some of the pathologies that threaten communicative breakdown, chief among them unchecked emotions. As the narrative progresses, the importance of calming those emotions emerges ever more clearly. Listeners must learn to identify and resist 'plotting' forms of communication such as flattery (Mummu to Apsû) and emotional blackmail (the rebel gods to Tiamat). Speakers must rein in their own emotions and help others steady theirs. The poet presents this as the preferred approach even in situations of extreme confrontation. There are several attempts in the epic to 'soothe' Tiamat even after she has raised an army of monsters. Yet, not all situations admit of diplomatic solutions, and as the poem approaches its violent climax, Ea must yield to Marduk, who knows how to use speech as a weapon against the massed forces of chaos (Tablet IV). The possibility of justified violence notwithstanding, as king, Marduk initiates *milku* and incorporates the *ṭēmu* of his chief advisor (Tablet VI). Together, Marduk and Ea, the king and his advisor, ensure lasting peace among the gods, and hence the stability of the world at large.

## Further reading

George Kennedy (1998: 115–40), William Hallo (2004), and Andreas Johandi (2015) discuss rhetoric and persuasion in Babylonian culture. Carol S. Lipson and Roberta A. Binkley (eds, 2004, 2009) offer broader surveys of ancient rhetoric outside the classical world. For *Enuma Elish* in particular, see Bernardo Ballesteros-Petrella's discussion of assembly scenes (2017); and Johannes Haubold's work on character speech (2017, 2020). Sophus Helle in this volume discusses the power of speech to shape the cosmos. Karen Sonik (2020) looks at counsel (Akk. *milku*) and the emotions in *Gilgamesh*, in an important essay that, as I have argued here, throws light also on *Enuma Elish*. Gösta Gabriel (2014) explores *Enuma Elish* as a major statement of Babylonian political thought.

## Notes

1 There is a growing body of research on the spoken word in ancient Babylon, much of it focusing on literary texts. See, e.g. Kennedy (1998: 115–40), Hallo (2004), Johandi (2015), Haubold (2020), and Piccin (2021). For broader surveys of rhetoric in the ancient Near East, see also Lipson and Binkley (eds, 2004 and 2009).

2 According to my calculations, the total is 587 of 1096 lines (53.5 per cent) devoted to character speech. Other classics of Babylonian poetry yield similar figures. The three best-preserved tablets of the *Gilgamesh Epic*, for example, compare as follows: 158 of 300 lines (52.7 per cent) in Tablet I; 113 of 183 lines (61.7 per cent) in Tablet VI; and 275 of 328 lines (83.8 per cent) in Tablet XI. As Benjamin Foster (2005: 30) puts it, 'Akkadian narrative poetry, like other ancient narrative traditions, allots more space to direct speech than to narrative, with emphasis on action rather than description.'

3 The motif is taken from the Flood epic *Atra-hasis*; for discussion, see Wisnom (2020: 110–15).

4 Before the first speech in the poem comes the first silence: I 25–6.

5 Formulations of this kind are attested since the Old Babylonian period and are especially common in royal inscriptions; see, e..g., *Codex Hammurabi* I 1 and 27 (*inu … inūmīšu*).

6 Elaborate speech introductions are not common in *Enuma Elish*, by contrast with *Gilgamesh*, where they are the norm. Ancient readers would have been alert to such details; see Jiménez (2017: 92–4).

7 For noisy children in real life, and the connections that already ancient observers saw with the theme of pre-cosmic noise, see Heffron (2014).

8 Contrast *Gilgamesh*, where some of the most emotionally disruptive figures (Ishtar, the patron deity of Uruk, and Gilgamesh, its king) belong to civilized society.

9 For the theme of Tiamat's anger and its roots in ritual lament, see Selena Wisnom in this volume.
10 See I 38 (*urriš lā šupšuḫāku mūšiš lā ṣallāku*) and I 50 (*urriš lū šupšuḫāt*(*a*) *mūšiš lū ṣallāt*(*a*)). For the history of flattery in Western thought, see Kapust (2018).
11 It is difficult to gauge the precise tone of these lines, but we can safely say that they suggest excessive closeness at a point where Apsû would be well advised to keep his distance.
12 As if to confirm the extent of the problem, Anshar sends off a second god, Anu, to try his luck with Tiamat ('Soothe her feelings', *šupšiḫ kabtataš*, II 100) – again without success. For the Babylonian Ninurta epic *Anzû* providing a model for the scene, see Selena Wisnom in this volume, who also discusses the theme of 'soothing' Tiamat and its roots in lamentation literature.
13 The poet only uses it one other time in the text, in V 114, where the gods declare their loyalty to Marduk (*ka'inimmak dumqi u tešmê*). In first- and second-millennium Mesopotamia, *ka'inimmaku* (Sumerian **ka enim-ma**) served as a technical term for 'ritual spell, incantation', a form of speech whose origins were traced back to the gods; see Zgoll (2022: 295–8).
14 Although only copies from outside Mesopotamia are extant, the incipit already appears in an Old Babylonian catalogue as [*ši-me*]-*e mi-il-kam*, suggesting that this kind of language had high recognition value from early on; see Cohen (2013: 115–16) with earlier literature.
15 The only line in their speech, out of a total of sixteen, that does *not* contain a second-person singular form (in a verb, independent pronoun, or pronominal suffix) is IV 11.
16 Marduk 'scans' the world when he is born (*barû*, I 98); he 'scans' Tiamat's carcass after his victory over her (IV 135); and he 'scans' the minds of his fellow gods once he is king (VII 35). The verb *barû* is not used of any other character in the poem.
17 Confirmation of this reading comes in an inscription of the Neo-Assyrian king Assurbanipal, which contains multiple echoes of *Enuma Elish* IV (*RINAP* 5, Ashurbanipal 011, iii 78–81): *u šū damiqtu annītu ēpušuš imšī-ma ištene"â lemuttu eliš ina šaptēšu ītammâ ṭubbāti šaplānu libbašu kaṣir nērtu* ('but he forgot this good turn that I had done him and kept looking for evil. Above, on his lips, he spoke pleasant things but underneath his heart plotted murder.').
Notice *ina šaptēšu* – *ina šaptīša* (IV 72); *eliš* – *eliš* (IV 77); *ṭubbāti* – *ṭubbātu* (IV 77); *libbašu kaṣir nērtu* – *kapid libbakī-ma dekê ananta* (IV 78).
18 This time, Ea will listen and respond, as Marduk did in Tablet II. The reversal is further emphasized by the fact that Marduk speaks 'from his heart' (*ubbal libbašu*, VI 2), a formulation that he shares with no other character in *Enuma Elish* (see III 56 and 114, both said of Marduk).
19 See *Chicago Assyrian Dictionary*, s.v. *ṭēmu*. In *Gilgamesh*, *ṭēmu* refers to the 'knowledge from before the Flood' (including, presumably, the story of the Flood itself) that Gilgamesh brings back from his travels (I 8).
20 Marduk had planted the idea of bringing rest to the gods (VI 8), but the abstract concept of *tapšuḫtu* is still reserved for Ea, here and elsewhere in the poem (II 59).
21 Old Babylonian *Atra-hasis* I 198–260; for discussion see Wisnom (2020: 124–8). Significantly, the god from whose flesh human beings are made in *Atra-hasis* is himself endowed with *ṭēmu*; see Old Babylonian *Atra-hasis* I 223 and 239, with discussion in Wilcke (1999: 80–2).

22 Contrast the much more direct approach employed by Mummu (*ḫulliqam-ma*, I 49) and by the rebel gods (*epšī … epšī-ma … šuknī*, I 123–4).

23 Marduk is the only character in the epic who receives *ṭēmu*. In VII 112–14, he is also said to 'know' *ṭēmu* about the lives of human beings whom he created.

24 Even Ea's defeat of Apsû, which certainly has a violent outcome (*ināraššu*, I 69), is described in essentially non-violent terms; see I 63–5.

## Bibliography


Ballesteros-Petrella, B. (2017), 'Divine Assemblies in Early Greek and Mesopotamian Narrative Poetry', DPhil. diss., Oxford University.

Bartash, V. (2010), '*Puḫru*: Assembly as a Political Institution in *Enūma eliš* (Preliminary Study)', in L. E. Kogan, N. Koslova, S. Loesov, and S. Tishchenko (eds), *Language in the Ancient Near East*, 2 vols., Compte rendu de la Rencontre Assyriologique Internationale 53, Orientalia et Classica 30, 1083–108, University Park: Penn State University Press.

Cohen, Y. (2013), *Wisdom from the Late Bronze Age*, ed. A. R. George, Writings from the Ancient World 34, Atlanta: Society of Biblical Literature.

Foster, B. R. (2005), *Before the Muses: An Anthology of Akkadian Literature*, 3rd edn, Bethesda: CDL Press.

Freedman, L. (2022), *Command: The Politics of Military Operations from North Korea to Ukraine*, Oxford: Oxford University Press.

Gabriel, G. (2014), *'enūma eliš' – Weg zu einer globalen Weltordnung: Pragmatik, Struktur und Semantik des babylonischen 'Lieds auf Marduk'*, Orientalische Religionen in der Antike 12, Tübingen: Mohr Siebeck.

Hallo, W. W. (2004), 'The Birth of Rhetoric', in C. S. Lipson and R. A. Binkley (eds), *Rhetoric Before and Beyond the Greeks*, 25–46, Albany: State University of New York Press.

Haubold, J. (2017), 'From Text to Reading in *Enūma eliš*', *Journal of Cuneiform Studies*, 69: 219–43.

Haubold, J. (2020), 'Politische Redekultur im griechischen und akkadischen Epos', in C. Horst (ed.), *Der Alte Orient und die Entstehung der athenischen Demokratie*, Classica et Orientalia 21, 37–54, Wiesbaden: Harrassowitz.

Heffron, Y. (2014), 'Revisiting 'Noise' (*rigmu*) in *Atra-hasīs* in Light of Baby Incantations', *Journal of Near Eastern Studies*, 73: 83–93.

Jiménez, E. (2017), *The Babylonian Disputation Poems: With Editions of the 'Series of the Poplar', 'Palm and Vine', the 'Series of the Spider', and the 'Story of the Poor, Forlorn Wren'*, Culture and History of the Ancient Near East 87, Leiden: Brill.

Johandi, A. (2015), 'Public Speaking in Ancient Mesopotamia: Speeches before Earthly and Divine Battles', in P. Espak, M. Läänemets, and V. Sazonov (eds), *When Gods Spoke: Researches and Reflections on Religious Phenomena and Artefacts; Studia in Honorem Tarmo Kulmar*, Studia Orientalia Tartuensia Series Nova 6, 71–106, Tartu: University of Tartu Press.

Kapust, D. J. (2018), *Flattery and the History of Political Thought: That Glib and Oily Art*, Cambridge: Cambridge University Press.

Kennedy, G. A. (1998), *Comparative Rhetoric: An Historical and Cross-Cultural Introduction*, Oxford: Oxford University Press.

Lipson, C. S. and R. A. Binkley (eds, 2004), *Rhetoric Before and Beyond the Greeks*, Albany: State University of New York Press.

Lipson, C. S. and R. A. Binkley (eds, 2009), *Ancient Non-Greek Rhetorics*, West Lafayette: Parlor Press.

Piccin, M. (2021), *Linguistic Aspects of Persuasiveness in Akkadian: Petitions and Prayers*, Alter Orient und Altes Testament 446, Münster: Ugarit-Verlag.

Sonik, K. (2020), 'Gilgamesh and Emotional Excess: The King without Counsel in the Gilgamesh Epic', in S.-W. Hsu and J. L. Raduà (eds), *The Expression of Emotions in Ancient Egypt and Mesopotamia*, Culture and History of the Ancient Near East 116, 390–409, Leiden: Brill.

Wilcke, C. (1999), 'Weltuntergang als Anfang: theologische, anthropologische, politisch-historische und ästhetische Ebenen der Interpretation der Sintflutgeschichte im babylonischen *Atram-hasīs*-Epos', in A. Jones (ed.), *Weltende: Beiträge zur Kultur- und Religionswissenschaft*, 63–112, Wiesbaden: Harrassowitz, 1999.

Wisnom, S. (2020), *Weapons of Words: Intertextual Competition in Babylonian Poetry; A Study of 'Anzû', 'Enūma Eliš', and 'Erra and Išum'*, Culture and History of the Ancient Near East 106, Leiden: Brill.

Zgoll, A. (2022), 'Sacred Texts and the First Myth about the Creation of Writing', *Journal of Ancient Near Eastern Religions*, 22: 258–314.

8

# A mirror for queens: Gender, motherhood, and power in *Enuma Elish*

Karen Sonik

*Enuma Elish*, once widely known as the *Babylonian Epic of Creation*, is today read primarily as a political narrative rather than a creation myth (see the introduction to this volume). While it certainly encompasses a cosmogony of sorts, it chiefly serves to justify the god Marduk's ascension to divine kingship and, by extension, to establish the legitimacy of Babylon (Marduk's patron city) as the pre-eminent city in Mesopotamia. The means by which Marduk secures his rulership has traditionally been understood as follows: Marduk battles and defeats the dreadful female 'monster' Tiamat, completing a task that has daunted all Marduk's potential competitors for kingship, including the gods Ea (Marduk's father) and Anu (one of his forefathers). Subsequently, in a vividly described account, Marduk structures the cosmos from Tiamat's corpse. In other words, the composition might yet be said to be structured around a *Chaoskampf*, a battle against chaos (with Marduk in the role of heroic defender of order and Tiamat in the role of chaos monster), followed by cosmic creation. As I argue in this essay, however, close attention to the individual characters and composition of *Enuma Elish* suggests the narrative is centered around quite different themes.

*Enuma Elish* is certainly a political narrative, asserting Marduk's kingship over the gods and articulating the circumstances of his elevation (see Gösta Gabriel in this volume).[1] But these circumstances cannot be encapsulated as a simple *Chaoskampf* or a battle between order and chaos. Instead, they take the form also of a royal family drama, complete with a complex battle over succession and negotiation of what constitutes legitimate rulership. This essay begins by exploring early (mis-) interpretations of *Enuma Elish* that continue to shape many readings of the epic.[2] It goes on to examine several major and minor characters of *Enuma Elish* as individuals rather than archetypes (e.g. hero, monster), attending to the gendered frameworks within which many of these characters have been understood. The essay argues that *Enuma Elish* serves, in the manner of medieval and Renaissance 'mirrors for princes', as a literary exploration of models of rulership and the legitimate exercise of power.[3]

## Europe encounters *Enuma Elish*

Ancient Mesopotamia and its material remains gained the interest of Europeans from the early nineteenth century, significantly later than the familiar remains of ancient Greece and Rome. This interest was provoked in part by the remarkable antiquities collection acquired by Claudius James Rich, a British antiquarian and traveller who had served as the East India Company Resident in Baghdad and published rousing memoirs of his explorations of the Middle East (Rich 1818a, 1818b, 1836).

By the mid-nineteenth century, British and French excavations had begun at major Mesopotamian sites near Mosul. These excavations were led by Austen Henry Layard and Hormuzd Rassam at Kalhu (Nimrud) and Nineveh and by Paul-Émile Botta at Dur Sharrukin. All three sites were Neo-Assyrian capitals (*c.* 911–612 BCE) located in present-day Iraq. They captured the contemporary public imagination through their monumental arts and architectural remains,[4] which were placed on display in the British Museum and the Louvre,[5] as well as published in illustrated volumes (Botta and Flandin 1849; Layard 1849, 1853). Among the finds were large numbers of clay tablets and other artefacts bearing cuneiform. Attempts at deciphering these texts proceeded apace, with researchers finding particular success in the translation of Akkadian. Already in 1857, scholarly efforts – particularly those of the Irish philologist and clergyman Edward Hincks – had proceeded so far that the British Royal Asiatic Society deemed Akkadian to be understood. Accordingly, our knowledge (if rudimentary and incomplete) of some of Mesopotamia's most important surviving works of literature, including *Enuma Elish* and *Gilgamesh*, dates back nearly to the beginnings of the European rediscovery of Mesopotamia.

*Enuma Elish* was first excavated in 1849 during Layard's excavations at Nineveh: it was one of the first of Mesopotamia's great narrative compositions to be translated (Smith 1876), and it garnered early and widespread public interest for its apparent biblical connections. In 1895, the German Old Testament scholar Hermann Gunkel (1895) located in *Enuma Elish* the origins of the theme of *Chaoskampf*, battle against chaos, followed by cosmogony and acts of creation, that he had discerned in several key episodes of the Hebrew Bible, including the apparently peaceful creation account in Genesis. The central events described in *Enuma Elish* were key to Gunkel's argument: a battle between Marduk, representing order, and the female Tiamat, representing chaos, as well as Marduk's subsequent victory and act of creation – the structuring of the cosmos from Tiamat's corpse.

While Gunkel's idea of *Enuma Elish* as the original exemplar of *Chaoskampf* has long been confuted,[6] his ideas continue to colour interpretations of the narrative, particularly with respect to the roles played by Tiamat and her consorts, Apsû and Qingu. In particular, Tiamat and Apsû are often identified as 'monsters' and sometimes explicitly as 'chaos monsters'[7] – though, as I argue here, the narrative challenges any such flat characterizations.

Gunkel's treatment and analysis of *Enuma Elish* occurred against a late-nineteenth- and early-twentieth-century backdrop, during which several key developments arose that would further shape the reception and interpretation of Mesopotamian literature (Sonik 2024, forthcoming):

1. Mesopotamia's newly translated narratives were examined and valued for their perceived relationships with biblical narrative[8];
2. a burgeoning and broadly applied interest in scientific classification shaped approaches to the analysis and interpretation of narrative and character[9];
3. fantasy and fairy tale flourished and gained new and broad popular (adult) appeal – even as they were often explicitly deprecated as primarily for children (Silver 1999: 6 and passim; Levy and Mendlesohn 2016: 32);
4. twentieth-century literary theory evinced a 'retreat from characterization' (Woloch 2006: 295; 2003)[10] in favour of an emphasis on archetypes and narrative forms.

Below, I explore the significance of these developments for the reception of *Enuma Elish*.

## The reception and early interpretations of *Enuma Elish*

In his 1876 book, *The Chaldean Account of Genesis*, George Smith, the Assyriologist who first translated *Gilgamesh*, analysed both that famous narrative and *Enuma Elish* for their relationships with the Old Testament. Following Henry C. Rawlinson, the so-called Father of Assyriology, Smith (1876: 3) also pointed out 'several coincidences between the geography of Babylonia and the account of Eden in Genesis, and suggested the great probability that the accounts in Genesis had a Babylonian origin'.

Apparent connections between episodes from the newly translated Mesopotamian narratives and episodes from the Bible – seemingly proving the latter's veracity – electrified contemporary scholarly and public audiences (see, e.g. Delitzsch 1903). This had the benefit of drawing significant resources to bear on the study and interpretation of significant Mesopotamian narratives like *Enuma Elish*, but it also established these, from the beginning, as ancillary to the Bible rather than autonomous compositions worthy of appreciation and analysis in their own right.

An emphasis on scientific classification and organization during this same period, evident in multiple disciplines and aspects of late nineteenth- and early twentieth-century public life,[11] also witnessed new approaches to narratives and narrative analysis. The Russian formalist Vladimir Propp, focusing on folk- and fairy tales, sought to systematize and analyse diverse narratives by reducing them to their smallest structural units (Pirkova-Jakobsen 1968 [1958]: xx). Aspects of such approaches were similarly brought to bear on biblical and Mesopotamian narratives, as in Hermann Gunkel's application of 'form criticism' (*Gattungsgeschichte*) to and analysis of fairy tale motifs in the Old Testament and Babylonian literature.[12] As noted above, Gunkel's (1895) work also argued for a direct relationship between Mesopotamian and biblical narratives, identifying the Akkadian epic *Enuma Elish* as originating the *Chaoskampf* motif he observed in Genesis.

The early-twentieth-century interest in identifying formal similarities among distinct narratives, including those from diverse cultural contexts, reflects some of the larger intellectual concerns of the era.[13] But a corollary of such approaches was the elision of narrative independence, coherence, and difference. The unique features of individual stories, the idiosyncrasies of their characters, and the ways in which their elements worked together to create distinct and coherent compositions: all were flattened in the pursuit of such broader similarities across texts. Narratives were reduced to compilations of their smallest structural elements; characters were wedged into archetypes. Such approaches have arguably played a significant role in shaping traditional interpretations of *Enuma Elish* as a type of patchwork drawing on diverse earlier compositions: Wilfred G. Lambert (1986: 56), for example, penned an influential assessment of it as possessing a 'highly composite nature … [whose] author has combined numerous mythological threads into a single narrative'. While this remains a prominent and, in its own way, productive interpretation[14] – it is also one that limits recognition of or attention to *Enuma Elish* as an internally coherent composition.[15]

A rising interest in folk and fairy tales and, eventually, many diverse forms of narrative classified as speculative fiction also characterized the nineteenth and early twentieth centuries. The broad public appeal of such narratives did not preclude their designation as primarily suitable for children or the frequent disparagement of their fantastic elements and characters as primitive or unsophisticated.[16] The consequences of such denigration for scholarly approaches to much older narrative works, which might contain an abundance of fantastic characters and events, were taken up in a seminal 1936 lecture by J.R.R. Tolkien.

Tolkien's lecture challenged then-common deprecations of *Beowulf* – a monster-ridden Old English composition likely dating from the seventh to eighth century CE – for the perceived 'radical defect of [its] theme and structure', localized in the centrality of its monsters, which contrasted sharply with its generally acknowledged 'dignity, loftiness in converse, and well-wrought finish' (Tolkien 1936: 8).[17] For Tolkien, the monsters of *Beowulf* were not primitive frivolities or childish 'irrelevances' tastelessly situated at the centre of the narrative (p. 7)[18]: they were instead 'essential, fundamentally allied to the underlying ideas of the poem, which give it its lofty tone and high seriousness' (p. 17). In defending *Beowulf* as a coherent artwork, worthy of our interest and our analysis *because* of its monsters, not despite them, Tolkien challenged (and ultimately redirected) the scholarly *Zeitgeist* of the late-nineteenth and early-twentieth century.[19]

Related to the diverse developments outlined above was the 'dismissal of the literary character … in [favor of] a heightened attention to narrative form' (Woloch 2006: 295) in twentieth-century approaches to literary theory. Where literary characters *were* analysed, they were generally decoupled 'from their implied humanness … [as] the price of entry into a theoretical perspective on characterization' (Woloch 2006: 298). Such effacement, if it seemed to render narrativity itself more visible, came at significant cost: it diminished both the complexity and power that these same characters brought to the narratives in which they appeared.

All of these developments arguably had specific and enduring effects on how Mesopotamia's extant narratives, *Enuma Elish* included, have been interpreted and valued.[20] The mining of these works for relationships to biblical and other compositions (e.g. Gunkel's proposed relationship between *Enuma Elish* and Genesis); their stripping down to skeletal narrative and character types (e.g. *Enuma Elish* as *Chaoskampf*; the mutable Tiamat of *Enuma Elish* as mere monster[21]); and the general deprecation of their fantastic elements have made it difficult to see compositions like *Enuma Elish* as fundamentally coherent narratives.

The case study below analyses one of the central characters of *Enuma Elish*, Tiamat, and her relationships with Apsû, Qingu, and Marduk, offering new insight into the narrative's structure and meaning. Particular attention is paid to issues of gender, motherhood, and the exercise of legitimate rulership.

## Characters and characterization in *Enuma Elish*

In 1974, the French writer and literary critic Hélène Cixous (1974: 383) asserted that it is only 'with the removal of the question of "character" that the question of the *nature of fiction* comes to the fore' (see also Felski 2011). The concept of character, as she regarded it, was oppressive and repressive, restricting the infinite potential and 'open, unpredictable, piercing part of the subject' (Cixous 1974: 384). This derogation of character as 'cog in an antiquated literary machinery' (Felski 2011: v), or, somewhat more generously, as a quaint anachronism, remained prominent through the latter twentieth century. Fortunately, however, significant new approaches to character and characterization have appeared over the past two decades, including those undertaken by Alex Woloch.

Woloch (2006: 296) recognized the constraints imposed on characters – 'implied personalities' in all their infinite complexity – by the narrative form, which is necessarily and definitively delimited.[22] But he nevertheless viewed character and characterization as a critical focus of literary analysis, observing that narrative meaning emerges from the 'dynamic flux of attention and neglect' towards the characters that are contained – and hold different positions within – the narrative.[23] In seeking to pay all characters, including but not limited to the protagonist, the attention they deserve, Woloch outlined a method based in two narratological categories: (1) the *character-space*, denoting the 'particular and charged encounter between an individual human personality and a determined space and position within the narrative as a whole' (Woloch 2003: 14; 2006: 32); and (2) the *character-system*, denoting the 'arrangement of multiple and differentiated character-spaces … into a unified narrative structure' (Woloch 2003: 14). *Character-spaces*, Woloch observed, inevitably point towards a work's *character-system* since 'the emplacement (and final 'destiny') of a character within the narrative form is largely comprised by his or her relative position vis-à-vis other characters' (Woloch 2006: 302).

The case study below is a character-driven analysis of *Enuma Elish*, with a primary focus on Tiamat. However, any examination of Tiamat as a complex and unique personality rather than mere stereotype or archetype (e.g. 'chaos monster') necessarily entails a reevaluation of the three male figures with whom she has significant relationships: Apsû, Qingu, and Marduk.

## Tiamat and Apsû

The character of Tiamat in *Enuma Elish*, even when it escapes relegation to a mere monster, is frequently classified as the chief antagonist of the epic, the enemy to the hero Marduk. But at the opening of the narrative, Tiamat is no one's enemy and Marduk has not been born. Instead, *Enuma Elish* looks out onto the dawn of new world, one still tranquil and little differentiated (I 1–6). Here, two liquid primordial entities, Apsû and Tiamat, are mingling their waters together (I 5). As in all cosmogonies, action impels creation, setting in motion the process of differentiating and, here, naming different types of matter.[24] In *Enuma Elish*, the action taken by Apsû and Tiamat together, the mingling of their waters, is as notable for its mutuality (both Tiamat and Apsû are active participants) as for its sexual aspect, the latter reinforced by its outcome: it generates the first gods, the male Lahmu and the female Lahamu. Lahmu and Lahamu, once brought forth and named (I 10), engender their own divine children, Anshar and Kishar, initiating a line of new gods.

It is noteworthy that, at the opening of the epic, Apsû and Tiamat are *not* designated as gods: their names lack the divine determinative that identifies deities and that marks the names of Lahmu and Lahamu and all their divine descendants.[25] But if they are other-than-gods, this does not make them less-than-gods. On the contrary: the narrative recognizes their extraordinary consequence, explicitly identifying them as the progenitors of all. Apsû 'fathered them', while Tiamat 'gave birth to them' (I 3–4). Here, at the beginning of things, Apsû and Tiamat commence the process of giving shape to the world – even as the world shapes them back. Through the act of generating Lahmu and Lahamu (and the lineage of gods they generate in turn), Apsû and Tiamat are transformed into parents, acquiring the socially and culturally inflected obligations inherent in this role.[26] They are also situated in new roles vis-à-vis each other: Apsû is a father (and forefather) but now also a husband to Tiamat; Tiamat is a mother (and foremother) but now also a wife to Apsû. (The term 'consort' is generally preferred below, though it lacks specific gendered associations that are pertinent in some contexts.) But if the boundless and formless primordial entities with which *Enuma Elish* began are thus rapidly domesticated and constrained by their new roles, it is not clear whether they also acquire new physical forms as a result.

In subsequent scenes, both Apsû and Tiamat do seem to possess more explicitly anthropomorphic features: they sit and confer, taking counsel together (I 29–34); Apsû wears both sash and crown (I 67), attributes that will be seized as spoils by the god Ea; and Tiamat's body, dismembered for parts, is later described as possessing facial features (eyes, nostrils, as well as, presumably, a mouth to speak), breasts, and, less expectedly, a tail (V 50–9).[27] This progression may be compared to a theme well known from elsewhere in Mesopotamian literature: that of metamorphosis through sexual congress or marriage. In the Standard Babylonian version of *Gilgamesh*, for example, Enkidu undergoes a change in substance (if not form) through his intercourse with Shamhat (I 194–202): he is severed from the wild and initiated into the civilized world, though this is only the first step in his ultimate metamorphosis into a man of the city.[28] Elsewhere in the epic, Ishtar offers marriage to Gilgamesh (VI 1–79), and the hero's contemptuous refusal details the terrible metamorphosis that would attend such a union.[29] In the case of Apsû and Tiamat in *Enuma Elish*, any civilizing potential of sexual congress is surely limited by the fact that neither is *already* civilized (unlike Shamhat in the *Gilgamesh Epic*, who is explicitly an urban denizen): they are together initiated into their new domestic roles.

Unfortunately, Apsû rapidly fails to fulfil the obligations of fatherhood. The lineage of divine descendants that he and Tiamat generated has continued to expand: Lahmu and Lahamu give rise to Anshar and Kishar, who in turn give birth to Anu, who engenders the powerful Ea.[30] Many of these young new gods are noisy and vigorous,[31] and roil their parents ceaselessly. Apsû, resentful of his disturbed sleep and seeking a return to quietude, calls on his counsellor Mummu and the two go to seek counsel with Tiamat (I 29–32).

The conclave does not go well. Apsû proposes the destruction of the gods to restore the silence necessary for sleep (I 35–40). Tiamat, enraged and horrified, seeks to dissuade Apsû from his terrible plan, demanding, 'should we destroy what we ourselves created?' (I 45). But Mummu supports Apsû and the latter determines to forge ahead (I 47–54). However, the gods have been listening in, and Ea, traditionally associated with wisdom and magic, prepares a spell that, with delicious irony, lulls Apsû to sleep (I 59–65). Ea then kills him, strips him of the garments and *melammu* ('awe-inspiring radiance') that denote his status,[32] and establishes his sanctuary within Apsû's watery corpse (I 60–78). It is here that Ea and his consort Damkina (her lineage is not given) engender an extraordinarily powerful, physically exceptional, and very active new god, Marduk, the protagonist of the subsequent narrative (I 79–108).

The extraordinary events recounted in this section would seem sufficient for a standalone epic. But within the framework of *Enuma Elish*, they are only the preamble to the main action. The conflict between Apsû and Ea introduces and amplifies the subsequent action, in which a more intense and extended conflict between Marduk (son of Ea) and Tiamat (consort to Apsû) is played out. Similar structural parallelism is evident in *Gilgamesh*.[33] As a narrative strategy, it serves to establish an interlocking and resonant narrative, in which individual episodes are related to, as well as amplified and reinforced by, prior, current, or future action. More directly, the conflict between Apsû and Ea and its brutal outcome offers a rich backdrop for the subsequent conflict between Tiamat and Marduk, imbuing the latter characters and their battle with additional meaning.

## Tiamat as independent agent, wife, and mother

Before discussing Tiamat and Qingu, some key points regarding the portrayal of Tiamat in this early part of the epic are worth highlighting. Particularly significant is Tiamat's explicit agency, from her active participation in mingling her waters with Apsû's to her establishment as an independent power in the conclave with Apsû and Mummu. Apsû may independently plan a (disastrous) course of action, but he does not implement it without attempting to bring Tiamat on board. Her positioning as a power worth courting is rendered even more noteworthy by its contrast with the other female characters in the narrative – Lahamu, Kishar, and Damkina – who are voiceless, colourless, and passive, seemingly existing only in relation to their male consorts (and, in Damkina's case, her son, Marduk). Later in the epic, Tiamat is clearly recognized as an adversary more powerful than her dead consort when Ea, who slew Apsû, concedes that he is not her match (II 85–6). Anu, who is sent forth against Tiamat after Ea, is equally overmatched (II 109–10). The remarkable and full-blooded rendering of Tiamat in this context also serves to render Tiamat a meet opponent for Marduk.[34]

Tiamat as a powerful independent agent can and does dissent from Apsû's plan, so that Ea has no reason to attempt her destruction. But this situation also constitutes something of a cruel catch-22 for Tiamat: in refusing to support her consort, she abrogates her obligations as a dutiful and committed wife – and her failure directly results (or so one might argue) in Apsû's death. Within the framework of the narrative, Tiamat also notably fails here to fulfil her obligations as a mother: she refuses to participate in Apsû's plot but she takes no action to protect her children.[35]

Both the above failures, and Tiamat's own recognition of these, render her vulnerable to the 'sleepy' faction of her (and presumably Apsû's) divine descendants, those who are troubled – as she is – by Marduk's vigorous play (I 105–10). This faction notably encompasses a whole host of other (mostly unnamed) gods descended from Apsû and Tiamat,[36] albeit with unclear lineages. These gods ruthlessly upbraid Tiamat for abandoning Apsû to his death, accuse her of failing in her maternal duties to them, and ultimately demand that she prove her love for them by waging war on the noisy faction of the gods (I 113–23). This request is notable for its insistence that Tiamat *actively* participate in the conflict. Until this point, Tiamat has essentially remained a neutral party: while she refused to join Apsû, she also did not physically array herself against him – or warn or otherwise protect her children from him.

Tiamat's identities as wife and mother are in opposition here: in first siding with her children against her consort, she abandoned the former. Now her guilt over Apsû's death is leveraged against her and, faced with the discomfort and trouble caused by the noisy faction of her children, she is persuaded to destroy the latter. She contravenes thereby the fundamental bond of motherhood – albeit at the urging of her other children.[37] If Tiamat indeed becomes a monster – and this is by no means assured, though she certainly does take on the role of dangerous enemy – this is the critical turning point. But the choices and transgressions that lead her here are rendered possible only by the agency and raw power the narrative cedes to her.

## Tiamat, Qingu, and the Tablet of Destinies

As Tiamat takes on the role of chief antagonist, *Enuma Elish* shifts course: Tiamat allies with her sleep-seeking descendants and commits to destroying her noisy children, who include (at minimum) the line of gods descended from Lahmu and Lahamu. She gives birth, apparently parthenogenetically, to a series of terrifying monsters (I 133–44),[38] and then selects a new consort, the god Qingu, from among the faction of her descendants spurring her on to destruction (I 147–55). Critically, she marks Qingu's elevation to kingship over the gods by assigning him the Tablet of Destinies, which she affixes to his chest (I 157).

In the space of a few lines, the narrative of *Enuma Elish* has plunged into a thorny thicket of new issues that raise new questions of characterization and identity for Tiamat and Qingu – as well as for the monsters. To elucidate these effectively, a brief treatment of the Tablet of Destinies is necessary. Andrew George (1986: 138) characterized the Tablet of Destinies as the means through which legitimate power was exercised: 'the power invested in the *rightful* keeper of the Tablet of Destinies is that of the chief of the destiny-decreeing gods … which amounts in principle to kingship of the gods' (emphasis added).[39] It is noteworthy that mere possession of the Tablet does not confer legitimate divine kingship, a point that has been highlighted elsewhere in Mesopotamian literature, as in the Sumerian narrative *Ninurta and the Turtle* and the Akkadian epic *Anzû*.[40] In the latter, the monster Anzû seizes the Tablet of Destinies from its rightful keeper, the god Enlil, and flees to his mountain home. But Anzû's theft, while it hurls the cosmos into disarray, does not make him king of the gods.

In *Enuma Elish*, both Tiamat's possession of the Tablet of Destinies and her bestowal of it on Qingu, as well as the circumstances in which this bestowal occurs, are worth noting. Tiamat possesses the Tablet but does not seem to exercise its power, suggesting she is the (legitimate) medium through which the Tablet is bestowed but not its 'rightful keeper'. That she assigns it to Qingu immediately after taking him as her consort and elevating him to rulership suggests that legitimate possession of the Tablet of Destinies may be acquired through marriage to Tiamat – with the caveat that one must be the *right* god. And that Qingu acquires the Tablet of Destinies through legitimate means and yet *is the wrong god* is suggested later, during the confrontation between Marduk and Tiamat. At that time, Marduk will explicitly accuse Tiamat of wrongdoing in taking Qingu as her consort and assigning him dominion (IV 81–2),[41] encompassing, presumably, her assignment to him of the Tablet of Destinies. And later, during Marduk's confrontation with Qingu, he defeats (and ultimately slays) the latter and seizes from him 'the Tablet of Destinies that he *unrightly* held' (IV 121, emphasis added). The question of who would be the *right* god to receive the Tablet of Destinies, if Qingu is the wrong one, is addressed below.

## Tiamat as queen, mother of monsters, and (mere) woman

In this second phase of the epic, *Enuma Elish* shifts from a domestic drama (albeit on a cosmic scale) to a royal one. The narrative pivots to issues of rulership and legitimacy, and Tiamat emerges in a new guise: that of powerful queen moving against her (legitimate) divine heirs.

The gods from the lineage of Lahmu and Lahamu, the first gods to have been generated by Tiamat and Apsû, now emerge more clearly as the would-be – and, within the narrative confines, reasonably legitimate – ruling dynasty. Their assembly reveals them to be an insular group, comfortable in electing Marduk to be not only their champion in battle but also their king (II 136–62, III, IV 1–30). In moving against them and taking a new consort, after all, Tiamat has proven herself not only a bad mother but also a bad queen: she has disrupted the established order of things – an order that she and Apsû set in motion at the opening of the epic. Qingu, from this vantage point, is not only the interloping 'stepfather', but also a false king attempting to usurp the rightful throne and inheritance of Marduk.

Tiamat's choice to array herself on the *wrong* side is reinforced by her generation of ferocious monster soldiers (I 133–44), a set of eleven extraordinarily dangerous creatures including the *mushmahhu* (seven-headed snake [hydra]), *ushumgallu* ('prime venomous snake'), *bashmu* ('venomous snake'), *mushhusshu* ('furious snake'), *lahamu* ('hairy'), *ugallu* ('big weather' beast), *uridimmu* ('mad dog'), *girtablullu* ('scorpion-man'), *umu dabrutu* ('fierce weather' beast), *kulullu* ('fish-man'), and *kusarikku* ('bison').[42] Tiamat's monster children are remarkable in several significant ways:

1. They are not paired or gendered, and they are physically unique: many, indeed, are *Mischwesen*, composite figures like the 'scorpion-man'. Unlike the gods, who at least begin with male-female pairs (Lahmu–Lahamu; Anshar–Kishar) and presumably have a common form, the monsters are all 'male-seeming' (Dalley 2002: 117), and their capacity to reproduce or form family units – a foundational feature of civilization – seems limited at best. Social and familial alienation is, notably, a common feature of Mesopotamia's (and other) monsters (Sonik 2013b).
2. They have no (known) father. Unlike the gods, who are generated through Tiamat's intercourse with Apsû, Tiamat seems to generate the monsters independently. This point would be merely a curiosity except that monsters elsewhere in Mesopotamian literature are frequently marked through the absence of parental figures – especially fathers. In the Sumerian narrative *Lugal-e* (also known as *Ninurta and Azag* or *Ninurta and the Stones*), the monster Azag was born of Heaven's copulation with the Earth but he is described as 'a child who sucked the power of milk without ever staying with a wet-nurse, a foster-child … knowing no father' (l. 26–9).[43]
3. The monsters are attributed with *melammu*, the type of awe-inspiring aura commonly born by gods, temples, kings, cult objects, and other super-natural entities and things – including Apsû earlier in the epic. The possession of *melammu* is linked to the fact that Tiamat made the monsters godlike (*iliš umtaššil*, I 138 and passim). In emphasizing the monsters' power and terror, these lines underscore the extraordinary threat posed by Tiamat – while also reminding us that Tiamat herself gave birth to the enormously powerful gods she now seeks to destroy.

These points highlight not only the alterity of the monsters but also that of Tiamat, their mother and sole parent: she has come quite a way from the 'mother of (all the) gods'. We would do well to remember, however, that though Tiamat is the mother of all the gods, she is not herself a god: likewise, when she also becomes the mother of monsters, this does not make her a monster.[44]

This section is also notable for its explicit introduction of gender into the narrative. Once Tiamat turns against the noisy faction of her children, first Ea and then Anu attempt to quell her. Both fail, but as they make their reports to Anshar, they insist: 'My father, do not despair, send another against her! / Great as a woman's strength may be, it is no match for a man's' (II 91–2, 115–16).[45] These purportedly reassuring lines are notable for their deliberate expansion of the space Tiamat occupies within the narrative: she is evoked (for both the internal and external audiences), even if she is not present or active. They also function to simultaneously reinforce Tiamat's threat and alterity – because she is demonstrably *already* a woman whose strength is a match for a man's (at least if that man is Ea, who easily defeated Apsû, or Anu) – and cast her forthcoming battle with Marduk in explicitly gendered terms: Marduk is the man who will put Tiamat in her place.

## Tiamat and Marduk

In the third phase of the epic, Marduk offers himself as martial champion of the gods in the battle with Tiamat, an offer contingent upon their acceptance of his kingship (II 135–62). The narrative, notably, has already established Marduk's physical aptitude for the role of king, highlighting his extraordinary prowess and the perfecting of his body by Anu (I 89–92).[46] The circumstances of Marduk's birth have also been formulated to establish him as uniquely fit both to rule the gods and to defeat Tiamat. After all, Marduk's father, Ea, not only defeated Apsû and assumed the latter's implements and *melammu*, but also founded his sanctuary in Apsû's watery corpse – the very place where Marduk was born. If *Enuma Elish* is to be read as a royal family drama, the case might be made that this circumstance of birth re-routes the line of succession from Apsû, father of all gods, directly to Marduk. Marduk's ostensible forefathers are thereby bypassed: they may retain a right to respect but cannot rival the vigorous young god. Marduk's birth in the Apsû arguably has another significant consequence: it establishes a (necessary) distance between Marduk and Tiamat. Tiamat's body may have generated the gods – but Marduk was born in the body of Apsû.[47]

In the discussion of Qingu and the Tablet of Destinies, it was argued that the process whereby Qingu gained the Tablet of Destinies was a rightful one (i.e. Tiamat had the right to bestow it) but that Qingu was nevertheless the *wrong* god on whom to bestow it. The question of who the *right* god may be is here answered: by circumstance and capacity, it is Marduk. This point is underscored when Marduk, following his defeat of Qingu, seizes the Tablet of Destinies, seals it, and fixes it upon his own chest (IV 121–2). Marduk will later turn the Tablet over to Anu as a trophy (V 70), but there is no doubt about who exercises legitimate authority over the gods.

Prior to Marduk's confrontation with Tiamat, his request for kingship is formally approved by the gods. Anshar convenes an assembly and feast to which are summoned all the gods belonging to this faction, and he instructs his vizier Kaka to communicate to all the attendees the dire state of current affairs. The emphasis placed on Lahmu and Lahamu in this part of the narrative (III 68–70, 121–31) is noteworthy, given the divine pair has otherwise done little but procreate since being generated by Apsû and Tiamat. But it is notable that, once Tiamat is gone, it is they who will stand at the origin point of the gods as the ultimate divine ancestors. Their support of Marduk's request carries particular weight in this light, and, following Marduk's defeat of Tiamat, they will explicitly approve and presumably thereby legitimate his kingship (V 107–10).

## Tiamat, in her place

The confrontation between Tiamat and Marduk in Tablet IV of *Enuma Elish* offers a strikingly explicit culmination of many of the themes that have threaded through the epic. Marduk is at first discomposed by Tiamat's power (IV 65–70), but when he rallies, he wields not only his weapon (the Flood) against her but also his words. He accuses her, in brief but striking terms, first of being a bad (unnatural) mother and then of being a bad queen, one who seeks to displace the legitimate heirs of her union with Apsû and who fails to show the queenly (and womanly) quality of mercy[48]: 'The children cried out and harassed their fathers, / but you, who gave birth to them, refused mercy [*rēmu*]. / You named Qingu as your [consort] / and unrighteously assigned him dominion' (IV 79–82).[49] These words, which establish Tiamat's guilt and justify her death, precede Marduk's demand that she join with him in single combat. Driven to fury, Tiamat does so, and, in a remarkably graphic passage, is violently slaughtered and trampled by him (IV 93–104).

The savage death to which Tiamat is subjected is quite different from the swift and anesthetized execution of Apsû. It is also succeeded by her gutting – like a fish (IV 137) – and plundering for parts that Marduk then uses to structure the cosmos (IV 129–40, V 9–11, 47–66). Her powerful and mutable body, now stilled, is here endowed with both breasts and tail, underscoring both her femininity and her alterity (V 57, 59).[50] At last silenced, much like the other women of the epic, Tiamat is forced into her proper place as a passive participant in the work of creation, the raw matter from which the cosmos is structured.

## Conclusion: A mirror for princes – and queens

*Enuma Elish*, as read here, constitutes both a political narrative and a royal family drama. In the guise of the former, one might recognize it not only as a type of 'mirror for princes' composition, offering a series of models of kingship for its (royal) audience (Sonik 2008), but also as a 'mirror for queens'.

Diverse models of kingship are offered by Apsû, Qingu, and Marduk, with figures such as Anshar, Anu, and Ea offering more rudimentary behavioural sketches. Apsû, the 'bad king', is a legitimate but unwise ruler, and his brief reign is marked by the (failed) attempt to inappropriately exercise his power. Qingu, the 'false king', gains rulership through a legitimate process, becoming Tiamat's consort and having the Tablet of Destinies bestowed on him, but he stands outside the proper succession of power and is (arguably) little better than a usurper. The 'true king', Marduk, stands in contrast to his predecessors: his status is portended by the peculiar circumstances of his birth in the Apsû and by his own extraordinary physical prowess and divinely perfected beauty. He is 'elected' by the assembly of his forefathers, proves his martial prowess through the swift dispatch of his rivals, and, through his structuring of the cosmos from Tiamat's raw matter, initiates an orderly and prosperous reign over the new world he has created.

Models of queenship in *Enuma Elish* are primarily provided by the mutable Tiamat, who offers an extensive object lesson in how *not* to be a queen – and, on a more domestic level, how not to be a wife and mother. The narrative conspicuously situates Tiamat in an apparently no-win situation from the beginning: upon establishing her as a wife and mother, it places these two roles in diametric opposition, so that to uphold one would be to betray the other. Her only possible escape from this trap might be to *mediate* between consort and children, something she does not do: instead, she abruptly vanishes from the narrative action during the subsequent confrontation between Apsû (her consort) and Ea (representing her own and Apsû's noisy heirs). It is only in the aftermath of that confrontation that she reappears, and it is only then, having failed in her duties to both Apsû and her children, that Tiamat is goaded (or guilted) into finally choosing sides by her divided descendants (I 110–24) – and thereby also into betraying her obligations as mother to *all* her children.

Given the emphasis on gender in *Enuma Elish*, Tiamat's personal failures, those ill-suited to a woman or mother (as well as to a queen or queen mother), are also worth noting, not least because they have political implications. In choosing Qingu as her new (and inappropriate) consort, for example, Tiamat does not merely take a new mate but rather establishes what is essentially a new ruling dynasty, one that displaces her original heirs. Perhaps worse, she continues to independently exercise both voice and agency – she *acts* of and on her own accord – in a world in which the women otherwise do little except give birth. Thus Damkina, Marduk's mother, is barely visible in *Enuma elish*, notable primarily for delivering Marduk, whom Ea begat or created (I 83–4): the closest she comes to independent action is in exclaiming with joy (her actual words are not recounted) over Marduk following his vanquishing of Tiamat (V 81) and providing him with a spotless robe (V 82).

As dangerous as her agency are Tiamat's exceptional fecundity and generative abilities, which give rise first to the gods and then to the monsters. The degree to which these powers threaten her mostly male heirs is evident primarily in the brutality with which they are stripped from her: Marduk guts and dismembers her, forcing her into passivity and compliance. And, subsequently, when the male Marduk conceives the idea for human beings, the task of creating them devolves not to a mother goddess, as it does in similar acts of creation in Mesopotamian literature,[51] but to the male god Ea (VI 1–38). Tiamat's powers of creation, along with Tiamat's body itself, have here been wholly usurped by her male heirs. As Tikva Frymer-Kensky (1992: 76) perspicaciously observed of Tiamat's ultimate fate, 'We live in the body of the mother, but she has neither activity nor power.'

## Further reading

For approaches to the gendered dynamics of *Enuma Elish*, see Sonik (2009), Cooper (2017), and Helle (2020a). Pioneering approaches to women in Mesopotamian literature, including in *Enuma Elish*, were undertaken by Frymer-Kensky (1992) and Harris (2000); while these remain important contributions, they include much outdated and contested material and should be approached critically. For conceptions of motherhood in Mesopotamia, see Couto-Ferreira (2016) and Stol (2016). For the political ideology of *Enuma Elish*, see Sonik (2008) and Gabriel (2014). For methodological issues relating to the study of characters in literature, see Woloch (2003). For Tiamat's monsters, see Wiggermann (1992); and for historically significant approaches to monsters more generally, see Tolkien (1936) and Cohen (1996).

## Notes

1 On the political logic of *Enuma Elish*, see also Johannes Haubold and Gösta Gabriel in this volume.

2 On the epic's modern reception, see also Gina Konstantopoulos in this volume.

3 Seleucid-era sources attest the recitation of *Enuma elish* during the Babylonian *akitu* (New Year) Festival, which was closely associated with the king and kingship. For the identification of the (human) king with Marduk in his role as vanquisher of Tiamat, see the Neo-Assyrian era SAA 3, 37 in Livingstone (1989), also posted online through Oracc at http://oracc.museum.upenn.edu/saao/corpus. So-called 'mirror of princes' or 'mirrors for princes' compositions (Latin *specula principum* or *speculum principis*; German *Fürstenspiegel*) are sometimes distinguished as a literary or political writing genre; e.g. Blaydes, Grimmer, and McQueen (2018). For a global approach to these, see the contributions in Perret and Péquignot (2023); for Islamic examples, see Marlow (2023, 2013), also Luce (2010); for diverse other contexts, see, e.g. Hellerstedt (2018) and Bratu (2010).

4 For accessible explorations of the cultural impact of these discoveries on Victorian Britain, see Kertai (2021) and McGeough (2021, 2015–21).

5 For the integration of Assyria's material remains into Europe's public museums and their aesthetic, political, and intellectual receptions, see the discussion (with extensive references) in Sonik and Kertai (2023).

6 Among the issues with Gunkel's hypothesis are the following: Mesopotamian conflict narratives significantly older than *Enuma Elish* have long since been translated (e.g. the Sumerian *Lugal-e*); the necessity for *Chaoskampf* to include both conflict and creation has been repeatedly challenged; and the translation of texts such as the Ugaritic *Baal Cycle* has significantly complicated the question of whether and how the so-called *Chaoskampf* tradition was introduced into biblical materials. See further Tsumura (2005) and Ballentine (2015).

7 These characterizations of Tiamat and Apsû have been sharply challenged in Sonik (2008, 2009, 2013a). Important early treatments of Tiamat in Frymer-Kensky (1992), Harris (2000), and Metzler (2002) established the significance of Tiamat as worthy of study in her own right, though I strongly disagree with various of the approaches and conclusions of these studies.

8 The biblical associations of Mesopotamia's visual arts were similarly highlighted; see, e.g. Russell (1997: 27–52); Sonik and Kertai (2023).

9 On the scientific classification and analysis of folktale, for example, see Pirkova-Jakobsen (1968 [1958]): xx. For a discussion of how this affected the reception of Mesopotamian literature, see Sonik (forthcoming).

10 Woloch focuses primarily on the retreat from characterization with respect to the theory of the novel, but this same development is unsurprisingly evident in theoretical approaches to other forms of narrative. Its consequences for Mesopotamia's narratives are discussed at greater length in Sonik (2021: 779–801; forthcoming).

11 The Enlightenment legacy of esteem for scientific ideals and organization as they applied to the development of nineteenth-century public museums in England, for example, is discussed in Jenkins (1992), the contributions in Paul (2012), Delbourgo (2017: 258–342), and, with particular attention to Assyrian collections, Sonik and Kertai (2023).

12 Influences of the Folkloristic School and Near Eastern archaeology on Gunkel's methods are discussed in Mihelic (1951: 120–9) and Carus (1901a, 1901b). See also Gunkel (1901, 1917).

13 Vladimir Propp's (1968 [1928]) early application of structuralism to Russian fairy tales specifically set the stage for its broader application to narrative, myth, and culture by later theorists including Algirdas Greimas, Claude Lévi-Strauss and Roland Barthes.

14 The relationships between *Enuma Elish* and other narrative compositions have been explored in a number of more recent studies, including Machinist (2005) and Wisnom (2020), relating *Anzû*, *Enuma Elish* and *Erra*, as well as Seri (2014), addressing diverse Akkadian narratives. For the need to balance intertextual and typological studies with focused analyses of individual narratives and characters, see Sonik (forthcoming) and Sonik and Shehata (forthcoming).

15 For an important book-length exception, see Gabriel (2014).

16 A forthright challenge to this marginalization was issued by J.R.R. Tolkien in his 1938 Andrew Lang lecture on Fairy Stories at St. Andrews (published in expanded form in 1947): 'It is true that in recent times fairy-stories have usually been written or "adapted" for children. But so may music be, or verse, or novels, or history, or scientific manuals … Any one of these things would, if left altogether in the nursery, become gravely impaired … Fairy-stories banished in this way, cut off from a full adult art, would in the end be ruined'; Tolkien (1966 [1947]: 59).

17 A number of subsequent treatments have built on this recognition: of particular interest here are those that have re-examined the significance of Grendel's mother (an ambiguous 'mother of monsters' like Tiamat), including, among many others, Alfano (1992), Burdoff (2014), and Chance (2019).

18 Tolkien is here explicitly challenging the then-prominent derogation of *Beowulf*'s 'main story' (and monsters) published in Ker (1904: 253).

19 Tolkien's recognition of monsters as worthy of both our interest and our analysis laid the foundations for the establishment of 'monster theory' as a flourishing field of contemporary academic research – e.g. Cohen (1996), Mittman and Hensel (2018a, 2018b) – as well as for my own work on the monsters of Mesopotamia's visual arts and literature.

20 The status of Sumerian narratives as fairy tales was examined, though with ambiguous results, in Edzard (1994: 7–14); see, more recently, George (2007: 50–3) and Sonik (forthcoming).

21 Mesopotamia's monsters are numerous and remarkable and should not be misattributed to the realms of fantasy, folk- or fairy tale; see Sonik (2013b: 103–16).

22 This contrasts sharply with the rather more pessimistic view articulated in Cixous (1974).

23 Woloch (2003: 2). Key approaches to character, including those developed in Woloch's (2003) and Frow's (2014) important volumes, are thoughtfully explored in Anderson, Felski, and Moi (2019).

24 The critical significance of the act of naming in Mesopotamia, as well as the link between name, identity, and *presence*, with extensive references, is explored in Sonik and Kertai (2021: 40–7 and passim). See also Radner (2005) and Seri (2006) on the

names of Marduk in *Enuma Elish*, as well as Sophus Helle and Marc Van De Mieroop in this volume.

25 The divine determinative (a DINGIR sign) is not used for the god Anshar as it would be redundant: the name Anshar is already written with an opening DINGIR sign (An).

26 On perceptions, duties, and obligations of motherhood in Mesopotamia, see, e.g. Couto-Ferreira (2016) and Stol (2016: 155–9).

27 On the gradual anthropomorphization of Tiamat, see Helle in this volume.

28 For discussions of this and other forms of metamorphosis, such as social integration through marriage, one might look to the Sumerian *Marriage of Martu* or the Sumerian *Gilgamesh and Huwawa* A; see, further, Sonik (2021, forthcoming).

29 See the discussion of this episode in Sonik (2012a: 391–3).

30 Anu's consort is not mentioned within the framework of the narrative: it is possible he engenders Ea independently (as Tiamat does the monsters), or that his consort belongs to another lineage (as the goddess Damkina may do) or is omitted for some other reason.

31 The connection between noise and creation (as opposed to silence, passivity, and stagnation) was established in Michalowski (1990: 381–96).

32 The concept of *melammu* (Akkadian) / **melam** (Sumerian) in literary contexts has been examined in Aster (2012); Sonik (2023: 487–524; 2022: 541–44). The stripping of Apsû, and this episode more broadly, was examined in Sonik (2008).

33 See, further, Sonik (2009; 2021: 794–5; forthcoming). This type of structural parallelism has been independently observed (and more globally explored) in Helle (2020b: 190–224).

34 Tiamat indeed proves a more dangerous opponent than Apsû in the subsequent action. This point was linked to different male and female aging patterns – with the former becoming more passive and the latter more active – in Harris (2000: 84–5), an interpretation I do not find persuasive. See, further, Sonik (2009) and Cooper (2017).

35 Tiamat's refusal to join Apsû at this juncture does not make her, as has sometimes been suggested, a 'good mother', nor are her actions an example of 'motherly compassion', as suggested in Frymer-Kensky (1992: 16–17). It is worth comparing her actions here – or, rather, her failure to act – to those of the independently powerful mother goddess Namma in the Sumerian narrative *Enki and Ninmah*. Namma, unlike Tiamat, actively mediates between disaffected minor gods and the great gods (her heirs) to avert catastrophe; see, further, Sonik (2012b: 388–9).

36 These unnamed gods name Tiamat as their mother (I 112), and it is from among their number that Tiamat selects Qingu to be her new consort (I 148).

37 Tiamat bears some similarities to other wrathful (mother) goddesses like Ninhursag, who curses the god Enki for eating the plant that grows from his own seed in the Sumerian narrative *Enki and Ninhursag* – but Ninhursag ultimately relents when Enki is in real danger and rushes to save him. Tiamat shows no such mercy, suggesting a comparison to the transgressive, easily enraged, and unforgiving Ishtar may be more pertinent; for the equating of Tiamat with Ishtar of Durna, see SAA 3 39 in Livingstone (1989) or online through Oracc at http://oracc.museum.upenn.edu/saao/corpus.

38 I do not regard Tiamat's apparently independent creation of the monsters as evidence for any inherently monstrous aspect of her own or of female generative capacities more generally; instead, the monsters seem ideally designed to their purpose as warriors and weapons in her battle against her (divine) heirs. For a different view, see Helle (2020a: 69).

39 The significance of the Tablet of Destinies as a narrative device in *Enuma Elish* was explored in Sonik (2012b).

40 For an accessible translation and transliteration of *Ninurta and the Turtle*, see ETCSL (Electronic Text Corpus of Sumerian Literature) 1.6.3, and Alster (1971: 120–5). For an accessible translation of *Anzû*, see Foster (2005: 555–78). For critical editions, see Vogelzang (1988) and Annus (2001). For electronic access, see SEAL (Sources of Early Akkadian Literature) nos. 1512 and 1514: https://seal.huji.ac.il.

41 I have characterized Qingu as Tiamat's consort rather than merely her lover (or puppet) as Tiamat's attempt to formally legitimize him is, I think, critical to how we understand the narrative.

42 Tiamat's monsters are extensively discussed and elucidated in the magisterial work of Wiggermann (1992). Several of Tiamat's monsters are commonly called 'demons', a classification I do not support: see the taxonomical discussion of monsters and demons in Sonik (2013b).

43 Translation from ETCSL 1.6.2; see also the edition in van Dijk (1983).

44 I would reiterate here the importance of recognizing Tiamat as other-than- instead of less-than-a god.

45 For recent interpretations of how these lines might work within the framework of the narrative, see Cooper (2017); Helle (2020a: 69).

46 For the perfection of the body of (human) kings, see, e.g. Winter (1989, 1996) and Sonik (2022).

47 One cannot quite argue that Marduk is not 'of woman born', as he is explicitly born of Damkina and Ea. But the location of his birth, the Apsû (naming both Apsû's powerful corpse as prepared by Ea, as well as Ea's sanctuary there), is explicitly emphasized in the narrative (I 81–4). This line of reasoning was previously considered in Sonik (2008, 2013a).

48 The roles of pity, compassion, empathy, and mercy in Sumerian and Akkadian sources have recently been considered in Katz (2023), Ziegler (2023), and Sonik and Steinert (2023: 17–19). Particularly relevant here is Ziegler's (2023: 756–8) exploration of pity (*rēmu*) in relation to women, especially royal women, in Old Babylonian Akkadian sources: this offers multiple rebukes of female figures – comparable to Marduk's rebuke of Tiamat (IV 80) – for failing to show compassion. See also the discussion of motherhood in Mesopotamia, with particular attention to the rebukes of mothers by their sons, in Couto-Ferreira (2016).

49 That Qingu was not worthy of being named Tiamat's consort is clear: whether Marduk might rightfully have fulfilled this role is less so. Tiamat is mother of all the gods, raising issues of incest (for her union with Qingu also), but Marduk's birth in the Apsû (despite the fact that Ea and Damkina are his progenitors) may put him on equal footing with Tiamat and also distance him sufficiently that incest is not be a concern. Themes of incest and murder (of prior generations) are perhaps best known from the *Theogony of Dunnu* – in which successive generations engage in murder of their fathers (and mothers) and incest with their mothers (and sisters) – published in Lambert (2013: 387–95).

50 I am not persuaded here that the tail attributed to Tiamat is a necessary signifier of her monstrosity in her lifetime, despite the strange matter of her corpse (IV 136), which in this volume's translation is read as *serkuppu*, 'watery mass', rather than *kūbu*, 'premature or stillborn child' or 'monstrous shape'; see my own prior discussions in Sonik (2009: 95–6; 2013a: 16–17), as well as Helle (2020a: 68) for a slightly different view on Tiamat's monstrosity.

51 In the Standard Babylonian *Gilgamesh Epic*, for example, while the god Anu has the idea for Enkidu's creation, it is still left to the goddess Aruru to actually do the *work* of creation – not surprising given how closely it resembles an act of childbirth; see the discussions in Frymer-Kensky (1992: 49, 75); Stol (2000: 74–83); and Sonik (2021).

## Bibliography

Alfano, C. (1992), 'The Issue of Feminine Monstrosity: A Reevaluation of Grendel's Mother', *Comitatus: A Journal of Medieval and Renaissance Studies*, 23 (1): 1–16.

Alster, B. (1971), 'Ninurta and the Turtle', *Journal of Cuneiform Studies*, 24: 120–5.

Anderson, A., R. Felski, and T. Moi (2019), *Character: Three Inquiries in Literary Studies*, Chicago: University of Chicago Press.

Annus, A. (2001), *The Standard Babylonian Epic of Anzu: Introduction, Cuneiform Text, Transliteration, Score, Glossary, Indices and Sign List*, State Archives of Assyria Cuneiform Texts 3, Helsinki: The Neo-Assyrian Text Corpus Project.

Aster, S. Z. (2012), *The Unbeatable Light: Melammu and Its Biblical Parallels*, Alter Orient und Altes Testament 384, Münster: Ugarit-Verlag.

Ballentine, D. S. (2015), *The Conflict Myth and the Biblical Tradition*, Oxford: Oxford University Press.

Beaulieu, P.-A. (2018), *A History of Babylon, 2200 BC–AD 75*, Malden: Wiley Blackwell.

Blaydes, L., J. Grimmer, and A. McQueen (2018), 'Mirrors for Princes and Sultans: Advice on the Art of Governance in the Medieval Christian and Islamic Worlds', *Journal of Politics*, 80 (4): 1150–67.

Botta, P. É. and E. Flandin (1849), *Monument de Ninive*, Paris: Imprimerie nationale.

Bratu, C. (2010), 'Mirrors for Princes (Western)', in A. Classen (ed.), *Handbook of Medieval Studies*, 1921–49, Berlin: De Gruyter.

Burdoff, S. F. (2014), 'Re-Reading Grendel's Mother: *Beowulf* and the Anglo-Saxon Metrical Charms', *Comitatus: A Journal of Medieval and Renaissance Studies*, 45: 91–103.

Carus, P. (1901a), 'The Fairy-Tale Element in the Bible', *The Monist*, 11 (3): 405–47.

Carus, P. (1901b), 'The Fairy-Tale Element in the Bible (Concluded)', *The Monist*, 11 (4): 500–35.

Chance, J. (2019), 'Reading Grendel's Mother', in H. Scheck and C. E. Kozikowski (eds), *New Readings on Women and Early Medieval English Literature and Culture: Cross-Disciplinary Studies in Honour of Helen Damico*, 209–25, Leeds: Arc Humanities Press.

Cixous, H. (1974), 'The Character of "Character"', *New Literary History*, 5 (2): 383–402.

Cohen, J. J. (ed., 1996), *Monster Theory: Reading Culture*, Minneapolis: University of Minnesota Press.

Cooper, J. S. (2017), 'Female Trouble and Troubled Males: Roiled Seas, Decadent Royals, and Mesopotamian Masculinities in Myth and Practice', in I. Zsolnay, *Being a Man: Negotiating Ancient Constructs of Masculinity*, 112–24, New York: Routledge.

Couto-Ferreira, M. E. (2016), 'Being Mothers or Acting (like) Mothers? Constructing Motherhood in Ancient Mesopotamia', in S. L. Budin and J. M. Turfa (eds), *Women in Antiquity: Real Women across the Ancient World*, 25–34, London: Routledge.

Dalley, S. (2002), 'Evolution of Gender in Mesopotamian Mythology and Iconography with a Possible Explanation of Ša Rešen, "the Man with Two Heads"', in S. Parpola and R. M. Whiting (eds), *Sex and Gender in the Ancient Near East: Proceedings of the 47th Rencontre Assyriologique Internationale, Helsinki, July 2–6, 2001*, vol. 1, 117–22, Helsinki: Neo-Assyrian Text Corpus Project.

Delbourgo, J. (2017), *Collecting the World: The Life and Curiosity of Hans Sloane*, London: Allen Lane.

Delitzsch, F. (1903), *Babel and Bible: Two Lectures on the Significance of Assyriological Research for Religion, Embodying the Most Important Criticisms and the Author's Replies*, trans. T. J. McCormack and W. H. Carruth, Chicago: Open Court Publishing Company.

Edzard, D. O. (1994), 'Sumerian Epic: Epic or Fairy Tale?', *Bulletin of the Canadian Society for Mesopotamian Studies*, 27: 7–14.

Felski, R. (2011), 'Introduction', *New Literary History*, 42 (2): v–ix.

Foster, B. R. (2005), *Before the Muses: An Anthology of Akkadian Literature*, 3rd edn, Bethesda: CDL Press.

Frow, J. (2014), *Character and Person*, Oxford: Oxford University Press.

Frymer-Kensky, T. (1992), *In the Wake of the Goddesses: Women, Culture and the Biblical Transformation of Pagan Myth*, New York: The Free Press.

Gabriel, G. (2014), '*enūma eliš*' – *Weg zu einer globalen Weltordnung: Pragmatik, Struktur und Semantik des babylonischen 'Lieds auf Marduk'*, Tübingen: Mohr Siebeck.

George, A. R. (1986), 'Sennacherib and the Tablet of Destinies', *Iraq*, 48: 133–46.

George, A. R. (2007), 'The Epic of Gilgameš: Thoughts on Genre and Meaning', in J. Azize and N. Weeks (eds), *Gilgamesh and the World of Assyria: Proceedings of the Conference Held at Mandelbaum House, the University of Sydney, 21–23 July 2004*, 37–66, Leuven: Peeters.

Gunkel, H. (1895), *Schöpfung und Chaos in Urzeit und Endzeit: Eine religionsgeschichtliche Untersuchung über Gen 1 und Ap Joh 12*, Göttingen: Vandenhoeck und Ruprecht.

Gunkel, H. (1901), *Genesis*, Göttingen: Vandenhoeck & Ruprecht.

Gunkel, H. (1917), *Das Märchen Im Alten Testament*, Tübingen: J. C. B. Mohr.

Harris, R. (2000), *Gender and Aging in Mesopotamia: The Gilgamesh Epic and Other Ancient Literature*, Norman: University of Oklahoma Press.

Helle, S. (2020a), 'Marduk's Penis: Queering *Enūma Eliš*', *Distant Worlds Journal*, 4: 63–77.

Helle, S. (2020b), 'The Two-Act Structure: A Narrative Device in Akkadian Epics', *Journal of Ancient Near Eastern Religions*, 20: 190–224.

Hellerstedt, A. (2018), 'Cracks in the Mirror: Changing Conceptions of Political Virtue in Mirrors for Princes in Scandinavia from the Middle Ages to c.1700', in A. Hellerstedt (ed.), *Virtue Ethics and Education from Late Antiquity to the Eighteenth Century*, 281–328, Amsterdam: Amsterdam University Press, 2018.

Jenkins, I. (1992), *Archaeologists & Aesthetes in the Sculpture Galleries of the British Museum, 1800–1939*, London: British Museum Press.

Katz, D. (2023), 'Compassion, Pity, and Empathy in Sumerian Sources', in K. Sonik and U. Steinert (eds), *The Routledge Handbook of Emotions in the Ancient Near East*, 741–53, New York: Routledge.

Ker, W. P. (1904), *The Dark Ages*, New York: Charles Scribner's Sons.

Lambert, W. G. (1986), 'Ninurta Mythology in the Babylonian Epic of Creation', in K. Hecker and W. Sommerfeld (eds), *Keilschriftliche Literaturen*, Compte Rendu de la Rencontre Assyriologique Internationale 32, Berliner Beiträge zum Vorderen Orient 6, 55–60, Berlin: Dietrich Reimer Verlag.

Lambert, W. G. (2013), *Babylonian Creation Myths*, Mesopotamian Civilizations 16, Winona Lake: Eisenbrauns.

Layard, A. H. (1849), *Nineveh and Its Remains: With an Account of a Visit to the Chaldaean Christians of Kurdistan, and the Yezidis, or Devil-Worshippers; and an Inquiry into the Manners and Arts of the Ancient Assyrians*, London: John Murray.

Layard, A. H. (1853), *Discoveries in the Ruins of Nineveh and Babylon; With Travels in Armenia, Kurdistan and the Desert: Being the Result of a Second Expedition Undertaken by the Trustees of the British Museum*, London: John Murray.

Levy, M., and F. Mendlesohn (2016), *Children's Fantasy Literature: An Introduction*, Cambridge: Cambridge University Press.

Livingstone, A. (1989), *Court Poetry and Literary Miscellanea*, State Archives of Assyria 3, Helsinki: Helsinki University Press.

Luce, M. D. (2010), 'Mirrors for Princes (Islamic)', in A. Classen (ed.), *Handbook of Medieval Studies*, 1916–20, Berlin: De Gruyter.

Machinist, P. (2005), 'Order and Disorder: Some Mesopotamian Observations', in S. Shaked (ed.), *Genesis and Regeneration: Essays on Conceptions of Origins*, 31–61, Jerusalem: Israel Academy of Sciences and Humanities.

Marlow, L. (2013), 'Among Kings and Sages: Greek and Indian Wisdom in an Arabic Mirror for Princes', *Arabica*, 60 (1–2): 1–57.

Marlow, L. (2023), *Medieval Muslim Mirrors for Princes: An Anthology of Arabic, Persian and Turkish Political Advice*, Cambridge: Cambridge University Press.

McGeough, K. (2015–2021), *The Ancient Near East in the Nineteenth Century*, 3 vols, Hebrew Bible Monographs, Sheffield: Sheffield Phoenix Press.

McGeough, K. (2021), 'Assyrian Style and Victorian Materiality: Mesopotamia in British Souvenirs, Political Caricatures, Theatrical Productions, and the Sydenham Crystal Palace', in K. Sonik (ed.), *Art/ifacts and ArtWorks in the Ancient World*, 415–46, Philadelphia: University of Pennsylvania Press.

Metzler, K. A. (2002), 'Tod, Weiblichkeit und Ästhetik im mesopotamischen Weltschöpfungsepos *Enūma elîš*', in S. Parpola and R. M. Whiting (eds), *Sex and Gender in the Ancient Near East*, Compte Rendu de la Rencontre Assryiologique Internationale 47, 393–411, Helsinki: Neo-Assyrian Text Corpus Project.

Michalowski, P. (1990), 'Presence at the Creation', in T. Abusch, J. Huehnergard and P. Steinkeller (eds), *Lingering Over Words: Studies in Ancient Near Eastern Literature in Honor of William L. Moran*, Harvard Semitic Studies 37, 381–96, Atlanta: Scholars Press.

Mihelic, J. L. (1951), 'The Influence of Form Criticism on the Study of the Old Testament', *Journal of Bible and Religion*, 19 (3): 120–9.

Mittman, A. S. and M. Hensel (eds, 2018a), *Classic Readings on Monster Theory, Volume One*, Leeds: Arc Humanities Press.

Mittman, A. S. and M. Hensel (eds, 2018b), *Primary Sources on Monsters: Demonstrare, Volume Two*, Leeds: Arc Humanities Press.

Paul, Carol (ed., 2012), *The First Modern Museums of Art: The Birth of an Institution in 18th- and Early-19th-Century Europe*, Los Angeles: The J. Paul Getty Museum.

Perret, N.-L. and S. Péquignot (eds, 2023), *A Critical Companion to the 'Mirrors for Princes' Literature*, Leiden: Brill.

Pirkova-Jakobsen, S. (1968 [1958]), 'Introduction to the First Edition', in *Morphology of the Folktale, by Vladimir Propp*, 2nd edn, xix–xxii, Austin: University of Texas Press.

Propp, V. (1968 [1928]), *Morphology of the Folktale*, 2nd ed., trans. L. Scott, Austin: University of Texas Press.

Radner, K. (2005), *Die Macht des Namens: Altorientalische Strategien zur Selbsterhaltung*, Wiesbaden: Harrassowitz.

Rich, C. J. (1818a), *Memoir on the Ruins of Babylon*, 3rd edn, London: Longman, Hurst, Rees, Orme, and Brown.
Rich, C. J. (1818b), *Second Memoir on Babylon, Containing an Inquiry into the Correspondence Between the Ancient Descriptions of Babylon and the Remains Still Visible on the Site*, London: Longman, Hurst, Rees, Orme, and Brown.
Rich, C. J. (1836), *Narrative of a Residence in Koordistan, and on the Site of Ancient Nineveh; with Journal of a Voyage Down the Tigris to Baghdad and an Account of a Visit to Shirauz and Persepolis*, ed. M. Mackintosh Rich, London: James Duncan.
Russell, J. M. (1997), *From Nineveh to New York: The Strange Story of the Assyrian Reliefs in the Metropolitan Museum of Art and the Hidden Masterpiece at Canford School*, New Haven: Yale University Press.
Seri, A. (2006), 'The Fifty Names of Marduk in "*Enūma Eliš*"', *Journal of the American Oriental Society*, 126 (4): 507–19.
Seri, A. (2014), 'Borrowings to Create Anew: Intertextuality in the Babylonian Poem of "Creation" (*Enūma eliš*)', *Journal of the American Oriental Society*, 134 (1): 89–106.
Silver, C. G. (1999), *Strange and Secret Peoples: Fairies and Victorian Consciousness*, Oxford: Oxford University Press.
Smith, G. (1876), *The Chaldean Account of Genesis, Containing the Description of the Creation, the Fall of Man, the Deluge, the Tower of Babel, the Times of the Patriarchs, and Nimroud; Babylonian Fables, and Legends of the Gods; from the Cuneiform Inscriptions*, London: Sampson, Low, Marston, Scarle, and Rivingston.
Sonik, K. (2008), 'Bad King, False King, True King: Apsû and His Heirs', *Journal of the American Oriental Society*, 128 (4): 737–43.
Sonik, K. (2009), 'Gender Matters in *Enūma eliš*', in S. Holloway, J. Scurlock and R. Beal (eds), *In the Wake of Tikva Frymer-Kensky*, 85–101, Piscataway: Gorgias Press.
Sonik, K. (2012a), 'Breaching the Boundaries of Being: Metamorphoses in the Mesopotamian Literary Texts', *Journal of the American Oriental Society*, 132 (3): 385–93.
Sonik, K. (2012b), 'The Tablet of Destinies and the Transmission of Power in *Enūma Eliš*', in G. Wilhelm (ed.), *Organization, Representation, and Symbols of Power in the Ancient Near East*, Compte Rendu de la Rencontre Assyriologique lnternationale 54, 387–95, Winona Lake: Eisenbrauns.
Sonik, K. (2013a), 'From Hesiod's Abyss to Ovid's *rudis indigestaque moles*: Reading Chaos into the Babylonian Epic of Creation', in J. Scurlock and R. Beal (eds), *Creation and Chaos: A Reconsideration of Gunkel's Chaoskampf Hypothesis*, 1–25, Winona Lake: Eisenbrauns.
Sonik, K. (2013b), 'Mesopotamian Conceptions of the Supernatural: A Taxonomy of Zwischenwesen', *Archiv für Religionsgeschichte*, 14: 103–16.
Sonik, K. (2021), 'Minor and Marginal(ized)? Re-Thinking Women as Minor Characters in the Epic of Gilgamesh', *Journal of the American Oriental Society*, 41 (4): 779–801.
Sonik, K. (2022), 'The Distant Eye and the Ekphrastic Image: Thinking Through Aesthetics and Art for the Senses (Western | Non-Western)', in K. Neumann and A. Karmel Thomason (eds), *The Routledge Handbook of the Senses in the Ancient Near East*, 530–57, New York: Routledge.
Sonik, K. (2023), 'Awe as Entangled Emotion: Prosociality, Collective Action, and Aesthetics in the Sumerian Gilgamesh Narratives', in K. Sonik and U. Steinert (eds), *The Routledge Handbook of Emotions in the Ancient Near East*, 487–524, New York: Routledge.
Sonik, K. (2024), 'Gilgamesh and Tiamat Abroad: (Mis-)Reading Mesopotamian Epic', in P. Lothspeich (ed.), *The Epic World*, 104–117, New York: Routledge.

Sonik, K. (forthcoming), 'Characterization and Identity in Mesopotamian Literature: The *Gilgamesh Epic*, *Enuma elish*, and Other Sumerian and Akkadian Narratives', in D. Shehata and K. Sonik (eds), *Contemporary Approaches to Mesopotamian Literature: How to Tell a Story*, Leiden: Brill.
Sonik, K. and D. Kertai (2021), 'Entangled Images: Royal Memory, Posthumous Images, and the Afterlives of Assyrian Rock Reliefs', in J. Ben-Dov and F. Rojas, *Afterlives of Ancient Rock-Cut Monuments in the Near East: Carvings In and Out of Time*, 39–68, Leiden: Brill.
Sonik, K. and D. Kertai (2023), 'Between Science and Aesthetics in the Nineteenth-Century Public Museum: The Elgin Marbles, The Chain of Art, and the Victorian Assimilation of Assyrian Sculpture', in J. C. Howard (ed.), *The Reliefs of Ashurnasirpal II: Architecture, Iconography, and Text*, 105–38, Leuven: Peeters.
Sonik, K. and D. Shehata (forthcoming), 'Mesopotamian Literature: Issues, Theories, and Methods of Sumerian and Akkadian Narrative Analysis', in D. Shehata and K. Sonik (eds), *Contemporary Approaches to Mesopotamian Literature: How to Tell a Story*, Leiden: Brill.
Sonik, K. and U. Steinert (2023), 'Emotions in the Ancient Near East: Foundations for a Developing Field of Study', in K. Sonik and U. Steinert (eds), *The Routledge Handbook of Emotions in the Ancient Near East*, 1–24, New York: Routledge.
Stol, M. (2000), *Birth in Babylonia and the Bible, with a Chapter by F.A.M. Wiggermann*, Cuneiform Monographs 14, Groningen: STYX Publications.
Stol, M. (2016), *Women in the Ancient Near East*, trans. H. Richardson and M. Richardson, Berlin: De Gruyter.
Tolkien, J. R. R. (1936), *Beowulf: The Monsters and the Critics*, Folcroft: The Folcroft Press.
Tolkien, J. R. R. (1966 [1947]), 'On Fairy-Stories', in C. S. Lewis (ed.), *Essays Presented to Charles Williams*, 38–89, Grand Rapids: William B. Eerdmans Publishing Company.
Tsumura, D. T. (2005), *Creation and Destruction: A Reappraisal of the* Chaoskampf *Theory in the Old Testament*, Winona Lake: Eisenbrauns.
van Dijk, J. J. A. (1983), *Lugal ud me-lám-bi Nir-g̃ál: Le récit épique et didactique des Travaux de Ninurta, du Déluge et de la Nouvelle Création*, 2 vols, Leiden: Brill.
Vogelzang, M. E. (1988), *Bin šar dadmē: Edition and Analysis of the Akkadian Anzu Poem*, Groningen: Styx Publications.
Wiggermann, F. A. M. (1992), *Mesopotamian Protective Spirits: The Ritual Texts*, Cuneiform Monographs 1, Groningen: Styx.
Winter, I. J. (1989), 'The Body of the Able Ruler: Toward an Understanding of the Statues of Gudea', in H. D. Behrens, D. Loding and M. T. Roth (eds), *Dumu-e$_2$-dub-ba-a: Studies in Honor of Åke W. Sjöberg*, Occasional Publications of the Samuel Noah Kramer Fund 11, 573–83, Philadelphia: University Museum.
Winter, I. J. (1996), 'Sex, Rhetoric and the Public Monument: The Alluring Body of Naram-Sin of Agade', in N. B. Kampen, *Sexuality in Ancient Art*, 11–26, Cambridge: Cambridge University Press.
Wisnom, S. (2020), *Weapons of Words: Intertextual Competition in Babylonian Poetry; A Study of 'Anzû', 'Enūma Eliš' and 'Erra and Išum'*, Cultue and History of the Ancient Near East 106, Leiden: Brill.
Woloch, A. (2003), *The One vs. the Many: Minor Characters and the Space of the Protagonist in the Novel*, Princeton: Princeton University Press.
Woloch, A. (2006), 'Minor Characters', in F. Moretti (ed.), *The Novel*, 2, 295–323, Princeton: Princeton University Press.
Ziegler, N. (2023), 'Pity and Suffering in Old Babylonian Akkadian Sources', in K. Sonik and U. Steinert (eds), *The Routledge Handbook of Emotions in the Ancient Near East*, 754–67, New York: Routledge.

9

# *Enuma Elish*, knowledge of the heavens, and world order

Francesca Rochberg

Knowledge of the heavens and description of world order, or what might be called astronomy and cosmology, are central to the poetic work *Enuma Elish* for achieving its main aim, which was to glorify the Babylonian national god Marduk by celebrating his creative acts. The gods made Marduk their king in order that he rule over 'the entirety of the whole of everything' (*kiššat kal gimrēti*, IV 14, translation modified).[1] The 'whole of everything' as the domain of Marduk's command referred to the entire expanse of heaven and earth, above, below, and all that was between. The body of that created world was measured and proportionate, characterized by the symmetry of counterparts and correspondences. This world body outwardly manifested divine order, regulation, and propriety. Divine propriety was achieved by stationing the gods in their cosmic places, but the ultimate symbol of divine control was completed by the creator god Marduk when he established himself in the centre of the new earth at the temple Esagil in Babylon and gave himself an astral manifestation as Neberu in the centre of the new heaven.

Because the very structure and interconnections of world parts – heaven, earth/netherworld and Apsû – were the product of Marduk's creative work, the description and understanding of the whole of these parts, as given in the poem, were necessarily a description and understanding of the world as a whole. The poem's mapping of the world's architecture describes symmetry, balance, and the proportionality of world parts. Thus the poem may be understood as a statement of cosmology in addition to cosmogony.

*Enuma Elish* reflects a certain basic knowledge of the heavens, detailed in the discussion to follow, a knowledge which, we can only assume, was the common property of the highly educated scribes of the period, among whom we can surely count the authors and copyists of *Enuma Elish*. The astronomical content of the poem is therefore circumscribed by the text's own aims, which were not to investigate or understand astronomical phenomena per se, as Wilfred G. Lambert (2013: 454) already said. On the contrary, the poem had a distinct interest in the structure and workings of the world as the god Marduk's creation. As a consequence, the narrative setting and frame of the work was the realm of the divine and the world of divine creation, from the heavens to the netherworld and the earth of human beings in between.

As Lambert's commentary makes clear, the place of the text in the history of astronomy is limited to its reflection of a certain early period in descriptive astronomy, neither quite observational nor predictive although based on a knowledge grounded in observing the heavens over a long period of time. This early Babylonian astronomy, attested prior to *c.* 600 BCE, is generally exemplified by the texts of the so-called Astrolabe tradition and astronomical compendium titled *MUL.APIN*.

The Astrolabe designates an originally late second millennium tradition of texts the purpose of which, principally, was to assign the risings of certain stars (heliacal risings[2]) to each of the twelve months of a schematic year in which those risings occurred.[3] Texts of the Astrolabe tradition, in both circular or ring form, and list form, stem from the reign of the Middle Assyrian king Ninurta-apil-Ekur (1191–1179 BCE), and continued to be copied into the Seleucid period in the third century BCE or later. Its purpose was to assign thirty-six fixed stars, constellations, and even planets to various parts of the sky for the twelve months of the ideal year, three stars per month. Each star represents a heliacal rising in its assigned month and in its assigned path, the outer ring for the path of Enlil, the middle ring for the path of Anu, and the inner ring for the path of Ea. The incipit of the Astrolabe text tradition was 'Three Stars Each' (mul$^{\text{meš}}$ 3$^{\text{TA.ÀM}}$), at least as far as we know from its two attestations (Horowitz 2014: 9). The intertextual relationship between the Astrolabe and *Enuma Elish* is discussed in Horowitz, *Three Stars*, 1–8.

*MUL.APIN* is a more extensive astronomical compendium in a two-tablet series from the early first millennium BCE that catalogued and systematized a wide variety of celestial phenomena.[4] *MUL.APIN* takes its incipit from the name of the first star of this list, *Epinnu* (written MUL.APIN) or 'Plow Star', which has been identified as Triangulum Boreale with γ Andromedae (Reiner and Pingree 1981: 10). *MUL.APIN* compiles the list of the stars in the paths of Enlil, Anu, and Ea (in that order), although it does not limit its list to twelve stars in each path. MUL.APIN tallies the numbers of stars in the paths as 33 Enlil stars (there are only 31 marked with DIŠ to signify new or separate entry in the list), 23 Anu stars (there are 20 entries with DIŠ) and 15 Ea stars (13 have DIŠ; Hunger and Steele 2019: 165). *MUL.APIN* includes each of the five planets within its list: Jupiter is assigned to the path of Enlil and Venus, Mars, Saturn, and Mercury are in the path of Anu. There is, therefore, overlap and difference in the names and ordering of the stars of the various paths in *MUL.APIN* as compared with the Astrolabe tradition, which is itself not standard in every case.

In describing the orderly nature of the world, *Enuma Elish* is reasonably consistent with the form and content of the knowledge of the heavens reflected in those two texts. This chapter, therefore, seeks to elucidate the knowledge of the heavens reflected in the poem's astronomical, calendrical, and cosmographical elements. As these astronomical, calendrical, and cosmographical elements constituted Marduk's great acts, their description was essential to the poem in order to achieve its goal of establishing the Babylonian national god's supremacy over the divine pantheon and his centrality for the world itself. The portions of the poem relevant to a discussion of knowledge of the heavens are mainly to be found in Tablet V, which is devoted to Marduk's organization of the newly created order of things. Tablets IV and VII are also of interest for a number of other elements, discussed below.

## Marduk and his astral manifestations

The god Marduk is the central figure of the poem and supreme deity of the Babylonian pantheon. Over the span of ancient cuneiform scholarship, Marduk had several names for his astral manifestations, but in *Enuma Elish* he has only one: Neberu (Akkadian *Nēberu)*. In Tablet V 1–8 and VII 124–31, references are made to the astral functionary called Neberu, whose name means 'crossing (point)' and whose job it was (in Tablet V) to set a boundary of some kind, by assuming a position at the midpoint between the three paths[5] of the fixed stars (also found in the Astrolabe tradition) and in Tablet VII to 'hold the crossing between heaven and earth' (*nēberet šamê* (*u*) *erṣeti lū tamiḫ*, VII 124).

The identification of Neberu with a particular celestial body is complicated by the fact that the god Marduk had two planetary identities, Jupiter and Mercury. These are only attested from the Neo-Assyrian period onwards. The identification of Marduk's star with Mercury is found in Neo-Assyrian reports: 'The star of Marduk, Mercury, is going beyond its (normal) position and ascends' (SAA 8 93, rev. 3), and 'If the star of Marduk becomes visible at the beginning of the year: that year his furrow will prosper. (This means) Mercury becomes visible in Nisannu' (SAA 8 503, 1–3). A commentary to *Enuma Anu Enlil* 56 iii 29a explains 'If a planet becomes visible in Nisannu (this refers to) Jupiter, variant: Mercury' (Reiner and Pingree 1981: 43–3; Hunger 1976: no. 90:1).

The passages in *Enuma Elish* concerning Neberu (Tablet V 1–8 and VII 124–31) are not easily reconcilable with one another. Indeed, they seem to refer to two different situations. Without specification of reference points, the 'boundary' and the 'crossing' are difficult to identify. Modern scholars have pursued many and various avenues for identification. To discuss them all would take this essay far afield, but the most recent investigation of this problem is found in Horowitz (2014: 22–3) with previous literature (also on p. 151 sub 36). Horowitz (2014: 22–3 with n. 114) argued for an identification of Neberu with the planet Mercury, both in *Enuma Elish* and in Astrolabe B, recognizing that later texts more often take Marduk's star to be Jupiter. Horowitz's identification of Neberu with Mercury faces the problem that Mercury is the most difficult of all the planets to observe due to its proximity to the Sun. This makes the planet visible only as an evening or a morning star, close to the western horizon in the evening or the eastern horizon in the morning where it is sometimes susceptible to problems of visibility in the half light of dawn or dusk. The innermost planet never appears high in the sky against the darkness of night, but will only be observable close to the horizon, either at dusk low in the western sky when the Sun has sunk sufficiently below the horizon, or before dawn low in the eastern sky before the Sun's light is too great. The reading of Mercury's name $GU_4$.UD as *Šihtu* 'The Jumper', that is, the sheep that 'jumps', calls to mind the erratic nature of its appearances due to its not being often or easily visible. At the vernal equinox, or some time in Nisannu, when the ecliptic stands at its greatest angle to the horizon, Mercury has its best chance of reaching a higher altitude, but it remains tethered closely to the sun with the greatest elongation (angular distance from the sun) between 18° and 28°. This planet's synodic period is 116 days (nearly four months long) between appearances of the same kind (e.g. as a first rising), so its appearance in Nisannu is not a marker for the beginning of the year.

In view of the problems with Mercury's visibility, Horowitz's suggestion to make Mercury 'divide the old year from the new year' in Astrolabe B and *Enuma Elish* V 1–8 is insufficiently clarified, nor does V 1–8 suggest a function for the planet Mercury to mark 'the organization of the stars':

*ubaššim manzāza ana ilī rabûti*
*kakkabī tamšīlšunu lumāšī ušziz*
*u'addi šatta miṣrāti umaṣṣir*
*šinšeret arḫī kakkabī šulu[š]ā ušziz*
*ištu ūmī ša šatti uṣṣ[ir]u uṣurāti*
*ušaršid manzāz nēberi ana uddû riksīšun*
*ana lā epēš anni lā egû manāma*
*manzāz enlil u ea ukīn ittīšu*

He fashioned positions for the great gods
and established the constellations, the images of the stars.
He marked out the year, drawing its outline,
and established the twelve months, with three stars each.
After he had planned out the year,
he fixed Neberu's station to mark the organization of the stars,
and so that they would not err or be remiss in any way,
he set up alongside it the positions of Enlil and Ea.

(V 1–8, translation modified)

The 'position' (*manzāzu*) of Neberu is most certainly in the path of Anu, which represents the path of the fixed stars lying closest to the celestial equator (see note 9) and running from east to west through the middle of the sky. On either side of this central position, Marduk fixed the other 'positions' (synonymous, presumably, with the paths) of Enlil and Ea (*manzāz enlil u ea*). Mercury's appearance in the path of Anu could in theory 'mark the organization of the stars', but given how erratic Mercury's appearance tends to be and how relatively dim and low on the horizon it frequently appears, Jupiter seems the better candidate for Neberu in *Enuma Elish*. Further discussion of Neberu continues in the section below, under 'Knowledge of the Heavens in *Enūma Eliš*'.

In the first millennium – that is, later than both *Enuma Elish* and the Astrolabe tradition – Marduk was astralized in the form of the planet Jupiter, whose name was most often $^{d}$SAG.ME.GAR, but also sometimes 'Brilliant Youth' ($^{d}$*Šulpae*), or 'Heroic One' ($^{d}$*Dāpinu*, written $^{MUL/d}$UD.AL.TAR), or indeed, 'The Crossing (Point)' ($^{d}$*Nēberu*), which were alternative or code names for Jupiter (Rochberg 2007: 433–40). It seems that the various names applied in different specific situations, as in the following explanation given to the King of Assyria by the scholar Nabû-mushesi, prompted by the sighting of a halo around the Moon and Jupiter and the constellation Scorpius within it: 'The star of Marduk at its appearance is (called) "Brilliant Youth". When it rises to (a height) of one double-hour it is (called) SAG.ME.GAR. When it stands in the middle of the sky it is (called) "The Crossing"' ([$^{m}$]$^{ul.d}$amar.utu *ina tāmartišu* $^{d}$*šul-pa-e*$_{3}$ 1 *bēru išaqqama* $^{d}$SAG.ME.GAR *ina qabal šamê* (murub$_{4}$ an-*e*) *izzizma* $^{d}$*Nēberu*, SAA 8 147 7–rev. 1). When it stands in the middle of the sky it is (called) The Crossing ($^{d}$*Nēberu*).

Marduk had other astral manifestations and other names, namely 'the King' ($^{d}$*Šarru*, $^{mul}$lugal, the star we have identified as Regulus) (SAA 8 170 rev.3) and 'The Crook' ($^{d}$*Gamlu* = the constellation we have identified as Auriga) (SAA 8 170 rev.1). When called $^{d}$*Šarru*, the 'King Star,' the reference is unequivocally to the status of Marduk as king of all the gods. Similarly, the metonymic $^{d}$*Gamlu* 'Crook' was a weapon of Marduk (*Chicago Assyrian Dictionary* s.v. *gamlu* c 6′), thus symbolic of the god himself. The pretext for Marduk's ascent to kingship (IV 5–10) and act of creation was that he was to be the avenger of the gods against the villainy of Tiamat together with her spouse and partner in crime, Qingu. When the transfer of power to Marduk was complete, the final demonstration came in the form of the destruction and remaking of a constellation:

*ušzizzū-ma ina birīšunu lumāša ištēn*
*ana marduk bukrīšunu šunu izzakrū*
*šīmatka bēlu lū maḫrat ilī-ma*
*abātu (u) banû qibi liktūnā*
*epšu pîka li’’abit lumāšu*
*tūr qibīšum-ma lumāšu lišlim*
*iqbī-ma ina pîšu i’’abit lumāšu*
*itūr iqbīšum-ma lumāšu ittabni*
*kīma ṣīt pîšu īmurū ilū abbūšu*
*iḫdû ikrubū marduk-ma šarru*

They set up among them one constellation,
and said to him, to Marduk their child:
'Your fate, Lord, shall equal the gods:
command destruction or creation, and it shall be done.
At the working of your words, let the constellation[6] be destroyed,
command again and let the constellation be made whole.'
He commanded, and at his word the constellation was destroyed,
he commanded again and the constellation was created anew.
When the gods his fathers saw the effect of his utterance,
they rejoiced and acclaimed: 'Marduk is king!'[7]

(IV 19–28)

Marduk's power to destroy and create by his verbal command alone was demonstrated in the starry heaven with the destruction and restoration of a constellation, the symbol par excellence of enduring permanence, if not eternity. In the recitation of the fifty names of Marduk the fiftieth name, Lord of the Lands, which is a well-known epithet of Enlil,[8] reflects the complete transfer of the power and station of the former god of creation, Enlil, to Marduk:

*aššu ašra ibnâ iptiqa dannina*
*bēl mātāti šumšu ittabi abu Enlil*

Because he created heaven[9] and fashioned the netherworld,[10]
Father Enlil has named (him by) his own name,[11] Lord of the Lands.

(VII 135–6, translation modified)

The twelfth name given to Marduk, Asaralimnunna ($^{d}$*asar-alim-nun-na*), has cosmological reference in the epithet 'who implements the decrees of Anu, Enlil and Ea' (*muštēšir têrēt* $^{d}$*Anu* $^{d}$*Enlil u* $^{d}$*Ea*, VII 6, translation modified), as the three great gods who inhabit the three principal parts of the world, heaven, earth, and Apsû. The paths of heaven that serve to organize, even map, the risings of stars in the Astrolabe, *MUL. APIN*, and in V 6–8, are named for these principal gods. Echoing the introduction to the celestial omen series, *Enuma Anu Enlil* is the conclusion to the eclipse omen section Tablet 22 (Rochberg-Halton 1988: 270–1; source E, 14′–20′), which makes clear what the decrees of Anu, Enlil, and Ea are (breaks are not indicated):

> *enūma Anu Enlil u Ea ilāni rabûti šamê u erṣeta ibnû u'addû giskimma ukkinnū manzāza ušaršidū gisgalla ilāni mušīti u- … uza''izū harrānī kakkabī tamšīlšunu īṣirū lumāšī mūša ūma kakku sakku … arha u šatta ibnû … šamê u erṣeti iprusū*(?) *purussî*(?)
>
> When Anu, Enlil and Ea, the great gods, created heaven and earth and made manifest the celestial signs, they fixed the stations and established the positions of the gods of the night … they divided the paths of the stars and drew the constellations as their (the gods') likenesses. They created night, day, abstruse omens(?), …., month and year. They decided(?) the decisions(?)[12] of heaven and earth.
>
> (Source E, 14′–20′)

The implementation of all this was conferred upon Marduk with the name Asaralimnunna, explained in a commentary text as 'light of Anu, Enlil, and Ea' (STC 1 216–17, l. 2, see Jiménez 2015). The passage in the opening of *Enuma Elish* V 1–8 appropriates the role of Anu, Enlil, and Ea to fix the stations and establish the positions of the gods of night (i.e. the stars) to Marduk as Asaralimnunna.

Finally, a reference to Marduk among the stars may be found in the section of *Udughul* known as Marduk's Address to the Demons[13]:

> *anāku Asalluhi eršu itpēšu šá š*[*ūturu hasīsa:*] *ša kakkabāni* ($MUL_x$.$MUL_x$.$MUL_x$.$MUL_x$) $^{d}$*Ea hāsisi*: $^{d}$*Ea*
>
> I am Asalluḫi, wise, sagacious, of superior understanding: of the stars, Ea the wise = Ea.

## Knowledge of the heavens in *Enuma Elish*

The degree to which the poem reflects knowledge of the heavens is strictly limited to its express aim to show Marduk's role in establishing the heavenly markers of permanence for his creation and its organized rhythms and regularity. The Moon as the indicator of day, night, and the month is one such example:

*nannāra uštēpâ mūša iqtīpa*
*u'addīšum-ma šuknat mūsi ana uddû ūmī*
*arḫīšam lā naparkâ ina agê uṣṣir*
*ina rēš arḫim-ma napāḫi elâti*
*qarnī nabâta ana uddû zakāri ūmī*
*ina sebûti agâ* [*ma*]*šla*
[*š*]*apattu lū šutamḫurāt*(*a*) *mišil* [*arḫī*]*šam*
*e*[*n*]*ūma šamšu ina išid šamê ina*[*ṭṭal*]*ūka*
*in*[*a s*]*imti šutakṣibam-ma bini arkāniš*
*bub*[*bul*]*u ana ḫarrān šamši šutaqrib-ma*
[*ina šalā*]*šê lū šutamḫurāt*(*a*) *šamša lū šannāt*(*a*)

He brought forth the Moon, entrusting the night to him,
appointing him as the night-time jewel, so as to distinguish the days.
Monthly and without fail, he ennobled him with a crown:
At the beginning of each month, light up the height of heaven!
You shine with horns to mark the naming of the days.
On the seventh day, (your) crown halved,
on the fifteenth, halfway through each month, may you always face (one another):
when Shamash can see you on the horizon,
reaching your full size at the fitting time, then reverse your form.
On the day of disappearance, approach the path of Shamash,
on the thirtieth day, you will again equal Shamash.

(V 12–22, translation modified)

First the Moon, the 'jewel of night' (V 13), is appointed to distinguish the nights from the days. He is commanded to change the shape of his disk, literally 'crown', from first having horns, then to being half and then full, whereupon the Moon's shapes reverse until the day of disappearance when the Moon again meets up with the Sun. This passage parallels the description of lunar phases in the commentary series *I-na*$_8$ GIŠ.HUR AN.KI lines 1–10 (Livingstone 1986: 22–3),[14] which is unfortunately quite broken:

*enūma ultu tāmart*[*i* … ]
*ana* UD.7.KAM *agâ* [*mašla*(?) … ]
UD.14.KAM i- … […]
*šapattu* […]
UD.21.KA[M … ]
UD.27.[KAM … ]
UD.28!.[KAM … ] *itūr* … […]
*bubbu*[*lu* … ] … *ukīn* … […]

When, from the first appearance (of the Moon) […]
On the seventh day a [half] disk […]

On the fourteenth day it ... [...]
The fifteenth day[...]
The twenty-first day [...]
The twenty-seventh [day ... ] ... [...]
The twenty-eighth [day ... ] it returned. [...]
On the day of its disappearance [...] it firmly established. [...]

(l. 1–10)

The parallel between *Enuma Elish* and *I-na*$_8$ GIŠ.HUR AN.KI is important in testifying to the common tradition of knowledge to which these texts belong.

Finally, Marduk orchestrated the completion of the lunar month by commanding Sin to approach and meet up with Shamash: 'On the day of disappearance, approach the path of Shamash, on the thirtieth day, you will again equal Shamash' (V 21–2). Shamash is instrumental for his relation to the Moon's position, 'seeing' him on the horizon at full moon or in 'opposition', and being 'matched' or equal to the Moon on the thirtieth day, when they are together in 'conjunction' in the same direction of the sky. Opposition and conjunction are the two lunar phenomena of greatest interest to the ancients as eclipses occur at these times, the solar eclipse when sun and moon are in conjunction, meaning in the same direction in the sky, and the lunar eclipse when sun and moon are in opposition, meaning on opposite sides of the sky. At conjunction, the moon will not be visible for being too near the sun, which *Enuma Elish* V 21–2 expresses as 'the day of disappearance' for Sin.

The other key role in marking the new heavenly organization is taken on by Marduk himself in the form of his own heavenly manifestation, Neberu. Neberu is Marduk's 'star', set to stand at the 'centre' or 'midpoint of heaven' (*qabal šamê*, see SAA 8 147 rev. 1). This position set aside for Marduk's heavenly manifestation is also referred to as controlling the 'crossing place' (*nēbertu*) between heaven and earth' (*nēberu nēberet šamê* (*u*) *erṣeti lū tamiḫ-ma*, VII 124, translation modified). The terminology of 'the middle of heaven' (*qabal šamê*) and 'crossing place' (*nēbertu*) has no obvious astronomical referent or referents. What the designation 'middle' refers to, and similarly, what two places or positions are between the 'crossing' is not specified but seems to relate to the paths of Anu, Enlil, and Ea, where Anu's path is in the middle between the other two. Neberu's position 'in the middle of heaven' seems compatible enough with the path of Anu, but what 'the crossing between heaven and earth' in VII 124 might mean in an astronomical sense is most unclear. Its significance seems rather to convey qualitatively the central ruling position of Marduk as one of the brightest lights in heaven, whether in the middle of the sky, or at the 'crossing' from one direction to another, or perhaps from above to below. In addition to the ambiguous nature of the central point controlled by Neberu, the identification of Neberu with a celestial body representing Marduk was variable in the ancient texts themselves, as outlined above.

In his analysis of the Astrolabe tradition, Horowitz (2014: 21) points to the description in Astrolabe B of Neberu as being red and 'divid[ing] the heavens': 'The red star which stands at the rising of the south wind after the gods of the night have completed (their courses), (he) divides the heavens, this star is (called) "The Crossing," (that is,) Marduk' (*kakkabu sāmu ša ina tīb šūti arki ilāni mušīti ugdammirū-ma /*

*šamê izâzū-ma izzazzū-ma kakkabu šû* / *ᵈNēberu Marduk*, Astrolabe B II ii rev. 10–13; Horowitz 2014: 38, translation modified). Parallel to the passage in the Astrolabe is VII 124–31 (on the forty-ninth name of Marduk):

*nēberu nēberet šamê* (*u*) *erṣeti lū tamiḫ-ma*
*eliš u šapliš lā ibberū liqe''ûšu šâšu*
*Nēberu kakkabšu ša ina šamê ušāpû*
*lū ṣābit kunsaggêšunu šâšu lū palsūšu*
*mā ša* (*ina*) *qerbiš tiāmti ītebbiru lā nâḫiš*
*šumšu lū nēberu āḫizu qerbīšu*
*ša kakkabī šamāmī alkassunu likīn-ma*
*kīma ṣēni lirta'â ilī gimrassun*

Let Neberu control the crossing between heaven and earth:
they (the stars) shall not cross above or below but wait for him.
Neberu is his (Marduk's) star that he (Marduk) caused to shine in heaven,
Let him hold their crossing point[15]; let them look upon him,
saying: 'He who unrelentingly crosses back and forth inside Tiamat:
may his name be Neberu, he who seized her insides!
May he make the ways of the heavenly stars constant and eternal,
May he shepherd all the gods like sheep'.

(VII 124–31, translation modified)

The passage in lines 130–1 employs a well-known metaphor for the astral gods, the fixed stars as the livestock within the *tarbaṣu* or 'cattle pen', following their regular paths (Rochberg 2010b).

In addition to the intertextual connections between the poem and the Astrolabe just discussed, the opening lines of Tablet V (1–4) make further reference to the Astrolabe with its 'twelve months with three stars each'. As said before, chief among Marduk's creative acts was his establishment of the order and regularity of the starry heaven. In the opening lines of Tablet V Marduk divided the year and its twelve months by making the divisions correspond to an organized pattern of the appearances of certain stars. In each of the twelve months, three stars were assigned to mark the division of the heavens into three parts, namely, the paths of Ea, Anu, and Enlil, in that order (defined above in footnote 5). As the year in question was a schematic, or ideal year of twelve thirty-day months, three stars, one for each path, were assigned to each of the twelve months, and this group of thirty-six stars marked the passage of the year. The concept of the paths and the use of the schematic year were standard in the scribe-scholars' astronomical tradition, including in the omen series *Enuma Anu Enlil*, up to and even after the invention of mathematical astronomy in the fifth century BCE in some non-mathematical astronomical texts.

The thirty-day month originated in the ideal conception of the lunar month. The number thirty became a logogram for the divine name Sin. Thirty represented the ideal duration of the cycle of the lunar phases, which, for the Babylonians, began on the day of the Moon's first appearance following a brief period of invisibility. The day of this reappearance was designated as the first day of the month. The month was not always experienced as an ideal thirty-day period, as it is in fact twenty-nine and a fraction days, experienced as either twenty-nine or thirty days in length. The ideal thirty-day month was the basis for the administrative and then scholarly calendar used in all early Babylonian astronomical and celestial divinatory texts, such as the Astrolabes, *MUL.APIN*, and *Enuma Anu Enlil*.

The cosmographical unity of the Astrolabe tradition and that of *Enuma Elish* is chiefly in the use of the paths of Ea, Anu, and Enlil to divide the heaven into arcs of rising and setting of the fixed stars and the brightest planets, Venus, Jupiter, and Mars, whose risings on certain calendar dates are not fixed each year as are those of the fixed stars near to the ecliptic. The inclusion of the planets in the Astrolabe scheme in set months and set paths of the sky raises the question of the purpose served by representing the heavens in that way. The paths themselves functioned in a descriptive way, as Reiner and Pingree pointed out:

> the association of a constellation name with a particular ideal month does not signify that that constellation had its heliacal rising in that ideal month, and that the three paths do not correspond to bands located between certain circles parallel to the equator. The declinations of the representative stars that we have selected range between 43.5° and +8° for the path of Ea; between −12.2° and +36.9° for the path of Anu; and between 43.2° and +74.1° for the path of Enlil. We presume that these associations with ideal months and with the three paths arc influenced by mythological as much as by astronomical considerations.
>
> (Reiner and Pingree 1981: 3)[16]

In addition to the division of the heavens into paths for the fixed stars in their months, Astrolabe B contains a religious calendar. It assigns to the months activities dedicated to gods associated with the particular month, as in the following excerpt (Horowitz 2014: 33; Akkadian quoted from Reiner and Pingree 1981: 19–25):

> *Ajaru Zappu Sibitti petû erṣeti alpū ulteššerū ruṭubtu uptattâ epinnū irraḫḫaṣū araḫ* ᵈ*Ningirsu qarradi iššakki rabî ša* ᵈ*Enlil*
>
> Ajaru (is the month) of the Pleiades, the seven great gods. (The month of) the opening of the earth, (month in which) the oxen go in procession, the water sluices are opened, the plows are flooded. The month of Ningirsu, the hero, the great *iššakku*-priest of Enlil.

The month sections of the Astrolabe also contain numerical values (probably in time degrees, i.e. 1 degree = 4 minutes) for the variation in length of daylight through the year. In accordance with a linear zigzag scheme, the longest day, 4, falls in month III (=summer solstice), the shortest day, 2, in month IX (=winter solstice) and the mean values of 3 correspond to the equinoctial months VI and XII. The ratio of longest to shortest day is 2:1. This parameter was preserved in schematic astronomical texts through the Seleucid Period where it had a usage in the scheme for the rising times of the zodiacal signs (Rochberg 2004; Steele 2017; 2021: 272, 275).

In the early texts Astrolabes, *MUL.APIN*, and *Enuma Anu Enlil*, and evinced in the opening passage of *Enuma Elish* Tablet V, the paths of Ea, Anu, and Enlil served to mark the schematic solar progress around the sky over the course of a year. Just as in the case of the idealized thirty-day month, the ideal year was defined as the return of the sun to a certain position with respect to the heavenly paths after the completion of twelve ideal months (for a total of 360 'days') and the schematic change in the length of the daytime through the year. The calendrical concept of the ideal year stems from accounting practices attested from the earliest periods (Brown 2000: 113–14; Brack-Bernsen 2007; Britton 2007: 117–19). Of the local Sumerian calendars in the Ur III period, where real month lengths varied, the Nippur calendar month names became standard. They were thereafter common to the scholarly traditions of the astral sciences, both astrology (celestial and natal divination) and astronomy (Astrolabes and *MUL.APIN*). The scholarly use of the ideal 360-day year is clear in the statement made in the Diviner's Manual: 'twelve are the months of the year, 360 are its days' (Oppenheim 1974: 200, 205, l. 57). The ideal calendar placed the cardinal points of the 360-day year at the midpoints of months XII, III, VI, and IX. The Neo-Assyrian tradition shifted the calendar year so that the vernal equinox fell in the first month, Nisannu.

## *Enuma Elish* and world order

Not long after *Enuma Elish* was first edited by George Smith (1876), Peter Jensen's *Die Kosmologie der Babylonier* (1890) set the text within the wider scope of cosmology. It would be seventy-five years, however, before the first synthesis of a Babylonian cosmology in light of *Enuma Elish* was offered. This came in the form of Lambert's article, 'The Cosmology of Sumer and Babylon' in the edited volume *Ancient Cosmologies* (1975) and then he returned to the subject in his edition with translation and extensive elucidation of *Enuma Elish* in his *Babylonian Creation Myths*.

*Enuma Elish* belongs at the centre of any discussion of the Babylonian conception of world structures according to its first-millennium scribes. Lambert regarded it as the single systematic treatment of cosmology in the cuneiform corpus. He said: 'Other than *Enūma Eliš*, there is no systematic treatment of cosmology in Sumero-Babylonian literature. ... But this does not mean that *Enūma Eliš* presents all that is known of Babylonian cosmology. On the contrary, the Epic uses only a selection of the wealth of available material ... parallels to Marduk's work have to be collected from allusions and incidental comments' (Lambert 2013: 169). As Lambert implied, we should not burden *Enuma Elish* with representation of a single Babylonian world picture, nor expect that there was only one world picture in all of cuneiform tradition. Nor should that be of any concern to modern scholars, as in the Greek world there was more than one cosmology and even greater divergence among them as compared with the cuneiform textual evidence (Pythagorean, Milesian, Platonic, atomist, Aristotelian, Stoic, Ptolemaic). What is of critical difference as compared with the Greek cosmologies is the fact that unlike the Greek designated inquiries into the nature, structure, and material constituents of the cosmos, *Enuma Elish* focused rather on the birth, rise, and elevation to power of the Babylonian national god, Marduk, and as demonstration of his might, the tale of his creative power to make, shape, and rule the entire world. The description of world order, then, is primarily a vehicle for the glorification of Marduk and secondarily a detailing of the structural components of the world brought about by Marduk's creative acts.

The narrative of Marduk's creation in the form of a re-ordering of what already existed culminates in *Enuma Elish* Tablet IV as a moral tale. Marduk, the avenging hero, slays the watery goddess Tiamat, whose body he then uses for creating anew the heavens. The killing of Tiamat is, however, primarily an act of vanquishing treachery and improper divine rule. Her death and reestablishment as the watery heavens actualized the hero Marduk's victory. When after the Babylonian *Chaoskampf* the re-making of the world is finally mentioned in IV 135–6, the god Marduk rests and surveys the corpse of Tiamat, which has been rendered a lifeless 'marsh' (*sarkuppu* or *serkuppu*).[17] Having then fashioned the heavens from half of her body, Marduk kept her waters from escaping by installing watchmen, and proceeded to make heaven a counterpart surveyed and precisely measured to the size of the subterranean watery Apsû. A recapitulation of the act of creation comes later in Tablet V:

*iškun qaqqassa*... [...] *išpuk*
*nagba uptettâ mê ittešbi*
*iptē-ma ina īnīša pur*[*atta*] *idiglat*
*naḫīrīša upt*[*e*]*ḫḫâ*... *ītezba*
*išpuk ina ṣertīša š*[*ad*]*î bērūti*
*namba'ī* [*u*]*ptallīša ana babāl*[*i*] *kuppī*
*egir zibbassa durmāḫ*[*i*]*š urakkis-ma*
[...] ... *apsâ šapal šēpuššu*
[*iškun ḫ*]*allīša retât šamāmī*
[*mišil*]*ša uṣṣallila erṣeta uktinna*

He set up her head, he heaped up [...]
He flung open a chasm, it filled up with water,
he let the Euphrates and Tigris flow from her eyes,
he plugged her nostrils, leaving behind [ ]
He heaped her breasts into lofty mountains,
he bored springs to carry the well-water,
he twisted her tail, tying it up as the Durmahu,
[...] Apsû beneath his feet.
[He set up] her groin, keeping heaven in place:
he made a roof out of her second half, founding the earth.

(V 53–62)

In addition to remaking the body of the world, Marduk rectified the order of divine propriety in setting up shrines where the high gods were to have their residences (IV 141–6).

The major parts of the world that are created in order to house these deities and set the world aright are the heavens (home to Anu), earth (as Marduk's new residence), the Apsû (home to Ea), also called Eshgala, and Eshara (literally 'House of the All') for Enlil. The location of the city of Babylon and the site of Marduk's own temple Esagila there is established as a new world centre (V 129 and VI 57; George 1999). Marduk's residence in the temple Esagila situated Babylon at the centre of the vertical world structured with heaven and Apsû as the extreme limits.

Apsû's watery depths were associated with the abode and kingdom of the god Enki (Sumerian)/Ea (Akkadian), so closely associated with him that Enki/Ea's son, Marduk, was known as 'firstborn son of the Apsû'. Because of Enki/Ea's association with wisdom, magic, and incantations, the Apsû was the fount of wisdom and source of the secret knowledge of incantations. The temple of Ea in the oldest Sumerian city of Eridu was called the E-Abzu, 'House of the Abyss'. Marduk's temple Esagil in Babylon was said to be the counterpart (*miḫirtu*) of Apsû (VI 62),[18] and *Enuma Elish* places Eshara, the dwelling place of Enlil, as a counterpart, or likeness (*tamšīlu*, IV 142) of Eshgala, the 'great shrine'. The name of the ziggurat foundation, Etemenanki ('House, Foundation Platform of Above and Below/Heaven and Underworld'), is itself testimony to the idea of the complementarity of above and below as well as being called a copy (gaba-ri) of Eshara in the compilation *Tintir* (IV 2; George 1992: 58–9).[19]

As abundantly testified to by the passages already quoted, the organization of world parts in *Enuma Elish* reflects one of the principal themes of Babylonian scribal scholarship, namely the notion of counterparts. Marduk's 'house', the Esagil, is said to be the equivalent, or counterpart, to the great abyss, the Apsû, where Ea dwelled: 'They raised the peak of Esagil, a replica of the Apsû' (*ša esagil meḫret apsî ullû rēšīšu*, VI 62, translation modified), using the term *miḫirtu*, 'equivalent, counterpart'. The importance of the idea of measured counterparts, equivalents, is also clear in the following passage:

*šamê ībir ašrata iḫīṭam-ma*
*uštamḫir meḫret apsî šubat nudimmud*
*imšuḫ-ma bēlu ša apsî binûtuššu*
*ešgalla tamšīlašu ukīn ešarra*
*ešgalla ešarra ša ibnû šamāmī*
*ānu enlil u ea māḫāzīšun ušramma*

He crossed the sky, surveyed the heaven,
and made it a counterpart of Apsû, the home of Nudimmud.
The Lord measured out the shape of the Apsû,
then founded the Eshara, the equivalent likeness of Eshgala.
In the Eshgala, in the Eshara he created, and in heaven,
he installed Anu, Enlil, and Ea in their temples.

(IV 141–6, translation modified)

A further indication that the idea of counterparts played a thematic role in a cuneiform world description is the use of the term *maṭṭalātu*, from the verb *naṭālu*, meaning 'to look at, face, or point toward'. The word is relatively rare, occurring only in first-millennium scholarly or literary contexts. The clearest usage is no doubt the one found as the incipit of Tablet 16 of the liver omen series (*Barûtu*, 'the art of inspection'), which is: 'If the liver is an image/counterpart of heaven' (*šumma amūtu maṭṭalāt šamê*; CT 20 1:31). Another attestation of *maṭṭalātu* occurs in the account of the rebuilding of the temple Esagil by Esarhaddon. The description of the rebuilding of Marduk's temple sanctuary reflects the political and ideological reconciliation with Babylonia, which Esarhaddon, the son of the Assyrian king Sennacherib, who savagely destroyed the city of Babylon in 689 BCE, intended to effect with this rebuilding (see Sophus Helle in this volume). In his royal inscription, Esarhaddon says the temple Esagil is the counterpart of the Apsû (*maṭṭalāt apsî*) and the equivalent or likeness (*tamšīlu*) of Eshara, in direct reference to the Babylonian *Enuma Elish*.[20]

Further indication of the importance of the theme of counterparts and correspondence is found in *Enuma Elish* V 1–2, where Marduk establishes 'the stations' or celestial positions (*manzāzu*)[21] of the great gods for the constellations to take up as the gods' likenesses: 'He created the (celestial) stations for the great gods the stars, their (the gods') likenesses, he set up (as) constellations' (*ubaššim manzāza ana ilī rabûti / kakkabī tamšīlšunu lumāšī ušziz*, V 1–2, translation modified). Measured counterparts, correspondences, and proportionality are the tools Marduk used in ordering the world. Reasons for the god's choice of these tools, such as that they were 'good' or 'beautiful' (evoking qualities that are made explicit in two other major ancient cosmogonies, namely the Book of Genesis and Plato's *Timaeus*), however, are nowhere articulated.

Thus, as far as cosmology is concerned, the world order constructed in *Enuma Elish* has to do not only with the measured and proportionate body of the world, but also with the divine heavenly bodies as outward manifestation of the world's order and regularity and with the order and propriety of divine rule. Divine propriety was achieved by stationing the gods in their places, establishing the creator god himself, Marduk, in Esagil at the centre of the new world on earth and placing his astral manifestation as Neberu in the middle of heaven to control the regular sequence of the fixed stars in their paths and to maintain 'the crossing' point of heaven, whatever that may be.

## *Enuma Elish* in context

That the writers of the Book of Genesis were well aware of certain Babylonian ideas has been documented ever since the discovery of the 'Tablets of Creation' in the late nineteenth century. As this essay concerns astronomy and cosmology suffice it to say that, in terms of the structure of heaven, the relation of *Enuma Elish* to the narrative in the Book of Genesis is most directly apparent in the motif of the 'firmament in the midst of the waters' that 'divided the waters from the waters' on the second day of creation. The biblical waters below and above the firmament are a clear reference to *Enuma Elish*:

*iḫpīšī-ma kīma nūn mašṭê ana šinīšu*
*mišlušša iškunam-ma šamāmī uṣṣallil*
*išdud maška maṣṣara ušaṣbit*
*mêša lā šūṣâ šunūti umta''ir*

He split her in two, like a dried fish,
set half of her up as a roof above heaven,
stretched out her skin and appointed a watch,
ordering them not to let her waters escape.

(IV 137–40)

If there is an echo of *Enuma Elish* V 12–22 (cited above) on the biblical fourth day of creation, when God set the luminaries and the stars in the firmament (heaven) to rule day and night (Genesis I 14–19), it is a faint echo indeed, devoid of detail.

As compared with the Babylonian creation story, the Bible is not reflective of a body of knowledge of the heavens existing apart from it, in the same way that *Enuma Elish* reflects some of the content of the *Three Stars Each*. Even so, neither Genesis nor *Enuma Elish* was the deliberate rendering of a work of science into poetic form, such as was the case for the third-century BCE hexameter poem *Phaenomena* by Aratus. Aratus set out to rework in verse the fourth-century BCE *Phaenomena* of Eudoxus of Cnidus (Mastorakou 2020). The relation of Aratus's *Phaenomena* to Eudoxus's *Phaenomena* is nothing like the relation *Enuma Elish* has to the Astrolabe or *MUL.APIN*.

The reception history of the biblical text in the form of the Late Antique and medieval Christian hexameral treatises did, however, bring the Bible, together with the legacy of the 'waters above the firmament' of *Enuma Elish*, within the ambit of natural philosophy. For cosmographers in the Christian tradition, such as St. Basil of Caesarea, John Philoponus, or St. John of Damascus, the six days of creation had important ramifications for a world picture already influenced by the reception of Plato's *Timaeus* (Niehoff 2007). By then, the embedded Babylonian motif of the cosmological waters went entirely unnoticed (Rochberg 2010a: chap. 17).

## Further reading

Supplementary reading for the cosmological and astronomical aspects of *Enuma Elish* may be found in Horowitz's (1998) study of Mesopotamian cosmic geography; David Brown's (2000) analysis of first-millennium BCE astronomy-astrology; the editions of the epic by Wilfred Lambert (2013) and Leonard King (1902); and Francesca Rochberg's studies of Mesopotamian cosmology (2005), the relation between gods and the heavens in Mesopotamia (2011), and the astrological trope of 'the waters above the firmament' (2010: chap. 17).

## Notes

1 Modification of the translation from 'kingship over the entire world, all of it' is meant to convey the classic Akkadian genitive chain and emphasize how exactly the conception 'the entire world' was constructed. Similarly, the *Chicago Assyrian Dictionary* s.v. *gimirtu* translates 'kingship over all the universe'. The intentional meaning is clear in both non-literal translations, but the literal translation better reflects the construction of its extensional meaning.

2 The heliacal rising is a phenomenon characteristic of fixed-stars near the ecliptic, that is to say, near to the sun's own path traceable against the background of the stars. The heliacal rising designates the first appearance, or morning rising, of such a fixed-star after its brief period of invisibility due to its being too close to the sun (conjunction). This first visible rising of a star in the east just before sunrise is the first phenomenon in an ecliptical star's synodic cycle of phases.

3 The sources and variants for the Astrolabe tradition are detailed in Horowitz (2014).

4 A full summary of *MUL.APIN*'s contents may be found in Hunger and Steele (2019).

5 Definition and discussion of these three paths for the fixed-stars may be found in Hunger and Steele (2019: 3, 11 and passim). They define the location of the paths (Akkadian *harrānu*) in terms of rough areas of declination: 'The stars in the three paths fall roughly into three regions of declination: the Enlil stars to the north of about +17° declination, the Anu stars to between about +17° and −17° declination, and the Ea stars to the south of about −17° declination,' where declination means the angular distance north or south of the celestial equator. The celestial equator is the extension of the earth's equator onto the imaginary celestial sphere and functions as a line of reference for the equatorial coordinate system of declination (and right ascension) in astronomy. See also the remarks of Reiner and Pingree, below p. 22 and note 29.

6 The word is *lumāšu*, used in a number of ways to designate fixed stars or constellations, among them a poetic usage for 'star', which is illustrated in texts such as *Enuma Elish*, and Standard Babylonian literature such as prayers and some Sargonid royal inscriptions, see *Chicago Assyrian Dictionary* s.v. *lumāšu*.

7 The proclamation of Marduk's kingship is made a second time in Tablet V 87–8, after the conquest of Tiamat and Marduk, still covered with the dust of battle, has finished his creation and the Igigi and Anunnaki gather to kiss his feet, and 'to pay him obeisance, [they drew near,] stood, and bowed: "This is the king!"'; see Gösta Gabriel in this volume.

8 The divine epithet 'Lord of the Lands' (ᵈ*bēl mātāti*, written en kur-ra or en kur-kur-ra) is known for Enlil as well as other gods; see Tallqvist (1938: 48).

9 The word is *ašru*, 'place', not the usual word for heaven (*šamû*). A related poetic term for heaven is *ašrata* (*Chicago Assyrian Dictionary* s.v.), which is attested in IV 141 and V 121.

10 I follow *Chicago Assyrian Dictionary* s.v. *danninu* here in translating 'netherworld' on the basis of its lexical references to the place *Ganzir* (igi-kur or igi-kur-za). See also *Chicago Assyrian Dictionary* s.v. *ganzir*. The Neo-Babylonian commentary to this line (LTBA 2 2:2) explains *danninu* as *erṣetu*, meaning 'netherworld'. The place referred to as *danninu* (=*erṣetu*) is either earth or netherworld in the sense of the cosmic counterpart to heaven.

11 In VII 136, the possessive – *šu* in the word *šumšu* 'his name' can refer to Markduk's name, or indeed, Enlil's 'own name', as Lambert (2013: 131) translates it; see note 2 for Enlil's epithet ᵈ*bēl mātāti*, 'Lord of the Lands'.

12 This would mean that they determined the omens and their consequences.

13 I thank Mark Geller for drawing my attention to this reference. BM 47529+ line 11, see Geller (2014: 63), translated '[in the] middle of the stars', and Geller (2016: 396–7), where he translates 'I am Asalluḫi, wise, sagacious, superlative in intelligence: of Taurus, wise Idim = Ea.' The logogram $MUL_x$ (ÁB) carries the bovine metaphor for the stars, see Rochberg (2010: 347–59).

14 The title of this text series, as suggested by Panayotov, cited by Markham J. Geller (2018: 308, note to l. 31) is *i-na*$_8$ GIŠ.HUR.MEŠ AN *u* KI, rather than i-NAM GIŠ. HUR AN.KI (see Livingstone 1986: 22–3). According to Panayotov's intriguing interpretation, the title refers to the 'eyes' (*īnā*) of the plan of heaven and earth, with 'eyes' being a common metaphor in all Semitic languages for a 'spring' or 'source', which is parallel to two other expressions in KAR 44: 30–1: *kullat nagbi nēmeqi* and *pirišti lalgar*, both referring to sources or springs of secret or esoteric knowledge, and both accord well with the idea of *īnā uṣurāt šamê u erṣeti*, the 'sources of the plans of the universe'.

15 The translation of *kunsangû* as 'crossing point' follows the *Chicago Assyrian Dictionary*, s.v. *kunsangû*; but see also Lambert (2013: 491–2) for his notes to VII 127 and his suggested translation, 'cosmic staircase'.

16 See also the definition of Hunger and Steele, above note 9.

17 This word has also been read as *kūbu*, 'lump', that is of flesh, usually in reference to a stillborn or premature fetus or a monstrosity of some kind.

18 Esagil is also said to be the 'counterpart (lit.: copy) of the Apsû' (gaba-ri *ap-se-*(*e*)) in VAB 7 300, 10; cited in Lambert (2013: 200).

19 Confirming this idea of the complementarity of above and below in the Babylonian world order is the following passage from the seventh-century Diviner's Manual: 'The signs on earth just as those in the sky give us signals. Sky and earth both produce portents, though appearing separately, they are not separate (because) sky and earth are related.' See Oppenheim (1974: 200, 204, l. 38–40).

20 Leichty (2011: 198), no. 104, l. iii 41b–iv 1. See also p. 206, no. 105, l. iv 37b–v 15.

21 In an astronomical sense, *manzāzu* takes on the meaning of celestial position, but the basic meaning is a 'place where (something) stands', as reflected in its logogram ki-gub.

## Bibliography

Brack-Bernsen, L. (2007), 'The 360-Day Year in Mesopotamia', in J. M. Steele (ed.), *Calendars and Years: Astronomy and Time in Ancient Mesopotamia*, 83–100, Oxford: Oxbow Books.

Britton, J. P. (2007), 'Calendars, Intercalations and Year-Lengths in Mesopotamian Astronomy', in J. M. Steele, *Calendars and Years: Astronomy and Time in the Ancient Near East*, 115–32, Oxford: Oxbow Books.

Brown, D. (2000), *Mesopotamian Planetary Astronomy-Astrology*, Cuneiform Monographs 18, Leiden: Brill.

Geller, M. J. (2014), *Melothesia in Babylonia*, Berlin: De Gruyter.

Geller, M. J. (2016), *Healing Magic and Evil Demons*, Die babylonisch-assyrische Medizin in Texten und Untersuchungen 8, Berlin: De Gruyter.

Geller, M. J. (2018), 'The Exorcist's Manual (KAR 44)', in U. Steinert (ed.), *Assyrian and Babylonian Scholarly Text Catalogues: Medicine, Magic and Divination*, Die babylonisch-assyrische Medizin in Texten und Untersuchungen 9, 292–312, Berlin: De Gruyter.

George, A. R. (1992), *Babylonian Topographical Texts*, Orientalia Lovaniensia Analecta 40, Leuven: Peeters Publishers.

George, A. R. (1999), 'E-sangil and E-temen-anki, the Archetypal Cult-Centre', in J. Renger (ed.), *Babylon: Focus mesopotamischer Geschichte, Wiege früher Gelehrsamkeit, Mythos in der Moderne*, 67–86, Saarbrücken: SDV Saarbrücken.

Horowitz, W. (1998), *Mesopotamian Cosmic Geography*, Mesopotamian Civilizations 8, Winona Lake: Eisenbrauns, 1998.

Horowitz, W. (2014), *The Three Stars Each: The Astrolabes and Related Texts*, Archiv für Orientforschung Beiheft 33, Vienna: Institut für Orientalistik der Universität Wien.

Hunger, H. (1976), 'Astrologische Wettervorhersagen', *Zeitschrift für Assyriologie und Vorderasiatische Archäologie*, 66: 234–60.

Hunger, H. (1992), *Astrological Reports to Assyrian Kings*, State Archives of Assyria 8, Helsinki: Helsinki University Press.

Hunger, H. and J. Steele (2019), *The Babylonian Astronomical Compendium MUL.APIN*, London: Routledge.

Jensen, P. (1890), *Die Kosmologie der Babylonier: Studien und Materialien*, Strassburg: Verlag Karl J. Trübner.

Jiménez, E. (2015), 'Commentary on Cento of Literary Texts (CCP 7.2.u93)', *Cuneiform Commentaries Project*. Accessed 15 April 2023, at https://ccp.yale.edu/P469976. DOI:10079/6hdr85p.

King, L. W. (1902), *The Seven Tablets of Creation, or the Babylonian and Assyrian Legends Concerning the Creation of the World and of Mankind*, 2 vols., London: Luzac.

Lambert, W. G. (1975), 'The Cosmology of Sumer and Babylon', in C. Blacker and M. Loewe, *Ancient Cosmologies*, 42–65, London: Allen and Unwin.

Lambert, W. G. (2013), *Babylonian Creation Myths*, Mesopotamian Civilizations 16, Winona Lake: Eisenbrauns.

Leichty, E. (2011), *The Royal Inscription of Esarhaddon, King of Assyria (680–669 BC)*, Royal Inscriptions of the Neo-Assyrian Period 4, Winona Lake: Eisenbrauns.

Livingstone, A. (1986), *Mystical and Mythological Explanatory Works of Assyrian and Babylonian Scholars*, Oxford: Clarendon Press.

Mastorakou, S. (2020), 'Aratus and the Popularization of Hellenistic Astronomy', in A. C. Bowen and F. Rochberg (eds), *Hellenistic Astronomy: The Science in Its Contexts*, 383–97, Leiden: Brill.

Niehoff, M. R. (2007), 'Did the *Timaeus* Create a Textual Community?', *Greek, Roman, and Byzantine Studies*, 47: 161–91.

Oppenheim, A. L. (1974), 'A Babylonian Diviner's Manual', *Journal of Near Eastern Studies*, 33: 197–220.

Reiner, E. and D. Pingree (1981), *Babylonian Planetary Omens*, ii: *Enūma Anu Enlil: Tablets 50–51*, Bibliotheca Mesopotamica, 2 (2), Malibu: Undena Publications.

Rochberg, F. (2004), 'A Babylonian Rising-Times Scheme in Non-Tabular Astronomical Texts', in C. Burnett, J. Hogendijk, K. Plofker, and M. Yano (eds), *Studies in the History of the Exact Sciences in Honour of David Pingree*, Islamic Philosophy, Theology and Science: Texts and Studies 54, 56–94, Leiden: Brill.

Rochberg, F. (2005), 'Mesopotamian Cosmology', in D. C. Snell (ed.), *A Companion to the Ancient Near East*, 316–29, Oxford: Blackwell.

Rochberg, F. (2007), 'Marduk in Heaven', *Wiener Zeitschrift für die Kunde des Morgenlandes*, 97: 433–42.

Rochberg, F. (2010a), *In the Path of the Moon: Babylonian Celestial Divination and Its Legacy*, Studies in Ancient Magic and Divination 6, Leiden: Brill.

Rochberg, F. (2010b), 'Sheep and Cattle, Cows and Calves: The Sumero-Akkadian Astral Gods as Livestock', in E. Frahm, W. R. Garr, B. Halpern, T. P. J. van den Hout, and I.

Winter (eds), *Opening the Tablet Box: Near Eastern Studies in Honor of Benjamin R. Foster*, Culture and History of the Ancient Near East 42, 347–59, Leiden: Brill.

Rochberg, F. (2011), 'The Heavens and the Gods in Ancient Mesopotamia: The View from a Polytheistic Cosmology', in B. Pongratz-Leisten (ed.), *Reconsidering Revolutionary Monotheism*, 117–36, Winona Lake: Eisenbrauns.

Rochberg-Halton, F. (1988), *Aspects of Babylonian Celestial Divination: The Lunar Eclipse Tablets of Enūma Anu Enlil*, Archiv für Orientforschung Beiheft 22, Horn: Ferdinand Berger und Söhne.

Smith, G. (1876), *The Chaldean Account of Genesis*, New York: Scribner, Armstrong & Co.

Steele, J. M. (2017), *Rising Time Schemes in Babylonian Astronomy*, Cham: Springer Nature.

Steele, J. M. (2021), 'The Continued Relevance of MUL.APIN in Late Babylonian Astronomy', *Journal of Near Eastern History*, 8: 259–77.

Tallqvist, K. (1938), *Akkadische Götterepitheta*, Studia Orientalia 7, Helsinki: Societas Orientalis Fennica.

Part Four

# Poetics and Hermeneutics

10

# Soothing the sea: Intertextuality and lament in *Enuma Elish*

Selena Wisnom

Intertextuality is fundamental to *Enuma Elish*. From the construction of its plot to the behaviour of its characters and the overall ideology it expresses, intertextuality is consistently at work throughout the poem as it reshapes its readers' understanding of a whole host of Mesopotamian traditions, reconfiguring them to demonstrate Marduk's ultimate power and control over the universe. As we will see, *Enuma Elish* alludes to well-known poems in both Akkadian and Sumerian, as well as other genres of Mesopotamian scholarship, to make its point in a variety of ways: Marduk is supreme and outdoes all competitors.

Studies of intertextuality in this poem have mostly focused on allusions to other narrative poems, although debts to other scholarly traditions have also been recognized. This chapter will survey these allusions and their significance, including some newly identified ones, and then will argue for hitherto unnoticed parallels with ritual texts, specifically Sumerian lamentations. It emerges that lamentation is a major force in the poem. Tiamat is consistently portrayed as an angry god in need of pacification, in ways that specifically evoke the Mesopotamian strategy of appeasing these deities: ritual lament. Elements of style, language, and specific vocabulary work together to create these resonances, and set up expectations in the reader who is familiar with these traditions about what they will mean. But expectations are there to be subverted, and in a manner typical of *Enuma Elish*, the poem surprises us by overturning them.

## Intertextuality: Concept, context, and scope

The study of intertextuality is the study of how texts relate to each other. The word was coined by Julia Kristeva (1980) to express the idea that no text can be created *ex nihilo* but is always to a greater or lesser degree drawing on other sources or ideas in a culture (for a history of the term, see Seri 2014: 89–91). Every text is 'a mosaic of quotations' dependent on ideas that have been expressed before, but the mosaic is not necessarily made by simply copying other words verbatim (Kristeva 1980: 66). Rather, phrases and ideas are altered in the process to create something new.

The word intertextuality is derived from the Latin *intertexo* meaning 'I weave', encompassing the idea that any new creation requires earlier ideas as raw materials. The metaphor of weaving for literary creativity is common across a range of different cultures and has been shown to be integral to the concept of authorship in Mesopotamia, with the same word meaning 'to weave' and 'to compose' (Helle 2020: 107–12). The metaphor is particularly apt for the intertextuality of *Enuma Elish*. The poem draws on a wide range of different sources and weaves together motifs to create an entirely new tapestry. Its use of earlier material is skilful and not merely a matter of stitching together, but also of transforming its sources. The threads are discernible, but they have created something very different from the original compositions (see also Katz 2011: 127).

Although the term 'intertextuality' is a product of postmodern philosophy, the concept of texts drawing on and referring to others has always been a staple of literary scholarship.[1] For example, Roman and Greek authors frequently alluded to earlier works in their writings and expected their audiences to recognize the borrowings. The similarities and differences between the new and earlier text are a crucial part of creating new meaning, since the audience is implicitly invited to compare the two, as has long been recognized in secondary scholarship.[2] But literary allusion is common to most literary cultures from ancient China to the Hebrew Bible and the romantic poets of English literature, to take just a few examples.[3] Ancient Mesopotamia is no exception, and *Enuma Elish* is one of the most intertextual of all Babylonian poems.

The poem alludes to a huge range and variety of other texts. This is perhaps because, more clearly than any other work of Akkadian literature, it has a specific aim: to establish the dominance of Marduk over all other gods and hence the supremacy of his city, Babylon. In so doing, the poem rewrites mythological history to establish an august genealogy for its protagonist, to portray him as the first and most powerful warrior god, and to show him as the god responsible for fundamental acts of creation, all of which justify his new position as king of the gods. In reality, Marduk was not the first to achieve any of these things and there are precedents for all of his actions in Mesopotamian mythology. For the argument to be credible, then, Marduk must outdo his predecessors and emerge as supreme in his power and ingenuity in as many areas as possible. The poem accomplishes this by alluding to those other episodes in previous works of literature and modelling Marduk's deeds upon them, but in each case also improving upon them, showing Marduk to be superior to all those who came before him. The Mesopotamian audience would have recognized these allusions to earlier texts and recognized both the similarities and differences between them and *Enuma Elish*. It is in these comparisons that the agenda most strongly emerges.

Another reason for *Enuma Elish*'s density of allusion is its scholarly context. The poem most likely originated among the priests of Marduk who had a vested interest in promoting the god they served. Mesopotamian temples were centres of scholarly activity, often containing libraries that held texts in a variety of genres – literary, ritual, lexical, theological, magical, and divinatory (see Robson 2011). The poem thus emerged from an environment steeped in tradition and among specialists who had a deep knowledge of Babylonian scholarship. The poem itself refers to this context at the end, where it stipulates that Marduk's names should be discussed among scholars

(VII 146–7). Scholars thus make up a key part of the intended audience as well as of its authorship.

The allusions work on many levels, and different audiences would have perceived them differently. Some of the more obvious parallels to well-known stories could have been picked up by anyone, regardless of their level of education. One example of this is the resemblance between Marduk's battle against Tiamat and the battle of the warrior god Ninurta against the monster Anzû, as told in the poem of the same name. As has been argued elsewhere, the song-like structure of both poems makes it likely that they were performed in entertainment contexts as well as cultic ones (Wisnom 2023), but their significance to Mesopotamian culture is such that ordinary people would have known the stories in one form or another: as they were narrated either in these poems or in more informal retellings. But knowledge of the details as presented in the texts enabled the audience to understand the meaning of the allusions on more and more levels. In most cases, the signposts for the comparisons are specific words and phrases that are adapted from earlier works. A scholar who recognized these would be able to recognize not only the broad similarities but all the individual details that enriched the comparison. Furthermore, the poem alludes to some highly technical texts that only specialists would have known, such as god-lists explaining the significance of Marduk's names and the creation of the universe as described in the astrological treatise *Enuma Anu Enlil*. A general audience would probably have known which gods were responsible for this act, but not the specific wording found in the text, while the list of Marduk's names depends on elaborate puns in Sumerian, a language that only specialists knew. The deeper one's knowledge of Babylonian traditions, the more one can appreciate the depth of *Enuma Elish*'s engagement with them and all the layers of meaning it creates.

The range of texts that *Enuma Elish* is so far known to allude to includes narrative poems in both Akkadian and Sumerian and various other traditions including creation myths, scholarly explanatory texts, incantation literature, and as will I argue here for the first time, ritual lamentations. The list will surely expand as further parallels are discovered.

Intertextual references can be made both to specific texts and to broader traditions represented by them. For instance, Andrea Seri argues that the exchange between Marduk and Ea before the creation of humankind in *Enuma Elish* VI 1–16 echoes the dialogues between Marduk and Ea that are found in many incantations, especially *Udughul* (Seri 2014: 101). But *Udughul* is not the only text to contain this scene – it is so common to incantations that Falkenstein dubbed it the 'Marduk-Ea type' (Falkenstein 1931). The dialogue between Marduk and Ea in *Enuma Elish* thus recalls a well-known scenario that we can access through *Udughul*, but the specific details on the textual level are not as important as the broader situation it portrays. Another example may be the tradition of god-lists, which set out various names of deities and in some cases comment on their meaning. Marduk's list of names at the end of *Enuma Elish* is certainly related to this genre. Lambert compared it to material from one particular triple-column god list (Lambert 2013: 142–4), as well as the widely known *An=Anum*, since the last fourteen names of Marduk in *Enuma Elish* occur in this text in the same order and with the same explanations.[4] However, this triple god-list is only known from Neo-Assyrian manuscripts and so might be drawing on *Enuma Elish*, rather than the other way round (Wisnom 2020: 92 n. 59), or both may depend on a common source (Lambert 2013: 159).

In other cases, a tradition may manifest in several texts and yet it can still be possible to allude to a specific one of them (see Wisnom forthcoming). This may be the case with the celestial omen series *Enuma Anu Enlil*, which describes Anu, Enlil and Ea establishing the positions of gods and stars and measuring out the length of the days, months, and years.[5] Such a tradition is also known from the bilingual exaltation of Ishtar dating to the Kassite period (l. 25–30),[6] which describes the same gods creating night and day by assigning positions to the moon, sun, and stars, which must have been a well-known idea. But when Marduk establishes the positions of the gods and sets up the celestial bodies the wording parallels that of *Enuma Anu Enlil*.[7] Since *Enuma Anu Enlil* is the definitive scholarly work on the organisation of the heavens, it would make sense for *Enuma Elish* to refer to this account specifically. In *Enuma Elish*, however, it is Marduk who is responsible for marking out the courses of the stars and hence the calendar, rather than Anu, Enlil, and Ea – indeed, he goes one step further and establishes their place for them (Vanstiphout 1992: 55; Lambert 2008: 23–4; Seri 2014: 100). By alluding to the most authoritative account, *Enuma Elish* would be making a statement that its version of events supersedes this ancient tradition. This suggestion must be caveated by the fact that we do not know the exact date of composition of the omen series, and it is possible that it may work the other way round, with *Enuma Anu Enlil* perhaps actually referring to *Enuma Elish*. In this scenario it would be expressing a tradition well-established in divinatory texts in general, but using the wording of this particular poem to express it. Leaving broader traditions aside, however, frequently the reference most definitely is to the wording of a particular text and the details of that text matter, as will be explored further below.

The allusions to other poems that have so far been identified in *Enuma Elish* compare Marduk to three high-ranking deities – Ninurta, Enlil, and Ea – and show him surpassing them in their traditional roles (Vanstiphout 1992: 44–8). These gods are also connected to important cultic cities in Mesopotamia, Nippur, and Eridu, which in the ideology of the late second millennium had also been superseded by Babylon – Nippur was the home of Ninurta and Enlil, while Eridu was Ea's traditional cultic centre, but now Babylon was presented as the new Nippur (Lambert 1992; George 1997; Katz 2011), while Eridu became the name of a district in Babylon and was sometimes used as a synonym for the city itself (George 1992: 19). Nippur was thus supplanted by, and Eridu incorporated in, the newly ascendant Babylon. The prominence of cities and their patron deities are thus closely linked. *Enuma Elish* systematically invites us to compare Marduk with these other gods through a web of allusions to three major narrative poems: *Anzû*, *Atra-hasis*, and *Lugal-e*. Allusions to these poems are frequent throughout *Enuma Elish*, resulting in a sustained engagement with them that reminds the informed audience at every turn of how superior Marduk's deeds are to those of other gods. Allusions to more technical texts crop up at specific moments to highlight particular points, but nevertheless work towards the same end. The allusions have been presented poem by poem in detail elsewhere (Wisnom 2020); here I summarize them character by character (following the lead of Vanstiphout 1992) and give an overview of the allusive techniques in play.

## Marduk as the new Ninurta

Marduk is presented as the new supreme warrior god via allusions to two major poems celebrating the prowess of the warrior god Ninurta – the Akkadian *Anzû* poem and the Sumerian *Lugal-e*. *Anzû* tells the story of Ninurta's battle against a demon with an eagle's body and a lion's head, while *Lugal-e* recounts his defeat of the demonic Asag and his army of stones. The most famous of these allusions is the blood on the wind that announces Marduk's victory over Tiamat, adapting a couplet from Akkadian *Anzû* where Anzû's feathers are carried on the wind to announce Ninurta's victory.[8] But this is just the tip of the iceberg. Peter Machinist first recognized that the whole structure of *Enuma Elish* is based on the structure of *Anzû*, a disturbance of order that leads to a struggle for supremacy, a battle to defeat the monster of disorder, and the reintegration of the champion into the realm of the gods of order (Machinist 2005: 37–40). Within this overall structure, there are similarities of detail that also connect them, such as the enemy possessing the Tablet of Destinies.[9] I have argued elsewhere that adaptations to the structure are also meaningful and meant to be noticed. For example, *Anzû* contains repeated passages where a description of the battle is carried back and forth between Ninurta on the battlefield and Ea, who has been approached for advice (II 70–147); *Enuma Elish* imitates the structure by repeating the description of Tiamat's fearful horde, but this time, the message is ferried between Ea, Anshar, the messenger Kaka, and another group of gods, none of whom can do anything about the threat, serving to emphasize their panic and inability to act in contrast to Marduk and his decisiveness (II 5–126; Wisnom 2020: 96–7, see also Labat 1935: 31; Foster 2005: 438). Structural similarities extend to the beginning and end of both poems, since both end with a list of names (Katz 2011: 132; Wisnom 2020: 93–4), and both begin by situating their action earlier in time than the poems they are competing with (for details, see Wisnom 2020: 91–2).

Such structural imitations set up the basic framework for a comparison that individual words and phrases keep bringing us back to. Ninurta's epithets are used of Marduk from his very first appearance in Tablet II: 'The mighty heir, avenger of his father, who hastens into battle, Marduk the hero' (*aplu gašru mutirru gimilli abīšu ḫā᾿iš tuqmāti marduk qardu*, II 127–28). Lambert first pointed out that 'avenger of his father' is a traditional Ninurta epithet (Lambert 1986: 59) while I have extended this (Wisnom 2020: 71–2) to show that 'hero' and 'the one who hastens' feature prominently in the *Anzû* prologue (I 13–14). When Marduk makes his proposal to the gods, saying that he will fight Tiamat in exchange for kingship, he again uses Ninurta's epithet, 'your avenger' (*mutīr gimillīkun*, II 156), which the gods themselves then use to address him as they urge him into battle (IV 13). And in the oft-repeated description of Tiamat's army, the venomous monsters may be compared with Ninurta's metaphorically poisoned arrows, echoing the exhortation of Ninurta's mother to 'let the arrow become poison to him!' (II 10; Wisnom 2020: 88–91).

Echoes of *Lugal-e* can also be heard in Marduk's battle against Tiamat. Before setting out, Marduk arms himself with a vast array of weapons, one of which is the bow and arrow with which Ninurta killed Anzû. But as Lambert (1986: 59) observed, the bow is given the name 'Longwood' (*iṣu arik*, VI 89), an Akkadian translation of Ninurta's spear named 'Longwood' (ĝeš-gid$_2$-da) in *Lugal-e* (l. 78). Other weapons also have a direct connection. Marduk carries a mace (IV 37) which he uses to crush Tiamat's skull at IV 130, harking back to Ninurta's battle companion Shar-ur, who is a personified mace in *Lugal-e* (Wisnom 2020: 132–8), and arms himself with winds and a weapon called 'the deluge' (IV 49), which may be the name of the mace in *Lugal-e* (l. 82; Wisnom 2020: 139–40).

However, the most detailed parallels come after the battle, where we get additional nuances to those gained from a comparison with *Anzû*. These allusions to *Lugal-e* focus on creation, in particular Ninurta's role as a god of agriculture and creator of order. Ninurta's battle against Asag and his army of stones occurs exactly halfway through the poem, just like Marduk's battle against Tiamat. Afterwards, Ninurta engages in a programme of re-establishing order. He creates a cosmic region, the netherworld, out of the dead body of his enemy (l. 329); repurposes the defeated stones by piling them up to block the waters, thereby inventing irrigation (l. 334–55); and decrees destinies for the stones, either cursing or blessing them according to their conduct (l. 416–644). The same sequence occurs in *Enuma Elish*. Marduk creates the world out of his enemy's dead body (IV 135–V 46; see also van Dijk 1983: 10; Horowitz 1998: 112; Wisnom 2020: 144–6); holds back Tiamat's waters by stretching out her skin to stop it escaping, but also creates sources of water by opening up springs from her eyes (V 47–58; Wisnom 2020: 146–51); and punishes those who fought against him by killing Qingu and turning other defeated gods into images guarding the gate of his temple (IV 119–22; V 73–6; see also Jacobsen 1976: 167). One important detail is that the number of enemies for whom Ninurta decrees destinies is fifty – the same number of names bestowed upon Marduk as a reward for his victory (Wisnom 2020: 151–4). We have here a reversal where, instead of being the one to decree destinies as we might expect, Marduk has destinies decreed for him, a fitting honorific climax to a poem that is all about elevating him to the highest position.

Marduk as the new Ninurta, then, is not only a great warrior, but a creator god who fashions order from chaos, transforming rebellious enemies into constructive parts of the cosmos, and both Akkadian and Sumerian traditions are used to create this image.

## Marduk as the new Enlil

*Enuma Elish* shows Marduk becoming the new king of the gods, supplanting Enlil, who traditionally held this role. This elevation is most prominent in the climax where Marduk receives fifty names, which corresponds to Enlil's symbolic number: as he is given these names, Marduk is also symbolically taking over from Enlil as head of the pantheon, taking his number fifty for his own (Röllig 1971: 500; Lambert 1984: 3; Seri 2006: 507). But the poem finds many other ways to slight Enlil in comparison with Marduk, especially through allusions to *Atra-hasis*.

*Atra-hasis* narrates the story of the Flood, how humankind was first created and then very nearly destroyed by a great deluge sent by the gods. In this poem Enlil is responsible for this catastrophic act – the noise of newly created human beings disturbs his sleep, and so in a fit of rage, he decides to wipe them out (I 354–9).[10] The same scenario plays out in *Enuma Elish*, when the newly created gods disturb Apsû and Tiamat with their noise (I 21–4). Unable to sleep, Apsû declares his intention to destroy his offspring (I 37–40). This is not only a similarity in terms of plot;[11] the same verbs are used in both poems (*šabû* and *adāru*), meaning that the specific wording echoes the older text (Wisnom 2020: 110–15). Thus a comparison between Apsû and Enlil is drawn. I have argued that when Apsû is murdered, we are to understand that Enlil is symbolically deposed also (Wisnom 2020: 105–30), and the rash thoughtless king who endangered the gods themselves by sending the deluge without thinking it through is taken out of the picture, clearing the way for Marduk to take his place as a good and compassionate king (Sonik 2008). But *Enuma Elish* does not only invoke *Atra-hasis* to make this point, it also alludes to the depiction of Enlil in *Anzû*. When Apsû is killed, his crown and aura are stripped off (I 67–70), which echoes the description of Enlil undressing for his bath just before Anzû steals the Tablet of Destinies from him (*Anzû* I 79–82). Since Enlil depends on the tablet for his authority, this is a reference to another instance of the chief god losing his supreme power (Wisnom 2020: 117–19). Thus allusions to two different poems are woven together in service of the same aim.

The specificity of references to an original text can further be illustrated with two newly identified allusions to *Atra-hasis*. In Tablet VI of *Enuma Elish*, Marduk asks the gods to build Babylon and they do so in a passage that is very reminiscent of the earlier poem:[12]

*anunnakkū itrukū alla*
*šattu ištât libittašu iltabnū*
*šanītu šattu ina kašādi*
*ša esagil meḫret apsî ullû rēšīšu*
*ibnû-ma ziqqurrat apsî elīta*
*ana āni enlil ea u šâšu ukinnū šubta*

The Anunnaki swung the hoe,
for one year they prepared the bricks.
When the second year arrived,
they raised up the top of the Esagil, the Apsû's counterpart.
They built the soaring ziggurat of the Apsû,
and established homes for Anu, Enlil, Ea, and him.

(VI 57–64)

Here, the Anunna gods are voluntarily engaging in manual labour to build Marduk's city and temple. This is a direct reversal of the situation at the beginning of *Atra-hasis*, which is set in a primordial time where the gods are forced to work on digging the channels for the first rivers and rebel against their toil. In *Atra-hasis*, this work was imposed by Enlil and is referred to as 'the work of Enlil' (*šipir enlil*, I 196; Lambert and Millard 1969: 56). Marduk uses the same word here to refer to the building of

Babylon but casts it as 'the work you desired' (*ša tērišā šipiršu*, VI 57) – far from being imposed unjustly this time, it is something that the gods themselves requested to do. Furthermore, in *Atra-hasis*, it is the Igigi who are forced to toil, a lower class of gods than the Anunna (I 5–6), but here the Anunna themselves freely offer their services, which stands to Marduk's credit. The number of years worked is also significant. *Enuma Elish* has the gods working for simply one year, in stark contrast to the forty years that the Igigi laboured for before they revolted, which is explicitly labelled as 'excessive' (*atram*, I 37).[13] The wording of *Enuma Elish* V 60–2 also plays with our expectations as compared with certain patterns in the phrasing of *Atra-hasis*, which marks the passing of time during which the people are suffering from famine as follows:

*ištêta šattam īkula la*[*rda*ˀ]
*šanīta šattam unakkima*ˡ *nakkamt*[*a*]
*šaluštum šattum illik*[*am-ma*]
*ina bubūtim zīmūšina* [*ittakru*]

For one year they ate couch grass,
for the second year they suffered from itching.
The third year came
[and] their faces [were changed] by starvation.
(II iv 9–12; Lambert and Millard 1969: 78)

The pattern continues up to the sixth year in this case. Such passages elongate the suffering by drawing it out year after year and describing its progressive worsening. When one comes across the phrase 'for one year they made bricks', in *Enuma Elish* and the second line begins with the second year as well, one perhaps expects the pattern to continue in a similar vein, but it does not. For one year they made the bricks, but that is all, and when the second year arrived, the gods built the ziggurat and that was the end of it. There is no third year of suffering, and the pattern has been cut short.[14] Although this particular passage in *Atra-hasis* refers to the suffering of human beings rather than gods, the gods also worked for year upon year, and there is a similar pattern describing the length of their toil in the Assyrian version of *Atra-hasis*, although there the first half of the lines containing the numbers is broken (manuscript S, l. 10–13; Lambert and Millard 1969: 45). All this shows that the work done for Marduk is much lighter and more lenient than the unbearable toil imposed by Enlil or the suffering that it resulted in, drawing a contrast between the two rulers.

Another specific allusion to *Atra-hasis* is found in the list of names at the end of *Enuma Elish*. Marduk's very first name, 'Marduk', is accompanied by a list of his attributes and achievements including the statement that he 'captured the clamorous with his weapon, the Flood' (*ša ina kakkīšu abūbi ikmû šāpûti*, VI 125). This is in a prominent place, as it is the second line after Marduk's first name, and so would be sure to draw attention. The use of the word 'clamorous' directly recalls the noise of human beings that so disturbed Enlil in *Atra-hasis*, which there is expressed with the same verb, *šabû*: 'The land clamoured like a bull' (*m*[*ātum kīma li*]'*î išabbu*, I 354; Lambert and Millard 1969: 66). The Flood was the weapon that Enlil used against these noisy beings. Earlier in *Enuma Elish*, the Flood is the name given to Marduk's mace which he uses to finish off Tiamat (IV 49). *Enuma Elish* is therefore repurposing a weapon that was used thoughtlessly and inappropriately by the previous king of the gods, Enlil, for a much better cause: the noisy beings referred to here are the army of monsters that threatened to oust the gods, meaning that Marduk's use of it was meant to 'rescu[e] the gods his fathers from anguish' (VI 126). Finally, Marduk is said to have imposed the toil of the gods on human beings so that the gods could rest (VI 129–30). This point was also made earlier, at the time when human beings were created (VI 33–4; Wisnom 2020: 126–8). Marduk's first name thus includes a summary of the ways in which Marduk has taken over from Enlil, driving the message home.

Marduk's ascent to the position of supreme god means he does not only replace Enlil, but the traditional triad of Anu, Enlil, and Ea, who ruled the universe together. The poem accomplishes this triple replacement through its allusions to *Enuma Anu Enlil*, as discussed above, but also by adaptating the structure of *Anzû*. In *Anzû*, three gods approach the monster and fail before Ninurta makes his attempt, whereas only two gods set out against Tiamat prior to Marduk in *Enuma Elish*. But in *Anzû*, three warrior gods make the first attempts (Adad, Girra, Shara), whereas in *Enuma Elish*, it is Anu and Ea who set out but turn back. The third god we would expect in this grouping is Enlil, but he is conspicuously missing. Thus, Enlil is side-lined yet again by omission, and an intertextual reading alerts us to that fact (Wisnom 2020: 98–100).

## Marduk as the new Ea

The god Ea is treated differently from Ninurta and Enlil, since he is not written out of the poem but still retains an active and significant role (Vanstiphout 1992: 45–7). Marduk does take over many of Ea's traditional functions; but since Ea is Marduk's father, this can be seen as a kind of inheritance. The son outgrows his father, following the pattern established at the opening of the poem, with each generation of gods successively becoming greater than their parents. Everything Ea does early in the poem, Marduk does later on a grander scale. And many things that Ea has done in earlier poems, Marduk will now do in *Enuma Elish*.

In Mesopotamian mythology, Ea is often associated with creation and problem-solving. For instance, in *Atra-hasis*, he has the idea to create human beings to toil instead of the gods, thus solving the problem that provoked their strike. In *Enuma Elish*, Marduk also takes over this role and shows himself to be supremely clever, explicitly outranking his father. *Enuma Elish* also contains an account of the creation of humankind, but now it is Marduk who has the idea and simply delegates the task of creation to Ea (Foster 2005: 469, 2016: 95; Seri 2006: 515). Furthermore, the switch in hierarchy is underlined by the similarities with dialogues between Marduk and Ea in incantation literature such as *Udughul*: traditionally, Ea is the one to give instructions to Marduk, but now Marduk is giving instructions to Ea (Seri 2014: 101).

This programme is also reinforced by intratextuality, whereby the poem references other parts of itself. Marduk's activities parallel Ea's earlier on in *Enuma Elish*: the defeat of Tiamat and Qingu parallels Ea's murder of Apsû and Mummu, the creation of Marduk's dwelling in the form of the temple Esagil parallels Ea's creation of his own dwelling out of Apsû, and Marduk's creation of the world from the body of Tiamat outdoes Ea's creation of his abode from the body of the dead Apsû.[15] Thus Marduk systematically improves upon his father's deeds both within *Enuma Elish* itself and through references to other poems.

## A new perspective: Sumerian lamentations

One area that is ripe for intertextual investigation in Mesopotamian literature more widely is the relationship between poetry and more technical textual genres. We have already surveyed some of the interconnections between *Enuma Elish* and scholarly literature in the form of divination texts, incantations, and explanatory lists. But connections with ritual have not yet been explored. To take just one genre as a starting point, *Enuma Elish* is suffused with the language of ritual lamentation, which is used to describe the anger of Tiamat and the approaches of the gods who try to pacify her. As we will see, an appreciation of how this language is deployed in ritual lamentations brings out a new aspect of Marduk's opponent and gives a new dimension to his battle against her.

The influence of the Sumerian lamentation tradition on Akkadian texts is increasingly being recognized in modern scholarship. Samuel Chen has shown that the Akkadian Flood poem *Atra-hasis* owes much to Sumerian lamentations, not only using them as a source for the imagery of Flood destruction but also transforming their motifs to create new meaning from them (Chen 2013). Nathan Wasserman (2020: 142–3) focuses on the lament of the birth goddess in the same poem and also compares it to Sumerian ritual laments. Allusions to Sumerian laments are also commonly found in Assyrian royal inscriptions; for example, Amitai Baruchi-unna has found the language of lament in Assurbanipal's L4 inscription (Baruchi-Unna 2013). Elsewhere I have shown that two other Akkadian poems – *Anzû* and *Erra and Ishum* – allude to this tradition, as well as *Enuma Elish* itself (Wisnom 2020: 59–62, 216–44 and 2021). Marduk's use of the net to capture Tiamat echoes the motif of Enlil the Fowler, the terrifying hunter who sets traps for the people in Sumerian lamentations. While Enlil's nets ensnare ordinary people, Marduk's is used solely against the enemy, showing him to be more benevolent than Enlil.

Laments were sung in the Sumerian language as part of the cult from as early as the third millennium BC and right up to the last phases of cuneiform culture (Delnero 2020: 32–5). The most abundant textual evidence comes from the first millennium, probably after the composition of *Enuma Elish*, but the evidence stretches back to the Old Babylonian period and many first-millennium laments exist also in Old Babylonian copies. The first-millennium versions are bilingual, with an accompanying Akkadian translation underneath each line of the original Sumerian. The purpose of these laments was to appease the wrath of the gods. They were sung both at special occasions and on a regular basis as part of the cultic calendars to pre-empt divine rage by lamenting in advance the destruction that the Mesopotamians knew the gods to be capable of causing. By acknowledging the power of the gods in this way, it was hoped that the gods would not feel the need to demonstrate it, and the outpouring of their anger would thus be averted. At first sight, it might seem like this theme has little to do with *Enuma Elish*, but as we will see, the poem uses the motifs of lamentation poetry subtly and cleverly to underscore the seriousness of the threat posed by Tiamat and her army, turning the motifs on their head. Usually, lamentations are addressed to all-powerful gods, and applying the motifs to Tiamat herself is an unexpected way of elevating and acknowledging her terrifying power.

The Flood as an agent of destruction is famous in Mesopotamian literature. Today it is best known from *Gilgamesh*, but this is just the culmination of millennia of tradition. The story of a great Flood that nearly wiped out all of humanity was told in the Akkadian poems of *Atra-hasis*, and a Sumerian Flood poem existed also (see respectively Wasserman 2020; Civil 1969), but throughout the Mesopotamian tradition, floods are found as agents of destruction and metaphors for catastrophe. That the main opponent in *Enuma Elish* is a massive body of water who threatens the annihilation of the established order would inevitably recall this tradition.

The ritual laments frequently compare the gods to raging floods or to the angry sea. Ninurta, Nergal, and Adad are especially frequently depicted this way,[16] but Ishtar and Enlil are as well.[17] Nor is this vocabulary strictly limited to laments – Nergal is called 'the angry sea' (**ab ḫu-luḫ**) in two hymns.[18] Ninurta, Nergal, and Adad are of course warrior deities that serve as models for Marduk. The prologue to *Anzû* refers to Ninurta as a 'wave of battle' (*agê tuqmāti*, I 7) invoking this aspect of him as a powerful flood, showing that the metaphor was found in the Akkadian traditions as well. 'Flood Which Drowns the Harvest' is the name of a well-known lament to Nergal that describes his destructive powers (Cohen 1988: 500–22). Closest of all to what we find in *Enuma Elish* is perhaps the lamentation 'Oh Angry Sea' addressed to and describing the chief god Enlil (Cohen 1988: 374–400), which was later adapted to address Marduk (Kutscher 1975, see also the table at the start of Cohen 1988).

If there is one adjective that characterizes Tiamat in *Enuma Elish*, it is 'angry'. Her name is frequently accompanied with a word for rage, beginning in line I 42 onwards, when she reacts to Apsû's intention to destroy their offspring ('she was angry', *īzuz-ma*, followed in the next line by the description, 'alone in her fury', *uggugat ēdiššīša*). In II 12, Ea tells Anshar that 'she has convened an assembly, seething with rage' (*puḫra šitkunat-ma aggiš labbat*). In his reply, Anshar refers to Tiamat as 'whom you enraged' (*ša tušāgigu*, II 56), and later in the same speech refers to her anger yet again: 'may her rage soon be driven out by your spell' (*uggassa lū … šūṣ*[*ât sur*]*riš ina šiptī*[*ka*], II 78). These mentions of the angry sea bring to mind the terrifying forces of destruction that the gods unleash in the laments, alluding to the looming disaster that Tiamat threatens.

I will focus now on a passage from Tablet IV where references to lamentation seem to cluster, a key moment leading up to the battle between Marduk and Tiamat. At this point in the narrative, the gods have dispatched Marduk to battle with words echoing Ninurta's mission in *Anzû* (*Enuma Elish* IV 31–2; *Anzû* III 22–3), and he has armed himself with an impressive array of weapons borrowed from Ninurta: the bow and arrow he uses in *Anzû* (*Enuma Elish* IV 35–6, *Anzû* II 59–67) and the mace, winds, and storms he uses in *Lugal-e* (*Enuma Elish* IV 37–50; Wisnom 2020: 138–40). Now he approaches his enemy:

*uštēšir-ma bēlu urḫašu ušardī-ma*
*ašriš tiāmti ša uggugat pānuššu iškun*

*ina šaptīšu tâ ukalla*
*šammi imta bullî tamiḫ rittuššu*
*ina ūmīšu idullūšu ilū idullūšu*
*ilū abbūšu idullūšu ilū idullūšu*
*iṭḫē-ma bēlu qabluš tiāwati ibarri*
*ša qingu ḫā'irīša iše''â šibqīšu*
*inaṭṭal-ma eši mālakšu*
*sapiḫ ṭēmašū-ma seḫât epšessu*
*u ilū rēṣūšu ālikū idīšu*
*īmurū-ma qarda ašarēda niṭilšun īši*
*iddi t[âš]a tiāmtu ul utār kišāssa*
*ina šaptīša lullâ ukalla sarrāti*

The Lord made straight and pursued his way,
toward raging Tiamat he set his face.
He was holding a magic spell ready upon his lips,
a plant, antidote to venom, he was grasping in his hand.
At that moment the gods were wandering, wandering about him,
the gods his fathers were wandering about him, the gods wandering about him.
The Lord drew near, to see the battle of Tiamat,
he was looking for the stratagem of Qingu her spouse.
As he looked, his advance turned to confusion,
his thinking was disconcerted and his actions panicky,
and as for the gods his allies, who went at his side,
when they saw the valiant vanguard, their sight failed them.
Tiamat cast her magic spell point-blank,
falsehood, lies she held ready on her lips.

(IV 59–72, translation modified)

Tiamat is again described as 'raging', *ša uggugat*, in IV 60, the battle framed as one against the angry sea. In the next line, Marduk has ready on his lips an incantation, the traditional weapon against an angry god. The other gods, clearly frightened and not knowing what else to do, wander about. In IV 63–4, we have a curious instance of repetition where the same word *idullūšu*, 'they wandered about', occurs four times in just two lines. This happens nowhere else in the poem. But the trope of wandering about occurs frequently in Sumerian laments, where it is used of the gods who are not paying attention to the plight of their despairing people or who are despairing themselves as they are unable to do anything about it.[19] Repeating the same word in consecutive lines is a fundamental part of the literary style of Sumerian laments, where it is common to repeat the same idea with slight variations in subject in long passages that can reach over ten lines or more. This burst of four 'wandering abouts' in a row, unusual for Akkadian poetry, may then be a nod to the Sumerian ritual poems, along with the word that evokes their content. A close parallel can be found in 'The Defiled Apsû' where the goddess Damgalnunna cries, 'I wander about the place that has been pillaged, I wander about, I wander about the place that has been pillaged' (l. 90–1; Cohen 1988: 47–64).

Two other lamentations show a similar pattern with the word for 'wanders about', **di-di-ra**, occurring three times in just four lines: 'The Honoured One Who Wanders About' (l. 1–4) and 'Honoured One, Wild Ox' (section e, l. 144–7), both dedicated to Enlil (Cohen 1988: 176, 279). Thus the laments even use this same style of repeating the same verb four times in a couplet as well as in block passages.

The gods wandering about perhaps highlights their lack of engagement in the battle. Like the gods in the laments who stand by and do nothing while the people suffer, so most of the gods stand back and do nothing during Marduk's combat with Tiamat. In some laments, the gods are unwilling to intervene, in others they are unable. Either way, the aimless wandering of the other gods contrasts with Marduk, who takes action and is never hesitant to intervene, consistent with the poem's portrayal of him as a greater warrior than any of his predecessors.

In IV 71, Tiamat casts her spell, and the text states, with an unusual phrase, that 'she did not turn her neck'. This phrase has a very strong connection with laments, particularly the *ershahunga* genre.[20] As Baruchi-Unna has shown, one of Assurbanipal's inscription also uses this phrase which directly links it to Sumerian laments (L4, l. ii 30), leading him to claim that 'the picture that emerges … leads one to suspect that any such occurrence in Akkadian prayer has a link with Sumerian texts' (Baruchi-Unna 2013: 619–20). The context in *Enuma Elish* is rather different – here we do not have a prayer, but we do have an imminent attack of a powerful supernatural being, which is the scenario that lamentations are designed to counter. All known attestations of the phrase in Akkadian are concerned with angry deities who are either beseeched to relent[21] or refusing to do so (see, e.g. *Enuma Elish* VII 153), except for Neo-Assyrian inscriptions where kings borrow this language to describe their own rage.[22] For Tiamat to not turn her neck, then, casts her in the role of an angry god who will not be pacified.

The gods do attempt to appease her in traditional ways before sending Marduk into battle. Anshar first sends Ea out against her and instructs him to 'Go before Tiamat, pacify her attack, may her rage be driven out quickly by your incantation' (*alik-ma muttiš tiāmti tēbâša šup*[*šiḫ*] / *uggassa lū* (…) *šūṣ*[*ât sur*]*riš ina šiptī*[*ka*], II 77–8). The verb used in l. 77 for 'pacify' is the very one commonly used of appeasing divine wrath, *pašāḫu* (Gabbay 2015: 5), while the next line gives the usual method of doing so: an incantation. But Ea fails to soothe Tiamat's rage. In fact, he does not even try: once he approaches her, he concludes that 'I found out her course, but my spell is no match for her' (*mālakša eše''ē-ma ul imaḫḫar šiptī*, II 86). Anshar then asks Anu to try, twice using the verb 'to pacify' again: 'pacify her mind, let her heart relax' (*šupšiḫ kabtataš libbuš lippuš* II 100), and 'speak words of obeisance that she may be pacified', (*amāt unnenni atmēšim-ma šī lippašḫa*, II 102). The same verb is then used twice in Anshar's instructions to Anu, who comes back with the same response as Ea, repeated in exactly the same way: 'I found out her course, but my spell is no match for her' (II 110). Even when Anshar sends Marduk, he asks the same thing: 'Pacify Tiamat with your sacred spell' (*tiāmta šupšiḫ ina têka elli*, II 150).

From the start of the rebellion right up to the battle, Tiamat is portrayed as an angry god in need of appeasement. Despite having an incantation ready on his lips (IV 61), however, Marduk does not attempt to appease her. His speech to her before the battle lists the terrible things she has done: she had no compassion, her sons cried out and harassed their fathers,[23] she inappropriately raised up Qingu to the highest level of power, and she stirred up trouble against the very king of the gods (IV 79–84). The exchange is interesting because prayers to pacify angry gods usually do accuse them of not caring and list the horrors they have inflicted in this way, because acknowledging their power to destroy can be a form of praise (Wisnom 2020: 238–43). But Marduk's intention seems not to be to pacify her – he ends his speech by telling her to gird on her weapons and declaring that the two of them will do battle (IV 85–6), and in response, Tiamat goes into a frenzy, loses her mind, and cries out fiercely (IV 87–90). Marduk's solution is not appeasement of the enemy but stirring her up for a battle he easily wins.

As is well known, the battle between Marduk and Tiamat is modelled on the battle between Ninurta and Anzû. But the lamentation resonances also work intertextually between these two compositions. Anzû's spell uses motifs that are common to Sumerian lamentations, but in its original context they describe the destruction wrought by the great gods, one of whom is Ninurta himself (Wisnom 2020: 59–62). Anzû's allusions to lamentations place him on the same level as an angry Ninurta but use language traditionally used to pacify that god as a weapon to enrage him further (Wisnom 2020: 62). This is a reversal on two levels: a role reversal of the figure acting as the angry deity (not the god but his opponent), and a reversal of the purpose of the lamentation (not to pacify but to infuriate). *Enuma Elish* uses these lamentation motifs slightly differently from *Anzû*: Tiamat herself does not perform any kind of lament like Anzû does, but is the target of it. Nonetheless, we have a similar pair of reversals – Tiamat is set up as being like an angry god in need of pacification (not the god but his opponent) and the words spoken to her do not soothe but instead stoke her rage (not to pacify but to infuriate).

Anyone who remembers *Anzû*'s use of lamentations might expect Tiamat's spell to be somewhat more powerful than it actually is. In IV 71 we are told she cast her spell and did not relent. L. 73 and 74, which may make up the contents of that spell, are unfortunately incomplete and difficult to understand, but it clearly has no effect on Marduk. This is in contrast to Anzû's spell, which causes serious problems for Ninurta. Despite the huge build-up leading to the battle itself, when Marduk is confronted by Tiamat, she is easier to defeat than expected, which contributes to the picture of Marduk easily outdoing Ninurta (Wisnom 2020: 101–2).

At the end of the poem, the unusual phrase about the 'turning the neck' occurs again. After the gods have given Marduk fifty names, there is a short passage of praise, including the couplet: 'If he glowers in anger he does not turn his neck, when his anger is inflamed, no god can face him' (*ikkelemmū-ma ul utār kišāssu / ina sabāsīšu uzzašu ul imaḫḫaršu ilu mamman*, VII 153–4, translation modified). This is the same phrase previously used of Tiamat, not only the turning of the neck but also 'no god can face him', as each god who approached her before Marduk said that their incantation could not face her (II 86 and 110). For a Babylonian audience, it would be unexpected for this language to be used of a monster – but now that Tiamat has been defeated, it is more conventionally used of a high god of the legitimate pantheon. As the poem comes to a close, the proper order has been restored.

## Conclusions

To read intertextually is to read in context – to be aware of the literary background that an original audience would have known, and of the ways this would shape their understanding of the poem. As we have seen, a knowledge of a whole range of Mesopotamian traditions in both Akkadian and Sumerian would influence the interpretation of *Enuma Elish*.

The references to lamentations discussed here are not necessarily aimed at any one specific composition, since the motifs are shared across several texts of this genre. But an awareness of how Sumerian ritual laments deploy this language transforms our understanding of how it is used in *Enuma Elish*. These words and phrases carry a cultural baggage that is inevitably imported and serves to highlight the seriousness of Tiamat's rage. Thinking about what else may be imported, we may also consider who these laments were originally addressed to. The classic angry sea in lamentations was the chief god Enlil, who was often described in this way. Tiamat is therefore the literalization of a metaphor strongly associated with Enlil, which may not have been lost on the original audience. As we have seen, *Enuma Elish* does away with Enlil via indirect intertextual strategies, such as allusion by omission, and through the murder of Apsû who represents him. Perhaps Marduk's battle with the angry sea is another indirect way for him to confront Enlil without Enlil himself being present, and defeat the old idea of the angry sea outright instead of placating it.

Yet this is not the only option. Another notable omission from *Enuma Elish* is the goddess Ishtar, one of the most important goddesses in all Mesopotamian religion. Ishtar also has an important role in the mythology of lament. According to one text from the early second millennium BC, the very figure of the lamentation priest was created specifically to calm the heart of Inana, an earlier name for the goddess.[24] The practice of lamenting, then, was thought to have been instituted specifically to soothe the rage of this prominent female deity. Tiamat is the only notable female figure in *Enuma Elish*, and it may be that Marduk's battle with her may also be an indirect way of him gaining dominance over Ishtar/Inana by defeating a representation of her rage. We do not necessarily have to choose between these interpretations, since Mesopotamian literature uses 'multiple reference' where one line or image can resonate with more than one previous composition simultaneously (Wisnom 2020: 22–3, 249). Tiamat as the angry sea may resonate both with the replacement of Enlil and with the side-lining of Ishtar at the same time, doing away with two angry deities in a single stroke.

Most readings of the poem overlook the centrality of divine rage – Tiamat's name is not written with the divine determinative, implying that she is not considered a goddess in the same way as other deities. Yet those great gods are themselves just as scared of Tiamat as mortals are of them, and initially attempt to pacify her in the same way their own rage would be pacified by human cultic specialists. Viewed in this way, *Enuma Elish* is not just a monster killing story but a reflection on the appeasement of divine anger and its limits. Ultimately, nothing will pacify Tiamat. Marduk recognizes this and does not attempt to soothe her, but goes straight in for the kill. As she is not an ordinary deity, the normal rules of engagement do not apply, and she will not be contained by the same strategies that work for other gods.

Yet since the poem is set at the beginning of time, these strategies have yet to be established by human beings in the first place (see Johannes Haubold in this volume). Tiamat is the first angry god, the first instance of terrifying divine rage, and the gods are faced with the difficulty of appeasing it. The mother of all gods is not subject to the same expectations as her descendants, but perhaps her transgression of limits is what leads those expectations to be set. In later mythological times, gods who are addressed with words of pacification will indeed calm down. Marduk himself is terrifying to behold when he is angry, but his fourth name Mershakushu describes him as 'angry but deliberative, furious but relenting' (*eziz u muštāl sabuš u tayyār*, VI 137). Unlike Tiamat, whose anger knows no bounds, Marduk is the one who has created the world order and knows the proper place of everything, his own rage included.

## Further reading

The classic studies on this topic are by Lambert (1986, 2013) and Herman Vanstiphout (1992). Andrea Seri (2014) gives a good summary of various types of intertextual references in the poem, while Dina Katz (2011) gives an account of the political dimensions of the allusions, and explores the origins and significance of Tiamat. Machinist (2005) sets *Enuma Elish* in the context of other combat poems that deal with cosmic order, while elsewhere I expand upon this (Wisnom 2020) and treat the intertextuality of the poem in full, concentrating especially on its competitive agenda.

## Notes

1 The difference lies in the degree of intentionality assumed – postmodern intertextual readings do not require the author to have planted these references deliberately, whereas more traditional approaches assert the author's intention. My own approach embraces both – an interpretation is justified so long as there is evidence for it in the text without us having to speculate about what the author intended, but when that evidence becomes overwhelming, we are equally justified in supposing it was deliberate.

2 See e.g. Pasquali (1951: 11–20), Giangrande (1967: 85–97), Russell (1979), Fowler (1997), and Hinds (1998).

3 Hu (2021), Fewell (ed., 1992), Zevit (ed., 2017), and Labbe (2015).

4 Lambert (1964: 4 and 1984: 3–4); see also Seri (2006: 516). Sommerfeld (1982: 175) has also suggested *An = Anum*.

5 Edited in Rochberg-Halton (1988: 270–1). For the relationship between *Enuma Elish* and astronomical texts, see also Francesca Rochberg in this volume.

6 Edited in Foxvog (2014); see Horowitz (1998: 144–5). For the date, see Jiménez et al. (2020: 232–3) and Enrique Jiménez in this volume.

7 Landsberger and Kinnier-Wilson (1961: 172). *The Exaltation of Ishtar* may of course be later than *Enuma Elish*, since all of its copies are Neo-Assyrian or later, but since it does differ in some details it seems to represent a slightly different tradition rather than being dependent on this poem. In *The Exaltation of Ishtar*, the moon and sun seem to keep the stars on course, whereas in *Enuma Elish* this is the responsibility of Marduk's star Neberu; see Horowitz (1998: 145).

8 Lambert (1986: 59), Seri (2014: 99), and Wisnom (2019, 2020: 75–8).
9 Lambert (1986: 59), Machinist (2005: 39), and Wisnom (2019: 278–9, 2020: 78–88).
10 Unless otherwise stated, all references to *Atra-hasis* are to its Old Babylonian version.
11 Labat (1935: 29), Moran (1971: 56–7, fn. 8), Jacobsen (1976: 167), Michalowski (1990: 389), Machinist (2005: 40), Seri (2012: 17), Sonik (2008: 741), and Katz (2011: 129), and Kvanvig (2011: 79).
12 The overall parallel was spotted by Wisnom (2020: 126–8), but is developed in detail here.
13 The exact number of years is disputed due to the text being damaged; see Shehata (2001: 32).
14 Cf. above on how the poem abbreviates the motif in *Anzû* of three gods approaching the monster to only two.
15 Vanstiphout (1992: 47), Talon (2001: 266), Machinist (2005: 43), Gabriel (2014: 190–7) Wisnom (2020: 122–30), and Katz (2011: 129–30).
16 See, for example, no. 20 and 28 in Gabbay (2015: 250–1), Cohen (1988: 436 and 596), and Maul (1988: 160 and 196–7).
17 See no. 61 in Gabbay (2015: 436 and 596).
18 *Shu-ilishu A*, l. 14, and *Nergal C*, l. 54.
19 See e.g. *Elum didara*, l. 1–10; *Udam ki amus*, l. f+224; *Mutina nunuz dima*, l. a+49 and a+149, a+159, 163, 167, 171, 175, 179, 183, 187, 191, and 195; and *Elum gusun*, e+141–8; all edited in Cohen (1988).
20 See Gabbay (2015: 136), and Maul (1988: 415). The bilingual translations of the events tend to use both *târu* and *saḫaru* in the Akkadian, both of which are well known equivalents of the Sumerian **gi**$_4$; see *Chicago Assyrian Dictionary*, s.v. *târu* and *saḫaru.*
21 See e.g. l. 47 in the prayer to pacify an angry god published by Lambert (1974); rev. 39 in the prayer to Ishtar published by Reiner and Güterbock (1967); and l. 23 in the prayer to Damkina, K 8105.
22 See e.g. Esarhaddon 33, i 33.
23 It is unclear who she was supposed to have compassion on – the sons or the fathers.
24 Forsyth (1981: 20–6) and Kramer (1981: 2–3). Other Inana myths associate this goddess with the lamentation priest: in the Sumerian *Descent of Inana*, the **gala** is also created by Enki to rescue her from the netherworld (ETSCL c.1.4.1, 223–5). The phrase used in the Akkadian version is 'when she calms' (*ultu libbaša innuhu*, l. 96; Setälä 2022), using the same vocabulary of soothing angry gods that we find in laments; Setälä (2022). See Gabbay (2015: 77–8), Shehata (2008), and Mirelman (2021: 131).

## Bibliography


Baruchi-Unna, A. (2013), 'Genres Meet: Assurbanipal's Prayer in the Inscription L4 and the Bilingual Communal Lamentations', in L. Feliu, J. Llop, A. Millet Albà, and J. Sanmartín (eds), *Time and History in the Ancient Near East: Proceedings of the 56th Rencontre Assyriologique Internationale at Barcelona*, 611–23, University Park: Pennsylvania State University Press.

Chen, Y. S. (2013), *The Primeval Flood Catastrophe: Origins and Development in Mesopotamian Traditions*, Oxford: Oxford University Press.

Civil, M. (1969), 'The Sumerian Flood Story', in W. G. Lambert and A. Millard (eds), *Atrahasis: The Babylonian Story of the Flood*, 138–45, Oxford: Clarendon Press.

Cohen, M. (1988), *The Canonical Lamentations of Ancient Mesopotamia*, 2 vols, Potomac: Capital Decisions.

Delnero, P. (2020), *How to Do Things with Tears: Ritual Lamenting in Ancient Mesopotamia*, Berlin: De Gruyter.

Falkenstein, A. (1931), *Die Haupttypen der Sumerischen Beschwörung*, Leipzig: J. C. Hinrichs.

Forsyth, N. (1981), 'Huwawa and His Trees: A Narrative and Cultural Analysis', *Acta Sumerologica*, 3: 13–30.

Foster, B. R. (2005), *Before the Muses: An Anthology of Akkadian Literature*, 3rd edn, Bethesda: CDL Press.

Foster, B. R. (2016), 'On Speculative Thought in Ancient Mesopotamia', in K. Raaflaub (ed.), *The Adventure of the Human Intellect: Self, Society, and the Divine in Ancient World Cultures*, 89–104, Hoboken: Wiley.

Fowler, D. (1997), 'On the Shoulders of Giants: Intertextuality and Classical Studies', *Materiali e discussioni*, 39: 13–34.

Foxvog, D. (2014), 'The Late Bilingual Exaltation of Ištar (Inannas Erhöhung)'. Available at: https://www.academia.edu/4297790/The_Late_Bilingual_Exaltation_of_I%C5%A1tar_Inannas_Erh%C3%B6hung_.

Gabbay, U. (2015), *The Eršemma Prayers of the First Millennium*, Heidelberger Emesal-Studien 2, Wiesbaden: Harrassowitz.

Gabriel, G. (2014), '*enūma eliš*' – *Weg zu einer globalen Weltordnung: Pragmatik, Struktur und Semantik des babylonischen 'Lieds auf Marduk'*, Tübingen: Mohr Siebeck.

George, A. R. (1992), *Babylonian Topographical Texts*, Orientalia Lovaniensia Analecta 40, Leuven: Peters.

George, A. R. (1997), 'Marduk and the Cult of the Gods of Nippur at Babylon', *Orientalia*, 5: 65–70.

Giangrande, G. (1967) '"Arte Allusiva" and Alexandrian Imitation', *The Classical Quarterly*, 17 (1): 85–97.

Helle, S. (2020), 'The First Authors: Narratives of Authorship in Ancient Iraq', PhD. diss., Aarhus University.

Hinds, S. (1998), *Allusion and Intertext: Dynamics of Appropriation in Roman Poetry*, Cambridge: Cambridge University Press.

Horowitz, W. (1998), *Mesopotamian Cosmic Geography*, Winona Lake: Eisenbrauns.

Hu, Y. (2021), 'Translation of Chinese Classical Poetry in the Perspective of Intertextuality', *International Journal of Frontiers in Sociology*, 3 (3): 61–5.

Jacobsen, T. (1976), *The Treasures of Darkness: A History of Mesopotamian Religion*, New Haven: Yale University Press.

Jiménez, E., A. C. Heinrich, A. Hätinen, Z. J. Földi, and T. Mitto (2020), 'From the Electronic Babylonian Literature Lab 8–15', *Kaskal*, 17: 231–79.

Katz, D. (2011), 'Reconstructing Babylon: Recycling Mythological Traditions Towards a New Theology', in E. Cancik-Kirschbaum, M. van Ess and J. Marzahn (eds), *Babylon, Wissenkultur in Orient and Okzident*, Topoi 1, 123–34, Berlin: De Gruyter.

Kramer, N. S. (1981), 'BM 29616 – The Fashioning of the gala', *Acta Sumerologica*, 3: 1–12.

Kristeva, J. (1980), *Desire in Language: A Semiotic Approach to Literature and Art*, ed. L. S. Roudiez, trans. T. Gora, A. Jardine and L. S. Roudiez, New York: Columbia University Press.

Kutscher, R. (1975), *Oh Angry Sea (a-ab-ba hu-luh-ha): The History of a Sumerian Congregational Lament*, Yale Near Eastern Researches 6, New Haven: Yale University Press.

Kvanvig, H. S. (2011), *Primeval History: Babylonian, Biblical, and Enochic; An Intertextual Reading*, Supplements to the Journal for the Study of Judaism 149, Leiden: Brill.

Labat, R. (1935), *Le Poème babylonien de la creation*, Paris: Adrien-Maissonneuve.

Labbe, J. (2015), 'Romantic Intertextuality: The Adaptive Wave', *The Wordsworth Circle*, 46 (1): 44–8.
Lambert, W. G. (1964), 'The Reign of Nebuchadnezzar I: A Turning Point in the History of Ancient Mesopotamian Religion', in. S. McCullough (ed.), *The Seed of Wisdom: Essays in Honor of Theophile James Meek*, 1–13, Toronto: University of Toronto Press.
Lambert, W. G. (1970), 'Fire Incantations', *Archiv für Orientforschung*, 23: 39–45.
Lambert, W. G. (1974), 'Dingir.šà.dib.ba Incantations', *Journal of Near Eastern Studies*, 33 (3): 267–322.
Lambert, W. G. (1984), 'Studies in Marduk', *Bulletin of the School of Oriental and African Studies*, 47 (1): 1–9.
Lambert, W. G. (1986), 'Ninurta Mythology in the Babylonian Epic of Creation', in K. Hecker and W. Sommerfeld (eds), *Keilschriftliche Literaturen: Ausgewählte Vorträge der XXXII. Rencontre assyriologique internationale, Münster, 8–12.7.1985*, 55–60, Berlin: D. Reimer.
Lambert, W. G. (1992), 'Nippur in Ancient Ideology', in M. deJong Ellis (ed.), *Nippur at the Centennial*, Occasional Publications of the Samuel Noah Kramer Fund 14, 119–26, Philadelphia: Samuel Noah Kramer Fund.
Lambert, W. G. (2008), 'Mesopotamian Creation Stories', in M. J. Geller and M. Schipper (eds), *Imagining Creation*, 15–59, Leiden: Brill.
Lambert, W. G. (2013), *Babylonian Creation Myths*, Winona Lake: Eisenbrauns.
Lambert, W. G. and A. Millard (1969), *Atrahasis: The Babylonian Story of the Flood*, Oxford: Clarendon Press.
Landsberger, B. and J. Kinnier-Wilson (1961), 'The Fifth Tablet of Enuma Eliš', *Journal of Near Eastern Studies*, 20: 154–79.
Machinist, P. (2005), 'Order and Disorder: Some Mesopotamian Reflections', in S. Shaked (ed.), *Genesis and Regeneration: Essays on Conceptions of Origins*, 31–61, Jerusalem: Israel Academy of Sciences and Humanities.
Maul, S. (1988), *Herzberuhigungsklagen: Die sumerisch-akkadischen Eršaḫunga-Gebete*, Wiesbaden: Harrassowitz.
Michalowski, P. (1990), 'Presence at the Creation', in T. Abusch, J. Huehnergard, and P. Steinkeller (eds), *Lingering over Words: Studies in Ancient Near Eastern Literature in Honour of William L. Moran*, Harvard Semitic Studies 37, 381–96, Atlanta: Scholars Press.
Mirelman, Sam. (2021), 'Mesopotamian Ritual Laments, "Music Therapy", and the Role of Song in the Conception of the Deity', in R. Eichmann, and D. Shehata (eds), *Music Beyond Cultural Borders: 33rd Deutscher Orientalistentag. Jena, 19–20 September, 2017, Studien zur Musikarchäologie 12, Orient-Archäologie 43*, 129–35, Rahden: Leidorf.
Moran, W. L. (1971), 'Atrahasis: The Babylonian Story of the Flood', *Biblica*, 52: 51–61.
Nolan Fewell, D. (ed., 1992), *Reading Between Texts: Intertextuality and the Hebrew Bible*, Louiseville: Westminster/John Nox Press.
Pasquali, G. (1951), *Stravaganze quarte e supreme*, Venice: N. Pozza.
Reiner, E. and H. G. Güterbock (1967), 'The Great Prayer to Ishtar and Its Two Versions from Boğazköy', *Journal of Cuneiform Studies*, 21: 255–66.
Reisner, G. (1896), *Sumerisch-babylonische hymnen nach thontafeln griechischer zeit*, Germany: Spemann.
Robson, E. (2011), 'Reading the Libraries of Assyria and Babylonia', in J. König, K. Oikonomopolou and G. Woolf (eds), *Ancient Libraries*, 38–56, Cambridge: Cambridge University Press.
Rochberg-Halton, F. (1988), *Aspects of Babylonian Celestial Divination: The Lunar Eclipse Tablets of Enūma Anu Enlil*, Horn: Ferdinand Berger und Söhne.

Röllig, W. (1971), 'Götterzahlen', *Reallexikon der Assyriologie und vorderasiatischen Archäologie*, 3: 499–500.
Russell, D. A. (1979), 'De Imitatione', in D. West and T. Woodman (eds), *Creative Imitation and Latin Literature*, 1–16, Cambridge: Cambridge University Press.
Saggs, H. W. F. (1986), 'Additions to Anzu', *Archiv für Orientforschung*, 33: 1–29.
Seri, A. (2006), 'The Fifty Names of Marduk in *Enūma eliš*', *Journal of the American Oriental Society*, 126 (4): 1–13.
Seri, A. (2012), 'The Role of Creation in *Enūma eliš*', *Journal of Ancient Near Eastern Religions*, 12: 4–29.
Seri, A. (2014), 'Borrowings to Create Anew: Intertextuality in the Babylonian Poem of "Creation" (Enūma Eliš)', *Journal of the American Oriental Society*, 134 (1): 89–106.
Setälä, A. (2022), 'Descent of Ištar', with contributions by Z. J. Földi, A. Hätinen, E. Jiménez and G. Rozzi. Translated by Benjamin R. Foster. *electronic Babylonian Library*. https://www.ebl.lmu.de/corpus/L/1/8/SB/-.
Shehata, D. (2001), *Annotierte Bibliographie zum altbabylonischen Atramḫasīs-Mythos: Inūma ilū awīlum*, Göttinger Arbeitshefte zur altorientalischen Literatur 3, Göttingen: Seminar für Keilschriftforschung Göttingen.
Shehata, D. (2008), 'On the Mythological Background of the Lamentation Priest', in A. A. Both, R. Eichmann, E. Hickmann, and L.C. Koch (eds), *Studien zur Musikarchäologie VI, Orient-Archäologie 22*, 119–27, Rahden: Leidorf.
Sommerfeld, W. (1982), *Der Aufstieg Marduks: Die Stellung Marduks in der babylonischen Religion des zweiten Jahrtausends v. Chr.*, Kevelear: Butzon und Bercker.
Sonik, K. (2008), 'Bad King, False King, True King: Apsû and His Heirs', *Journal of the American Oriental Society*, 128 (4): 737–43.
Studevent-Hickman, B. (2010), 'Language, Speech, and the Death of Anzu', in J. Stackert, B. Nevling Porter, and D. P. Wright (eds), *Gazing on the Deep: Ancient Near Eastern and Other Studies in Honor of Tzvi Abusch*, 273–92, Bethesda: CDL Press.
Talon, P. (2001), '*Enūma Eliš* and the Transmission of Babylonian Cosmology to the West', in R. Whiting (ed.), *Mythology and Mythologies: Methodological Approaches to Intercultural Influences*, 265–77, Helsinki: The Neo-Assyrian Text Corpus Project.
van Dijk, J. A. (1983), *Lugal ud me-lám-bi nir-ĝál: Le récit épique et didactique des travaux de Ninurta, de Déluge et de la nouvelle creation*, Leiden: Brill.
Vanstiphout, H. L. J. (1992), 'Enuma Elish as a Systematic Creed: An Essay', *Orientalia Lovaninesia Periodica*, 23: 37–61.
Wasserman, N. (2020), *The Flood: Akkadian Sources; A New Edition, Commentary, and a Literary Discussion*, Orbis Biblicus et Orientalis 290, Leuven: Peeters.
Wisnom, S. (2019), 'Blood on the Wind and the Tablet of Destinies: Intertextuality in Anzû, Enūma eliš, and Erra and Išum', *Journal of the American Oriental Society*, 139 (2): 269–86.
Wisnom, S. (2020), *Weapons of Words: Intertextual Competition in Babylonian Poetry; A Study of 'Anzû', 'Enūma Eliš', and 'Erra and Išum'*, Culture and History of the Ancient Near East 106, Leiden: Brill.
Wisnom, S. (2021), 'Marduk the Fisherman', *Journal of the American Oriental Society*, 141 (1): 211–14.
Wisnom, S. (2023), 'The Dynamics of Repetition in Akkadian Epics', in G. Konstantopoulos and S. Helle (eds), *The Shape of Stories: Narrative Structures in Cuneiform Literature*, Cuneiform Monographs 54, 112–43, Leiden: Brill.
Zevit, Z. (ed., 2017), *Subtle Citation, Allusions and Translation in the Hebrew Bible*, Sheffield: Equinox.

11

# The shape of water: Content and form in *Enuma Elish*

Sophus Helle

*The Shape of Water* – the title of an Oscar-winning film by Guillermo del Toro – is an oxymoron. Water has no fixed shape; it is the fluid material with which most humans are most familiar. What the phrase captures is a conceptual tension between form and flow, and my claim in this chapter is that this same tension pervades *Enuma Elish*. The epic tracks a transformation from the watery formlessness of the world's beginning to the realm of everyday experience: a landscape of distinct shapes to which we assign names and meaning. *Enuma Elish* depicts the world as a fundamentally fluid matter that was bound by Marduk into shapes that then acquired their identity in language, meaning that language, according to the epic, carves out specificity from an originally shapeless state. But because the epic is itself made of language, it does not chart this transition neutrally: it is actively invested in the world of words, and I will argue that the epic recreates in its own poetic form the shift from liquid to language, participating in the creation of order out of water.[1]

The epic's epilogue shows how central the poetry of water, and especially the contrast between water and language, is to *Enuma Elish*. As first noted by Benjamin Foster (1991, 2019), a recurrent feature in cuneiform narratives is that they tend to end by describing their own composition – a poetic motif that I have elsewhere dubbed the 'self-referential climax' (Helle 2023) – and *Enuma Elish* is no exception. In its final passage, it describes its own creation as follows:

*taklimti maḫrû idbubu pānuššu*
*išṭur-ma ištakan ana šemî arkûti*
*šīmat marduk ša u[ll]û ilū igīgū*[2]
*ēma mû iššattû šumšu lizzakrū*
*inannam-ma zamāru ša marduk*
*ša tiā[mta i]kmû-(ma) ilqû šarrūta*

This is the revelation that 'the first one' recited before him (Marduk),
wrote down and set up for future generations to hear:
the fate of Marduk, whom the Igigi exalted.
Wherever water is drunk, may his name be invoked.

This now is the song of Marduk,
who bound Tiamat and received kingship.

(VII 157–62)

Nestled between the lines that refer explicitly to the poem we have just been reading – the revelation of Marduk's fifty names, the exaltation of his fate, and the song of his triumph – is the seemingly incongruous comment: 'Wherever water is drunk, may his name be invoked.' But in fact, the comment is anything but incongruous. It invites us to rethink an action we perform every day as a miniature re-enactment of the epic's main narrative, Marduk's battle against Tiamat: as he subdued the sea, so we swallow the stuff of which Tiamat was made. Drinking water becomes a *lieu de mémoire*, a regular occasion on which to recall a foundational myth (Nora 1984: vii–viii).[3] Tellingly, we are to recall not just Marduk's glory, but his name, which comes to stand in triumphant opposition to Tiamat's watery form. But what is the relation between the water that is drunk and the song that is performed? Or, in other words, what is the relation between the content of the epic – the shaping of the sea-like Tiamat and Apsû to create the world order – and the epic's own literary form? I will argue that *Enuma Elish* casts creation in textual terms, presenting cosmogony as the emergence of a language-like structure from a primordial fluidity that defied all words and writing. This allows the epic to depict itself as the culmination of the process by which the cosmos came into being, taking the reader on a journey from the beginning of time to its own composition.

## Unbound by meadows

*Enuma Elish* begins in an age before shapes, names, and fates, an age beautifully captured in the opening lines: 'When on high heaven had not been named, and the ground below not given a name … ' (*enūma eliš lā nabû šamāmū* / *šapliš ammatu šuma lā zakrat*, I 1–2). In this state, Tiamat and Apsû are free to mingle their waters together, since 'they had not yet bound meadows or lined the reedbeds' (*gipāra lā kiṣṣurū ṣuṣâ lā šē'ū*, I 6). As noted by Giorgio Buccellati (1990: 125), this mention of meadows and reedbeds alludes to the landscape of southern Mesopotamia, which was a checkerboard of grassland and canals; on the banks between them stood clusters of reeds, marking the boundaries between land and water. Before the formation of these natural borders, the two seas are free to mix and so form a single, shapeless mass. Because everything was fluid, and distinct forms had not emerged, there could be no names either, as emphasized in the opening couplet. The epic thus reaches back to a past before the words it uses to describe that past.[4] The primordial scene can only be described through negation – the word *lā*, 'not', appears seven times in the first eight lines – because names depend on the separation of the things they name, and that separation has yet to happen. In the beginning was no word.[5]

It is not that the universe has not been created at this point, but that it has not yet been separated out into shapes. To exist, in the logic of *Enuma Elish*, is to be an entity distinguishable from the surrounding cosmos. The epic spells out the three elements that are required for existence according to its worldview, again relying on the force of negation: 'when none of the gods had been brought forth, had not been given names and had not decreed destinies' (*enūma ilū lā šūpû manāma / šuma lā zukkurū šīmāti lā šīmū*, I 7–8). To exist, one must be 'visibly manifest', *šūpû*, have a 'name', *šumu*, and be assigned a 'fate', *šīmtu*: the epic juxtaposes these three elements and concatenates them in our mind through the repetition of *š*-. Shapes, names, and fates are thus depicted as fundamentally interconnected, and their absence from the beginning of the story foreshadows what the world will be like at the end of it. Marduk will have split apart Tiamat's body and shaped it into the landscape we know, replete with mountains, rivers, cities, and temples, and each separate thing will be given a name and a role to play within the world order, that is, a destiny.

This differentiation of the world into separable, nameable objects is the foundation for existence as we know it, and it is also the foundation for poetry. Without words and distinct shapes, there can be no narration, and *Enuma Elish* as a text is thus implicated in the story it tells: the transition from water to language also makes the epic itself possible. Consider again the description of Tiamat and Apsû as being unbound by meadows and unlined by reedbeds. For the scribes of ancient Iraq, the banks of canals and the reedbeds that lined them also carried another meaning. They were the places where, at least ideally, the scribes would gather the clay they shaped into tablets and the reed styluses with which they wrote on those tablets. As noted by Jon Taylor and Caroline Cartwright (2011: 297), the clay used by ancient scribes 'most readily came from the sediments in riverbanks and canals'. Not only does the primordial scene lack names, it also lacks the materials with which those names could be written, meaning that *Enuma Elish* begins, literally, *avant la lettre* – before the possibility of writing.

Tablet I tracks the gradual emergence of language from this primordial state (see also Michalowski in this volume). First, the newly created gods make a wordless noise, described with the rare term *naṣīru*, 'clamour', which disturbs Apsû and keeps him awake (I 22). Apsû then utters the first word: *mummu* (I 30). The concept of *mummu* is central to *Enuma Elish*, but difficult to translate, being equated in Commentary I with both *nabnītu*, 'creation', and *rigmu*, 'noise', while also being used as an epithet of Tiamat and as the name of Apsû's minister.[6] In the battle against Apsû, Ea speaks what we may call the first magical words, that is, the first speech that acts directly upon the world, namely 'his sacred spell' (*têšu ellu*, I 62), which allows him to subdue, bind, and kill Apsû and then turn him into a cosmic region.[7] When Ea has shaped Apsû's waters into a definite form, he then carries out the first act of naming: 'he called it Apsû, "the shrines are made known"' (*imbīšum-ma apsû u'addû ešrēti*, I 76). The first name is here immediately followed by the first interpretation, as Apsû's name is unfolded into the phrase 'the shrines are made known', according to a set of hermeneutic principles to which I return below (see also Van De Mieroop in this volume). Gradually, then, language comes into being, moving from wordless clamour towards magic and meaning. The process culminates, at the end of Tablet I, with the creation of the Tablet of Destinies, *tuppi šīmāti*, the ultimate symbol of linguistic power over the world (I 157).

Over the course of Tablet I, language comes to look much like it did to ancient scribes: it consists of distinct words, efficacious speech, meaningful names, and powerful writing. But again, the text relating to this story is itself made of language. The poem is tracking the emergence of its own medium, thus fusing its form (words, names, and writing) with its content (the creation of words, names, and writing). The interlinked trajectories of form and content culminate in the recitation of Marduk's names in Tablet VII, followed by the self-referential epilogue quoted above. The namelessness that characterized the primordial scene has thus been replaced by an overabundance of names, namely the fifty names given to Marduk and the cosmic functions that accompany them. As noted by Piotr Michalowski (1990: 396), the final Tablets of *Enuma Elish* describe a world where everything carries significance, for everything is in some way connected to Marduk and his many-meaning names: at this point in the epic, 'the universe had become a library'. For example, Marduk assigns a fixed path to the heavenly bodies, and any deviation from that path is seen as an omen to be interpreted, littering the sky with signs (see Rochberg in this volume). Reminders of Marduk's greatness are everywhere, even and especially in the water we drink.

Finally, just as the initial lack of forms foreshadows their later creation, and just as namelessness gives way to namefulness, so the (obliquely expressed) non-existence of reed and clay in the beginning is resolved by the writing of the epic itself, as the author 'wrote it down and set it up for future generations to hear' (*išṭur-ma ištakan ana šemî arkûti*, VII 158). The narrative arc of *Enuma Elish* culminates in the creation of *Enuma Elish*, since the absences that defined the primordial world are doubly resolved, once in the storyline (the seas are separated out, water is bound into shape, Marduk is hailed with fifty names, signs are strewn across the skies) and once in the medium through which the story is told (the existence of the text proves that writing, names, and words have now become possible). *Enuma Elish* is a story about the creation of world order that is, at the same time, about the creation of its own text and textuality at large. The two levels – word and world, song and cosmos – are interwoven throughout the story, as the following sections explore in more detail.

## To bind the sea

Words cannot exist in the opening scene because there are no separable entities for them to refer to, so for language to emerge, the primordial waters must be shaped into distinct forms. The epic repeatedly describes this process with the language of *binding* (*kamû*), and it is worth noting what a curious metaphor that is. To bind water with a rope would normally be an exercise in futility, but not so in *Enuma Elish*, where Ea binds Apsû (I 69 and 73) and Marduk binds Tiamat (IV 103 and 128) to mark their respective triumphs. In both cases, the act of binding is immediately followed by an act of reshaping, as the gods seize the newly defeated enemies and use their bodies to create, in Ea's case, a definite part of the cosmos, and in Marduk's case, the whole world order (Gabriel 2014: 190–2). The gods shackle the seas into shapes and arrange those shapes into ordered wholes, in a clear illustration of the conceptual tension that underlies the epic: forms emerge from fluids, shapes are made from water.

Just as it is odd for water to be bound, so it is odd that Marduk defeats Tiamat with a net (IV 95). Again, it seems an almost proverbially senseless thing to do. Nets are used for catching fish precisely because they do not retain the water in which fish swim.[8] The seeming mismatch between weapon and foe has been explained as a conflation of the two myths on which *Enuma Elish* draws: Baal's battle against the sea god Yam in the Ugaritic tradition and Ninurta's battle against the monstrous bird Anzû in an older Akkadian tradition.[9] Birds are indeed hunted with nets, but are we really dealing with a thoughtless mashing of sources? The intelligence that is everywhere evident in the epic's composition suggests otherwise, especially given the contrast between shapes and shapelessness that underlies the plot. Perhaps, then, Marduk's defeat of Tiamat relies precisely on his magic ability to fix her in place *as form*. The divine power he wields over her in his moment of triumph is the power to turn her into a delimited, tangible object that can be captured by a net and shaped according to his needs – rather than the limitless, formless expanse she once was.

Throughout the epic, Tiamat's form is hard to define (Lambert 2013: 459–60; Gabriel 2014: 118, n. 41, with references to previous literature). In some passages, she is clearly understood as a cosmic sea. This is the case in the opening scene and in I 107–10, where Marduk's winds roil Tiamat's belly, the watery world in which the gods live: it is because her body is shaken by his storms, tossing like a rough sea, that the gods inside her cannot sleep or lie still (I 119–20). But elsewhere, she is described in what seem to be anthropomorphic terms, as when Apsû comes to sit before her (I 33–4). Many of her actions are difficult to conceptualize if one does not mentally assign to her a human form: what would it mean, for example, for a sea to take Qingu as its lover or to fix the Tablet of Destinies on his chest (I 167)? As Wilfred Lambert (1994: 104) puts it, 'At times she is presented as a solid-bodied monster, at other times as a mass of water.' There are several references to Tiamat's *karšu*, 'belly', and *libbu*, 'heart', but in Akkadian, these words can signify (1) concrete body parts, (2) the interior of her waters, and (3) her mood and mind, making the picture more rather than less obscure.[10] Later, the epic mentions that Tiamat has a tail (V 59); other sources depict her as a dromedary or equate her with the constellation of the Goat-Fish.[11] In a relief from the Temple of Bel at Palmyra, she is depicted with snakes for legs, like a monstrous octopus; as Lucinda Dirven (1999: 150) concludes in an analysis of that relief, 'it is difficult to arrive at a precise picture of her' (see also Frahm in this volume). But that may be precisely the point. In the first half of the epic, Tiamat is fluid in a double sense of the word, again conflating content and form: she is fluid in that she is, among other things, a body of water (content), and she is fluid in that she is also other things, as the text does not allow us a firm grasp on her but presents us with conflicting information, keeping her shape unsettled in our minds (form).[12]

All this changes after Tiamat's battle with Marduk. In the lines leading up to their duel, reference is made to her 'neck', *kišassa*, which she does not turn back in defeat, and to her 'lips', *šaptīša*, in which she holds falsehood and lies (IV 71–2). These are human features, but figuratively used, and the text soon afterwards states that Tiamat 'shook all over, down to her depths' (*šuršiš malmališ itrurā išdāša*, IV 90). Though some translators render *išdā*, 'depths', in anthropomorphic terms (Lambert 2013: 91 renders it as 'all her lower members', Kämmerer and Metzler 2012: 335 as 'ihre beiden Beine', 'both her legs'), it literally means 'foundation' and is most often used of buildings. Though it can apply to people – typically referring to the stability of their stance[13] – it is a strikingly non-human metaphor. At this point, Tiamat still seems more water than woman, but just five lines later, Marduk traps her with his net, and her physiognomy begins to change. At no point so far are Tiamat's limbs described in any detail, but in the eight lines after she is captured in Marduk's net, we are treated to a volley of anatomical specificity: her mouth (IV 97, 100), lips (98), belly (99, 101), insides (100), entrails, and heart (102) are mentioned in quick succession, as Marduk's weapons tear through her body. In a grim conclusion, Marduk binds her (*kamû*, 103) and steps on her corpse (104), declaring victory. The battle is thus a process by which Marduk makes Tiamat into a body he can bind.

The battle unfolds at the precise midpoint of the epic, and in its second half, Tiamat's body will be further bound into textual fixity, through a detailed and often violent exploration of her limbs; as Lambert (2013: 459) writes: 'beyond question, in these passages, Tiāmat is a monstrous animal, not a body of water'. Marduk manipulates her limbs and fixes them in place, arranging a once shapeless sea into discrete body parts, each of which becomes a cosmic region: we are subjected to one more torrent of limbs, as the text mentions her head (V 53), eyes (55), nostrils (56), breasts (57), tail (59), and groin (60). That is not to say that Tiamat entirely ceases to be fluid.[14] The text seems to conceive of the world as a giant air bubble within her endless waters, and the water that humans know, such as rivers and well-water, flows into this bubble through the regulated channels established by Marduk. But Marduk has brought Tiamat's fluidity under control, transforming her from a formless flow into an agriculturally useful force.[15] The list of Marduk's names and destinies in Tablets VI and VII frequently mentions his role as the creator of farming and master of waterways, doling out Tiamat's waters in a managed and therefore productive manner (VI 124, VI 1, and 57–69).

According to *Enuma Elish*, the world was thus created through a violent imposition of form onto Tiamat's previously shapeless body. Kai Metzler points out the implicit misogyny of this account, noting the connection between death, femininity, and the aesthetic formation of objects. It is because Tiamat's body is made passive, pliant, and unresisting that it can be shaped aesthetically (i.e. according to a premeditated design; see Metzler 2002). Earlier in the text, Tiamat is herself a source of creation, since she gives birth to the gods; but her fertility is then shown to be potentially threatening, as she also gives birth to an army of monsters. Subduing Tiamat means subduing her creative force, making her the material of the male god's design. The imposition of form on formlessness, which is the precondition for world order, is thus also an act of gendered violence, especially in the scene where Tiamat's limbs are gruesomely anatomized: the misogynist force of her dismemberment is underscored by the mention of her groin and breasts, which are roughly and offputtingly handled by Marduk (on the misogynist logic of *Enuma Elish*, see Sonik in this volume).

As I have argued elsewhere (2020: 63–77), *Enuma Elish* is driven by a patriarchal paranoia that is most powerfully manifested in Marduk's constant need to control Tiamat's body, which reaches a fever pitch in his forty-ninth name, Neberu (VII 124–34). Neberu is the name of Marduk's astral manifestation (see Rochberg in this volume), and it literally means 'crossing'. The text takes this 'crossing' to refer to Marduk's path through the night-sky, and since the night-sky was made from Tiamat's corpse, the crossing is seen as perpetuating the primordial moment of violence: 'He who unceasingly crosses back and forth inside Tiamat: let his name be *Neberu*, he who seized her waist!' (*ša qerbiš tiāmti ītebbiru lā nâhiš / šumšu lū nēberu āhizu qerbīšu* VII

128–9). The gendered violence implicit in the poem is here made especially clear. The planet's movement 'inside' (*qerbiš*) Tiamat is interpreted as Marduk seizing 'her waist' (*qerbīšu*), but why would Marduk seize the waist, specifically? Because the waist is also the site of Tiamat's womb (the closely related word *qerbītu* can mean 'womb'), meaning that Marduk is here neutralizing her dangerous fertility. Jupiter's orbit is reimagined as an eternally renewed restraint on Tiamat's body and particularly on her reproductive organs, with the planet's path through the sky becoming an enormous rope holding her in place: 'Let him bind (*kamû* again) Tiamat, let her breath be kept short and shallow' (*likmi tiāmta napištaša lisīq u likri*, VII 132). The text emphasizes that the movement should go on forever, that Marduk should keep binding Tiamat again and again in perpetuity (133–4). Patriarchal paranoia knows no end: even with Tiamat dead and disremembered, the female body is seen as always potentially dangerous and in need of control. Crucially, the female body must not just be controlled, but *bound* anew: Jupiter's rope-like orbit holds back Tiamat's waters, which always threaten to rush back in. For the world to be kept safe, Tiamat must be continuously kept from becoming fluid again. The form that Marduk forced upon her waters must be forever re-imposed.

At this point, the text has achieved a complete reversal of the primordial scene in which Tiamat and Apsû mingled their waters. Tiamat is initially a fluid concept, but the text gradually fixes her in place, separating her into limbs and making her form clearer in our minds through cascades of body parts. The text does what Marduk does, transforming Tiamat from a mostly fluid to a mostly fixed shape. It seems to me that, at least metaphorically, Tiamat is also bound through the writing and narrative progression of the epic, which restricts her primordial fluidity: the text's description of her is thus complicit with Marduk's defeat of her. This confluence of her textual and physical restrictions is also highlighted by an echo between the description of Jupiter and the epilogue that follows shortly thereafter. As Neberu, Marduk is said to 'grasp' the orbit of the stars and 'seize' Tiamat's waist (*ṣābit* and *āhizu*, VII 127 and 129); just sixteen lines later, the reader is encouraged to 'grasp' the fifty names, and fathers are encouraged to let their sons 'seize' them in their mind (*liṣṣabtū* and *lišāhiz*, VII 145 and 147; Helle 2020: 73). In both cases, the words appear in the same order (*ṣabātu* then *aḫāzu*) and are separated by precisely one line, making the symmetry especially clear. In yet another parallel between content and form, the readers' actions are made to mimic Marduk's: as he keeps Tiamat in check, so we commit the text to memory.

But if *Enuma Elish* traces the gradual emergence of shapes out of water, and ties those shapes to the emergence of language, then what does the appearance of language mean, according to the text itself?[16]

## From word to world

Ea's defeat of Apsû exemplifies the epic's understanding of language.[17] Ea subdues Apsû with his spell and puts him to sleep; Apsû is killed, bound, and then given a fixed form, as Ea shapes him into a cosmic region. As noted above, Ea then assigns a name to this region, which is accompanied by an epithet: he 'called it (*nabû*) Apsû, "the shrines are made known"' (*imbīšum-ma apsû u'addû ešrēti*, I 76). Jean-Marie

Durand (1994) has shown that this epithet is an etymographic interpretation of the name 'Apsû', which is written ZU-AB, since ZU is equated with *u'addû*, 'they make known', and AB (through the reading $e\check{s}_3$) with *ešrēti*, 'shrines'. The line foreshadows the much longer epithets that will accompany each of Marduk's fifty names, with each epithet again being linked to the corresponding name through a complex set of linguistic equations, following the principles of Babylonian hermeneutics (Van De Mieroop in this volume). But the epithets are not just honorific titles: they describe a cosmic role that Marduk performs – that is, a destiny. As Asari he creates farmland, as Ziku he makes the wind blow, as Suhrim he subdues monsters, and so on. The fifty names are also fifty fates, and the hermeneutic ties between them establish a connection between *šumu* and *šīmtu* (Gabriel 2014: chap. 5). In Apsû's case, the name and corresponding fate are assigned immediately after the moment in which he is bound into a (visible) form, simultaneously realizing the three aspects of existence that were juxtaposed in the opening passage – *šūpû*, *šumu*, and *šīmtu*.

The same is true of Marduk's fifty names. Before they begin reciting his names, the gods say: 'Let us give him (*nabû*) fifty names (*šumu*), so that his ways may be brought forth (*šūpû*), and likewise his doings' (*i nibbī-ma hamšā šumīšu / alkatuš lū šūpât epšetuš lū mašlat*, VI 121–2). Again, the three aspects of existence are interconnected: there is an inherent link between giving Marduk a name, 'bringing forth' his being, and assigning him a cosmic role. In turn, the world order that Marduk creates combines the same three aspects of existence. A telling example is the role he assigns the Moon. Instructing it to wax and wane at the appropriate time of the month, he says, 'You shine with horns to mark the naming of the days' (*qarnī nabâta ana uddû zakāri ūmī*, V 16). The line relies on a pun between *nabû*, here meaning 'to shine', and *nabû*, 'to name', setting up a direct link between them: the course of the lunar cycle allows for the days to be distinguished and named as the seventh, fifteenth, and thirtieth day of a given month. The naming of the days relies on their separability, which the regular changes in the moonlight provide (see Rochberg in this volume).

According to *Enuma Elish*, names are invested with a profoundly creative power. Addressing Marduk, the gods refer to '[Babylon], which you have named' ([*bābili*] *ša tazkura šumšu*, V 137). Marduk did not only name Babylon, he also built it; but the two actions are so closely interlinked in the poem that they can be used interchangeably.[18] Names do not only describe the act of creation but actively participate in it, as stated explicitly in one of the commentaries to the epic. Commentary II analyses the meaning of Marduk's names and connects each word of their interpretation in the text – which, I have argued, amounts to the destinies bestowed on the god – to a syllable or sound in the name they accompany (Bottéro 1977; Van De Mieroop in this volume). To connect the name Tutu-Ziku to the word 'named' (*imbû*, VII 19), the commentary links the sound /tu/ in Tutu to the sign $DU_3$, meaning *banû*, 'to create', and that word to *nabû*, meaning 'to name' (l. 19).[19] The equation between *banû* and *nabû* relies on a similarity of sound but also expresses the principle at work in *Enuma Elish* more broadly, where names are an inextricable part of creation. The moment when an object that is coming into being is named, it acquires the form and function that sets it aside from all other objects.

Further, since fifty names and destinies help to maintain the world order that Marduk created, the list also represents his control over the cosmos – making the plants grow and the rain fall, keeping the gods in line and the wicked at bay, healing the righteous and feeding the hungry. The names map directly onto Marduk's activities, and since those activities sustain and shape the world we know, they also map out the fabric of the cosmos. By interpreting all natural phenomena as the result of Marduk's actions, and those actions (or destinies) as linked to his many names, the epic makes language central to the universe. Associations at the level of sounds, signs, and syllables provide the key for grasping the connections that control our world. That is exactly the kind of analysis that is carried out in Commentary II. By explaining the meaning of Marduk's names, the commentary also analyses the impact of the names on the world. The hermeneutic analysis is also, according to its own logic, an ontological analysis, since it sets out to reveal something about the nature of creation (Van De Mieroop 2016: 9).

Again, we should keep in mind that the epic itself is made of language. The importance it assigns to sounds, signs, and syllables is an importance it assigns to its own medium. When the epilogue invites its readers to study the fifty names – 'let the wise and the learned discuss them together' (*enqu mūdû mitḫariš limtalkū*, VII 146) – it is inviting us to study both the text of *Enuma Elish* and what that text will reveal about the world Marduk created. Assigning such cosmic weight to the list of names results in a final conflation of content and form, as the epic draws a direct connection between its own textual structure and the world order described in it. These connotations should be at the back of our minds when we come, in the epilogue, to the line, 'Wherever water is drunk, may his name be invoked' (VII 160). Speaking Marduk's name whenever we drink water celebrates his triumph over Tiamat but also reflects the narrative arc of *Enuma Elish*, in which the world of water gives way to a name-bound cosmos.

## Returning to water

The relation between water and text in *Enuma Elish* can be compared to another key myth of Babylonian culture: the Flood. As noted by Hans-Peter Müller (1985: 295), in both biblical and cuneiform literature, the story of creation and of the Flood stand in an antithetical relation, serving as myth and anti-myth, respectively.[20] The Old Babylonian epic *Atra-hasis* exemplifies this tension, as the first half of the poem tells of humanity's creation, the second half of its near-total destruction in the waters of the Flood. Given this symmetrical relation, it is telling that accounts of the Flood use a set of tropes also found in *Enuma Elish* – but develop these tropes in the opposite direction. The Flood story, especially as told in the Standard Babylonian version of *Gilgamesh*, relies on the same contrast between water and form and the same association between form and text, but depicts destruction rather than creation.[21] I am not arguing that *Gilgamesh* directly reverses the themes found in *Enuma Elish*, since the chronological relation between the two epics is uncertain. Indeed, they may both be drawing on a set of pre-existing concepts regarding form, language, and fluidity. But whatever the nature of their connection, the contrast between them is telling.

As the gods unleash the Flood over the human population, the world is returned to the aboriginal state of shapelessness that is described in *Enuma Elish*. The winds and rainfall destroy all human structures and cover the world with an endless expanse of water, described as an *ušallu*, 'flood plain' (XI 136). All distinctions dissolve: as in the opening passage of *Enuma Elish*, the boundaries between land and rivers disappear, allowing water to flow freely once more. One line tellingly states that 'Erra ripped out the mooring poles; Ninurta walked by and made the weirs overflow' (*tarkullī errakal inassaḫ / illak Ninurta miḫrī ušardi*, XI 102–3; George 2022). The 'mooring poles', *tarkullī*, would normally stand on the river banks and so mark the border between water and earth, like the reedbeds in *Enuma Elish*, so when they are torn out by Erra – here called by his byname Errakal, to allow for a pun with *tarkullī* – it is implied that this border also disappears. Meanwhile, Ninurta, as the inventor of agriculture, destroys his own creation by letting the torrents of the Flood tear through the weirs, which are small dams used to regulate the flow of water through the fields.[22]

In *Enuma Elish*, Marduk charges the Moon with creating distinctions between days and so allow for their naming, and again this logic is reversed by the Flood. The clouds of the Deluge upend the normal flow of time by creating darkness during the day: 'all that was bright turned into darkness' (*mimma namru ana da'ummat utterru*, XI 107; George 2022; see also Worthington 2019: 209–10). *Gilgamesh* repeatedly refers to the moment when night turns to day with the phrase, 'in the first lighting of dawn' (*mimmû šēri ina namāri*, VII 90 and *passim*; George 2022), and the lexical parallels between the two lines (*mimma / mimmâ* and *namru / namāri*) show that the Flood undoes the usual flow of time, reversing the distinction imposed by the dawn and thus rendering time shapeless again. All things lose their appearance in the Flood, including humans: 'A brother could not find his brother, people could not be recognized in the slaughter' (*ul immar aḫu aḫāšu / ul ūtaddâ nišū ina karāši*, XI 112–13; George 2022). In the chaos and confusion of the Deluge, people cannot be told apart, because everyone looks like everyone else. Shapelessness reigns once more; the world of separable forms has reverted to the fluidity from which it came.

As we would expect after reading *Enuma Elish*, the disappearance of forms also leads to the disappearance of language. Not only does the cataclysm leave silence in its wake (XI 106), the Flood is also a specifically *anti-textual* event.[23] Since clay, the preferred medium of cuneiform writing, is water-soluble, all written records are dissolved in the Flood, or as the mother goddess Belet-ili more poetically puts it, 'the past has truly turned to clay' (*ūmu ullû ana ṭiṭṭi lū itūr-ma*, XI 119; George 2022), meaning that all historical remains have been deformed and now resemble a lump of unshaped clay. As the Flood returns the world to its original fluidity, writing can no more exist than it could in the age before meadows and reedbeds. Since writing was the main medium for ancient people to know their past, the Flood also imposes a historical limit: history, according to cuneiform sources, was split into a time 'before the Flood' and 'after the Flood', *lām abūbi* and *arki abūbi*, and the former was all but impossible to access. In *Gilgamesh*, the Flood's destruction of writing resonates in complex ways with the writing of the epic itself, especially as the text refers to itself as a tablet made of lapis lazuli, a sturdier material which might have survived the Flood.[24] In the story of the Flood recounted by Berossus – a Babylonian priest writing the history of cuneiform culture in Greek around the third century BCE – it is said that Ea instructed Atra-hasis, there called Xisouthros, to bury the tablets so as to protect them from the Flood (Burstein 1978; Haubold et al. 2013; and Frahm in this volume). This detail adds a different implication to the story – Berossus stresses the continuity of tradition and *Gilgamesh* the epochal divide – but preserves the contrast between the Flood and the writing that would have been obliterated by it. In both texts, as in *Enuma Elish*, we see a recurrent contrast between water and words, fluid formlessness and texts. We may understand this grid of contrasts and connections as the underlying cultural logic that determined how each text would depict cosmic creation and destruction: as, respectively, the shaping of fluids into identifiable forms and the returning of those forms to an aboriginal, shapeless, nameless substance.

This concept of destruction is enshrined in Sennacherib's account of the sack of Babylon that he carried out in 689 BCE as punishment for the revolt that deposed his son Ashur-nadin-shumi, who was serving as regent of the city (see Reynolds and Frahm in this volume). In a text known as the Bavian Inscription, Sennacherib describes the vengeful desolation he wrought upon the city:

> I destroyed, devastated, and burned the city and its buildings, from its foundations to its crenelations. I removed the bricks and earth, as much as there was, from the inner wall and outer wall, the temples, and the ziggurat, and I threw it into the Arahtu river. I dug canals into the centre of that city and thus levelled their site with water. I destroyed the outline of its foundations and thereby made its destruction surpass that of the Deluge. So that in the future, the site of that city and its temples will be unrecognizable, I dissolved it in water and annihilated it, making it like a flood plain.
>
> (50–4)[25]

What is remarkable about this account is the thoroughness with which Sennacherib destroys, not just the city, but its form. Reading the passage is like reading *Enuma Elish* backwards, as Sennacherib reverts Babylon to its primordial formlessness. While explicitly alluding to the Deluge, he says that he destroys not just Babylon but the 'outline of its foundation' (*šikin uššēšu*, l. 52). He tears down the city to the point that it becomes impossible to recognize (*lā muššî*, l. 54), just as the people in the Flood could not identity one another; and he leaves the city as a 'flood plain', using the word *ušallu* that also described the water covering the world at the end of the Flood (Finn 2017: 92). Finally, Sennacherib dissolves what is left of Babylon in water (*ina māmī ušḫarmiṭsū-ma*, l. 54), because water – according to the cultural logic traced in this essay – is the antithesis of identity. And as such, it is also the antithesis of textuality, since the act of physical violence is matched by a simultaneous and interlinked moment of textual violence: as Babylon's identity disappears into the water, so does its name. Sennacherib's inscription calls the city by name in line 49, the destruction begins in line 50, and after that, Babylon is only referred to as 'that city' (*ālu šuātu*, l. 52). A flooded city can have no form and thus no name; it has been returned to the mythical state described in the opening lines of *Enuma Elish*.

## Conclusion

In his devastation of Babylon, Sennacherib adhered to the logic of the epic that celebrated its superiority: he destroyed Babylon on its own terms, as it were.[26] By reversing the logic of *Enuma Elish*, Sennacherib actually confirmed the ontological assumption behind it, namely that all we see around us consists of a primordial water that has been bound, if only temporarily, into shapes that allow it to acquire names, fates, and identities. We are all made of a fundamentally fluid matter, but to return to that original fluidity would mean to stop existing. Our physical form is derived from, dependent on, but also opposed to the primary shapelessness of the water we drink.

*Enuma Elish* traces a narrative arc that leads from the namelessness of the world's beginning to the fifty names bestowed on Marduk, from fluidity to order, and from the absence of language to the text itself. The trajectory of this arc is based on a contrast between fluidity and the domain of forms, names, and fates, and what the epic recounts is the process by which Ea and Marduk created one out of the other. The story thus puts a unique twist on the trope of the self-referential climax – the tendency for cuneiform narratives to end by describing their own composition – as the trope is folded into the text's account of creation. As the world order gradually emerges, so does the material, both physical and linguistic, of which the epic will be made. *Enuma Elish* thus draws a line from the beginning of time to its own composition, presenting itself as the natural conclusion to a cosmic process of separating, binding, fixing, and naming the shapeless waters. In sum, the textually inflected account of creation allows the epic to present our reading experience as a miniature recreation of Marduk's battle. Just as we must remember Marduk's triumph whenever we drink water, so our reading of *Enuma Elish* is – in a deep, structural sense – parallel to the mythical events described in it.

## Further reading

The epic's self-reference is discussed by Foster (1991, 2019), who shows that this is a more widespread feature of cuneiform poetry. For the relation between the text's cosmogonic content and poetic form (i.e. between the world order presented in the epic and the literary techniques used to do so) see especially the studies by Hermann Vanstiphout (1992), Gösta Gabriel (2014), and Karen Sonik (2013). Michalowski (1990) emphasizes the strongly linguistic slant of the epic's account of creation; and in an analysis of Commentary II, Jean Bottéro (1977) describes the kinds of linguistic analysis that are used to unfold Marduk's names. The practice of Babylonian hermeneutics is presented more broadly by Frahm (2011: chap. 4) and Van De Mieroop (2016: chap. 1); and Radner (2005) discusses the importance of names in cuneiform cultures. Selena Wisnom (2020) explores the relation between *Enuma*

*Elish* and the Flood narrative. For references to *Enuma Elish* in later cuneiform texts see Reynolds in this volume; for the gendered dimension of the epic, see Sonik in this volume.

## Notes

1 For previous studies of the relation between the cosmogony and the textual form of *Enuma Elish*, see Gabriel (2014) and Vanstiphout (1992).

2 Note the elegant construction of this couplet. Apart from the repetition of *išt-*, it cleverly connects *ana šemî arkûti*, 'for future (generations) to hear', with *šīmat marduk*, 'Marduk's fate', the object of that hearing: especially if the name Marduk was pronounced *marūtuk*, there is a near-anagrammatic linking of the two words.

3 Note also that, as argued by Michalowski in this volume, the syllable *mu* recurs throughout the epic as an aural figure for creation: in this line, *mû* is the word for 'water' and MU the sign for 'name'.

4 As pointed out to me by Johannes Haubold, the epic avoids using the word 'earth' (*erṣetu*) until the earth is created in V 62, using instead the rare synonym *ammatu*, here translated 'ground', in the opening couplet.

5 See also Michalowki's analysis of the opening passage in this volume. In this initial state, Apsû and Tiamat already have names and thus seem to exist as separable entities, but the text also states that their waters were mingled *ištēniš*, 'together' or literally 'into one' (I 5), meaning that the separation between them must be partial or potential. On the commingled duality of their initial existence, see Gabriel (2014: 116–17).

6 On the meaning of *mummu*, see Frahm (2013: 104–12), with references to previous literature. On the equations in Commentary I, see Lambert (2013: 60), l. 4 for *nabnītu* and 134, l. 121 for *rigmu*. On the commentaries to *Enuma Elish*, see Frahm (2011: 112–17), and Reynolds in this volume.

7 Gabriel (2014: 190–1) emphasizes that Ea's binding, shaping, and naming of Apsû represents the creation of the first defined cosmic region, creating the template for Marduk's later creation of the entire cosmic order.

8 It may be relevant that Marduk will later split Tiamat in two 'like a dried fish' (*kīma nūn mašṭê*, V 137).

9 For the net as a weapon inherited from *Anzû*, see Lambert (1986: 59); on its adaptation to *Enuma Elish*, see Seri (2012: 15, 20–3) and Wisnom in this volume.

10 Before the battle in Tablet IV, Tiamat's *karšu* is mentioned in I 23, 44, and 116; her *libbu* is mentioned in I 117, II 100, and IV 78.

11 Tiamat is depicted as a dromedary (*ibilu*) in the Assyrian commentary text KAR 307 r. 13–15. This association likely relies on the cuneiform spelling of that word as $^{\text{anše}}$a-ab-ba, since a-ab-ba could also be read *tâmtu*; see Livingstone (1986: 89). On the association between Tiamat and the goat-fish (*suḫurmašû*), see Reynolds (1995: 369–78). Again, it relies on the syllable ab, meaning 'sea': $^{\text{iti}}$ab means 'the month Tebet', and the star of that month is the goat-fish.

12 For other parallels between the content and literary form of *Enuma Elish*, see Michalowski in this volume.

13 The *Chicago Assyrian Dictionary*, s.v. *išdu*, lists several instances of *išdu* being used to refer to the instability of one's stance, especially when due to terror or tipsiness.

14 Tellingly, the word *išdu*, 'foundation', reappears as a description of Tiamat in IV 129, after the battle: 'the Lord trampled upon the depths of Tiamat' (*ikbus-ma bēlu ša Tiāmat išissa*). Likewise, in IV 136 Tiamat's corpse is described with the rare word *serkuppu*, which may mean 'marsh' or the like; it is translated above as 'watery mass'.

15 Wisnom (2020: 146–51) shows that *Enuma Elish* is here drawing on the older *Lugal-e*, the story of Ninurta's defeat of the demon Asag and his subsequent invention of agriculture. In both stories, the defeat of the monstrous opponent is followed by the transformation of water from a destructive to a domesticated force.

16 On the importance of names in cuneiform cultures, see Radner (2005); on the interpretation of Marduk's names, see Bottéro (1977) and Van De Mieroop in this volume.

17 On the many parallels that link the stories of Ea and Marduk in *Enuma Elish*, see the references collected in Helle (2021a: 195–8).

18 Lambert (1998: 192–3) argues that the use of *nabû* to describe creation is a poetic circumlocution, based on the idea that 'having a name is to exist'. Though it does function as a circumlocution in this line, the significance of names in *Enuma Elish* clearly extends beyond a metonymic description of creation. On the creative power of language in the poem, see also Michalowski and Van De Mieroop in this volume.

19 The word is in fact written *ne*$_2$*-bu-u*$_2$, but as the text is commenting on the word *imbû*, the infinitive form *nabû* must be meant.

20 See likewise Kvanvig (2011: 210): 'What we find in the flood narrative is the creation told in reverse; the chaotic waters take the earth back.'

21 On specific intertextual connections between *Enuma Elish* and the Flood narrative, see Wisnom (2020: chap. 3). Wisnom notes, among other things, the motif of sleep leading to the ruler's rage in both accounts, and the contrast between Marduk's control of Tiamat's water in *Enuma Elish* and Enlil's release of water in the Flood story, illustrating Marduk's superiority over the previous ruler of the pantheon (p. 110–15).

22 I owe the point that Ninurta, as inventor of agriculture, is here shown destroying his own creation to Selena Wisnom (personal communication).

23 See Haubold (2013: 64–71), who notes the parallel opposition between water and storytelling in *Gilgamesh* and the *Iliad*.

24 On the relation between Uta-napishti's Flood narrative and the *Gilgamesh* epic in which it is contained, see Michalowski (1996: 187–90; 1999: 79–82) and Helle (2021b: 191–200).

25 The translation is taken, in a lightly revised form, from the edition in Grayson and Novotny (2014: 316–17, no. 223). On the cultural logic of the inscription, see Van De Mieroop (2003: 3–23). The Bavian Inscription celebrates Sennacherib's construction of a hydraulic system that would provide Nineveh with water; as Van De Mieroop notes, the water-based destruction of Babylon is presented as the mirror image of his work on behalf of Nineveh.

26 See already Van De Mieroop (2003: 14), who noted that through the parallelism between his treatments of Nineveh and Babylon, Sennacherib tacitly admits to the equality between the two cities, suggesting that the destruction of Babylon was also a recognition of the city's unique status. Likewise, Michalowski (1990: 396) argues that, in their attempts to expurgate Marduk's name from *Enuma Elish* and replace him with Ashur, the Assyrian scholars ended up reaffirming the superiority of Babylon.

## Bibliography

Bottéro, J. (1977), 'Les noms de Marduk, l'écriture et la "logique" en Mésopotamie ancienne', in M. de Jong Ellis (ed.), *Essays on the Ancient Near East in Memory of Jacob Joel Finkelstein*, Memoirs of the Connecticut Academy of Arts and Sciences 19, 5–27, Hamden: Archon Books.

Buccellati, G. (1990), 'On Poetry – Theirs and Ours', in T. Abusch, J. Huehnergard and P. Steinkeller (eds), *Lingering over Words: Studies in Ancient Near Eastern Literature in Honor of William L. Moran*, Harvard Semitic Studies 37, 105–34, Atlanta: Scholar's Press.

Burstein, S. M. (1978), *The Babyloniaca of Berossus*, Sources for the Ancient Near East I/5, Malibu: Undena Publications.

Dirven, L. (1999), *The Palmyrenes of Dura-Europos: A Study of Religious Interaction in Roman Syria*, Leiden: Brill.

Durand, J.-M. (1994), '*Enûma Eliš* I 76', *Nouvelles assyriologiques brèves et utilitaires*, 1994 (4): 91, no. 100.

Finn, J. (2017), *Much Ado about Marduk: Questioning Discourses of Royalty in First Millennium Mesopotamian Literature*, Studies in Ancient Near Eastern Records 16, Berlin: De Gruyter.

Foster, B. R. (1991), 'On Authorship in Akkadian Literature', *Annali dell'Istituto Universitario Orientale di Napoli*, 51: 17–32.

Foster, B. R. (2019), 'Authorship in Cuneiform Literature', in I. Berensmeyer, G. Buelens and M., Demoor (eds), *The Cambridge Handbook of Literary Authorship*, 13–26, Cambridge: Cambridge University Press.

Frahm, E. (2011), *Babylonian and Assyrian Text Commentaries: Origins of Interpretation*, Guides to the Mesopotamian Textual Record 5, Münster: Ugarit-Verlag.

Frahm, E. (2013), 'Creation and the Divine Spirit in Babel and Bible: Reflections on *mummu* in *Enūma eliš* I 4 and *rûaḥ* in Genesis 1:2', in D. S. Vanderhooft and A. Winitzer (eds), *Literature as Politics, Politics as Literature: Essays on the Ancient Near East in Honor of Peter Machinist*, 97–116, Winona Lake: Eisenbrauns.

Gabriel, G. (2014), '*enūma eliš*' – *Weg zu einer globalen Weltordnung: Pragmatik, Struktur und Semantik des babylonischen 'Lieds auf Marduk'*, Orientalische Religionen in der Antike 12, Tübingen: Mohr Siebeck.

George, A. R. (2022), 'Poem of Gilgameš', with contributions by E. Jiménez and G. Rozzi, *electronic Babylonian Literature*. https://www.ebl.lmu.de/corpus/L/1/4.

Grayson, A. K. and J. R. Novotny (2014), *The Royal Inscriptions of Sennacherib, King of Assyria (704–681 BC), Part 2*, The Royal Inscriptions of the Neo-Assyrian Period 3 (2), Winona Lake: Eisenbrauns.

Haubold, J. (2013), *Greece and Mesopotamia: Dialogues in Literature*, Cambridge: Cambridge University Press.

Haubold, J., G. B. Lanfranchi, R. Rollinger and J. M. Steele (eds, 2013), *The World of Berossos*, Classica et Orientalia 5, Wiesbaden: Harrassowitz.

Helle, S. (2020), 'Marduk's Penis: Queering *Enūma Eliš*', *Distant Worlds Journal*, 4: 63–77.

Helle, S. (2021a), 'The Two-Act Structure: A Narrative Device in Akkadian Epics', *Journal of Ancient Near Eastern Religions*, 20 (2): 190–224.

Helle, S. (2021b), *Gilgamesh: A New Translation of the Ancient Epic*, New Haven: Yale University Press.

Helle, S. (2023), 'The Return of the Text: On Self-reference in Cuneiform Literature', *Journal of Cuneiform Studies*, 75: 93–107.

Kämmerer, T. R. and K. A. Metzler (2012), *Das babylonische Weltschöpfungsepos 'Enūma elîš'*, Alter Orient und Altes Testament 375, Münster: Ugarit-Verlag.
Kvanvig, H. S. (2011), *Primeval History: Babylonian, Biblical, and Enochic; an Intertextual Reading*, Supplements to the Journal for the Study of Judaism 149, Leiden: Brill.
Lambert, W. G. (1986), 'Ninurta Mythology in the Babylonian Epic of Creation', in K. Hecker and W. Sommerfeld (eds), *Keilschriftliche Literaturen*, Compte Rendu de la Rencontre Assyriologique Internationale 32, Berliner Beiträge Zum Vorderen Orient 6, 55–60, Berlin: Dietrich Reimer Verlag.
Lambert, W. G. (1994), 'A New Look at the Babylonian Background of Genesis', in R. S. Hess and D. T. Tsumura (eds), *'I Studied Inscriptions from Before the Flood': Ancient Near Eastern, Literary, and Linguistic Approaches to Genesis 1–11*, 96–113, Winona Lake: Eisenbrauns.
Lambert, W. G. (1998), 'Technical Terminology for Creation in the Ancient Near East', in J. Prosecký (ed.), *Intellectual Life of the Ancient Near East*, Compte Rendu de la Rencontre Assyriologique Internationale 42, 189–93, Prague: Academy of Science of the Czech Republic.
Lambert, W. G. (2013), *Babylonian Creation Myths*, Mesopotamian Civilizations 16, Winona Lake: Eisenbrauns.
Livingstone, A. (1986), *Mystical and Mythological Explanatory Works of Assyrian and Babylonian Scholars*, Oxford: Oxford University Press.
Metzler, K. A. (2002), 'Tod, Weiblichkeit und Ästhetik im mesopotamischen Weltscöpfungsepos *Enūma elîš*', in S. Parpola and R. M. Whiting (eds), *Sex and Gender in the Ancient Near East*, Compte Rendu de la Rencontre Assyriologique Internationale 47, 393–411, Helsinki: The Neo-Assyrian Text Corpus Project.
Michalowski, P. (1990), 'Presence at the Creation', in T. Abusch, J. Huehnergard and P. Steinkeller (eds), *Lingering over Words: Studies in Ancient Near Eastern Literature in Honor of William L. Moran*, Harvard Semitic Studies 37, 381–96, Atlanta: Scholars Press.
Michalowski, P. (1996), 'Sailing to Babylon, Reading the Dark Side of the Moon', in J. S. Cooper and G. M. Schwartz (eds), *The Study of the Ancient Near East in the Twenty-First Century: The William Foxwell Albright Centennial Conference*, 177–93, Winona Lake: Eisenbrauns.
Michalowski, P. (1999), 'Commemoration, Writing, and Genre in Ancient Mesopotamia', in C. S. Kraus (ed.), *The Limits of Historiography: Genre and Narrative in Ancient Historical Texts*, Mnemosyne Supplements 191, 69–90, Leiden: Brill.
Müller, H.-P. (1985), 'Das Motiv für die Sintflut: Die hermeneutische Funktion des Mythos und seiner Analyse', *Zeitschrift für die alttestamentliche Wissenschaft*, 97 (3): 295–316.
Nora, P. (1984), 'Présentation', in P. Nora (ed.), *Les lieux de mémoire*, 1, vii–xiii, Paris: Gallimard.
Radner, K. (2005), *Die Macht des Namens: Altorientalische Strategien zur Selbsterhaltung*, Santag 8, Wiesbaden: Harrassowitz Verlag.
Reynolds, F. (1995), 'Stellar Representations of Tiāmat and Qingu in a Learned Calendar Text', in K. V. Lerberghe and G. Voet (eds), *Languages and Cultures in Contact: At the Crossroads of Civilizations in the Syro-Mesopotamian Realm*, Compte Rendu de la Rencontre Assyriologique Internationale 42, Orientalia Lovaniensia Analecta 96, 369–78, Leuven: Peeters.
Seri, A. (2012), 'The Role of Creation in Enūma eliš', *Journal of Ancient Near Eastern Religions*, 12: 4–29.

Sonik, K. (2013), 'From Hesiod's Abyss to Ovid's *rudis indigestaque moles*: Chaos and Cosmos in the Babylonian "Epic of Creation"', in J. Scurlock and R. H. Beal, *Creation and Chaos: A Reconsideration of Hermann Gunkel's Chaoskampf Hypothesis*, 1–25, University Park: Penn State University Press.

Taylor, J., and C. Cartwright, (2011), 'The Making and Re-Making of Clay Tablets', *Scienze dell'Antichità*, 17: 297–324.

Van De Mieroop, M. (2003), 'Revenge, Assyrian Style', *Past & Present*, 179: 3–23.

Van De Mieroop, M. (2016), *Philosophy before the Greeks: The Pursuit of Truth in Ancient Babylonia*, Princeton: Princeton University Press.

Vanstiphout, H. L. J. (1992), 'Enuma Elish as a Systematic Creed: An Essay', *Orientalia Lovaniensia Periodica*, 23: 37–61.

Verbrugghe, G. and J. M. Wickersham (1996), *Berossos and Manetho, Introduced and Translated: Native Traditions in Ancient Mesopotamia and Egypt*, Ann Arbor: University of Michigan Press.

Wisnom, S. (2020), *Weapons of Words: Intertextual Competition in Babylonian Poetry; A Study of 'Anzû', 'Enūma Eliš', and 'Erra and Išum'*, Culture and History of the Ancient Near East 106, Leiden: Brill.

Worthington, M. (2019), *Ea's Duplicity in the Gilgamesh Flood Story*, London: Routledge.

12

# The sound of creation: The revolutionary poetics of *Enuma Elish*

Piotr Michalowski

*No, poetry is glory and revelation and mystery*
*suddenly unveiled,*
*poetry is not inherited,*
*poetry*
*is not given.*
*Poetry is what no one knows.*
– Robert Kelly[1]

## Introduction[2]

For decades Mesopotamian literature was thought to have been ruled by a 'stream of tradition', as defined many years ago by Leo Oppenheim (1960), with long periods of statis and redactional activity dominating the scribal realm. Not everyone has subscribed to this way of looking at ancient literary production, leading to critical voices as our knowledge base increased exponentially. Most eloquent was Eleanor Robson (2019: 10–48), who has offered a detailed analysis of the debate and a historicizing critique of this notion, focusing on differences in scribal education and the acquisition and preservation of knowledge. Insightfully, Eckart Frahm (2019) has provided a nuanced overview of the complexities of late second and first millennium poetic and scientific textual production, documenting the divergent trajectories of genres, broadly defined, as well as individual texts and general trends of focus on invention, antiquarianism, and redactional activity. Such studies have served to restore a balance in our views on Mesopotamian textual production, allowing us to appreciate better the dynamic interplay between innovation and tradition and to define more clearly moments of modernization, reinterpretation, traditionalism, and reinvention that had lasting cultural consequences.

While the flow of literary creation in the years preceding it is significantly obscured by the paucity of recovered materials, the last three centuries of the second millennium seem to have been particularly fruitful as one such period of creative reshaping of the content, aesthetics, poetics, and language of literary and scholarly traditions. Texts that were likely composed during this time include one of the finest Babylonian poems, *Ludlul*, as well as the *Babylonian Theodicy* and the structurally and thematically innovative syncretistic hymn extolling the goddess of healing, conventionally designated as *The Gula Hymn of Bullussa-rabi* (see most recently Frazer 2013; Frahm 2019: 20). Significantly, Zsombor Földi (2019) has persuasively argued that Bullussa-rabi was likely a woman, and later tradition assigned three other works to her stylus.

This brings us to the approximate time when *Enuma Elish*, the poem that is the focus of this book, was composed, sometime between *c.* 1300 and 1100 BCE.[3] It has long been recognized that many aspects of this innovative work are unique, as expressed by Wilfred G. Lambert (2013: 465), who knew it better than anyone:

> [I]t appears that toward the end of this millennium, the author, either starting or following a new trend among the priests of Marduk, composed a highly original work which ran counter to previously accepted opinion in most of the country. During the first millennium, the basic ideas of the poem, though not always its particular expression of them, made considerable headway in ousting other conceptions. But tradition died hard, and even the political supremacy of the city Babylon did not result in the suppression of deviant myths.

The 'highly original' *Enuma Elish* was thus crafted during a period of intense literary creativity, and yet I would go further and argue that it was thematically, theologically, structurally, and intertextually revolutionary and transgressive, programmatically reshaping Akkadian poetics and poetic language for multiple purposes in a manner that was unique even for those times. The elaborate novel vision of the creation of the world and the rise of its divine master Marduk and his city Babylon that forms the central narrative of *Enuma Elish* asserted claims of new religious, cultural, and political realities projected unto the timeless semantic universe of myth, where the story happened, was happening, and would happen forever. To achieve these goals the creator of the poem worked with a new and unique personal poetics that exploited the full potential of existing Babylonian literary language, expanding it in novel directions, having absorbed many innovations of his predecessors. In doing this, the author was particularly adept with language games, exploiting the potential of sound and aural patterning and word formation strategies of the Akkadian language, but also of Sumerian, its ancient literary ancestor, creating lexical neologisms or using rare words, some of which played with lexical equivalences from both, referencing the bilingual foundations of the Mesopotamian literary project. All of this was strikingly revolutionary, but not all of it was completely new, drawing on a long tradition of parallelistic poetics fundamental to Sumerian and Akkadian verbal art.[4] Rather, as Stuart Isacoff (2022: 4) has recently written, with radical moments in the history of Western music in mind, change 'usually didn't arise in a flash, like an unseen volcanic eruption, but instead unfolded as an arc: preceded by earlier hints and models and encompassing long-term aftereffects'.

## The poetics of creation

To illustrate these claims, I will focus on the first episode of *Enuma Elish*. While fully aware of the risk of anachronistic perspective, I would argue that the opening ten lines constitute an ancient equivalent of a poetic manifesto. Since the very foundations of Mesopotamian written literary production in the third millennium BCE, some magical charms and mythological works began with short passages describing the beginnings of the cosmos, usually initiated by the separation of the upper and lower regions. An unwritten rule required that, while the general themes were similar, each depiction had to differ in narrative structure and thematic detail, providing a canvas for expression of compositional skill. The poet of *Enuma Elish* took up this challenge to present something entirely new, challenging tradition on every level of language, be it phonology, syntax, or word choice, but also using the creation motif in an innovative manner and inventing a radically new story. To be sure, the rhetorical and poetic devices applied here, such as chiasmus or paronomasia, had featured in Mesopotamian verbal art for ages, but never in such an original and concentrated fashion. As the storyline of the poem develops, one must wait for the climax of a separate creation account to learn how the new god Marduk, after defeating his enemy Tiamat, split her in two to form the heavens and the earth – a drastically new vision of creation that went against the grain of all previous Mesopotamian origin accounts (Seri 2012). Therefore, the traditional cosmological introduction was now reshaped to narrate the complex unity of time and place before the heavens and the earth had even been named.

The beginning ten lines have been analysed again and again by too many scholars to count, and most translations differ in varying levels of detail.[5] More than any other part of the poem, this section has confounded analysis, raising unresolved questions concerning Akkadian syntax and lexicography, as well as matters of religion, symbolism, and cosmology. One distinguished scholar even resorted to tampering, rearranging the lines to conform with preconceived poetic notions (West 1997: 87).

Here, I will accept the challenge laid down by the poet and analyse how the dense and concentrated poetic texture of the opening lines created new cultural connotations, anticipated things to come, and projected structural organizational elements onto the whole poem. So, with Dylan Thomas, 'To begin at the beginning':[6]

*enūma eliš lā nabû šamāmū*
*šapliš ammatu šuma lā zakrat*
*apsûma rēštû zārûšun*
*mummu tiāmtu muʾallidat gimrīšun*
*mûšunu ištēniš iḫiqqūma*
*gipāra lā kiṣṣurū ṣuṣâ lā šēʾū*
*enūma ilū lā šūpû manāma*
*šuma lā zukkurū šīmāti lā šīmū*
*ibbanûma ilū qerebšun*
*laḫmu (u) laḫāmu uštāpû šuma izzakrū*

When above unnamed were the heavens,
below the lands uncalled by name
but freshwater marsh there was, initiator, their (future) progenitor,
and creatrix brackish marsh, the (future) birther of them all.
Yet while their waters mingled together
but did not pleat *reedbed*, nor matt canebrake.
At the time when no gods whosever had yet appeared,
none called by name, nor had (their) future ordained.
Then born were the gods within them:
Lahmu and Lahamu appeared and were called by name.

(I 1–10, translation modified)

At the very inception, the text proclaims its artistic status and radical narrative intentions. These are highlighted by the novel dense syntactic, semantic, morphological, and phonemic patterning of the lines. To explicate the revolutionary poetics of this opening passage, we will have to take it apart in pieces.

The first couplet is organized in a complex chiastic manner $(A_1B_1{\sim}B_2A_2 / C_1D_1{\sim}D_2C_2)$ that separately governs the halves of both lines:

| | | | |
|---|---|---|---|
| *enūma* | *eliš* | *lā nabû* | *šamāmū* |
| when | above | not named | heavens |
| $A_1$ | $B_1$ | $C_1$ | $D_1$ |
| *šapliš* | *ammatu* | *šuma* | *lā zakrat* |
| below | firmament | name | not named |
| $B_2$ | $A_2$ | $D_2$ | $C_2$ |

All the adverbs and nouns in this complex arrangement are antonyms, while the predicates are synonyms: they are negated and thus align with the opposing semantics of the former, invoking a cosmic void that is anticipatory by negation, summoning expectations of things to come. The opening *enūma*, 'when, in that time', invokes tradition and signals cosmological beginnings, alluding to texts that described the creation of the world and building expectations for what is to follow; yet any such anticipations are immediately confounded. As explained in more detail below, in traditional Babylonian practice, the next word after *enūma* should be either the name of the sky god Anu or the synecdochic *ilū*, 'gods', but their place is taken by *eliš*, 'above'. The latter is homonymic with *ilu* but is marked with the adverbial/locative suffix *-iš* that was characteristic of literary Akkadian, albeit not restricted to poetic language. Then follows a negative verbal phrase, *lā nabû šamāmū*, 'the heavens were not yet named', invoking the tradition of tropes of non-existence to designate the absence of the order of the universe, but in a radically novel manner: whereas in older poems about world beginnings things to come were said not to exist or not yet constructed,[7] here presence is equated with naming and the power of language, setting up a theme that will play a crucial role in the narrative.

The initial unfulfilled poetic expectations imply that the notion of presence in the first couplet of our introduction is *the presence of absence*: the missing sky god Anu is explained by the as-yet unnamed heavens; both he and the missing gods recall the opening lines of compositions where such gods do appear and that will function as prior texts in the narrative to come, including the story of *Atra-hasis* and the grand Babylonian compendium of astronomical omens, *Enuma Anu Enlil*, to which we shall return below. But there is more to these unfulfilled expectations. That the skies and earthly firmament are not yet here serves to upend tradition: all earlier Mesopotamian stories about creation began in some way with the often-noisy coupling of the two, sometimes preceded by their initial separation (Rubio 2013). Here, they are conspicuous by their non-existence, but also by the watery murmur or even quiet that contrasts with the older loud conception acts in which noise itself was a mark of creation and creativity (Michalowski 1990).

As concerns syntactic arrangement, the two first two lines begin with parallel nominal elements that provide contrast within limited semantic spheres, balanced in a chiastic mirror image that will appear elsewhere:

| | | |
|---|---|---|
| *enūma eliš* | : | *šapliš* |
| x A1 | | A2 |
| *apsûma* | : | *mummu tiāmtu* |
| B1 | | x B2 |

The noun at the end of the first line is the third surprise, as it is both familiar and strange. The word *šamāmū* is a very rare poetic one that doubled the final syllable of *šamû*, the standard Akkadian word for 'skies'. Similarly, the first noun below is equally innovative, redesigned to structurally mimic its antonym *šamāmū* and provide assonance with *enūma*. Thus, *mātu*, 'land, country, territory, etc.', was expanded by a mirror mechanism, doubling the first syllable rather than the last and reversing it (*ma:mātu* > *am:mātu* > *ammatu*); in both cases, these extremely rare words were brilliantly reimagined for dramatic poetic effect.[8] The chiastic reordering of elements on the lexical level (the added elements *-mā-* and *am-*) corresponds to the chiastic rearrangements in syntax. The significance of the added syllable is explicitly proclaimed at the outset of l. 5, with the appearance of *mû*, the Akkadian word for 'water', but also interlingually referencing **mu**, the Sumerian word for 'name', conspicuously hiding in Akkadian *šumu*, 'name', that appears in l. 2 – the homonym setting up an important synonymic statement.[9]

The second couplet takes up some of these structural orderings but introduces contrasting devices as well: the two parallel antonymic directional adverbs are now echoed by two nouns, *apsû* and *tiāmtu*, but just as those in the previous couplet were defamiliarized by morpho-phonological means, so these are defamiliarized by semantic innovation. The introduction of *apsû* and *tiāmtu* adds more anticipatory tension: unlike the unnamed skies and the firmament, they are present, but are they named? This is unlikely, because the patterning in the section defined by the first five couplets leads to the final naming at the very end of l. 10. The text demands that we view these terms as familiar and unfamiliar at the same time, common nouns that will morph into concepts and finally into proper names, when Apsû and Tiamat, once again as neologisms, will become active agents in the drama. Both will be killed and fashioned into territory: the former into the freshwater habitat of the god Ea, the latter to create the skies and earth below, whose anticipatory non-existence was signalled in the opening two lines. But there are many actions and battles to come before Apsû becomes the familiar place of Mesopotamian myth and ritual. Here the word is ambiguous; it seems to be a proper noun, but the previous line insists that no one and nothing has yet been named. Like the *tiāmtu* below, *apsû* must be a common noun, albeit used here, like most nouns that have preceded them, in a defamiliarized manner. As everything else here, Apsû and Tiamat are as much potential as present.

But what exactly were the referents of these words here? Ever since the discovery of *Enuma Elish*, scholars have assumed that *tiāmtu* was 'ocean, sea', and *apsû* referred to an expanse of sweet water. The experiential and emotive associations with these modern translations of *tiāmtu* have led to the supposition that Babylonian beliefs about origins included a concept of a primeval or cosmic 'ocean', presumably an expanse of open sea. But *tiāmtu* and its underlying Sumerian equivalent **a-ab-ba** were used by Mesopotamians to designate any large body of water or watery terrain, including marshes. Thus, during the seventh century BCE, a large wetland formed in the area of the city of Borsippa, *c.* eleven miles southwest of Babylon, and it was designated in native records as a *tiāmtu* (Cole 1994: 87). The deltaic area in which the southern Mesopotamian landscape met the Persian Gulf did not lead immediately to an open sea, but was a marshy area where fluctuating waters intermingled: fresh ones from the various estuaries of the rivers running from the north and tidal flushing from brackish salt water tidal basins that came and receded daily and in seasonal patterns – an ever-shifting environment of marshes, swamps, vast reed beds, and levies (e.g. Pournelle and Algaze 2014; Al-Hamdani 2020). Thorkild Jacobsen (1968: 107) was aware of this when he wrote, concerning *Enuma Elish*, 'in Mesopotamia, in Babylon, ... the sea is far away to the South behind extensive freshwater marshes and reed-thickets. It is no part of the basic everyday experience of the common man, plays no part in his world as he knows it of own experience.'

Unfortunately, Jacobsen and others following in his wake drew the wrong conclusions from this fact, contrasting such a vista with their concept of a vast open sea 'ocean', and so proposed that the Tiamat of *Enuma Elish* was an alien concept, borrowed from West Semitic mythemes. While this interpretation did not immediately convince many, subsequent discoveries in various languages led to a revival and acceptance of such ideas (see most comprehensively Ayali-Darshan 2020). Yet to the contrary, the imagery of *Enuma Elish* was local and harkened back to native Mesopotamian topographical realities and mental maps without any connection to myths of sea serpents and cosmic oceanic mêlées from Mediterranean areas.

Nonetheless, the watery primeval setting of *Enuma Elish* has no solid precedent in mainstream Mesopotamian writings. Some scholars have attempted to trace the motif of primordial aquatic origins back to early times, associating them with the goddess Namma, but as noted by Walter Sallaberger (2017: 97, with references to earlier literature), this is most unlikely. And yet, there is one eighteenth-century Old Babylonian Sumerian-language magical incantation that hints at relevant earlier traditions that existed on the margins of writing. The tablet, of unknown origin, is thus far unduplicated, but this is not unusual for the time, as most early incantation texts are documented by single exemplars (Wagensonner 2020). The opening line, which in Mesopotamia functioned as the title, was already known from a late Assyrian ritual, whose importance was recognized by Lambert (2013: 237), so if this is indeed the same incantation, it survived well past the time when *Enuma Elish* was composed (see also Wagensonner 2020: 120). The purpose of the charm is to expel disease-causing demons by somehow utilizing a fish and a bird that came from the sealand marshes; hence the text begins with this unique combination of words: 'The sealand, mother of the gods, is the grand habitation of divine Enki' (**a ab-ba ama diĝir-re-ne / ki-tuš mah $^{d}$en-⸢ki⸣-kam**, l. 1–4). The image of the marshy sealand, filled with reedy lagoons, is further illustrated in another Old Babylonian composition, *The Debate between Summer and Winter*: '(Winter) created lagoons midst the waters of the sealand, made bird and fish breed on their own in the sealand, and thickened all the canebrakes with mature reeds, reed shoots and … reeds' (**a ab-ba-ka abbar ba-ni-ib$_2$-dim$_2$-dim$_2$ / ab-ba ku$_6$ mušen ni$_2$-ba mu-un-u$_3$-tud / ĝiš-gi ki-šar$_2$-ba gi sumun gi henbur$_2$ gi BAD ba-ni-ib$_2$-gur-gur**, l. 30–2). It is likely that the theme of the sealand as the 'mother' of the gods and goddesses alludes to an early tradition concerning their birth on the Sacred Mound in the southern marshes, which is known to us only from oblique references.

One cannot posit that this specific magical charm was a prior text for the great poem, but the combination of the unique uses of 'sea' and 'marsh' evidences an old theme that, like many others in this passage, harkens back to ancient incantations. As such, it indicates, once again, the deep learning of the person who composed *Enuma Elish*, an erudition that went far beyond the standard teaching materials and professional library holdings of the late second millennium BCE.

With this topographic background to local imagination in mind, it might perhaps be more apposite to view the mention of Tiamat and Apsû as salty-brackish and freshwater marshes of the kind that constantly met and intermingled with each other in the southern Mesopotamian delta, rather than as salt and sweet expanses of water, more familiar to readers from other parts of the world. In standard usage, *apsû* was the name of the underground sweet water expanse that was the domain of the god Ea, who will play a major role in the narrative to come, and *tiāmtu* was the standard term for larger visible bodies of water such as the Persian Gulf or the Mediterranean Sea, which were filled with salt water, but also for Lake Urmia, which was not. Thus, the concepts first move from vertical to horizontal contiguity, but then it is immediately apparent that they have acquired new meaning, uniquely personified as masculine and feminine actors in the story, but never again in any other Mesopotamian narrative. At this moment they are all that *in potentia*, while functioning in a strange new manner that was hitherto unknown in Mesopotamian literature, as primeval bodies of gendered sweet and salt water, masculine and feminine, respectively.

For over a hundred years, the creation narrative of *Enuma Elish* has been characterized by many exegetists as one in which the 'primeval sea, ocean' represented primordial 'chaos', but both are chimeras of scholarly imagination.[10] Rather, the introduction of our poem describes a 'pre-order', as Peter Machinist (2005: 43) felicitously defined it, or, as I might suggest, a moment of entropy that will be disturbed by the noise of the younger deities 'to create the world that will eventually prevail, that is, the real and normal order, the one known to the author'.

But that is not all. Looking back at the chiastic syntax of the opening lines, we see that the elements *enūma* and *mummu* were criss-crossing elements additional to the patterns, marked as X. The meaning of the word *mummu* has been vigorously debated.[11] In line 4, in apposition, it qualifies *tiāmtu*, and both are parallel with *apsû-ma* in the previous line. It is generally assumed that the latter consisted of the (proper) noun expanded with the multifunctional particle *-ma*, which here either has a focus function or acts predicatively, creating a nominal sentence, 'Apsû it was' or the like. But in view of what has been argued above, it cannot be separated from the expansive use of the syllable *mu/ma* in the first two lines or from the word *mummu* that follows it. At this specific moment in this introductory passage, there can be little doubt that the poet is alluding to the noun *ummu*, 'mother' (< *mu-ummu*) as qualifying the feminine actor *tiāmtu*, while at the same time anticipating the coming of a homonymous character, Apsû's vizier, later in the story, as well as other associations that will be discussed below.

In the lexical tradition, going at least as far back as the eighteenth century BCE, Sumerian **mu$_7$-mu$_7$**, possibly to be read **mumu(n)**, was interpreted to mean 'noise, cry' (Akkadian *rigmu*), but also 'magical incantation' (Akkadian *šiptu*). One late bilingual list rendered it as *ḫuburru*, a synonym of *rigmu* and a word that will be used to qualify Tiamat in I 133 later in the text: once she becomes active, she is designated as *ummu ḫubur*, literally 'mother noise'. There was also a separate noun *mummu*, possibly a loan from Sumerian **umun$_2$**, that meant 'creator' or the like, meaning someone who crafted things, including texts, and was also used to designate a place where texts, perhaps more precisely musical ones, were composed and taught. All of this is implied here, but in its immediate context, the phonological resonance of the word gives it additional meaning and structural identity. Here *mummu*, echoing the two expanded nouns in the preceding lines, is likewise a neologism created by the addition of an /m/-phoneme, in this case *mu-ummu*, 'mother'. As line onsets, the assonance between *mummu* and *enūma*, which mimics their parallel positions, is offset by the relationship between the former and *šapliš*, 'below'. While markedly distinct in phonological terms, they are both construed as pseudo-palindromes (*enūma* ~ *amūne* / *šapliš* ~ *šilpaš*) while the full palindrome *ummu* is here disturbed by the prefixed *mu*. All of this resonates at once in a polyphony of linguistic play: appositional structural position, the combined meanings of three different semantic resonances – noise, creation, motherhood – and the anticipation of a named actor later in the poem, when Mummu will become Apsû's vizier. Others have commented on all these qualities and have sometimes kept them apart, but what is important here is the poetic invocation of them all at the same time. Moreover, the sonic imagery of *mu-ummu* is then reflected twice, first in **ama**, Sumerian for 'mother', inside the name of Ti-ama-t; and then in one of the synonyms of *mummu*, namely *rigmu*, 'noise', which is anagrammed in *gimrīšun*, 'all of them'.

A telling echo of this appears sometime later, after generations of deities have been born and assert their creative independence from their begetters, their presence and liberation symbolized by *their* productive noise, which is signalled by anagram and rhyme (in bold below). By now, Apsû and Tiamat have been named and are personified:

*lā našir apsû* ***rigimšun***
*u tiāmtu šuqammumat ina* ***maḫrīšun***

Apsû could not lessen their racket,
But Tiamat stayed silently still in their presence.

(I 25–6, translation modified)

Compare this to the couplet from the opening passage in which they are introduced:

*apsûma rēštû* ***zārûšun***
*mummu tiāmtu muʾallidat* ***gimrīšun***

But freshwater marsh there was, initiator, their (future) progenitor
And creatrix brackish marsh, the (future) birther of them all.

(I 3–4, translation modified)

The *rigmu*, 'racket, clamour', that Apsû is helpless to control emulates and appropriates Tiamat's *mummu* and its own enunciation, as anagrammed in *gimrīšun*. While the younger deities were making all this noise, Apsû spoke loudly to his wife Tiamat, complaining about the din and urging her to put an end to their activity. The fuming mother cannot bear this, raging against the very idea of the murder of her children. She is paradoxically answered not by her husband but rather by his vizier Mummu, the very incarnation of her creative potential in the silent primordial soundscape, encapsulated in a couplet that echoes the poetics of that beginning:

*īpul-ma mummu apsâ imallik*
*sukkallu lā māgiru milik mummīšu*

But it was Mummu who answered, advising Apsû
It was that of a treacherous vizier, the advice of his Mummu!

(I 47–8, translation modified)

The chiastic rearrangement of Mummu and of the verb and noun 'advising, advice' echo the poetics of the first quatrain, as does the wash of the sonorants /l/ and /m/, and, once again, an anagram of *rigmu* in *lā māgiru*, 'disobedient, treacherous'. After the ensuing battle, Apsû and Mummu will reappear, now conquered by the god Ea. The former has now morphed once again, back into a watery element, but different from its or his original state, as a place name that would remain as the domain of Ea, topped with the tied-up prisoner Mummu, symbolizing his vibrational creative force as master of all craft and of magical incantations (**mu**$_7$-**mu**$_7$ in Sumerian). Significantly, this creative force would eventually be transferred from father to son in *Erish Shummi*, a syncretistic hymn to Marduk that riffs on *Enuma Elish* VI–VII, where we read, '(Your name is) Ninshiku, creator, maker of everything, without whom nothing whatsoever was formed, sire of the gods, shaper of creatures, maker of wonders' (*ninšīku mummu bān kal šumīšu ša ullânuššu napḫar mimmāma lā ippatqu / muʾallid ilī kāṣir binûti mubannû niklāti*, IV

26–7; Fadhil and Jiménez 2022: 234–5). Here, Ninshiku, a well-attested by-name of Ea, is transferred to Marduk, explained in glorious detail as a 'creator' (*mummu*) of 'maker of all that has a name' (*bān kal šumīšu*), with the parallelism between *mummu* and *mu'allid ilī* as well as the repeated sonorous /m/'s echoing the description of the brackish waters, soon to be Tiamat in l. 4 of the introduction to *Enuma Elish*.

The trope of associations that metaphorically linked 'noise' with action, creativity, and creation has a long history in Mesopotamian literature, with strong intertextual implications for the study of *Enuma Elish* that can only be considered briefly here. In earlier poems such as the stories of *Anzû* and *Atra-hasis*, noise represents action while silence signals stupor, rest, sleep, and even destruction. In *Enuma Elish*, the symbolic use of such tropes is particularly salient in the introductory passage: recall that the murmuring aquatic origin theme was contrasted with the noisy loud splitting apart or coming together in procreative force of the upper and lower regions in earlier Mesopotamian origin stories, one of the many negations that were full of coiled up creative potential signalling the coming revision of the initial cosmic pre-origins.

With all of this in mind, we must look again at l. 26, already cited above. When the noise of the younger gods, which demanded recognition of their creative place in the world, disturbed the older generation, Apsû could not quiet them down, 'but Tiamat stayed silently still in their presence' (*u tiāmtu šuqammumat ina maḫrīšun*, I 26, translation modified). Here, but sixteen lines after our initial passage, the poet spells out a new element in the symbolic repertoire of the story, in the form of the verb *šuqammumu*, 'to be silent, still', used in *Enuma Elish* to denote a state of silent inactive stupor: the exact antonym of creative resonant *mummu*, with the latter chiastically embedded in the former (*šuq-ammum-u*).

But the silence of pre-origins is not total; hence, the stillness is metaphorical, embedded in the murmur of the aquatic setting. To understand this apparent paradox, I invoke the words of Adele Bardazzi (2014: 11) in the context of a discussion of the poetry of Eugenio Montale. Citing the composer John Cage's notes on his piece *4'33"* that marks the length of silence dictated to the performer, 'Cage states that the audience "missed the point [the meaning]. There's no such thing as silence [...] they thought [it] was silence because they didn't know how to listen". As paradoxical as it may seem, silence, according to Cage, does not exist. Silence does not exist in the sense that it is as eloquent as sound; it is, therefore, possible to speak on a metaphorical level of the sound – and meaning – of silence.' Thus, silence is anagrammed in the opening two couplets, this initial silence infused with the murmur of creation, ready to metamorphose into more creative noise, poetically inscribed in the descriptions of mother Tiamat, whose creative potential as *mu'allidat*, 'birther' will eventually be stifled still as *šuqammumat*, 'quiet'.[12] The world begins, according to *Enuma Elish*, with the low musical murmur of creation, the resonance of quiet lapping water, a soundscape that will slowly be transformed into landscape.

The vision of marshland topography is further developed in the third couplet: 'Yet while their waters mingled together, but did not pleat *reedbed*, nor mat canebrake' (*mûšunu ištēniš iḫiqqūma / gipāra lā kiṣṣurū ṣuṣâ lā šē'ū*, I 5–6, translation modified). The first word, *mû*, 'water', as already noted, explains the meaning of the labial sonorant phonetic texture of what preceded it, while the next one, *ištēniš* ('together'), picks up the adverbial form of the first half of the first two lines (*eliš* and *šapliš*). The next line, l. 6, introduces a new syntactic arrangement of two successive synonymic parallel phrases construed, once again, with rare, perhaps even novel words, reinforcing the power of the unusual linguistic coinages proclaimed in the opening couplet: 'But did not pleat *reedbed*, nor mat canebrake'. The explication of this line requires a brief lexicographical detour.[13] The Akkadian noun *gipāru*, borrowed from Sumerian, normally referred to a specific type of elite building, the residence of a high priestesses or priest, but here, as explained by the synonymic parallelism with *ṣuṣû*, 'canebrake, swamp', a word that is currently attested only twice before the time *Enuma Elish* was composed.[14] Assuming that the line is indeed construed as a synonymous parallelism, it must be an unrelated homonym, presumably designating a swampy area filled with reed (Sumerian **gi**). The word *ṣuṣû* was a synonym of Akkadian *apparu*, which, in turn, was a loan from Sumerian **abbar**. But the use of *gipāru* with the meaning 'swamp' or the like is otherwise undocumented in Akkadian, although some translations of this line render it as such without commentary. I would propose that Sumerian **abbar** was an archaizing construct, rarely encountered outside of literary language, made up of **ab**, 'sea', and **bar**, '(out)side' (formally parallel to the phrase, **ab ša$_3$**, 'the inside of the sea') and meant literally, 'on the borders of the sea(land)'.[15] It is thus conceivable that this *gipāru* was a learned artificial construct, made up in language-game fashion from Sumerian **gi**, 'reed', and **bar**, 'side', referring to the reed thickets bordering on lagoons in the sealand, as in the incantation cited above.[16] If this interpretation holds, the synonymic parallelism of the line would consist of a loanword followed by a synonymous native one, a poetic device well attested in ancient and modern Middle Eastern poetics (on such devices see Boeder 1991; Michalowski 1996: 148).

The third couplet of the introduction bridges the initial and final quatrains, as the fourth couplet (l. 7–8) refashions the parallelism of the opening line, including a structural reminder of the preceding l. 6, but with content taken from l. 2:

| | |
|---|---|
| (l. 1) *enūma eliš lā nabû šamāmū* | ('when above not named heavens') |
| (l. 7) *enūma ilū lā šūpû manāma* | ('when gods not appeared whosoever') |

| | |
|---|---|
| (l. 6) *gipāra lā kiṣṣurū ṣuṣâ lā šēʾū* | ('reedbed not pleated canebrake not matted') |
| (l. 2) *šapliš ammātu šuma lā zakrat* | ('below firmament name not named') |
| (l. 8) *šuma lā zukkurū šīmāti lā šīmū* | ('name not named fate not fated') |

Note how l. 6, with its internal parallelism between the two parts of the line, creates a form of semantic and phonic cesura, setting up two equally parallel sections. Most significantly, the naming of still non-existent vegetation is expressed without any of the watery sounds that otherwise permeate all lines in the introduction, adding expressive power to its liminal poetic status. The phonological fabric of this line sticks out as well, devoid of any labials but populated by stops (g, p), and repeated harsh emphatics (ṣ), but ending with a negated verb that has but one consonant, the voiceless sibilant /š/, sometimes described as hushed, that was articulated by the teeth and was continuous like the labials. Taking another look at the whole introduction, it is obvious that its hushed quality mingled with the aquatic /m's/ to set the murmurous mood, but also in combination with them anagramming the other creative force, the name and naming word *šumu* and with the /t/ of *zakrat* pointing to the associated concept that was chiastically linked with naming in line 8, 'fate not fated', *šīmāti lā šīmū*.

Much more could be said about this set of parallel constructions; here I will only point out how cleverly *manāma* picks up the emblematic /m/'s of *šamāmū*, and how the unfulfilled intertextual expectation of what should follow *enūma* at the very launch of the poem is partially fulfilled by a tip of the hat to the earlier poem of *Atra-hasis*, which began with the words *inūma ilū*, 'When the gods … ', that will be partially absorbed and transformed in the narrative to come.

The arrival of Lahmu and Lahamu in the final couplet marks the first major change in the widening mire: a combination of the first proper nouns and the first finite predicates as until now all these have been 'statives', that is nominal forms of the verb that denote static situations, rather than actions and are not marked for tense, aspect, or mood.[17] The finale of the section reverses the grammar and semantics, from non-finite verbs to finite ones and from negative to positive, enclosing the first origin narrative by means of naming, now denoting action as opposed to stasis even if their passive forms still signal a lack of specific agency in the developing world. Something has stirred in the murmuring soundscape.

But while the nouns are now more defined, they remain novel, peculiar, and strange. The Sumerian **la-ha-ma**, associated with the Apsû, are attested as far back as the time of Gudea of Lagash in the twenty-second century BCE, and are generally identified as bearded male figures with long hair, represented on cylinder seals and in other media and generally explained as guardian figures at entrances. But a pairing of Lahmu and Lahamu, masculine and feminine, never appears before the time of *Enuma Elish* other than in the god list *An* = *Anum*, where they are listed right at the beginning as **$^{d}$lah$_3$-ma** and **$^{d}$la-ha-ma** in two Middle Assyrian manuscripts of the list as part of the genealogy of the high god Anu.[18] It is difficult to provide a precise dating of these tablets; usually they are described as late thirteenth century, which is within the general time frame of the composition of *Enuma Elish*.[19] Thus, the feminine Lahamu is likely another innovation or example of an appropriation of a rare or esoteric word. Both names have been etymologized as Akkadian words meaning either 'muddy' or 'hairy', with a preference for the latter. 'Muddy', or mud seems to make more sense in the present context, as several scholars have argued in concert with ideas first proposed by Thorkild Jacobsen.[20] Dietrich, however, suggested that the words may refer to sea monsters.[21] It is possible that the pair refers obliquely to aquatic beings, without as yet any proper definition.[22] And just as was the case with *apsû*, *tiāmtu*, and *mummu*, these two nouns will be transformed into beings as the story evolves, when Lahmu and Lahamu reappear among the monsters created by Tiamat to battle Marduk.

To summarize, the first four lines of *Enuma Elish* depict an expanse of waters, with nouns that are expanded, in each case differently, by a combination of the consonant /m/ and a vowel. This creative murmur, to adapt the felicitous words of Anne-Caroline Rendu Loisel with reference to magical charms, invokes incantatory language and doubtless contributes to the melodies of the lines, but most significantly, it is motivated by the simple Akkadian term for 'water' – *mû* – which is anagrammed throughout the first couplets and then explicitly fronted in l. 5.[23] The consonants of the opening two lines consist only of labials (/m/, /n/, /p/), an additional sonorant (like /m/ and

/n/), /l/, and the hushed voiceless sibilant /š/, until the final *šuma la zakrat*, which is partially anagrammed in the next line as *rēštû zārûšun*, and of course, the repeated /m/ and /l/ sounds, particularly concentrated in l. 4, dominate the rest of the message. Significantly, such consonants, articulated with the lips, are not punctual, and the sound can resonate at length, just like vowels, creating melodic sequences. The element of water does not end with its explicit naming in l. 5, but permeates all five couplets, offering a complex soundscape of phonological symbolism. Looking again at the whole section, accentuating the /m/ syllables, the pattern becomes clear:

*enū**ma** eli**š** lā nabû **š**a**māmū***
***š**apli**š** **ammā**tu **šuma** lā zakrat*
*apsû**ma** rē**š**tû zārû**š**un*
***mummu** tiā**m**tu **mu**ʾallidat g**im**rī**š**un*
***mûš**unu i**š**tēni**š** iḫiqqū**ma***
*gipāra lā kiṣṣurū ṣuṣâ lā **š**ēʾū*
*enū**ma** ilū lā **š**ūpû **manāma***
***šuma** lā zukkurū **šīmā**ti lā **šīmū***
*ibbanû**ma** ilū qereb**š**un*
*laḫ**mu** (u) laḫ**āmu** u**š**tāpû **šuma** izzakrū*

Lest one argue that this is mere coincidence, similar poetic devices that allude to the sound of water operate once again in another scene of creation further down in the poem, when the victorious Marduk, usurping the traditional role of Enlil, Ea, and the mother goddess, proclaims:

*lušziz-ma lullâ lū amēlu šumšu*
*ubnī-ma lullâ amēla*

And so, I shall generate an unformed person, 'human' shall be its name.
So, I shall create the prototypical human being.

(VI 6–7, translation modified)

Creation and naming signal here a return to the very beginning of the poem. The complex word plays in the couplet are difficult to translate into English, as they involve a bilingual synonymic pair structurally similar to the alternation of two different words for 'canebrake', or the like in l. 6: one a loan from Sumerian and the other the native Akkadian, since *lullû* was adapted from Sumerian $\mathbf{lu}_2$-$\mathbf{lu}_7$, 'person, man'. But in poetry, this new word was nuanced to signify humans that were not yet fully socialized, such as very young infants, and here the two words are then combined into a new compound (*lullû amēlu*) to denote persons ready to be instructed and integrated into a role in society. In this passage, the poet has borrowed and modified a passage from *Atra-hasis*, but exploits it in a novel manner to revel in the resonance of the /l/ sound from *lullû* and *amēlu* as well as a the /m/ of the latter in a manner that harkens back to the sonic echoes of the opening lines of the work as well as the interlanguage games of a passage that introduces Marduk's name later in the same tablet (I 101–2).[24] The repetition of the nasal /m/ invokes the reverberation of the syllable /mu/ or /ma/ in the opening lines that anagrammed *mû*, the Akkadian word for water, sound symbolism that in this instance provided an allegory to the aquatic imagery of childbirth, so often invoked in incantations that were murmured at difficult birth moments.[25]

To put it succinctly: at the beginning of the beginning, everything is new and exceptional, as marked by the dense parallelistic syntax, the sound symbolism, and the fact that each noun is either extremely rare or is evoked in an innovative manner that for all practical purposes brands them as neologisms.[26] The only commonplace nouns are *šumu*, 'word', and *šīmtu*, 'future, destiny', but these belong with the verbs as it is part of the collocations or idioms *šuma zakāru*, 'to name', and *šīmta šâmu*, 'to determine destiny', that are complex predicates in Akkadian, with specific phrasal meanings. While some of these devices were not new, the sheer poetic density of the opening passage is not only boldly radical – it is unmatched in the millennia of Mesopotamian literature.[27]

## Structural projection: Intertextual references and naming names

The introduction is not just a poetic credo but also a harbinger of things to come; alluding, sometimes by absence, sometimes by presence, to the longer storyline that is yet to unravel. We have already witnessed how many of the nouns anticipate transformations into divine names and then, mostly in death, into place names (especially in the case of Apsû). But there are also other devices that structurally presage the well-thought-out poetic contents of the seven-tablet story, among them two that stand out with particular salience: the anticipation and realization of intertextual allusions and the recursive reference to naming that permeated the opening lines.

The dense poetic fabric of the opening words of *Enuma Elish* anticipates intertextual appropriations and recollections and signals its participation in the learned Sumero-Akkadian philological tradition, as does the use of interlingual word play. As already observed, the second word of the text confounds the reader, who expects the word *enūma*, 'when', to be followed by the name of the sky god Anu or the word *ilū*, 'gods'. In the Sumerian tradition, certain types of royal inscriptions began with the words, 'When An', describing the selection of a king for greatness, including monarchs such as Ur-Namma of Ur and Hammurabi of Babylon. The monumental stele of the latter, inscribed with legal provisions, taught to young students down to the first millennium, was the first of this kind expressed in Akkadian rather than Sumerian, and its opening words read *inu Anum* ... *Enlil*, 'When Anu ... and Enlil'. More important for the poet of *Enuma Elish* was the short bilingual introduction to the greatest Babylonian compendium of celestial omens, *Enuma Anu Enlil*, which would eventually serve as the defining work of Mesopotamian scholarship, so that the designation 'scribe of *Enuma Anu Enlil*' came to designate the highest level of intellectual achievement.[28] Indeed, that work includes two such stories, one at the very outset and another opening Tablet XXII, which begins *enu Anu Enlil u Ea*, 'When Anu, Enlil, and Ea'. The sole earlier poem that broke with this pattern was the one that moderns label *Atra-hasis*, which began *inūma ilū awīlum*, 'When deities were as if humans', but this described the universe as already created, but unpeopled. Our poem alludes to this as well, by sharing *enūma* and the assonance of *ilū* and *eliš*, signalling that the older story will be appropriated and cannibalized later in the narrative; certain astronomical omens will also be referenced as the piece unfolds (on these and other such appropriations of the textual tradition, see Seri 2014).

The second structuring element that radiates from the very first words is the trope of naming that is first referenced by its absence is then first realized with the creation and naming of Lahmu and Lahamu, and then reappears no less than twenty times at critical junctures in the story (for a list and discussion of these junctures, see Gabriel 2014: 268–70). Crucially, in the aftermath of the most important birth of the story, that of Marduk, the future king of the gods is described in an unexpected manner, as his naming is signalled by a radical poetic turn. At this juncture, such naming is not expressly described with the standard words for such acts but is only implied in a couplet of a poetic density that rivals that of the opening lines. Even though this passage has been analysed by others (see most recently Horowitz 2010: 89–90), it deserves another closer look (I 101–2).

*māri'utu māri'utu*
*māri šamšu Šamaš* (or *šamšu*) *ša ilī*

To grasp these lines fully, it is important to observe that Marduk's name was regularly written with a pseudo-logogram ᵈAMAR-UTU, that is, the normally unpronounced classifier **diĝir**, 'deity' (rendered by moderns as a superscriptᵈ), followed by the Sumerian words **amar**, 'calf, youngster', and **utu**, 'sun'. Marūtuku – for that is the Akkadian form of the name that we render as Marduk – was thus playfully represented as if it were Sumerian **amar utu-ak**, 'offspring of the Sun' (-**ak** being the Sumerian possessive suffix), with the sign combination interlingually anagramming the name of the god. The poet of *Enuma Elish*, harkening back to the poetics of the opening lines, takes this much further, once again referencing the bilingual nature of Sumero-Babylonian philology, and anticipating the extensive section that begins at the end of the sixth Tablet and continues to cover much of the last one, in which Marduk will be gifted with fifty Sumerian names and their Babylonian explanations (VI 123–VII 136). But the couplet also indirectly invokes the complex role of the sun and the sun god Shamash in Mesopotamian royal self-representation, with a rhetorical history reaching far back in time, thereby presaging Marduk's assumption of the kingship of the gods.[29]

The first line of the naming of Marduk orders the cuneiform signs of the name in an Akkadian pseudo-phonological rendering that, on first glance, makes little sense, but recalls the language games and lexical innovations of the opening passage, in the form of an artificial neologism, a play on an otherwise unattested **māri'ūtu*, with the abstract suffix *-ūtu* likely functioning here as a diminutive marker on the word for 'son', *māru*.[30] Serendipitously, we can exploit the English homonymity between 'son' and 'sun', so that this may be translated as 'sonny'. In the next line, the first word is probably *mārī*, with a different diminutive ending, now 'sunshine', in its endearing meaning of 'sweet little child', and Sumerian **utu**, 'sun', is replaced by its Akkadian equivalent *šamšu*, or in Babylonian manuscripts by Shamash, the name of the sun god. The repetitive symmetry of the first line is contrasted in the next one by the reversal of the word order in the second half, with 'of the gods' rendering in Akkadian the initial **diĝir**, 'deity', the aforementioned classifier that begins Marduk's name. The passage can thus perhaps be rendered as

> Sonny, sonny
> Sunshine, sun, Sun god (or: sun) of the gods! (translation modified)

Translation matters aside, the *tour de force* naming process for the new god implies a rooting in the bilingual learned tradition and thus in the very fabric of cuneiform writing, once again invoking the technical practices of scholarship and elite cultural tradition.

The culmination of the recursive trope of naming is found in the long passage that narrates Marduk's fifty esoteric Sumerian names and their Akkadian explications, exploiting various scholastic genres: god lists, lexical texts, and commentaries.[31] But the fifty names do not end the structural projection of naming. At the very end of the second origin story of *Enuma Elish*, Tiamat – now defeated and dismembered by Marduk, 'split in two like a fish for drying' (IV 137, translation modified), to create the upper and lower regions in her involuntary last act as a *mummu*, or murmur-agent of creation, is never again mentioned in an active role. The victorious new king of the gods 'order[ed] not to let her waters escape' (IV 140) from the part of the corpse that are now the skies (once again *šamāmu*), creating a mirror image of heavenly waters as a memento of Tiamat, with the relic of Apsû having become the sweet waters just under the firmament below: a perpetual commemoration of the aquatic origins that initiated *Enuma Elish* and the known world. At least one native commentator drew attention to this: in a later esoteric astronomical composition that cites the poem several times, *šamê*, 'skies', was cosmologically etymologized in playful fashion as *ša mê*, 'of the waters'.[32] An Old Babylonian omen already compares the skies to water, so such ideas might be much older (Rochberg 2010: 306, who invokes this very etymology).

Just before the very final lines of the poem, the poet returns the reader to the waters and repeats the trope of naming, bringing together, for one last time, the two thematic structural elements of the first quatrain of the story of creation, recapping the interlingual relationship between Akkadian *mû*, 'water', and Sumerian **mu**, 'name':[33] 'Wherever water is drunk, may his name be invoked. This now is the song of Marduk, who bound Tiamat and took kingship' (*ēma* ***mû*** *iššattû šu**m**šu lizzakrū / inanna**m**-**ma** za**m**āru ša **m**arduk / ša tiā**m**ta ik**mû**-(**ma**) ilqû šarrūta*, VII 160–2, translation modified). The final naming (*šumšu lizzakrū*) has now morphed into song (*zamāru*), and the murmuring sound of creation, inscribed with the deep labial resonance of /m/, continues to vibrate in the once and future dimension of myth, governed not by mundane time but by poetry.

The radical innovative poetics of *Enuma Elish*, in which motifs, structure, and progressive theme development exhibit a disciplined vision of a compositional whole, and whose elements echo throughout the long text, provide support for Lambert's (2013: 353) assertion that the poem was composed just as we have it by a single person at one time.[34] It may very well be that this was recognized and acknowledged by those who transmitted it in libraries and studied it in schooling, who guarded the integrity of the work and wrote it down with few substantive variants over the centuries. The revolutionary project of *Enuma Elish*, which harnessed poetics to create a new vision of the world that sought to absorb, incorporate, and reimagine the whole Babylonian literary universe, including lexical, magical, narrative, and mythological traditions, was clearly admired and respected, but had no obvious followers, even if some of its novel words gained currency in literary circles and some lines would be cited by others in years to come. It served as a prior text for others, with the introductory origin story inspiring a veiled response from the author of the first lines of Genesis, and thus indirectly, its echoes reached many other languages, resounding with us to this day (Frahm 2010 and Eckart Frahm in this volume). The astounding poetic density and subtle aurally vibrational force of its first ten lines bear the mark of one of the world's great poets, one who will forever remain anonymous but who revealed to us the lapping, murmuring sound of waters, coiled with the silenced potential for loud action – the very sound of creation.

## Further reading

The poetics of the opening lines has been explored most imaginatively, if somewhat differently by Giorgio Buccellati (1990) and many others listed in n. 5. For an exposition of Mesopotamian creation stories and their mythic functions, see Gonzalo Rubio (2013), followed more recently by Gioele Zisa (2020). Akkadian (and Sumerian) poetics have been explored in the essays collected by Marianna Vogelzang and Hermann Vanstiphout (1996) and lately by Sophus Helle (2014).

## Notes

1 Robert Kelly, '(An Anecdote as Preface)' (Kelly 1998: i).

2 I must thank Peter Machinist for years of fruitful discussions about some of the issues discussed here and for his generous comments on a draft. The analysis presented here was inspired by the studies of poetics by Roman Jakobson, his students and the pioneers of the Prague School but space precludes any discussion of these matters.

3 For the literary history of *Enuma Elish*, see the introduction in this volume.

4 On such matters see, most recently and insightfully, De Zorzi (2022: 368–94), with earlier literature.

5 For a comprehensive survey of the syntax of the passage and a selection of major modern renditions, see Kämmerer and Metzler (2012: 57–72). There are differing opinions on how to understand the scope and functions of the opening lines. For example, Gabriel (2014: 116) describes only the first six lines as 'prolog' and with l. 7 making a new section that stretches to l. 78. For relatively recent studies focused on these opening lines, with differing perspectives, see, e.g. Buccellati (1990: 125–8), Talon (1992), Streck (2014), and Maul (2015), 20–5.

6 Dylan Thomas, *Under Milk Wood: A Play for Voices* (Thomas 1954: 1).

7 For example, a Sumerian poem from Girsu from *c*. 2350 BCE relates 'At that time, the Enki and Ninki deities were not yet living, Enlil was not yet living, Ninlil was not yet

living ... daylight did not shine, moonlight was not rising (each night)'; see Rubio (2013: 5), l. ii 3–5 and iii 3–4.

8 Pre-*Enuma Elish* attestations of *šamāmu* are the fragmentary Ishtar text *VS* 10, 213, obv. 6', 7', and 10' (SEAL no. 7499); in the Middle Babylonian Ishtar poem *SEM* 117 iii; the Middle Assyrian 'Prayer of Tukulti-Ninurta I', *KAR* 128 rev. 32; and a royal grant stele (*kudurru*) from the time of the Babylonian King Nebuchadnezzar I (*c.* 1121–1100 BCE), that is, from around the time when *Enuma Elish* may have been composed – see the edition by Paulus (2014: 492), l. i 14. There are only two possible earlier attestations of *ammatu*, both in crasis contexts and subject to alternative interpretations: the Ishtar hymn mentioned above, VS 10, 213, l. i 7, *e-li-ia(-)matum*, for which see Wasserman (2003: 78 n. 84); and the 'Papuleagra Hymn', l. v 6 (*šar-ra(-)am-ma-tim*), the latter conceivably to be understood as *šarra mātim*; see Beaulieu and Mayer (1997: 167).

9 On the relation between water and language in *Enuma Elish*, see also Sophus Helle in this volume.

10 For a concise critical history of the ideas of primordial chaos in creation narratives in the Ancient Near East, see Sonik (2013).

11 Krebernik (1993), Michalowski (1990: 384–7), Frahm (2013a), and now Rendu Loisel (2016: 200–4; 2018).

12 The matter was succinctly described by Machinist (1983) and pursued further, with a focus on *Enuma Elish*, by Michalowski (1990).

13 The grammatical issues involved in the interpretation of this line have been investigated by Haubold (2017: 223–8); here I follow his guarded suggestion to take the predicates as active rather than passive.

14 Both attestations are unclear: an incantation to help catch fish edited in Cavigneaux and Al-Rawi (1994: 82, l. rev. 20); and a city lament prayer analysed by Wasserman and Gabbay (2005: 71), l. rev. 3' (restored).

15 Parallel to **an** $\textbf{ša}_3$, '(unseen) interior of the skies', etc. and **an bar**, likely '(visible) exterior of the skies'; see Ragavan (2010: 54, 105–7), with earlier literature.

16 There is another *gipāru*, meaning 'meadow' or the like, in the poem *Erra and Ishum* and an inscription of King Assurbanipal (see *Chicago Assyrian Dictionary*, s.v. *gipāru*), as well as the synonym list *Malku* II 115–16, where it is listed as equivalent to *rītu* and *tamirtu*, for which see Hrůša (2010: 60). A later commentary on *Enuma Elish* explains it as *erṣetu*, 'earth'; see Frahm and Jiménez (2015: 300). It is unclear how this word relates to the neologism posited here; Lambert (2013: 51) took them to be one and the same, translating the phrase 'before meadow-land had coalesced'. Note that in Sumerian poetry, the words **appar** and **sug**, equivalents of Akkadian *apparu* and *ṣuṣû*, were combined with the verb $\textbf{zu}_2$ **...** $\textbf{keš}_2\textbf{(d)}$, which was translated by *kaṣāru*, the Akkadian verb used here. This was drawn to my attention by Jerrold S. Cooper; for references see Herrmann (2010: 186–7).

17 See, most recently, Carver (2016). On the verbs in these lines, see Buccellati (1990: 127).

18 *An = Anum* I, l. 14–15 (Lambert and Winters 2023: 70), in texts α and ß, both written in Assur by the same scribe, Kidin-Sin. (ibid. 10–11).

19 On the date of these tablets, see, most recently, Wagensonner (2018: 237, n. 81).

20 'On the collective, often fifty, Lahama of the Abzu—rarely single—see George (2016, 61) with earlier literature. They represent, it would seem, silt which had formed in the waters'; Jacobsen (1946: 170). The various interpretations have been summarized by Gabriel (2014: 119, n. 42). See now also Van De Mieroop (2018: 382).

21 Dietrich (2006: 140: 140, fn. 26); apparently Lambert (2013: 424) came around to this interpretation, writing '*laḫmu* is the Akkadian, **laḫama** the Sumerian for "sea monster"'.
22 Note that Afro-Asiatic **laḫ-am* and its reflexes in various Semitic languages, as well as in ancient Egyptian, Chadic, and Kushitic, are all labels for marine creatures, including large fish such as sharks in Semitic; see most recently Militariev (2023: 286). Considering this, we may posit that these are still another set of neologisms in Akkadian, albeit revised from their Anu genealogy context, taken from Semitic, building upon a much older borrowing, designating primordial aquatic beings.
23 *Murmure créatrice*, Rendu Loisel (2016: 204). On the relation between water and language in *Enuma Elish*, see also Sophus Helle in this volume.
24 For a fuller exposition of these matters, including the relationship with the *Atra-hasis* and *Gilgamesh* stories, see Michalowski (forthcoming). See also Johannes Haubold in this volume.
25 On the poetic imagery of birth incantations in which the womb is sometimes metaphorically described as the 'sea' and the mother as a boat laden with precious cargo that represented the baby, see the insightful observations of Hätinen (2017).
26 To my knowledge, the only commentator to remark on this matter was Buccellati (1990: 126), who observed that '*šamāmu* is an "arcane" morphological formation, while *ammatum* has an "arcane" semantic range'.
27 For example, on the dense poetic exploitation of the sound patterns of *īlum*, 'god', *awīlum*, 'human, person', and *Wêila*, the name of the god whose blood was used to create humanity, and *ṭēmum*, 'intelligence', *eṭemmum*, 'ghost', and *damum*, 'blood', in *Atra-hasis* see Bottéro (1982: 28–31). Geller (1993) and most recently Abusch (2020: 71–2). Also note the multifaceted repetition of /m/ in the late version of *Gilgamesh* X 301–2, as analysed by Nurullin (2020: 561–3).
28 On the relation between *Enuma Elish* and *Enuma Anu Enlil* (and astrology more broadly), see Francesca Rochberg in this volume.
29 On 'my sun' as an epithet of deities and kings, see Dalley (1966: 98–9); for a survey of Shamash symbolism in early Mesopotamian royal ideology, see Charpin (2014) and for Assyria, Frahm (2013b).
30 The unique *māri'ūtu* would presumably literally mean 'sonship', understanding the final morphemes as the abstract formative *-ūt* followed by nominative *-u* expressing the vocative. In view of the language games employed here, it is possible that this form was meant to invoke an even more esoteric neologism, **māri'atu*, with the feminine -(*a*)*t*- marking diminutive ('sonny'), singulative ('*the* son'), or both. On these functions of the feminine nominal morpheme in Akkadian, see Hasselbach-Andee (2014: 330–1).
31 On names in *Enuma Elish*, see also Marc Van De Mieroop in this volume.
32 Livingstone (1986: 32), l. 6. The name of the composition I.NAM.ĜIŠ.HUR.AN.KI is now read *i-na*$_8$ ĜIŠ.HUR AN (*u*) KI, 'the "eyes" of the plans of the upper and lower regions'; see Panayotov apud Geller (2018: 308). See the important comments on this text by Rochberg (2010: 344).
33 Interestingly, the *Enuma Elish* poet does not use the rare *māmū* variant of the word 'water', known mostly from Neo-Assyrian royal inscriptions, but attested once earlier in the twelfth century BCE *Tukulti-Ninurta Epic*; see the references in the *Chicago Assyrian Dictionary*, s.v. *māmū*. On this passage, see also Sophus Helle in this volume.
34 For views that favour a history of redaction including posited mistakes or additions to the original composition, see, e.g., West (1997: 187), Abusch (2019), and Ayali-Darshan (2022).

# Bibliography

Abusch, T. (2019), 'Some Observations on the Babylon Section of *Enūma Eliš*', *Revue d'assyriologie et d'archéologie orientale*, 113 (1): 171–3.

Abusch, T. (2020), 'Ghost and God: Some Observations on a Babylonian Understanding of Human Nature', in T. Abusch (ed.), *Essays on Babylonian and Biblical Literature and Religion*, Harvard Semitic Series 65, 67–86, Leiden: Brill.

Al-Hamdani, A. (2020), 'The Settlement and Canal Systems during the First Sealand Dynasty (1721–1340 BCE)', in S. Paulus and T. Clayden (eds), *Babylonia under the Sealand and Kassite Dynasties*, 28–57, Berlin: De Gruyter.

Ayali-Darshan, N. (2020), *The Storm-God and the Sea: The Origin, Versions, and Diffusion of a Myth throughout the Ancient Near East*, Orientalische Religionen in der Antike 37, Tübingen: Mohr Siebeck.

Ayali-Darshan, N. (2022), 'The Editorial Technique of Resumptive Repetition: The Cosmogony and the Anthropogony in *Enūma Eliš*', in Y. Cohen, A. Gilan, L. Cerqueglini and B. Sheyhatovitch (eds), *'Carrying a Torch to Distant Mountains': The IOS Annual 21*, 50–70, Leiden: Brill.

Bardazzi, A. (2014), 'The Sound of Silence in Eugenio Montale: A Critical Analysis of *Ossi di seppia*', *HARTS & Minds: The Journal of Humanities and Arts*, 1: 1–19.

Beaulieu, P.-A. and W. R. Mayer (1997), 'Akkadische Lexikographie: CAD $Š_2$ und $Š_3$', *Orientalia Nova Series*, 66 (2): 157–80.

Boeder, W. (1991), 'A Note on Synonymic Parallelism and Bilingualism', *Studia Linguistica*, 45 (1): 97–126.

Bottéro, J. (1982), 'La création de l'Homme et son nature dans le Poème d'Atraḫasîs', in M. A. Dandamayev, I. Gershevitch, H. Klengel, G. Komoróczy, M. T. Larsen and J. N. Postgate (eds), *Societies and Languages of the Ancient Near East: Studies in Honour of I. M. Diakonoff*, 24–32, Warminster: Aris & Phillips.

Buccellati, G. (1990), 'On Poetry – Theirs and Ours', in T. Abusch, J. Huehnergard and P. Steinkeller (eds), *Lingering over Words: Studies in Ancient Near Eastern Literature in Honor of William L. Moran*, Harvard Semitic Studies 37, 105–34, Atlanta: Scholars Press.

Carver, D. E. (2016), 'The Akkadian Stative: A Non-Finite Verb', *Ancient Near Eastern Studies*, 53: 1–24.

Cavigneaux, A. and F. N. H. Al-Rawi (1994), 'Charmes de Sippar et de Nippur', in H. Gasche (ed.), *Cinquante-deux reflexions sur le proche-orient ancien: offertes en hommage à Léon De Meyer*, Mesopotamian History and Environment 2, 73–89, Leuven: Peeters.

Charpin, D. (2014), '"I Am the Sun of Babylon": Solar Aspects of Royal Power in Old Babylonian Mesopotamia', in J. A. Hill, P. Jones and A. J. Morales (eds), *Experiencing Power, Generating Authority: Cosmos, Politics, and the Ideology of Kingship in Ancient Egypt and Mesopotamia*, 65–96, Philadelphia: University of Pennsylvania Press.

Cole, S. W. (1994), 'Marsh Formation in the Borsippa Region and the Course of the Lower Euphrates', *Journal of Near Eastern Studies*, 53 (2): 81–109.

Dalley, S. (1966), 'The God Ṣalmu and the Winged Disk', *Iraq*, 48: 85–101.

De Zorzi, N. (2022), 'Parallelism and Analogical Thought in Babylonian Poetry: Case Studies from Ludlul bēl nēmeqi, the Babylonian Theodicy, and the Šamaš Hymn', *Wiener Zeitschrift für die Kunde des Morgenlandes*, 112: 368–94.

Dietrich, M. L. G. (2006), 'Das *Enūma eliš* als mythologischer Grundtext für die Identität der Marduk-Religion Babyloniens', in M. L. G. Dietrich and T. Kumar (eds),

*Significance of Base Texts for the Religious Identity – Die Bedeutung von Grundtexten für die religiöse Identität*, Forschungen zur Anthropologie und Religionsgeschichte 40, 135–63, Münster: Ugarit-Verlag.

Fadhil, A. A. and E. Jiménez (2022), 'Literary Texts from the Sippar Library III: "Eriš šummi", A Syncretistic Hymn to Marduk', *Zeitschrift für Assyriologie und vorderasiatische Archäologie*, 112 (2): 229–74.

Földi, Z. J. (2019), 'Bullussa-rabi, Author of the Gula Hymn', *Kaskal*, 16: 81–3.

Frahm, E. (2010), 'Counter-texts, Commentaries, and Adaptations: Politically Motivated Responses to the Babylonian Epic of Creation in Mesopotamia, the Biblical World, and Elsewhere', *Orient: Reports of the Society for Near Eastern Studies in Japan*, 45: 3–33.

Frahm, E. (2013a), 'Creation and the Divine Spirit in Babel and Bible: Reflections on *mummu* in *Enūma eliš* I 4 and *rûaḥ* in Genesis 1:2', in D. S. Vanderhooft and A. Winitzer (eds), *Literature as Politics, Politics as Literature: Essays on the Ancient Near East in Honor of Peter Machinist*, 97–116, Winona Lake: Eisenbrauns.

Frahm, E. (2013b), 'Rising Suns and Falling Stars: Assyrian Kings and the Cosmos', in J. A. Hill, P. Jones and A. J. Morales (eds), *Experiencing Power, Generating Authority: Cosmos, Politics, and the Ideology of Kingship in Ancient Egypt and Mesopotamia*, 97–120, Philadelphia: University of Pennsylvania Museum of Archaeology and Anthropology.

Frahm, E. (2019), 'Textual Traditions in First Millennium BCE Mesopotamia between Faithful Reproduction, Commentary, and New Creation', in W. Bührer (ed.), *Schriftgelehrte Fortschreibungs- und Auslegungsprozesse: Textarbeit im Pentateuch, in Qumran, Ägypten und Mesopotamien*, 13–47, Tübingen: Mohr Siebeck.

Frahm, E. and E. Jiménez (2015), 'Myth, Ritual, and Interpretation: The Commentary on *Enūma eliš* I–VII and a Commentary on Elamite Month Names', *Hebrew Bible and Ancient Israel*, 4 (3): 293–343.

Frazer, M. (2013), 'Nazi-Maruttaš in Later Mesopotamian Tradition', *Kaskal*, 10: 187–220.

Gabriel, G. (2014), '*enūma eliš' – Weg zu einer globalen Weltordnung: Pragmatik, Struktur und Semantik des babylonischen 'Lieds auf Marduk'*, Orientalische Religionen in der Antike 12, Tübingen: Mohr Siebeck.

Geller, M. J. (2018), 'The Exorcist's Manual (KAR 44)', in U. Steinert (ed.), *Assyrian and Babylonian Scholarly Text Catalogues: Medicine, Magic and Divination*, 292–312, Boston: De Gruyter.

Geller, S. A. (1993), 'Some Sound and Word Plays in the First Tablet of the Old Babylonian *Atramḫasīs* Epic', in B. Walfish (ed.), *The Frank Talmage Memorial Volume Volume 1*, 63–70, Haifa: Haifa University Press.

George, A. R. (2016), Mesopotamian Incantations and Related Texts in the Schøyen Collection, Cornell University Studies in Assyriology and Sumerology 32, Bethesda: CDL Press.

Hasselbach-Andee, R. (2014), 'Agreement and the Development of Gender in Semitic (Part II)', *Zeitschrift der Deutschen Morgenländischen Gesellschaft*, 164 (2): 319–44.

Haubold, J. (2017), 'From Text to Reading in Enūma Eliš', *Journal of Cuneiform Studies*, 69: 221–246.

Hätinen, A. (2017), '"I Am a Fully Laden Boat!" A Mesopotamian Metaphor Revisited', *Kaskal* 14: 169–86.

Helle, S. (2014), 'Rhythm and Expression in Akkadian Poetry', *Zeitschrift für Assyriologie und vorderasiatische Archäologie*, 104 (1): 56–73.

Herrmann, S. (2010), *Vogel und Fisch – Ein sumerisches Rangstreitgespräch: Textedition und Kommentar*, Philologia – Sprachwissenschaftliche Forschungsergebnisse 145, Hamburg: Verlag Dr. Kovač.

Horowitz, W. A. (2010), 'Name Midrashim and Word Plays on Names in Akkadian Historical Writings', in W. Horowitz, U. Gabbay and F. Vukosavovic (eds), *A Woman of Valor: Jerusalem Ancient Near Eastern Studies in Honor of Joan Goodnick Westenholz*, Biblioteca del Proximo Oriente Antiguo 8, 87–104, Madrid: Consejo Superior de Investigaciones Científicas.

Hrůša, I. (2010), *Die akkadische Synonymenliste* allku = šarru*: Eine Textedition mit Übersetzung und Kommentar*, Alter Orient und Altes Testament 50, Münster: Ugarit-Verlag.

Isacoff, S. (2022), *Musical Revolutions: How the Sounds of the Western World Changed*, New York: Knopf.

Jacobsen, T. (1946), 'Mesopotamia', in H. Frankfort, H. A. Groenewegen-Frankfort, J. A. Wilson, T. Jacobsen and W. A. Irwin (eds), *The Intellectual Adventure of Ancient Man: An Essay on Speculative Thought in the Ancient Near East*, 125–219, Chicago: University of Chicago Press.

Jacobsen, T. (1968), 'The Battle between Marduk and Tiamat', *Journal of the American Oriental Society*, 88 (1): 104–8.

Kämmerer, T. R. and K. A. Metzler (2012), *Das babylonische Weltschöpfungsepos Enūma Eliš*, Alter Orient und Altes Testament 375, Münster: Ugarit-Verlag.

Kelly, R. (1998), *The Time of Voice: Poems 1994–1996*, Santa Rosa: Black Sparrow Press.

Krebernik, M. (1993), 'Mum(m)u', *Reallexikon der Assyriologie und vorderasiatischen Archäologie*, 8: 415–6.

Lambert, W. G. (2013), *Babylonian Creation Myths*, Mesopotamian Civilizations 16, Winona Lake: Eisenbrauns.

Lambert, W. G and R. D. Winters (2023), *An = Anum and Related Lists*, God Lists of Ancient Mesopotamia, Volume I, Orientalische Religionen in der Antike 54, Tübingen: Mohr Siebeck.

Livingstone, A. (1986), *Mystical and Mythological Explanatory Works of Assyrian and: Babylonian Scholars*. Winona Lake: Eisenbrauns.

Machinist, P. (1983), 'Rest and Violence in the Poem of Erra', *Journal of the American Oriental Society*, 103: 221–6.

Machinist, P. (2005), 'Order and Disorder: Some Mesopotamian Reflections', in S. Shaked (ed.), *Genesis and Regeneration: Essays on Conceptions of Origins*, 31–61, Jerusalem: The Israel Academy of Arts and Sciences.

Machinist, P. (2011), 'Kingship and Divinity in Imperial Assyria', in J. Renger (ed.), *Assur–Gott, Stadt und Land*, 5. Internationales Colloquium der Deutschen Orient-Gesellschaft, 405-30, Wiesbaden: Harrasowitz Verlag.

Maul, S. (2015), 'Kosmologie und Kosmogonie in der antiken Literatur: Das sog. Babylonische Weltschöpfungsepos *Enūma Eliš*', in P. Derron (ed.), *Cosmologies et cosmogonies dans la littérature antique: huit exposés suivis de discussions et d'un epilogue*, Entretiens sur l'Antiquité classique 16, 15–49, Vandoeuvres: Fondation Hardt.

Michalowski, P. (1990), 'Presence at the Creation', in T. Abusch, J. Huehnergard and P. Steinkeller (eds), *Lingering over Words: Studies in Ancient Near Eastern Literature in Honor of William L. Moran*, Harvard Semitic Series 37, 381–96, Atlanta: Scholars Press.

Michalowski, P. (1996), 'Ancient Poetics', in M. E. Vogelzang and H. L. J. Vanstiphout (eds), *Mesopotamian Poetic Language: Sumerian and Akkadian*, 141–53, Groningen: Styx.

Michalowski, P. (forthcoming), 'First Humans', in R. de Boer and E. Zomer (eds), *Memorial Volume Wilfred Hugo van Soldt.*, PIHANS, Leiden: Nederlands Instituut voor het Nabije Oosten Leiden.

Militarev, A. (2023). 'Common Afrasian (Afro-Asiatic) Terms Related to the Magic, Supernatural, Spiritual and Mythic: Etymologies and Reconstructions', *International Journal of Afro-Asiatic Studies*, 27: 265–94.

Nurullin, R. (2020), 'On Birth, Death and Gods in the Epic of Gilgamesh: Two Notes on the Standard Babylonian Version', in I. Arkhipov, L. Kogan and N. Koslova (eds), *The Third Millennium: Studies in Early Mesopotamia and Syria in Honor of Walter Sommerfeld and Manfred Krebernik*, 547–68, Cuneiform Monographs 50, Leiden: Brill.

Oppenheim, A. L. (1960), 'Assyriology – Why and How?', *Current Anthropology*, 1 (5–6): 409–23.

Paulus, S. (2014), *Die babylonischen Kudurru-Inschriften von der kassitischen bis zur frühneubabylonischen Zeit: Untersucht unter besonderer Berücksichtigung gesellschafts- und rechtshistorischer Fragestellungen*, Alter Orient und Altes Testament 51, Münster: Ugarit-Verlag.

Pournelle, J. R. and G. Algaze (2014), 'Travels in Edin: Deltaic Resilience and Early Urbanism in Greater Mesopotamia', in A. McMahon and H. Crawford (eds), *Preludes to Urbanism: The Late Chalcolithic of Mesopotamia*, 7–37, Cambridge: McDonald Institute for Archaeological Research.

Ragavan, D. (2010), The Cosmic Imagery of the Temple in Sumerian Literature, Harvard University doctoral dissertation.

Rendu Loisel, A.-C. (2016), *Les chantes du monde: Le paysonage sonore de l'ancienne Mésopotamie*, Toulouse: Presses universitaires du Midi.

Rendu-Loisel, A.-C. (2018), 'Le prêtre incantateur est-il un scribe rate?', *Parcours anthropologiques*, 13: 94–109.

Robson, E. (2019), *Ancient Knowledge Networks: A Social Geography of Cuneiform Scholarship in First-Millennium Assyria and Babylonia*, London: UCL Press.

Rochberg, F. (2010), *In the Path of the Moon: Babylonian Celestial Divination and Its Legacy*, Ancient Magic and Divination 6, Leiden: Brill.

Rubio, G. (2013), 'Time before Time: Primeval Narratives in Mesopotamian Literature', in L. Feliu, J. Llop, A. M. Albà and J. Sanmartín (eds), *Time and History in the Ancient Near East*, Compte rendu de la Rencontre Assyriologique lnternationale 56, 3–17, Winona Lake: Eisenbrauns.

Sallaberger, W. (2017), 'Das göttliche Wesen des Kosmos: Zum Sitz im Leben von Weltentstehungsmotiven im frühen Mesopotamien', in R. A. Díaz Hernández, M. C. Flossmann-Schütze and F. Hoffmann (eds), *Antike Kosmogonien: Beiträge zum internationalen Workshop vom 28. bis 30. Januar 2016*, 9, 3–108, Tuna el Gebel 9, Vaterstetten: Verlag Patrick Brose.

Seri, A. (2012), 'The Role of Creation in *Enūma eliš*', *Journal of Ancient Near Eastern Religions*, 12 (1): 4–29.

Seri, A. (2014), 'Borrowings to Create Anew: Intertextuality in the Babylonian Poem of "Creation" (*Enūma eliš*)', *Journal of the American Oriental Society*, 134 (1): 89–106.

Sonik, K. (2013), 'From Hesiod's Abyss to Ovid's rudis indigestaque moles: Chaos and Cosmos in the Babylonian "Epic of Creation"', in J. Scurlock and R. H. Beal (eds), *Creation and Chaos: A Reconsideration of Gunkel's Chaoskampf Hypothesis*, 21–45, Eisenbrauns: Winona Lake.

Streck, M. P. (2014), 'The Beginning of the Babylonian Epic of Creation', in S. J. Wimmer and G. Gafus (eds), *'Vom Leben umfangen': Ägypten, das Alte Testament und das Gespräch der Religionen; Gedenkschrift für Manfred Görg*, Ägypten und Altes Testament 80, 391–5, Münster: Ugarit-Verlag.

Talon, P. (1992), 'Le premier épisode de l'Enūma Eliš', in M. Broze and P. Talon (eds), *L'atelier de l'orfèvre: Mélanges offerts à Philippe Derchain*, 131–46, Leuven: Peeters.
Thomas, Dylan (1954), *Under Mild Wood: A Play for Voices*, New York: New Directions.
Van De Mieroop, M. (2018), 'What Is the Point of the Babylonian Creation Myth?', in S. Fink and R. Rollinger (eds), *Conceptualizing Past, Present and Future: Proceedings of the Ninth Symposium of the Melammu Project Held in Helsinki / Tartu May 18–24, 2015*, Melammu Symposia 9, 381–92, Münster: Ugarit-Verlag.
Vogelzang, M. E. and H. L. J. Vanstiphout (eds, 1996), *Mesopotamian Poetic Language: Sumerian and Akkadian*, Cuneiform Monographs 6, Groningen: Styx.
Wagensonner, K. (2018), 'Sumerian in the Middle Assyrian Period', in J. Braarvig and M. J. Geller (eds), *Multilingualism, Lingua Franca and Lingua Sacra*, Max Planck Research Library for the History and Development of Knowledge Studies 10, 225–97, Berlin: Edition Open Access.
Wagensonner, K. (2020), 'Expelling Demons by the Use of a Fish and Bird', *Akkadica*, 141: 115–25.
Wasserman, N. (2003), *Style and Form in Old Babylonian Literary Texts*, Cuneiform Monographs 27, Leiden: Styx.
Wasserman, N. and U. Gabbay (2005), 'Literatures in Contact: The Balaĝ Úru Àm-ma-ir-ra-bi and Its Akkadian Translation *UET* 6/2, 403', *Journal of Cuneiform Studies*, 57: 69–84.
West, M. L. (1997), 'Akkadian Poetry: Metre and Performance', *Iraq*, 59: 175–87.
Wisnom, S. (2020), *Weapons of Words: Intertextual Competition in Babylonian Poetry; A Study of 'Anzû', 'Enūma Eliš', and 'Erra and Išum'*, Culture and History of the Ancient Near East 196, Leiden: Brill.
Zisa, G. (2020), '"In quel giorno, in quella notte, in quell'anno": Cosmogonie e cosmologie sumeriche e assiro-babilonesi', in I. E. Buttitta and A. La Barbera (eds), *L'uomo e il cosmo nella storia: paradigmi, miti, simboli; Atti del Convegno internazionale Palermo, 18–20 settembre 2019*, 83–119, Palermo: Fondazione Buttitta.

13

# Marduk's names and cuneiform hermeneutics

Marc Van De Mieroop

In his detailed retelling of *Enuma Elish* as a political parable that explains the rise of kingship in ancient Mesopotamia, the famous twentieth-century Assyriologist Thorkild Jacobsen (1976: 183) passed over the final part of the poem with a terse statement: 'The story ends with Anshar exhorting the assembled gods to name Marduk's fifty names, which they do, each name indicative of a power or a deed that characterizes him.' Jacobsen was not alone in his summary treatment of the passage. The recent commentary alongside a Spanish translation of the epic also summed it up in one sentence, while some discussions and translations have fully ignored it.[1] This may come as a surprise to those who have read the 1,100-line poem in its entirety, as they know that the enumeration of Marduk's names takes up the final 200 lines of it. No other subject receives as much attention in the epic: each name of the now supreme god is followed by an explanation that can take up to nine verses. Although the length of the passage and its position at the end of the text have inspired the idea that it was an awkward secondary addition to the poem and not essential to it, its intricate connections to the rest of the text (as shown below) suggest the opposite.[2] In fact, scholars today increasingly see the passage's meaning very differently, including some who were previously dismissive of it. A recent English re-edition of the text suggests that the epic's author considered it the 'true climax' of the poem, while to some it contains its main point.[3] This re-evaluation may be partly inspired by the fact that, across the humanities in general, the format of this passage – the list – is now seen as a fascinating literary device rather than a dull enumeration. Perhaps the best illustration of this new stance is that in 2009 the Louvre Museum in Paris invited Umberto Eco to curate an exhibition entitled 'Vertige de la liste'. The official English translation, 'The Infinity of Lists', renders the title imprecisely. Eco (2009a, 2009b) stressed the vertigo or giddiness that lists trigger rather than their limitlessness. But probably more important is the recent surge in interest among students of ancient Mesopotamia in the scholarship that their predecessors produced long ago. This ancient scholarship shows us that the contents of the passage are very significant and give us the key for their understanding.

On line 123 of the sixth Tablet of *Enuma Elish*, the gods begin to enumerate the names of Marduk at the instigation of Anshar, the great-grandfather of the newly elected king: 'Let us give him fifty names, so that his ways may be brought forth, and likewise his doings' (VI 121–2). In fact, they end up giving him fifty-one names, but the final one is of a different character; it is simply the name of Marduk's father's, Ea. The number fifty is not accidental; it was a numerical way to denote Enlil, the supreme god of the pantheon before Marduk's exaltation, indicating that the latter had now taken over Enlil's status. The fifty names are not all of equal standing, but a series of main alternative designations of the god Marduk set in different contexts, with many odd names thrown into the mix. Marduk was equated through a process of syncretism with the gods Asarluhi, the son of Ea (name 7); Tutu, the city-god of Borsippa (name 13); Enbilulu, a Sumerian god of agriculture (name 24); and an enigmatic Shazu, who may have been assimilated with Asarluhi (name 18). As Enbilulu, for example, he was given that name both by itself and in relation to the irrigation ditch (Enbilulu-Epudan), the canal inspector (Enbilulu-Gugal), and prosperity (Enbilulu-Hegal), giving him four distinct names (names 24–27). Such catalogues of divine names were not unusual in ancient Mesopotamian scholarship, nor were they limited to Marduk. We even know of texts that parallel the order given in *Enuma Elish*. Some were composed prior to *Enuma Elish* and may have inspired the poem's passage; others were written later and may have been intended as elaborations on it.[4] The general nature of *Enuma Elish*'s list was thus not exceptional, but what makes it unusual is that each name is followed by several verses that elaborate on what the name entails, such as: 'Enbilulu-Hegal, who piles up plenty for the people, who rains prosperity on the wide earth and makes plants grow in abundance' (VII 68–9). Such comments are not entirely unparalleled, although they are much shorter elsewhere.[5] The closest analogy known so far appears in a passage of a hymn to Marduk in which the god is given the names of eleven others, unlike those in *Enuma Elish* all leading gods in the pantheon, with an explanation of what that entails spanning several lines of text. For example, as Adad he is a storm god whose clamour can shake mountains and stir up seas and as Shamash he lights up heaven and earth. That hymn is indebted to *Enuma Elish* for some of its formulations, but still it lacks the systematic name analysis that poem presents (Fadhil and Jiménez 2022: 229–74).

What was the basis for the extensive and unique comments in *Enuma Elish*'s final passage? They are not just elaborations on the main ideas recorded in the names, as the example just cited may suggest. The analysis goes much deeper, as ancient Mesopotamian scholarship itself shows us. In the great seventh-century library of King Assurbanipal at Nineveh were two manuscripts that contained a detailed exploration of Marduk's names as listed in Tablet VII of *Enuma Elish* (names 10 to 51). Neither manuscript is fully preserved, but the system behind the text is clear. They belong to a genre of scholarship that we call commentaries, which list interpretative cruxes in a given text, often in a column on the left of the tablet, and provide clarifications, often in the right column.[6] The commentary on *Enuma Elish* systematically lists Marduk's names in the left column, breaks them up into their constituent parts, and provides Akkadian translations of these elements in the right column, as in the following example.[7]

| | |
|---|---|
| [ASA]R-RI | *ša$_2$-rik* |
| RU | *ša$_2$-ra-ku* |

| | | |
|---|---|---|
| | SAR | *me-reš-tu* |
| | A | *is-ra-tu* |
| SI | RA$_2$ | *ka-a-nu* |
| RU | DU$_3$ | *ba-nu-u* |
| | SAR | *še-em* |
| | SAR | *qu-u*$_2$ |
| MA | MA$_4$ | *a-ṣu-u*$_2$ |
| | SAR | *ar*$_2$*-qu* |

This analysis justifies the explanation of Marduk's tenth name, Asari, as 'giver of farmland, who established the watered fields, creator of grain and flax, who brings forth plants' (*šārik mērešti ša israta ukinnu / banû še'am u qê mušêṣu urqēti,* VII 1–2). How did this detailed explanation of the name come about? We do not have to assume that the author(s) of the commentary knew exactly what the poet of *Enuma Elish* had in mind, but we can see that they all used the same hermeneutic practices. These were grounded in the basic characteristics of the cuneiform writing system, a logo-syllabic script rather than an alphabetic one, in which each cuneiform sign had multiple readings and each of these readings could have various meanings. The multiplicity of the potential readings of a sign was essentially the outcome of the fact that the script was rooted in bilingualism, as each sign had meanings in both Sumerian and Akkadian. Each sign indicated one or more Sumerian words, each of which had one or more Akkadian translations. Moreover, signs could have homophones, that is, other signs with the same pronunciation but a different meaning.[8]

The ancient scholars expanded these principles to increase the number of possible interpretations massively. They explored all sorts of phonetic and semantic similarities to give individual signs more meanings. A closer look at the example cited above shows how they worked. The entry starts with the name Asari, which, although not written with syllabic signs, was divided into three parts, each of which was considered an individual sign to be studied separately: A, SAR, and RI. The final sign RI had no useful Akkadian equivalent, but its near-homophones, RU and RA, did (vowels were considered less important than consonants). RU had the Akkadian translation *šarāku*, 'to give', which allowed for it to indicate 'the giver', *šārik* in Akkadian. The same syllable could be written with the RU$_2$ sign, which also can be read as **du**$_3$, the Sumerian word for 'to create', Akkadian *banû*, thus rendering 'the creator'. The syllable RA, when written out with the RA$_2$ sign, had the alternative reading DU; the latter had an alternate reading, **gin**, a Sumerian verb that was translated into Akkadian as *kânu*, 'to establish'. By interpretating RI as RU and RA and including their various alternative readings, the analyst could connect the signs to 'the giver', 'the creator', and 'who established' in the text of *Enuma Elish*.

In this commentary, **a**, a very common word in Sumerian meaning 'water', is equated with Akkadian *isratu*, usually translated as 'plan' or 'design'. In *Enuma Elish* it indicates watered fields, however, because, as a separate commentary to *Enuma Elish* tells us, *isratu* can be the synonym of *eqlum* 'field', a term commonly written with the Sumerian **a-ša**$_3$ (Frahm and Jiménez 2015: 308).

The author(s) of the commentary gave the sign SAR, the central element in the name, the most attention. Its basic meaning had to do with gardens (when read sar) and orchards (when read $kiri_6$), which are both semantically related to 'farmland', *mēreštu*. Because of SAR's connection to agriculture, then, it was taken to indicate two main agricultural crops, 'grain' (*še'um*) and 'flax' (*qû*). The sequence $u_2$-sar meant 'vegetables' (*arqu*), and thus 'greenery' (*urqētu*) in general. Finally, the sign SAR could also be read $ma_4$, which had the Akkadian equivalent *aṣû*, 'to come out'. SAR thus justified the elements 'farmland', 'grain', 'flax,' 'who made grow', and 'plants' in *Enuma Elish*'s interpretation of the name Asari.

Proceeding in this way, the commentary systematically explained all the names of Marduk and their elaborations as they appeared in Tablet VII of *Enuma Elish*. The analysis explored the various readings of each sign – for example, sar and $kiri_6$ for SAR – and expanded them to include semantically related readings, such as 'farmland' and 'grain'. The author(s) used the signs' homophones, near-homophones, and multiple readings; thus RI's near-homophone $RA_2$ led to inclusion of the latter's alternate reading DU, and an alternative reading of DU made GIN an acceptable interpretation for RI. The author(s) saw single elements of complex signs as rendering the whole, so that A could stand for A-$ŠA_3$ and SAR for $U_2$-SAR. Elsewhere in the commentary, they further expanded their range of options by taking other creative steps. Because the final letter /m/ had been dropped from case endings at some point in the history of the Akkadian language – a fact that the first-millennium scholars seem to have known – Sumerian words ending in /m/ could stand for those without it: TUM for TU, RUM for RU, etc. All the Akkadian translations of RU thus applied to RUM as well. And although the Sumerian version of the name was the starting point of the analysis, sometimes its Akkadian translation could also justify an equation. The name 'Lord of the Lands', **en-kur-kur** in Sumerian (name 50), was considered to include the syllable **ma**, because the name's Akkadian translation, *bēl mātāti*, contained that syllable. Taking **ma** as a Sumerian word in turn allowed for a translation of it into several new Akkadian words. In another name, A-gilim-ma (name 32), the final sign MA was equated with the Sumerian $\mathbf{mu_9}$, which, when written with the simpler sign MU, was the Akkadian word for 'water'. In one case, in the interpretation of the name Tutu-Ziku (name 15), the Akkadian word *banû* is taken as equivalent to its anagram *nabû* (Frahm 2011: 116; Talon and Anthonioz 2019: 215). All this work was done through systematic reasoning, which often involved a series of intermediate steps: DU was translated as *kânu*, not because that was common practice, but because when read gin, it meant *kânu* in Akkadian. There was always a logic behind each step.

Every element of Marduk's names was thus accounted for in the commentary, but the author(s) stressed those that they considered to be the most important for each name. In the case of Asari, the sign SAR received most attention because that name showed Marduk's role as benefactor of agriculture. The next name, Asar-Alim, focused on counsel and advise, so the author(s) parsed it differently in order to elaborate on that aspect. Here SA rather than SAR became the crucial element and was given six different connotations: *bītu*, 'house', *milku*, 'counsel' (twice), *atru*, 'superb', *uqqû*, 'to pay heed', *adāru*, 'to fear', and *aḫāzu*, 'to learn'. Only two other elements in the name were each given a single Akkadian translation. It is clear that the author(s) wanted to justify how *Enuma Elish* came up with its interpretation of each name; even if they did not accurately repeat the original author's reasoning, they justified the explanations that followed each of Marduk's fifty names.[9]

The interpretative steps were not an invention by the author(s) of the commentary but part of the attitude towards the written word that can be found already at the invention of the cuneiform script. At that time, in the late fourth millennium, there appeared – alongside the administrative documents for which writing was invented – lists of words, which modern scholars call lexical lists. These began as monolingual collections of Sumerian words, which remained the basic word-signs in the script throughout its history. Over time, the lists came to include different readings of each sign and the multiple Akkadian translations of each of those readings, as in the following example (Civil 1979: 91, l. 66–9).

| Sumerian sign | Reading of the sign | Akkadian translation | (English translation) |
|---|---|---|---|
| $TUG_2$ | **mu** | *litbušu* | (to clothe oneself) |
| $TUG_2$ | **tu** | *ṣubātu* | (garment) |
| $TUG_2$ | **nam** | *rubû* | (prince) |
| $TUG_2$ | **umuš** | *ṭēmu* | (reason) |
| | | *milku* | (counsel) |

This passage indicates that the Sumerian word-sign $TUG_2$ could be pronounced in four different ways – **mu, tu, nam,** and **umuš** – each of which had at least one Akkadian translation. In this case, when read **umuš**, two translations are given.

In short, the lexical lists explored connections. The links were not only inspired by semantic meaning, but also by phonetic and graphic similarities. Some lists grouped signs together because they dealt with similar objects, such as wooden objects, animals, or body parts. Others noted associations because the signs looked similar: because they started with horizontal or vertical strokes, looked like boxes, or the like. Yet others grouped the signs together because they sounded alike when pronounced: words starting with the syllable **ša**, then **šu**, then **ši**, etc. In all of these groupings, they had one or more Akkadian translations, establishing a vast network of links that enabled logical interpretations like those found in the commentary on *Enuma Elish*, interpretations that on the surface seem irrational to us. One entry, for example, states that the Sumerian word for 'sun' could be translated 'donkey'. This required two intermediate steps: 'sun' in Sumerian, **utu**, sounds like **udu**, which means 'sheep'; and 'sheep' in Akkadian, *immeru*, sounds like *imēru*, 'donkey'. Thus, it is fully logical – according to the principles of the text – to translate **utu** as 'donkey' (Crisostomo 2019: 158).

There was an enormous variety in the structure, aims, and organization of the lexical lists, but they all shared the ultimate goal of exploring the possible interpretations of each cuneiform sign. The script remained a central part of cuneiform scholarship from its invention to its last occurrence in the first century CE.[10] Throughout that history, everyone who used the script was convinced that a cuneiform text was meaningful not just because of what it represented but also because of how it represented. A word written with one or more signs was not just a record of a word spoken or thought; its graphic appearance was meaningful too, as it allowed for multiple interpretations, and a full comprehension of a text required a consideration of all these possible understandings. The ancient Mesopotamian science of hermeneutics unearthed those potential meanings. Although the analyses that *Enuma Elish* provides are by far the longest and most systematic examples of this practice, evidence for it appears from the late third to the late first millennium BC (for other examples, see Glassner 2019: 580–1).

The basic characteristics of the cuneiform writing system in which each sign had various readings while words and syllables could be rendered with more than one sign led to the possibility that a text could be written in multiple ways, ostensibly rendering the same message. Examples of two versions of the same text appear in the early second millennium, some providing two Sumerian renderings, others combining Sumerian and Akkadian. The primary version follows common practices of sign choice, and the other one is highly artificial, seemingly trying to show off the scribe's knowledge of esoteric signs. In one example, a myth about the birth of the god Enlil, the standard and artificial versions of the text, both in Sumerian, are laid out on the tablet in an irregular way – like the pages in a book – in order to make the simultaneous consultation easier. For the artificial version the scribe selected synonyms of common words that were only found in lexical texts in order to rewrite the standard version sign-by-sign (Metcalf 2019: 30–4). The source text could also be in Akkadian, with the Sumerian version following that language's word order and rendering each word with an uncommon Sumerian term extracted from lexical lists (e.g. George 2009: 78–112). These artificial versions are incomprehensible to the modern reader on their own; the ancient scribes may have wanted to flaunt their lexical knowledge, but they also gave a deeper meaning to the text.

The concept that the written form of a text had significance beyond what the text said sounds unorthodox to those who use alphabetic scripts – although some mystical schools of interpretation, such as kabbalah, make similar claims for those scripts. Alphabets are usually considered to render spoken words or thoughts, the meaning of which is primary, and their limited repertoire of signs gives little opportunity to choose alternative ways of writing out words. As heirs of Socrates and the Platonic ideas of representation, we see writing as one step further from the truth, an extra layer that adds confusion – so Socrates, who never wrote down his thoughts but only lectured, tells us according to the notes of his student Plato. Those who used cuneiform writing, even in its most elementary form, believed the opposite: writing *added* meaning. When recording the basic word for 'house', **e**$_2$ in Sumerian, *bītu* in Akkadian, they did not attempt to render it phonetically, but used a sign originally based on the conventional drawing of a house, 𒂍. The word for 'waterskin', **ummud** in Sumerian, *nādu* in Akkadian, was rendered with a sequence of four signs that, when read literally, expressed the idea, 'a leather bag to carry water in the steppe', 𒋢𒀀𒂔𒇲, obviously much more time-consuming to write than a syllabic spelling would have been and only apparent to someone reading the text rather than hearing it spoken. From the beginning of their education, children who studied cuneiform were taught this principle; it was baked into the system. They would never write the word for 'house' with a sign that did not show the outlines of a house. But the few of them who went on to become scholars, composing and copying texts of higher learning, elaborated further on this idea by choosing signs carefully in order to add meaning to their texts, and their choices were oftentimes unconventional. In cleansing rituals, for example, the use of pure water was important, thus some highly educated scribes made sure to include the cuneiform sign indicating 'spring' (**tul**$_2$) when they wrote out the Akkadian statement, 'you cleanse them', *tullalšu*. When they prescribed the use of an oven (Akkadian *tinūru*) in rituals against witches, they used the sign for 'light' (Akkadian *nūru*), because witches fear light (see the detailed discussion in Maul 1999). There are even occasions where the visual shape of a written word strengthened the plot of a story. In the Sumerian tale *Lugalbanda in the Wilderness*, for example, a shelter that looks like a bird's nest plays an important part. The injured hero is left there with abundant food supplies by his companions who hope that he will survive until they return, but who also know that he may die. The monosyllabic Sumerian word for nest **gud**$_3$ is written with a sequence of signs that indicates its structure, 'the place where food is put down'. But if one breaks up the sequence, one can also read it as 'food on his grave'. Later in the tale, the reader will find out which of the two meanings will come true (Johnson 2013). In some cases the sign choice may have been whimsical in order to show off lexical knowledge (e.g. Civil 1972), but in general it was serious business. It was not just what you wrote that was important, but how you wrote it.

Conversely, when reading a text, the way in which it was written provided additional information to its contents. The polysemy or multiplicity of meanings in each sign expanded the message of the text. And the possibilities of interpretation seem almost without limit, as further connections could be established along the same principles of reasoning as were used to establish the basic relationships. This may sound ludicrous to someone used to consult dictionaries whose entries are listed in exact alphabetical order, and where definitions are given with a strict hierarchy – 1, 2a, 2b, 3, etc. In cuneiform scholarship, by contrast, the connections branched out in every direction. The final product was a *rhizome* – a presentation of knowledge that resembles the roots of a plant, growing horizontally and able to expand without limits – rather than a genealogical tree. Think of the algorithms that generate the results of an internet search. They state that the order is based on relevance, but there is no obvious hierarchy to the user. The principles behind them are hidden, yet somehow, we take the outcome as rational.

The author of *Enuma Elish* firmly believed in the validity of cuneiform hermeneutics. Every one of Marduk's fifty names was a combination of signs that could be interpreted in various ways and together revealed the name's full meaning. The poet did not make the interpretative choices explicit, so the author(s) of the commentaries tried to reconstruct those choices or developed them following the same methods of interpretation. Multiple options were sometimes possible: in the example of Asari given above, the idea that A stood for A-ŠA$_3$, that is, in Akkadian *eqlum* 'field', was paralleled with the suggestion that it stood for A-GAR$_3$, that is, in Akkadian *tamirtu* 'irrigated land' which also was a synonym of *isratu*, the word they needed to explain in *Enuma Elish* (Lambert 2013: 482; Frahm and Jiménez 2015: 308). They could have consulted lexical texts as the basis of some of the explanations – we find some of the equations in other preserved lists – but that was not necessary. Everyone knew the principles behind the underlying system and shared a belief in its value. We may find what they came up with 'ridiculous' (Lambert 2013: 167), but they did not.

There was also the danger that this type of name analysis could pose problems by suggesting options that were theologically impossible. This affected Marduk's name itself, which as traditionally written out amar-utu could easily be understood as 'bull-calf of the sun god Utu', while he was neither a solar deity nor the son of one. When Marduk was given his name early on in the poem (I 101–2) the author immediately precluded this misunderstanding by asserting that it meant that he was the 'sun of the gods' (*šamšu ša ilānī*), that is, their king. Some manuscripts took the precaution even further by writing out the word that could be read as 'sun god', Akkadian Shamash, in such a way that it referred to Shazu, 'the god who sees the heart' and a proper equivalent for Marduk. Several layers of exegesis were involved (Fadhil and Jiménez 2021: 217–18).

Through the analysis of his various names, it was possible to associate Marduk to many of the aspects of life and activities that had been explored in the preceding narrative of the poem. For instance, he had defeated Tiamat, the force of chaos, a fact that was repeatedly celebrated in his names. His thirty-sixth name, Lugalabdubur, was analysed as 'the king who disrupted the doings of Tiamat, who uprooted her weapon, whose foundation is firm, both before and behind' (VII 91–2). His military valour allowed him to counter all evil, so as Shazu-Zisi, his nineteenth name, he is 'he who silenced rebels, who expelled paralysis from the bodies of the gods his fathers' (VII 41–4). Also the elements of the universe that he had created earlier in the epic were embedded in his names. As Tutu-Zi-Ukkinna (name 14) he 'firmly established holy heaven for the gods, took hold of their ways and appointed their stations' (VII 16–17). He created stability (name 31), heaven and earth (name 32), grain and flocks (name 30), grasslands and watering holes (name 24), canals, dikes, and furrows (name 25), and flax and grain (name 10). He made sure that the gods had proper shrines (name 13) with regular food offerings provided to them (name 33). He supported 'the land, the city, and his people' (name 3, VI 135). Because of all these accomplishments he was supreme (name 41) and the lord of the lands (name 50). We can thus see how the names picked up elements of the poem's story and reinforced them.

The order of the names given to Marduk at the start of the long list parallels the events described throughout the poem. In the list, his first four names are variations on the name Marduk, that is, the birthname that his parents Ea and Damkina give him early on in the epic (I 81). The next two names in the list include the expression 'king of the gods of heaven and earth', Lugal-Dimmer-Ankia, a name that he was explicitly granted by the other gods later on:

> Marduk was once our beloved son,
> now he is your king – obey his command!
> Then they said, speaking together:
> 'Lugal-Dimmer-Ankia is his name – trust in him!'
>
> (V 109–12)

The next three names in the list invoke Asarluhi, the son of Ea, a name that Anshar assigned to him at the end of the epic's narrative section: 'Anshar made him supreme and gave him his name Asarluhi. "When his name is spoken, let us do obeisance"' (VI 101–2; Seri 2006: 510–11).

The interconnections between the epic's storyline and Marduk's names already implies that the latter's enumeration is not a mere ritual appendix to the text, meant to honour the god when *Enuma Elish* was recited. But the connections go even deeper. Naming is central to the epic and the process of it appears throughout the poem, which starts out with the statement that at the beginning of time 'when heaven on high had not been named and the ground below not given a name'. The absence of names means that nothing existed. Giving names is mentioned explicitly in nineteen verses, not just to Marduk, but also to other gods, places (Apsû and the city of Babylon), and Marduk's bow. In these other cases too, the names are followed by an analysis. When Ea named Apsû as his residence, the verse added the explanation 'that makes known the shrines' (I 76). The poet took ab to represent 'shrines' because an alternative reading of the sign, $eš_3$, had that meaning; zu indicated 'to make known' as this was the translation of a grammatical form of the Akkadian equivalent of the Sumerian verb **zu**, *uddû*, the D-Stem of *edû*. Marduk's bow received three names: '"Longwood" was the first, the second was "Striker", her third name was "Bow Star", he brought her forth in heaven, and made firm her orbit with the gods her brothers' (VI 89–91). Each one of these could be derived from the simple term 'bow', $^{giš}$**ban**, through the various hermeneutic techniques discussed above (Gabriel 2014: 268–307).

In Mesopotamian thought, the name was not accidental to the god, person, or object named, but contained their essence. When one gave a name, one assigned a destiny.[11] The names of Marduk's bow confirmed its efficacy, while the fifty names of Marduk legitimized his rise to kingship (Gabriel in this volume) and made him responsible for all aspects of his creation. The idea permeates the entirety of *Enuma Elish*: again and again, acts of creation are paralleled with acts of naming. Conversely, this meant that one could only grasp someone's or something's essence with a full understanding of their name; many texts explicitly state that it revealed someone or something's character introducing the analysis with the expression 'as his/its name (indicates)' (Jiménez 2018). And one needed to scrutinize the name in all its aspects to do so fully. The intricate investigation of Marduk's fifty names revealed how his actions had altered the universe in all its details.

The rationale for the name-analysis is thus clear: through it, we are able to understand Marduk in full. But why is the passage so long and placed at the end of the poem? It is the story's finale; it is the climax of the process of creation. The poet knew that humans were the audience of the work, and *Enuma Elish* tells us that humankind was fashioned out of the blood of Qingu, one of the gods who had assisted Tiamat. This happened at the very end of the story, after Marduk had created everything else, and humans were to act as servants so 'that the toil of the gods be imposed upon them' (VI 8). The epic treats their appearance almost as a minor detail, yet humans were the ones to whom it explained creation. And in this story of creation, the final passage tells us how we can understand what the gods do; it gives us the key to unlock their secrets. Mesopotamian gods were not inscrutable. They gave humans messages, but the challenge was to find out how to read them. In daily practice, this was done by diviners; it was their task to read the omens that the gods left in every aspect of the universe. In the first millennium BCE, celestial divination had become the most prominent form of omen readings, and Mesopotamians were famous as astrologers in the ancient Mediterranean world. In *De divinatione* (I.1.2) the Roman author Cicero described the

Assyrians and Chaldeans (i.e. Babylonians) as the most devoted readers of stars and their constellations. The special status of celestial divination is reflected in *Enuma Elish*. The poem devotes much attention to how Marduk assigned the gods their positions in the sky as celestial bodies (V 1–46, unfortunately a fragmentary passage) and one of the names given to Marduk's bow is 'Bow Star' (VI 89–91, cf. above), another celestial body (the bright winter stars of Canis Major). The naming of the bow may even have been the first celestial omen ever sent by the gods (Gabriel 2014: 299–306 and 2018). Astrology/astronomy was only one of many divinatory sciences, however. Omen lists interpreted every possible and impossible phenomenon in the sky and on earth, in the human body and in that of animals, in nature and in the built environment as a sign of the gods. The importance of divination is clear from the fact that close to half of the Babylonian literary and scientific tablets in the library of Assurbanipal as we know it contained omen series. Of those tablets, 48 per cent were astronomical, 14 per cent dealt with extispicy, and 10 per cent contained terrestrial omens.[12]

Divinatory signs were considered to be written signs. The patterns of celestial bodies in the sky were called 'heavenly writing', *šiṭir šamê* in Akkadian, and the sun god Shamash, among others, was praised for communicating through the livers of sacrificed sheep. 'You inscribe omens in sheep', states a Neo-Assyrian incantation to Shamash, while King Sargon II asserted, 'Shamash the warrior caused an unambiguous omen to be inscribed for me on the liver (of the sacrificial animal)' before he ordered an attack on an enemy.[13] And just as the reader had to apply hermeneutical principles to understand a written text, the diviner had to follow the same rules to comprehend the message of the gods. Each ominous sign had more than one reading depending on the context, as omen lists laid out in great detail. Just as a lexical list enumerated the multiple readings of a Sumerian cuneiform sign and their translations, the omen list pointed out that a sign of the gods could mean different things. A cat was not just one sign; its meanings were multiple, depending on its colour:

> If a white cat is seen in a man's house – (for) that land hardship will seize it.
> If a black cat is seen in a man's house – that land will experience good fortune.
> If a red cat is seen in a man's house – that land will be rich.
> If a multicolored cat is seen in a man's house – that land will not prosper.
> If a yellow cat is seen in a man's house – that land will have a year of good fortune.
> (Guinan 1997: 424)

*Enuma Elish* tells us that upon creation, the gods had granted humans the ability to discover their plans, giving them the key to unravelling the messages that they left behind everywhere. To do so required special skills, but the final passage of *Enuma Elish* showed us those principles in practice. That was the point of the entire poem.

## Further reading

Bottéro (1977) gives a detailed analysis of Marduk's names (in French), briefly summarized in English in Bottéro (1992: 94–6). Gabriel (2014: 268–307) explores naming practices throughout the poem (in German). For a history of the lexical corpus and its principles, see Veldhuis (2014), more briefly Taylor (2007). For Mesopotamian commentary texts, see Frahm (2011). Van De Mieroop (2015) explores the importance of the written word in Babylonian hermeneutics. On celestial divination as a reading exercise, see Rochberg (2004), more briefly Rochberg (2011). For Mesopotamian divination in general, see Maul (2018).

## Notes

1 Feliu and Albà (2014: 23–4) sum the passage up in one sentence; Lambert (2008: 15–59) retells the story in detail without any mention of the list; Foster (1997: 390–402) translates the entire epic except for the fifty names.

2 Lambert (1968: 108) considers it an addition; Dalley (1989: 230) states that it is 'not essential to the poem'.

3 Lambert (2013: 147) calls it the epic's climax; Van De Mieroop (2018: 381–92) claims that it contains the poem's main message.

4 See Lambert (2013: 147–60) for other lists. He thinks that *Enuma Elish* drew upon an existing list. Beaulieu (2020: 109–28) discusses a list that he takes to explore further aspects of Marduk ignored by *Enuma Elish*.

5 Seri (2006: 512–14) edits a list that does so more briefly and compares its statements to those in *Enuma Elish*.

6 For a detailed discussion of commentary texts, see Frahm (2011). The composition analysing Marduk's names is discussed there on pp. 114–16.

7 Talon and Anthonioz (2019: 211–30) reproduce the commentary in full.

8 When rendering a cuneiform text into the Latin alphabet, modern scholars distinguish the homophones with subscript numbers, for example, ša, $ša_2$, and $ša_3$.

9 See Bottéro (1977) for a detailed analysis of the commentary and its interpretative practices. Bottéro (1992: 94–6) gives a brief summary in English.

10 See Veldhuis (2014) for a detailed survey of the genre; and Taylor (2007: 432–46) for an overview.

11 Radner (2005) studies the importance of names in Mesopotamian thought in general; Gabriel (2018) discusses the importance of names in *Enuma Elish*.

12 See Maul (2018) for a detailed survey of Mesopotamian divination. Fincke (2003–4) gives statistics on the genres represented in Assurbanipal's library.

13 For an in-depth study of the ideas behind *šiṭir šamê*, see Rochberg (2004). Foster (2005: 744, 807) gives the quotations about Shamash.

## Bibliography

Beaulieu, P.-A. (2020), 'The God List CT 24 50 as Theological Postscript to Enūma eliš', in U. Gabbay and J. J. Pérennès (eds), *Des polythéismes aux monothéismes: Mélanges d'Assyriologie offerts à Marcel Sigrist*, 109–28, Leuven: Peeters.

Bottéro, J. (1977), 'Les noms de Marduk, l'écriture, et la "logique" en Mésopotamie ancienne', in M. DeJong Ellis (ed.), *Essays on the Ancient Near East in Memory of Jacob Joel Finkelstein*, 5–28, Hamden: Archon Books.

Bottéro, J. (1992), *Mesopotamia: Writing, Reasoning, and the Gods*, trans. Z. Bahrani and M. Van De Mieroop, Chicago: University of Chicago Press.

Civil, M. (1972), 'The Anzu-Bird and Scribal Whimsies', *Journal of the American Oriental Society*, 92: 217.
Civil, M. (1979), *Ea A* = nâqu, *Aa A* = nâqu, *with Their Forerunners and Related Texts*, Materials for the Sumerian Lexicon 14, Rome: Biblical Institute Press.
Crisostomo, C. J. (2019), *Translation as Scholarship: Language, Writing, and Bilingual Education in Ancient Babylonia*, Studies in Ancient Near Eastern Records 22, Berlin: De Gruyter.
Dalley, S. (1989), *Myths from Mesopotamia*, Oxford: Oxford University Press.
Eco, U. (2009a), *Vertige de la liste*, Paris: Flammarion.
Eco, U. (2009b), *The Infinity of Lists: From Homer to Joyce*, trans. Alastair McEwen, London: MacLehose.
Fadhil, A. A. and E. Jiménez (2021), 'Literary Texts from the Sippar Library II: The Epic of Creation', *Zeitschrift für Assyriologie und vorderasiatische Archäologie*, 111: 191–230.
Fadhil, A. A. and E. Jiménez (2022), 'Literary Texts from the Sippar Library III: 'Eriš šummi', A Syncretistic Hymn to Marduk', *Zeitschrift für Assyriologie und vorderasiatische Archäologie*, 112: 229–74.
Feliu Mateu, L. and A. M. Albà (2014), Enūma eliš *y otros relatos babilónicos de la creación*, Madrid: Trotta.
Fincke, J. C. (2003–2004), 'The Babylonian Texts of Nineveh: Report on the British Museum's Ashurbanipal Library Project', *Archiv für Orientforschung*, 50: 111–49.
Foster, B. R. (1997), 'Epic of Creation', in W. W. Hallo (ed.), *The Context of Scripture*, vol. 1: *Canonical Compositions from the Biblical World*, 390–402, Leiden: Brill.
Foster, B. R. (2005), *Before the Muses. An Anthology of Akkadian Literature*, 3rd edn, Bethesda: CDL Press.
Frahm, E. (2011), *Babylonian and Assyrian Text Commentaries: Origins of Interpretation*, Guides to the Mesopotamian Textual Record 5, Münster: Ugarit Verlag.
Frahm, E. and E. Jiménez (2015), 'Myth, Ritual, and Interpretation: The Commentary on *Enūma eliš* I–VII and a Commentary on Elamite Month Names', *Hebrew Bible and Ancient Israel*, 5: 293–343.
Gabriel, G. I. (2014), *'enūma eliš' – Weg zu einer globalen Weltordnung: Pragmatik, Struktur und Semantik des babylonischen 'Lieds auf Marduk'*, Orientalische Religionen in der Antike 12, Tübingen: Mohr Siebeck.
Gabriel, G. I. (2018), 'Decreeing Fate and Name-Giving in Enūma eliš: Approaching a Fundamental Mesopotamian Concept with Special Consideration of the Underlying Assumptions and of the Condition of Possibility of Human Knowledge', in P. Attinger, A. Cavigneaux, C. Mittermayer and M. Novák (eds), *Text and Image: Proceedings of the 61e Rencontre Assyriologique Internationale*, Orbis Biblicus Orientalis 40, 163–78, Leuven: Peeters.
George, A. R. (2009), *Babylonian Literary Texts in the Schøyen Collection*, Cornell University Studies in Assyriology and Sumerology 10, Bethesda: CDL Press.
Glassner, J.-J. (2019), *Le devin historien en Mésopotamie*, Ancient Magic and Divination 16, Leiden: Brill.
Guinan, A. J. (1997), 'Mesopotamian Omens', in W. W. Hallo (ed.), *The Context of Scripture*, vol. 1: *Canonical Compositions from the Biblical World*, 423–26, Leiden: Brill.
Jacobsen, T. (1976), *Treasures of Darkness: A History of Mesopotamian Religion*, New Haven: Yale University Press.
Jiménez, E. (2018), '"As Your Name Indicates": Philological Arguments in Akkadian Disputations', *Journal of Ancient Near Eastern History*, 5: 87–105.
Johnson, J. C. (2013), 'Indexical Iconicity in Sumerian *belles lettres*', *Languages and Communication*, 33 (1): 26–49.

Lambert, W. G. (1968), 'Myth and Ritual as conceived by the Babylonians', *Journal of Semitic Studies*, 13: 104–12.
Lambert, W. G. (2008), 'Mesopotamian Creation Stories', in M. J. Geller and M. Schipper (eds), *Imagining Creation*, 15–59, Leiden: Brill.
Lambert, W. G. (2013), *Babylonian Creation Myths*, Mesopotamian Civilizations 16, Winona Lake: Eisenbrauns.
Maul, S. M. (1999), 'Das Wort im Worte: Orthographie und Etymologie als hermeneutische Verfahren babylonischer Gelehrter', in G. W. Most (ed.), *Commentaries - Kommentare*, 1–18, Göttingen: Vanderhoeck and Ruprecht.
Maul, S. M. (2018), *The Art of Divination in the Ancient Near East: Reading the Signs of Heaven and Earth*, trans. B. McNeil and A. J. Edmonds, Waco: Baylor University Press.
Metcalf, C. (2019), *Sumerian Literary Texts in the Schøyen Collection. Volume I: Literary Sources on Old Babylonian Religion*, Cornell University Studies in Assyriology and Sumerology 38, University Park: Eisenbrauns.
Radner, K. (2005), *Die Macht des Namens: Altorientalische Strategien zur Selbsterhaltung*, Santag 8, Wiesbaden: Harrassowitz.
Rochberg, F. (2004), *The Heavenly Writing. Divination, Horoscopy, and Astronomy in Mesopotamian Culture*, Cambridge: Cambridge University Press.
Rochberg, F. (2011), 'Observing and Describing the World through Divination and Astronomy', in K. Radner and E. Robson (eds), *The Oxford Handbook of Cuneiform Culture*, 618–36, Oxford and New York: Oxford University Press.
Seri, A. (2006), 'The Fifty Names of Marduk in "Enūma eliš"', *Journal of the American Oriental Society*, 126 (4): 507–19.
Talon, P. and S. Anthonioz (2019), *Enūma eliš: Lorsqu'en haut* ..., Littératures anciennes du Proche-Orient 22, Paris: Éditions du Cerf.
Taylor, J. (2007), 'Babylonian Lists of Words and Signs', in G. Leick (ed.), *The Babylonian World*, 432–46, London: Routledge.
Van De Mieroop, M. (2015), *Philosophy before the Greeks: The Pursuit of Truth in Ancient Babylonia*, Princeton: Princeton University Press.
Van De Mieroop, M. (2018), 'What Is the Point of the Babylonian Creation Myth?', in S. Fink and R. Rollinger (eds), *Conceptualizing Past, Present and Future: Proceedings of the Ninth Symposium of the Melammu Project Held in Helsinki / Tartu May 18–24, 2015*, Melammu Symposia 9, 381–92, Münster: Ugarit-Verlag.
Veldhuis, N. (2014), *History of the Cuneiform Lexical Tradition*, Guides to the Mesopotamian Textual Record 6, Münster: Ugarit Verlag.

# Index

Achaemenid 122–4
Adad 104, 151, 155–6, 162 n.11, 269, 321
advice 204–5, 207–10
*aganutillû*-disease 17, 102–6, 107 n.7, 108 n.9, 108 n.11
agriculture 157, 264, 288, 292 n.15, 292 n.22, 321, 323
*akītu* (New Year's festival) 3, 13, 115–22, 124, 125 n.2, 125 n.10, 129–32, 134–9, 142–3, 152–4, 166, 174
alliteration 8
*amēlu* 104, 187, 194 n.13, 208
ancestor 5–6, 27 n.4, 89 n.141, 151, 225, 297
anger (rage) 6, 133, 202–3, 268–9, 272–4
Anshar 6–7, 143, 153, 155, 182–3, 185–92, 203–5, 207, 212 n.12, 220–1, 224–5, 230 n.25, 263, 269, 271, 320, 327
Anu (An) 3, 6–7, 123–4, 130, 139, 141, 155, 182, 190, 202, 212 n.12, 215, 221–2, 224–6, 232 n.51, 238–40, 242, 244–8, 267, 271, 299–300, 309
Anunnaki 81 n.113, 186, 252 n.7
Anzû (monster) 105, 223, 261, 263–5, 272, 283
*Anzû* (text) 16, 20 n.9, 105, 184, 198, 223, 263–5, 267–9, 272, 305
Apsû (also *Abzû*) 5–7, 9–11, 19 n.8, 103, 143, 145, 155–6, 158, 167, 170–2, 182, 185, 187–90, 193, 199–204, 207–10, 212 n.11, 216, 220–7, 228 n.7, 230 nn.34–5, 242, 248–50, 265, 267–70, 273, 280–3, 285–6, 301–5, 311, 328
Asarluhi 189, 321, 327
Ashur 13, 67 n.91, 119–20, 124, 151–5, 160–1
assembly 6–7, 16, 115, 154, 182–6, 188–9, 191–2, 205–6, 209, 211, 223, 225–6
assonance 8, 300, 303, 310
Assurbanipal, King 102–3, 138, 167, 212 n.17, 268, 271, 321, 329
  library of 12, 329
Assyria 13, 100, 118, 130, 135–7, 142, 145, 151, 153, 155, 240
Astrolabe ('Three Stars Each') 238–40, 242, 244–7, 251
*Atra-hasis* 7, 16, 20 n.8, 170, 176 n.15, 187–8, 209, 212 n.21, 264–9, 287, 289, 300, 305, 314 n.24
avenger 241, 263

Babylon 3–5, 7–8, 11–14, 17, 20 n.17, 100, 102, 104, 116, 118–25, 125 n.9, 129–32, 134–44, 151–4, 156–7, 160, 182, 185–8, 191, 207, 210, 215, 237, 247, 249–50, 260, 262, 265–6, 286, 289–90, 292 n.26, 297, 301, 309
Babylonian calendar treatise 115, 129–30, 144, 146
battle 5–7, 11, 13, 15, 105, 116–17, 119, 123–4, 132, 135, 138–9, 143–6, 152–4, 172, 182, 206, 215–16, 221, 223, 225, 261, 263–4, 268–73, 280–1, 283–4, 290, 301, 304, 307
Bel-Marduk 154–5
Bel-ushezib 144
*Beowulf* (Tolkien) 218
Berossus 14, 110 n.22, 156–8, 160, 162 n.16, 289
  *Babyloniaca* 156–7
Bible (Hebrew Bible) 14–15, 19, 118, 158–60, 216, 260. *See also* Old Testament
  Genesis 14–15, 19, 158–60, 168, 216–18, 250–1, 312
birth 5–6, 18, 173, 221–2, 224–7, 268, 284, 302, 309–10, 325
blood 105, 157–8, 171, 185, 187, 222, 263, 314 n.27, 328

bow (Marduk's) 188, 264, 328–9
  Bow Star 328–9

Cage, J. 305
Chaldean 14–15, 157, 329
*Chaldean Oracles* 155–6, 162 n.11
chaos 15, 119, 124, 132, 152, 169, 172–3, 201, 210, 215–16, 288, 302, 327
*Chaoskampf* 15, 215–17, 219, 228 n.6, 248
character-space 219
character-system 219
Cicero 328–9
Cixous, H. 219
clouds 207, 288
Commentary (on *Enuma Elish*)
  Commentary I 13, 120–1, 281
  Commentary II 8, 13, 286–7, 290
contractarianism 181, 191–3
counsel 17, 199–204, 207–10, 220–1, 323
cult
  at Esagil 130, 132, 134, 137, 139, 141
  of Marduk 11, 17, 115, 118, 120–4, 139, 141, 143, 151
cuneiform
  culture 14, 19, 116, 123–4, 139, 151, 153, 174, 268, 289
  literature 3, 5–6, 8, 12–15, 210, 287
  palaeography 100
  pantheon 3
  reception 129–30, 133–4, 146
  sign 10, 18, 136, 210, 322, 324, 326, 329
  writing system 153, 288, 311, 322, 325
*Cuneiform Commentaries Project (CCP)* 132

Damascius 14, 154–6, 158, 160
Damkina 5, 141, 143, 155, 221–2, 227, 231 n.47, 327
Darius 14
death 13–14, 105–6, 116, 119, 167–8, 171, 187, 222, 226, 248, 284, 309
deliberation 188, 193, 201, 209
Deluge 264–5, 288–9
destiny (fate) 8, 17, 134, 144, 182–3, 188, 191, 205, 219, 223, 227, 280–1, 286, 290, 309, 328
divine propriety 237, 248, 250
*Dungeons & Dragons* 173–4

Ea (Nudimmud, Enki, Ninshiku) 3, 5–7, 19–20 n.8, 103, 151, 155–6, 182, 185, 189–91, 202–5, 208–11, 212 n.18, 215, 220–2, 224–7, 230 n.37, 238, 240, 242, 246–7, 249, 261–3, 267–9, 271, 281–2, 285, 289–90, 301–2, 304–5, 308, 321, 327–8
Elam (Elamite) 11, 101, 132, 138, 145
*Electronic Babylonian Library (eBL)* project 15, 18, 132–3, 140, 146
  Fragmentarium 132, 140
emotions 17, 201–4, 207, 210
Enlil 3, 7–8, 16, 19 n.6, 106, 123–4, 130, 140–1, 151–2, 155, 188–91, 193, 223, 238–42, 244–7, 249, 264–9, 271, 273, 308, 321, 325
*Enuma Anu Enlil* 239, 242, 245–7, 261–2, 267, 300, 309
Eridu 167, 171, 249, 262
*Erish Shummi* 137, 304
Erra (god) 13, 137, 288
*Erra and Ishum* 13, 19, 129, 131–2, 134, 136–7, 268, 288
Esagil 7, 12, 17, 101–2, 118, 121, 123, 129–30, 132–45, 237, 249–50, 268
Esarhaddon 13, 103, 130, 138, 144, 250
Eshara 63 n.75, 77 n.106
Eshgala 63 n.75
Eudemus of Rhodes 14, 156
Europe 216–17

Ferocious Lord 101
flattery 201–2, 204, 207, 210, 212 n.10
Flood (Deluge) 19 n.6, 188, 266–7, 269, 287–9
Frahm, E. 131–2, 139–40, 144

Gabriel, G. 5–6, 16, 291 n.7
gender 7, 15–16, 215, 220, 224, 227, 284–5, 302
*Gilgamesh* 14, 99, 105, 160, 167–9, 198, 201, 211 n.8, 216–17, 220–1, 287–9
*gipāru* 306, 313 n.16
Gula 104
Gunkel, H. 15, 216–17

Hammurabi 3, 309
heaven 7, 17, 63 n.73, 77 n.106, 102, 132, 136, 138, 143, 145, 157, 159, 169,

186, 199, 237–51, 262, 280, 282, 298–300, 311, 321, 327–9
Hellenistic Babylon 122–4
henotheism (henotheistic) 151
Hobbes, T. 192
Homer 14, 162 n.13
*Iliad* 4, 162 n.13, 169
Horowitz, W. 239–40, 244–5
Horton, R. 99
humanity 7, 9, 186–8, 261, 265, 267, 269, 287, 328

Igigi 145, 186, 252 n.7, 266
*Inamgishhurankia* 131, 136
intertextuality 132, 259–63
Ishtar (Inana) 13, 121, 125 n.9, 152, 174, 175 n.3, 220, 230 n.37, 262, 269, 273, 275 n.24
Isin II 11, 100, 102, 105–6

Jacobsen, T. 16, 18, 181, 189, 194 n.4, 307, 320

Kaka 205, 225, 263
Kassite (dynasty, period) 11, 99–103, 105–6, 107 n.4, 110
kingship 6–7, 16, 117, 122, 124, 129–30, 134–5, 137, 144–5, 181–6, 188–9, 193, 198, 206–7, 210, 215, 222–3, 225–6, 241, 252 n.7, 263, 328
Kishar 155, 220–1
Kislimu 122, 131, 141
Kutir-Nahhunte 11

Lahmu and Lahamu 155, 186, 194 n.8, 194 n.15, 205, 220–5, 307, 310
Lambert, W. G. 8, 10–16, 20 n.17, 100–1, 107 n.3, 110 n.22, 110 n.24, 116, 131, 133, 168, 218, 237–8, 247, 261–4, 283–4, 292 n.18, 297, 302, 311
lamentation 268–72
*Leviathan* (Hobbes) 192
Lovecraft, H. P. (*Necronomicon*) 171
*Ludlul* 9, 12, 99, 101, 297
Lugal-Dimmer-Ankia 75 n.102, 186, 327

mace 264, 267, 269
*Mahabharata* 4
Marduk 3–19, 225. *See also* Ea (Nudimmud, Enki, Ninshiku); Enlil; Ninurta (Ningirsu)
argumentative challenge 189–91
and astral manifestations 239–42
in Babylon 122–4
contractarianism 191–3
cult of 11, 17, 115, 118, 120–4, 139, 141, 143, 151
rise to power 182–3
and the sea 104–6
self-curse and naming 188–9
submission and naming 185–8
treaty 183–5
and water disease 102–3
*Marduk Ordeal* 13, 17, 116, 119, 130–1, 133–4, 139, 143–4
*maṭṭalātu* 249–50
meadows 280–2
*melammu* (aura) 31 n.16, 221, 224–5, 230 n.32, 265
Meli-Shipak 106
Mercury 238–40
Mershakushu 274
Mesopotamia 16, 99, 101, 105–6, 109 n.14, 110 n.24, 116, 118, 123, 125, 131–2, 134, 141, 146, 151–2, 154–5, 160, 166–75, 216–18, 220, 223–4, 227, 259–62, 267–9, 273, 296–8, 300–2, 305, 309–10, 320–1, 325, 328, 330
Michalowski, P. 17, 19, 292 n.26
monsters 6–7, 105, 110 n.22, 152, 154, 157, 159, 173, 182, 201–2, 210, 215–16, 218–20, 222–4, 227–8, 229 n.19, 229 n.21, 230 n.38, 231 n.42, 261, 263, 267, 272–3, 283–4, 286, 307
Moon 104, 157–8, 240, 242–5, 286, 288. *See also* Sîn (god, Nanna)
mother 6–7, 155–6, 182, 202–3, 206–7, 220, 222–4, 226–7, 231 n.49, 274, 288, 302–5, 314 n.25
*MUL.APIN* 238, 242, 246–7, 251
mummu 5, 155–6, 158, 201–2, 204–5, 207, 221, 281, 291 n.6, 303–5, 307, 311
music (song) 17, 166–7, 171–3, 181, 187, 191–2, 280, 297, 311

Nabû 117–18, 121, 130, 132–3, 137, 152, 154, 240, 286, 292 n.18
naming 119, 159, 181–2, 185–9, 220, 281, 286, 288, 290, 299–300, 306–11, 328–9
  fifty names of Marduk 171, 241, 328
*namru* 83 n.120, 288
Namtila 83 n.118
Nari-Lugal-Dimmer-Anki 83
Neberu 7, 65 n.79, 93 n.155, 237, 239–40, 244–5, 250, 284–5
Nebuchadnezzar I 11, 16, 101–2, 106, 145, 313 n.8
Neoplatonic philosophy 154–6
Nergal 269
net (Marduk's) 57 n.55, 268, 282–4
Nineveh 12–13, 121, 125 n.9, 133, 138, 142–4, 152–3, 167, 216, 292 nn.25–6, 321
Ninurta (Ningirsu) 12, 16, 105, 132, 140, 152, 184, 246, 261–4, 267, 269, 272, 288
Nippur 3, 123–4, 130, 140–2, 144, 152, 247, 262
Nisannu 115, 117, 122, 129, 131, 133–4, 136, 138–9, 141–3, 153, 239, 247
noise 5, 20 n.8, 199, 265–6, 281, 300, 302–5
Notley, A. 169–70

Oannes 157–8
obedience 185
offerings 7, 120, 141, 208, 219, 226, 308, 327
Old Testament 217. *See also* Bible (Hebrew Bible)
omens 124, 242, 245, 249, 262, 282, 300, 309–11, 328–9

Palmyra 14, 118, 153–4, 160, 283
Peterson, J. 15
philosophy 134, 154–6, 192, 251, 260
plotting 199–203, 205–7, 210
poetics of creation 298–309
poison 263
Pongratz-Leisten, B. 116–17, 120, 125, 132

Qingu 6–7, 123, 132, 138, 145, 167, 171, 182, 187, 190, 206, 209, 216, 219, 221–7, 231 n.49, 241, 264, 267, 270, 272, 283, 328

rebellion 153, 185, 188, 202, 205–6, 271
reception 4, 13–15, 17, 129–37, 139–42, 146, 166–75, 175 n.1, 217–19, 251
  Neo-Assyrian 131–9
rejoicing 241
*rhizome* 326
ritual 3, 12–14, 17, 115–25, 129–35, 138–46, 152–3, 155, 160, 259–61, 268–70, 273, 301–2, 326
royal inscriptions 9, 101, 118, 131–2, 135, 138–40, 146, 250, 268, 309

*Sagig* 103
SAG.ME.GAR 240
*šamāmū* 300, 311, 313 n.8
Sargonid (dynasty, rule) 118–19, 169
Sargon II, King 102, 118, 138, 329
Sennacherib, King 13, 116, 119, 129–30, 134–5, 137–9, 143–4, 153–4, 158, 250, 289–90, 292 nn.25–6
Shamash 65 n.85, 244, 310, 321, 327, 329
silence 6, 155, 182, 191, 198–9, 203–5, 221, 226, 288, 305, 312, 327
Sîn (god, Nanna) 103–4, 106, 117, 130, 140, 244–5. *See also* Moon
Sippar Collection 135–6, 142
*šīqu*-disease 104
sleep 5, 11, 18, 200, 202–3, 208, 221–2, 265, 283, 285
Smith, G. 14–15, 167–8, 175 n.6, 217
Sommerfeld, W. 100, 106–7
Sonik, K. 14, 16–17, 201
spell, magic 5–6
stars (constellation) 6–7, 157, 183, 207, 238–42, 245–6, 250–1, 252 n.5, 262, 283, 329
statue 7, 11, 101, 129, 131, 133, 135, 137–9, 141–5
Susa 11

Tablet of Destinies (Tablet of Fates) 6–7, 222–3, 225–6, 263, 265, 281, 283
*tārītu* 120

temple 7, 12, 17, 102, 115–21, 123, 125 n.9, 129–30, 132, 135, 143, 153–4, 156–7, 249–50, 260, 264–5, 268, 281, 289
throne 124, 181, 183, 190–1, 224
Tiamat 3, 5–7, 9–11, 13, 15–18, 19 n.2, 104–6, 110 nn.22–3, 116–19, 121, 123–4, 132, 134–9, 141–6, 154–9, 167, 169–74, 176 n.20, 182, 184–7, 190, 192, 199, 202–10, 215–16, 219–28, 230 nn.34–5, 230 n.37, 231 nn.49–50, 248, 263–5, 267–74, 280–5, 287, 298, 301–5, 307, 311, 327–8
*tiāmtu* 300–4
toil 187, 265–7, 328
Tolkien, J. R. R. 218, 229 nn.18–19

Ubshu-ukkinnaku 6
*Udughul* 140, 171, 242, 261, 267
Ur III period (Third Dynasty of Ur) 247
Uruk 104, 123–4, 130–1, 139, 141, 175 n.3
Usmû 122, 141

war 13, 18, 129, 136–7, 182, 190–2, 209, 222
water 5–7, 9, 17–18, 143, 157–9, 169–71, 220–1, 248–51, 264, 269, 279–85, 287–90, 291 n.5, 301, 304–9, 311–12, 322–3, 325–7
water disease 102–6
weapons 7, 106, 174, 207, 210, 226, 241, 264, 266–7, 269–70, 272, 282, 284, 327
weather 224
winds 6–7, 104–6, 182, 202, 263–4, 269, 283, 286, 288
wisdom 156, 221, 249
Wisnom, S. 12, 16–17, 132, 169, 194 n.18
Woloch, A. 219, 228 n.10

Zgoll, A. 117, 122, 124, 125 n.4, 184
ziggurat 249, 266, 289

www.ingramcontent.com/pod-product-compliance
Lightning Source LLC
Chambersburg PA
CBHW050332230426
43663CB00010B/1833
*9781350297197*